IMPLEMENTATIONS
OF DISTRIBUTED
PROLOG

WILEY SERIES IN PARALLEL COMPUTING

SERIES EDITORS:

R.G. Babb, *Oregon Graduate Center, USA*

J.W. de Bakker, *Centrum voor Wiskunde en Informatica, The Netherlands*

M. Hennessy, *University of Sussex, UK*

R. Oldehoeft, *Colorado State University, USA*

D. Simpson, *Brighton Polytechnic, UK*

Carey (ed.): Parallel Supercomputing: Methods, Algorithms and Applications

de Bakker (ed.): Languages for Parallel Architectures: Design, Semantics, Implementation Models

Axford: Concurrent Programming: Fundamental Techniques for Real-Time and Parallel Software Design

Gelenbe: Multiprocessor Performance

Treleaven (ed.): Parallel Computers: Object-oriented, Functional, Logic

Williams: Programming Models for Parallel Systems

Raynal and Helary: Synchronization and Control of Distributed Systems and Programs

Eliëns: DLP—A Language for Distributed Logic Programming: Design, Semantics and Implementation

Kacsuk and Wise (eds): Implementations of Distributed Prolog

IMPLEMENTATIONS
OF DISTRIBUTED
PROLOG

Edited by

Peter Kacsuk
KFKI Research Institute for Measurement and Computing Techniques, Hungary

and

Michael Wise
University of Sydney, Australia

JOHN WILEY & SONS
Chichester · New York · Brisbane · Toronto · Singapore

Copyright © 1992 by John Wiley & Sons Ltd.
Baffins Lane, Chichester
West Sussex PO19 1UD, England

All rights reserved.

No part of this book may be reproduced by any means,
or transmitted, or translated into a machine language
without the written permission of the publisher.

Other Wiley Editorial Offices

John Wiley & Sons, Inc., 605 Third Avenue,
New York, NY 10158-0012, USA

Jacaranda Wiley Ltd, G.P.O. Box 859, Brisbane,
Queensland 4001, Australia

John Wiley & Sons (Canada) Ltd, 22 Worcester Road,
Rexdale, Ontario M9W 1L1, Canada

John Wiley & Sons (SEA) Pte Ltd, 37 Jalan Pemimpin 05-04,
Block B, Union Industrial Building, Singapore 2057

British Library Cataloguing in Publication Data

A catalogue record for this book is available
from the British Library

ISBN 0 471 93116 0

Printed and bound in Great Britain by
Courier International Limited, East Kilbride, Scotland

Contents

Foreword	xi
List of Contributors	xviv
PART I OR-PARALLEL IMPLEMENTATIONS OF PROLOG	**1**

1 OR-Parallel Logic Computational Models 3
   S. A. Delgado-Rannauro

1. Concepts and methods — 3
2. The shared binding environment family — 6
3. The closed binding environment family — 16
4. Recomputation family — 20
5. Summary — 24
   Acknowledgements — 26

2 Parallel Prolog on a Scalable Multiprocessor 27
   S. Raina, D. H. D. Warren and J. Cownie

1. Introduction — 27
2. Parallel Prolog implementations — 28
3. MIMD multiprocessors — 29
4. Related work on scalable architectures — 30
5. The Data Diffusion Machine — 31
6. A Transputer-based emulation of the DDM — 32
7. Aurora and Andorra-I on the DDM emulator — 41
8. Conclusion and future work — 43
   Acknowledgements — 44

3 OPERA: OR-Parallel Prolog System on Supernode 45
   J. Briat, M. Favre, C. Geyer and J. Chassin de Kergommeaux

1. Introduction — 45
2. Architecture of the Supernode — 47
3. The OPERA computational model — 48
4. Scheduling of work — 54
5. Implementation and preliminary results — 59
6. Related work — 61
7. Conclusion — 63
   Acknowledgements — 63

4 A Distributed Interpreter for Inherent AND/OR Parallelism   65
M. Avvenuti, P. Corsini and G. Frosini

1. Introduction   65
2. The parallel execution model   66
3. Implementing the interpreter   72
4. Performance evaluation   79
5. A model optimization   83
6. Conclusions and future work   85
   Appendix 1: The benchmark programs   86

5 Distributed Data Driven Prolog Abstract Machine   89
P. Kacsuk

1. Introduction   89
2. Graph representation of Prolog programs   90
3. Parallel execution   92
4. General view of the 3DPAM   97
5. Machine registers and data structures   98
6. Abstract instruction set   101
7. Variable binding   112
8. Comparison with related research   115
   Conclusions   117
   Acknowledgements   118

PART II   AND- AND AND/OR-PARALLEL IMPLEMENTATIONS OF PROLOG   119

6 Restricted AND- and AND/OR-Parallel Logic Computational Models   121
S. A. Delgado-Rannauro

1. Restricted AND-Parallel logic models   121
2. AND/OR-Parallel logic models   132
3. Summary   140
   Acknowledgements   141

7 An AND-Parallel Distributed Prolog Executor   143
A. Verden and H. Glaser

1. Introduction   143
2. An example execution   145
3. Communicating variable bindings   146
4. The Execution scheme   147
5. Clause level intelligent backtracking   151
6. Evaluation of our implementation   153
7. Conclusions   156
   Appendix   157

8 The OPAL Machine — 159
J. S. Conery

1. Background: OPAL and the AND/OR model — 159
2. Modules of an OPAL implementation — 161
3. Control: processes and continuations — 165
4. Unification: closed environments — 171
5. Performance — 179
6. Acknowledgements — 181
7. The OM instruction set — 182

9 The Reduce-OR Process Model for Parallel Logic Programming on Non-shared Memory Machines — 187
L. V. Kalé and B. Ramkumar

1. Introduction — 187
2. The Reduce-OR process model — 188
3. The Binding environment — 191
4. Compiled execution — 205
5. Performance — 207
6. Summary — 212

10 An Actor-oriented Computer for Logic and its Applications — 213
C. Percebois, N. Signès and L. Selle

1. Committed-choice languages vs non-deterministic systems — 213
2. The COALA goal rewriting system — 215
3. Implementation of the parallel execution model — 219
4. Independent AND-Parallelism — 223
5. SEARCH-Parallelism — 227
6. The CIAM abstract machine — 228
7. Preliminary results — 234
   Summary and conclusion — 235
   Acknowledgements — 235

PART III   COMMITTED CHOICE LANGUAGES — 237

11 Stream AND-Parallel Logic Computational Models — 239
S. A. Delgado-Rannauro

1. Concepts — 239
2. CCND languages — 241
3. Architectural models for CCND languages — 246
4. Summary — 256
   Acknowledgements — 257

12 Logical Occam — 259
D. Cohen, M. M. Huntbach and G. A. Ringwood

1. Introduction — 259
2. The producer–consumer prototype — 261
3. Synchronous from asynchronous — 267
4. The client–server prototype — 272
5. Semantics — 275
6. Open worlds — 277
7. Implementation issues — 279
8. Meta-interpretation and partial evaluation of Occam — 281
9. Conclusions — 284

13 A Distributed Implementation of Flat Concurrent Prolog on Multi-transputer Environments — 287
U. Glässer

1. Introduction — 287
2. Concurrent logic programming — 289
3. Design of an abstract FCP machine — 293
4. Concepts for a distributed implementation — 295
5. A multi-transputer implementation of FCP — 304
6. Conclusions — 309

14 Distributed Implementation of KL1 on the Multi-PSI — 311
K. Nakajima

1. Introduction — 311
2. GHC and KL1 — 312
3. Architecture of the Multi-PSI — 313
4. Intra-PE processing — 316
5. Inter-PE processing — 319
6. Programming environment support — 327
7. Evaluation — 328
8. Conclusion — 332
   Acknowledgements — 332

PART IV PROCESS-ORIENTED PROLOG LANGUAGES — 333

15 Delta Prolog: A Distributed Logic Programming Language and its Implementation on Distributed Memory Multiprocessors — 335
J. C. Cunha, P. D. Medeiros, M. B. Carvalhosa and L. M. Pereira

1. Introduction — 335
2. The programming model — 335
3. Operational semantics — 339
4. Implementing the parallel models — 352
5. Conclusions and future work — 355
   Acknowledgements — 356

16 CS-Prolog: A Communicating Sequential Prolog — 357
Sz. Ferenczi and I. Futó

1. Introduction — 357
2. Concepts of CS-Prolog — 358
3. Ensuring distributed completeness — 368
4. Examples — 370
5. System simulation in CS-Prolog — 374
6. Implementation issues — 375
7. Assessment of CS-Prolog — 377
   Acknowledgements — 378

17 PMS-Prolog: A Distributed, Coarse-grain-parallel Prolog with Processes, Modules and Streams — 379
M. J. Wise, D. G. Jones and T. Hintz

1. Introduction and desiderata — 380
2. Assumptions underlying PMS-Prolog — 383
3. Preliminaries — adding modules to Prolog — 385
4. Adding processes and streams — an overview — 386
5. A simple example: the producer–consumer problem — 388
6. More details on *fork, transmit* and *receive* — 389
7. Two other built-ins — 393
8. Uniprocessor and multiprocessor PMS-Prolog — 393
9. Discussion of the longer example — 399
10. Related work — 400

18 PADMAVATI Prolog — 405
X. de Joybert and J. J. Monot

1. Introduction — 405
2. The PADMAVATI machine — 406
3. Prolog parallelism model — 407
4. Implementation of parallel aspects — 409
5. Implementation of sequential aspects — 414
6. Padmalog through examples — 415
7. Discussion of performance — 423
8. Conclusion — 423
   Acknowledgements — 427

References — 429

Index — 459

Foreword

Even in the earliest days of computing technology, designers aimed at the idea of coupling multiple computing elements into a single, integrated machine that would both be much more powerful than any single element and capable of solving problems significantly more complex than possible on a single element. Early versions of such machines were usually called multiprocessors. In these machines, multiple processors were integrated into a system into which the remaining resources (memory, tape drives, disks, etc.) were shared by the multiple central processors. The main goal of these machines almost always focused on increasing throughput — the number of jobs completed per second — rather than on solving increasingly larger problems. In so doing, however, the time required to execute some or even all jobs was often significantly increased. Thus while the throughput of the machine went up, the execution time of jobs also often went up, and users of such machines often experienced unpredictably longer delays in receiving the answers to their computations. Unfortunately, the jobs that tended to experience this lengthening of execution time were frequently the very large jobs, the ones that took immense amounts of computing cycles to being with and whose answers were not expected to be produced before several days, even in the best case. Back in school, when I was a systems programmer on a powerful dual CDC 6600/6400 system, we frequently had in the job queue one or more very long jobs belonging to a particular computational chemist on campus, and it was not uncommon to see that his jobs had not received any compute cycles in days, as they were continually demoted in priority due to their size and passed over by the system's scheduler in order to crank through the small jobs that would keep the system throughput high. We felt so bad for him that every few days, we'd give him a gratuitous priority increase for a few minutes; but he still would rarely finish.

Multiprocessors were fairly successful as throughput increasers, but they were not very successful with respect to the second goal. When it came to solving problems significantly larger than could be solved on a single computing element, they were almost a total failure. It was easy to hope that with multiple central processors available in a single machine, a single program could somehow be decomposed into separate pieces that could then be executed simultaneously on the multiple processors. While moderate success was achieved, significant success was elusive. Several problems can be pointed to, but those most generally acknowledged are inadequate programming language and operating system support and inadequate hardware synchronization, communication, and data sharing support.

In addition to these early multiprocessor efforts, there were other efforts aimed at designing multiple processor machines that, unlike multiprocessors, were specifically oriented to executing a single, large program in much less execution time than possible on a single processor system. These machines usually cared little for increasing overall system throughput. In fact, they were at first usually dedicated machines, capable of running only a single program at any one time, even when not all resources in the machine were used by that program. These machines were called parallel processors, as opposed to multiprocessors. With parallel processors, the intent was that a single program would be decoupled into multiple, interdependent pieces, all of which would execute simultaneously (in parallel) on all the available processors. If the machine contained N processors, then the hoped for execution time would be only 1/Nth of that on a single processor. These machines contained special-purpose hardware extensions aimed directly at supporting the parallel execution of a single program, and new languages, language features, and parallel computation models for these machines began to proliferate. A great many machines were designed, and a significant number were built (mostly by government and university research labs). Although most of these machines are now extinct, the pioneering work that went into these efforts made possible the current age of commercially available parallel processing.

Although the field of parallel processing is actually quite old, the number of years in which parallel processors have been commercially available is really quite small; yet it is already uncommon to find a leading R&D center anywhere in the world without access to one. Numerous international scientific conferences are held each year on various aspects of parallel processing, and several international journals dedicated to parallel processing are regularly published. When the IEEE Computer Society recently began publishing its *Transactions on Parallel and Distributed Systems*, the paper submission rate to this journal surprisingly rose within two years to exceed that of any other IEEE Computer Society journal. Certainly there is a great deal of emphasis and interest in parallel processing today.

But how successful is it? Measured by a great many standards, parallel processing has been greatly successful. In some domains (mostly scientific), problems that were ten years ago considered thoroughly impractical or too expensive (in cost and/or time) are now routinely solved on large-scale parallel processors costing only fractions of large, mainframe, multiprocessors or vector processors. Parallel processors containing thousands of integrated processors are now available from multiple commercial vendors. Through high-speed networks, these machines are being made available to researchers all over the world. At the other end of the spectrum, very powerful, small-scale parallel processor boards are available for immediate insertion into personal computers, and at prices sometimes rivaling those of television sets.

Measured by several other standards, however, parallel processing has a long way to go before it can be considered greatly successful. For example, parallel processing remains critically expensive to exploit in terms of code development, debugging time, and performance tuning, especially when conventional, sequential programming languages with extensions for parallelism are used. New languages, designed especially for expressing parallelism, also involve heavy costs, such as waging battles of acceptability against skeptical management, generally weaker compilers and programming support environments, and a too-frequent inability to interface with existing corporate data-sets. The 1980s, for example, were replete with significant R&D accomplishments that failed to transfer into the commercial arena simply because they were written in a non-standard (read 'wrong') language (read 'Lisp'). Finally, many large, existing programs simply cannot be parallelized due to the many outdated programming practices previously engaged in (and still in use!) that prevent parallelization by even today's most powerful parallelizing compilers. And yet so many of these programs are precisely the ones that companies would pay dearly to have parallelized. Buying a powerful parallel processor won't help them if their programs cannot be parallelized, yet recoding or even modifying these programs is often beyond the financial or technical means of the companies.

It is straightforward to observe that the vast majority of parallel processing activities are occurring in the research lab; many of the greatest successes in the field have occurred with prototype applications using synthetic data. Others have occurred in the national research labs, but the number is significantly less. It is anecdotal that several of the most commercially successful parallel processor systems find that they are mostly used as multiprocessors instead of parallel processors, with each single processor being dedicated to a single user or program. Parallel processing is certainly absent from the great majority of corporate centers; yet many corporations can readily point to one or more life-blood programs on which their futures depend and that require orders of magnitude performance increases to reach their full potentials.

Why isn't parallel processing providing the solutions? Clearly this question can (and should) be debated at great length. But first, consider that very few applications programmers have any formal training in 'thinking' parallel; thus, for the vast majority of programmers, developing parallel programs is difficult, time consuming, and error prone (and debugging them is a leading cause of hair loss). Programmers are trained to consider correctness, not performance (as it should be). Most programmers were taught to decompose their programs according to either data flow or information hiding principles, whereas program parallelization is generally a control flow issue, and control flow decomposition may easily run orthogonal to data flow or information hiding techniques. Also, many studies have shown that predicting performance problems is a task that even most experts have difficulty doing, and yet parallelizing code involves parallelizing exactly those code segments with the performance problems. If we follow the programming methodology approaches taught in school, we will first develop our program and ensure its correctness; only then will we go back and try to tune it; but by this time, it may be too late to inject parallelism, and we may be doomed to a sequential implementation. So with parallel processing, we must consider performance, control flow, and program behavior perhaps long before we even begin to worry about correctness issues.

This means we must analyze the problem specification and candidate parallel algorithms in order to determine what types of and how much parallelism we can find. We must then chose a parallel computation model and a parallel programming language. If we are in a research center, perhaps the job is over; but if we work in some company or government center that is relying on us to ensure that, after tens of millions of dollars and tens of person-years, we will deliver to them a robust, parallel implementation of the corporate jewels, running at least one order of magnitude faster than it currently does, then we will have to persuade management that our choices are both wise and correct. This may be difficult.

But what makes the task all the more difficult is that there is no leading approach to parallel processing today. There are so many models of parallel computation that everyone can pick his or her own favorite; in fact, you can pick two or three and, using some unique twist, combine them into your own personal model. And you can pick your own favorite parallel processing language as well, or you can again invent your own, because no single existing parallel processing language has yet emerged as the clear leader. Sure, there are lots of them out there, and some even have small groups of devotees, but none can by any measure be claimed to be 'adopted' by either the scientific or commercial sectors. One reason for this state of affairs is that there is no IEEE, ANSI, BCI, or any other kind of standard for parallel processing (except for Ada, hmmm!). Without these, corporations and government centers are unlikely to invest tens of millions of dollars into equipment and tens of person-years of salaries rewriting their corporate life-blood programs in some new, strange, parallel programming language if that programming language is not based on some formal standard; they have seen too many programming languages come and go, and they know the cost of maintaining obsolete code and compilers.

But unfortunately, it is still probably too soon to consider standards in this field; too many significant problems remain to be solved in nearly every single approach to parallel processing. Automatic extraction of parallelism from programs is very tough, especially when irregular code or irregular data structures are involved, and dynamic extraction and management of parallelism is even tougher. Mapping task-structured computations and shared data elements onto homogeneous systems is tough, especially when non-uniform latencies are involved. Tuning and debugging parallel programs are beyond tough. Determining which form of parallelism best lends itself to a particular problem is often quite tough, and answers to this question often become machine or architecture specific.

There isn't even general agreement as to whether discovering and expressing the parallelism have to (should) be the responsibilities of the programmer or whether the compiler and run-time system can (should) perform these jobs. If parallelism is made the responsibility of the programmer, we can expect far less exploitation or parallel processing technologies, as parallel processing would, due to its incredibly tough demands on the programmer, remain a guru technology in a world with too few gurus; this would be disappointing. But even if the decision is made to rely on the compiler and run-time, there is no agreement on whether this can be done using existing conventional languages, or perhaps existing conventional languages with extensions for parallelism, or whether new languages and whole new computing paradigms will be required.

Other concerns enter into the debate, including SIMD versus MIMD versus SPMD versus whatever, shared memory versus message passing, synchronous versus asynchronous, explicit versus implicit data sharing, loosely coupled versus tightly coupled, systolic versus data parallel versus task-structured, massively parallel versus modestly parallel, shared address space versus separate address spaces, and the list goes on.

What we see today is an increasing number of proposed new languages, extensions to languages, and increasingly sophisticated models of parallel computation supported by entirely new languages. Given the fantastic proliferation of parallel languages, it is difficult to compare and contrast them with one another in order to identify the best languages and language features. What often makes it difficult to assess the contributions of a specific parallel language proposal are all the language's impure, side-effective, and non-functional expressions that usually accompany the sequential aspects of the language. There is so much sequential syntax and semantics involved, in addition to all the proposed parallel syntax and semantics, that the assessment job gets pretty tough. For example, COMMON block statements obfuscate many an otherwise straightforwardly parallelizable FORTRAN subroutine. Furthermore, many parallel language proposals are presented by embedding them within C. The problems with that approach should be obvious.

If we know precisely what we want to do and how to do it, we can certainly try to embed some if not all of our model into a conventional, sequential language such as C. Then we can develop parallelizing compilers and parallel run-time systems and host them on some set of parallel machines and then pray that they will catch on. One very impressive example of this approach is Gehani's Concurrent C, of which I am a fan; everything so far has worked well except for the praying part. There are other examples of this approach as well, but again, none have reached the state of formal acceptance by a large enough segment of the parallel processing community to make then a *de facto* standard.

If we assume that the praying part generally fails simply because there remain too many unsolved problems within parallel processing, then we must conclude that perhaps it is premature to restrict all of our research to embedding known parallelization techniques into the constrictive environments of existing, sequential, procedural languages. Rather, perhaps we should continue to examine entirely new language approaches that more adequately lend themselves to parallel processing, languages in which the central issues of parallel processing are readily exposed and thus allow more serious analysis of the approaches and problems. Then, in order to make more progress in studying all the various alternative approaches to parallel processing, it would be nice to see parallel processing language proposals presented using algorithms without all the other stuff that makes it so hard to see what is going on in the parallel processing domain. Sure, we eventually have to understand *what* is being computed, but for assessing the proposed language or extension, we are initially far more interested in understanding *how* it is being computed. So a language or language shell with minimal syntax and constructs would seem nearly ideal for exploring language, compiler, run-time, and even architectural issues, as it would allow us to present our parallel execution ideas with a minimum of baggage.

Consider logic programming. Sure, we can argue all day long as to whether logic programming is a good computational paradigm, and whether logic programming languages, such as Prolog, are worthy of notice. But that is not the point here (nor of this book you are about to read). We are not yet to (or perhaps we are past) the point of 'praying for adoption'. For now, let's ignore the question of whether logic programming, as a programming paradigm, is good or bad, superior or inferior, brilliant or dumb; instead, let's focus on whether logic programming is superior oin any way for presenting and examining proposals for parallel processing. One aspect of logic programs that is so very nice, at least with respect to the cited goal, is the almost total absence of syntax and semantics; few languages have fewer. Also, there is one and only one name scoping rule for all program statements, and it is as simple as you can get. There is a single sequencing construct, there is a single statement format, and there is a minimal number of data types and data structuring operations. And whereas many logic programming languages, such as Prolog, define a strict execution sequencing semantics, logic programs themselves are frequently devoid of any inherent sequencing constraints. Thus they are neither sequential nor parallel, and we can examine them free of any sequential semantics baggage. Finally, logic programs are easily parallelized, making automatic parallelization by compilers relatively simple.

Given all this, it becomes quite easy to propose and describe a novel method of parallel execution, and this proposal can usually be presented quite straightforwardly. We can read the parallel code examples and concentrate on the proposed parallel execution model without having to reconcile our thoughts with a remembered, formal, sequential execution model. Furthermore, new syntactic constructs stick out like sore thumbs, so they are not easily confused with the old constructs. When Hoare presented his Communicating Sequential Processes (CSP), he did so within the framework of a programming language *shell*, stating that a full language was neither necessary nor desirable for understanding the communication and synchronization aspects of his proposal. Similarly, we can view a logic program as a shell language for exploring parallel processing; but we can also view it as a complete parallel programming language, or we can view it as both, depending on the need.

Lately, my own research interests have involved speculative computation and throttling of parallelism. Even though the concepts and solution techniques are applicable to almost any language (even to C), I have found studying the problems in the realm of logic programming to be the most straightforward and natural. The concepts can be studied with minimal imposition by a programming language, and I can treat the logic programs as parallel processing shells rather than as useful computation (even if they are so). When I present the ideas to others, I sometimes resort to presenting them within C or Pascal or whatever, but when I study them, I mostly study them within logic programming, no doubt about it.

Similarly, this book describes the research of many leading parallel processing experts. The many intriguing, novel concepts presented herein are all presented within the framework of logic programming, from scheduling, to compilation, to algorithm expression, to performance issues. Hopefully, by the time you finish reading this book, you too will be convinced of this superior aspect of logic programming. The fact that the concepts are all presented within the logic programming framework allows you to relax and focus strictly on how the computations are performed rather than on what is being computed. The syntax and semantics will be almost totally dedicated to the parallel portion, not to the sequential.

To narrow the scope of the book, only distributed implementations of parallel logic programming models are presented. However, even with this restricted domain, full coverage is made of nearly all important issues in the field. As you will see, the papers are quite naturally divided into four sets. Each builds upon the others, and so multiple readings of several papers may prove valuable. If you decide that you like one of the proposed parallel computation models, the authors would be very happy; if you decide even further that you like the language, they would be even happier. But that has not been the goal of this book. If, as a result of having studied them within the logic programming arena, we all come to a better understanding of some of the many complex issues inherent in parallel processing, we will *all* be happy.

Doug DeGroot
March, 1992

List of Contributors

Marco Avvenuti
Dip. di Ingegneria dell'Informazione
Universitá di Pisa
Via Diotisalvi, 2
I-56126 Pisa
Italy
marco@iet.unipi.it

Jacques Briat
CMaP Project
LGI-IMAG
46 Avenue Félix Viallet
F-38031 Grenoble Cedex
France
briat@imag.fr

Manuel B. Carvalhosa
Universidade Nova de Lisboa
Departamento de Informática
2825 Monte da Caparica
Portugal

Jacques Chassin de Kergommeaux
CMaP Project
LGI-IMAG
46 Avenue Félix Viallet
F-38031 Grenoble Cedex
France
chassin@imag.fr

Daniel Cohen
Dept Computer Science
Queen Mary and Westfield College
Mile End Road
London E1 4NS
England
dc@dcs.qmw.ac.uk

John S. Conery
Department of Computer and Information Science
University of Oregon
conery@cs.uoregon.edu

Paolo Corsini
Dip. di Ingegneria dell'Informazione
Universitá di Pisa
Via Diotisalvi, 2
I-56126 Pisa
Italy
corsini@iet.unipi.it

James Cownie
Meiko Limited
650 Aztec West
Almondsbury
Bristol BS12 4SD
England
jim@uk.co.meiko

José C. Cunha
Universidade Nova de Lisboa
Departamento de Informática
2825 Monte da Caparica
Portugal
jcc@fct.unl.pt

Xavier de Joybert
THOMSON-CSF/DOI
Parc d'activites Kleber
160 Bd. de Valmy
BP 82 / 92704 Colombes Cedex
France
xj@thcsf.thomson-doi.fr

Laxmikant V. Kalé
Department of Computer Science
University of Illinois at Urbana-Champaign
Urbana, IL 61801
kale@cs.uiuc.edu

Pedro D. Medeiros
Universidade Nova de Lisboa
Departamento de Informática
2825 Monte da Caparica
Portugal
pm@fct.unl.pt

Jean-Jacques Monot
THOMSON-CSF/DOI
Parc d'activites Kleber
160 Bd. de Valmy
BP 82 / 92704 Colombes Cedex
France
jj@thcsf.uucp

Katsuto Nakajima
Computer and Information Systems
    Laboratory
Mitsubishi Electric Corporation
5-1-1 Ofuna, Kamakura
Kanagawa 247
Japan
nak@isl.melco.co.jp

Christian Percebois
Institut de Recherche en Informatique
    de Toulouse
Université Paul Sabatier
118, route de narbonne
31062 Toulouse Cedex
France
perceboi@irit.fr

Luís Moniz Pereira
Universidade Nova de Lisboa
Departamento de Informática
2825 Monte da Caparica
Portugal

Sanjay Raina[†]
Department of Computer Science
University of Bristol
Queens Building
University Walk
Bristol BS8 1TR
England
raina@uk.ac.bristol.compsci
† *Seconded from Meiko Limited
    Bristol, UK*

Balkrishna Ramkumar
Coordinated Science Laboratory
University of Illinois
    at Urbana-Champaign
Urbana, IL 61801
ramkumar@crhc.uiuc.edu

Graem Ringwood
Dept Computer Science
Queen Mary and Westfield College
Mile End Road
London E1 4NS
England
gar@dcs.qmw.ac.uk

Luc Selle
Institut de Recherche en Informatique
    de Toulouse
Université Paul Sabatier
118, route de Narbonne
31062 Toulouse Cedex
France
selle@irit.fr

Nathalie Signes
Institut de Recherche en Informatique
    de Toulouse
Université Paul Sabatier
118, route de Narbonne
31062 Toulouse Cedex
France
signes@irit.fr

LIST OF CONTRIBUTORS

Sergio A. Delgado-Rannauro
Laboratorio Nacional de Informática
 Avanzada, A.C
A.P. 696 Rébsamen 80
91000 Xalapa
Veracruz
México
LANIA01@mtecv1.mty.itesm.mx

Michel Favre
CMaP Project
LGI-IMAG
46 Avenue Félix Viallet
F-38031 Grenoble Cedex
France
favre@imag.fr

Szabolcs Ferenczi
MULTILOGIC Computing Ltd
H-1119 Budapest, Vahot u. 6.
Hungary
h1088fer@ella.hu

Graziano Frosini
Dip. di Ingegneria dell'Informazione
Universitá di Pisa
Via Diotisalvi, 2
I-56126 Pisa
Italy
frosini@iet.unipi.it

Iván Futó
MULTILOGIC Computing Ltd
H-1119 Budapest, Vahot u. 6.
Hungary
h1086fut@ella.hu

Cláudio Geyer
Instituto de Informática
Universidade Federal do Rio Grande do Sul
Av. Oswaldo Aranha, 99
CAIXA Postal 1501
90001 Porto Alegre – RS
Brasil
geyer@vortex.ufrgs.br

Uwe Glässer
Dept of Mathematics and Computer Science
Paderborn University
Warburger Str. 100
D-4790 Paderborn
Germany
glaesser@uni-paderborn.de

Hugh Glaser
Dept of Electronics and Computer Science
University of Southampton
Southampton
SO9 5NH
England
hg@uk.ac.soton.ecs

Tom Hintz
School of Computing
University of Technology, Sydney
P.O. Box 123
Broadway, N.S.W. 2007
tom@socs.uts.edu.au

Matthew Huntbach
Dept Computer Science
Queen Mary and Westfield College
Mile End Road
London E1 4NS
England
mmh@dcs.qmw.ac.uk

David G. Jones
c/o Michael J. Wise
Department of Computer Science, F09
Sydney University, N.S.W. 2006
Australia
michaelw@cs.su.oz.au

Peter Kacsuk
MTA-KFKI
Research Institute for Measurement and
 Computing Techniques
H-1121 Budapest
Konkoly Thege ut 29-33
Hungary
h2633kac@ella.hu

Andrew Verden
Dept of Electronics and Computer
    Science
University of Southampton
Southampton
SO9 5NH
England
arv@uk.ac.soton.ecs

David H. D. Warren
Department of Computer Science
University of Bristol
Queens Building
University Walk
Bristol BS8 1TR
England
warren@uk.ac.bristol.compsci

Michael J. Wise
Department of Computer Science, F09
Sydney University, N.S.W. 2006
Australia
michaelw@cs.su.oz.au

PART I OR-Parallel Implementation of Prolog

The first part of this book is concerned with the OR-parallel implementation of Prolog on distributed memory multicomputers. The concept of OR-parallelism is explained in detail in Chapter 1, which is an overview of OR-parallel computational models. It surveys implementation schemes for OR-parallelism, not just on the distributed memory multicomputers but on shared memory systems as well. After reading Chapter 1 the reader will be familiar with three main approaches of implementing OR-parallel Prolog systems:

(a) Shared Binding Environment model
(b) Closed Binding Environment model
(c) Recomputation model

The Shared Binding Environment model is better suited to shared memory computers and is therefore not thoroughly investigated in this book. Nevertheless a significant representative of the Shared Binding Environment model, the research on Aurora and Andorra-I, is presented in Chapter 2. Performance results from these projects prove that the Shared Binding Environment model is a viable and feasible alternative. However, the limited number of processors in the available shared memory multiprocessors, such as the Sequent Symmetry, restricts the achievable parallelism. The research described in Chapter 2 investigates the possibility of porting the Shared Binding Environment OR-parallel Aurora system and AND-parallel Andorra-I system to a novel scalable shared data architecture, called the Data Diffusion Machine, which represents a step towards distributed memory computers. The Data Diffusion Machine is actually emulated on a Meiko Computing Surface containing 24 Transputers.

Chapter 1 classifies OR-parallel systems according to the way they manage the binding environment. This metric is really one of the most crucial points in the design of a parallel Prolog system. However, another important metric described in Chapter 1 is scheduling, i.e. the way work is allocated to idle processors. This metric has a great influence on the performance of parallel computers and is particularly important in the case of distributed memory systems. In a wider sense scheduling also includes the problem of controlling granularity. This issue is thoroughly investigated in Chapter 3, which describes a Recomputation model based OR-parallel system, called OPERA, implemented on a Supernode computer containing 16 Transputer nodes. In OPERA the scheduler is based on an approximate representation of the state of the system in order to avoid costly synchronisations and to reduce the number of expensive inter-processor messages.

Closed Binding Environment models are particularly important in distributed memory systems. Chapter 4 and 5 describe two projects based on the Closed Binding Environment model. Both approaches originate from Conery's AND/OR process scheme and restrict it by applying only pipeline AND-parallelism instead of independent AND-parallelism. The latter represents a restricted version of real AND-parallelism (see Part II), since AND processes work on partial results of the same resolution in parallel. However, in the case of pipeline AND-parallelism distinct AND processes work on different resolutions in parallel, which is equivalent to a form of OR-parallelism, which is why these chapters are placed in this part of the book.

Chapter 4 explains in detail the principles of the AND/OR process model and introduces an interpreter for implementing the model on a multi-transputer system. The main emphasis is on the problem of implementing a dynamic process creation scheme in a static language environment, like Occam. The Occam code of the OR and AND processes shown in Chapter 4 nicely illustrates the concepts of the AND/OR process model.

Chapter 5 describes a data driven distributed Prolog abstract machine called 3DPAM. The design of the 3DPAM was driven by the basic recognition that the AND/OR process model is a message driven computational model that can be considered as a generalised data driven model. A systematic rethinking of the AND/OR process model from the dataflow point of view resulted in an innovative novel approach to implementing Prolog on distributed memory systems.

The chapters of Part I represent all the main approaches to implementing Prolog systems on distributed memory multicomputers. For beginners in parallel Prolog implementations Chapter 1 is highly recommended as a lead into the field. Readers expert in parallel Prolog systems might find the most interesting path is to browse Chapter 5, which offers a novel scheme for extending the Warren Abstract Machine towards distributed memory systems. Readers particularly interested in applying distributed techniques for the implementation of Prolog might enjoy Chapters 2, 3 and 4.

1 OR-Parallel Logic Computational Models

S.A. Delgado-Rannauro
Laboratoire Nacional de Informática Avanzada, Mexico

ABSTRACT

An important property of logic languages is the single assignment of variables per proof. Thus, to represent multiple bindings, the binding of variables must remain consistent during the execution of each proof. Variable bindings are valid or only hold relative to subtrees of the search space. An efficient OR-Parallel computational model should strive for a clear and efficient distinction of the scope of these bindings.

This chapter reviews the OR-Parallel logic computational models. As part of this review, the different OR-Parallel variable binding schemes are also described. In fact, the OR-Parallel models are classified according to the type of binding scheme. The following section defines the basic concepts of OR-Parallel models; in addition, some metrics are established for the analysis of the different OR-Parallel computational models. In sections 2, 3 and 4, the different models which have been proposed recently are reviewed by the the classification provided in section 1.

1 CONCEPTS AND METRICS

1.1 Concepts

Pure OR-Parallel computation may be represented solely by an OR-tree. The space represented only accounts for relation calls (OR-nodes). The execution of AND-nodes is sequential and is implicit in the OR-tree. A relation call can give rise to several distinct search paths; an OR-node represents a relation call, a downward directed arc in the OR-tree represents an inference step; the mgu of the inference step is related to the directed arc. There are two different types of OR-nodes, non-deterministic and determinate. The determinate nodes represent sequential execution, whereas the non-deterministic ones can represent either sequential or parallel execution. In this OR-tree representation, several directed arcs spring from non-deterministic nodes; whereas only one directed arc springs from a determinate node. Fig. 1 shows a logic program and the OR-trees for two queries.

Note that for the query ?- p(1,2), as shown in Fig. 1(b), only determinate computation exists, and the generated OR-tree therefore contains only determinate OR-nodes. In Fig. 1(a), all the variables in clause p have multiple binding instances. X is bound to $\{1,2\}$, Z to $\{2,3\}$ and Y to $\{3,4\}$. Within the context of OR-Parallelism, variables which can have multiple bindings are named *OR-shared*. A variable is **OR-shared** if it is still unbound after the detection of alternative search paths, i.e. it is to be *shared* by more than one search path.

Assume the program in Fig. 1 is executed in parallel for the query ?- p(X,Y) (Fig. 1(a)) and two processors, P_1 and P_2, each computes a different branch. Their view of

```
p(X,Y):- a(X,Z),b(Z,Y).
a(1,2).
a(2,3).
b(2,3).
b(3,4).
```

A logic program

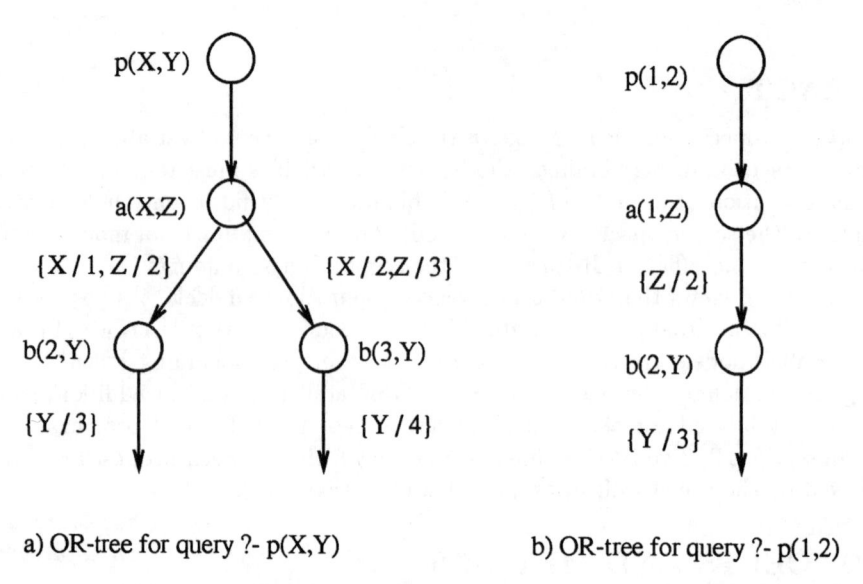

a) OR-tree for query ?- p(X,Y)

b) OR-tree for query ?- p(1,2)

Figure 1: OR-trees for the queries ?- p(X,Y) and ?- p(1,2)

the variables X and Z must be unbound at the beginning of each search path. When P_1 binds X to 1 and Z to 2, those bindings must have their scope restricted to P_1's view of the search space; otherwise, if they were made global then they would conflict with P_2's view of the search space. Therefore, any OR-Parallel binding scheme should strive for an efficient representation of the multiple bindings and a clear distinction of the scope of these bindings of OR-shared variables.

1.2 Metrics

This section presents a series of metrics to analyse the relative efficiency of the models to be reviewed. This analysis aims at discussing common features in logic languages that could affect their performance. The models are discussed in terms of memory usage for variable bindings, dereferencing of terms and scheduling operations. These metrics have been chosen because, due to their abstract nature, they can be isolated from implementation details.

1.2.1 Memory Management. Memory usage has always been an important management issue in any computational model; it is particularly true in models for declarative languages. The high memory consumption in these languages has normally required a garbage collection algorithm to recover the space no longer used. Concerning the evaluation of the memory management for OR-Parallel models, the intention is to discuss the amount of memory required for the representation of the multiple bindings of OR-shared variables. There are other issues related to memory management of an OR-Parallel Logic system, such as the space required at run time for the parallel system, which will not be discussed in this chapter.

1.2.2 Dereference of Terms. Terms must be dereferenced before unification. A reference link of a reference chain is formed while unifying two distinct variables. The constant term dereferencing induces short reference chains at the expense of extra overhead. Empirical studies of Prolog architectures indicate that 99% of the length of reference chains is less than 2 [Tick88c].

In OR-Parallel models, term dereferencing may not show the same behaviour of sequential Prolog. Some OR-Parallel models make the cost of dereferencing higher. Most of the OR-Parallel models use extra data-structures to maintain and represent the multiple variable bindings. These extra data-structures can slightly increase the dereferencing cost of non-shared variables compared to WAM. However, the dereferencing cost of OR-shared variables can be potentially unbound depending on the binding scheme, it can be either constant, proportional to the length of the currently active search path, or proportional to the number of bindings made to the OR-shared variable.

In the present analysis, the metrics for term dereferencing are based on these simple observations: their minimal cost, whether they are constant or proportional to a given data structure.

1.2.3 Scheduling. The last metric to apply in the evaluation phase is the freedom the particular computational model has to allocate idle work to idle processors. The relative freedom of the model for scheduling may be directly influenced by the representation of OR-shared variable bindings, as it will be discussed in the following sections. This freedom of scheduling is important; the more freedom an OR-Parallel model has, the easier is to map it to different parallel architectures; conversely, the less freedom the more it is tight to specific machine configurations. Freedom of scheduling should also be related to the cost of thread[1] switching. The higher the cost, the more constrained for scheduling a given model should be.

1.3 OR-Parallel Computational (OPC) Model Families

Following the tendencies in the reported research, this section presents a classification of the different OPC models. They can be classified as:

- the shared environment family,
- the closed environment family and
- the recomputation family.

The shared environment family arises from developments of the shared binding environment used in sequential Prolog. The closed environment corresponds to mechanisms based on environment copying and the recomputation family on recomputing the search path or selective copying of the inherited computational state of the search path.

---

[1] The term *thread* is used instead of task. Each piece of sequential execution in the search space can be seen as a thread of computation.

2 THE SHARED BINDING ENVIRONMENT FAMILY

These mechanisms are based on the notion of shared environment used in sequential Prolog, i.e. on WAM-based Prolog[Warr83a]. In an OPC model in the Prolog binding style, all the descendant nodes share the parent's environment. When an unbound variable created in the parent's environment is to be bound in any of the descendant nodes, the variable cannot be bound directly because the binding may conflict with the other active descendants. A shared binding mechanism should avoid these conflicting bindings. Each descendant must have a virtual copy of the parent's environment, so that bindings in different scopes cannot be recognised by the descendant nodes.

Most of the shared binding mechanisms have auxiliary data structures, to the WAM, to represent the virtual copy. In those data structures only OR-shared variable bindings are recorded. A Prolog like binding method can be used to detect an OR-shared variable; a variable is OR-shared if it was created before the current non-deterministic OR-node. The names defined in [Warr87b] are used to describe bindings. A **conditional** binding is made when the variable is OR-shared, otherwise the binding is **unconditional**. It is assumed that an OR-shared variable is not overwritten unless this is specified by the binding method.

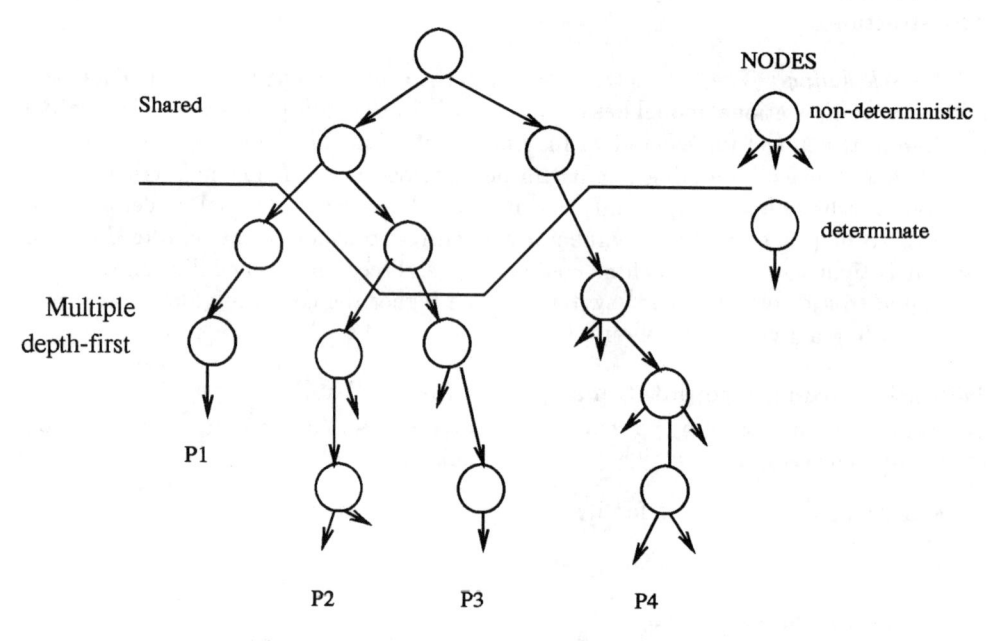

Figure 2: Multiple depth-first execution

The majority of the parallel computational models presented in this section proceed with the execution of the search tree in a multiple depth-first fashion. In this execution model, several processors may be active at same time, each one executing a depth-first search. Fig. 2 represents the execution state of an OR-tree in a parallel machine with four processors. The shared part of the tree represents non-deterministic nodes with no more alternatives left, these nodes are *shared* until the computation in their subtrees is completed. The multiple depth-first execution is being performed by processors P_1 to P_4. P_1 at that moment is performing determinate computation; whereas the others have created non-deterministic computation. The further parallel expansion of the OR-tree will stem from nodes created by processors P_2, P_3, P_4. If there were no requests for parallel execution, the currently unexplored path of the remaining subtrees would be solely computed by the processors which created them. The main reasons for performing the execution in this form are:

- to take advantage of the well-known and efficient compilation techniques developed for sequential Prolog [Warr83a],

- to achieve large thread granularity. Each processor, when active, is engaged in a depth-first search of the inherited path, but taking the necessary provisions for the management of OR-shared variables. As each processor executes its inherited path sequentially, most of the work created may be performed locally by the processor. Consequently, gains in locality of reference are to be expected.

- thus the distribution of work follows a processor demand-driven approach, in which only idle processors seek work. Active processors are only concerned with the computation of the OR-tree search and to produce parallel threads.

In the rest of this section, the multi-sequential execution model is assumed unless it is specified otherwise.

2.1 Directory Trees

Ciepielewski and Haridi [Ciep83a] were among the first to introduce a solution for the management of shared variables in OR-Parallelism. They were also the first to present a detailed account of a memory management model for OR-Parallelism. The inclusion of this model in this classification is rather controversial due to the use of a hybrid scheme. The model has both a shared and a copy mechanism. Since it shares environments it is included here.

In [Ciep83a] a multiple binding scheme, called directory trees, is described. The basic idea is that any term is accessed by a two stage memory model. In the first stage, *environment directories*, are used to access *contexts*, the second stage. Contexts are frames containing terms for a particular OR-node in the tree. The environment directories contain pointers to all the contexts in the current search path (see Fig. 3).

To protect the single assignment property of a shared variable, ancestor contexts (i.e. any context pointed to via the environment directory) with unbound variables are copied to the current directory. Thus bindings to any variable within that context always become local. These contexts are called *uncommitted*. Contexts containing only ground terms are called *committed* and are considered to be shared. Fig. 3 shows the relationship between OR-nodes and their environment directories. Uncommitted contexts, in the figure, are those with U entries; with U representing an *unbound* term.

In the directory tree model, for every OR-node in the tree, a directory needs to be created and initialised. The initialisation procedure is proportional to the depth of the OR-node in the tree, i.e. to the number of relation calls made in the path. Committed contexts are installed by pointing to them, uncommitted contexts are copied and the entry in the directory points to the new copy.

The advantage of this method consists in the fact that access to terms takes constant time, once the directory is fully initialised. The main disadvantage is the excessive usage

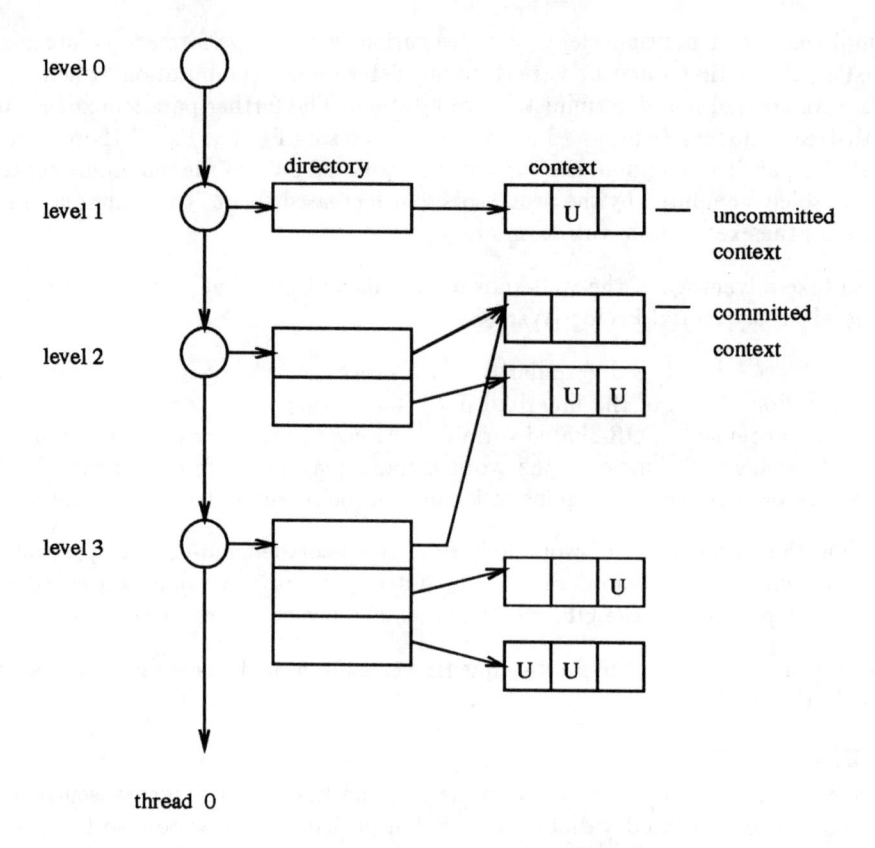

Figure 3: Directory trees

of memory and the time penalty of initialising the directory, when only few contexts are normally accessed per OR-node.

As an optimisation, a demand-driven approach for the management of the directories is proposed [Ciep86a]. It improves the technique described above, by only updating the directory entries on request, i.e. lazy evaluation. The access of an OR-shared variable is no longer a constant time operation. It always starts in the current directory. When dereferencing, if the variable's context pointer is not found, then the pointer is looked up until either the context pointer is found or the context's home directory is reached. In any case, if the context is committed, the context pointer may be placed in all the directories consulted; otherwise a copy of the context is made and only the current directory is updated with the new context.

Discussion: The main advantage of this binding scheme is that it uses a structured form for the addressing of context pointers. The main disadvantage is still the cost of creating directories; even in the demand-driven approach the cost is proportional to the number of contexts used for a particular path. Context copying avoids overwriting variable cells, but increases memory consumption.

In general, the original model has large memory consumption and the locality of reference due to directory initialisation is not high [Cram85a]. Some locality of reference can be gained in distributed memory architectures when the search path is large and a delayed copying of contexts is used [Ciep86a]. The scheduling algorithm would need to be guided to clauses that share most of the directory entries, i.e. contexts with no variables, to minimise the copying costs.

2.2 Hash-Windows

This model uses hash tables as the auxiliary data structures to manage multiple bindings of OR-shared variables. This binding mechanism was developed by [Borg84a], and subsequently used in Argonne National Laboratory's parallel Prolog [Butl86a] and in ECRC's PEPSys [West87a].

In this scheme every non-deterministic OR-node[2] has a hash table or *hash-window* to store the OR-shared bindings. The hash-windows are linked towards the root node, forming a tree of tables. Thus, any processor from any tip in the tree can look up the OR-shared bindings formed in its active search path (Fig 4).

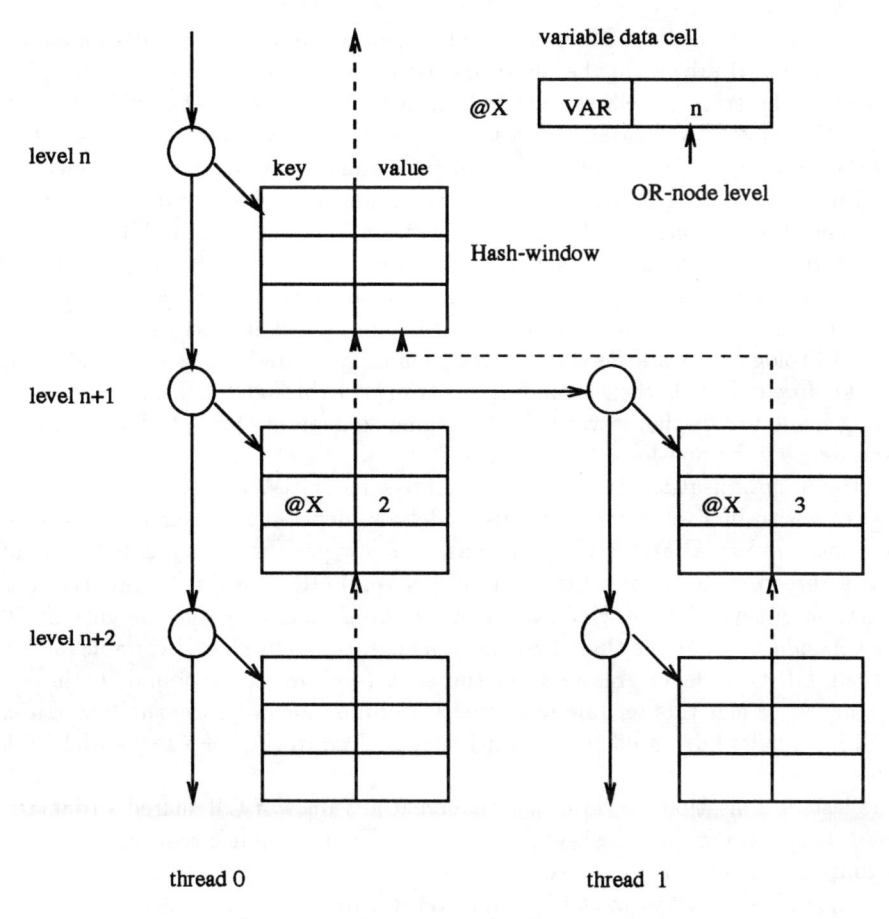

Figure 4: OR-tree with hash-windows

An **OR-node level** is defined to distinguish the scope of the variables, OR-shared

---
[2]Since the opportunities for OR-Parallelism stem from non-deterministic OR-nodes, they will be called simply OR-nodes from now on.

or unshared, (see Fig. 4). The OR-node level represents the depth of the search branch. Each new variable is tagged with its corresponding OR-node level. A variable is OR-shared if its OR-node level is smaller than the current OR-node level. In this case, a *conditional* binding is made through the hash-window in the current OR-node. Unconditional variable binding is made by overwriting the variable cell.

The dereference algorithm for OR-shared variables starts looking for OR-shared variable bindings in the current OR-node's hash-window. If the OR-shared variable binding is not found there, then the algorithm continues looking up in the chain of ancestor OR-nodes until the binding is found or the OR-node level of the OR-shared variable is reached. Assume the current OR-node level is $n+3$ and an OR-shared variable created at level n needs to be dereferenced. The dereference algorithm starts looking at the current level, $n+3$. If the OR-shared binding is not found there, the algorithm looks into the next ancestor level, i.e. $n+2$. This step is repeated until the binding is found or until the hash-window of level $n+1$ has been looked up. If the search through the hash window chain is not successful, it is established that the OR-shared variable is unbound.

A hash-window needs to be created only when a binding to an OR-shared variable is required. However, in the above mentioned simplified model, for most of the OR-nodes in the tree, a hash-window will need to be created. This will render the model inefficient for two reasons: i) a long chain of hash-windows would have to be searched constantly, giving a potentially unbound limit to the dereferencing operation; ii) constant initialisation of hash-windows. Several optimisations have been proposed to overcome these problems and to render the model more efficient and attractive.

In ([Butl86a],[West87a]), the concept of *shallow binding* is introduced within the context of hash-windows. A shallow binding can only be performed to OR-shared variables by the same processor which created them and it follows the same rules of sequential Prolog (i.e. trail the variable upon binding and undo it upon backtracking). A *deep binding* is called when a binding is performed through the hash-windows, i.e. a binding made to OR-shared variables belonging to another thread[3]. These variables are considered to be non-local to the thread.

A further optimisation, found in the PEPSys model [West87a], is to reduce the number of hash-windows created. In this model, the depth-first traversal of the search tree is considered as a *thread*. Only one hash-window per thread is created. The lifespan of a thread could involve the creation of several OR-nodes, therefore saving the initialisation of several hash-windows. The improved model records the current OR-node level, *split node*, at the thread creation time. All the OR-shared variable bindings with their OR-node level greater than the split level are to be found in the local hash-window. When this technique is used in conjunction with the shallow binding, the PEPSys model has an efficiency which comes close to that of a sequential Prolog machine.

The last optimisation concerns the dereferenced values of OR-shared variables. If they are cached in the local hash-window, the dereference chain is reduced further and the locality of reference is increased.

The optimised PEPSys model has, on average, the dereference chain of non-local OR-shared variables proportional to the distance of the last level the variable was accessed. In the majority of cases this is one, the hash-window of the current thread.

---

[3] The term used in [West87a] is *process*. In this context, *thread* is used in order to avoid any confusion with the term *process* used in the process based models.

In [Chas89a] detailed measurements of performance of the PEPSys model were made. These measurements indicate the high locality of reference that the hash-window model yields, over 80% of the hash-window accesses are always local to the hash-window of the currently active thread.

Discussion: In the PEPSys optimised model, the cost of thread creation depends only on the initialisation of the hash-window, i.e on the number of entries per table. The total cost of thread creation increases as the thread granularity of the system decreases, therefore, the size of hash-windows should not be large for systems with a large number of processors[4]. Thus, the memory usage for the management of OR-Parallel environments of the PEPSys model is conditioned by the thread granularity size. Problems with large search space are more efficiently represented with this scheme than, for example, the directory trees, where the amount of memory depends on the depth of the search space rather than on the thread granularity size.

The optimised management of the hash-windows also makes term dereferencing for OR-shared variables nearly constant and highly localised. Although dereferencing is still potentially unbound, its frequency is so small that its effects could be considered close to nil.

This computational model imposes little restriction on a scheduling strategy when performing the search for work, because the inherited OR-shared bindings are only copied as needed. Thus, a demand-driven approach reduces the amount of context required to initiate any given path.

2.3 Binding Array Method

The Binding Array Model was first proposed in [Warr84a] and subsequently used and adopted by the Gigalips project as the SRI-Model ([Warr87b],[Warr87a]), and the BRAVE implementation [Reyn87a].

The management of OR-shared variables in this model depends on two auxiliary data structures. One is global and shared, the OR-shared variable *binding tree*, and the other one is local to each processor, the *binding array*. OR-shared variable cells are not overwritten; conditional bindings are performed with the aid of the auxiliary structures.

Fig. 5 depicts currently active two processors in the OR-tree, the computational state of each processor reflects the execution of a thread.

The nodes in the binding tree have two entries: the OR-shared variable identifier and its binding. A processor making a conditional binding to an OR-shared variable creates an entry in the tip of the current branch of the binding tree. The binding tree resembles the shape of the OR-tree search. Every OR-node in the OR-tree is related to a node in the binding tree. Such relationship indicates the inherited OR-shared variable bindings from the current search path.

Each processor uses the binding array as a cache for OR-shared variable bindings of its current search path. The use of the binding array when it is completely updated makes OR-shared variable access a constant time operation. The binding array of the processor is updated at thread creation[5] with all the inherited OR-shared bindings of the parent OR-node.

---

[4] This same behaviour is expected from all OR-Parallel systems herein described. As soon as the thread granularity diminishes the overhead increases due to parallel computation.

[5] A thread is created when a processor has found available work in the OR-tree, i.e an untried alternative of a non-deterministic OR-node in the OR-tree.

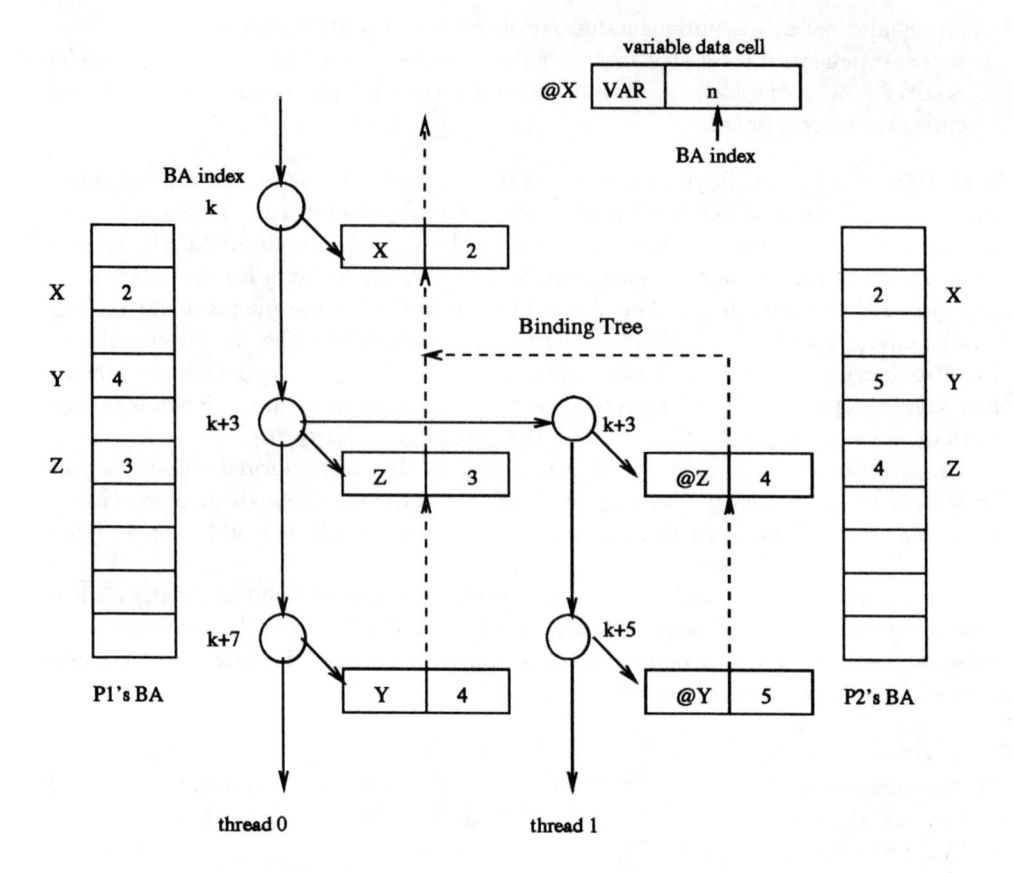

Figure 5: Binding tree and Binding Arrays.

The scope of variables can no longer be detected as in sequential Prolog, simply by comparing the addresses of the variables. Such a model implies a linear relationship between the addresses of the variables in the system. Obviously this cannot be maintained any longer in a parallel environment. Although the space is global and shared, each processor may have a different address space which does not correspond to the seniority rule of sequential Prolog.

Instead, in the binding array model, the index to the binding array is used to detect the scope of variables. The index is used as a time stamp. Every time a variable is created, its value is assigned with an index to the array. At the beginning of the query, the index value is set to zero. The index is increased every time a variable is created. The index is saved in every OR-node to detect the scope of the variable. Then, if the index of a variable is smaller than the index of the OR-node, the variable is declared OR-shared. The index is a time stamp and it is always relative to the root OR-node. When a processor obtains work from an OR-node, it inherits the index from the OR-node.

A *conditional* binding is made as follows: i) the creation of an entry in the binding tree, and ii) the OR-shared binding is installed in the binding array. An OR-shared variable is declared to be unbound if its entry in the binding array is nil. Therefore, the binding array now plays a similar role as the variable cell in sequential Prolog. While backtracking, the untrail operation has to clear the OR-shared variable bindings from the binding array with the aid of the binding tree. The untrail operation in the Binding Array model is an extension of sequential Prolog's untrail operation, the binding tree and the binding array form an extended trail.

The binding array model has several advantages, such as its relative simplicity, a constant access time operation for OR-shared variables and an efficiency very similar to that of sequential Prolog for one processor.

The main disadvantage is the management of the binding array at thread or context switching which, in its simplest implementation, would normally require a complete de-installation of bindings in the array of the current path and the installation of bindings in the array of the new path, i.e. a pseudo-untrailing and a pseudo-trailing operations of the WAM. In order to maintain the constant access time for OR-shared variables, the binding array needs to be completely updated at thread switching. Therefore, to minimise the cost of thread switching, a scheduling strategy that attempts to pair idle processors with work closest to their current state is desirable. Several approaches following such a policy for scheduling have already been implemented, ranging from a centralised mechanism to a pseudo breadth-first mechanism ([Cald89a],[Butl88a]).

Discussion: The management of the binding array at thread switching is the main overhead of the model. A centralised scheduling algorithm [Cald89a] is bound to cause severe bottle-necks as the number of processors increases. The other scheduler [Butl88a] is more distributed and likely to give a better performance in larger machines. In the discussion of the hash-window model it was said that: large parallel systems have smaller thread granularity and, consequently, parallel overheads grow. The same applies to the binding array model. As the system grows, the management of the binding array becomes crucial. Thus, a scheduling algorithm which can minimise the costs of the management of the array at thread switching is essential for an efficient binding array model.

2.4 Time Stamping and Inheritance Binding Mechanism

This mechanism is presented in [Tink87a] as a high-performance Butterfly OR-Parallel Prolog (BOPLOG). BOPLOG's execution model was designed with the following considerations: i) access to local variable cells should be fast, as in WAM, ii) small delays should be permissible for dealing with non-local variable cells, iii) thread set up should be fast, and iv) the access time for a specific value of a OR-shared variable should be proportional to the number of its shared bindings.

The execution model is tailored to be implemented on BBN's Butterfly parallel machine. The Butterfly is a distributed memory machine that has a global addressing scheme; therefore, the execution model attempts to achieve high locality of reference by increasing the accesses to each processor's local memory.

The multiple binding scheme is based on a *time stamp* mechanism to detect the validity of OR-shared variable bindings. The time stamp is spread in the search tree in a similar fashion to the hash-window **OR-node level**. Spawned threads inherit the parent's thread time stamp. However, the management of the time stamp is rather different, it is not increased with every new OR-node. The time stamp is increased by two methods: i) every time an OR-node is created by the thread and ii) every time an alternative is taken from the OR-node. For example, if an OR-node with 3 alternatives is created at time 10, then after all the alternatives have been taken, the current time stamp would be 13. If the thread generates another OR-node, the time stamp is increased further and would then be 14. The child threads inherit the time stamp at the time of the thread migration and use it as their initial time stamp.

Variables are tagged with the current stamp when created. Only local threads are allowed to overwrite variables but their tags must be modified to the current time stamp. Threads are not allowed to overwrite non-local variables since the execution model implies non-local variables to be OR-shared.

An extra data structure is needed to detect the validity of variable bindings, called the *ancestor stack*. This stack is the history of the computation for the current path, and must be made available to the child threads at migration time; it is part of the thread migration procedure. Each entry in the stack consists of the span and the ancestor (thread number). The span is used to detect the validity of bindings made by the corresponding ancestor thread. For example, assuming the following ancestor stack:

thread	span
T_2	0-2
T_3	2-4

Thread T1 is dereferencing a variable created by thread T2. The value cell is tagged currently with time stamp 3, such a binding is invalid since it was made after T2's span.

The lower bound span is determined by the thread migration or by the time an alternative is taken from the current OR-node. The upper bound is the time at which the thread created its next OR-node. Then an unconditional binding is made to variables created within the current span. A conditional binding is made to variables outside the current span.

The conditional bindings of the same OR-shared variable are linked by a double circular list. One loop links the threads which have bound the OR-shared variable and the other one links the conditional bindings made by the same thread, the thread's *local binding list*. Fig. 6 shows the binding status of the OR-shared variables X, Y, Z of the program in section 1. The instances bound by thread T_1 (in processor P_1) were performed at time stamp with value 0. The thread T_2 inherits its current search path with time stamp 1 and all its bindings are recorded with this time stamp.

The time for the dereferencing operation for OR-shared variables in this model is proportional to the number of alternative bindings made to an OR-shared variable. The dereferencing starts from the OR-shared variable address and continues until either a valid binding is found, i.e. it falls within the span of that thread in the ancestor stack or the double linked list is completely searched. In the latter case, the variable is declared as unbound and the current process is allowed to create a new binding entry in the list.

Discussion: This particular binding scheme uses all the global address space extensively. Very little attention is paid to obtain better locality of reference. Although the execution model induces locality of reference, the management of OR-shared variable bindings can increase the number of non-local accesses since most of the double linked list elements may be in other processor nodes. In order to reduce the number of non-local accesses due to the dereferencing of OR-shared variables, a system with remote dereferencing mechanism could be used.

Another disadvantage in this binding method is the synchronisation required for the management of the double circular list. Although the competition for gaining exclusive access to these data structures may not be large, several levels of synchronisation will tend to affect the system's overall performance.

OR-PARALLEL LOGIC COMPUTATIONAL MODELS

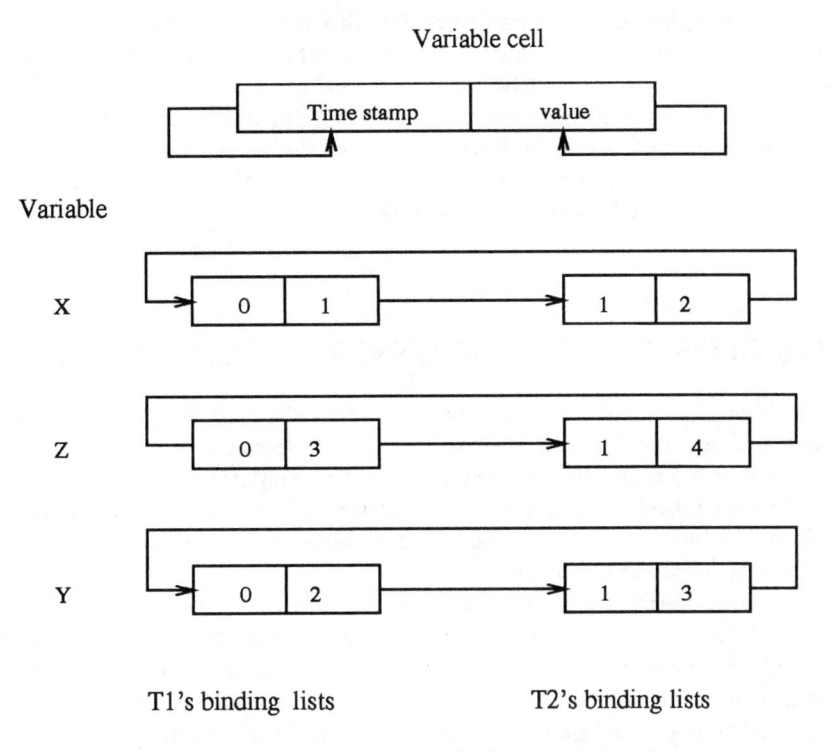

Figure 6: Inheritance Binding Mechanism

An advantage of this method is the relative freedom of the system scheduler to choose the next thread. Indeed, this was one of the aims of its development, but this freedom may not result in any outstanding improvements due to the overheads caused by the dereferencing of OR-shared variables.

2.5 Versions-Vector Binding Mechanism

This mechanism creates a binding environment similar to the binding array, but instead of one array per processor, it uses a vector of instances per shared variable [Haus87a].

The multiple bindings to OR-shared variables are solved by introducing a version-vector per OR-shared variable. Each vector has the same number of entries as there are processors in the system, and it must be accessible to all processors in the system. When the first conditional binding is made to a shared variable a *Versions-Vector* (VV) is created. The variable is tagged as VV and the conditional binding is stored in the processor's vector entry. The rest of the VV is updated with unbound variables. The conditional binding is also trailed as in the binding array model, i.e. in a binding tree.

The problems with this method are very similar to the problems of the binding array model, except that an extra overhead is caused by the need for synchronisation whenever a versions-vector is created; the binding array does not require such a feature for the management of OR-shared variables. The cost of creating the VV increases with the number of processors in the system which, as a side effect, also gives increasingly bad utilisation of the assigned space in the vector. It is unlikely that all the processors in the system would bind the same OR-shared variable.

The same scheduling features of the binding array apply in the Versions-Vector.

In addition to the thread switching overheads, this binding method is more sensitive to different implementations of shared memory machines. The Versions-Vectors can be implemented better on a tightly coupled shared memory machine (e.g. Sequent's Symmetry) than on a distributed memory machine (e.g. BBN's Butterfly). The latter depends more on locality than the former where all the access to shared memory bear the same cost. Hence, the management of the Versions-Vectors may not induce the expected locality in a distributed memory machine.

3 THE CLOSED BINDING ENVIRONMENT FAMILY

The closed binding methods assume a distributed architecture for the underlying computational models. The binding environments to be described in this section restrict the bindings seen by any OR-node while unifying two environment frames. The environments are organised in such a way that all the information needed for unification can be found in two frames. One frame corresponds to the parent environment and the other to the local environment.

These binding mechanisms avoid unrestricted access to environments that occurs in the shared binding environments, where a variable can be directly accessed from any OR-node in the search tree. This unconstrained memory access in distributed architectures, where non-local accesses are expensive and unbound would render such computational models inefficient. On the other hand, if the binding scheme provides isolated and self-contained environments, then most of the accesses will only require the parent environment as its source of external communication, giving the desired locality of reference and independence of computation required for distributed architectures.

The computational model of these closed schemes is process based. OR-nodes are now OR-processes in which the computation of the search tree follows explicit communication during forward and backward computation. Communication is always restricted between parent and child processes. These process models trade self-contained environments for extra computation when compared with the shared binding environments. The extra computation is due to the procedure to isolate the environments. For example, when a goal call is made, the calling environment must be protected against binding its variables (which could be OR-shared) when unifying with the matching clause. Bindings can only be returned to the calling environment, the parent OR-process, after the subtree of the child OR-process has been completed. When the process subtree of the parent is completed it also sends its binding back to its parent and so forth.

Some of the assumptions made in the shared binding family could also hold for these models, such as the way to further increase locality of reference is to attempt a demand-driven scheduling approach. This would imply a pseudo multiple depth-first computation as the overall strategy.

These models allow great flexibility in the design of scheduling operations. An efficiency problem arises in these models if the distance between the processing nodes is not uniform in the underlying architecture. An extra level of complexity is introduced taking this distance into account. Notions of neighbourhood between processing nodes may need to be established in order to achieve the desired load balancing and locality of reference.

OR-PARALLEL LOGIC COMPUTATIONAL MODELS

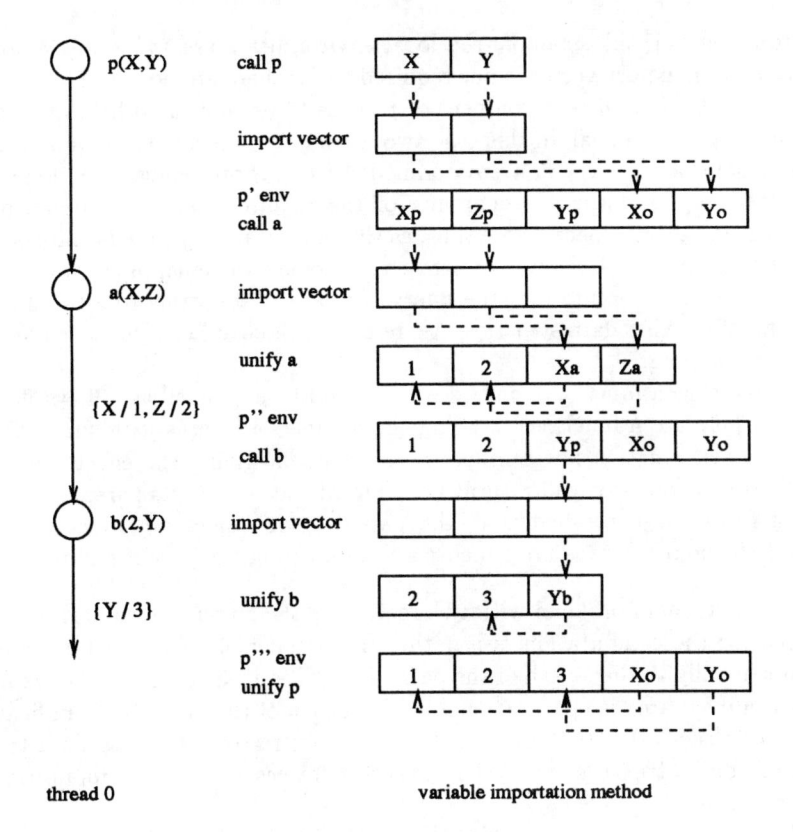

Figure 7: Variable Importation Vector

3.1 Variable Importation Method

With this method developed in [Lind84a], the operations involve forward and backward unification. In forward unification, an argument vector is created for each clause executed. Unification is made between the argument vector of the ancestor goal and of the matched clause. If the ancestor vector is free of unbound variables, no modification of its content is implied by unification. However, if there are unbound variables, an import vector is created. The import vector isolates the variables of the ancestor vector by providing links for each unbound ancestor variable to newly created variables in the local vector. Thus, the unification of the unbound variables in the ancestor vector is achieved via the new variables in the the local vector.

Backward unification takes place when the computation of a body goal is completed. In this method, a new parent frame is created to include the bindings of the solution of the recently completed goal. The remaining unbound variables in the solution are exported, using an export vector. A similar technique to the import vector case is used but now the export vector links the appended variables in the ancestor vector.

Fig. 7 illustrates an example with the logic program given in section 1; it only describes one of the search paths. In this example each variable is annotated as X_i; where i is the environment of the goal i. The annotation means that variable X_i ranges in that environment. After each goal call an *import vector* is created. Each import vector provides links to the OR-shared variables which are appended in the local environment (In this example the local environments are: *p'*, *unify a*, *unify b*). The creation of an export vector is not required, since there are no variables left in the solved goals. Note that the environment of *p* needs to be replicated for every solution being returned per each goal; in this case two extra environments are required, one for each goal. Note that in every new environment *back unification* has been done.

The latter step performs a remapping of the required bindings to continue the exploration of the search space. Note that, as the computation proceeds and gets closer to the root OR-process of the process tree, the amount of remapping grows. This is specially evident if the solution of the query is a large data structure. In addition to the overhead of copying data structures there is also the overhead due to environment copying or remapping.

This scheme has a functional nature which could be explained as follows: for every relation call there are n functions, *n* being the number of clauses with successful head unification. Each function has a different environment giving the effect required for OR-Parallelism. A function call returns its environment back to its parent. Since there could be n functions per called goal, the parent environment must also reflect this functional behaviour which is implemented by replicating the parent environment.

Discussion: The main problem with this method is the amount of environment copying required for the computation of a path. The number of environments copied can grow proportionally to the length of the path. In addition, the operations to remap the path's environment are also proportional to the length of the path (back unification as described in [Wise82a]). Furthermore, there is an extra overhead, the data traffic of the imported data structures created in ancestor frames when the computation is in another processor.

The dereference operations in this scheme seem to be of constant time. However, the binding algorithm depicted indicates only constant access to one level structures. Access to partially instantiated data structures may mean several levels of access to the uninstantiated variables of the data structure. The solution to this non-constant dereference operation is described in the following section.

Apparently this model imposes no restriction on the scheduling of work but, due to the non-constant dereference, it may require a locality biased scheduling algorithm.

3.2 Closed Binding Environments

This method discussed in ([Cone87b],[Kale88a]) is a direct descendant from the variable importation mechanism. Each process sees at any time two frames in which unification is to be performed. The close binding scheme uses less memory space and conceals the environments completely. It achieves by means of a two-pass isolating algorithm. The first pass arranges for the parent process environment to avoid binding any of its unbound variables, and the second pass isolates the unbound variables of partially instantiated data structures.

Memory usage is less due to the elimination of the importing and exporting vectors used in the variable importation method [Lind84a]. With the second pass, dereferencing operations are now done in constant time.

A regular variable referencing mechanism is used, variables are only created in the environment. Partially instantiated data structures have only pointers to the variables in the environment which makes the second pass of the isolating algorithm simple and cheap.

OR-PARALLEL LOGIC COMPUTATIONAL MODELS

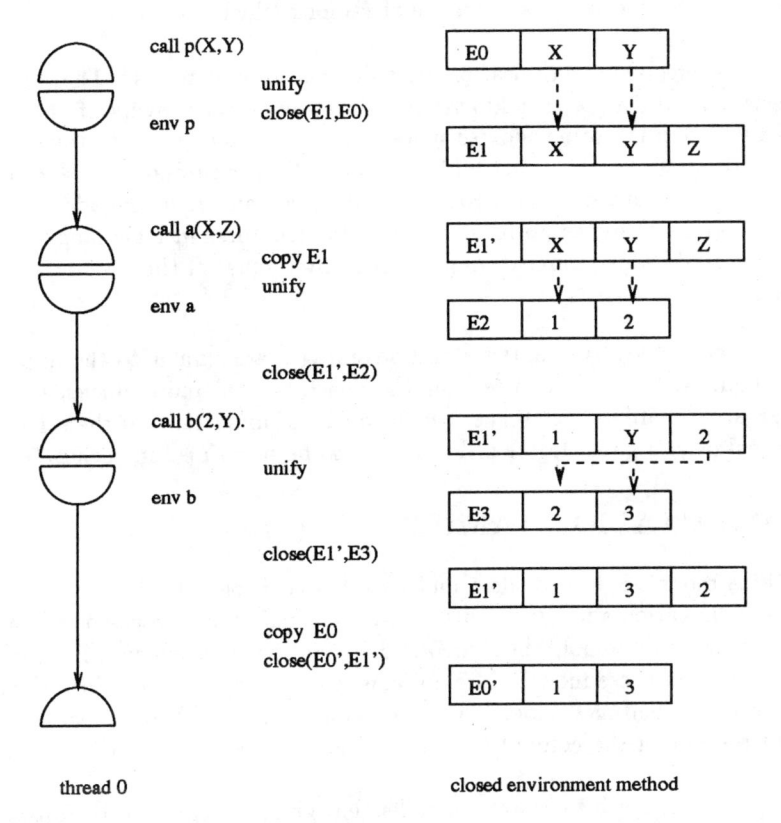

Figure 8: Closed Environment Method

The basic operations made in this method are: (i) to unify a goal g with the head of matching clause c, (ii) to close the environment between the goal g and its matching clause c. In case that more than one clause should match with the goal g, one copy must be made of the environment of g for each matching clause.

The closed environment algorithm ensures that no reference to any other environment exists after unification between two environments. An environment frame is closed with respect to any other frame if there is no reference in the *closed* frame to any other frame.

Fig. 8 illustrates the closed environment method with the logic program given in section 1. In this example only one of the search paths is presented. The environments used for the proof of the query are denoted with E_i where i is the environment number. An environment denoted as E_i' corresponds to the first copy of E_i. In Fig. 8 the environment E_0 corresponds to the query ?- p(X,Y). Initially, this environment is closed since its variables are unbound. After unification and closing the environment, E_1 is closed with respect to E_0 (denoted by close(E_1, E_0)) since there is no reference from E_1 to E_0. When the goal a is called, a copy of E_1 is made to prevent it from being overwritten. The copy E_1' is unified and closed with respect to E_2. Once all the body goals of the clause have been executed, the environment of the called goal, E_0 in this case, is closed with respect to the environment of the clause, E_1. Since there will be several copies of E_1, a copy must be made of E_0 for each closing of the environment to prevent overwriting.

In [Kale88a] there is an optimisation that detects ground terms. These ground terms are assigned with a global address; thus intensive local copying of these data structures is avoided in the same address space. However, copying is not avoided if the ground terms are required in another address space. This optimisation is very useful if the computation is realised in one processor, taking advantage of the address space within the processor. However, in most cases, data structures in logic languages are partially instantiated. Thus, a mayor improvement by the use of this technique is not to be expected.

Discussion: Most of the disadvantages and advantages are similar to the importing variables method, with the difference that the space is used more efficiently. This results in a greater locality of reference, which can be of importance if the scheduling strategy can maintain a good degree of local work to be performed in each processor.

4 RECOMPUTATION FAMILY

The aim of these models is to provide a multi-sequential Prolog machine in which the amount of communication and synchronisation is minimal. Each processor is mapped to the same address space to hold the shared Prolog binding environment. The problem of multiple bindings in these models does not exist since every processor in the system basically executes sequential Prolog. They use, as in sequential Prolog, backtracking as a means of rebuilding the computational state at the previous point in the search space.

The basic mechanism has a central controller that gives directions to the processors for the selection of the proper subtree, i.e. a processor farm. This avoids mechanisms that compete for memory and communication resources. The difference between the models presented in the literature consists in how the controller directs the processors in the system and how recomputation takes place.

A problem of these Prolog systems is how to implement meta-predicates to control the search, e.g. cut, or the implementation of negation as failure. In [Ali87a] a method was presented in which parallelism was restricted to allow for the proper implementation of these Prolog features. In that method the execution of these meta-predicates is semantically similar to Prolog. An implementation without restricting the parallelism may demand the use of a complex synchronisation mechanism.

The scheduling capabilities of these models vary. There is a centralised scheme which can be a potential bottle-neck if there is a large number of processors in the system. If the scheduling operations are rarely needed, then the maximum number of processors can be increased. However, these models seem to be suitable for machines with a few tens of processors, or with larger numbers for very large applications where the amount of parallelism is sufficient to keep the scheduling operations and copying operations, in some of the models, relatively low.

4.1 Prolog Multi-Sequential Machine

[Ali87b] discussed a recomputation method based on a machine with a selective broadcasting communication network. The basic idea of this computational model is that all processors start computing the query concurrently and as soon as OR-nodes are created, i.e. as soon as the processors start computing different paths. Each processor selects its alternative paths without any communication; a specially designed distributed splitting algorithm provides such a feature.

The basic split algorithm ensures that all branches are computed and that all processors are busy whenever there is enough parallelism. There are several possibilities for the split algorithm: balanced, right biased and left biased. The balanced algorithm tries to split the branches almost evenly within the group of processors working in a given subtree. For example, a group of 3 processors create an OR-node with 6 branches, each processor is assigned two different branches and the computation is split forming three different search paths.

The right and left biased schemes mirror each other. Thus, it is only necessary to explain briefly the right biased scheme. The split is made on a processor basis and according to the group size and number of branches of an OR-node. There are three cases for the different values of group size (**g**) and the number of branches (**b**).

- **g > b**: When the number of processors exceeds the number of branches. The first (b-1) processors take one alternative each and the rest forms a new group of size (g-b) with the last branch of the choice point. The newly formed group starts computing the last branch together until another OR-node is found.

- **g = b**: Each one of the processors in the group gets one branch, and starts computing independently the different search paths.

- **g < b**: In this case, the first (g-1) processors get one branch each and the last processor gets the other branches of the OR-node.

The split algorithm uses two local variables to enable each processor to make the correct decision about which branch to select. These variables are the *virtual processor (vp)* number, and the *number of processors (np)* in each group. These variables are set up for all processors at system start up or for a new group every time the Local Manager (the central controller) schedules work to a group of idle processors. In a machine with n processors at system start up, the local variables for each processor$_i$ are given the following values: $vn_i = i$ and $vp_i = n$.

For a newly formed group of size m, the vp of each processor is assigned one value from 2 to m and the np of every processor is set to m. When a processor is working alone in a path, its vp and np are set to 1, i.e. to a group of size 1.

If processors become idle, they report to the Local Manager. They remain idle until a threshold value k is reached. There is no clear definition about which values k can take. It is assumed that it should be directly related to the size of the system and also the size of the program. Correspondingly, a small system will have a proportionally smaller k and so forth. The choice of an adequate value for k seems to have important consequences on the performance of the computational model. A badly chosen k (i.e. a small value in a large configuration solving a small problem) may mean an extreme amount of copying which could deteriorate the performance of the system considerably.

When the number of idle processors has reached k, the Local Manager chooses a busy processor to distribute its environment via the broadcast network. The recipient processors (idle) together with the busy processor form a new group, assigning the corresponding vp and np values before they continue computing together. They follow any of the above described split algorithms for the selection of the independent search space.

The Local Manager makes the decision from which busy processor it is going to obtain work, based on information about the status of the active processors. The information status is based on whether the active processor is in a subtree with untried branches, working alone or in a group. The allocation of work to idle processors in this model, hihgly depends on the value of k, as briefly mentioned in the paragraph above.

Discussion: The multi-sequential approach herein described is expected to perform reasonably well for machines with small configurations, i.e. computation of large granularity. However, as the system starts increasing its configuration the thread granularity will be lower which means an increase in the amount of broadcasts. The Local Manager does not itself represent a severe bottle-neck for this machine but the amount of broadcasting operations can affect the overall performance. Mechanisms which could avoid using the same processor constantly to act as the broadcaster may improve the performance when larger configurations are used.

4.2 The Muse Model

This model is a development of the Prolog Multi-sequential machine described above, and of the BC-Machine [Ali88a]. The **Multi-senquential (MUSE)** Prolog engines model [Ali90a] follows the same basic principles of its predecesors, but the aim is to reduce the copying overhead caused by the non-communicating distributed split algorithms. To minimise the overhead, the Muse model uses both shared and local memory, and an incremental copying scheme. The shared memory is not frequently accessed and is used to hold control frames and globalised OR-nodes. The local memory still holds the working memory of a processor. The incremental copying scheme is used to reduce the amount of copying while scheduling a new thread for an idle processor.

The computation at the beginning of the query proceeds in one processor, say P, the other processors are idle until P creates local OR-nodes. One idle processor, say Q, requests P work. P gives a piece of work to Q by sharing its local OR-nodes as follows:

- For each local OR-node, P creates a global OR-node in the shared space. The global OR-node contains the unprocessed alternatives corresponding to the local OR-node.

- Each of P's local OR-nodes is made to point to the corresponding global OR-node.

- P copies its state to Q; both processors have now identical states and share all the work.

Both processors, P and Q, work in the same subtree to finish the shared unprocessed alternatives (threads). Each processor executes a thread exactly as in a standard sequential Prolog engine. When a processor P creates local OR-nodes and there is an idle processor Q, P makes its local OR nodes shared with Q, as described previously.

The incremental copying scheme is used to make the recipient processor Q keep the part of its state that is consistent with P's state, and only to copy the parts that are different between the states of the two processors.

The scheduling mechanism of the Muse model attempts to minimise the main sources of overhead, these are: (1) copying processor states, (2) making local OR-nodes shareable, (3) taking a piece of work from a shared OR-node (a thread), (4) selecting a busy processor for an idle processor, and (5) selecting a position in the tree for an idle processor.

The scheduling strategy opted in the Muse system is as follows: (a) sharing of work takes several OR-nodes at a time, this maximises the number of shared threads and tends to reduce the copying frequency; (b) threads are released from the bottommost shared OR-node with available work in the current path; (c) an idle processor is responsible for selecting the best busy processor.

The Muse Parallel Prolog system is running on different platforms and operating systems[Ali90a]. The Muse system is based on the Sicstus Prolog system (V0.6). The performance results, on a shared memory multiprocessor machine, show that the average overhead of the Muse system, on a single processor, is 5% of the Sicstus Prolog system (V0.6).

Discussion: The Muse Parallel Prolog system is one of the most advanced OR-Parallel Prolog systems. It has very low overhead compared to a sequential Prolog system. The Muse model has two distinct and important features: (1) an incremental copying scheme between two processors sharing work, and (2) a scheduling strategy that attempts to minimise the overhead and frequency of copying.

4.3 The Delphi Model

This model controls the alternative search paths by a set of bits strings, called *oracles*. These oracles indicate to a processor which path to follow. One of the design goals in this model is that the computational state should not be copied [Cloc86a, Alsh88a]. The oracles provide the information to compute incomplete search paths. A processor, upon receiving an oracle, can generate three outputs: a solution, failure or a new oracle. For the model to work with oracles, the search tree is preprocessed into a binary search tree.

The basic model implies a central controller which sends oracles to idle processors. If the processor generates a partial proof, it reports the new oracle back to the central controller. As the search space is explored, the number of oracles and their size grow. Also their management increases and becomes excessive, it involves the transmission of large oracles and substantial amount of recomputation.

A more practical method has been developed by [Alsh88a]. It uses a bounded-depth backtracking approach in which the amount of recomputation and the amount of transmitted oracles is reduced considerably. A processor follows the oracle sent by the controller. When the oracle is completed, the processor enters in a new phase which adopts depth-first search with backtracking. Whenever a specified depth is reached, the processor sends the generated alternatives, a set of oracle strings, to the controller in order to distribute work to idle processors. At the same time, the processor continues execution in its current search path. If the bounded depth is not reached, the processor declares itself idle.

The bounded-depth backtracking model provides a class of implementation. A wide range of control strategies can be tested with this method. Theoretical studies demonstrate that setting the backtracking depth bound equal to the length of the oracle received from the controller has low recomputation and communication overheads. Furthermore, the percentage of recomputation decreases as the problem complexity and the amount of non-determinism increases. The method has similar characteristics to sequential depth-first iterative deepening [Korf85a] (such as completeness, and efficiency of finding some solution).

The model has been implemented with three methods for the bounded-depth search: *fixed*, *double* and *local*. The fixed bounded-depth sets the depth to a constant value.

This has the advantage of less idle time but at the expense of more recomputation and more oracle communication. The double depth-bound sets the depth to twice the size of the received oracle. The local depth-bound is the same as the double but avoids transmitting the oracles until a local buffer is full.

Discussion: The Delphi computational model has evolved but there is still no clear description of how the load distribution can be made fair. Trying to avoid excessive recomputation and communication of oracles implies reducing the amount of potential work which can be assigned to any idle processor. The main goal is to find the right balance between these two contradictory characteristics which may require substantial experimentation.

4.4 Kabu Wake Model

This method is based on environment copying with selective backtracking to allow processors to compute alternative paths [Kumo86a]. In this model communication is only generated on request. An active processor computes in a similar manner to sequential Prolog. The only difference consists in the handling of OR-shared variables. In this model a time stamp is used to record bindings to shared variables.

Work is only split on request by an idle processor; otherwise a processor computes sequentially. Load distribution is performed eagerly by idle processors selecting their parent processor. Once it has chosen a busy processor to be its *parent*, an idle processor waits to receive the environment it requires for starting the computation of the new path. The parent processor stops computing once it is selected and resumes its computation after the thread has been sent to the child processor. Part of the splitting procedure requires the parent processor to backtrack *'temporarily'* to the splitting point, so that the shared variables bindings created before the splitting point are *'undone'*. In order to recognise the validity of bindings, the system records the binding time in each variable cell. While backtracking 'temporarily', the parent processor untrails the variables according to the recorded binding time. After this pseudo-backtracking the thread is sent to the child processor.

Discussion: This execution model performs well if the thread granularity is large and the amount of copying is minimal. If a program does not generate enough parallelism or its search tree is shallow, the performance of the model can degrade considerably because the constant requirement of thread splitting represents a considerable overhead for busy processors.

The description of the model fails to indicate if there is any decision process for the selection of a busy processor. A disadvantage of this mechanism is the processing time lost by each processor when splitting a thread. It may be better to send the thread first and continue with the computation. This allows the child processor to *simulate* the backtracking by undoing any variable it needs to (Fig. 9).

5 SUMMARY

In this chapter, the different strategies for the management of OR-Parallelism in logic languages have been reviewed. A classification of the field was presented, the different approaches were grouped into three distinctive families: Shared Binding Environments, Closed Binding Environments and Recomputation.

KABU WAKE Model

```
[ c ][  sp  ][ s ][ c ]                    parent processor

[     i     ][ r ][ cn ][c]                child processor
```

MODIFIED Model

```
[ c ][ s ][       c        ]               parent processor

[  i  ][ r ][ cn ][ sp ][c]                child processor
```

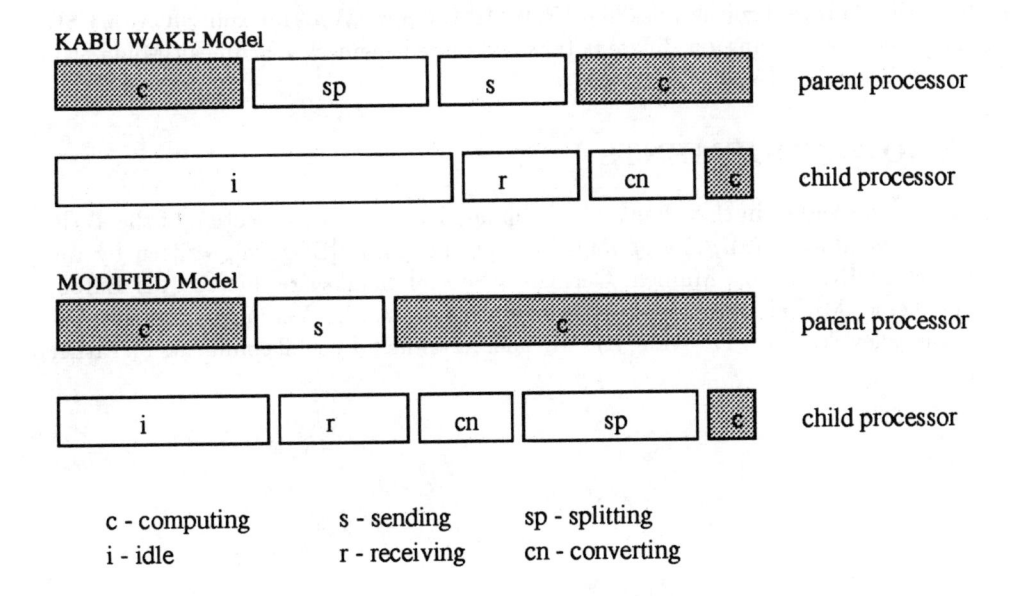

c - computing   s - sending   sp - splitting
i - idle   r - receiving   cn - converting

Figure 9: A modified thread splitting procedure for the Kabu Wake model

The Shared Binding Environment family regards the computation of the OR-tree as shared space. The majority of these models avoid expensive synchronisation for the management of multiple bindings; OR-shared variables are rarely rewritten and auxiliary data structures are used to maintain the different bindings that each OR-shared variable can have. Several implementations based on the Shared Binding Environment approach have been made: the Aurora Prolog by the Gigalips Project ([Lusk88a], [Szer89a]), ECRC's PEPSys ([Chas88a],[Baro88b], [Chas89a]), ECRC's ElipSys [Vero91a] and BRAVE [Reyn87a]. The executing time overhead of these implementations for one processor is about 25% with respect to a sequential implementation of Prolog (running on the same machine).

The Closed Binding Environment family considers the computation as a tree of independent processes where each process has an independent and self-contained view of its environment. The self-contained view is restricted to the active part of the process in the search space. Modifications to this partial view are local to each process; explicit communication is required when this partial view needs to be *shared*. Normally, the process tree is formed by explicit parent-child relationships. Consequently communication is only restricted between these levels of relationship.

The Recomputation models have a different view of the computation of the search space. These models attempt to perform recomputation or selective copying of the search space, instead of having shared or independent views of the search space. The motivations are purely implementational. They try to reduce the amount of communication, synchronisation and more complex binding schemes that are observed in the other two families. The reported overhead of the Muse system due to parallel processing in a single processor is about 5% in [Ali90a].

The stage of development of the OR-Parallel computational models for logic languages has reached its maturity, there are fully operational OR-Parallel Prolog systems, such as the Aurora Prolog [Lusk88a], ECRC's ElipSys [Vero91a] and SICS' MUSE [Ali90a] that are running on different types of shared memory machines ([Muda89a], [Szer89a], [Delg91a], [Ali90a]).

ACKNOWLEDGEMENTS

The review presented in this chapter is an updated version of one section of the Tech. Report *Computational Models of Parallel Logic Languages*[Delg89a], written by the author at ECRC GmbH, Munich, Germany. Special thanks are due to: Uri Baron, Andy Cheese, Michel Dorochevsky, Kees Schuerman, André Véron, Jiyang Xu, Andrzej Ciepielewski, Kam-Fai Wong and Michael Ratcliffe for useful comments on earlier drafts.

2 Parallel Prolog on a Scalable Multiprocessor

S. Raina[†], D. H. D. Warren[†] and J. Cownie[‡]
[†]University of Bristol, UK
[‡]Meiko Ltd, Bristol, UK

ABSTRACT

Shared data access is a natural requirement of parallel Prolog systems that regard the search tree as a large data structure which is cooperatively explored by a number of processing agents. Aurora and Andorra-I are two such Prolog systems that currently run on shared-memory multiprocessors. Currently available shared-memory multiprocessors, like the Sequent Symmetry, have limited scalability. The Data Diffusion Machine is a novel scalable shared data architecture which is characterised by the lack of any physical home location for data items. We describe a Transputer-based emulation of the DDM including a link-based coherence protocol and additional support for synchronisation. Both Aurora and Andorra-I have been ported to the emulator without significant change and, despite emulation overheads, real speedups have been achieved. The results obtained from the emulator so far indicate very low miss rates and modest network traffic in the DDM hierarchy.

1. INTRODUCTION

Parallel Prolog implementations generally regard a search tree as a large data structure with a number of processing agents exploring parts of the tree. The existence of a shared address space is therefore the most natural requirement of such implementations. As a result, many parallel Prolog systems have been implemented on physically shared-memory machines [Baro88b, Lin88b, Lusk88a]. Typically, such machines only scale up to a limited number of processors. Implementations on distributed memory machines, which are considered to be generally scalable, also regard the tree as a large data structure which is partitioned and distributed amongst the processors' local memories. Access to shared parts of the tree is enabled by copying portions of the tree from the address space of one processor to that of another. This clearly means additional burden on the programmer. We believe that no more should be expected of programmers than what they are best at - i.e. writing correct, efficient programs. The control and harnessing of parallelism should be left to the combination of the underlying model and the hardware that it is implemented on. The only noticeable difference that the programmer should experience is the speed of execution.

The requirement of a shared address space need not imply that the underlying hardware should have physically shared-memory. All that is required is a virtual address space that is directly accessible (via some abstraction) to all the processing agents or *workers*. The actual mapping of a data item from this virtual space to a physical location should be handled by hardware automatically and dynamically. The programmer or the software, therefore, has no control on the physical placement of data.

In this paper we describe an architecture called the Data Diffusion Machine (DDM) [Warr88a] that fulfills such requirements, i.e. it provides a shared virtual address space and at the same time is arbitrarily scalable. It localises communication by physically moving data to where it is needed. The DDM is intended to be a general purpose architecture, however, it is particularly suited to applications whose data referencing behaviour follows a write-once-read-many-times pattern and is capable of exploiting the good temporal locality offered by the DDM.

In this paper we describe a Transputer-based realisation of the DDM and discuss how existing shared-memory implementations of two parallel Prolog systems, namely Aurora and Andorra-I, have been run on such a platform without any significant change. We present results that confirm the suitability of the DDM for both Aurora and Andorra-I, which exhibit low miss rates and low traffic ratios in the DDM hierarchy. We also present results that show that despite the software overheads of emulation we can achieve real speed-ups on the Transputer-emulated DDM.

2. PARALLEL PROLOG IMPLEMENTATIONS

A large number of execution models and implementations of parallel Prolog are in existence today. Aurora and Andorra-I are two recent prototype systems that transparently exploit parallelism in Prolog programs. The following two sections give an overview of each of the two systems.

2.1 Aurora - An Or-parallel Prolog System

Aurora [Lusk88a] is an or-parallel Prolog system based on the SRI model [Warr87a]. It supports full Prolog including cut and side-effects. The SRI model involves cooperative exploration of a Prolog search tree by a collection of workers. Each worker explores a portion of the search tree, extending (thus creating more tasks for workers to explore) and contracting the branches. Whilst executing a task, a worker behaves very much like a sequential Prolog engine, creating bindings and backtracking as it goes along within the subtree. Branches common to the subtrees of workers are shared between the workers. Each worker keeps record of shareable bindings in a *binding array*, giving immediate access to to the binding of a variable. The basic Prolog operations of binding, unbinding and dereferencing are constant-time operations just as in Prolog with little overhead. The only major overhead incurred is when a worker switches its context to a different part of the tree — the binding array has to be updated in accordance with the movement of the worker. The system consists of two components - the *engine* and the *scheduler*. The prototype system currently runs on a number of shared-memory multiprocessors including Sequent Symmetry and BBN Butterfly.

2.2 Andorra-I - Combination of Dependent And and Or-parallelism

The Andorra-I system [Cost91a] is based on an extension of the SRI model called the Basic Andorra Model where, in addition to or-parallelism, goals can be executed in and-parallel as soon as they become determinate. In Andorra-I workers are grouped into teams with each team exploring a different or-branch. Inside a team, workers explore the branch in and-parallel. Andorra-I also uses the concept of binding array to provide fast access to variable bindings. However, unlike Aurora, a binding array is shared by the members of a team. In addition to the binding array, each team also contains a run-queue to support and-parallel execution by the members of a team. The scheduler is responsible for the appropriate matching of tasks to available workers. A prototype of Andorra-I currently runs on the Sequent Symmetry multiprocessor.

3. MIMD MULTIPROCESSORS

A variety of MIMD multiprocessors are currently available. These range from the small-scale Uniform Memory Access (UMA) architectures like the Sequent Symmetry and Encore Multimax to larger-scale Non-Uniform Memory Access (NUMA) systems like the BBN Butterfly and IBM RP3, so classified because of the nature of their access to remote data. Both types, however, have the capability to access common memory. In contrast to shared-memory systems, distributed memory machines like the Intel Hypercube and Transputer-based multiprocessors do not provide the processors with the capability of accessing any remote memory directly. Instead, data movement is achieved explicitly via message passing.

3.1 The Dichotomy of Shared Memory vs Message Passing

The debate over shared-memory versus distributed memory is a long standing one. Shared memory machines are ultimately limited in their scalability due to the common interconnect bandwidth bottleneck. They, however, do relieve the programmer of the burden of explicit coordination and management of data. Since processors communicate (implicitly) in a single address space, data can be passed by reference.

Distributed memory systems are generally scalable and hold promise for building large scale multiprocessors. However the existence of multiple address spaces necessitates additional work from the programmer to provide for the movement of data. The programmer has to be aware, at all times, of the layout of the application code and data across the processors.

3.2 Shared Virtual Address Space

As far as the software is concerned an address is an entity that identifies a data item. The physical location of the data is irrelevant to the software. Shared physical memory machines as well as uniprocessors hide the physical location by providing some translation mechanism from a virtual to a physical address. This translation is often determined by the operating system and/or additional hardware and is quite rigid. However we believe that (especially in multiprocessors) this mapping from the virtual address of a data item to its physical location should be dynamic and sensitive to the data referencing demand of the application software. In particular, the mapping should be such that the data is located close to where it is most in demand, instead of being located at a fixed position for the entire duration of the program run.

As mentioned earlier, the actual physical organisation of the hardware is immaterial so long as the software can perceive the architecture as a collection of processes with global access to a single address space. Indeed most existing shared-memory machines provide this view *directly*. However, it is possible to facilitate this even on hardware without any physically shared-memory with the help of a layer of abstraction (software, hardware or a combination of both). This results in a combination of the benefits of both shared-memory (i.e. programability) as well as distributed memory (i.e. scalability). The address space is a single coherent one that is physically distributed amongst processors and each processor's local memory behaves rather like a cache even though there is no common memory. Typically, each local memory contains a subset of the entire virtual address space at any given time. Memory controllers on each node ensure coherence of replicated data as well as mapping between physical and shared virtual addresses.

3.3 Data Consistency

The existence of multiple copies of data items raises the question of data coherence. The problem is similar to the multi-cache consistency problem as found in most cache-based multiprocessor systems. The latter has been an area of active investigation in its own right [Arch86a]. The problem of coherence is essentially to ensure that a reference originating from anywhere in the network is returned the most recently modified copy of a data item. Cache coherence is maintained between various cached copies and the main memory copy by tagging blocks of memory with state information. Using the state, a protocol then ensures that an update to a data item is reflected everywhere else (other caches as well as the main memory). On a write, cache coherence protocols either invalidate all other cached copies (write-invalidate) or broadcast the update to all other caches (write-update). The former generates less network traffic [Arch86a] and helps to distribute data (only) where it is needed. Protocols are also classified as either snoopy or directory-based. Snoopy protocols rely on a broadcast medium of interconnection (e.g. a bus). All coherence transactions are visible to all the caches as well as the main memory. Such protocols can be seen in most bus-based shared-memory machines today. Directory-based protocols [Chai90a] on the other hand maintain a map (centralized or distributed) of cached items, and transactions are directed rather than broadcast. Such protocols are suitable for general interconnection networks that do not have the broadcast capability.

4. RELATED WORK ON SCALABLE ARCHITECTURES

At present a number of researchers are investigating scalable architectures utilising cache-coherency techniques to provide a shared address space on essentially physically distributed hardware. Some of the proposals include the Stanford University DASH multiprocessor project [Leno90a], the MIT J-machine [Dall89a] and Li's shared virtual memory proposal [Li89a]. The DASH multiprocessor consists of a number of processing node clusters connected via an interconnection network and features a distributed directory-based coherence protocol. The J-Machine consists of a 3-D mesh network of processing agents and efficient message communication and buffering mechanisms to support multiple programming paradigms including shared-memory, actors and dataflow. Li's proposal consists of page-level implementation of shared virtual memory and has been implemented on a hypercube. The DDM, described in detailed in the next section, differs from most related approaches in that the virtual address of data is completely decoupled from its physical location. The data has no single home location and is constantly migrating. Also, unlike many other proposals, the DDM has a hierarchical physical organisation.

5. THE DATA DIFFUSION MACHINE

The Data Diffusion Machine [Warr88a] is a scalable multiprocessor architecture that offers a shared virtual address space. The address space is truly shared in that shared-memory applications can be ported to the DDM with no change. The address space is also virtual in that memory is physically distributed across different processors.

In the DDM a datum has no fixed home location and the virtual address is completely decoupled from its physical location. Where data resides at any given time is entirely dependent upon where it is most in demand. Copies of data with the same virtual address can co-exist in different parts of the machine and a request to a data item will return its nearest copy. Communication due to data access is thus localised only in the parts of the machine that are actively using the data.

The hardware organisation of the DDM is hierarchical as shown in Figure 5.. At the tips are the *worker* processors, each with a large, local set-associative memory. This is the sole form of main memory in the system. The memory is connected to the local bus via a *memory controller* and the local bus is connected to a higher bus

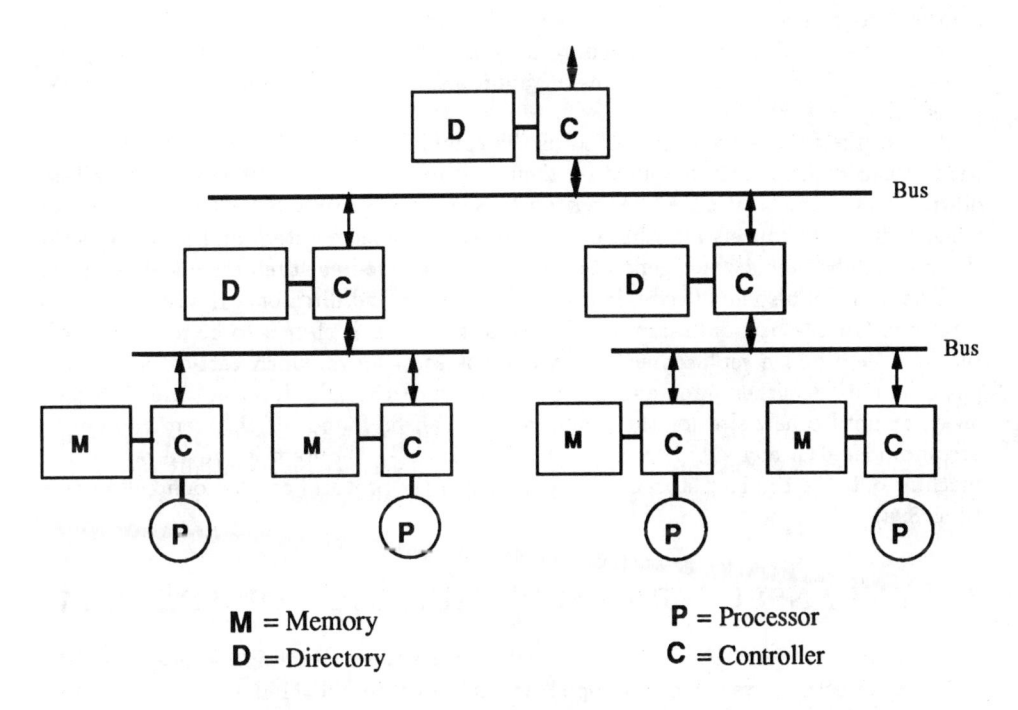

Figure 1: Hardware organisation of the DDM

via a *directory controller*. The directory controller also has access to a set-associative directory. The root-directory has a disk attached to it which holds overflow data (not shown in the figure). The machine can be arbitrarily scaled by increasing the number of levels in the hierarchy. The unit of data storage is an *item*, the size of which is fairly small (of the order of a few words). A directory stores state information for the items in the subsystems below it. The existence of multiple copies of data requires the consistency of data to be maintained. A write-invalidate protocol ensures consistency by allowing multiple readers and a single writer for an item of data.

Most references generated by a processor are satisfied by the local memory. Non-local accesses are propagated on higher buses until another memory responds to the request. As a result, data is fetched from the nearest memory that holds a copy and communication is limited only to the parts of the machine where the data exchange is taking place.

5.1 Cache Coherence Protocol of the DDM

The cache-coherence protocol of the DDM is a hierarchical snooping protocol based on write invalidation [Hage89a]. Read accesses result in replicated data items whereas write accesses require that all other copies be erased before the value can be updated. The protocol is implemented by associating a *state* with each item which determines whether the item is the only copy (*exclusive*) or one of several copies (*shared*).

An item can be non-existent (invalid), the only copy (exclusive) or one of many copies (shared). Besides these *stable* states an item can be in one of the transient states while waiting for a response. Read and write accesses from the application are turned into *read* and *erase* transactions. These are responded to by *data* and *exclusive* transactions respectively. Other transactions (e.g. *inject, out, leave etc.*) are used for replacement. The protocol is enforced by a controller which watches (snoops) the transactions above and below, makes the appropriate state change and forwards a new transaction.

One of the features of the protocol is the combining of multiple reads to the same item. Read requests are combined on their way up, and read responses on their way down. The protocol also handles write-race conditions correctly. The first erase to reach a directory cancels all other erase requests to the same item and proceeds with the erase. Subsystems which generated the other erases re-issue their erase transactions.

The protocol also handles replacement in memory and directory. If a set that is to accommodate the new data item is full, one of the items is chosen to be replaced with the new item and a replacement transaction is sent above which carries on moving upwards until it either finds another copy, in which case the item is simply thrown away, or until a new site for the replaced item can be found. If the item cannot be accommodated in any subsystem (i.e. all sets are full), the item is moved out of the machine onto a secondary storage. More details of the protocol can be found elsewhere [Hage89a].

6. A TRANSPUTER-BASED EMULATION OF THE DDM

As part of our efforts to realise and evaluate the abstract design concepts of the DDM architecture, we have developed an emulator on the Meiko Computing Surface - a Transputer-based multiprocessor. The emulator is intended to run existing large shared-memory applications, modelling the functionality of the DDM closely and efficiently. In this section we describe the design and implementation of the emulator.

6.1 Objectives

The techniques for performance evaluation of an architecture range from hardware monitors to simulation and analytical modelling. A discussion on existing methods of performance evaluation appears in [Stun91a]. Hardware monitors can be highly accurate but have the drawback of inflexibility and high cost. Software simulators are generally trace driven and simulate the hardware characteristics of the architecture in software. Such schemes are highly flexible but lack the accuracy of hardware tools. Analytical models are driven by synthetic address traces and are only suitable for a shallow indication of the performance of the system. The last category, multiprocessor emulation, though less widely used [Rain90a, Sven90a], combines the accuracy of hardware based techniques and the flexibility of software techniques.

In order to evaluate the DDM and study its characteristics a uniprocessor simulation may seem sufficient. However, while a simulator is necessary for studying the detailed behaviour of a specific hardware realisation, it is likely to be limited in terms of performance, size of the machine and applications that can be simulated, and in the accuracy with which the timing of events (such as locking) is modelled. We feel that an emulator on a multiprocessor, on the other hand, will enable us to get a clear picture of the overall behaviour of a full-scale DDM running real applications. An emulator, therefore, can provide us with an accurate realisation of the DDM, close to a hardware realisation, and yet be flexible enough for observing the behaviour of the machine by allowing certain system parameters to be varied.

6.2 Design of the Emulator

The original conception of the DDM and its snoopy cache-coherence protocol assumed that members of a subsystem are connected to a higher level directory by a bus. However the functionality of the bus is only to provide a means of interconnection in the hierarchy and is by no means indispensable. A general purpose multiprocessor like the Transputer-based Meiko Computing Surface gives us the opportunity to consider alternative interconnect media (i.e. point-to-point links, in our case) to replace buses in the DDM. Moreover, rather than simulate the functionality of the bus (and consume link-bandwidth) a more efficient and equally realistic representation of the DDM is possible if a link-interconnect is assumed instead of a bus-interconnect. This involves a modification of the snoopy protocol to cater for links instead of buses.

6.2.1 A Link-based Protocol As mentioned earlier, coherence protocols are generally divided into two classes, *snoopy* protocols and *directory-based* ones. With the advent of bus-based shared memory machines, snoopy protocols have become prominent. However, for machines based on point-to-point interconnections, directory-based protocols are more appropriate. Accordingly, we have modified the snoopy protocol of the DDM to give it a directory-based flavour. In the modified protocol transactions are *directed* rather than *broadcast* thus eliminating the snooping and broadcast overhead. The memory protocol (at the caches) remains the same as the original protocol, however the protocol at the directory level is significantly different. It is essentially an approximation of a full map directory coherence scheme [Chai90a, Cens78a]. Such a modification results in better utilisation of the Transputer links by eliminating superfluous traffic generated if the snoop and broadcast capability of the bus is modelled.

In the link-based protocol, distinction is made at each directory, between the *stable* and *transient* states of an item. An item is in a transient state if there is a request outstanding for it; otherwise it is in one of the stable states. A bit-vector is associated with each type of state, where each bit corresponds to a memory/directory below (see figure 2). Whenever the directory-controller receives a transaction, the bit-vector helps

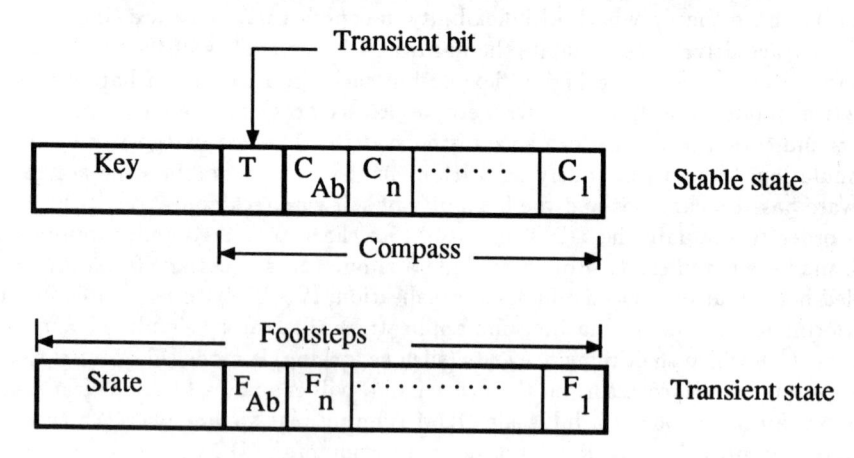

Figure 2: *Directory entries*

resolve which link the new transaction should be sent on. The stable- and transient-state bit-vectors are referred to as *compass* and *footsteps* respectively, where the least significant bit corresponds to the first (rightmost) sub-system below. Thus the ith bit in the bit-vector corresponds to the ith subsystem below (from right to left). For a directory with n sub-systems below, the $n+1$th bit (C_{Ab} and F_{Ab} in figure 2) indicates the status of the item outside the sub-system. The most significant bit in *compass* (called the transient-bit) indicates whether the item is in stable or transient state where the most significant bits (2 bits in the current implementation) in *footsteps* encode the transient state. To illustrate the mechanics of the protocol, let us go through an example. Consider a subsystem with three leaf processors P_1, P_2, and P_3 and a directory D. Suppose the P_1 tries to read an item which is present in P_3 (and nowhere else), then the initial state of the item in memories and directory is given by:

$$P_3 :: EXCLUSIVE;\ P_2 :: INVALID;\ P_1 :: INVALID$$

$$D :: compass = \langle stable, 0, 1, 0, 0\rangle,\ footsteps = \langle\rangle$$

After receiving the read transaction from below the directory changes the state of the item to :

$$D :: compass = \langle transient, 0, 1, 0, 0\rangle\ footsteps = \langle READING, 0, 0, 0, 1\rangle$$

It forwards the *read* to P_3 and asserts the transient state as *reading*. Subsequently, P_3 will reply with a *data* transaction after changing the item state to *SHARED*. The directory now remembers which processor had generated the read and forwards the *data* transaction to P_1. The resulting state of the item will be as follows:

$$P_3 :: SHARED;\ P_2 :: INVALID;\ P_1 :: SHARED$$

$$D :: compass = \langle stable, 0, 1, 0, 1 \rangle,\ footsteps = \langle \rangle$$

Notice that no more traffic is generated than is necessary to perform the state changes. P_2 carries on uninterrupted without ever knowing about the exchange of transactions between P_1 and P_3. This would not be the case if snooping were modelled.

We also hope to explore the possibility of combining the link and bus-based schemes to provide a hybrid interconnection topology for the DDM in order to overcome the problem of saturation in higher-level buses. The bandwidth and size requirements of buses and directories will be greater as one goes up the hierarchy creating potential bottlenecks in the top part of the DDM. To avoid this problem buses can be split at higher levels with different buses handling different parts of the address space. The same effect can be achieved by splitting links provided the race-free nature of the network is preserved (e.g. by time-stamping transactions).

6.2.2 Synchronisation Support In order to run shared-memory programs, it is imperative to provide some form of synchronisation primitives in addition to the basic protocol. A large number of shared-memory multiprocessors provide spin-locks as a basic synchronisation primitive to guarantee mutually exclusive access to critical sections. Typically an atomic or indivisible instruction reads and updates a memory location (i.e. a lock), inhibiting simultaneous attempts by other processors to acquire the lock. While a lock is held by a processor, other processors simply busy-wait until the lock is relinquished.

The rationale behind spinning is that most current parallel machines are used to run applications in essentially rigid environments with reasonably small critical sections. In such situations spinning is favoured because the waiting processors usually have no other work to do and the cost of switching tasks is far greater than the gain in utilising the small duration of the critical sections. However, processors with fast context switching are becoming increasingly popular and, as parallel processing matures people, will want to run multiple applications on multiprocessors. So as the spin-time becomes increasingly run-time dependent and processors with fast context switches become widely available, spin-waiting may be replaced by block-waiting.

As far as our experimental set-up is concerned, the choice of block-waiting over spinning is almost a necessity since each Transputer is running a controller process (which could use the processor cycles otherwise wasted in spinning) alongside the application. Fortunately the Transputer also has a very fast process switch $\approx 1\mu sec$ [INMO88b] as very little state needs to be saved. So, block-waiting is more suitable for a system based on Transputers.

A `test-and-set` operation is an example of an atomic instruction that acquires a lock. Spinning on pure `test-and-set`, as implemented on commercial bus-based multiprocessors like the Sequent Symmetry, generates excessive bus traffic because the lock value is modified irrespective of the availability of the lock. An optimisation of spinning on a read before attempting to `test-and-set` (known as `test-and-test-and-set`) has found its way into most commercial multiprocessors in existence today. It, however, cannot prevent the burst of transactions that results whenever a lock is released and several processors attempt to do a **test-and-set** simultaneously. The excess traffic generated is due to the processors trying to acquire the lock with all but one competing to update the lock unsuccessfully on each lock release. The traffic generated due to such write-competition can be $O(n^2)$, for an n processor system.

To alleviate the problems of simple test-and-set synchronisation, several improvements to the basic spin-locking algorithms have been proposed in the literature [Ande90a], with the intent of reducing network bandwidth consumption and contention. Such algorithms invariably result in increased software and/or hardware complexity.

Our synchronisation protocol is an extension of the basic emulator protocol and is implemented with additional transactions (i.e. **lock** and **unlock**) and transient states (i.e. **lock_waiting** and **lock_promised**). The mechanisms are similar to the locking extensions of the snoopy DDM protocol. The main characteristic of the locking mechanism is that at any given time only one (exclusive) copy of the lock item is allowed to exist and, instead of the processors repeatedly trying to acquire the lock (and all but one failing), the above directory keeps a record of the requests and satisfies them one by one.

As a directory receives lock requests from below, it keeps track of the subsystems that requested the lock (with the help of *footsteps*, cf. section 6.2). When a processor receives a lock request from above, it can either forward the item above and erase its local copy (if the item is **unlocked**), or change the state to **lock_promised** (if the the item is **locked**), indicating that the lock item will be granted above as soon as an **unlock** is received. When a directory receives a response to a lock request, it arbitrates and selects one of the waiting subsystems to give the lock to. If there happens to be more than one subsystem waiting, the directory keeps the state as **lock_waiting** and waits for a response to arrive from the most recently selected system. The advantage of such a scheme is that, unlike a normal exclusive ownership operation, no invalidations need to be sent and the heavy competition for the lock is reduced by the directory controller.

Replacement of lock items is handled just like ordinary data items. As a result, a lock item while in **lock_promised** state may be moved to a processor other than the one which acquired the lock. In such a case the lock will be released on receipt of an **unlock** from above (the lock-holding processor) rather than from below (the lock hosting processor).

The $O(n^2)$ traffic is a feature of not only locking operations, but in general any situation with heavy write contention (e.g. barrier synchronisation). In future we plan to extend the locking mechanism described above into a more general *exclusive read* operation which will help reduce the burst of traffic due to write-contention.

6.2.3 Coupling Applications to the Emulator New architectures are often evaluated using simulators, rather than the direct emulation approach that we have adopted. Simulators are usually trace-driven, operating on address traces as input. A number of techniques exist for generating address traces, e.g. hardware monitoring, microcode modification and program instrumentation. One of the problems with trace-driven techniques is that address traces tend to be excessively large. Trace filtering and compaction schemes alleviate this problem but result in lower accuracy. Accuracy is also impaired by the fact that in simulating multiprocessor architectures , address traces by themselves cannnot capture the non-deterministic information like acquiring /releasing a lock. Such information has to be additionally fabricated. An alternative to trace-driven simulation is execution-driven simulation where an application program (i.e. the trace-generator) is run alongside the simulator. Such a technique reduces the storage requirement and improves the accuracy of a simulator.

Compared with simulation approaches, DDM emulator is execution-driven and is closely coupled to the application program. The coupling between the application and the emulator is achieved by augmenting the assembler source of the application before generating the object code. The augmented code then calls the emulator on every shared-memory access. Identifying the instructions that can access shared-memory is easier than it might appear at first sight due to the simplicity of the Transputer instruction set [INMO88b]. Memory accesses are either *local* - relative to the *workspace pointer* or *non-local* - relative to the A register. Non-local access instructions are used to access variables with non-local scope with the help of static links. Since the scope of shared-memory access never includes local accesses, the instructions that can potentially access shared-memory are:

- ldnl
- stnl
- move
- lb
- sb

There are also some floating point instructions that fall into this category.

We perform program instrumentation by replacing the occurrences of the above *non-local* memory access instructions by code that transfers control to the emulator, prior to actually performing the access. Figure 3 shows a snapshot of the instrumented program and how it calls the emulator. It must be noted that library routines do not go through this mechanism. An augmented version of the C-library has been developed which needs to be linked with any application that is to run on the emulator.

The disadvantage of the above technique is that it is sensitive to the way a particular C compiler generates code. Any change in code generation strategy means that the set of replacement instructions for those listed above will have to be changed. The other problem is that of efficiency. The emulator is slowed down on *all* occurrences of the above instructions, even though, some of these occurrences they can never access the shared address space. By careful analysis of the program some of these transformations can be avoided.

6.3 Implementation on the Computing Surface

A version of the emulator on the Computing Surface and is now operational. It uses an augmentation program that transforms the original source of the application and a configurer have been implemented. As shown in figure 4 the source is first compiled to generate assembler code which is then instrumented and fed to the configurer which in turn loads it together with the emulator onto a network of Transputers.

6.3.1 The Meiko Computing Surface and its Software Development Environment The Meiko Computing Surface is a general-purpose distributed-memory multiprocessor computer that consists of a modular, reconfigurable array of Transputers. The Computing Surface at our site is currently populated with 24 processors in all. Each T800/20 processor is rated at 10 MIPS with cycle time of 50 ns and memory cycle-time of 200 ns. Each processor also has 4 Mbytes of on-board memory and 4 links that operate at 20 Mbits/sec.

Instrumented application program

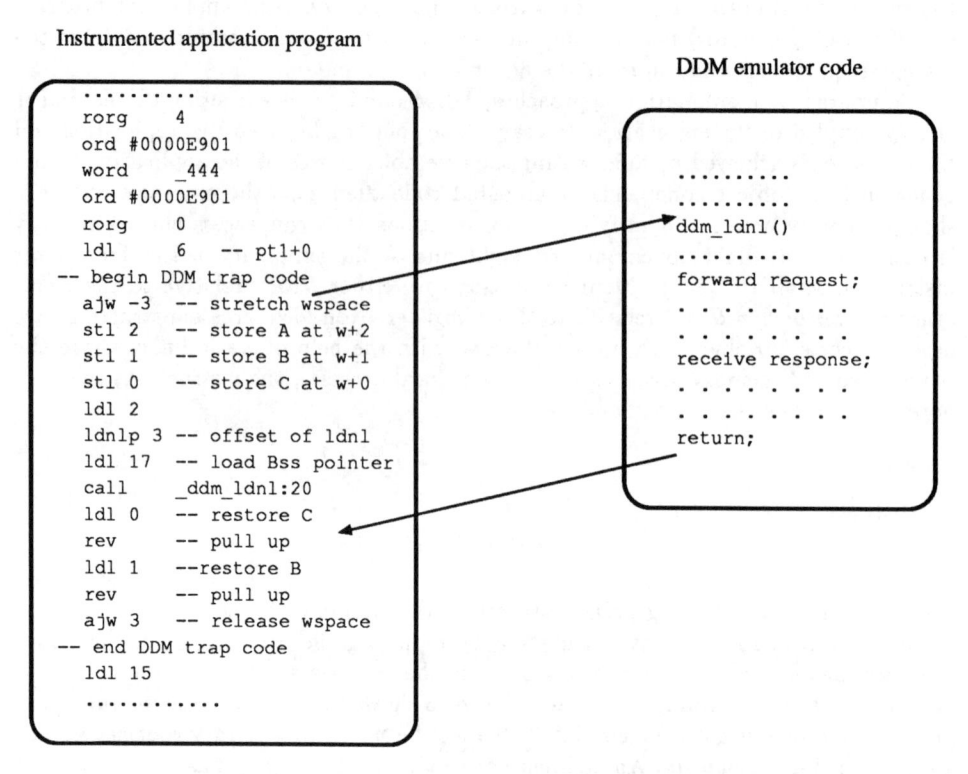

```
         . . . . . . . . . .
   rorg     4
   ord  #0000E901
   word     _444
   ord  #0000E901
   rorg     0
   ldl      6    -- pt1+0
-- begin DDM trap code
   ajw  -3      -- stretch wspace
   stl  2       -- store A at w+2
   stl  1       -- store B at w+1
   stl  0       -- store C at w+0
   ldl  2
   ldnlp 3      -- offset of ldnl
   ldl  17      -- load Bss pointer
   call         _ddm_ldnl:20
   ldl  0       -- restore C
   rev          -- pull up
   ldl  1       --restore B
   rev          -- pull up
   ajw  3       -- release wspace
-- end DDM trap code
   ldl  15
         . . . . . . . . . . . .
```

DDM emulator code

```
         . . . . . . . . . .
   ddm_ldnl()
         . . . . . . . . . .
   forward request;
         . . . . . . . . .
         . . . . . . . . .
   receive response;
         . . . . . . . . .
         . . . . . . . . .
   return;
```

Figure 3: *Instrumented program to divert control to the emulator*

The development environment provided on the Computing Surface is a cross-development toolset called CSTools. Parallel programming in CSTools is based on Communicating Sequential Processes. The toolset enables mixed-architecture parallel programming with a common user-level interface. More details about the toolset can be found in [Meik90a].

Communication services provide an interface between the programmer and the physical hardware. Two levels of interface are provided, namely, the *Transport* library and the *Channel* library. The Transport library provides a higher level interface with the help of *CSN* (the *C*omputing *S*urface *N*etwork), giving the programmer a view of fully connected system. A *CSN* is a background process which resides on every processor that requires its services. The *CSN* processes collectively provide virtual links between application processes. Application processes communicate via a *CSN* process, which handles message retransmission, multiplexing and buffering as required. The Channel library provides more direct and "raw" form of low-level communication primitives whose semantics are the same as those of **occam** channels. As expected, however, channels only allow fully synchronised communication.

Conventional operating system services like file and screen I/O etc. are provided by *R*un *T*ime *E*xecutives (RTEs) which reside on each Transputer. A system request is satisfied locally or remotely (by the host).

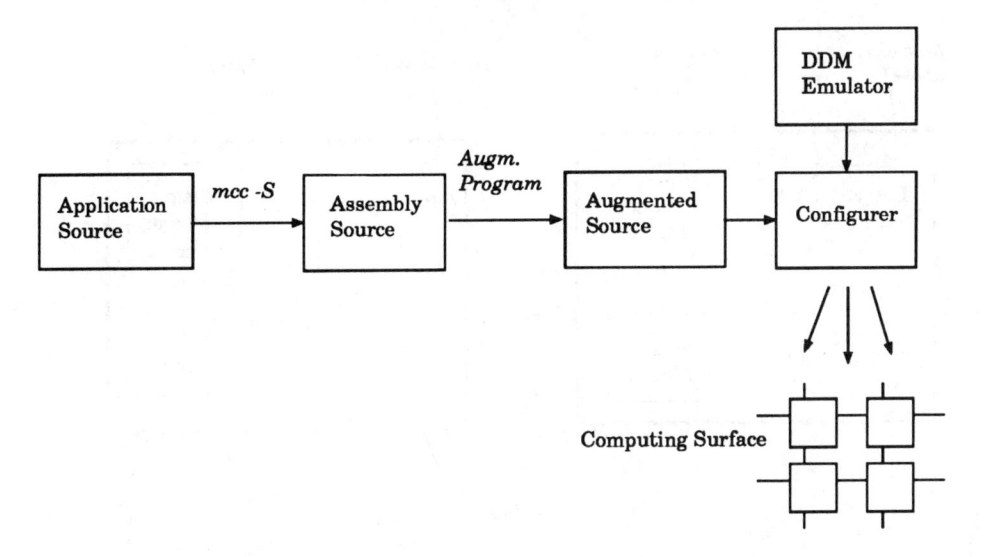

Figure 4: *Configuring the emulator and instrumented application*

The *cs_build* library can be used to write configuration programs tailored to the specific needs of a user application. The library allows complete freedom over placement of user code and data onto the Computing Surface resources. Alternatively one can use a generic utility called the *parfile* loader by specifying the layout of the application in a text file (parfile).

The emulator has been implemented using the channel library and the configurer uses the cs_build library. Since the application processes are statically loaded by the configurer, it is imperative to simulate the dynamic behaviour of the Unix *fork* correctly. The *BSS* section of each "forked" process is placed at a pre-determined address on each Transputer and its contents copied from the forking (parent) process to the child processes.

6.3.2 The Process Structure of the Emulator Topologically, the DDM consists of a hierarchy of nodes. At the tips of the hierarchy are the processors with the physical memory and a memory-controller each. We will refer to such nodes as *memory nodes* and the higher level nodes (comprising a directory and a controller each) as *directory nodes*. Each node in this topology is mapped on to a Transputer with a number of processes per Transputer dedicated to particular functions of the DDM.

The memory processor models a tip node in the DDM. This node essentially generates memory references, listens to the network above and performs the protocol translation. The above activities are implemented by the following three processes on a Transputer as shown in Figure 5(a).

application : This is the worker process that runs the application and generates memory references. A non-local request is pushed into the transaction queue and the worker then awaits the response from above.

memory_controller : This process has access to the state-memory and implements

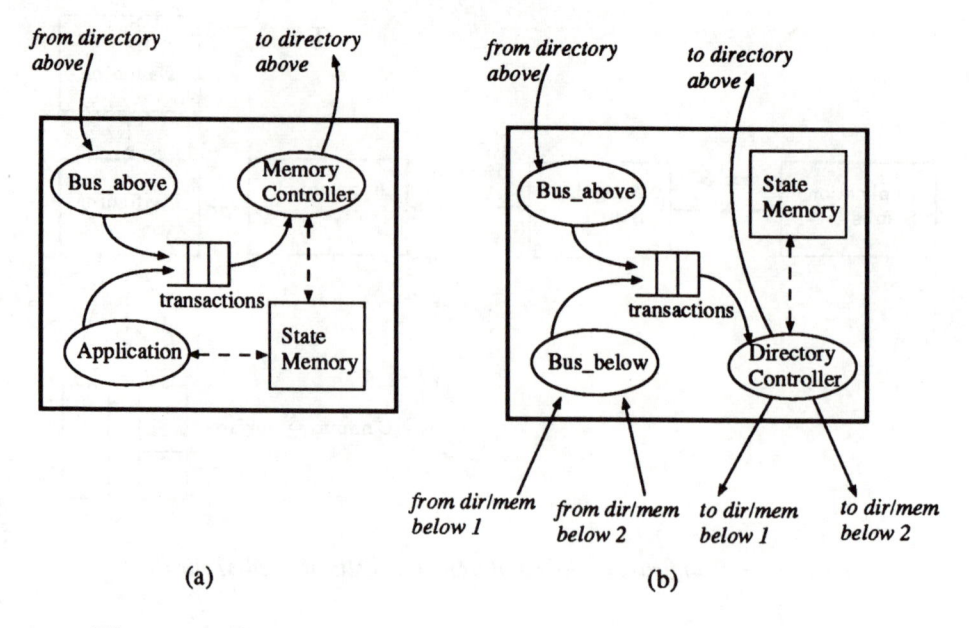

Figure 5: The memory-processor node (a) and the directory node (b)

the protocol machinery. The controller pops a transaction off the transaction queue and filters it through the protocol state-machine making any necessary state changes.

bus_in_above : A process which receives transactions from above and buffers them in the transaction queue.

A directory processor is responsible for listening to network above and below and also for performing protocol translation (see Figure 5(b)). The following three processes are hosted on the directory processor.

bus_in_below : A process for handling transactions below and queueing them.

directory_controller : A process which implements the protocol machinery and has access to the state directory at that node. A transaction is popped off the transaction queue and, depending on the protocol, any necessary state changes are made.

bus_in_above : A process to handle transactions arriving from above and queueing them.

In order to process transactions asynchronously, a queue data structure is maintained to buffer incoming transactions. The queue is maintained as a circular buffer. At the memory node the *application* and the *bus_in_above* processes queue transactions, which are then processed by the *memory_controller*. Similarly at the directory processor, *bus_in_below* and *bus_in_above* processes queue requests, which the *directory controller* then processes.

7. AURORA AND ANDORRA-I ON THE DDM EMULATOR

The shared-memory implementations of Aurora and Andorra-I were designed to run on the Sequent Symmetry multiprocessor. Both Aurora and Andorra-I now run on the emulator. We have also ported Sicstus Prolog (the engine component of Aurora) as well as sequential versions of Aurora and Andorra-I to the Transputer. Tables 1 and 2 show the base performance of Sicstus, Aurora and Andorra-I on a Transputer relative to Sun/3 and Symmetry implementations.

Table 1: *Sicstus and Aurora run-times on a T800 relative to Sun 3/50 and Sequent Symmetry*

benchmark	Sicstus Sun 3/50	Sicstus T800	Aurora (1 worker) Sequent Symmetry	Aurora (1 worker) T800
salt_mustard	1.0	1.37	1.0	1.77
zebra	1.0	1.15	1.0	1.48
tina	1.0	1.39	1.0	1.77

Table 2: *Andorra-I (1 worker) run-times on a T800 relative to Sequent Symmetry*

benchmark	Sequent Symmetry	T800
map	1.0	1.65
fibonacci	1.0	1.81
mergesort	1.0	1.81

The addition of the DDM emulator machinery incurs an overhead which can slowdown the basic execution speed by a factor of up to 8 (table 3). Most of this slowdown

Table 3: *Aurora run-times on a T800 with and without the DDM emulator*

benchmark	T800	T800+DDM
ham	1.0	7.41
zebra	1.0	7.05
turtles	1.0	7.78

is due to the software trap on every potentially shared-memory access leading to a call to, and a return form the emulator.

One of the basic factors that determines the overall performance in a hierarchical memory system is the miss-rate in the lowest level memory. The effective access time in a hierarchical memory system is characterised by the following.

$$T_{access} = R_{hit} \times T_{hit} + R_{miss} \times T_{miss} \qquad (1)$$

The hit-time (T_{hit}) is the time to access the lowest level memory, i.e. cache or local memory and is typically of the order of a few cycles. The miss-time (T_{miss}) is the time required to access main or remote memory. The miss-rate becomes even more significant in memory systems with non-uniform access times including the DDM.

Miss rate depends on a number of factors including the cache-size, line-size, degree of associativity and locality of programs. In general increasing any of these parameters results in a reduced miss rate. Table 4 describes the miss rates observed at the local memories (tip-processors) for Aurora and Andorra-I, including the total number of references made and the fraction of different types of transactions. As seen from the

Table 4: *Miss rates at the local memories*

	Aurora			Andorra-I	
	query	tina	nand	houses (-S3)	houses (-M4)
Total	655987	4503573	775204	1239816	682029
Miss (%)	0.28	0.22	0.2	0.27	0.81
Write (%)	0.51	10.32	15.0	0.36	8.88
Locks (%)	0.11	0.042	0.0417	0.49	1.38
Replace (%)	0.0028	0.00392	0.00187	0.022	0.19

table both Aurora and Andorra-I exhibit low miss rates although in Andorra-I it is slightly higher. Also, synchronisation in Andorra-I generally tends to be higher than in Aurora because of the finer granularity of tasks.

Apart from the miss rate, another factor that determines the effective memory access time is the traffic generated at various levels in the DDM hierarchy. Any contention in the network can increase the latency and therefore the average access time resulting in degraded overall performance. Table 5 describes the mean traffic observed on each link in the DDM hierarchy. The figures are averaged over the four

Table 5: *Traffic on each link in the hierarchy*

	Aurora			Andorra-I	
	query	tina	nand	houses (-S3)	houses (-M4)
Dir-to-Top	0.43	0.27	0.33	1.0	1.6
Top-to-Dir	0.43	0.27	0.37	1.1	1.6
Mem-to-Dir	0.95	0.51	0.41	4.5	2.3
Dir-to-Mem	0.98	0.53	0.45	4.6	2.5

processors and the two directories and represent the number of transactions per 100 shared-memory references at an application processor. For instance, in the case of Aurora (on 'query'), every 100 shared-memory references generated by a tip processor result in 0.95 transactions sent above by the memory-controller and 0.43 transactions sent by the directory-controller to the top-controller. In order to make any general conclusions about network traffic we need to perform more extensive experiments on larger configurations of the DDM.

Despite the software overheads and the long access-latency of the emulator we have been able to observe near linear speed-ups in Aurora when run on the emulator. This is mainly due to the good locality and low communication which is characteristic of Aurora. Table 6 presents the execution times on a four processor configuration of the emulator. Figure 6 depicts the speed-ups observed in the above benchmark programs run with Aurora on the DDM emulator. We expect similar results from Andorra-I on the emulator.

Table 6: *Run-times on 4-processor emulator*

benchmark	No. of DDM Processors			
	1	2	3	4
ham	1.0	0.54	0.38	0.32
zebra	1.0	0.59	0.40	0.32
turtles	1.0	0.56	0.41	0.32

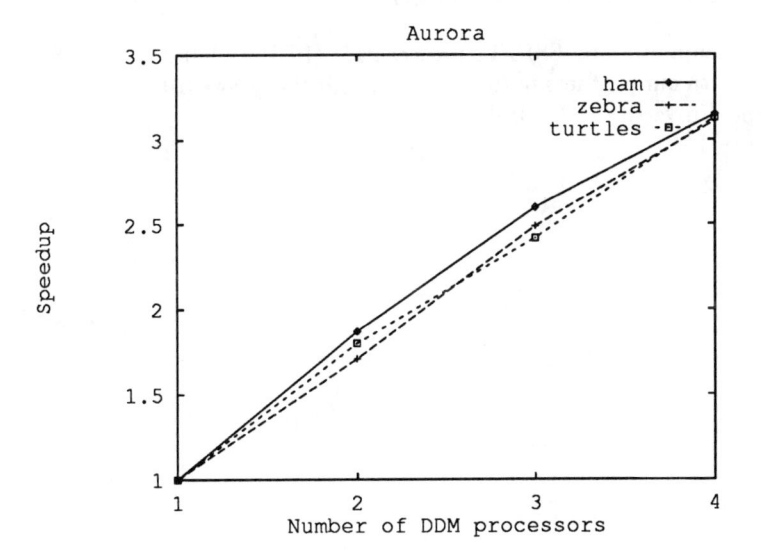

Figure 6: *Aurora on the 4-processor emulator*

8. CONCLUSION AND FUTURE WORK

We have described the Data Diffusion Machine - a scalable shared virtual memory architecture which is well suited for parallel Prolog implementations like Aurora and Andorra-I. We have also described a software emulation of the DDM on a Transputer-based multiprocessor. We have been able to port Sequent Symmetry shared-memory implementations of both Aurora and Andorra-I to the emulator without any significant change. The emulator also runs a collection of numerical applications called SPLASH

[Sing91a] as part of a wider evaluation strategy. Both Prolog systems on the emulator have shown very low miss rates and network traffic which compares favourably with the non logic programming applications. Also, despite emulation overheads we have demonstrated real speed-ups in Aurora programs.

In future we will optimise and tune the emulator towards better performance and we will also study larger DDM configuration. In the longer term we plan to eliminate a large proportion of emulation overhead by exploring future hardware enhancements to a Transputer like processor. We have shown how shared-memory implementations of parallel Prolog systems like Aurora and Andorra-I can be supported on future scalable coherent multiprocessor architectures. We have demonstrated this by describing a scalable shared virtual memory architecture and its software realisation on an existing distributed memory multiprocessor. We view the DDM emulation as an intermediate stage towards the ultimate goal of supporting parallel Prolog systems on large scale multiprocessors. A more realistic implementation of the DDM can be realised by eliminating the software overheads with more efficient hardware support.

9. ACKNOWLEDGEMENTS

This work is supported by ESPRIT project 2471 (PEPMA) and has benefited from collaboration with our partners in the project, particularly Swedish Institute of Computer Science and University of Madrid.

3 OPERA: OR-Parallel Prolog System on Supernode

J. Briat[†], M. Favre[†], C. Geyer[‡] and
J. Chassin de Kergommeaux[†]
[†] LGI-IMAG, Grenoble, France
[‡] Universidade Federal de Rio Grande do Sul, Brazil

ABSTRACT

The OPERA project aims at implementing efficiently Prolog on scalable, reconfigurable, distributed memory architectures. The OPERA computational model exploits OR-parallelism following a multisequential approach: each processor executes a complete Prolog engine; inter-processor communication is reduced to work installation and no more parallelism is created than required by the available resources. The implementation of the Prolog engine is based on the Warren Abstract Machine (WAM). When an idle processor is granted work from an active one, the complete state of the active Prolog engine is copied onto the idle one, the copy operation being optimized to avoid any disturbance of the already active processor. Scheduling of work must keep the workers busy while limiting the overhead arising from parallel activities. These goals are particularly difficult to achieve in a scalable distributed architecture such as Supernode, because of the potentially high number of workers and the significant cost of inter-processor communication. In OPERA, scheduling is performed by a hierarchy of specialized processors, operating in parallel to the workers. To avoid costly synchronisations, schedulers use an approximate representation of the state of the system. Because of the important overhead of task installation in a distributed memory architecture, only workers having a large amount of work to execute can give work to idle workers. The prototype implementation of OPERA on transputer-based Supernode reaches effective speed-ups in parallel over efficient sequential Prolog systems.

1. INTRODUCTION

The aim of the OPERA project is to use the significant computing power offered by scalable distributed memory multiprocessors to execute efficiently Prolog programs in parallel. The Transputer architecture is suited to the building of inexpensive massively parallel architectures such as the dynamically reconfigurable Supernode [Harp86a], in the development of which part of the OPERA team was involved. Prolog has been chosen as a parallel programming language because of its inherent parallelism, which allows the execution of ordinary Prolog programs in parallel. Contrary to the Concurrent Logic Languages approach [Shap89a], which aims at developing new languages for parallel processing, the goal of OPERA is to speed-up the computation of "standard" Prolog programs by using parallelism. Among the potential sources of parallelism offered by Prolog programs, OPERA exploits the OR-parallelism, expected to require less communication than AND-parallelism and therefore be more suitable for existing distributed-memory architectures with slow communications, such as the Supernode.

The computational model of OPERA is multisequential: each processor (worker) executes a Prolog engine which computes portions of the search tree defined by the program. Parallelism is initiated by otherwise idle workers: no more parallelism than available resources is generated. The OPERA Prolog engine is based on the most efficient compilation techniques used for Prolog, known as the *Warren Abstract Machine* (WAM) [Warr83a]. The WAM has been extended into a "TWAM" (*Transputer Warren Abstract Machine*), tailored to the Transputer and a distributed memory architecture. When an "idle" worker takes work from an active one, the stacks describing the state of the computation are **copied** from the active to the "idle" worker. Such copying being a potential source of important overhead, the TWAM extends the WAM data structures (stacks) to allow an efficient copy operation. Specific features of the Transputer-based Supernode multiprocessor architecture, used for the implementation of OPERA, have been taken into account for these extensions.

Scheduling is one of the most important issues to be solved by parallel Prolog systems. The scheduler must keep the workers as busy as possible while limiting the overhead generated by parallelism. The first constraint implies generating enough parallelism but the second one implies that the granularity of each new parallel activity should remain bigger than the overhead that it introduces. Scheduling is more difficult in distributed-memory than in shared-memory architectures because of the higher cost of task creation and the lack of global state for the parallel Prolog system, unless extremely costly synchronisation algorithms are used. The computational difficulty of task scheduling increases with the number of processors used by the multiprocessor, since the amount of exploited parallelism should increase as well. Because of the difficulty of scheduling, significant computing resources are devoted to schedule tasks in OPERA. The structure of the OPERA scheduler is hierarchical and mimics the architecture of the control network of the Supernode, used for the implementation. Specialized scheduler processes keep an approximate record of the states of their slave schedulers or workers and balance the workload among these slaves. Several load balancing strategies, based on dynamic criteria, have been designed and are currently being tested.

A prototype of OPERA has been implemented on Supernode. The sequential efficiency of this implementation is one of the best sequential Prolog implementations on the Transputer. First experimental results indicate good performance speed-ups of parallel computations over sequential ones, for programs providing a large enough search space.

The organisation of this chapter is the following. After this introduction, the main features of the Supernode architecture are presented. The following section outlines the OPERA computational model and its implementation called TWAM (Transputer Warren Abstract Machine). The scheduling issues and their solutions in OPERA are then described. The next section is dedicated to the preliminary results obtained by the OPERA prototype, implemented on a Supernode. The two last sections compare OPERA to similar approaches and conclude the chapter.

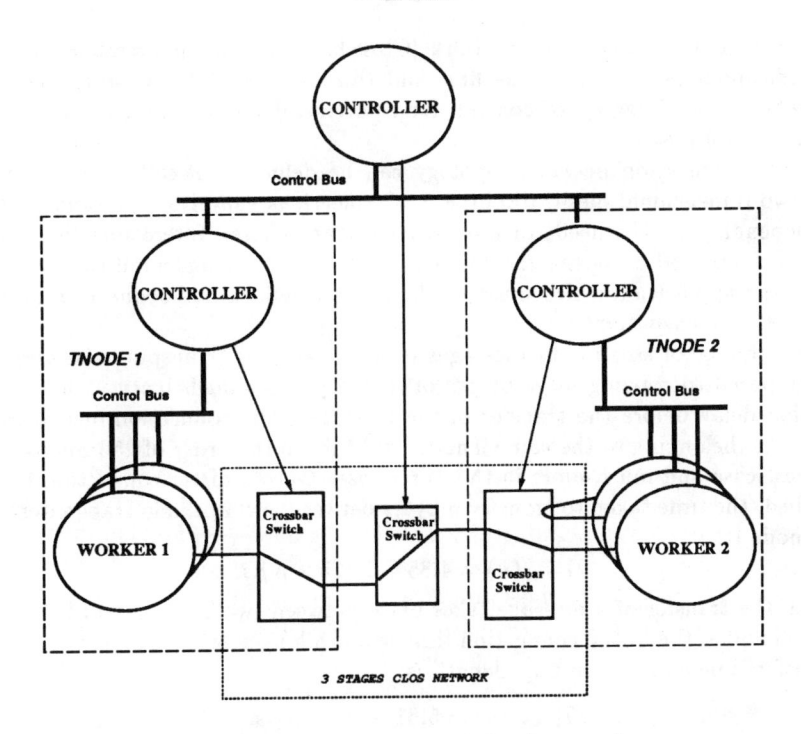

Figure 1: *Architecture of the Supernode*

On request from two processing Transputers, the control Transputer T414 connects them directly through the crossbar switch. Sixty four links connect each Tnode to the external world, interconnecting the Tnodes to obtain a Meganode. The Meganode architecture is scalable up to 1024 T800 processors.

2. ARCHITECTURE OF THE SUPERNODE

The target multiprocessor architecture of the OPERA project is the Supernode [Harp86a], developed in the ESPRIT project 1085. The Supernode architecture is a dynamically reconfigurable array of Transputers. It is based on a general purpose parallel processor, T800 floating point Transputer, together with a special programmable switch allowing dynamic reconfiguration of the links between worker Transputers. The Supernode architecture is a two-level architecture, where Meganodes are built of Tnodes.

A basic Tnode module is composed of 16 working Transputers in the basic version and 32 Transputers in the "tandem" version. Interprocessor communication is provided by a crossbar switch controled by a specialized control Transputer. Working Transputers are connected to the control Transputer by a dedicated control bus, used to pass communication requests as well as miscellaneous control commands for the working Transputers (initialization, termination, etc.). A 16 Transputer Tnode is represented on Figure 1.

Several Tnodes can be interconnected by a second-level network of crossbar switches to build a Meganode. The structure of the network of switches of a Meganode is organized as a three stage Clos network [Clos84a] in which the crossbar switches of the Tnode modules participate as first and third stages. The network of switches is controled by a hierarchy of control Transputers interconnected by a hierarchy of identical control buses.

The interconnection network topology can be defined statically as an arity four graph: two dimensional mesh, toroid, etc. Connections can also be modified dynamically, depending on the needs of the working Transputers. Interconnection requests are then transmitted using the control bus. In any case, the control of the connections is left to the application which must implement a deadlock-free connection algorithm in the control Transputers.

The exchange of small data messages between working Transputers is very inefficient compared to copying large blocks of memory. This inefficiency stems from the connection delay before the transfer of the message. The connection of two working Transputers, belonging to the same Tnode, will take in the order of 250 micro-seconds in the best case and much more in the worst case. Once a direct connection has been established, the time taken to transfer n bytes between two working Transputers in the same Tnode is:

$$T_{trans}(n) = 4.85 + 1.125 \times n \ \mu s.$$

When the transfer of a message takes place between two Transputers belonging to different Tnodes, the initial connection time is much longer, while the relation between the transfer time and the message length is:

$$T_{trans}(n) = 5.61 + 2.2 \times n \ \mu s.$$

Because of the inefficiency of the dynamic interconnections at the second level, OPERA uses static interconnections between Tnodes.

Transfer of messages is performed in parallel to normal computation by the sender and receiver working Transputers, using DMA mechanism. DMA accesses to memory being indeed interleaved with local accesses, the overhead of the copy operation remains limited for both Transputers.

The software environment available for the Supernode at the beginning of the OPERA project was very limited. Therefore, important efforts had to be devoted to basic system work at the beginning of the project [Bria89a] to be able to use the Supernode.

3. THE OPERA COMPUTATIONAL MODEL

3.1 Language supported by OPERA

The language supported by OPERA is "standard" Prolog including cut and some Input/Output predicates. The Prolog "data-base" predicates, modifying the program, are not considered in the first version of OPERA. No special declarations are used to distinguish "parallel" predicates, which can be used to generate parallelism, from "sequential" ones, where the alternative clauses will be executed on backtracking. Therefore any choice-point can be used to create a new task.

3.2 Overview of the OPERA computational model

The computational model of OPERA is multi-sequential: each processor executes a Prolog Abstract Machine on a local copy of the Prolog program. This Abstract Machine called TWAM for Transputer Warren Abstract Machine is based on the WAM [Warr83a], regarded as the most efficient technique used in sequential Prolog implementations. No parallelism is explicitly created by active workers. Idle workers request work from active workers having untried alternatives, recorded in choice points. An idle worker becomes active when granted from the scheduler a choice point of an active worker. OPERA executes sequential (deterministic) programs at the efficiency of the TWAM implementation, close to the best sequential Prolog implementations based on the WAM. In the best case, speed-ups provided by parallel over sequential execution can be linear in the number of processors.

When receiving work from an active worker, an idle worker copies a complete resolvent, that is the state of the active TWAM when the choice-point providing work was created. Variables created before this choice-point but bound after (and therefore trailed) must be unbound. To avoid going through the trail stack to unbind these variables, all the bindings are tagged with a time-stamp (see below 3.4). The TWAM defined for OPERA uses basically the "standard" WAM instruction set but extends the WAM data structures to improve the efficiency of the copy operation. Other solutions performing sharing of stacks cannot be applied [Warr87a] [West87a] because of the inefficiency of passing small messages in a distributed memory architecture such as the Supernode, compared to copying of large chunk of data.

3.3 Process structure of a worker (TWAM)

A worker is a Transputer executing a complete TWAM engine. Due to the lack of a virtual memory management unit or relocation registers in the Transputer, it is only possible to execute a single TWAM on each working Transputer. Each worker is composed of four processes: the *Solver*, the *Exporter*, the *Importer* and the *Spy* (see Figure 2). The Solver implements the TWAM sequential Prolog engine. The Exporter transfers stacks when exporting work to the Importer of an idle worker (see section 3.5). The Spy informs the scheduler of the state of the TWAM (see section 4.).

3.4 TWAM data structures

The TWAM extends the number of WAM data structures to allow a more efficient copy operation of the relevant portions of the stacks, from an active to an idle worker. The local and global stacks of the WAM have been reorganized into four stacks in the TWAM.

Contrary to the WAM, where clause activation records and choice points are interleaved in the local stack, choice points are managed in a special stack of the TWAM, such as in [Ali90a]. The main advantage of this solution is to isolate the communication with the outside world, which takes place when an untried alternative is taken by an idle worker. The second advantage is a better memory behaviour, since choice-points can be discarded as soon as they are no longer being used, which is not always possible when they are interleaved with environments. In OPERA, the choice-points stack is actually a double-linked list, giving much greater freedom for its management.

Another additional data structure of the TWAM is the variable stack, similar to a data structure proposed in [Wars84a], used to store all the Prolog variables that would otherwise be initialized free and pushed onto the local or global stack. An entry, pointing to the location of the variable in the variable stack, is still created in the local or global stack. Constant terms, corresponding to input parameters of imperative

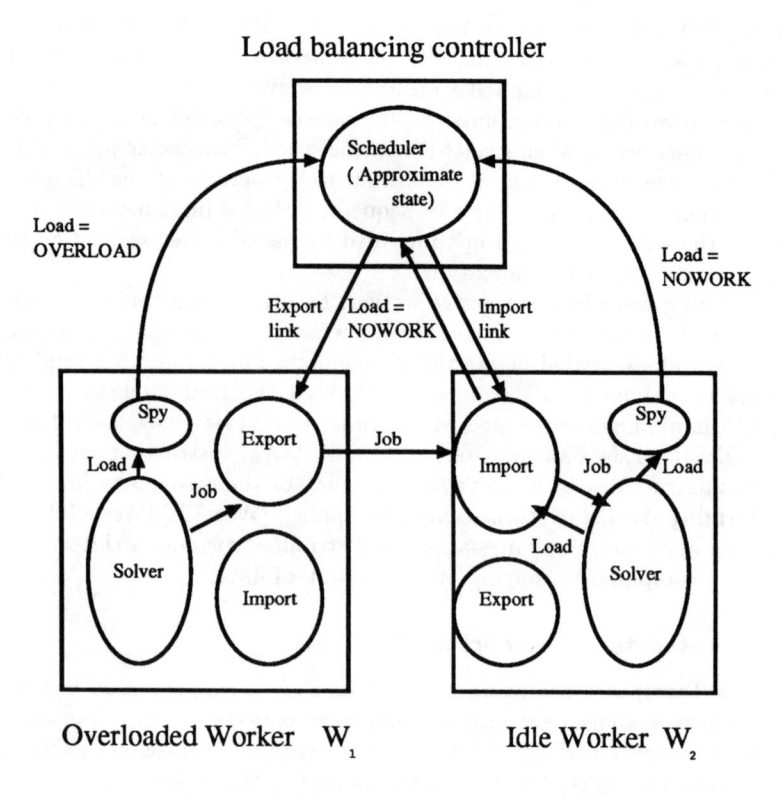

Figure 2: *Software structure of OPERA*

languages, are stored in the local or global stack, depending on whether they are complex or not. As in the Kabu-Wake [Masu86a] and PEPSys [West87a] models, each variable of the variable stack is tagged with a "time stamp", which is actually the depth of the current OR-node in the search tree. Figure 3 shows the TWAM stacks for a tutorial example. Variable stacks are used to speed-up work installation on idle processors as explained in paragraph 3.5.

3.5 Copying of the stacks

When backtracking, the Solver of a worker W_2 may find an empty choice point stack and therefore becomes *idle*. The Importer of W_2 then requests work from the scheduler and waits until it is granted an untried choice-point from an export worker W_1 (see section 4.). The relevant portions of the stacks of W_1 are then copied to W_2. The order of the copy operations is as follows (see Figure 2) :

1. The transfer of stacks using DMA mechanisms is initiated by the Exporter of W_1 and the Importer of W_2.

2. The portion of the variable stack existing at the creation of the choice-point having given work is copied from the workspace of W_1 to the workspace of W_2. The use of time-stamps allows the Solver of W_1 to remain active during the whole

Program example:
(Cl1) ...   ← ..., p(X, Y), ...
(Cl2) p(Z, f(b))   ← ...
(Cl3) p(Z, f(c))   ← ...

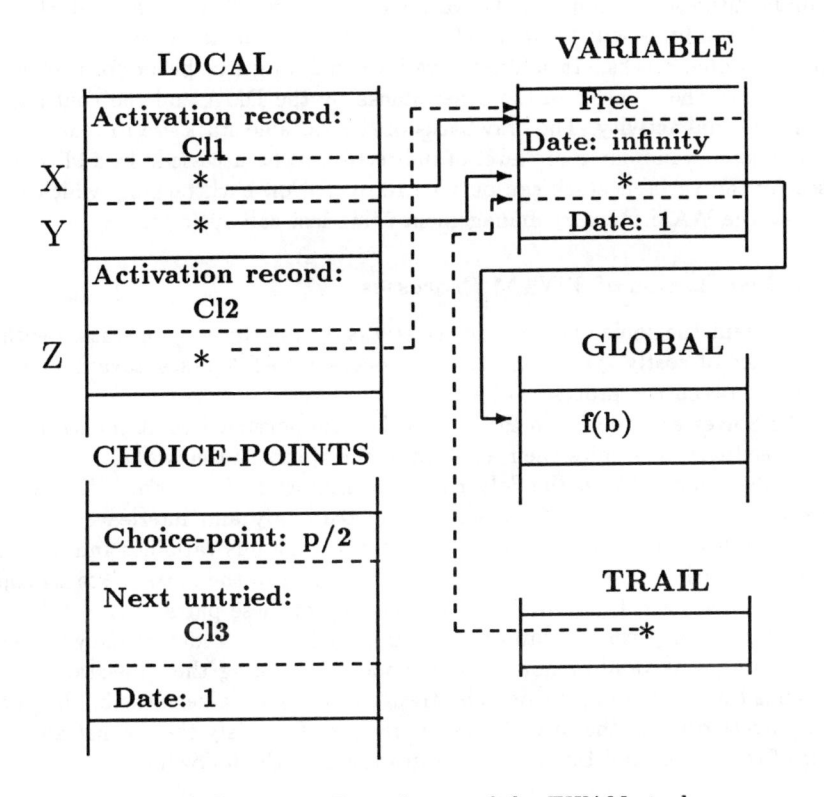

Figure 3: *Example use of the TWAM stacks*

*If the choice-point is used to give work from an active worker W_1 to an idle worker W_2, all the bindings the date of which is **greater or equal** to the creation date of the choice-point (1), will have to be unbound by W_2. This operation will be performed by W_2 **simultaneously** to the copying of the global and local stacks and the continuation by W_1 of its normal activity.*

copy operation, without requiring any costly synchronization, when binding a variable found on one of its copied stacks (see section 3.6).

3. The portions of the local and global stacks existing at the creation of the choice-point having given work are copied from the workspace of W_1 to the workspace of W_2 while, **simultaneously**, the Importer of W_2 tests the time-stamp of each variable copied in phase 2 to check whether it belongs to the resolvent being copied. Variables bound after the creation of the seminal choice-point of W_1, are

reset by the Importer of W_2.

4. When the transfer is over, the Exporter of W_1 and the Importer of W_2 acknowledge the transfer to the scheduler and the Solver of W_2 resumes work from the granted choice point.

The main interest of grouping the variables in a special stack is that checking the validity of bindings will be more efficient than if variables were spread out in the local and global stacks. In addition, validity checking can be performed by W_2 simultaneously to the transfer of the other stacks by the DMA and the continuation by W_1 of its normal activity. The drawbacks of the variable stack are to require more memory and to demand one more level of indirection to be accessed. In addition, the space used by the variable stack can only be recovered on backtracking, which is less efficient than the WAM memory management using last call optimization.

3.6 Synchronization of TWAM Processes

To keep consistent the copied portions of the stacks during the copy operation without paying the price of costly synchronization protocols, OPERA takes advantage of the relationships between the processes of a worker.

Since the Solver and the Importer of a worker are never active at the same time, there is no need to synchronize their accesses to the stacks of the worker.

It is not the same between the Solver and the Exporter of a worker. The accesses of the Exporter to the stacks of the worker are read-only and interleaved with the read/write accesses of the Solver. The Solver binds or unbinds variables and pushes or pops frames on stacks. To avoid corruption by the Solver of the parts of stacks copied by the exporter, we need to maintain the consistency of these parts.

The Importer of any worker importing work must be able to determine whether an "imported" binding is valid or not. This is done by checking the time-stamp of the binding. Thus this time-stamp needs to be always valid. The value of the binding needs also to be correct **only** in the case of a valid binding. To satisfy these constraints, the behaviour of the Solver and Exporter processes must be the following:

- Solver:

  1. set/reset to **infinity** the time-stamps of all free variables,
  2. when binding a free variable, update the time-stamp of the variable cell **after** binding its value; do the opposite when unbinding a bound variable.

- Exporter: transfers first the date of a variable cell.

There is no problem when pushing a new frame onto a stack since it is always younger than the currently exported part of the stack. On the other hand, when the Solver backtracks to a choice-point being transferred or an older one, it needs to pop parts of stacks currently being copied by the Exporter. In OPERA, this popping is delayed until the end of the copy; the Solver checks that it is not backtracking to the currently exported choice-point or to an older one. A more complex solution is to cancel the whole copy operation, notify failure to the Exporter and backtrack. The Exporter must warn the remote Importer to request other work from the Scheduler.

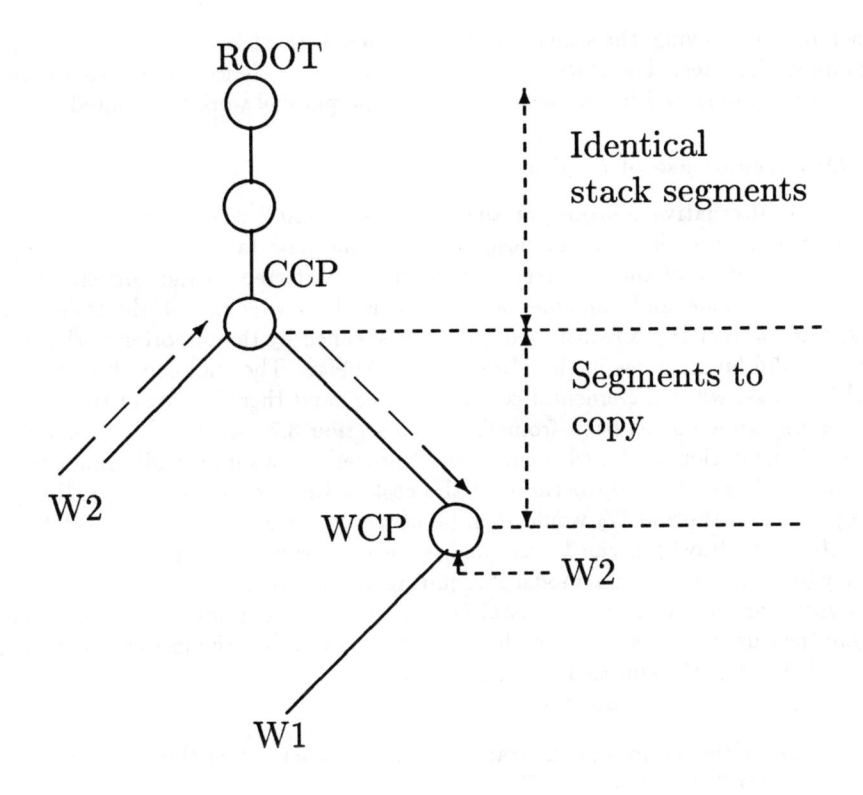

Figure 4: *Incremental copying of the stacks*

The nodes of the tree represent choice-points (figure inspired by [Ali90a]).

3.7 Optimization: incremental copying of the stacks

The overhead of stack copying can be reduced by remarking that any idle worker always shares a part of the program search tree with any active worker. So, when an idle worker W_2 becomes active, there is no need to copy the complete stacks of the selected active worker W_1, since W_1 and W_2 already share a part of the program search tree. This optimization is successfully used by the Or Parallel Prolog System Muse [Ali90a].

When incremental copying is used between an idle worker W_2 and an active worker W_1, W_2 backtracks to the last common choice point (CCP) before copying the segments of the stacks of W_1 that are **younger** than CCP and **older** than the choice-point WCP used to give work (see figure 4). In addition, bindings performed by W_1 in the common parts of the stacks, between the creations of CCP and WCP, must be installed in the stacks of W_2. In OPERA, this will involve the cooperation of W_1, which uses its trail stack to send to W_2 the bindings necessary to update the previously transfered stacks.

The last common choice-point has usually been removed from the choice-point stack of the active worker giving work, when it has been sent to an idle worker. To implement the incremental copying, the scheduler (see section 4.4) must keep track of the shape of the computation tree. The stack pointer registers of each choice point, used to create parallel work, are stored by the scheduler when the parallel work is initiated.

3.8 Discussion: use of a value trail

There is an alternative solution for the worker importing work. To discard invalid bindings behind the choice-point used to create the new task, the importer worker uses the trail stack of the exporter worker, not transferred in the current OPERA computational model and implementation. In this alternative model, the trail stack of the exporter worker W_1 is transferred and later scanned by the importer worker W_2 to discard invalid bindings, as in the Muse model [Ali90a]. The trail can also be used to install bindings, when incremental copying is used, and therefore avoid the overhead of requesting some cooperation from W1 as in section 3.7. However, contrary to the Muse implementation on shared-memory multiprocessors, a simple trail cannot be used to install bindings efficiently because of the cost of small messages: one exchange of message between W_1 and W_2 would then be necessary to get the value of each binding to install. This drawback can be avoided by using a value trail, to keep the current property of the computational model of requiring a single exchange of messages between the importer and the exporter to install a new task. The binding values stored in the trail are then used to install the bindings performed between the last common choice-point and the choice-point used for task creation.

The copying operation becomes:

1. transfer of the sections of the trail and variable stacks older than the choice-point used for task creation, from W_1 to W_2.

2. Tidying up and installation of bindings in the variable stack of W_2, using the value trail, **in parallel** with the transfer of the relevant sections of the other stacks from W_1 to W_2.

Compared with the current solution using time-stamps, the value trail solution introduces the space and time overhead of storing the values of the trailed bindings while removing the overhead of dating the bindings. The current solution seems well suited to the efficient creation of a new task from a choice-point located at top of a deep branch of the search tree: in this case the trail stack can be expected to be long and scanning a long trail stack to discard invalid binding, can be expected to take longer than scanning the dates of a small variable stack. However, should incremental copying be used frequently, using a value trail would probably be more efficient than the current solution, which introduces some overhead for the exporter worker in installing the bindings behind the last common choice-point.

Only experimental comparison will establish if one solution is consistently better than the other or if the most efficient depends on the benchmark program.

4. SCHEDULING OF WORK

Scheduling is important in OPERA because of the high cost of task creation on the target Supernode architecture. The structure of the OPERA scheduler is hierarchical: specialized master schedulers schedule slave workers or schedulers. The schedulers of

OPERA are designed to use an approximate representation of the system, to avoid costly synchronizations.

4.1 Task granularity issue

It is possible to give the conditions under which it is worthwhile to export work in an OR-parallel Prolog system, where the computation of both the exporter and the importer workers will proceed independently, i.e. without any synchronization or communication. Let T be the time necessary for a worker W_1 to complete a task. Let us assume that this task can be split in two subtasks of durations T_1 and T_2, let E_2 be the overhead caused to W_1 by exporting the task T_2 from W_1 to W_2, and let I_2 be the time required for W_2 to import the task T_2. Obviously: $T = T_1 + T_2$. In order for the parallel computation of T_1 and T_2 to terminate faster than the sequential computation of T, the two following inequalities must hold :

$$T > (T - T_2) + E_2 \text{ (time necessary for } W_1 \text{ to complete)}$$
$$T > I_2 + T_2 \text{ (time necessary for } W_2 \text{ to complete)}$$

These inequalities can be simplified as :

$$E_2 < T_2 \quad I_2 < T_1 = T - T_2$$

These constraints mean that the granularities of both the exported and remaining tasks depend on the time taken to transfer (export and import) a new task. This transfer time depends a lot on the multiprocessor architecture. It is much longer on a distributed-memory than on a shared-memory architecture. In the Supernode, DMA accesses to the memory are interleaved with local accesses and therefore the export time overhead E_2 can be expected to be low. By contrast, the speed of the links - 1 MegaByte per second - is limited compared to the speed of a standard bus (such as VME for example) and the import time I_2 can therefore be expected to be fairly important. To limit both the export and import times, the scheduler must select, among the possible exportable tasks, the task requiring the smallest stack transfers. In addition, because of the second inequality above, the scheduler should ensure that an active worker, giving work to an idle worker, keeps enough work to remain active after the initialization of the new task.

Since import and export times depend linearly on the size of the transferred data, they can be estimated at runtime; it is not the same for the execution time of the exported task and of the task remaining on the exporting worker. An heuristic is required for predicting the lifetimes of these tasks (see section 4.3.2).

To stress the importance of the task granularity problem, early measurements indicate that, on average, it takes as long to connect and initiate a task transfer between two Transputers of the same Tnode module, as to execute 200 inferences with a TWAM Prolog engine. This problem is going to be even more serious in a Meganode, since the time required to set up a connection between two Transputers of different Tnode modules is much longer.

4.2 Structure of the OPERA scheduler

Several possible structures have been considered for the OPERA scheduler:

centralized: scheduling is then performed by a unique process. This is the simplest solution to implement, although the scheduler process may become a bottleneck, especially in a scalable multiprocessor including a potentially high number of processors, such as the Meganode.

distributed: scheduling is then distributed among the workers. This solution is more difficult to implement since there are no shared data. In addition, it generates some traffic control overhead on the communication links.

hierarchical: scheduling is implemented as a hierarchy of specialized scheduler processes. At the lower level, inside a Tnode module, this solution is equivalent to the centralized structure. In a Meganode, the schedulers of the Tnode modules are hierarchically connected, mimicing the architecture of the machine. The hierarchical structure does not introduce any bottleneck since each scheduler controls a limited number of workers or schedulers of a lower level. This structure also creates a limited overhead since the control traffic, on the control buses, remains independent of the data traffic on the links.

The hierarchical structure, being best suited to the scalable distributed memory architecture in general and to the architecture of the Supernode in particular, has been chosen for the OPERA scheduler.

In the current OPERA Tnode prototype, there is one Scheduler process placed on the Tnode control Transputer (see figure 1). For the planned implementation on a 128 Transputer Meganode built with eight basic modules, we need eight first level Schedulers (one for each Tnode). To schedule work between Tnodes, a second level scheduler is necessary. This second level scheduler can be either centralized on the second level control Transputer or distributed among the eight Schedulers of the first level.

4.3 Work selection strategies

4.3.1 Classification of workers and clusters

On each worker, the Spy process (see section 3.3) informs the scheduler of the activity of the worker. Three classes of workers have been defined:

idle: an idle worker does not have any Prolog task to compute and after having sent a request for work to its scheduler, it is expecting an import authorization.

quiet: a quiet worker is active but does not have enough work to share with an idle worker without taking the risk of becoming rapidly idle. As long as it remains quiet, a quiet worker does not communicate with the rest of the system.

overloaded: an overloaded worker is active and has enough work to share with an idle worker.

The Spy estimates the workload of the active workers. Workers are classified as quiet or overloaded depending on whether they are below or above a threshold. If all workers are quiet or overloaded during the whole program execution, more workers should be allocated to the program (if resources exist). If some workers are idle, too many workers are used. Maximum efficiency in the use of the multiprocessor is reached when all the workers are quiet.

This classification is generalized to the Tnode modules of a Meganode; the threshold between quiet and overloaded Tnodes is of course different.

4.3.2 Evaluation of workload

There are no simple and exact criteria to evaluate the load of a worker. Compile time analysis of the granularity of Prolog programs is currently an active research topic [Herm90a]. In OPERA, the evaluation of workload is performed dynamically. The simplest heuristic, used in the current OPERA prototype implementation, is to measure the workload by the number of choice points held by the worker. This measure is maintained by the Spy process and transmitted to the Scheduler. The threshold between quiet and overloaded workers is then simply a number of choice points.

4.3.3 Evaluation of a global state

Maintaining the exact state of a distributed memory system amounts to the costly problem of global synchronization in a message passing architecture [Rayn88a]. Therefore a more pragmatic solution was devised for OPERA. The OPERA strategy is first described for a Tnode and then generalized to a Meganode.

On each worker, the Spy process samples the number of choice-points and filters the "noise" caused by small variations of the load. The filtered values are then transmitted to the Scheduler. The sampling frequency is adjusted to limit the overhead for the Solver. The filtering of workload reduces the number of messages from the Spies to the Scheduler, to avoid saturation of the Scheduler.

Because of the filtering and the transmission delays from the Spies to the Scheduler, the global state managed by the Scheduler can only be approximate. The discrepancy between the approximate and the real state of the system may be the origin of inappropriate scheduling decisions: an overloaded worker may become quiet or idle after it has been selected by the scheduler to give work to an idle worker. Experimental results indicate that the number of occurrences of this case depends on the value of the threshold and remains very low for reasonable threshold values. On the other hand, a high frequency of such inappropriate decisions corresponds to a high frequency of fine-grained OR branches which, if exported, could not increase the speed-up (see section 4.1).

The solution described above can be generalized to the Meganode, where the Schedulers of the Tnode modules play the part of the Spies of the workers, reporting to the second-level Scheduler.

4.3.4 Communication protocol between Scheduler, Importer and Exporter

To cope with the relative inaccuracy of state information maintained by the Schedulers, a protocol has been defined between the three entities involved in the creation of a new task. This protocol can be decomposed into four major steps (see figure 2):

1. A Scheduler receives, via the control bus, a request for work from the Importer of a worker W_2 and an overload signal from the Spy of W_1.

2. The Scheduler establishes a communication link through the crossbar switch (switches in the case of a Meganode). It then sends export and import authorizations to W_1 and W_2, giving the identification of the ports to use for sending and receiving the TWAM stacks.

3. Transfer of the stacks between W_1 and W_2 takes place (see section 3.5). In case where W_1 has become quiet or idle in between, W_1 simply sends a NOWORK signal to W_2.

4. After completion of the transfer, or the transmission of a NOWORK signal, both the Exporter of W_1 and the Importer of W_2 release their communication link by sending their **precise load** (neither sampled nor filtered) to the controller/Scheduler.

At the end of step 4, receiving the exact load values of both W_1 and W_2 allows the Scheduler to update its approximate state and avoid consecutive inappropriate decisions. In particular, if no task could be transferred (NOWORK signal in step 3), the Scheduler classifies W_1 as quiet or idle, depending on its load, W_2 remaining idle. If a transfer took place, the state of W_1 may remain overloaded or become quiet, while the state of W_2 is changed from idle to quiet. As a consequence, the more scheduling decisions made, the more accurate the state of the system maintained by the scheduler.

4.3.5 Selection of work Idle workers obtain from their scheduler the address of a choice point (of an active worker) containing at least one untried alternative. Two criteria are used by the scheduler to select work in the search tree:

1. maximize the benefit provided by the selected work, which is equivalent to maximizing the granularity of this work. To reach this goal the OPERA scheduler selects the highest possible work in the tree, following the heuristic that " higher the work, larger the granularity".

2. minimize the overhead generated by the initialization of the new task. This can be obtained by selecting, among the possible work, the piece that minimizes the size of the stack segments to be copied, at the possible expense of the granularity. To further minimize the copying overhead, which mainly derives from initializations of transfers, several choice-points can be used to create a new task. This number of choice-points must be carefully chosen to leave enough work for the overloaded worker.

Finding the best possible compromise being an open problem, the current prototype selects the highest work in the search tree, the height in the search tree being measured by the count of choice-points.

4.4 Representation of the branching tree on a Scheduler process

The incremental copying optimization can only be performed if the Scheduler processes can compute the parts of the computation tree common to workers exchanging work. This is possible if the Schedulers keep a representation of the public part of the OR tree.

There exists several possible representations of the public OR tree. The simplest one uses an $N \times N$ matrix, where N is the number of workers controlled by a scheduler process. Stacks are stored at the same addresses on each worker. Each element E_{ij}, where $i \neq j$, stores the stack pointers of the deepest node of the tree common to workers i and j. The matrix is used to compute the identity of the overloaded worker i such that the amount of stack transfers required to give work to worker j is minimized. The matrix is updated at each creation of a new task.

This simple solution is not practical when the number of processors increases, since the size of the matrix grows as the square of the number of processors. A better solution is to use a binary tree, the leaves of which describe the memory state of each worker. Each intermediate node of the tree describes the common part, inherited from the lower nodes of the tree. The size of this tree is limited to 2N - 1, where N is the number of processors of the multiprocessor. The tree is split at each task creation and pruned at each task termination, in order to discard the unnecessary common parts.

This operation is performed in parallel to the computation of the parallel program and therefore does not introduce any additional overhead for the active workers. However, some overhead for the scheduler process and idle workers is introduced in the selection of the best exporter for a given idle worker. Experiments will establish if it is balanced by the gain provided by incremental copying.

The OR-tree contains the control information needed to implement *cut* as a parallelism inhibitor. This role increases with parallel control structures such as parallel *bagof* or *cut* used for pruning speculative work [Haus89a].

5. IMPLEMENTATION AND PRELIMINARY RESULTS

5.1 Implementation

A prototype of OPERA is currently running on a Supernode basic module. Because of the lack of software environment available on this machine, a lot of basic system work has been necessary, prior to the implementation of OPERA [Bria89a]. In spite of this difficulty, special care has been taken to begin with a very efficient sequential implementation in order to provide **effective speed-ups** over efficient sequential Prolog systems. Therefore the WAM code generated by the compiler is expanded into a mixture of inline code and runtime subroutine calls, both written in the assembly code of the Transputer, instead of being emulated as in most of the existing compiled Prolog systems.

The existing OPERA prototype executes on a single Tnode module. Cut and side-effects have not yet been included. In addition, incremental copying being not yet available, the scheduler always selects the top-most work available in the search tree in order to minimize the amount of copying and maximize the granularity of the tasks.

5.2 Sequential efficiency

The TWAM is one of the most efficient existing Prolog implementations on the Transputer. Measured on the standard *naive-reverse* benchmark, OPERA runs at 34 KLIPS (Kilo Logical Inferences per Second). This performance is confirmed by the results of several other classical benchmarks. Because of the uniqueness of the Transputer architecture (T800), it is difficult to relate the performances of OPERA with the performances of other Prolog systems running on different hardware. The Transputer delivers 10 RISC Mips, if all program and data are located in the internal RAM of 4 KBytes.[1] Processor address and data paths being multiplexed, the actual efficiency of

---

[1] Which is **not** a cache memory but an ordinary memory explicitly addressed by the programmer.

Table 1: *Sequential performances of the TWAM*

In the following performance figures, T1 is a TWAM where all code and data are located in the main memory. In the T2 implementation, the compiled Prolog benchmark program is stored in the internal RAM. In T3, the TWAM registers and part of the run-time system are loaded in the internal RAM. Performances are given in milliseconds and Klips.

Program	T1 Ms	T1 Klips	T2 Ms	T2 Klips	T3 Ms	T3 Klips
fib (15)	209	23	143	34	143	34
deriv	1353	7	1285	8	813	13
hamilton	35593	13	34116	14	20335	24
nrev (30) *100	39979	19	26953	21	23123	34
queens1 (4)	284	24	269	25	179	38
query	155	14	148	15	104	22
quickdiff	1933	15	1872	16	1139	26
quicksort	346	17	327	18	204	29
farmer *100	3729	8	3542	8	2112	14
map	1795	13	1693	13	1009	22
queens1 (8)	5787	18	5440	19	3663	28

this Transputer architecture is much lower for programs using external memory intensively such as Prolog systems. Moreover the Transputer architecture is optimized for context switching, at the expense of sequential performance: few registers are available and bit fields manipulations intensively used for tag management are very expensive. Altogether, Transputers do not execute Prolog systems better than 1 Mips CISC processors. The actual efficiency of the TWAM depends a lot on the use of the internal RAM (see Table 1). In the fastest sequential version of the TWAM, it is used to store the TWAM registers and part of the runtime System. In the parallel TWAM, used for the measurements of Table 2, only the TWAM registers are stored in the internal RAM.

5.3 Parallel benchmarks

Several benchmarks, mainly provided by ECRC, have been used to measure the efficiency of OPERA running in parallel. The four programs used in Table 2 are:

hamilton: the problem is to find a closed path in a graph. The graph used in the benchmark includes 20 vertices and 60 edges. All solutions are computed (460,000 inferences).

map: computes all solutions to a small map colouring problem (22,800 inferences).

queens1: this is a solution to the *queens* problem where the rows and columns already used in a partial solution are recorded to avoid using them again and therefore reduce the search space. All solutions (92 for eight queens) are computed (103,000 inferences for eight queens).

Table 2: *Execution times of benchmarks running in parallel*

The first line gives the execution time, measured in milliseconds. The second line is the speedup of parallel execution relative to the parallel system running on a single processor. The measures of OPERA on a Tnode of 16 working Transputers and one control Transputer (not counted as a working Transputer in the top-line figures) are compared to Quintus Prolog release 2.4.2 running on a 1.5 MIPS SUN3/50 and on a 12.5 MIPS SUN4/60.

Program	1	4	8	16	Quintus Sun3/50	Quintus Sun4/60
ham	31271	8122	4320	2791	27100	6000
	1	3.85	7.24	11.2	1.15	5.2
map	1568	515	378		1350	300
	1	3.04	4.15		1.16	5.2
queens1-8	3890	1112	682	540	4350	930
	1	3.50	5.70	7.20	0.89	4.2
queens1-10	90926	23029	11663	6433	103300	21900
	1	3.94	7.79	14.13	0.88	4.15
queens2-8	8571	2380	1319	933	8650	1867
	1	3.60	6.50	9.18	0.99	4.6

queens2: this is a more "natural" solution to the *queens* problem, where each possible row is tested for each column. All solutions (92 for eight queens) are computed (approximately 233,000 inferences for eight queens).

Contrary to the measures of other OR-parallel Prolog systems [Chas89a] [Szer89a] [Ali90a] [Bosc90a], the benchmarks are **plain** Prolog programs, without any parallel declarations. Any choice-point can therefore be used to create a new task. Nevertheless, the OPERA prototype running in parallel provides effective speed-ups over sequential execution, these speed-ups being nearly linear when the size of the problem is sufficient (*queens(10)*). For the "smallest" benchmarks (*map, queens(8)*), the speed-ups level off rapidly.

6. RELATED WORK

A large number of models have already been proposed to parallelize Prolog. In this section, we will concentrate on the OR-parallel Prolog systems that have been successfully implemented following the multisequential approach.

The OPERA model is mainly inspired from the Kabu-Wake system [Masu86a], which was the first to copy stacks when a task is created and to use time-stamps to avoid active workers sending invalid bindings to idle ones. In Kabu-Wake, the worker giving work suspends its execution to copy its stacks into the idle worker's local memory (apparently without the incremental optimization). The scheduling is distributed and performed by otherwise idle workers. The Kabu-Wake implementation, on special purpose hardware, provides nearly linear speed-ups for large problems computed in parallel. However, it is based on a rather slow interpreter.

The closest approach to the Opera scheduler is probably followed by the multi-level load balancing scheme implemented for the Multi-PSI [Furu90a].

In the Muse model [Ali90a], active workers **share**, with otherwise idle workers, several choice points containing unprocessed alternatives. Sharing is performed by the active worker, which creates an image of a portion of its choice-points stack, in a workspace **shared** among workers. The stacks of the active worker are then copied from its local memory to the local memory of the idle worker, most of the copying being performed in parallel by the two workers, using the incremental copying optimisation (see section 3.7). Unwinding and installation of bindings in the shared section uses the trail stack instead of dates in Kabu-Wake and OPERA. The Muse implementation on a commercial shared-memory multiprocessor is based on SICStus Prolog [Carl88a]. It combines a very low overhead (5%) with good parallel speed-ups over SICStus.

The PEPSys [West87a] and SRI [Warr87a] models avoid copying of the WAM stacks by sharing their common parts. In spite of the sharing of the stacks, the PEPSys model can be implemented on distributed memory architectures [Baro88a], which is not the case of the SRI model, optimized for shared-memory architectures. Bindings to shared variables are performed in *hash-windows* (PEPSys) or *binding arrays* (SRI model), the latter being similar to the variable stack of OPERA. Accessing the contents of a variable is a constant time operation in the SRI model, which is not the case in PEPSys, where it may be necessary to follow a chain of hash-windows. Initializing of work in the SRI model is similar to the initialization of the variable stack in OPERA, while it is very cheap in PEPSys. Both models have been efficiently implemented on a commercial shared memory multiprocessor, the Aurora implementation [Szer89a] of the SRI model usually providing better speed-ups than the PEPSys system [Chas89a] when the granularity of tasks is sufficient. Limited work has been devoted to scheduling in the PEPSys implementation since the cost of task installation is independent of the respective positions of the idle and active workers in the search tree. This is not the case in Aurora where four schedulers have been implemented [Butl88a, Cald89a, Bran88a, Beau90a] for limiting the binding array installation overhead. Compared to the scheduler of OPERA, the schedulers of Muse, Aurora and PEPSys share the characteristics of being executed by otherwise idle workers and using an exact representation of the search tree located in a shared memory. These systems implement the complete Prolog language including side-effects and cut. Both PEPSys and Aurora run sequentially slower than Muse: around 20% for Aurora, 25% for PEPSys. They provide good speed-ups in parallel execution, compared with SICStus Prolog, although they remain slower than Muse.

K-LEAF [Bosc90a] is a parallel Prolog system implemented on a Transputer-based multiprocessor. Contrary to multisequential systems, processes are created **eagerly**. Combinatorial explosion of the number of processes is avoided by using some language constructs of the K-LEAF language to ensure sufficient grain size of parallel processes. K-LEAF has been implemented on an experimental Transputer-based multiprocessor providing a virtual global address space. This implementation is based on the WAM and uses a combination of binding arrays and binding lists. The WAM code is either emulated or expanded into C, and then compiled using a commercial C compiler, the latter solution being five times more efficient than the former.

OPERA runs sequentially approximately three times faster than the emulated version of K-LEAF[2]. OPERA seems also to be more efficient than Muse, Aurora and

---

[2] assuming that *queens1* and *queens2* of K-LEAF are respectively *queens2* and *queens1* from ECRC

PEPSys, although it is difficult to compare a processor of a Sequent to a Transputer! In parallel, the speed-ups of OPERA are lower than the speed-ups provided by the other systems. Several reasons may explain these lower results. The main reason is probably the high cost of inter-processor communication in the Supernode compared to shared-memory or fully connected multiprocessors. Another possible explanation is the high efficiency of the sequential Prolog engine of OPERA, which increases the relative overhead of task scheduling and requires larger benchmarks (the speed-ups of queens1(10) are good) to deliver good speedups. The experimental conditions are also different, since, contrary to the other systems, all programmer annotations of "parallel" predicates have been removed from the benchmarks used by OPERA, which are **plain** Prolog programs. In addition, a large number of optimizations have not yet been included in the current OPERA prototype, such as incremental copying of the stacks and giving several choice points to idle workers, to reduce to the task installation overhead.

7. CONCLUSION

The OPERA project aims at implementing Prolog efficiently on scalable, distributed memory architectures. Prolog is a good candidate for parallel programming because of the inherent parallelism of Prolog programs. OPERA exploits OR-parallelism, expected to provide coarser-grained parallelism than AND-parallelism and is therefore more suitable to distributed memory architectures. The computational model of OPERA is based on efficient sequential Prolog engines running almost independently on each processor. Scheduling is performed by specialized processors, structured hierarchically. Each scheduler controls several slave workers executing a Prolog engine or several slave schedulers at a lower level. To avoid costly synchronizations, the schedulers use an approximate representation of the state of the system, using sampled and filtered measurements performed by their slaves. In spite of the lack of software on the Supernode, an efficient prototype of OPERA has been implemented on a Tnode, a 16 Transputers Supernode basic module. The efficiency of the sequential Prolog engine is close to the best existing Prolog implementations while parallel execution provide good speed-ups for large search space programs.

Current developments of OPERA include extensions and improvements of the existing prototype. Sequentially, a better use of the internal RAM memory will almost double the speed of the basic Prolog engine. More important is the extension of the basic Prolog engine of OPERA to support more standard Prolog predefined predicates in parallel execution, especially cut or commit, to allow running a larger number of existing Prolog programs. The overhead of task creation will be decreased by using the incremental copying optimization. The most challenging development will be to explore the scheduling issues raised by executing OPERA on a 128 Transputer Meganode, composed of eight interconnected Tnodes.

Acknowledgements

Jacques Eudes, Philippe Waille and Miguel Santana contributed to the implementation of the software environment of the Supernode and Patrick Poissonnier implemented the measurement tools.

---

and considering that the *hamilton* problem of K-LEAF, using a ten nodes graph, is much smaller than the *hamilton* problem of ECRC, using a 20 nodes graph.

4 A Distributed Interpreter for Inherent AND/OR Parallelism

M. Avvenuti, P. Corsini and G. Frosini
Universitá di Pisa, Italy

ABSTRACT

An attractive feature of Prolog programs is their inherent parallelism, which enables us to design models that automatically process them in parallel. This chapter presents the implementation of a parallel execution model exploiting inherent AND/OR parallelism at interpretation level. The model adopted exploits the full OR-parallelism and a restricted form of AND-parallelism (*pipeline AND-parallelism*), by decomposing programs into a dynamic set of communicating processes. A distributed interpreter working in accordance with such a model and running on a message-passing parallel machine, is therefore allowed to speed up the execution. The interpreter behaves in a user-transparent way and maintains the depth-first, left-to-right search strategy of sequential Prolog.

Occam and the Transputer were chosen for the implementation and evaluation of the interpreter. First, general implementing issues on a multi-Transputer machine are reviewed, then an Occam description of processes is given. A strategy to handle the side-effects of the CUT predicate on a distributed environment is also proposed. Finally, factors influencing the performance and the actual degree of parallelism that the interpreter can recover are discussed.

1 INTRODUCTION

The inherent parallelism of Prolog programs makes them attractive for parallel processing, especially when one desires to speed up execution by using a parallel machine in a way that is invisible to the programmer, i.e. without adding any explicit, possibly machine-dependent parallel construct to the standard language. For this purpose, AND/OR forms of parallelism allow the computation to be easily splittable into concurrent activities suitable for execution on a parallel machine.

The design of a parallel execution model exploiting inherent AND/OR-parallelism involves efforts to overcome difficulties related to the control of multiprocessing overhead and to the management of binding environments.

One difficulty, known as the *binding conflicts* problem, arises with AND-parallelism when two or more literals contain terms which share a variable, since only one of them should be allowed to bind it. An effective way to preserve the consistency in the environment is to restrict the AND-parallel execution of literals to those yielding conflict-free substitutions. Models for *restricted* AND-parallelism [Degr84a], [Herm86a] avoid binding conflicts by placing a read/write discipline on the variables [Cone87a], or using compile-time analysis [Chan86a], [Fagi90a].

Although OR-parallelism is implementationally simpler, because the clauses under consideration are logically independent, the parallel exploration of alternative branches of the search space leads to difficulties in how to represent and manage *multiple binding environments* [Lind84a], [Warr87b]. The solutions to this problem mainly depend on the nature of the underlying parallel machine (i.e. shared-memory or message-passing) and characterize different models for OR-parallelism [Cram85a], [Borg84a].

The research described in this chapter is concerned with the design of a distributed interpreter exploiting the inherent AND/OR parallelism of standard Prolog programs. Our proposal is aimed at achieving an effective implementation, where the problems mentioned above are solved by preferring design simplicity to the full exploitation of parallelism. Based on Conery's AND/OR Process Model [Cone87a], the parallel execution scheme adopted exploits the full OR-parallelism and a restricted form of AND-parallelism (*pipeline AND-parallelism*) by generating a dynamic set of communicating processes. From an external point of view, the interpreter exploits parallelism in a user-transparent way, and maintains the classical depth-first, left-to-right search strategy, i.e. the solutions are always produced in the same order a sequential interpreter would produce them.

Pipeline AND-parallelism [Cors89a] is an effective scheme for solving the binding conflicts problem at interpretation level. Literals are considered in the order they appear in the clause body, and a solution produced by a given literal $L(i)$ is used to solve the literal $L(i+1)$, at same time as further solutions are produced by the literal $L(i)$. The exploited parallelism is not the maximal one, but no run-time overhead is required to check the program in order to find out about properties such as clause independence. Clearly, no advantage is taken of the pipeline AND-parallelism if backtracking never occurs, since in this case body literals are solved sequentially.

The chapter is divided into six sections. In Section 2 an informal description of the parallel execution model and the management of environments are given, and a computational example explained. Section 3 describes the Occam implementation for the distributed interpreter on a multi-Transputer machine, while in Section 4 the performance results of the interpreter running on a fully connected network of four Transputers are presented and discussed. Possibilities for simplifying the model and future work are suggested in Sections 5 and 6.

2 THE PARALLEL EXECUTION MODEL

The basic idea to exploit the inherent parallelism of logic programs involves splitting the computation into independent activities and carrying these out using sets of cooperating processes. In our model, the evaluation of goal statements is performed by two types of processes. An *AND process* is created to solve the body of a clause, which is a conjunction of one or more literals; an *OR process* is created by an AND process to solve just one of those literals, i.e. to find every set of variable bindings resulting from the reduction of the literal to the null clause. Processes communicate only via messages and are logically connected as in Figure 1.

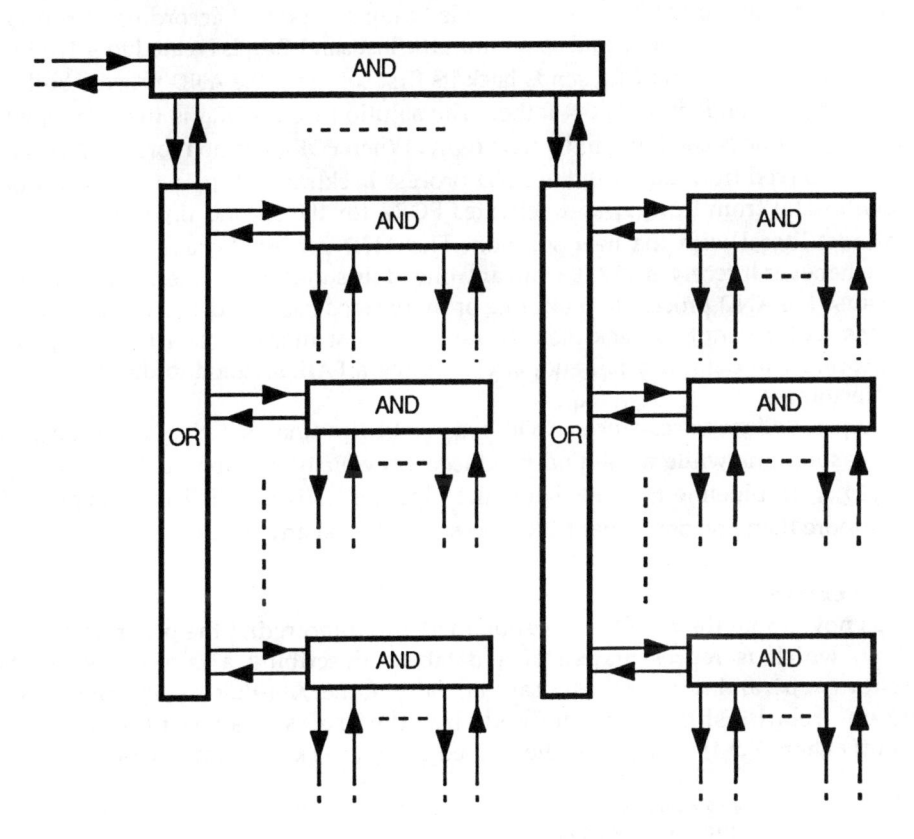

Figure 1 Process hierarchy in the model

2.1 OR Processes

An OR process is started with the literal to be solved, and a list of variable bindings. The process scans the database linearly, from top to bottom, to find all the clauses unifiable with the literal. For each unifiable clause, not corresponding to a fact (unit clause), it creates a son AND process with the aim of solving the body of the clause itself. As soon as an AND son produces solutions, it sends them to the OR father, which in turn re-orders the solutions received from all its sons and forwards them to its AND father, according to the standard depth-first order of sequential Prolog. Before terminating, the OR process sends a FAIL solution to its father.

The parallelism arises since multiple AND processes are created to solve alternative clauses. Thus, the OR-parallelism is exploited when more than one descendant AND process is active at any time.

2.2 AND Processes

The call parameters of an AND process are the index of the clause whose body must be solved, and a set of variable bindings that have been generated during the unification of the head of the clause. The AND process creates the first son OR process, say POR$_1$, to solve the leftmost literal in the clause body. As soon as a solution is received from the first son, the AND process creates a new son, say POR$_2$, to solve the next literal (with a list of variable bindings updated according to the solution returned from POR$_1$), and so on until the last son POR$_n$ is created to solve the rightmost literal. When POR$_n$ sends back its first solution, the AND process builds a solution and sends it to its OR father. The solution from POR$_n$ is then dropped, and the next one is used to build a new reply. When POR$_n$ has no more solutions (a FAIL is received from the son), the AND process backtracks. It gets a new solution (if one exists) from POR$_{n-1}$ and activates POR$_n$ for the second time to solve the rightmost literal with the new solution. The AND process behaves in the same way whenever it receives a FAIL from any one of its son OR processes. Backtracking can cause the AND process to make one or more steps backward and in the end the process will attempt to backtrack through the first literal. When this happens, the process will definitely fail and, after sending a FAIL solution to the OR father, will terminate.

The parallelism arises since an OR process POR$_i$ remains active and produces further solutions while a solution produced previously is elaborated by POR$_{i+1}$, POR$_{i+2}$,..., in pipeline fashion. Thus, the pipeline AND-parallelism is exploited when more than one descendant OR process is active at any time.

2.3 An Example

Let us now apply the parallel execution model to interpreting the program shown below, which is representative of a database describing a family tree. Facts father(a,b) and mother(a,b) say that 'a' is father/mother of 'b'; some well-known relationships are defined by the rules parent(U,V) and grandfather(X,Y); the query is then posed to find mark's grandfathers:

1. father(alex,mark).
2. father(horace,grace).
3. mother(grace,mark).
4. mother(anne,grace).
5. parent(U,V) :- father(U,V).
6. parent(U,V) :- mother(U,V).
7. grandfather(X,Y) :- father(X,Z), parent(Z,Y).
   ?- grandfather(X,mark).

The following processes are created:

PAND1	for solving the initial goal statement;
POR1	for solving the unique literal grandfather(X,mark);
PAND2	for solving the goal father(X,Z), parent(Z,Y);
POR2$_1$	for solving the first literal father(X,Z);
POR2$_2$	for solving the second literal parent(Z,Y);
PAND3	for solving the goal father(U,V);
PAND4	for solving the goal mother(U,V);

POR3   for solving the unique literal father(U,V);
POR4   for solving the unique literal mother(U,V).

A possible time evolution of the processes involved in the interpretation is shown in Figure 2, where the time durations quoted are solely explanatory. Communications between processes are indicated as arrows, where tags indicate the instantiations sent by a father to each son and the solutions returned. A continuous line indicates a process that is active, performing unification or processing a message, while a dashed line means a process is waiting for a message. Note that processes POR2$_2$, PAND3, PAND4, POR3 and POR4 are activated two times. The behaviour of the most significant AND process, i.e. PAND2, is as follows:

1. it activates POR2$_1$ with instantiation {Y=mark}, and waits for a reply message from POR2$_1$;
2. when it receives from POR2$_1$ the solution {X=alex,Z=mark}, it activates POR2$_2$ with instantiations {Y=mark,Z=mark}, and waits for a reply message from POR2$_2$;
3. when it receives from POR2$_2$ the solution FAIL, it takes the second solution {X=horace,Z=grace} from POR2$_1$ (already arrived), re-activates POR2$_2$ with instantiations {Y=mark,Z=grace}, and waits for a reply message from POR2$_2$;
4. when it receives from POR2$_2$ the solution SUCCESS, it sends to its father the solution {X=horace}, and waits for a further reply message from POR2$_2$;
5. when it receives from POR2$_2$ the solution FAIL, it takes a further solution from POR2$_1$ (already arrived); since this time the solution is a FAIL, it sends to its father the solution FAIL and terminates.

The first time the OR process POR2$_2$ is activated, it tries to solve the literal parent(mark,mark) as follows:

1. it unifies the literal with the head of clauses 5 and 6, activates PAND3 and PAND4 with instantiations {U=mark,V=mark}, and waits for reply messages from children;
2. since solutions from both PAND3 and PAND4 are FAIL, it sends to its father the solution FAIL and terminates.

The second time POR2$_2$ solves the literal parent(grace,mark) as follows:

1. it unifies the literal with the head of clauses 5 and 6, activates PAND3 and PAND4 with instantiations {U=grace,V=mark}, and waits for reply messages from the children;
2. when it receives from the first son PAND3 the solution FAIL, it drops the corresponding clause in the procedure;
3. when it receives from the second son PAND4 the solution SUCCESS, it forwards the solution to its father, and waits for a further reply message from PAND4;
4. when it receives from PAND4 the solution FAIL, it sends to its father the solution FAIL and terminates.

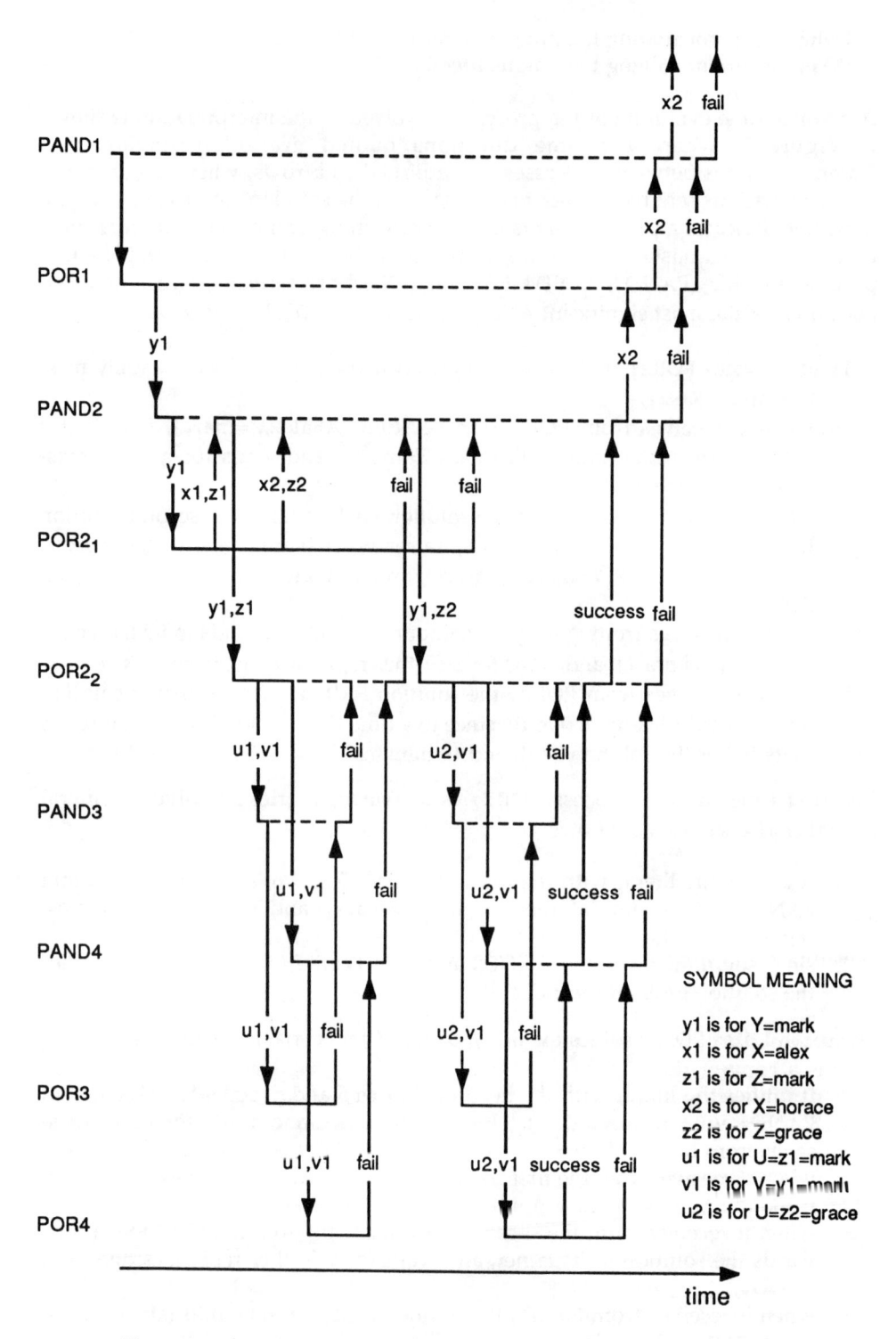

Figure 2 A possible time evolution of the above PAND and POR processes

From the time evolution graph given in Figure 2, it should be noted that OR-parallelism is exploited in those intervals in which multiple AND sons of a given OR process are simultaneously active (as with processes PAND3 and PAND4). The pipeline AND-parallelism is exploited when multiple OR sons of a given AND process are simultaneously active (as with processes POR2$_1$ and POR2$_2$).

2.4 The Environment

Fast and memory-efficient techniques to store and update the environments have been developed for sequential implementations [Warr83a]. Unfortunately, they are not applicable in parallel implementations [Warr87b], where either shared or multiple binding environments must be managed [Cram85a], [Herm89a]. Since the model described here falls within the message-passing paradigm, there are no shared variables between processes, but multiple copies of the same variable exist during the exploitation of the OR- and the pipeline AND-parallelism.

In our model, the *environment* of a clause is a data structure storing the current value of each variable in the clause. For each variable, it contains a cell describing the binding type (e.g. atom, integer, variable, structure, free) and zero or more cells for representing the bound value.

Handling the environment in AND processes. An AND process is invoked with a set of variable bindings that have been generated during the unification of the head of the clause. To this set, the process adds one cell (initialized to a free value) for each local variable (i.e. a variable occurring only in the clause body). The augmented set of variable bindings becomes the current environment for the process, and is sent to the first OR son together with the literal to be solved. In the case of success, the son will reply with an updated copy of the environment, where new instantiations are possibly present. The reply environment of the first son becomes the current environment, and is sent to the second OR son. The sequence is repeated until the last son is activated. The solution to be sent to the OR father is built from the reply environment of the last OR son, by replacing chains of variable-variable bindings with their terminal values (*dereferencing*), and removing the local variable cells.

Handling the environment in OR processes. An OR process is started with the literal to be solved and a copy of the environment from its AND father. For each attempt to unify the given literal with a clause head, a working table is built, made up of two data structures: a *unification table* and a *link table*. The *unification table* is a copy of the father environment, while the *link table* contains a cell for each variable in the clause head, initialized to a free value. During the unification, bindings of father variables are written into the unification table, while those of head variables are written into the link table. After a successful unification, the OR process invokes an AND son with a dereferenced copy of the link table. It should be noted that undesired growth of data structures is prevented by sending to the son only the dereferenced environment contained in the link table, instead of the entire binding environment.

A reply from a successful AND son is a copy of the invocation environment, possibly containing new values for free variables. When an OR process receives a reply from one of its sons, it creates a message for its father by comparing the reply with the content of the link table. Each cell in the link table is dereferenced, together with the corresponding cell in the reply. If the terminal value derived from the link table is a free cell in the unification table, the unification table is filled with the value derived from the reply. Then, the updated copy of the unification table is sent as a reply to the parent process. In this way, bindings are propagated towards the calling process.

2.5 Unification

During head matching, the OR process invokes the *unification procedure*, which possibly binds father variables and head variables, whose instantiations update the unification table and link table respectively. Corresponding arguments of the literal and of the clause head are in turn dereferenced, and the following decisions are taken depending on the terminal values:

- **constant & constant**: unification succeeds if, and only if, constants are of the same type and value;
- **constant or structure & free variable**: unification always succeeds with the variable being instantiated to the other object;
- **free variable & free variable**: unification always succeeds with one of the two variables being bound to the other. When the variables belong to different tables, the head variable is bound to the father one (not vice versa);
- **structure & structure**: if structures have the same functor and arity, the unification procedure is recursively applied to their arguments.

Figure 3 shows the messages and the data structures involved in the unification process discussed above. An activation message (1) is sent to an OR process by its AND parent. A working table (2) is then built during unification with each matching clause head. Successful unification causes the working table to be updated. The activation message for the AND son (3) is derived by dereferencing the right part of the working table. The current environment (4) is sent to the first OR son, which returns an updated copy (5) if successful. The environment (6) is then modified and returned by the last OR son. The reply (7) is dereferenced and cleaned up of local variable cells, then it is sent to the OR father (8). Here, instantiations of father variables are derived by comparing the working table (2) and the solution received. Then, the updated copy of the unification table (9) is sent to the AND father.

3 IMPLEMENTING THE INTERPRETER

An interpreter for standard Prolog, working in accordance with the parallel execution model described above, appears at the system level as a dynamic tree of independent processes communicating only via messages (such a tree of processes represents exactly the search tree developed by the Prolog inference mechanism). Since the number of processes is closely related to the nature of the program to be solved and may vary in a wide range, the interpreter requires *dynamic creation of processes*. In any case, a large number of processes is required to remain in existence, but direct communications are only between parent and children.

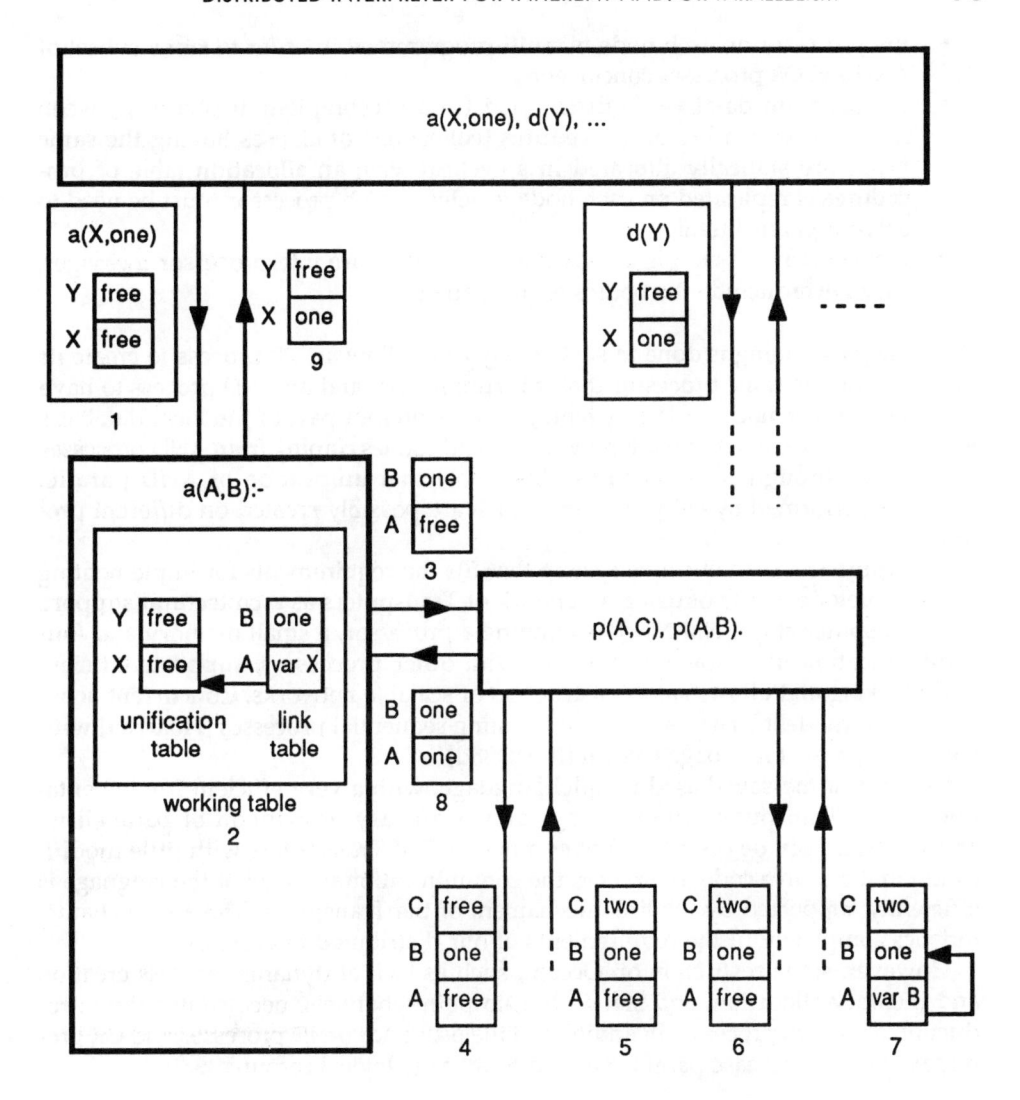

Figure 3 *Message and data structures in the unification process*

The most natural implementation of the interpreter is provided by a message-passing parallel machine, where each node is a computer element with a processor, a private memory and communication links. Ideally, true multi-processing can be provided by a sufficiently large number of nodes, so as to assign every process to a new node, while a particular node may act as an interface between the system and the external world. Messages are delivered by an interconnection network on the basis of explicit node naming.

Since a practical parallel architecture has a limited number of nodes, a limited memory size on each node and a limited communication bandwidth, the requirements for the interpreter can be fulfilled by putting forward the following assumptions:

- the processor on each node is multi-programmed in order to run a subset of AND and OR processes concurrently;
- the program database is distributed (in a precompilation phase) between nodes, to which Prolog procedures (collections of clauses having the same head) are statically allocated in a cyclical way; an allocation table of procedures is replicated on each node to select which processor must be used to solve a given literal;
- messages are as simple as possible and, if they are interprocessor messages, they never include the bodies of the clauses.

Database partitioning is done in such a way as to allow an OR process to create its AND sons on the same processor that it is running on, and an AND process to have OR sons on other nodes if the matching clauses are not part of the local database. As a consequence, AND activation messages and replies coming from AND processes never flow through physical links. Also, note that unification of AND-parallel literals is performed by OR processes, which are possibly created on different processors.

Our approach to an effective system that fits the requirements for implementing the interpreter consists of using a network of Transputers as architectural support. The Transputer chip [INMO88c], containing a processor, a small memory and four communication links for data transfer with other processors, supports efficient multi-tasking and allows easy construction of scalable networks. Concurrent activities can be modelled as sets of communicating sequential processes [Hoar78a] written in the parallel language Occam [INMO88d].

Occam is a message-based parallel language, with a very efficient implementation on the Transputer. The language allows an easy description of parallelism, and processes can be distributed over a network of Transputers with little modification to the source code. Moreover, the communication protocol of the language is efficiently supported by the link mechanism of the Transputer. The above characteristics completely fit the requirements of our distributed interpreter.

However, some restriction on Occam, such as lack of dynamic process creation and memory allocation, and static point-to-point channels, necessitates the introduction of system processes in addition to the user ones (AND processes and OR processes), both to increase parallelism and to manage logical resources.

3.1 Resource Management

As stated above, in the implementation it is necessary to create processes dynamically because the number of sons of each process can only be defined at run-time, depending on the evolution of the program. Channels, connecting a father process to its newly created sons, cannot be statically allocated. Finally, for performance reasons, it is important that channels are buffered to let processes produce multiple solutions before blocking because previous solutions have not yet been used.

Dynamic creation of processes and channels has been simulated by introducing resource manager processor on each node (see Figure 4). Collections of AND and OR processes are statically created and remain in an idle state until an activation message is received. Process activation is administered by a Process Manager (PM), that wakes up the required process when needed. Whenever a process has to create a son, it sends an activation message (containing activation parameters for the son)

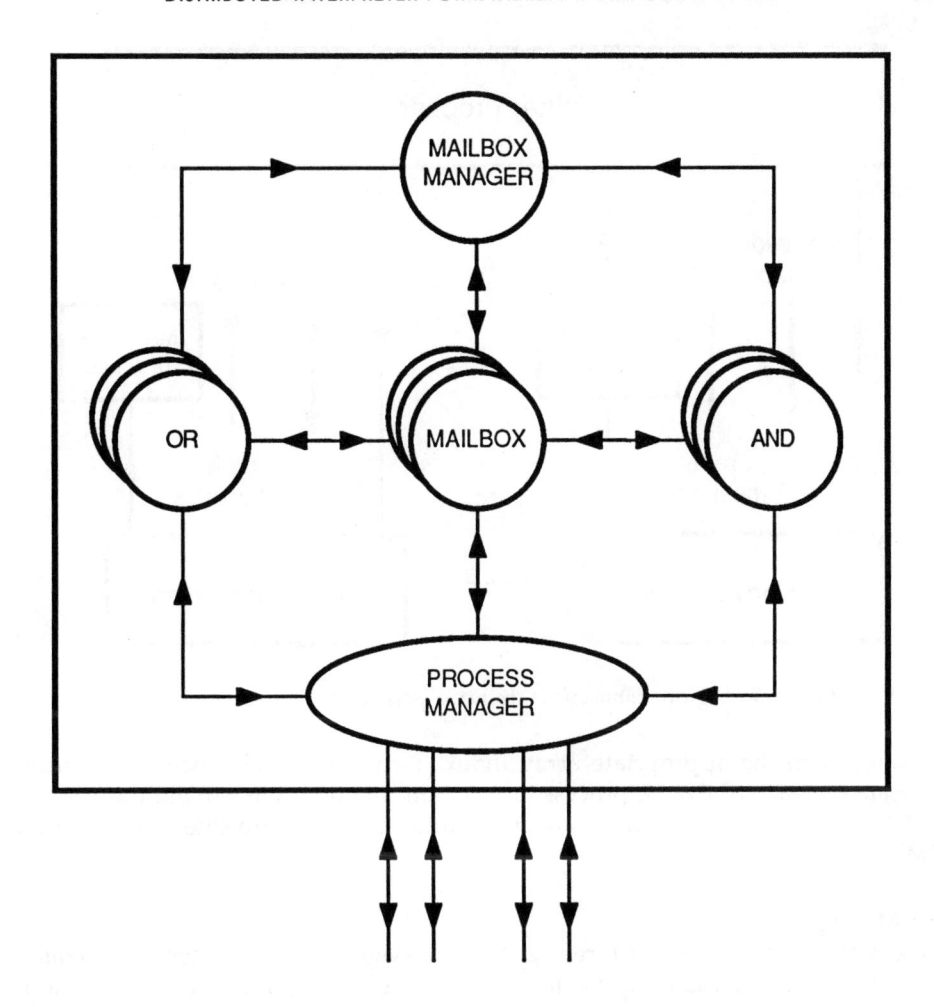

Figure 4 Set of processes on each node

to the PM. The PM selects an idle AND/OR process, wakes it with a message on a dedicated channel, then sends it the activation message. The PM is notified when a process has terminated its task, so that the process can be restarted later with a new task. By means of the database allocation table, the PM also selects the processor on which new OR processes must be created when the clauses involved are resident on another node.

Buffering on channels has been achieved by means of additional MAILBOX processes on each reply channel (see Figure 5). With such a scheme, a process can produce reply messages that are stored in the first-in/first-out queue of the MAILBOX if the requesting process is not ready to use them. MAILBOX processes are activated in the same way as AND/OR processes by a Mailbox Manager (MM) on each node.

The MM is also responsible for allocating channels dynamically. Each AND/OR process has access to some channel arrays through which it is connected to the MAILBOX processes. Each entry is allocated to a sender and to a receiver process by

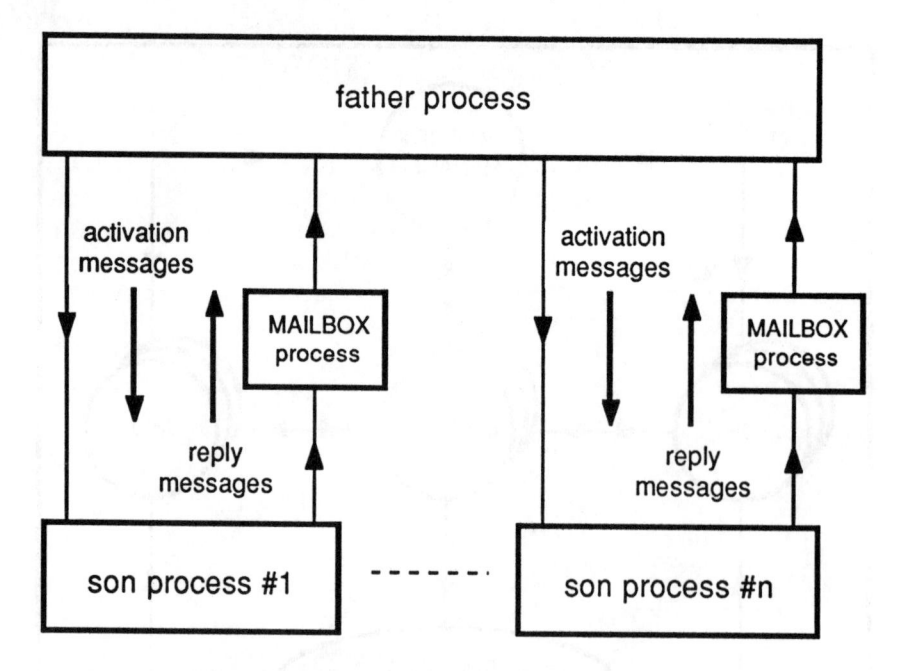

Figure 5 Logical connections between parent and children processes

passing them the appropriate array index. Two pairs of channels are statically allocated to each AND/OR process to communicate with the PM and the MM. The PM has direct access to the Transputer links that communicate with the other PM's.

3.2 Messages

Processes communicate via three types of messages: *activation, reply* and *termination*. Messages are made up of three sections: a header, a control section, and a data section. The message header identifies its type and length, and corresponds to an Occam protocol. Control and data sections depend on the message type, as described below:

- An **activation** message is sent to the PM by an AND/OR process which has to create a descendant OR/AND process. The control section indicates type and identifier of the sender process, and a reply queue identifier. The data section of an AND activation message contains the index of the clause whose body must be solved, and all the variables that are present in the clause head with their current bindings. The data section of an OR activation message contains the literal to be solved and the environment of the calling process.

- A **reply** message is sent through the MAILBOX by a process to its parent. The control section contains the destination node and queue identifier for the message. The data section is either a copy of the original environment with fresh instantiations derived during the resolution of the goal, or a FAIL token.

- **Termination** messages are sent by processes to the PM to signal they are ready for a new task. It is made up of the header section only.

3.3 The AND Process

An Occam-like description of an AND process is given in Figure 6. The process is woken by the PM with a message on channel andin. Then it receives the activation message from its father, creates (throughout the PM) its first OR son and waits for a solution. Then a loop is entered where success solutions cause the process to activate the next OR son, while FAIL messages induce backtracking (the current solution of the previous literal is skipped and a new one is received).

```
PROC and
   WHILE TRUE
     SEQ
       andin ? ANY
       < receive an AND activation message >
       son.index := 1
       < request a queue to the mailbox manager >
       < send an OR activation message >
       < wait reply message from OR son >
       WHILE (NOT (solution = FAIL) AND (son.index = 1))
       | SEQ
       |    WHILE solution <> FAIL
       |    | SEQ
       |         IF
       |    |    | son.index <= number.literals
       |              SEQ
       |    |    |    son.index := son.index + 1
       |    |    |    < request a queue to the mailbox manager >
       |    |    |    < send an OR activation message >
       |              TRUE
       |    |    |    < prepare and send reply message to father >
       |         < wait reply message from OR son >
       |    WHILE (solution = FAIL) and (son.index > 1)
       |         SEQ
       |         < dispose queue >
       |         son.index := son.index -1
       |         < wait reply message from OR son >
       < send FAIL message to father >
       < send termination message to process manager >
:
```

Figure 6 Structure of an AND process

3.4 The OR Process

The body of an OR process is made up of two sections (Figure 7). In the first, unification of the literal with clauses in the database is attempted and AND sons are created. The second section receives the solutions from its sons and sends them back to the AND father according to the standard ordering of sequential Prolog. Note that, in the case of a fact, the corresponding AND son is not created; instead, the solution is directly computed by the OR process and stored into factarray[], from which it is then sent to the father.

```
PROC or
  WHILE TRUE
    SEQ
      SEQ i = [0 FOR factarray.dim]
        factarray[i] := FALSE
      orin ? ANY
      < receive OR activation message >
      son.index := 0
      SEQ clause.index = [1 FOR clause.number]
        SEQ
        |   < try unification >
            IF
        |   | is.unifiable
              SEQ
        |   |   | son.index := son.index + 1
                < determine whether the clause is a fact>
        |   |   | IF
                  is.a.fact
        |   |   |   factarray[son.index] := TRUE
                  TRUE
        |   |   |   < send an AND activation message >
              TRUE
        |   |   SKIP
      SEQ k = [1 FOR son.index]
      | IF
          factarray[k] = TRUE
      |     < prepare and send a reply to the father >
          TRUE
      |   | SEQ
              < wait reply message from son >
      |   |   WHILE solution <> FAIL
                SEQ
      |   |       < prepare and send a reply to the father >
                  < wait reply message from son >
      < send FAIL message to the father >
      < send termination message to the manager >
:
```

Figure 7 Structure of an OR process

3.5 Handling the CUT

The effect of a CUT predicate is to alter the way backtracking works afterwards, so that certain literals cannot be resatisfied. In our parallel execution model this turns out to be a limitation on exploiting parallelism. When an AND process encounters a CUT in the body of a clause, pipeline AND-parallelism must be limited to only literals following the CUT, and the OR-parallel evaluation of those preceding it should be broken. The father OR process must also be notified so that it can drop solutions from sons following the one by which the CUT has been found. Handling this event in a distributed environment requires the forced termination of some processes. Forced termination of processes is also useful to break infinite loops, that might occur in programs having the following structure:

```
a.
a:-a.
?-a,!,other_literals.
```

An OR process is created to solve the first query literal. It immediately finds a matching fact, and also creates an AND son to solve the body of the second clause. The son process creates a new OR son that, in turn, finds a solution with the first fact and creates another AND son for the second clause. The chain of process creation will never stop unless some external actions are taken. The top-level AND process, after receiving the first solution, encounters the CUT, which means that no more solutions are needed. Although termination of the son process is not necessary in principle, the son would otherwise produce an infinite number of processes that would saturate the system. Thus, it must be possible to force the termination of processes.

Multi-tasking on a Transputer is done by hardware, not by some sort of operating system. This implies that living processes cannot be aborted, unless an explicit communication protocol for forced termination is established within the system. Thus, the following strategy should be applied to solve the problem:

- an AND process that encounters a CUT sends a CUT message to its father, and an ABORT message to the sons solving the literals before the CUT;
- an OR process that receives a CUT message sends an ABORT message to all its sons that follow the one from which the cut message has been received;
- an OR process that receives an ABORT message broadcasts it to its living sons and terminates;
- an AND process that receives an ABORT message broadcasts it to its living sons and terminates.

For this protocol to work, it is necessary that OR processes issue a non-blocking receive for an ABORT message before attempting to create sons. It is also necessary that ABORT and CUT messages have priority over reply messages.

Although such a technique works in principle, the check for the abort message in OR processes seems to be extremely costly. So, ABORT messages are sent directly to the PM and a copy to the MM, that prevent further creations of sons and allocation of MAILBOX's for the aborted process and its descendants.

4 PERFORMANCE EVALUATION

The Occam & Transputer implementation for the distributed interpreter has been tested by running several benchmark programs, with the aim of evaluating the actual exploitation of parallelism inherent in programs and of finding which class of programs can favourably use such an execution model.

4.1 The Hardware architecture

The interpreter was mapped onto three hardware configurations, consisting of 1, 2 and 4 working nodes respectively. The 4-node system consists in all of five Transputers (T414-20) connected as shown in Figure 8. The node T0 is set on a mono-Transputer B004 board and runs a user.manager process performing the I/O required to load the database from the host computer and to communicate with the user through the console. The node T0 also runs the AND process related to the initial goal-statement. The working nodes reside on the four Transputers of a B003 board; each of them runs the set of processes as shown in Figure 4. The 1-node and the

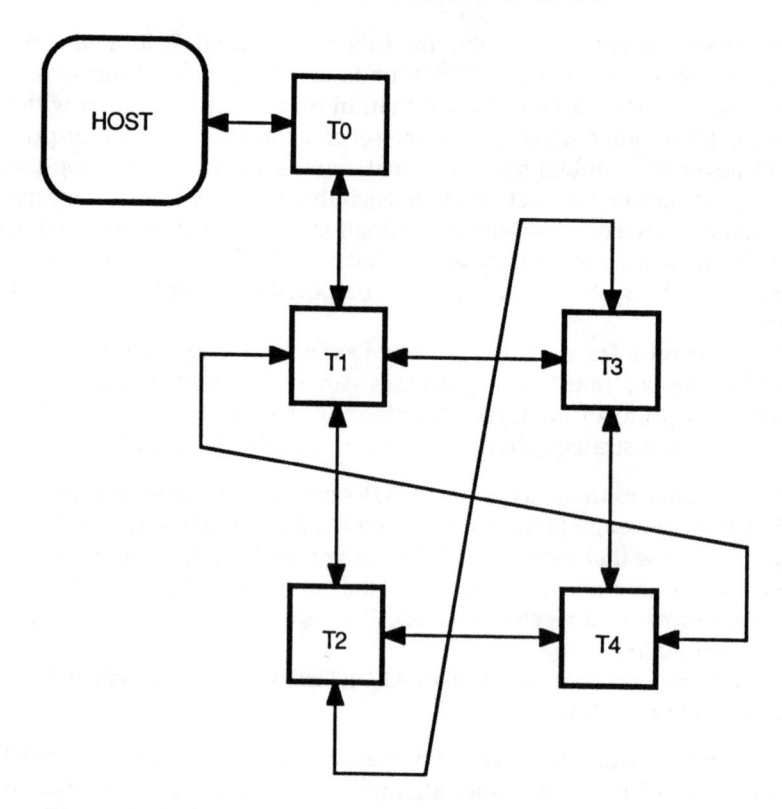

Figure 8 Transputer-based architecture for the 4-node interpreter

2-node configurations are obtained as subsets of the 4-node configuration and consist of T0-T1 and T0-T1-T2, respectively. The 1-node configuration, which performs a sequential interpretation, has been used for purposes of comparison with the parallel configurations.

Note that the tetrahedral topology of the network T1-T2-T3-T4 implies point-to-point links between nodes. Because of this property, additional overhead for message routing can be avoided. However, since full connection between five Transputers is impracticable (one of the four links of T0 is used to connect it to the host system), node T1 must include an additional task to route messages from/to T0.

4.2 Benchmarks

A total of eight benchmarks were examined, each of them giving different opportunities to exploit AND-parallelism and OR-parallelism. The benchmark programs used are listed in Appendix 1. They are non-trivial and make use of typical Prolog paradigms, such as recursion, non-determinism and processing of recursive data structures. Permute, Reverse, Query and Min_route code classical problems, while the other four have been expressly designed to test the interpreter's ability to exploit parallelism.

Table 1 summarizes the speed-up figures obtained by running the benchmark programs on the multi-node configurations of the interpreter. Speed-ups were defined as the ratio of the execution time reported on the 1-node configuration to those reported on the multi-node configurations. It should be noted that a wide range of speed gains were obtained. General factors limiting and differentiating the performance were found to be:

- *Type and amount of parallelism inherent in programs.* The different nature of benchmarks offers the interpreter varying opportunities for exploiting parallelism. Moreover, as discussed in the next section, the two forms of parallelism speed up the execution differently. The Reverse benchmark, for which speed-up lower than 1 was obtained, is an extreme case. Inspection of this benchmark shows that at any point only one clause exists that can be unified, and that backtracking never occurs. As a result, neither OR-parallelism nor pipeline AND-parallelism are exploitable.
- *Parallelization overhead.* A percentage degradation of performance with all the benchmarks is due to time-consuming operations such as multi-processing, communication, synchronization of processes, management of replicated data structures. The amount of overhead largely depends on the number of AND/OR processes involved and on the complexity of data structures processed. In fact, the more complex data are (e.g. recursive structures), the larger the environments; the larger the number of processes is, the more times environments are communicated in the system, affecting the efficiency.
- *Constraints imposed by the search strategy of Prolog.* As observed by Fagin [Fagi90a], a limited average speed-up is common in parallel implementations of standard Prolog, either compiled or interpreted, due to the depth-first, left-to-right search strategy. Since such a strategy is preserved under our parallel execution model, even though the interpreter carries out the search concurrently, the solutions are produced in the same order a sequential interpreter would produce them. This constitutes a severe limit on the exploitation of parallelism, because the production of a solution must be deferred until all the previous paths in the search tree have been explored.

Table 1 *Speed-up on the Transputer systems*

Program	Speed-up 2-node	Speed-up 4-node
Reverse	0.9	0.9
Permute	1.1	1.4
Query	1.5	2.2
Deep_back	1.5	2.8
Test_OR.2	1.1	3.1
Test_OR.4	1.2	2.7
Min_route	1.3	1.8
Tree	1.4	2.3

4.3 Parallelism Exploitation

In the following graphs speed-up figures are plotted by gathering benchmark programs on the basis of the type of parallelism exploitable (AND, OR, and blended

AND/OR). The *linear* trend (representing the theoretical maximum speed-up) has been drawn for sake of comparison. Generally, the gradient of the curve gives some idea of the actual possibilities of exploiting parallelism: the further from the linear a gradient is, the smaller the improvements that will be gained by increasing the number of nodes.

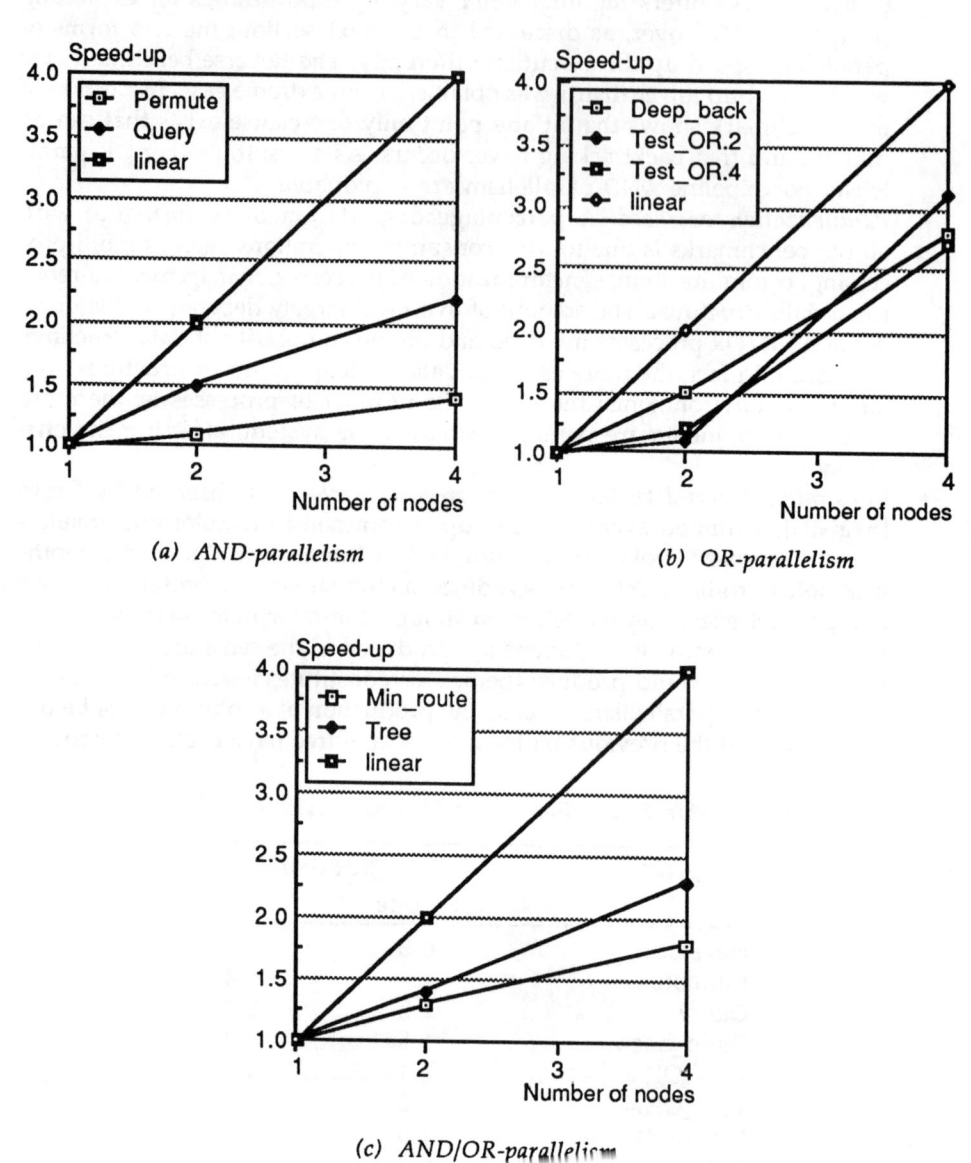

(a) AND-parallelism

(b) OR-parallelism

(c) AND/OR-parallelism

Figure 9 Parallelism exploitation

Figure 9a shows the performance improvement obtainable with AND-parallelism. In Permute the pipeline AND-parallelism is exploited by forcing backtracking with the fail predicate in the query statement, while the OR-parallelism is absent because at any point only one clause can be unified. It is the same with Query, where an intensive backtracking is required for the query(..) rule, but OR-parallelism is absent even if multiple clauses are unifiable each time the literals pop(..) and area(..) are attempted. This is because the unified clauses are facts, and no son AND processes are activated. The OR-parallelism exploitation is shown in Figure 9b. Remarkable speed gains are obtained with the three benchmarks, which use OR-parallelism at an increasing depth. Finally, Figure 9c shows performance improvement for the benchmarks where both AND-parallelism and OR-parallelism are exploited. The results obtained from blended parallelism are significant because the Tree and Min_route benchmarks can be considered as templates for serious programs with complex databases.

The above results indicate that good candidates for the execution model are programs where genuine OR-parallelism is present and all solutions are required, or the desired solution is not on the immediate left of the search tree.

5 A MODEL OPTIMIZATION

From late analysis on the basic AND/OR process model, we identified some changes that can be introduced to improve the execution efficiency of the interpreter. In particular, it should be noted that the role of an AND process mainly consists in coordinating the activities of a set of descendant OR processes created to solve the body of a clause. Without affecting the parallelism exploited by the model, we may by-pass the AND process by connecting descendant OR processes in a pipeline fashion and providing a direct communication between them (a similar communication criterion is also adopted between the AND operators of ECDAM-2, as described by Kacsuk in [Kacs91a]). As a result, a simplified version of the execution model can be defined, where a single type of process (SOLVER process) plays the roles of both an OR and an AND process.

The SOLVER process extends OR processes by adding to ability to forward solutions, as AND processes do in the current model. Such an extension is achieved by modifying the mechanism a process uses to transmit the solutions, which is now based on the position of the literal within the body of the clause.

Like an OR process, the SOLVER process is an interpreter created to search for all the solutions of a given literal. Each time a rule clause is found to be unifiable with the literal, the SOLVER starts a new pipeline of descendant processes devoted to the solution of its body. To do this, it only creates the leftmost SOLVER of the pipeline (i.e. the process solving the leftmost body literal). Then, the pipeline will grow automatically, as each component process will become able to create the next element, i.e it will have a solution to forward. As an example, let us consider the following clauses:

```
p :- a,b,c.
p :- d,e.
    .
    .
    .
?- p.
```

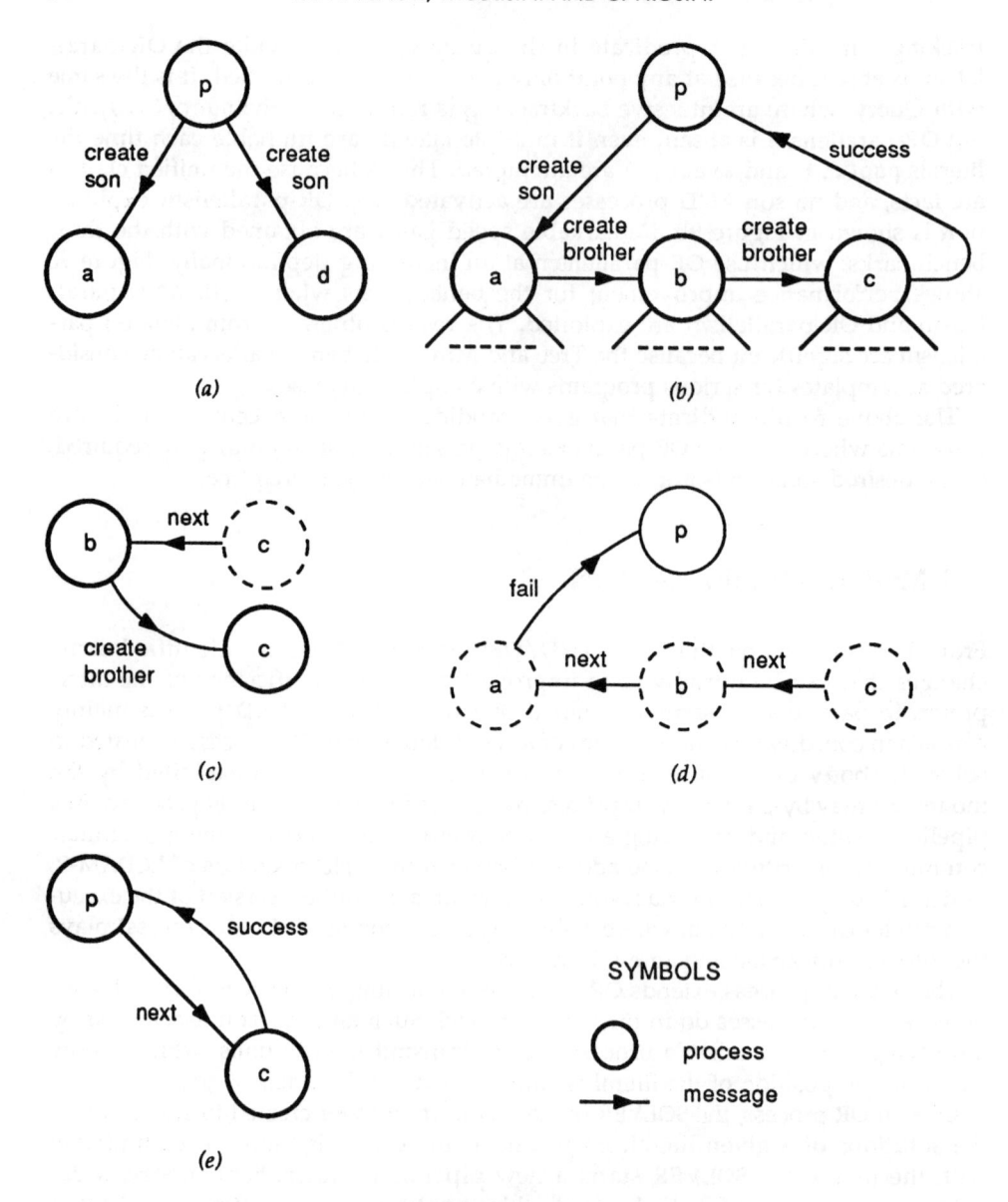

Figure 10 Parallel execution with SOLVER processes

Figure 10 shows the relationships between some processes involved in the interpretation (processes are tagged with their literals). The process dealing with the query literal p, creates a *son* process to solve the leftmost body literal of each unifiable clause (Figure 10a). As soon as a son process finds a solution, it creates a *brother* process to solve the second body literal, and so on to the rightmost body literal. Eventually, the SOLVER dealing with the rightmost literal sends its solutions to the *father* process directly (Figure 10b). In such a way, the binding environment flows through the pipeline of sibling SOLVER's, is updated at every turn with the partial solutions produced by each process, and is finally returned to the father.

The forward flow through the pipeline of processes described above breaks off when a SOLVER is unable to provide solutions. In this case, the failing process requests the next solution from its predecessor brother and terminates. If the request can be satisfied, the forward flow resumes with the creation of a new brother (Figure 10c), otherwise the request is propagated backward, until a process is able to satisfy it. If the backtracking reaches the leftmost process and this one is unable to provide a new solution, a FAIL solution is sent back to the father, causing the clause under consideration to be dropped and the next one to be considered (Figure 10d). The backtracking can also be forced by the father by means of an explicit request for the next solution to the descendant process solving the rightmost literal (Figure 10e).

In such a way, pipeline AND-parallelism is exploited when multiple sibling SOLVER's are active within the set solving the body of a clause. OR-parallelism is exploited when multiple sets of descendant SOLVER's are simultaneously solving the bodies of different clauses unifiable with a given literal.

Such an optimization in the model meets the need for controlling the parallelization overhead. In fact, the number of active processes becomes smaller, communication is reduced and management of binding environments is simplified. An Occam implementation for an interpreter based on the improved model is under development [Avve91a].

6 CONCLUSIONS AND FUTURE WORK

In this chapter we have shown an effective method for parallelizing the interpretation of Prolog programs. The execution model exploits OR-parallelism and pipeline AND-parallelism by decomposing Prolog programs into a collection of communicating processes. A realistic implementation of a distributed interpreter is given on a message-passing parallel machine based on Transputers. Experiments on the interpreter have been conducted on an Occam implementation running on a network of four Transputers. The aims were: to evaluate the actual parallelism exploited in the model; to understand the limiting factors for parallelism, both in the model and in the Prolog search strategy; and to identify a class of programs that can take advantage of the parallelism of the system. An optimization of the execution model for controlling the parallelization overhead and the number of active processes has also been given.

Future work might focus on improvements to be made in the implementation of the interpreter. Optimization of techniques for representing and managing the binding environments may lead to shorter message size and more efficient execution. A dynamic work-load balancing strategy could be established in a system where either the size of local memory allows the replication of the entire database on each node, or a cache-based memory management exists. Finally, the limit on the number of processors up to which a better performance can be achieved should be evaluated for a wide variety of programs (note that the structure of processes and their organization on each node allow for the system to be easy scalable).

Acknowledgements

The interpreter and its underlying message-passing multi-node architecture were developed at the University of Pisa, Italy, as part of a national research project on Logic Programming Dedicated Processors. The research was supported in part by the Italian Research National Council.

APPENDIX 1: THE BENCHMARK PROGRAMS

/*reverse */
  reverse([X | L0],L) :- reverse(L0,L1), concatenate(L1,[X],L).
  reverse([],[]).
  concatenate([X | L1],L2,[X | L3]) :- concatenate(L1,L2,L3).
  concatenate([],L,L).
  ?- reverse([1,2,3,4,5,6,7,8,9,10,11,12,13,14],L).

/* permute */
  permute([],[]).
  permute(L,[H | T]) :- append(V,[H | U],L), append(V,U,W), permute(W,T).
  append([],L,L).
  append([X | L1],L2,[X | L3]) :- append(L1,L2,L3).
  ?- permute([1,2,3,4,5],X), fail.

/* query */
  query(C1,D1,C2,D2) :-
       density(C1,D1), density(C2,D2), D2<D1, A is (20*D1), B is (21*D2), A<B.
  density(C,D) :- pop(C,P), area(C,A), D is (P/A).
  /* it follows the "population & area" database for 25 nations */
  pop(italy,55).
   .
   .
  area(italy,120).
   .
   .
  ?- query(A,B,C,D),fail.

/* deep_back */
  /* the following clauses are replicated 4 times */
  p(X,Y,Z) :- q1(X,Y,a).   p(X,Y,Z) :- q2(X,Y,a).
  p(X,Y,Z) :- q3(X,Y,a).   p(X,Y,Z) :- q4(X,Y,a).
  p(X,Y,Z) :- q5(X,Y,a).   p(X,Y,Z) :- q6(X,Y,a).
  p(X,Y,Z) :- q7(X,Y,a).   p(X,Y,Z) :- q8(X,Y,a).
  p(X,Y,Z) :- q9(X,Y,a).   p(X,Y,Z) :- q10(X,Y,a).
  /* the following clauses are unique */
  p(a,b,c).
  q1(X,Y,b).   q2(X,Y,b).   q3(X,Y,b).   q4(X,Y,b).   q5(X,Y,b).
  q6(X,Y,b).   q7(X,Y,b).   q8(X,Y,b).   q9(X,Y,b).   q10(X,Y,b).
  ?- p(X,Y,Z).

/* test_OR.2 */
a(1) :- b(X), X=2.
a(1) :- b(X), X=2.
a(1) :- b(X), X=2.
a(2) :- b(X), X=2.
/* the following clause is replicated 14 times */
b(1) :- c(X), X=4.
b(2) :- c(X), X=4.
/* the following clause is replicated 14 times */
c(1).
c(4).
?- a(X), X=2.

/* test_OR.4 */
a(1) :- b(X), X=2.   b(1) :- c(X), X=2.   c(1) :- d(X), X=2.
a(2) :- b(X), X=2.   b(2) :- c(X), X=2.   c(2) :- d(X), X=2.
d(1) :- e(X), X=2.   e(1).
d(1) :- e(X), X=2.   e(1).
d(1) :- e(X), X=2.   e(1).
d(2) :- e(X), X=2.   e(2).
?-a(X), X=2.

/* min_route */
member(Z,[Z|_]).
member(Z,[_|A]) :- member(Z,A).
pen_ins(X,[Y],[X,Y]).
pen_ins(X,[Y|A],[Y|B]) :- pen_ins(X,A,B).
min(P1,L1,P2,L2,P2,L2) :- L1=0.
min(P1,L1,P2,L2,P2,L2) :- L2<L1.
route(N,N,X,Y,L) :- distance(X,Y,L).
route(V,N,X,Y,L) :-
    distance(X,Z,I), not(member(Z,V)), pen_ins(Z,V,M), route(M,N,Z,Y,J), L is (I+J).
min_route(X,Y,P1,L1,P2,L2) :-
    route([X,Y],P3,X,Y,L3), min(P1,L1,P3,L3,P4,L4), !, min_route(X,Y,P4,L4,P2,L2).
min_route(_,_,P,L,P,L).
distance(a,b,5).   distance(a,c,3).   distance(a,d,1).   distance(b,c,5).
distance(b,d,3).   distance(b,a,1).   distance(c,d,5).   distance(c,a,3).
distance(c,b,1).   distance(d,a,5).   distance(d,b,3).   distance(d,c,1).
?- min_route(a,b,[],0,P,L).

/* tree */
p([],[]).
p([_|X], [alfa|A]) :- do_something, p(X,A).
p([_|X], [beta|A]) :- do_something, p(X,A).
p([_|X], [gamma|A]) :- do_something, p(X,A).
do_something :- list(X), list(Y), X=Y.
list([1,2,3,4,5]).
?- p([1,2,3],X), X=[gamma,gamma,gamma].

5 Distributed Data Driven Prolog Abstract Machine

P. Kacsuk

KFKI Research Institute for Measurement and Computing Techniques, Hungary

ABSTRACT

A modified version of the Warren Abstract Machine (WAM) designed for executing Prolog programs on distributed memory multicomputers is described. This new machine, the Distributed Data Driven Prolog Abstract Machine (3DPAM) shows many similarities with the WAM mainly in the unification oriented subpart of the instruction set but significantly differs from it as to the control instructions. These instructions serve for exploiting OR-parallelism and pipeline AND-parallelism using a data driven execution scheme. A distinctive feature of the 3DPAM is that it generates all possible solutions for a query, i.e. it works as an all-solutions Prolog machine. A detailed description of the registers, main data structures and instruction set of the 3DPAM are given. Transformation of Prolog programs into 3DPAM code is carefully investigated and shown how they are executed based on the data driven semantics.

1 INTRODUCTION

Dataflow models ([Denn74a],[Arvi82a]) are first class candidates for exploiting inherent parallelism without using explicit parallel constructs in programming languages. This is particularly true for Prolog which itself offers different kinds of implicit parallel execution methods (OR-, AND-, stream-, search-parallelism). However, dataflow execution mechanism turned out to be rather inefficient due to the large number of tokens generated even in the case of a relatively small program and the significant administration time of matching tokens and enabling nodes fire.

It is generally accepted that for sequential execution of Prolog programs the Warren Abstract Machine (WAM) is a highly efficient execution scheme. The main advantage of the WAM comes from an optimized use of machine registers supporting unification and backtracking.

The present chapter describes a modified version of the WAM designed for executing Prolog programs on distributed memory multicomputers based on the data driven semantics. This new machine, the Distributed Data Driven Prolog Abstract Machine (3DPAM), shows many similarities with the WAM mainly in the unification oriented subpart of the instruction set, but significantly differs from it as to the control instructions. These instructions serve for exploiting OR-parallelism and pipeline AND-parallelism using a data driven execution scheme. In order to exploit pipeline AND-parallelism, 3DPAM works as an all-solutions Prolog machine generating all possible solutions for any query.

As a first step, a generalized dataflow model called Extended Cellular-Dataflow Model (ECDAM) was developed and described in [Kacs90a]. Based on ECDAM Prolog programs can be transformed into a Dataflow Search Graph (DSG) which defines a high level Parallel Prolog Abstract Machine (PPAM). In Section 2 and 3 a short overview of ECDAM-2 (a revised version of ECDAM) is given describing how Prolog programs can be transformed into DSGs and how OR- and pipeline AND-parallelisms can be exploited within the model (for more details see [Kacs91a]).

The DSG represents an Intelligent Logic Network Layer applied for connecting independent WAMs realising the inherently sequential subparts of Prolog programs [Kacs91a]. In the WAM/3DPAM concept each Prolog program should be organised into sequential and parallel modules. Sequential modules are compiled into the WAM, while parallel modules into the 3DPAM. This module organisation of Prolog programs makes it possible for the user to control granularity for a given distributed memory multicomputer and to combine dataflow and controlflow semantics at the machine level to reduce the token administration overhead of usual dataflow computers.

The remaining sections of the chapter describe the 3DPAM in detail. Section 4 gives a general view of the work of the 3DPAM. Section 5 enumerates the registers of the 3DPAM and its main data structures. The instruction set of the 3DPAM is shown in Section 6, which also explains how to transform Prolog programs into this instruction set. The implementation of the closed environment scheme of Conery [Cone87b] in the 3DPAM is shown in Section 7. Comparison of the 3DPAM with related works is given in Section 8.

2 GRAPH REPRESENTATION OF PROLOG PROGRAMS

Dataflow computational models derive a dataflow graph from a program to be executed on a parallel computer. Nodes of the graph represent computational tasks, while the directed arcs connecting the nodes demonstrate the data communications paths among computational nodes. From node X an arc is directed to node Y, if Y uses data produced by X. Data are packed into tokens moving along the arcs. The computation is data driven controlled by the so called firing rule. In the pure static dataflow model (1_arc_1_token model) the firing rule is as follows [Denn74a]: A node can fire, if all of its input arcs contain one token and there is no token on the output arcs. The firing activity consists of three steps:
    1. consumption of input tokens
    2. execution of the function associated with the node
    3. emitting output tokens (results of the executed function) on the output arcs

In the dynamic (1_arc_N_token) models more than 1 token are allowed to be on an arc at the same time. However, in this case a token colouring scheme is needed to distinguish the input tokens of a node that belong to the same activation of a procedure. The different activations are represented by different colours and the firing rule is modified according to the colouring scheme [Arvi82a]: A node can fire, if all of its input arcs contain a token with the same colour.

ECDAM-2 (Extended Cellular-Dataflow Model) which was introduced for the dataflow based parallel execution of Prolog programs is based on the colouring scheme as well but the firing rule is modified towards enabling descriptions of compound nodes. For compound nodes the following firing rule (Extended Transition Function) is applied [Kacs90a]:

(next_state, <out_tokens>) := f(state, <inp_tokens>, <functions>)

The ETF states that a node can have inner state which can be modified during firing. The firing can take place if in a given state a given input token set is available on the input arcs and then <functions> should be executed by consuming <inp_tokens>. As a result of firing <out_tokens> are generated on a set of output arcs and the node enters into <next_state>. Compound nodes defined in this way can be built-up from ordinary nodes defined upon the firing rule of the dynamic model (see Section 6.1).

In ECDAM-2 Prolog programs are represented by the Dataflow Search Graph (DSG) containing the following node types (graphically shown in Figure 1):

UNIFY:	for executing unification of non-unit clause heads and entering binding results into clause bodies
UNIT:	for executing unification on unit clause heads
AND:	for connecting body goals
OR:	for connecting alternative clauses of a procedure
BUILTIN:	for executing built-in procedures
CALL:	for calling shared procedures
PRED:	for sharing procedures among multiple calls
SEQ:	for sequential execution of a subprogram

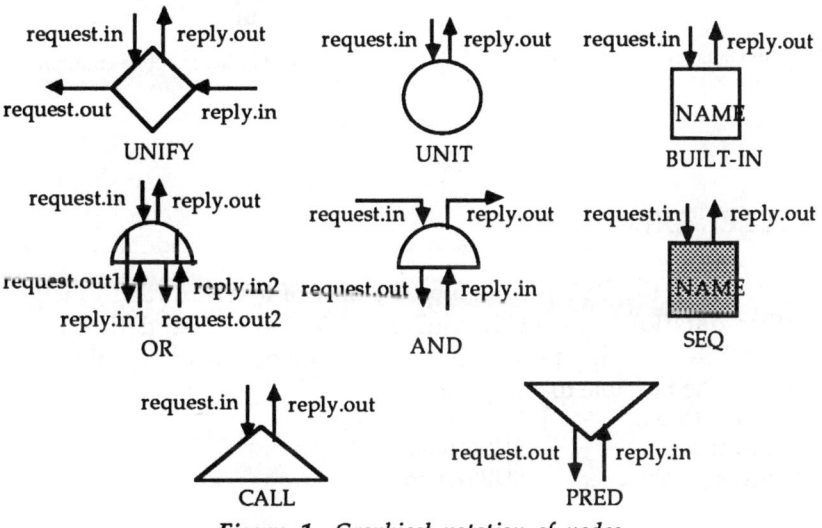

Figure 1 Graphical notation of nodes

Each Prolog program can be translated into a DSG based on the nodes given above. The transformation rules are given in [Kacs91a], here they are only briefly summarised:

1. A procedure consisting of N unit-clauses is represented by a single UNIT node.
2. A clause with body is represented by the UNIFY/AND ring (Figure 2.a).
3. DSGs of clauses within a procedure containing at least one rule-clause are connected by OR nodes (Figure 2.b).
4. If a procedure is called from several places of a program, only one copy of the DSG representation of the procedure is included in the graph of the program. In this case the DSG representation of the procedure starts with a PRED node and CALL nodes are used in the calling positions.
5. Inherently sequential subprograms can be packed into SEQ nodes and will be executed by sequential techniques (WAM). Database operations like assert and retract have no parallel operational semantics and therefore they cannot be mapped in the dataflow graph representation. However, if their scope can be included in a SEQ node, they can be used as well.

(a) Non-unit clause representation

(b) Predicate representation

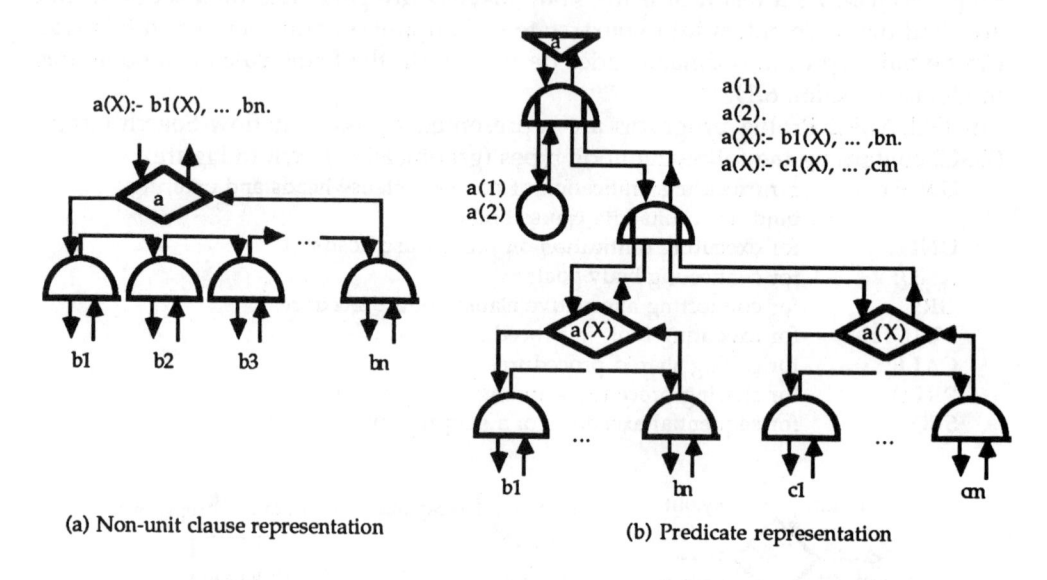

Figure 2   DSG representations

3 PARALLEL EXECUTION

The computation in the DSG is driven by the flow of tokens through the graph just like in other dataflow models [Denn74a],[Arvi02a]. After defining the static structure of DSGs of Prolog programs, the dynamic behaviour should be specified by introducing the possible token types:
    1. request token: DO (<env>,<args>)
    2. reply tokens: SUCC (<env>), FAIL
    3. request/reply token: SUB (<env>)

The computation is based on the concept of token streams. In reply to a request token each node will produce a token stream. A token stream is a series of tokens consisting of either N consecutive SUCC tokens or N consecutive SUB tokens closed by one terminating FAIL token. The empty stream consists of only a single FAIL token.

The DSG of a Prolog program works as a pipeline. After sending a request token to the DSG, a second one can immediately be sent again without waiting for the result token stream of the first one. Token streams belonging to different request tokens are distinguished by colours. As a reply for a request token, the DSG of the Prolog program will send back all possible solutions packed in a token stream. SUB or SUCC tokens in the stream represent proper solutions. If there is no answer for the goal, the empty stream, i.e. a single FAIL token will be sent back.

Based on the DSG representation and dataflow semantics, OR-parallelism and pipeline AND-parallelism can be exploited in Prolog programs. Now an informal description of the major nodes is given to show how Prolog programs are executed in parallel based on the DSG.

3.1 UNIT and BUILT_IN nodes

All the leaves of the DSG are UNIT or BUILT-IN nodes. Thus, they are responsible for initiating result token streams going upwards in the graph. A UNIT node represents N unit-clauses of a given predicate by storing the arguments of the clauses in local storage. A DO token represents a goal, where the arglist of the DO token corresponds to the arglist of the goal. Therefore, whenever a UNIT node receives a DO token, it sequentially unifies the arguments of the token (goal arguments) and the stored arguments (head arguments). The results of the successful unifications are packed into SUCC tokens and sent back to the caller node through the reply.out arc of UNIT. Failed unifications do not result in any reply token. When all the unifications are completed, a FAIL token is generated on the reply.out arc as an end_of_stream token.

The BUILT-IN nodes work similarly but instead of doing unification they execute the corresponding function upon the arglist of the DO token.

3.2 OR node and OR-parallelism

The OR node is the source of OR-parallelism in the DSG. It works by copying the incoming DO token on both request.out arcs. This way two new DO tokens are generated and as a result two subparts of the DSG will work in parallel. The reply token streams arriving back from the activated subparts are merged into a single token stream by the OR node (Figure 3).

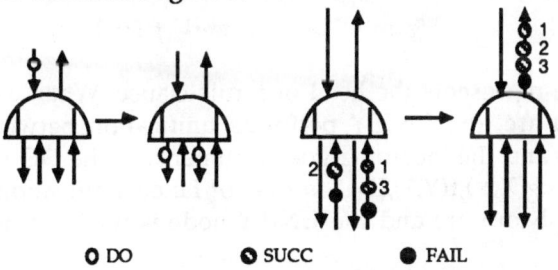

○ DO ◐ SUCC ● FAIL

Figure 3 Stream merge by OR node

3.3 UNIFY/AND ring

The head of a clause is represented by a UNIFY node and the body by a chain of AND nodes. These nodes work in a ring called *UNIFY/AND ring* where only SUB token streams can move. Neither DO nor SUCC tokens are permitted here. For illustrating the work of a UNIFY/AND ring consider the following simple example:

```
a(g(X,Y), f(Y,1), Z):- b(Z,U), c(X,U).
b(6,b1).            c(c1,b1).
b(5,b2).            c(c11,b1).
b(6,b3).            c(c3,b3).
?- a(g(S,5),T,6).
```

The generated DSG and its dynamic behaviour represented by tokens are shown in Figure 4. In the present section a detailed explanation of the work of UNIFY and AND nodes is given.

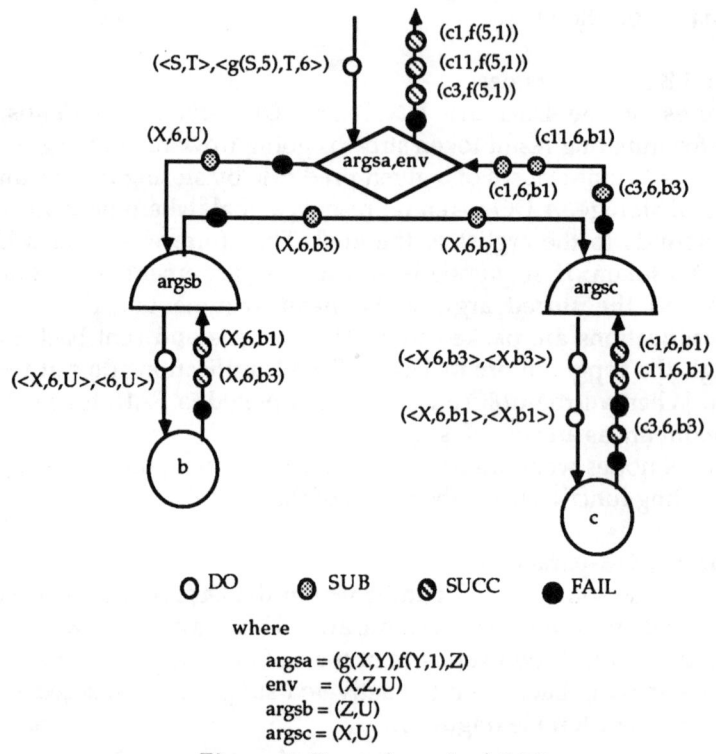

Figure 4 Dynamic work of DSG

where
argsa = (g(X,Y),f(Y,1),Z)
env = (X,Z,U)
argsb = (Z,U)
argsc = (X,U)

The UNIFY node represents the head of a rule-clause. When a DO token arrives on the request.in arc, the UNIFY performs unification between the associated clause arguments and the incoming goal arguments of the DO token. (In Figure 4 <g(S,5),T,6> and <g(X,Y),f(Y,1),Z>.) In case of failed unification, a FAIL token is placed on the reply.out arc and the UNIFY node is ready to accept another DO token.

During a successful unification, the environments of both the caller clause and the current clause might be modified by instantiating variables. In the example above the DO token conveys S and T in the environment field. These are bound to X and f(5,1) respectively. The caller environment with the new variable instantiations is saved in the local storage of the UNIFY node, meanwhile a SUB token is generated and placed on the request.out arc ((X,6,U) in the example). The arguments of the SUB token represent the updated environment of the current clause. They are either the permanent variables in the order of their appearance in the clause or the binding values of the permanent variables that were instantiated during the unification.

Receiving a reply SUB token stream on the reply.in arc, the UNIFY node transforms it into a SUCC token stream. The preceeding transformation of SUCC tokens into SUB tokens by AND nodes does not affect the environment field of tokens. However, in the UNIFY node transforming SUB tokens into SUCC tokens means the restoration of the original saved caller environments and updating them by binding values of the incoming SUB tokens. (For example in Figure 4 SUB(c1,6,b1) is transformed into SUCC(c1,f(5,1)).)

An AND node represents a goal in the clause body by locally storing the arguments of the goal. When a SUB token arrives on the request.in arc of the first AND node of the UNIFY/AND ring, the AND node creates a DO token on its request.out arc containing the incoming environment and the updated goal arguments. (In Figure 4 the first AND node creates the DO(<X,6,U>,<6,U> token from SUB(X,6,U).) The incoming SUCC token stream from the reply.in arc is transformed into a SUB token stream and placed on the reply.out arc. Notice that reply SUCC tokens contain an updated version of the environment field of the original activating SUB token of the AND node.

The SUB token stream arrives to the next AND node on its request.in arc. This AND node works as described for the first one but now the token stream might contain more than one SUB token. In this case the AND node temporarily stores the number of incomming SUB tokens and generates a DO token for each SUB token on its request.out arc. The connected subpart of the DSG (the "c" UNIT node in Figure 4) will send back as many token streams as many DO token was created by the AND node. These token streams should be merged into a single SUB token stream by the AND node. This is done by absorbing the FAIL tokens of the incomming SUCC streams and counting them. When the number of the SUCC streams is equal to the stored number of the SUB tokens, an end_of_stream FAIL token is placed by the AND node on its reply.out arc. (See in Figure 4 the merge of SUCC(c1,6,b1), SUCC(c11,6,b1) and SUCC(c3,6,b3) streams into the SUB(c1,6,b1), SUB(c11,6,b1), SUB(c3,6,b3) stream.)

3.4 Pipeline AND-parallelism

Each $goal_i$ of a clause body can generate more than one solutions for a given query and these solutions are transported to the next $goal_{i+1}$ of the body. After $goal_{i+1}$ is activated by the first solution derived from $goal_i$, the two goals can work in parallel: $goal_{i+1}$ is working on the first possible solution, while $goal_i$ is working on the second possible solution. In ECDAM-2 the goals of a body (represented by AND nodes) are organized in a pipeline. The input of the pipeline is the request.out arc of the UNIFY node, while the output is the reply.in arc of the UNIFY node. The elements of the pipeline are the AND nodes of the UNIFY/AND ring. Partial solutions are forwarded from AND_i to AND_{i+1} and assuming that they are mapped onto different processing elements, they can work in parallel on different partial solutions belonging to the same initial query (DO token). This kind of parallelism is called *pipeline AND-parallelism* and should be clearly distinguished from independent AND-parallelism where goals of the body can work in parallel on the same solution of a query.

In order to realise pipeline AND parallelism, the different token streams flowing through the DSG in an overlapped way should be identified and distinguished. For this purpose the colour (context field) of tokens are introduced in dataflow models [Denn74a], [Arvi82a]. Tokens belonging to the same token stream have the same colour, while tokens of different token streams have distinct colours.

Token colours are administrated by context tables in the 3DPAM. Each node has a context table to save the colour of the incomming token and to generate a new colour for the corresponding output token. The colour is simply realized by an index in 3DPAM. The colour of the incomming token is saved in the first free position of the corresponding context table (UNIFY, AND, AND1, OR). The new colour is the index of this free position in the context table. To demonstrate this *Save-and-Restore token colouring scheme,* Figure 5 shows how the colours are saved and generated by context tables. (The interested reader can find a more detailed description in [Kacs91b].) Notice that the AND Context Table contains an extra field for counting the incomming SUB tokens.

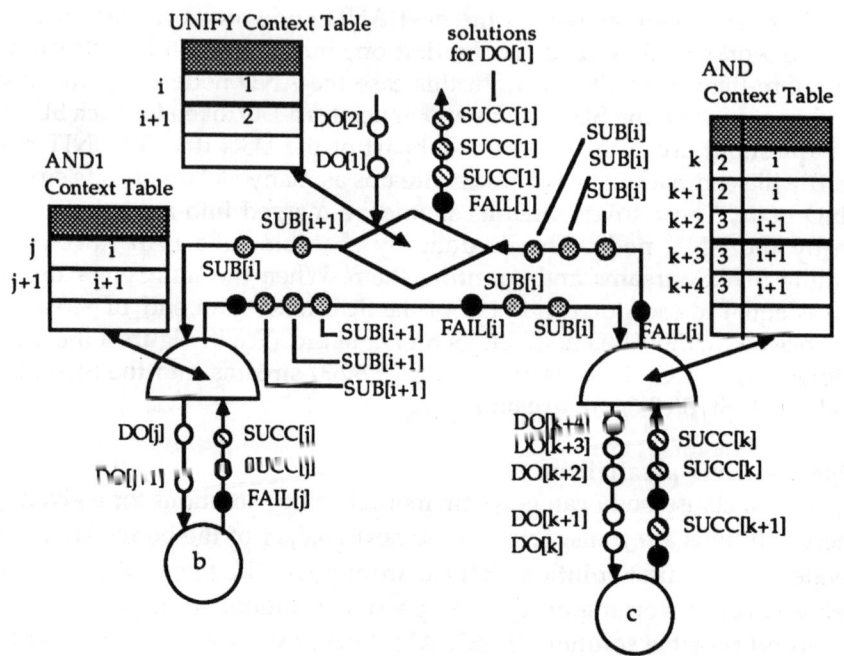

Figure 5   *Save-and-Restore token colouring scheme*

4 GENERAL VIEW OF THE 3DPAM

As it was shown in the previous section a Prolog program can be transformed into a DSG. This DSG is distributed among the Processing Elements (PEs) of the parallel system. One or more segments of the DSG are loaded into each PE. A Distributed Data Driven Prolog (3DP) engine is placed on each PE of the distributed system. The 3DP engine emulates the data driven execution of the DSG allocated on the given PE. The general view of the 3DPAM on each PE is shown in Figure 6.

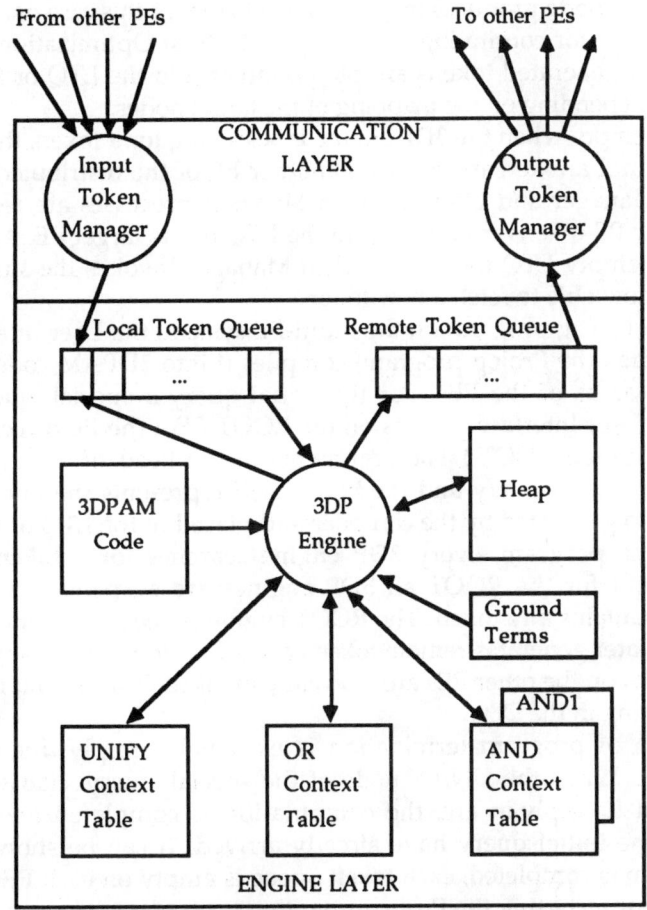

Figure 6 *Structure of the 3DPAM on PEs*

Unlike usual data flow machines, a remarkable feature of the ECDAM-2 based DSG is that one token is always enough to make a node fire. As a consequence, the matching store of dataflow machines can be omitted in the 3DPAM resulting in a very fast and efficient selection of firable nodes. It is sufficient to select an available token, the node to be activated by that token can immediately fire.

The available tokens are stored in the Local Token Queue (LTQ), therefore the 3DP engine takes a token from LTQ whenever it runs out of work. The fetched token points the address of the code of the dataflow node whose input arc contains the fetched token. The 3DP engine starts the execution of the node code from that address. As a result of executing a node function one of the following situations appears:

a/ The node does not produce any output token. In this case after finishing the execution of the node function the 3DP engine runs out of work and therefore searches for another token in the LTQ.

b/ The firing node produces exactly one token. The 3DP engine continues the emulation of the DSG by using the currently generated token. (This Depth First Optimization is similar to the one introduced in the Flat Concurrent Prolog Abstract Machine [Tayl86a].)

c/ The activated node produces more than one token. In this case one token is kept by the 3DP engine for continuing its work (Depth First Optimization), meanwhile the other newly generated tokens are placed either into the LTQ or RTQ (Remote Token Queue) depending on the mapping of the target nodes.

If the LTQ is empty when the 3DP engine is searching for a token, the 3DP engine is suspended until a token arrives from another PE of the distributed system. The Input Token Manager and Output Token Manager processes are responsible for delivering inter-PE tokens from a RTQ to the LTQ of the target PE. After placing a token into the empty LTQ the Input Token Manager invokes the suspended 3DP engine that is now able to fetch a new token.

For starting a Prolog program on the multi-PE system, the User Interface process on the Host reads the Prolog program, compiles it into 3DPAM code and loads it into the Code areas of the PEs. For the initial query a special 'query' clause is created by the User Interface process on the ROOT PE. (The PE directly connected to the Host is called ROOT.) The arguments in the head of 'query' contain the variables of the initial query and the body itself represents the query. An initial DO token is also generated by the compiler and placed in the LTQ of the ROOT.

At starting the program, every 3DP engine searches for a token in its LTQ. However, except for the ROOT all 3DP engines are suspended since only the ROOT's LTQ contains any token. The ROOT engine processes the initial DO token and sooner or later generates remote tokens according to the mapping of the DSG. The 3DP engines on the other PEs are gradually invoked as more and more inter-PE tokens are moving in the DSG.

The detection of program termination is extremely simply due to the token stream concept. When the UNIFY node of the special 'query' clause receives the FAIL token on its reply.in arc, the computation is completed and all possible solutions for the initial query have already arrived. It can be shown that when the computation is completed, each token queue is empty on each PE, therefore all PEs are ready for restarting the Prolog program.

5 MACHINE REGISTERS AND DATA STRUCTURES

5.1 Token Representation

The current token handled by the 3DP engine is represented by the following set of registers:

Token context registers
    TID   Token Id
    TRPE   Token Return Processing Element

TSR	Token Successful Return (Address of the sender CALL node)
TFR	Token Fail Return
TTPE	Token Target Processing Element
TADDR	Token Address (Address of the target node's code)

The first four registers identify the source of the token and specify where to send the corresponding reply tokens. The TTPE and the TADDR identify both the target PE and the arc of the DSG where the token to be placed.

Token environment registers
TEN	Token Environment Number
TE1	Token Environment 1
TE2	Token Environment 2
:	

Token argument registers
TAN	Token Argument Number
TA1	Token Argument 1
TA2	Token Argument 2
:	

The TEi registers can be used as temporary registers too. In this case they are refered to by Xi in the 3DPAM instruction set. Those variables which appear only in the head are called temporary variables and are stored in Xi. Partial results of unification for subterms of nested compound terms are also stored in Xi registers.

Local Token Queue and Remote Token Queue. The current token processed by the 3DP engine is placed in the token register pad. Other tokens are stored either in the LTQ or in the RTQ. These queues are implemented by linking DO token records, FAIL token records and SS (SUB/SUCC) token records.

DO token record: A DO token record consists of a pointer and a DO token slot. The pointer serves for linking used records in one of the token queues or free records in the Free DO queue. The DO token slot contains three fields to save the context field, environment field and argument field of the current token.

FAIL token record: A FAIL token record consists of a pointer and a FAIL token slot. The pointer serves for linking used records in one of the token queues or free records in the Free FAIL queue. The FAIL token slot contains three fields to save the TID, TTPE and TADDR registers of the current token.

SS (SUB/SUCC) token record: An SS token record consists of a pointer and an SS token slot. The pointer serves for linking used records in one of the token queues or free records in the Free SS queue. The SS token slot contains fields to save the environment field and the TID, TTPE, TADDR registers of the current token.

5.2 Data Representation
Data objects in the environment and argument fields of tokens consist of tags and values. In the 3DPAM the following tags are applied:
UNDEF:	Uninstantiated variable where the value is meaningless.
GREF:	Reference to a variable stored in the goal's environment.

CREF: Reference to a variable stored in the clause's environment.
INT: Integer where the value represents the integer value.
A/F: Atom or functor where the value has two fields. The first one points to the Symbol table, while the second one defines the arity (=0 in the case of atoms).
STR: Structure pointer - the value points to the structure stored in the Heap.
LIST: List pointer - the value points to the list stored in the Heap.
GND: Ground term pointer - the value points to the ground structure or ground list stored in the Ground Term Table.

Notice that instead of using only REF type variable pointers two different kinds of references (GREF and CREF) are applied to distinguish the variables in the caller goal's environment from those held in the clause's environment (see Section 7).

Compound ground terms of the program text are created at compile time and placed in the Ground Term Table (GTT) that is loaded in each PE on the same address at load time. Ground data structures are represented by their ground term pointer (GND data type) to the Ground Term Table that is locally accessible by all PEs at run time Thus, instead of sending large ground terms it is sufficient to send their unique GTT address in inter-PE messages.

5.3 Data structures for context handling

The actual contents of the various context tables depend on the role of the associated nodes.

UNIFY Context Table. UNIFY nodes allocated on a given PE use the UNIFY Context Table as a common resource which contains u_context records consisting of one pointer and one u_context slot. The pointer serves to maintain a list of free u_context records. In the u_context slot the following fields are used to save token registers of the incoming DO token:
- TID, TSR, TFR, TRPE: describing the origin of the DO token and the target of the reply tokens
- TEN, TE1, ..., TEi: describing the environment of the caller goal

AND1 Context Table. First AND nodes of the UNIFY/AND rings allocated on a given PE use the AND1 Context Table as a common resource which stores a1_context records consisting of one pointer and one a1_context slot. The pointer serves to maintain a list of free a1_context records. The TID register of the incoming DO token is saved in the a1_context slot.

AND Context Table. The AND Context Table stores a_context records consisting of a pointer and an a_context slot. The pointer serves to maintain the list of free a_context records and link the a_context slots of the same AND node. Recall that an AND node can receive several overlapped SUB streams and for each SUB stream it should maintain a separate slot. The a_context slot contains the following fields:
- TID: describing the colour of the incoming SUB token stream
- TC: Token counter representing the state of the AND node for the specific TID colour

- TC state: indicating if the ending FAIL token of the SUB token stream has arrived
- New TID chain: pointer to the chain of new TID colours allocated for the new DO tokens

The AND Context Table should also be handled as a common, dynamically allocatable resource. However, to find a particular a_context record belonging to an incoming reply token would require an associative and therefore tremendously time-consuming search. In the case of the AND Context Table, the token colour does not identify the location of the stored record. Though the search can not be perfectly avoided it can significantly be reduced by storing the starting address of the chain of records belonging to that particular AND node. For this purpose the so-called AND Table is introduced. The i-th item of the table contains the chain address of the i-th AND node.

OR Context Table. OR nodes allocated on a given PE use the OR Context Table as a common resource which contains or_context records consisting of one pointer and one or_context slot. The pointer serves to maintain a list of free or_context records. In the or_context slot the following fields are used :
- TID, TSR, TFR, TRPE: describing the origin of the DO token and the target of the reply tokens
- State: that can be WAIT, WAIT1 or WAIT2

5.4 Registers
Token registers. These registers are used to maintain the current token. Whenever the 3DP engine selects a token from the LTQ the components of the token are installed into these registers before the actual processing of the token begins (see Section 5.1).

General purpose registers. playing similar role to the corresponding WAM registers:
- PC: program counter of 3DPAM code
- FC: fail continuation (pointer to the 3DPAM code)
- HP: top of heap
- SP: structure pointer (has the same role as in the WAM)

Token queue registers: for administrating queues containing tokens [Kacs91b].
Context Table registers: for administrating context tables described in Section 5.3 [Kacs91b].

6 ABSTRACT INSTRUCTION SET

6.1 Head Unification and Term Handling
Unification Instructions. Unifications are performed either by UNIFY or UNIT nodes in the 3DPAM. The most general way of executing unification by the UNIFY node is described here, and the work of UNIT nodes is discussed later in Section 6.5. Unification is realised by 'get' and 'unify' instructions as in the WAM, however, some slight modifications have been introduced into their semantics.

The 'get' instructions describe the head arguments of a clause:

```
get_var      TEi,TAj              get_value    TEi,TAj
get_const    C,TAi                get_struct   F,TAi
get_list     TAi                  get_nil      TAi

get_sub_struct      F,Xi          get_sub_list        Xi
get_gr_struct       F,TAi,P,Cgr   get_gr_list         TAi,P,Cgr
get_gr_sub_struct   F,Xi,P,Cgr    get_gr_sub_list     Xi,P,Cgr
```

where **TEi** is a Token Environment register, **TAi** is a Token Argument register, **Cgr** is an address in the 3DPAM Code Memory, **C** is a constant, **F** is a functor and **P** is a pointer to a ground term in the Ground Term Table.

The 'unify' instructions describe the head arguments within a compound term:

```
unify_void    N                   unify_var    TEi
unify_value   TEi                  unify_const  C
unify_nil
```

The main difference between the WAM and 3DPAM instructions is in the handling of nested and ground terms of the program text. The sub_struct and sub_list instructions were introduced because they work on temporary registers instead of the argument registers.

Recall that the compound ground terms are created by the compiler and placed in the Ground Term Table (GTT). Besides reducing the communication time, a further advantage of this optimisation is that unification can be significantly shortened by introducing special ground term oriented instructions (get_gr_struct, etc.). If the dereferenced value of TAi is a variable, the reconstruction of the ground term in the Heap can be avoided and the variable is simply bound to the stored ground term by placing its P pointer in the variable. An example for handling ground structures is shown in Figure 12.

Context Handling Instructions. The Save_and_Restore technique described in Section 3.4 is realised by the following context handling instructions of the 3DPAM:

```
3DPAM INSTRUCTION                           NODE/INVOKING TOKEN
    save_u_context                              % UNIFY/DO
    close_u_context                             % UNIFY/DO
    restore_u_context                           % UNIFY/SUB
    restore_free_u_context                      % UNIFY/FAIL

    save_a1_context                             % 1st AND/SUB
    restore_a1_context         PEi,C            % 1st AND/SUCC
    restore_free_a1_context    PEi,C            % 1st AND/FAIL/rep

    save_a_context             AND_ID           % AND/SUB
    restore_a_context          AND_ID,PEi,C     % AND/SUCC
    restore_free_a_context     AND_ID,PEi,C     % AND/FAIL/rep

    save_or_context                             % OR/DO
    restore_or_context                          % OR/SUCC
    restore_free_or_context                     % OR/FAIL
```

The 'save' instructions save the corresponding token registers in the Context Tables and set the state of nodes in the case of AND and OR nodes. The 'restore' instructions restore the saved token registers, while the 'restore_free' instructions free the given context record for reuse after restoring the saved token registers. Recall that the Token Environment registers are not modified by the OR and AND nodes and hence they are not saved in the OR and AND Context Tables. The Token Argument registers never have to be saved. 'close_u_context' validates the current u_context record if the unification is successful.

Encoding UNIFY Operators. The instructions used for realising UNIFY nodes in addition to the 'save_and_restore', 'get' and 'unify' instructions are:

```
        allocate  M              fail_unify  Cfail
        close_env
        succ_return              fail_return
```

A UNIFY node is represented by 3 segments of code in the 3DPAM Code Memory as shown in Figure 7.

C_DO/request.in segment: Before starting a unification, the environment of the caller goal should be saved and a new environment should be created for the invoked clause. In the WAM this is executed by opening a new frame in the Local Stack. In the 3DPAM, the environment of the goal is packed in the Token Environment registers (parts of the current DO token). These should firstly be saved in the selected u_context record along with the Token Id, TSR, TFR, TRPE registers. This saving function is realised by the 'save_u_context' instruction.

As a next step the environment of the called clause should be created. This environment will to travel around the UNIFY/AND ring as a SUB token. The new environment is created by the 'allocate' instruction that sets TE1-TEM as empty variables and sets TEN to be equal to M.

The 'fail_unify' instruction defines where to pass control to in case of any failed unification. Notice that in the WAM this instruction is not needed since failed unification always results in backtracking to the last choice point. The unification is executed between the TAi registers that hold the arguments of the DO token and the head arguments encoded as a series of 'get' and 'unify' instructions. Notice that the "locally stored arguments" of the UNIFY node are actually realised by the 3DPAM code and therefore it is not necessary to store them inside the node nor to pack them in another incoming token as it was suggested by [Bisw88a].

To handle the token environments in a distributed system, 3DPAM uses the "closed environment" concept suggested by Conery [Cone87b]. In the 3DPAM the 'close_env' instruction is used for closing the environments.

Finally, after a successful head unification, the u_context record should be closed against other use. If the unification failed on one of the 'get' or 'unify' instructions, the control is directly passed to the Cfail address where a 'fail_return' is executed. In this case the saved u_context is not closed and therefore it can be reused for another DO token.

C_SUB/reply.in segment: If the UNIFY node receives a SUB token on its reply.in arc, the control is passed to the C_SUB/reply.in address (PC := C_SUB/reply.in) and the 'restore_u_context' instruction is executed. This closes the saved goal environment as it was proposed by Conery [Cone87b] and then restores the saved u_context. The 'succ_return' instruction generates a SUCC token and sends it back to the emitter node of the invoking DO token.

C_FAIL/reply.in segment: In the case of a FAIL token the saved u_context is not needed anymore, hence, the corresponding item of the UNIFY Context Table is freed by the 'restore_free_u_context' instruction for reuse. With the restored u_context, a FAIL token is generated and sent back to the emitter node of the invoking DO token.

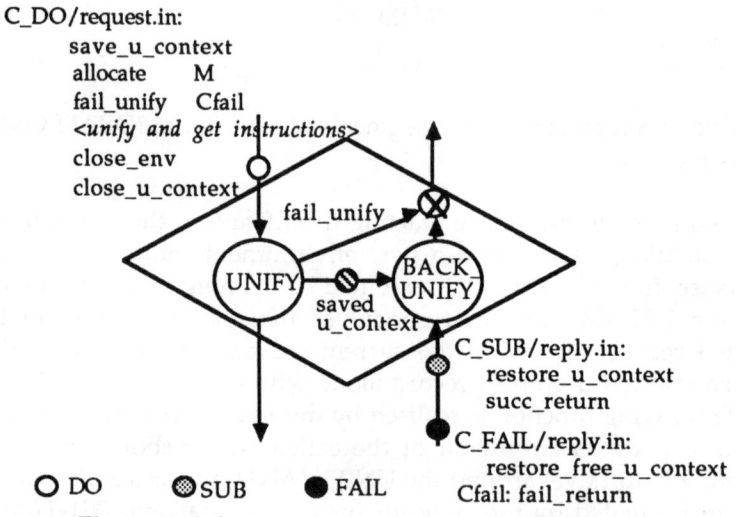

Figure 7 Code sements representing the UNIFY node

UNIFY as compound node. As it was mentioned in Section 2 the compound nodes of ECDAM-2 can be constructed by simple nodes. Figure 7 illustrates that the compound UNIFY node can be constructed from 3 simple nodes: UNIFY, BACK_UNIFY and UNION. The simple UNIFY node executes the unification. In the case of a failed unification it generates a FAIL token and sends it directly to the UNION node. In the case of a successful unification, simple UNIFY generates two tokens: a SUB token and a special u_context token which is invisible outside the compound UNIFY node. The u_context token is available on the first input arc of BACK_UNIFY, which waits until the corresponding SUB or FAIL token arrives on its second input arc (identical with reply.in of the compound UNIFY). When both input arcs contain matching tokens BACK_UNIFY executes either the C_SUB/reply.in or the C_FAIL/reply.in code segment depending on the type of the incomming token and places the result token on the second input arc of the UNION. Whenever a token is available on any input arcs, the UNION copies it on its output arc (identical with reply.out of the compound UNIFY). Notice that u_context tokens are implemented by the records of the UNIFY Context Table shared by all UNIFY nodes allocated on the same PE. This implementation is much more efficient than sending the u_context tokens through the whole UNIFY/AND rings.

6.2 Handling of Body Goals

Body goals are connected by AND nodes in the UNIFY/AND ring. The AND nodes have two major tasks. The first one is to prepare arguments for body calls and the second one is to merge reply token streams (see Section 3.4) for realising pipeline parallelism.

Argument Preparation Instructions. For the argument preparation, the 'put' instructions are used like in the WAM. However, instead of using 'unify' instructions for creating goal arguments inside compound terms rather a modified version of the 'put' instruction called 'write' is introduced, since the machine is always in WRITE_MODE (see WAM) during the execution of these instructions.

The 'put' instructions describe the goal arguments outside structures or lists:

```
put_var      TEi, TAj        put_value    TEi, TAj
put_const    C, TAi          put_struct   F, TAi
put_list     TAi             put_nil      TAi

put_sub_struct      F, Xi         put_sub_list      Xi
put_gr_struct       F, TAi, P     put_gr_list       TAi, P
put_gr_sub_struct   F, Xi, P      put_gr_sub_list   Xi, P
```

The 'write' instructions describe the goal arguments inside structures or lists:

```
write_void   N                write_var    TEi
write_value  TEi              write_const  C
write_nil
```

The 'write' instructions work on the heap guided by the SP register. In the case of 'put' instructions the advantage of using the ground term optimization instructions (put_gr_struct, etc.) is even more obvious than in the 'get' instructions. TAi or the term element in the Heap shown by SP simply gets the P pointer of the ground term. Here even the generated code is shortened since there is no need for generating code for the subterms of the ground term. As an example, let us consider the following clause:

```
a(X,f(11,aa),Y) :- b(g(X,h(bb,cc),Z)), c(Z,Y,X).
```

The 3DPAM code for creating the arguments of goal b:

```
put_gr_sub_struct    h/2, X4, @h      % h(bb,cc)
put_struct           g/3, TA1         % g(
write_value          TE1              %   X,
write_value          X4               %   h(bb,cc)
write_var            TE3              %   Z)
```

Notice that h(bb,cc) ground structure is represented by its pointer (@h) and there is no need to create it at run time by any series of instructions.

AND Operators. The instructions used for realising AND nodes, in addition to the 'put' and 'write' instructions, are as follows:

```
save_a_context              AND_ID
close_token_counter         AND_ID, PEj, C_Un_fail
restore_a_context           AND_ID, PEi, C_next_SUB/req
restore_free_a_context      AND_ID, PEi, C_next_FAIL/req
```

An AND node is represented by 4 segments of code in the 3DPAM Code Memory. These segments correspond to the following token/input_arc combinations:

```
C_SUB/request.in:                                          % 1st segment
    save_a_context           AND_ID
    <'put' and 'write' instruction for creating goal arguments>
C_FAIL/request.in:                                         % 2nd segment
    close_token_counter      AND_ID, PEj, C_Un_fail
C_SUCC/reply.in:                                           % 3rd segment
    restore_a_context        AND_ID, PEi, C_next_SUB/req
C_FAIL/reply.in:                                           % 4th segment
    restore_free_a_context   AND_ID, PEi, C_next_FAIL/req
```

1st segment: SUB *token arrives on the request_in arc.* The 'save_a_context' instruction checks if there is any a_context record containing the current token_id (i.e. if any other SUB token arrived from the same stream). If there is, TC is incremented in the a_context record (see Section 5.3) and a new TID is allocated and linked to the new TID chain. The newly created TID is loaded into the TID register of the output DO token. The TAi arguments of the output DO token are loaded by the put and write instructions. All other token registers are unchanged, hence, inherited from the incoming SUB token.

2nd segment: FAIL *token arrives on the request_in arc.* The token_counter (TC) should be closed indicating that no more SUB token need to be considered ('close_token_counter' instruction). If there is no SUB token before the incoming FAIL token, no solution is possible for the given TID, hence, the control is directly passed to the reply.in arc of the UNIFY node. Notice this is an optimization for preventing empty SUB streams (containing only the end_of_stream FAIL token) in traveling through the UNIFY/AND ring. After closing TC no token is generated, therefore, the scheduler should be invoked.

3rd segment: SUCC *token arrives on the reply_in arc.* A SUB token is generated with the TID restored by the 'restore_a_context' instruction. If the next AND node of the underlying UNIFY/AND ring is allocated on another PEi, the created SUB token should be placed in the RTQ with the following parameters:
```
    TTPE  := PEi
    TADDR := C_next_SUB/req
```

4th segment: FAIL *token arrives on the reply_in arc.* Whenever a reply stream is ended on the reply.in arc (by receiving a FAIL token), the TC is decremented in the a_context record and the corresponding item in the new TID chain is removed by the 'restore_free_a_context' instruction. If TC is closed and has reached zero, the merge of reply streams can be finished, therefore, a FAIL token is generated on the reply.out arc by placing a FAIL token in the RTQ with the following parameters:
```
    TID   := TID from a_context record
    TTPE  := PEi
    TADDR := C_next_FAIL/req
```

Moreover, the a_context record is removed from the AND chain and linked to the list of free a_context records.

First AND Operators. As it is shown in Section 3.4 the first AND nodes of the UNIFY/AND rings always receive 1-length token streams on their request.in arc, therefore, they do not need to count the reply streams. Consequently, the UNIFY nodes do not have to send end_of_stream FAIL tokens to the first AND node, hence, their code does not contain the C_FAIL/request.in segment. The other 3 segments are the same as in the other AND nodes except that they handle a1_contexts not containing token_counters.

6.3 3DPAM Code of Rule Clauses

After showing how to represent UNIFY and AND nodes in the 3DPAM, we can study the representation of complete rule clauses (UNIFY/AND rings). A further instruction is needed for realising the CALL node of the body goals:

```
call  PROC_ID, ARG_NO, PEi, C_fail
```

The 'call' instruction creates a local or remote DO token depending on the result of comparison between PEi and the current PE. If they are equal a local token is created with

```
TAN := ARG_NO
TSR := PC + 1      % the next instruction is to be executed after success
TFR := C_fail      % C_fail is to be executed after failure
```

and the control is passed to PC := PROC_ID to execute the called procedure. If the called procedure is mapped onto another PE, a remote token is created and placed in the RTQ with the following values:

a/ Token environment is copied from the current token
b/ Token arg is copied from the current token
c/ TAN := ARG_NO
c/ Token context:
```
    TID is copied
    TRPE := current PE
    TSR := PC + 1      % the next instruction is to be executed after success
    TFR := C_fail      % C_fail is to be executed after failure
    TTPE := PEi
    TADDR := PROC_ID
```

Notice, the called procedure can result in either success or failure. In the former case the instruction following the 'call' is executed according to TSR, while in the latter case the instruction placed on C_fail is executed according to TFR. This is one of the main differences between the WAM and the 3DPAM. In the WAM the control is passed to the last choice point in the case of failure, while in the 3DPAM an extra argument of the 'call' instruction specifies where to continue the execution after a failure occured.

There are several possible ways of mapping the UNIFY/AND ring onto a distributed system. Here we suppose a mapping technique that allocates the UNIFY and the first AND node on the same PE while the other AND nodes are mapped on different PEs. For brevity also assume that the rule contains only 2 body goals as shown in Figure 8. The scheme can easily be generalized to any number of body goals.

```
save_u_context
fail_unify      Cfail
allocate        3                           Ccu:
get_struct      g/2,TA1                       restore_u_context
unify_var       TE1                           succ_return
unify_var       TE4                         Ccuf:
get_struct      f/2,TA2                       restore_free_u_context
unify_value     TE4                         Cfail:
unify_const     1                             fail_return
get_var         TE2,TA3
close_env
close_u_context
```

PE1

PE1   PE2

```
save_a1_context                     Cac: save_a_context        c
put_value       TE2,TA1                  put_value       TE1,TA1
put_var         TA3,TA2                  put_value       TE3,TA2
call            Cb, 2, PE1, Cbf          call            Cc, 2, PE2, Ccf
restore_a1_context  PE2, Cac             restore_a_context   c,PE1,Ccu
Cbf:                                Cacf: close_token_counter  c,PE1,Ccuf
    restore_free_a1_context PE2, Cacf   Ccf: restore_free_a_context c,PE1,Ccuf
```

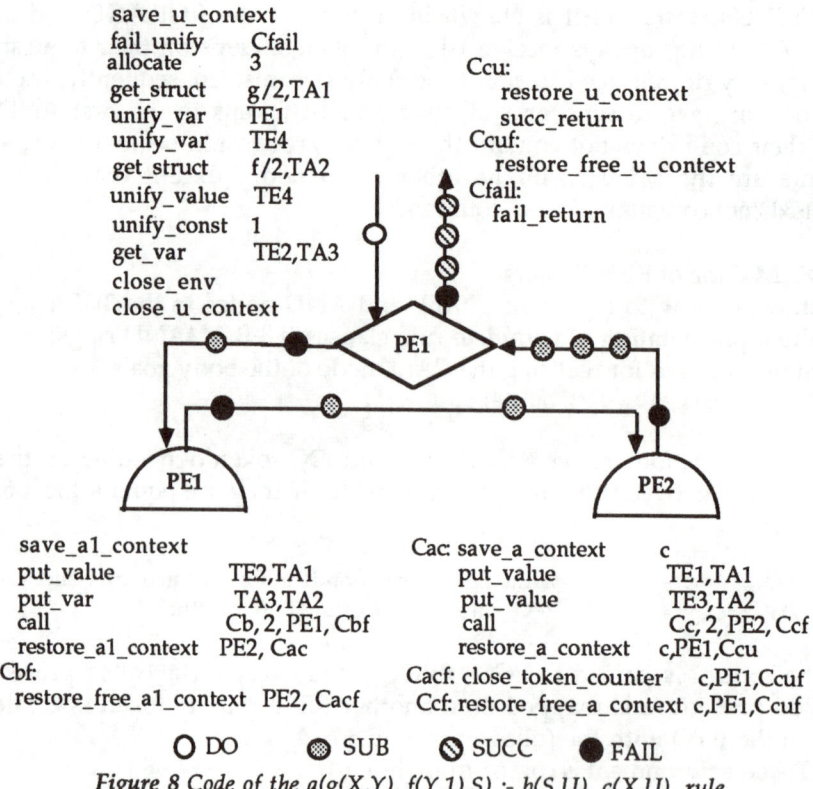

○ DO   ◉ SUB   ⊘ SUCC   ● FAIL

Figure 8 *Code of the a(g(X,Y), f(Y,1),S) :- b(S,U), c(X,U). rule*

Now based on Figure 8 let us observe how the dataflow graph is actually mapped in the distributed processor space and coded in the 3DPAM Code area. The arc connecting the UNIFY and first AND node is simply realised by placing the AND1 code segment directly after the UNIFY 1st code segment, i.e. 'save_a1_context' directly follows 'close_u_context' in the code memory. In this way moving the SUB token from the UNIFY to the first AND node does not require any token handling overhead. The arc between the two AND nodes is realised by two remote-token emitter instructions:

```
restore_a1_context       PE2, Cac
restore_free_a1_context  PE2, Cacf
```

The first argument identifies the PE where the second AND node is mapped and the second argument identifies the position in the code area where the corresponding code segment of the AND node is loaded. In the general case similar instructions ('restore_a_context' and 'restore_free_a_context') are used for connecting the other AND nodes of UNIFY/AND rings and for connecting the last AND node with the output code segment of the UNIFY node. The CALL node is represented by the 'call' instruction. The arcs between the AND and CALL nodes

6.4 3DPAM Code of OR-Alternatives

The instructions used for realising OR nodes in addition to the 'save_and_restore' instructions are as follows:

```
or_create_do      PE_ID, C_clause
check_or_state    C_OR_Wait_1_2
set_or_state      STATE
```

Alternative rules of a procedure are connected by an OR-chain as shown in Section 3.2 (Figure 2). In order to exploit real OR-parallelism the distinct OR-branches of each OR node should be mapped on different PEs. A very simple compile time algorithm assures this mapping. Let us suppose that PEs are ordered and numbered from 1 to N. The mapping algorithm allocates the left branch of an OR node being on PE[i] to the same PE, while the right branch to PE[i+1] mod N. Figure 9 illustrates for a simple example how to generate code for OR alternatives in the 3DPAM.

Each OR node starts by using the 'save_or_context' instruction to save the or_context of the caller DO token and to set TRPE, TSR and TFR in the following way:

```
TRPE := current_PE
TSR  := C_OR_Succ
TFR  := C_OR_Fail1
```

The 'or_create_do' instruction creates a remote DO token placed in the RTQ with the following parameters:

```
TRPE  := current_PE
TSR   := C_OR_Succ
TFR   := C_OR_Fail2
TTPE  := arg1
TADDR := arg2
```

The token environment parameters are copied from the current token registers.

On the current PE processing of the current DO token continues on the next instruction, that represents the left branch clause. Meanwhile the remote DO token is transferred to the LTQ of the target PE where the right branch clause is allocated. As soon as the 3DP engine of the target PE fetches the DO token the OR-parallel execution starts.

The OR branches deliver SUCC or FAIL tokens to the OR node. Suppose that a SUCC token is conveyed on one of the reply.in arcs and the 3DP engine processes this token. Control is passed to the C_OR_Succ address (gained from TSR) where a 'restore_or_context' instruction restores the saved or_context. The next 'succ_return' instruction sets PC, based on the TSR and TRPE registers.

If a FAIL token activates an OR node, the PC is set to either C_OR_Fail1 or C_OR_Fail2 depending on the conveying arc. At these addresses 'check_or_state' tests the state of the OR node. If the node is in WAIT state, i.e. no FAIL token has arrived, the next 'set_or_state' instruction is executed. This includes a search for another token in the LTQ since the OR node does not create any token at this point.

Otherwise PC is set to C_OR_Wait_1_2 meaning that the incoming FAIL token is the second one and therefore the merge of the two reply streams should be terminated by generating a FAIL token ('fail_return'). For the FAIL token the saved or_context should be restored and since no more reply tokens can appear the or_context record can be freed by 'restore_free_or_context'.

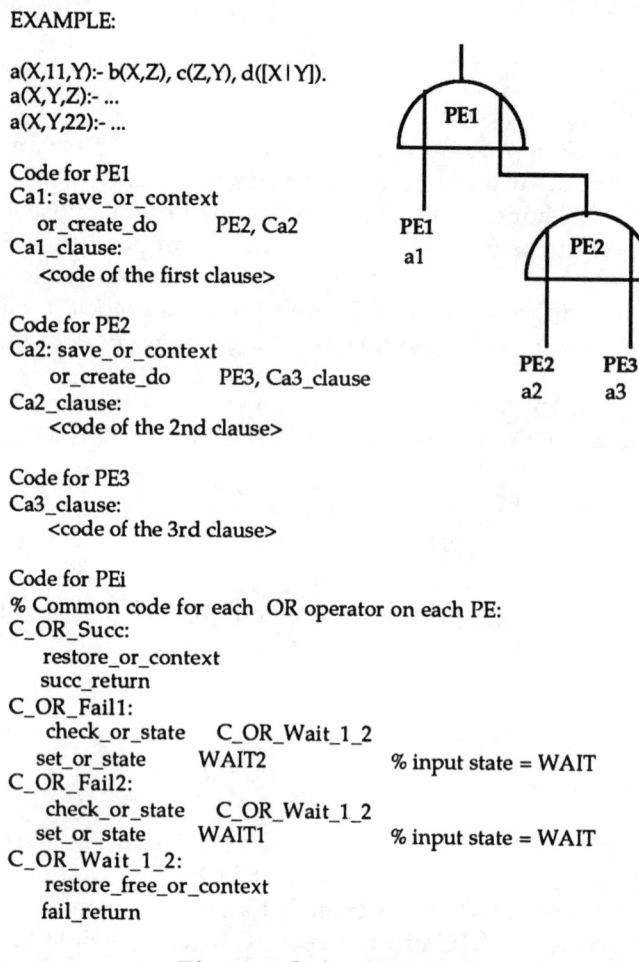

EXAMPLE:

a(X,11,Y):- b(X,Z), c(Z,Y), d([X|Y]).
a(X,Y,Z):- ...
a(X,Y,22):- ...

```
Code for PE1
Ca1: save_or_context
     or_create_do      PE2, Ca2
Ca1_clause:
     <code of the first clause>

Code for PE2
Ca2: save_or_context
     or_create_do      PE3, Ca3_clause
Ca2_clause:
     <code of the 2nd clause>

Code for PE3
Ca3_clause:
     <code of the 3rd clause>

Code for PEi
% Common code for each OR operator on each PE:
C_OR_Succ:
     restore_or_context
     succ_return
C_OR_Fail1:
     check_or_state    C_OR_Wait_1_2
     set_or_state      WAIT2           % input state = WAIT
C_OR_Fail2:
     check_or_state    C_OR_Wait_1_2
     set_or_state      WAIT1           % input state = WAIT
C_OR_Wait_1_2:
     restore_free_or_context
     fail_return
```

Figure 9 Code of OR-chain

Notice that the request.out1 arc of the OR node is simply realised by placing the code of the connected clause directly after the request.in (Cai) code segment. The request.out2 arc is realised by the 'or_create_do' instruction. The reply.in1 and reply.in2 arcs are represented by the common code of the OR nodes (C_OR_Succ, C_OR_Fail1 for reply.in1 and C_OR_Succ, C_OR_Fail2 for reply.in2). The reply.out arc is realised by the 'succ_return' and 'fail_return' instructions using the TRPE, TSR and TFR registers to describe the target node connected to the reply.out arc of the OR node.

6.5 UNIT Operators

The instructions used for realising UNIT nodes are as follows:

```
save_env              resave_env
restore_env           restore_close_env
create_succ           create_fail
```

A procedure containing N unit clauses is realised by a single UNIT node that eagerly generates all possible responses for a DO token by packing them in a reply token stream. A UNIT node executes as many unifications as many unit clauses are included in it. In the case of successful unifications, SUCC tokens are generated while failed unifications simply invoke the next unit clause unification. Finally, a FAIL token is generated indicating the end of the reply token stream. The general structure of the code of a UNIT node is as follows:

```
C1:    save_env
       fail_unify         C2
       allocate           M              % if there are M variables in the head
       <'get' and 'unify' instructions>
       restore_close_env                 % if there is any variable in the head
       create_succ
C2:    resave_env
       fail_unify         C3
       <'get' and 'unify' instructions>
       restore_env                       % if there is no variable in the head
       create_succ
  :
CN:    resave_env
       fail_unify         Cend
       <'get' and 'unify' instructions>
       restore_env                       % if there is no variable in the head
       create_succ
Cend:  create_fail
```

Since the environment of the invoking DO token is used in several consecutive unifications and the environment can be modified in any of these unifications, the invoking environment should be saved before the first head unification ('save_env') starts and should be restored ('resave_env') before any other unifications are executed within the UNIT node. These instructions are applied before each head unification and they are responsible for loading the caller goal arguments into the current free u_context record. In this way, the same 'get' and 'unify' instructions can be applied in the UNIFY and UNIT nodes.

If the unification is successful for each argument of the current head, a SUCC token is generated by 'create_succ' either in LTQ or RTQ depending on the value of TRPE. Before creating the SUCC token the goal environment should be restored to the TEi registers. This is done by the 'restore_env' or 'restore_close_env' instructions. The latter is used if the head contains any variable since in this case the goal environment frame should be closed with respect to the clause environment frame [Cone87b].

If the unification of any argument has failed, the control is passed to the beginning of the next head unification. This address is set by the 'fail_unify' instruction. A FAIL token is generated by 'create_fail' only when all the head unifications have been finished. The FAIL token is placed either in LTQ or RTQ depending on the value of TRPE.

7. VARIABLE BINDING

One of the major problems of implementing Prolog in a distributed memory environment is the efficient handling of variable bindings. A genuine method called environment closing has been described in [Cone87b]. The same method is used in 3DPAM. Here we outline the implementation of the method in the world of data-driven nodes. Environment closing is radically different from those methods used for shared memory implementations. The main ideas of closed environments are as follows:

1. A closed environment does not contain any reference that points out from the environment. As a consequence unification of two closed environments can be done perfectly locally without referring to any other environments placed in the local memory of other PEs.

2. No variables are ever placed in the heap. Whenever a structure containing a variable is built up in the heap, the variable is replaced by a reference pointing to the variable stored in the current token environment. (For distinguishing the variables stored in goal and clause token environments GREF and CREF tags are used respectively in the variable references). As a consequence the same compound term can be shared by different environments.

The environment close algorithm has two steps [Cone87b].:

1. Reverse the direction of all variable references pointing from CE to RE, where CE is the frame to transform into closed form and RE is the reference frame.

2. Extend CE with a new unbound variable for every unbound variable of RE referenced by any term belonging to CE.

In 3DPAM there are two cases for closing environments:
    1. Before entering a clause body (in UNIFY nodes after unification).
    2. Before exiting a clause (in UNIFY and UNIT nodes).

For illustrating the implementation of closed environments the following simple example is used in the present section:
```
a(X, f(Y, 1), Z) :- b(X, Y, Z).
b(g(7, 5), Y, 6).
b(g(17, 5), Y, 6).
? a(g(S, 5), T, 6).
```

Figure 10 illustrates the phases of work (preparing unification, unification, environment closing) in UNIFY nodes before entering a clause body. Figure 11 and 12 shows the work of UNIFY and UNIT nodes respectively before exiting a clause. In all of these figures GREF is simply denoted by G and CREF by C.

7.1 Environment closing before entering a clause body
Two token environments take part in each unification inside the UNIFY node:
    1. Goal token environment (GTE) arriving in a DO token
    2. Clause token environment (CTE) created during unification for SUB token

During unification only CREF references are created and placed in any token environment or in the heap. This means each references are directed from GTE to CTE and therefore the first step of Conery's close algorithm can be omitted. However, after unification CTE can contain structures that have GREF references (for example X is bound to g(S,5) in Figure 10), therefore the second step of the close algorithm should be executed for CTE before entering the clause body (generating the SUB token). The reference frame is obviously GTE. As a result of the close algorithm executed by the 'close_env' instruction of UNIFY, CTE and all its structures will contain only CREF references, thus CTE is closed (see Figure 10). Notice that GTE can contain CREF references, thus it is unclosed. However, GTE is frosen in this state and will be closed when the UNIFY node receives a reply SUB token (see Figure 11).

Entering into the body, the CTE should appear as a goal environment for the body goals and hence a CTE->GTE transformation is executed by the UNIFY node before emitting the SUB token. The CTE->GTE transformation exchanges all CREF tags into GREF tags in the whole environment. This means that the current GTE, conveyed in SUB tokens within the UNIFY/AND ring, is closed.

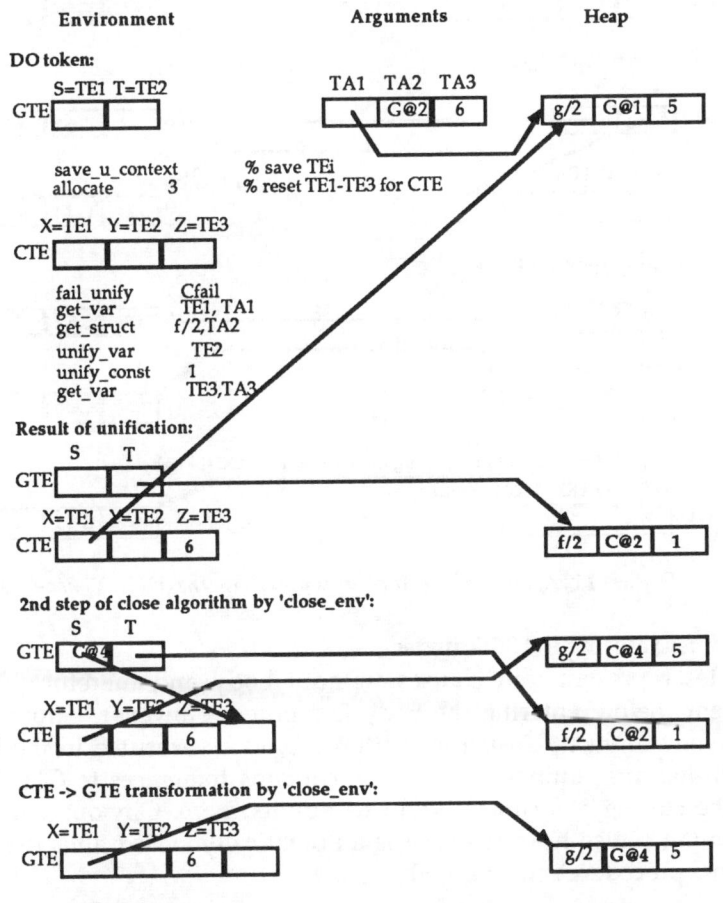

Figure 10 Actions in UNIFY after receiving a DO token

7.2 Environment closing before exiting a clause in UNIFY nodes

When a SUB token arrives to the reply.in arc of a UNIFY node the saved GTE (stored in the UNIFY Context Table) should be closed with respect to the incomming GTE as reference frame. Recall that the incomming GTE was originally the CTE of the UNIFY node. Hence, before executing the close procedure, a GTE->CTE transformation is needed on the incomming GTE (all GREF tags are exchanged into CREF tags).

Since the unification of GTE and CTE could result in references in GTE pointing to CTE both the first and second steps of Conery's algorithm should be applied. The resulting environment is a closed GTE packed in a SUCC token to be conveyed to an AND or OR node. All of these actions are done by the 'restore_u_context' instruction of the UNIFY node and they are summarised in Figure 11.

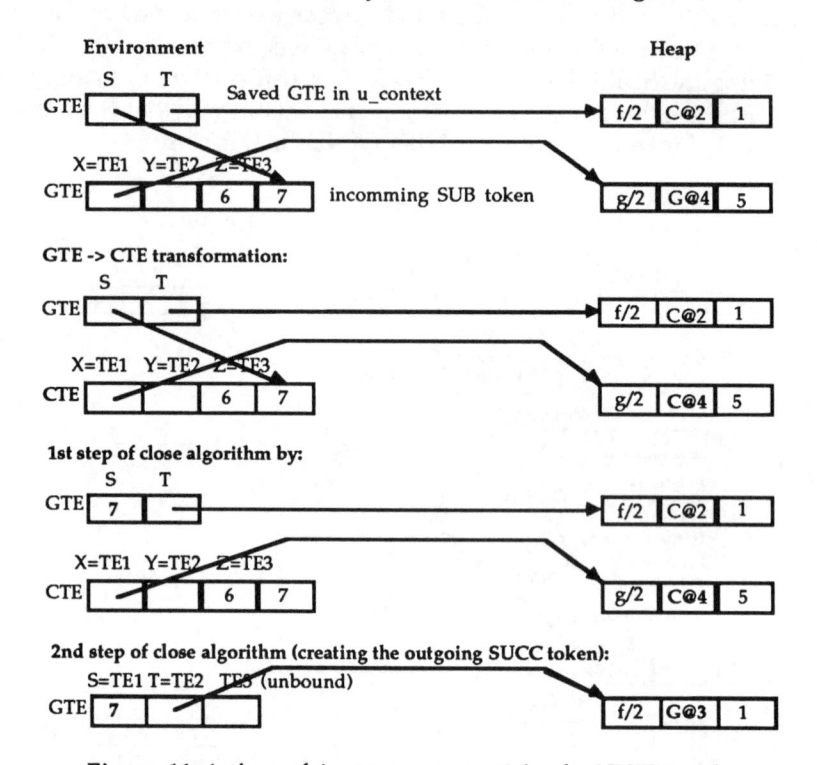

Figure 11 Actions of 'restore_u_context' in the UNIFY node

7.3 Environment closing in UNIT nodes

UNIT nodes represent unit clauses without body and therefore the close of environment before entering the body is omitted. However, before exiting the clause, the environment closing algorithm should be executed in the UNIT node too. Recall that after unification the GTE contains references to CTE, hence both steps of the closing algorithm should be applied here. Obviously if there is no variable in the clause head the GTE is automatically closed after the unification and the close procedure is not needed.

Figure 12 shows the steps of processing DO tokens in UNIT nodes. Notice that in the given example the UNIT node generates two SUCC tokens sharing the g(5,5) term on the heap. This structure sharing technique is useful as far as the tokens are processed on the same PE. However, if they are moved onto other PEs the term structure is copied for each token.

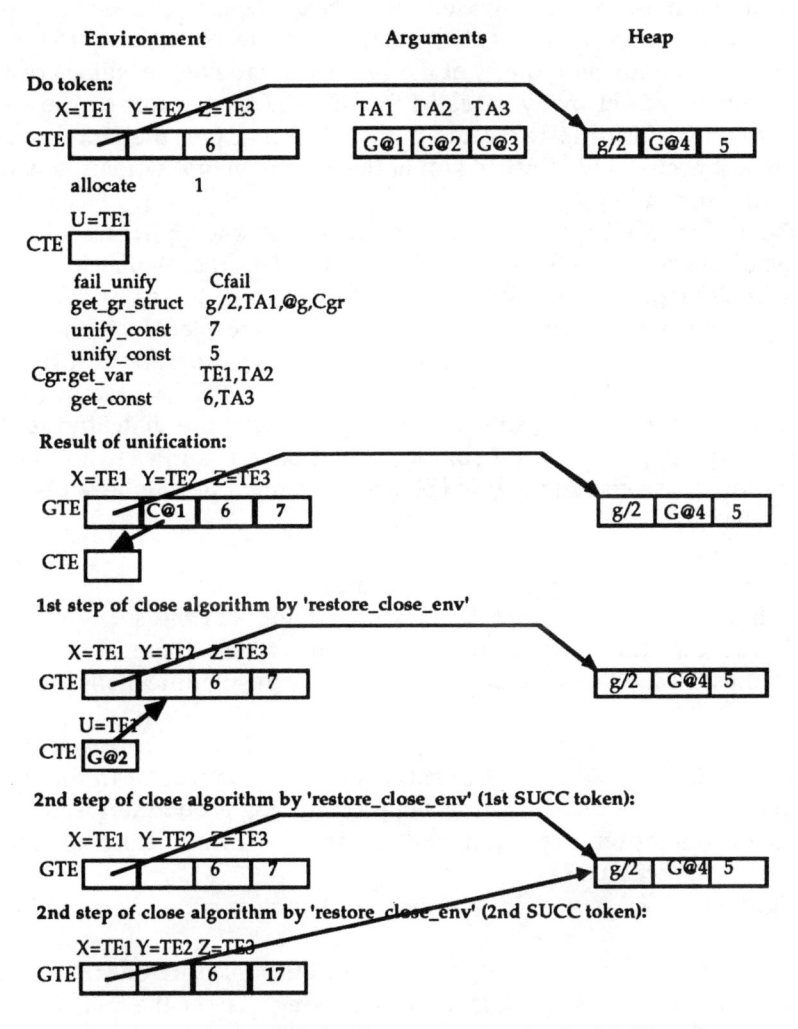

Figure 12 Steps of DO token processing in the UNIT node

8 COMPARISON WITH RELATED RESEARCHES

The introduced distributed data-driven Prolog abstract machine is closely related with the following researches:

1. Prolog dataflow models
2. Prolog abstract machines
3. Distributed implementation techniques

8.1 Comparison with Prolog Dataflow Models
The main difference with other dataflow models [Wise82a], [Hali86a], [Bisw88a] are as follows:

1. The other dataflow models are aimed at to be implemented on real dataflow computers and therefore no WAM-like abstract machine was proposed for them.

2. From similar reasons, those models create real tokens after executing any node functions. These tokens should again go through the whole administration process (and corresponding function units) of the proposed dataflow machines resulting in significant overhead. In many cases in the 3DPAM as a result of the work of a node, the new token is directly created in the token registers, therefore, can be used by the next connected node (instruction in the code memory) without any dataflow oriented administration.

3. All the other models enable nodes with more than one input arcs and apply the firing rule of the pure dataflow model [Denn74a]. This means that in the case of a practical implementation, a matching unit is needed in the dataflow machine to select those tokens that have the same colour and are placed on the arcs of the same node. This is a time-consuming associative operation introducing a significant overhead into the dataflow systems. In the 3DPAM, each node can fire even if only a single arc contains a token. In this way the matching unit can be omitted and the application of a simple token queue is sufficient to find fireable nodes. It should be remarked that in [Bisw88a] a similar technique is used to avoid the use of the matching unit.

8.2 Comparison with Prolog Abstract Machines
In the definition of the 3DPAM the starting point was the study of the WAM [Warr83a]. In fact the unification related instructions of the 3DPAM are very similar to those of the WAM, though there were some modifications introduced as follows:

1. *Introduction of 'ground' version of the 'get' and 'put' instructions handling compound data terms.* This can be considered as an optimization in the distributed environment to reduce the size of messages containing ground terms. It turned out that this optimization even can reduce the execution time of unification instructions (see Section 6.1).

2. *Application of the 'write' instructions as it was proposed in the KL1 abstract machine [Kimu87a].*

The failure mechanism of the 3DPAM is significantly different from that of the WAM since in the 3DPAM there is no backtracking. Rather the failure mechanism is realised by distinguishing the success return address and failure return address of tokens. According to this, there is no need for the Trail in the 3DPAM. However, the Heap of the 3DPAM plays the same role as the Heap of the WAM. The Local Stack of the WAM is substituted by the UNIFY Context Table of the 3DPAM.

Although the basic semantics of an all-solution Prolog and of a guarded Horn clause (GHC) language like FCP and KL1 are quite different, there are surprisingly many similarities in their abstract machine based implementations. Both in the 3DPAM and in the abstract machines of GHC languages ([Kimu87a],[Hour87a], [Tayl86a], [Fost90a]), the computation is based on a queue of information packages representing executable pieces of work. The main difference is that in the GHC abstract machines this queue contains processes (representing executable goals), meanwhile in the 3DPAM this queue contains tokens. In the GHC abstract machines there is no obligation on the order of processes in the process queue. Similarly in the 3DPAM the order of tokens is basically irrelavant except for the stream ending FAIL tokens. These should be handled only after the consumption of the other tokens in the token stream. Finaly, the depth-first optimization (or tail-recursion optimization) of the GHC processes can be applied for the 3DPAM tokens as well.

8.3 Distributed Implementation Techniques
The four main problems of implementing logic programming languages in a distributed environment are:
1. handling of binding environments
2. distributed handling of compound terms
3. controling granularity
4. mapping

For the first problem an efficient solution called closed environments was proposed in [Cone87b] and the same method is applied in the 3DPAM.

The handling of compound terms in distributed environments poses the question whether the eager or the lazy communication of the terms is the most efficient. Eager communication means that the whole term is communicated to the consumer PE while in case of lazy communication only those terms and even only those parts of the terms are actually sent to the consumer PE that are explicitly requested by the consumer. In the distributed implementation of Flat Parlog [Fost90a] and FCP [Tayl86a] the lazy communication scheme was used, meanwhile in the 3DPAM the eager scheme is applied. In [Verd90a] it was shown that any scheme has superiority over the other one since the communication cost is highly depending on the actual size of the compound terms.

For controling granularity in [Ramk89a] a method similar to the use of SEQ nodes (based on sequential predicates and modules) of the 3DPAM [Kacs91a] is introduced.

Unlike the other proposals the 3DPAM is based on a static mapping scheme. It avoids the time consuming run time decisions of dynamic mapping systems like [Bria91a], but results in reduced performance in case of unbalanced loading. However, in the case of large Prolog programs, the system is likely to be statistically well-balanced.

CONCLUSIONS

The main results of the present research can be summarized as follows:

1. A Prolog program can be compiled into a dataflow graph (DSG). Subparts of the DSG can be mapped onto different PEs. The node functions and node connecting arcs are represented by the instructions of the 3DPAM.

2. Unification and term handling instruction of the 3DPAM are closely related to those of the WAM. However, the indexing and procedural instructions of the WAM targetted for realising the sequential execution mechanism are fully replaced in the 3DPAM by instructions realising the data driven execution scheme.

3. There are several possible mapping schemes of DSG into a distributed processor space. Herein a mapping scheme was introduced which supports the full exploitation of OR-parallelism and pipeline AND-parallelism.

4. The execution mechanism of the 3DPAM is token oriented unlike the implementation of committed choice languages [Tayl86b] which are process oriented. The token oriented execution scheme can efficiently be implemented in a distributed memory system without the matching store of dataflow systems since one token is sufficient to make any node of the DSG fire.

5. The hibryd dataflow/controlflow implementation scheme assures that inherently sequential subprograms can be executed based on the most effective WAM implementation, while inherently parallel subprograms are handled by a data driven abstract machine (3DPAM) optimised for executing Prolog on distributed memory systems.

Due to lack of space many important questions of a real implementation (like handling of 'cut', built-in procedures and others) have not been addressed in this chapter. The interested reader can consult [Kacs91b] where all these questions are described in detail.

ACKNOWLEDGEMENT

This work was supported by an SERC research grant titled "Study of the Implementation of Prolog on Mixed Architecture Parallel Computers". I would particularly like to thank Prof. Heather Liddell for making possible and encouraging this research and Jonathan Hill for writing an experimental Prolog compiler for this project.

PART II AND- and AND/OR-Parallel Implementation of Prolog

The structure of the second part of this book is very similar to that of Part I. The initial chapter surveys the distinct AND-parallel and AND/OR-parallel schemes for implementing Prolog on parallel computers. This chapter is recommended for novice Prolog users and implementors, but even readers familiar with the parallel implementation techniques of Prolog might find it useful to get a systematic overview of the field. Chapters 1 and 6 together can also be considered as a basis for teaching parallel implementation of Prolog at universities.

Further chapters in Part II illustrate specific approaches to implementing Prolog on distributed memory multicomputers and explain in detail special techniques. Chapter 7 describes an AND-parallel distributed Prolog executor based on the independent AND-parallel execution scheme. This executor is derived from the schemes of Hermenegildo and Lin by extending the WAM with some special data structures for administrating potential AND-parallelism. The backward execution algorithm also makes it possible to exploit clause level intelligent backtracking.

Chapters 8, 9 and 10 describe three different approaches to investigating both OR- and AND-parallelism on distributed memory multicomputers. The AND/OR process model, familiar from Part I, is the subject of Chapter 8, which describes an abstract machine, called the OPAL Machine. The instruction set of the OPAL Machine is carefully investigated and explained. The unification algorithm used in this model is based on the closed environment concept introduced in Part I. It is interesting and instructive to compare the instruction set of the 3DPAM described in Chapter 5 and that of the OPAL Machine. The former is a data driven, while the latter is a message driven, implementation of the same execution model. However, while the 3DPAM handles only OR-parallelism the OPAL Machine can cope with both OR- and AND-parallelism.

Chapter 9 describes in detail the Reduce-OR Process Model. Special attention is paid to a two-phase unification scheme, which represents an optimisation of Conery's closed environment method. The two-phase unification scheme makes it possible to retain structure-sharing techniques in distributed memory environments by introducing molecules for shared structures. Another interesting part of this chapter is the description of the Join Algorithm used for incremental collection of partial results deriving from parallel, independent subgoals. Some compilation techniques are also mentioned in Chapter 9, which also outlines the most important features and instructions of a corresponding abstract machine. Finally, impressive performance results prove the feasibility of the model for different distributed memory multicomputers like Intel's iPSC/2 and the NCUBE 2.

The third project implementing AND/OR parallel Prolog represents a radically different approach. This is based on Kowalski's AND/OR connection graph and is described in Chapter 10. The model is inherently distributed, but unfortunately requires a large number of messages to administer the step-by-step reduction of the connection graph. The necessary message types and their use in the distributed interpretation scheme are thoroughly investigated in the COALA execution model, which enables the exploitation of OR-parallelism independent AND-parallelism and SEARCH-parallelism. The design of an abstract machine, called CIAM (COALA Inference Abstract Machine), is also described in detail in Chapter 10.

A common feature of chapters in Part II is that abstract machines are defined and described for implementing AND/OR parallel Prolog systems. As a consequence the whole part can be highly recommended to readers interested in constructing abstract Prolog machines for parallel computers.

6 Restricted AND- and AND/OR-Parallel Logic Computational Models

S. A. Delgado-Rannauro
Laboratoire Nacional de Informática Avanzada, Mexico

ABSTRACT

In this chapter, a review of Restricted AND-Parallel logic and AND/OR-Parallel logic computational models is presented. The Restricted AND-Parallel (RAP) logic models exploit parallelism by executing in parallel only those body goals that do not share any variables, i.e. independent. Different mechanisms have been designed to exploit this kind of parallelism. They are based on analysis made of the body goals in a clause. The analysis can be either static, dynamic or hybrid. The AND/OR-parallel models reviewed in this chapter evaluate logic programs by exploiting a combination of Restricted AND-Parallelism and OR-parallelism.

1 RESTRICTED AND-PARALLEL LOGIC MODELS

In this section a review of the different approaches taken for the realisation of independent AND-parallelism, commonly referred to as *Restricted AND-Parallel (RAP)* models, is presented. There are two clearly distinct approaches to RAP: a static and a dynamic one. The static approach is based on program analysis (compile time analysis) for the detection of the data-flow between the goals in the clause body. The dynamic approach uses run-time tests to determine the applicability of parallel execution, but sometimes at considerable costs. There are two different approaches to be found in the literature: the work described in [Cone83a] and in [Lin88c]. A third, intermediate or hybrid, approach has also been mentioned ([DeGr84a],[Herm86c]); it tries to combine the advantages of the static and dynamic schemes.

All these methods designed to exploit RAP, use a data-dependency graph of goals in the clause body. In these computational models, *don't know* non-determinism is also supported. The backward execution mechanisms need to obtain information from the data-dependency graph. The backward literal or backtracking point follows the dependency path of the graph. These schemes, besides exploiting a restricted form of AND-parallelism, also attempt to avoid recomputation by *"intelligently"* backtracking to the proper literal in the execution graph rather than using the ordering rule of Prolog.

1.1 Concepts

Restricted AND-parallelism was developed, as well as stream AND-parallelism, as an alternative to unrestricted AND-parallel models. The notion of Restricted or Independent AND-parallelism aims at evaluating conjunctions in parallel only if their execution is independent. As it was briefly mentioned in the paragraphs above, there are basically three methods to detect independency among the body goals of a clause:

- **Dynamic:** The data-flow dependency among subgoals can be detected at run-time ([Cone83a],[Lin88c]). These methods change the execution graph dynamically according to the availability of data. In [Cone83a] a set of algorithms is used for the dynamic management of the graph which may involve the recomputation of the complete graph. The approach by [Lin88c], uses a set of tokens to detect the data-flow dependencies. There is no need to recompute the execution graph after the proof of each goal in the clause body. Both schemes can have expensive tests to determine whether variables are completely grounded or independent.

- **Static:** The static dependency analysis [Chan85b] is the complete opposite of the dynamic approach. It is a compiler-based mechanism in which, by extensive mode analysis of the program, the worst case execution graph is always selected. The idea is to eliminate all the run-time tests. With this scheme, several cases of parallel evaluation may be overlooked by the static analysis. Only one data-flow dependency graph can be generated by this method.

- **Hybrid:** This scheme represents a compromise between the previous two. It attempts, by means of compilation techniques, to evaluate an approximation to the maximal parallelism [DeGr84a]. It also provides simple and efficient run-time tests for the evaluation of the data-flow graph. The compilation technique produces one expression graph which could produce different execution graphs depending on variable instantiations.

1.2 Dynamic Data Dependency

1.2.1 Lin's Bit-vector

The detection of the data-flow graph in this method [Lin88c] follows a partial order based on the syntactic definition of a clause. The detection of the data-flow graph is based on a producer-consumer approach. A forward execution algorithm is used to control the dynamic creation of the data-flow graph. The algorithm can be viewed as a token passing scheme. Where a token is created for each variable appearing in the execution of each clause. Each newly created token (for variable **V**) is given to the leftmost goal **G** which has **V** in its environment. A goal **G** is selected as the generator of **V** if it holds the token for **V**. A goal **G** becomes executable when it has received all the tokens for the shared variables in its current environment.

The backward execution algorithm performs backtracking at a clause level. Each goal G_i, the i-th goal in a clause, dynamically maintains a list of goals denoted as B-list(G_i). This list consists of the goals in the clause which could be used to backtrack upon failure of G_i. The goals G_k in each B-list have a descending order of k (according to their position in the clause). The contents of B-list(G_i) are those goals which have contributed to the binding of the environment of G_i. If G_i fails, the selected backtracking goal G_j is then taken from the head of the B-list(G_i)[1]. The tail of the list is now B-list(G_j), so that in case of failure, the goal G_j can direct the backward algorithm to the right point in the graph. In the case that the selected backtracking goal G_j has several children depending on the current set of bindings. All the goals G_k such that $k > j$, and their related children need to be cancelled.

---

[1] In this partially ordered data-dependent graph, a failed goal G_i will normally have a backtracking point G_j such that i > j, which will be within the current clause. When the backtracking point is the head literal G_0, the current clause is considered as failed.

Conceptually, the above defined model can be implemented on either a shared or distributed memory architectures. The former follows a philosophy similar to [Herm86c], in which the abstract machine design is based on the WAM; whereas the latter is a process-based model similar to Conery's AND-/OR-process model [Cone83a].

In [Lin88b] an implementation on a shared memory multiprocessor is described. A slightly modified token-passing scheme has been implemented with bit-vectors. Each AND-shared variable **V** in a clause has an associated *bit-vector*, the length of the vector corresponds to the number of goals in the clause body. Each element in the vector represents a goal G_i in the clause, the leftmost goal G_1 in the clause is the most significant bit in the vector. The *i-th* bit is 1 if the goal G_i can contribute or has contributed to bind variable V. A goal G_i is executable on the condition that for every AND-shared variable V in its environment there is no unsolved goal G_j *(j<i)* such that *j-th* bit in the vector is 1^2. For example, consider the following clause of the quick sort program.

```
qsort(L,SL):-
  partition(L,L1,L2),
qsort1(L1,SL1),
qsort2(L2,SL2),
append(SL1,SL2,SL).
```

After the unification of the head, variable L has its bit-vector set up to {1000}, variable L1 as {1100}, variable L2 as {1010}, SL1 as {0101}, SL2 as {0011} and SL as {0001}. The bit-vector of L1 {1100} means that partition (G_1) and qsort1(G_2) can contribute to bind it. In terms of the token scheme, *partition* has tokens for variables L, L1, and L2. Thus, it can be executed. At the end of the execution of any goal the bit-vectors of the variables involved need to be updated.

Note that the bit-vector of a given variable V has only the scope of the clause involved; for every new call where a variable is involved a new bit-vector will be associated with it, thus this scheme needs to have environments for every called goal, which does not fit completely in the WAM environment allocation policy. The latter may mean that another data area is needed for the management of the bit-vectors.

In order to check when a given goal G_i is executable, each goal has **bit-vector mask** associated with it to obey the precedence rule. G_1 (partition) has a bit-vector mask of {0000}, G_2 has {1000}, G_3 has {1100} and G_4 has {1110}. For each clause a *finish bit-vector* is used to detect whether the goal G_j has completed its execution. For example, after the head unification of qsort, the finish bit-vector is {1111}. The successful execution of G_k is represented by having the *k-th* bit set to 0. Thus, the following tests are performed to determine if a goal G_i is executable, for every AND-shared variable V in G_i:

$DD(V,G_i) \leftarrow \wedge$ (bit-vector of V) $\wedge$ (bit-vector mask of G_i)
$Ready(V,G_i) \leftarrow DD(V,G_i) \wedge$ finish-vector

If for any V in G_i Ready(V,G_i) is non-zero, the goal G_i cannot be executed because there is an unsolved goal G_j such that $j < i$, which violates the partial execution order of the scheme. Therefore, the execution of G_i needs to be delayed until its test for execution succeeds.

---

[2] The implementation of the bit-vector scheme provides a simple solution to the partial ordering of the goals in the clause body. All the operations only require simple bit-wise and equality comparisons.

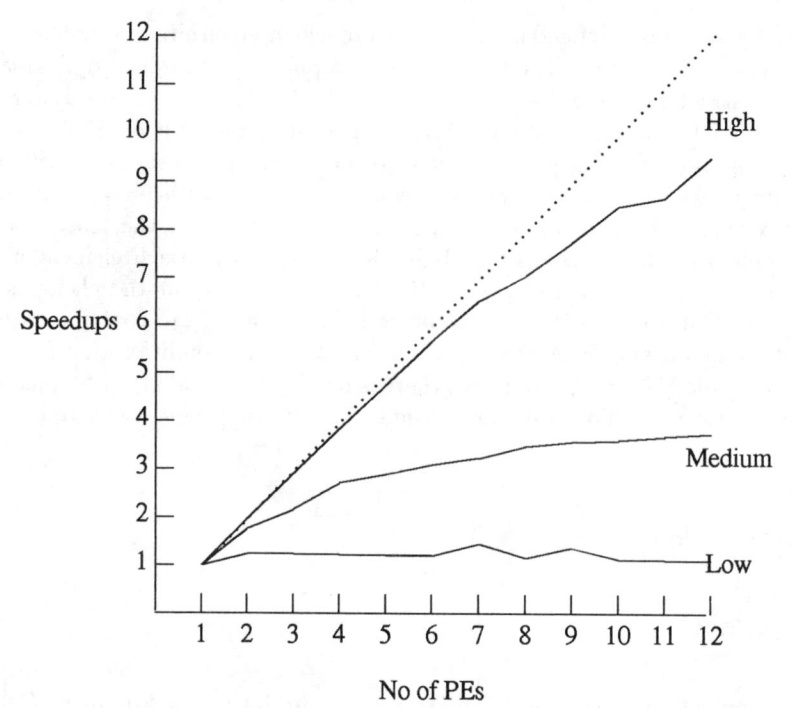

Figure 1: Performance results of the Bit-vector model

The implementation of the backtracking algorithm is also based on the bit-vector scheme, for each B-list(G_i) a bit-vector is associated. In fact, the DD(V,G) bit-vector represents the list of goals that have contributed to bind the variable V. Thus, the DD(V,G) of all the shared variables in G represent the B-list of G (a logical OR operation on all the DD(V,G) gives the sorted B-list(G)). The execution of the backward execution algorithm is given by the order of the less significant bits of the B-list bit-vector. The implementation of the backtracking algorithm forces a sequential order in the selection of the backtrack point if several processors are involved. A processor, which has detected a non-local backtracking point, signals to all the other processors in the system to stop the computation until the backward execution is completed. Normally this case does not occur with large problems, in these situations most of the backtracking is done locally.

Some results from the implementation of the Bit-vector model have been reported. Fig. 1 shows the performance of the model with a benchmark suit. The benchmark programs used are from a typical set, they are known to have AND-parallelism and good behaviour on "intelligent" backtracking. These speed up curves show the average performance improvement with different types of benchmarks. The high curve represent programs with large amount of RAP, the medium with middle size RAP, and low curve represents generate and test type programs, e.g. queens.

The experiments were run on different set of parameters. Among these some experiments were observed that measured the relationship between task granularity and the number of data-dependency checks. It turned out that the latter affected the parallel computation of goals. Therefore, if the number of parallel goals is reduced likewise is the need for data-dependency checks (due to the induced sequential execution). This

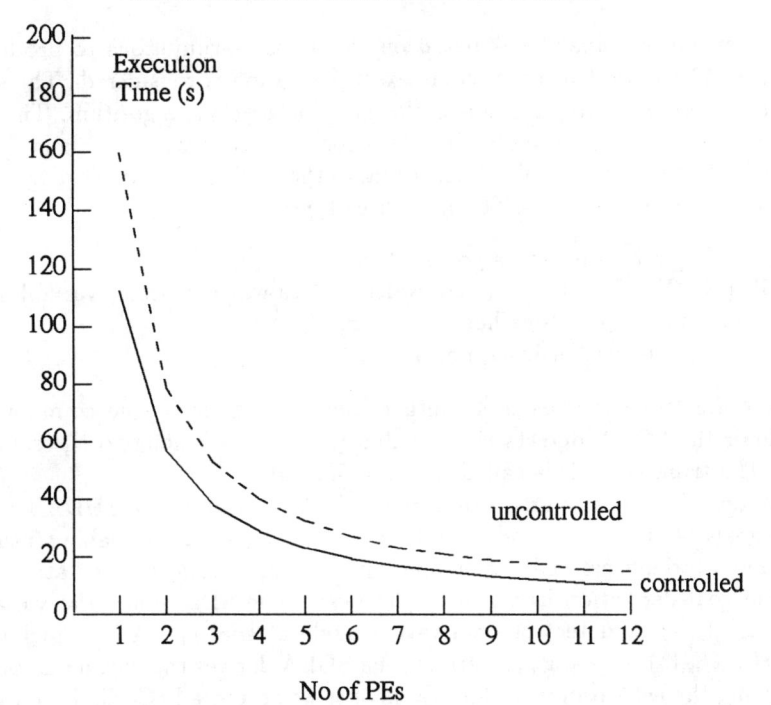

Figure 2: Relationship between dependency-check and task granularity optimisation in the Bit-vector model.

relationship can only last as long as the amount of computation is large and enough task granularity can be induced. It may, however, not be possible to maintain it if the number of processors in the parallel machine grows. Fig. 2 shows the relationship between the dependency-check and task granularity. The *uncontrolled* graph represents an implementation that eagerly generates parallel processes, whereas the *control* curve presents an implementation with controlled generation of parallel tasks, i.e. only on demand.

Discussion: This scheme has reduced the run-time overhead for the dynamic data-dependency analysis of Restricted AND-parallelism. The implementation of the token passing scheme using bit-vector is good but there is a constant overhead for its management. For every successful computation of a goal, the bit-vectors of each of its related shared variables need to be updated, so that the proper execution of the data-dependency graph can be determined. The overhead can be minimised if the number of shared variables is small and a compile-time analysis is used to avoid performing dependency checks. In addition, it can also be optimised with task granularity control.

1.3 Static Data Dependency Analysis (SDDA)

The method described in [Chan85c] uses a technique similar to the automatic mode analysis of Prolog programs [Mell84a]. Instead of detecting the mode of arguments, it uses the information to generate a data-flow dependency graph for each clause in the program. The SDDA eliminates the need for run-time independency tests. The minimal information that the user must supply are the modes of the top-level query to the system.

The dependency analysis is based on worst-case assumptions to produce safe independent AND-parallelism; only one execution graph is considered. The system also generates information for a *"semi-intelligent"* backtracking algorithm. The backtracking points considered by the algorithm are confined to be within a clause [Chan85b].

In SDDA, goals are examined according to the Prolog execution order, left to right. Variables in a clause are classified into three types:

G - { V | V is bound to a ground term }
C - { V | V ∈ EC, EC is an equivalence class which contains variables that
  may be coupled together }
I - { V | V is neither in G, nor in C }

There are two variables in C, either they have at least one common, unbound variable or the SDDA detects the possibility that they belong to the same coupling group. The triple (C,G,I) is called the *variable status*.

The data-dependency graph of a clause is derived after the SDDA has examined all the goals of the clause and kept track of the worst-case variable status. During derivation a variable can only be on one type at a time, however, its status may change from one goal derivation iteration to the next. The SDDA uses the variable status $(C_{i-1}, G_{i-1}, I_{i-1})$ to detect the activation mode of goal g_i. After the final variable status (C_n, G_n, I_n) of goal g_n is derived, the SDDA derives the exit mode of the clause by coupling the activation variable status of the clause head (C_0, G_0, I_0) on to the final variable status (C_n, G_n, I_n).

The worst-case analysis is extended to a relation call since the call may invoke all the candidate clauses. They have to be processed in the same manner in order to get the exit mode of the procedure call for a given activation. The exit mode for the relation is the worst-case combination of the exit modes of all the candidate clauses.

The data-dependency graph is generated after the activation and the exit modes of clauses in the program have been generated. With this information, the static analysis can now generate the data-dependency for each clause in the program. The generation of the data-dependency graph starts by assuming goal ordering in the clause of the program. The left-most goal g_1 is considered the generator of its variables. For every goal in the clause, a *data-dependency list* is created by the SDDA. The data-dependency list of goal g_i describes the preceding goals of goal g_i. As part of the analysis, the backtrack goals for each goal g_i are also generated in a list. Every element in the *backtrack list* of goal g_i represents a different type of backtracking.

The backward execution algorithm of this scheme distinguishes three types of backtracking situations but without recording the history of each execution path for the analysis of the cause of failure. The three types of backward execution supported by the SDDA are:

1. A shallow backtracking occurs if a goal is called in forward execution. In this case, goal g_i has to backtrack to its closest predecessor in the data-dependency list. If the closest predecessor of g_i has several common dependent goals, they also have to be removed.

2. In forward execution, goals of the same level of the data-dependency graph are independent. However, during backward execution this may not be the case. Assume that the execution of the data-dependency graph is on its third level, furthermore a goal g_k in the third level, which is a direct descendent of goal g_i,

fails immediately after it is called. If goal g_i cannot satisfy the backtracking request of g_k, g_i must make all its other descendents to abort their computation (type 1 backtracking), and start a backtracking procedure. If g_i decides to backtrack "*intelligently*" to its predecessor, then all siblings of g_i also need to be aborted (again, type 1 backtracking). However, such decision can make the search incomplete, i.e. a solution may exist in the neglected search space. The proposed solution in this scheme is to backtrack sequentially to the right siblings of goal g_i, so that all the space is completely searched.

3. This backtracking type is naive, it backtracks sequentially through all the alternative search paths.

In [Chan85c], a sequential and a parallel implementation are described. The sequential implementation is based in the WAM, and has extensions for the different types of backtracking discussed above. The measurement of the sequential implementation indicates that the scheme is good for naive programs which generate an excessive amount of recomputation. It fails, however, to achieve good performance for better written programs and generate-and-test programs, e.g. queens.

The parallel execution model is a process-based model in which the forward and backward execution of the scheme is achieved by means of messages. Simulation results of a modified parallel execution model are presented in [Fagi87a]. The expected performance of that simulator is very poor, this is due to the process model overhead and to the wrong simulation assumptions.

Discussion: The SDDA attempts to extract enough safe information for the execution of independent AND-parallelism. This compiled approach does not need any run-time tests for exploiting the parallelism. However, as we have repeatedly said, it fails to exploit all the available parallelism due to the worst-case analysis performed for the activation of procedure calls. The complexity of the scheme is comparable to the standard compilation of the same program.

As a side effect, the SDDA can also generate information for a more sophisticated backtracking algorithm; modifications to the basic abstract machine, the WAM, are required for such an implementation. The different backtracking alternatives do not attempt to avoid recomputation completely. Thus, on average, this *semi-intelligent* backtracking mechanism is not expected to perform extremely well over the naive sequential backtracking method.

1.4 Hybrid Models

All the work in this area started with [DeGr84a] in which the initial definitions of the *Conditional Graph Expressions (CGE)* were made. Subsequent work by Hermengildo ([Herm86c],[Herm86b],[Herm86a],[Muth90a],[Herm90b], [Herm90a]) took the basic principle and defined more precisely an execution model for the Restricted AND-parallel (RAP) scheme. Another hybrid scheme has been proposed in [Xia88a], based on abstract interpretation to detect data-flow dependencies.

1.4.1 DeGroot's RAP Model This model was developed from observations on the work in [Cone83a]. The idea was to put the most expensive run-time tests of such a model into a compiled expression graph. This graph would also have some simple run-time tests for the detection of the correct execution graph at run-time. The system only generates one expression graph for each clause in the program, which at run-time, may produce one of several execution graphs.

Determining safe independence at compile time is simple but too restrictive; the scheme performs a worst-case analysis. In order to expand beyond the safe independence, some run-time tests are required. However, terms must be typed to identify their scope for the independence run-time test. Terms can have these three types: ground (**G**), non-ground (**NG**) and variables (**V**). Ground terms are completely instantiated structures, constants or integers. Non-ground terms are complex structures with uninstantiated variables in their body. Variable terms are unbound.

```
if type(arg1) equal G or type(arg2) equal G
   return(independent)
else
   if type(arg1) equal type(arg2) equal V and
      address(arg1) not equal address(arg2)
      return(independent)
   else
      return(dependent)
```

Figure 3: RAP Independence Test Algorithm

The scheme uses an efficient approximation method to obtain the compiled expression graph. The approximation method considers how type **V** terms can inherit type **G** or **NG** at run-time. The method uses the *"ground"* and *"independent"* predicates to perform the run-time tests. The ground predicate, $GPAR(X_1,...,X_n)$, succeeds iff all the tested terms are grounded. The independence predicate, $IPAR(X_1,...,X_n)$, succeeds iff all the terms are proved to be independent. In Fig. 3, the independent test algorithm for two terms is given. This algorithm has $O(n^2)$ complexity, where n is the number of terms to be tested for dependency. Note that the algorithm assumes that its arguments are completely dereferenced terms.

The compiled expression graphs are built from a set of six execution expressions:

1. G
2. (SEQ E_1 ... E_n)
3. (PAR E_1 ... E_n)
4. (GPAR($X_1,...,X_k$) E_1 ... E_n)
5. (IPAR($X_1,...,X_k$) E_1 ... E_n)
6. (IF E_1 E_2 E_3)

The compiler generates the CGE shown in Fig. 4 for the quick sort program. The call to partition is executed sequentially. The calls to qsort could be executed in parallel iff L1 and L2 are independent. From this CGE, two different execution graphs could be created at run-time.

In [DeGr87a], Prolog side-effects are discussed within the RAP model. Clauses and procedures are *pure* if they are free of side-effects. A compilation technique, similar to [Chan85b] detects pure clauses. The parallel execution of pure clauses is free of any ordering or sequencing constraints. However, if a clause body also has *impure* goals (i.e. subgoals with side-effects) a sequencing rule is adopted. All pure subgoals

```
qsort(L,SL):-
      partition(L,L1,L2),
      qsort(L1,SL1),
      qsort(L2,SL2),
      append(SL1,SL2,SL).
```
Conditional Graph Expression (CGE) for the qsort program

```
(SEQ
      partition(L,L1,L2)
      (IPAR(L1,L2)
            qsort(L1,SL1)
            qsort(L2,SL2))
      append(SL1,SL2,SL))
```

Figure 4: **The quick-sort program compiled to CGEs**

preceding an impure subgoal must be successfully completed before the impure goal can be executed. All subgoals following an impure subgoal may only be executed after the successful completion of the impure subgoal.

An impure goal affects the execution of the subtree where it is located, i.e. any subtree with an impure goal is also considered to be impure. Thus, the sequential execution order is propagated from the impure goal up to the root of the subtree containing it. Which, of course, is unacceptable. In order to remedy this behaviour, the graph expressions have been extended with synchronisation mechanisms.

The mechanism devised for this purpose uses a *synchronisation block* which can be considered as an evaluable predicate with two arguments, a *counter* and a *signal*. These two variables are passed down and are only valid for the subtree in which they were created, giving an uniform view of the synchronisation. The counter specifies the number of active pure goals preceding the impure goal. The signal is used to control the execution of the goals that follow the impure goal. If the counter reaches a zero value (i.e. if there are no more preceding pure goals to execute), the impure goal can be executed. As soon as the impure goal completes execution, the signal variable is updated with the value true and all the goals waiting for the impure goal can now be started.

When a wait-on-signal instruction is executed in an expression graph, it may be that the signal variable has not yet been set to true. Therefore, the execution of the expression must be suspended, entering in the suspended expression list. Reactivation of suspended expressions is attempted when a processor has run out of active expressions. The processor checks the suspension list to find one expression with its signal set to true. If none is found, the processor tries to assist other processors with their active expressions.

The RAP computational model has been implemented at Texas Instruments. There are two versions based on the TI Explorer II processor:

- loosely-coupled Explorer workstations.

- tightly-coupled shared memory NuBus cluster, with 6 processors.

The implementation is written in Lisp with some Prolog control predicates, the raw performance per processor is 128KLips. A preliminary backward execution algorithm has been completed with the mechanism considering backtracking over I/O. The management of side-effects has not yet been incorporated into the compiler. The main motivation of this research is to produce a system which:

- responds fast to balance load requirements. The scheduling scheme developed for this RAP implementation is demand-driven. Parallel tasks are only activated upon request. Special attention has been paid to an algorithm which is highly responsive to these requests.

- is fault tolerant. At present, their system is capable of restarting any lost or broken computation.

Discussion: As the author has stated, the present model fails in some cases to detect the maximum parallelism. In addition, due to the form the CGEs are evaluated, goals may need to wait for execution regardless of whether their terms are ready for evaluation. However, the aim of the project, as stated, is a compromise between efficiency and the amount of parallelism to be generated, which seems to be achieved. This early work did not make enough studies about the impact of backward execution. A step forward in this direction and in the specification of compiled code for the independence test is described in the following section.

The extension of the RAP model to handle Prolog side-effects is a safe approach and minimises the impact of restricting the parallelism even further. The extension of the expression graph includes synchronisation mechanisms to support the rapid reactivation of suspended expressions. However, the method used to reactivation is too simple, there is room for improvement in this area[3].

1.4.2 RAP-WAM The RAP, as specified by DeGroot [DeGr84a], is taken as the basis for an efficient parallel abstract machine RAP-WAM ([Herm86c], [Herm86a]). It incorporates the necessary abstract instructions for the proper parallel execution. The abstract memory model is stack-based, as in the WAM, and assumes a shared memory architecture. Performance results from a simulated system [Herm87a] and a parallel shared memory implementation [Herm90b] have been reported.

The work done in [Herm86a], besides developing an abstract machine for RAP, is a more in-depth study of the management of backtracking. The backward execution algorithm now needs to consider backtracking over Conditional Graph Expressions (CGEs). There are several cases, depending on whether the next backtracking point is in or over a CGE, or as in sequential execution. Only the first two cases need to be discussed. To illustrate the cases more clearly, assume the following clause is executed:

p:- a, (<conditions> | b & c & d), e.

where the expression inside the brackets is a CGE.

- **backtracking in a CGE:** Assume the execution of the clause is in the CGE, one of the parallel subgoals fails, namely **b**. Since the parallel subgoals are completely independent, there is no binding dependency. Thus, bindings produced by any of

---

[3]The signal variable could have an associated suspended list, similar to the CCND suspension on variable mechanism. Thus after the completion of the impure goal, all the goals could be placed in the active expression list.

the other parallel subgoals did not cause the failure of **b**. Therefore, the parallel evaluation of the CGE must be aborted, and the computation is resumed at the backtracking point immediately preceding the CGE.

- **backtracking over a CGE:** Normally during the execution of a CGE several alternative search patterns remain unexplored. Assuming, from the above clause, the execution of **e** fails. The backtracking in the CGE follows the left to right ordering of sequential execution. Thus, the system will first backtrack on unexplored alternatives of **d** and so forth. The model requires information about the remaining unexplored alternatives of each parallel goal, to conduct the backtracking in the proper sequence.

Discussion: Hermenegildo's work aims to implement efficiently RAP with minor modifications to WAM. It follows the same memory management and abstract machine design as the WAM. The backward execution algorithm used is simple and only requires small additional information to do backtracking. Recent developments ([Muth90a],[Herm90a]) have improved the amount of parallelism that may be obtained from a Restricted AND-parallelism. These achievements have been attained by means of new compilation techniques based on abstract interpretation and static analyses of logic programs.

1.4.3 Xia's Hybrid Model In conntecion with the basic work performed by DeGroot, another hybrid model is presented in [Xia88a]. The data-flow dependency analysis is also made at compile time using abstract interpretation which can produce a more efficient execution of RAP. In this model opportunities for parallelism can be explored where the RAP model would fail to find parallelism. Furthermore, the number of tests to declare goals independent is reduced.

The method is based on abstract interpretation to detect the input clause activation and the exit clause mode. The abstract analysis algorithm only requires one-pass through the clause to derive its exit mode, unlike the worst-case analysis of the SDDA [Chan85b] which requires several passes through the same clause to the detect the worst-case analysis.

The analysis is made on the assumption that variables of a goal call are neutral, i.e. independent. The application of the neutral activation modes yields the natural exit modes of a clause, derived from the information available in the program. The data-dependency is made at variable level rather than at argument level, as in [DeGr84a]. Each variable **V** has, at any given time, any of these four classes:

- **G** { V | V is bound to a ground term }

- **I** { V | V is either not instantiated or shares no variables with other variables }

- **C** { V_1, V_2 | V_1 shares variables with V_2 }

- **E** { V_1, V_2 | V_1 is equivalent to V_2 }

This set, which is richer in variable classes, helps the derivation procedure to obtain a more precise information about the possible instantiations of a variable. Furthermore, with the assumed neutral clause activation, all the activation and exit modes of a clause can be statically known. If only this information were used to generate AND-parallelism, the system could be as restrictive as the SDDA technique [Chan85b]. This scheme can, however, accept top-level activation modes to generate even more precise information about clause activation; or modify the exit modes of clauses at run time without deriving them again.

This hybrid scheme, in term, performs at run time a worst-case approximation to derive new exit modes of clauses. The method uses the new activation mode of a clause together with the previously derived exit mode of the clause. This worst-case approximation can restrict the parallelism but the authors claim that extreme cases, in which the parallelism could be restricted, occur rarely.

The detection of AND-parallelism in this scheme uses the data-dependency graph built with the compile-time analysis to produce static *variable-generator* relations. A variable-generator is a goal g_i that may contribute to the instantiation of a variable. In the hybrid scheme, AND-parallelism is detected at run time, after the head unification of a clause. At run time different activation modes for a clause are possible, the run time execution graph is constructed with the current activation mode of the clause and the static variable-generators relations of the clause.

Discussion: The hybrid model seems promising, it combines an efficient compile time analysis of the data-dependencies in the clauses of the program, which are independently constructed at clause level, not at relation level as in [Chan85b], with an efficient derivation of the run-itme execution graphs. The derivation of the run time execution graph is heavily dependent on the compile time analysis, but at the same time, in most of the cases optimal parallelism could be achieved.

The description of the backward execution algorithm can also be derived using the techniques described above, for the time being, there is no information available about the description of the algorithm nor the execution and the implementation models of this scheme.

2 AND/OR-PARALLEL LOGIC MODELS

The combination of AND and OR-parallelism presents the most difficult challenge for an efficient parallel computational model in logic programming. The parallel exploitation at all levels of the search space can easily generate a combinatorial explosion of concurrent events, which has deterred people from attempting to use it in practical systems. The complete parallel exploitation of a logic program represents the ultimate model, it offers elegant solutions to some of the restrictions (e.g. completeness, reduced search) introduced by models based only on a single parallel evaluation mode (OR, Restricted AND, stream AND).

From the recognised overhead of a full unrestricted AND-OR parallel model, the research has evolved towards a compromise to reduce this overhead of unnecessary computations. Such models are still by no means simple, but they present a step forward in the area. The purpose of this section is to give a coherent view of the Restricted AND-/OR-Parallelism models.

2.1 Concepts

The computational models to be presented in this section can be distinguished further by the explicit target architectures. Some models subsume a non-shared memory view of the computation, others follow a data-flow concept and others are based on shared memory view.

The first two kinds of models are process-based, with the search tree viewed as a process tree. The main feature of these process models is their procedural behaviour. All these models use back-unification [Wise82a] to propagate the consistent set of bindings up to higher levels of the process tree. This mechanism behaves similarly to the return value from function calls of procedural languages, e.g. "C", with the difference that here a process may have several active children, each potentially having a set of consistent bindings for the same variable. Thus, whenever the parent environments need to be preserved, several copies must be made to propagate back the different sets of consistent bindings.

The advantage of the process based models is the isolation of computation and the notion of independent working space, which suits architectures with message passing and distributed memory. However, they have several disadvantages:

1. Constant recomputation is required both in forward and backward execution of the process tree. In the forward execution (expansion of the process tree), the binding context has to be constantly isolated to ensure independent environments at every level in the tree. In backward execution, the back-unification is propagated at every level, the complexity is even increased further with the management of solution sets (eager OR-parallel evaluation).

2. Last call optimisation, a generalisation of tail recursive optimisation (TRO) [Warr80a], cannot be performed in these process models due to the restriction of passing the consistent set of bindings one level at a time up the tree.

3. Locality of reference studies in Prolog [Tick88c], indicates that normally the working set of Prolog involves 2 or 3 levels in the tree. Thus, the fine granularity supported by the process models may require high communication if they support unrestricted distribution of the computation.

On the other hand, the problems of computational models that rely on shared memory are well-known: contention, synchronisation and bottle-necks due to the Von Neumann effect. However, the simplicity of such models do make them attractive despite these problems. Furthermore, the concept of global memory space does not need a bus-based shared memory architecture, which is the common view. There are several architectures which can provide organisations of hundreds of processing elements and are still able to support a global memory space (Dally's jelly bean machine [Dall87a], IBM's RP3[Pfis85a]). In addition, AND-/OR-parallel models can also be supported in bus-based machines with tens of processors (Sequent's Symmetry, etc).

When a process-based computational model is referred to in the rest of this section, it must be understood that the execution is performed step by step in the process tree, and communication is explicit and restricted to parent and child processes. When a computational model is specified as a shared memory or shared environment model, its advantages and disadvantages should be understood from this introduction.

Due to the variety of computational models presented in this section, and their different requirements, it is difficult to put forward any coherent set of metrics to evaluate them; besides the different approaches described in the paragraphs above.

2.2 Restricted AND-/OR-Parallel Models

The restricted AND-OR models presented here group systems that use a form of Restricted AND parallelism, as defined by [DeGr84a], combined with OR-parallelism. The forms of the latter have been eager or lazy. Lazy OR-parallelism is only activated on demand, one solution at a time, similar to Conery's AND-OR process model [Cone83a], whereas eager OR-parallelism does not wait, but begins computing alternative solutions immediately.

There is a further distinction between the types of Restricted AND-Parallelism, and the way they are detected (see section 1, for a detailed account of the methods used). In this section, those distinctions are taken for granted and the review concentrates on the problems which arise when combining it with OR-Parallelism.

2.2.1 Reduce-OR Model The Reduce-OR model aims at exploiting all the extracted parallelism available in logic programs. To achieve such a goal efficiently, the model attempts to subdivide independent computations as early as possible (to reduce the communication problem). The idea is not to constrain the parallelism at the abstract model level, but to make it dependent on the characteristics of the system to be implemented [Kale87a]. The model is also aimed for large-scale parallelism and uses a non-shared memory organisation.

The Reduce-OR model is based on modified version of the AND-OR tree for the representation of the search space ([Kale85a],[Kale87a]). The Reduce-OR tree divides the search tree into independent subproblems. Each node in the tree has a partial view of the solution set for the tree, the so-called *partial solution set (PSS)*. So that at any given moment each node can produce work without being related to any other node.

The Reduce-OR tree consists of Reduce and OR nodes. The definition and relationship between these nodes follows a recursive relation. The Reduce nodes correspond to a query; in this context a query represents any head clause successfully matched and the body goals related to it. The initial query is the root node and is represented by a Reduce-node without head (implying no further communication). Every literal in the Reduce-node can generate OR nodes. For every alternative of a goal literal an OR-node is created. Every successful unification of OR-nodes generates a Reduce-node for the matched clause.

Restricted AND-parallelism is used in processing the Reduce-OR tree. It is achieved by establishing a *data-join graph (DJG)* among the conjunctive goals in a clause, i.e. the Reduce-node literals. A data-flow analysis is performed to create the DJG; arcs in the graph represent goal calls, and nodes represent the data generated by the arcs, which may need to be joined. A *conditional* DJG has been developed in [Kale85a] to minimise the amount of run-time checking and to overcome the limitations of statically assigned graphs. OR-parallelism is eager in the Reduce-OR model.

The computational model is abstractly viewed as an extension of the Reduce-OR tree. There are two types of processes: Reduce and OR which corresponds directly to the nodes in the tree. The model assumes a very fine grain computation. The underlying idea is to build *incrementally* the partial solution sets and to start processes as soon as they become available for execution.

Reduce-processes are complex entities. They not only need to spawn OR-nodes, but also to wait for the responses of their child OR-process, execute the DJGs, and pass the consistent sets of partial solution sets on to their parents, i.e. incremental construction of the partial solution sets. The execution of the literals in the Reduce nodes is performed according to their respective DJGs. Nodes in the DJG become available for execution as soon as their input data is completely instantiated.

The combination of AND-OR parallelism is solved by using two distinctive unification algorithms: the multiple binding and the join binding algorithms. The *multiple binding* algorithm is executed in the OR nodes and is based on Conery's closed binding environment (the method is fully described in ([Cone87b],[Kale88a])), but avoids copying when structures are **ground**. The *join binding* algorithm is used by a Reduce-process to match bindings produced by different independent AND-parallel goal calls that reach the same node in the DJG. The algorithm cannot simply match the corresponding members of different binding tuples (although being mutually exclusive), because the incoming tuples may contain new instantiated variables generated by a child OR-process or any of its descendents (part of the back unification in the model described in [Cone87b]). A renumbering procedure for variables in the tuples is needed to position the newly imported variables during the join operation. After the last node has been reached in the DJG, the bindings must be exported to the parent OR-node (the completion of the multiple binding scheme).

Discussion: Kale states, "enough parallelism must be generated to exploit all the concurrency available in logic programs, and a parallel computational model must not restrict available parallelism before its execution". However, parallelism should not be needlessly generated, as it seems to be the case with this scheme. The parallelism should be generated in sufficient quantity to fit the available machine resources and only if it is worthwhile.

The Reduce-OR execution model produces very fine grain computation. Each node in the search tree represents a process. The main problem with the scheme is the complexity of the algorithms to manage the join operations. The amount of work replicated at every level of the tree and nodes in the DJG can be considerable.

2.2.2 PEPSys Computational Model The PEPSys computational model is the first to implement a combined AND-/OR-Parallel approach with shared environments, although accessing environments is not only restricted to a shared memory implementation ([Hail86a],[West87a],[Chas87a],[Baro88a]).

The PEPSys language follows most of the features of sequential Prolog, such as its declarative semantics and all-solution predicates. *Property declarations* allow the user to declare the possible sources of parallelism, which may or may not be exploited at run time, depending on the availability of resources.

The aim is to develop a parallel Prolog system which evolves from the environment sharing scheme of sequential Prolog, and in which parallelism is generated according to the available resources. Parallel computation aims at large granularity so that execution should only bear the minimum overhead. For these reasons, the basic execution mode of the PEPSys model is sequential. Thus, the integration of *independent* AND-parallelism, full OR-parallelism and sequential backtracking is supported in this model.

The combination of independent AND-parallelism with the execution of "don't know" non-determinism requires the formation of cross-products of solution sets for the AND-parallel branches. In PEPSys, the solutions are *lazily* gathered in different *virtual bags*. Due to the interaction with OR-parallelism and sequential backtracking, the completeness of the cross-product needs to be guaranteed. The proposed management scheme for this interaction is rather complex.

The management of multiple bindings uses the *hash-window* scheme; the OR-level time stamp in PEPSys is called *OR-branch level (OBL)*. The binding mechanism used in PEPSys does not assume any particular memory organisation.

The computation in PEPSys is viewed as a set of active *threads*. The concept of thread used in PEPSys is not fine-grained, and it could have a life-span over several levels in the search tree (inducing larger thread granularity). There can be several threads per processor, only one may be active. Each processor computing an active thread is engaged in a depth first left to right execution of the search tree. If a procedure is declared as OR-parallel, it is made available for parallel execution by creating a *branch point*. Processors can backtrack over branch points whenever they have not been taken up by idle processors to continue with the basic search strategy.

The execution of AND-parallel goals supported is at the level of only one pair of goals at a time. If a user specifies three independent AND-parallel goals, the system will execute the goals in parallel, while forming their cross-product with two join operations (see Fig. 5). AND-parallelism is created on demand; if a processor encounters a set of body goals annotated for AND-parallel execution, only the right hand goal is made available for parallel evaluation. The processor executing the AND-parallel goals itself continues with the computation of the left goal.

Fig. 5 shows the execution of independent AND-Parallelism in PEPSys. In this diagram, the AND-parallel goals are assumed to be evaluated in parallel. When Processor P_1 has encountered the AND-parallel goals a#b#c, it will fork an AND-task and continue with the execution of goal **a**. Then, processor P_2 takes the AND-task. The execution of the thread will fork a second AND-task and continue with the execution of goal **b**. If, later, another processor, say P_3, takes the available AND-task, it starts the execution of goal **c**. In addition, to the forking of the AND-parallel goals, two different join operations are required to form the cross-product of the AND-parallel goals.

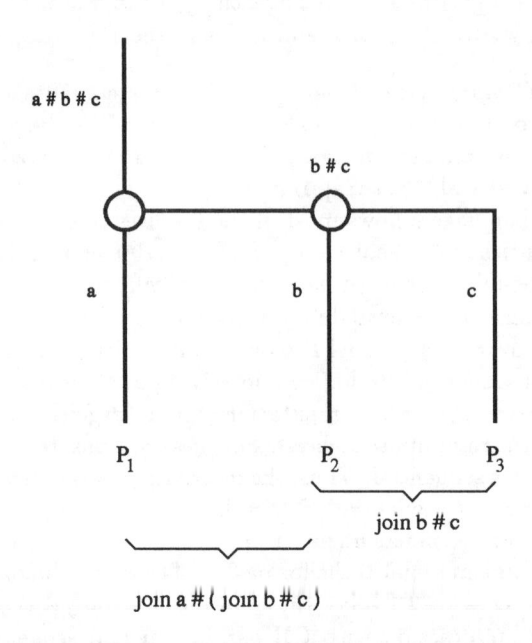

Figure 5: Independent AND-parallel execution in PEPSys

The possibility of OR-parallel processing with an AND-parallel computation produces several cases:

1. **AND-parallelism with one OR-parallel branch:** The OR-parallel branch proceeds in the normal OR-parallel execution mode, producing new OR-branches with their associated hash-windows. Whenever one of the OR-parallel branches

completes the search of the AND-parallel goal, it has to wait for the other side to deliver its partial solution. When it is available, it just continues with the parallel execution.

2. **AND-parallelism with full OR-parallelism:** Both sides of the AND-parallel computation have created branch points. In this case the cross product of the partial solutions found has to be formed lazily. Every new task created for the solution of any of the AND-parallel goals has one hash-window. The cross product is performed by pairing two hash-windows of tasks in the different AND-parallel branches. A *join cell* is used to pair them. This procedure is replicated to represent all pairings of the partial solutions from the two AND-parallel branches. The join cell only pairs two branches at a time (see Fig. 6).

3. **AND-Parallel goals on the same processor:** In this case no hash-windows are created, but bindings made on the left-hand side need to be distinguished from the right-hand side bindings, by incrementing the task's current OBL at the start of execution of the right AND-parallel goal.

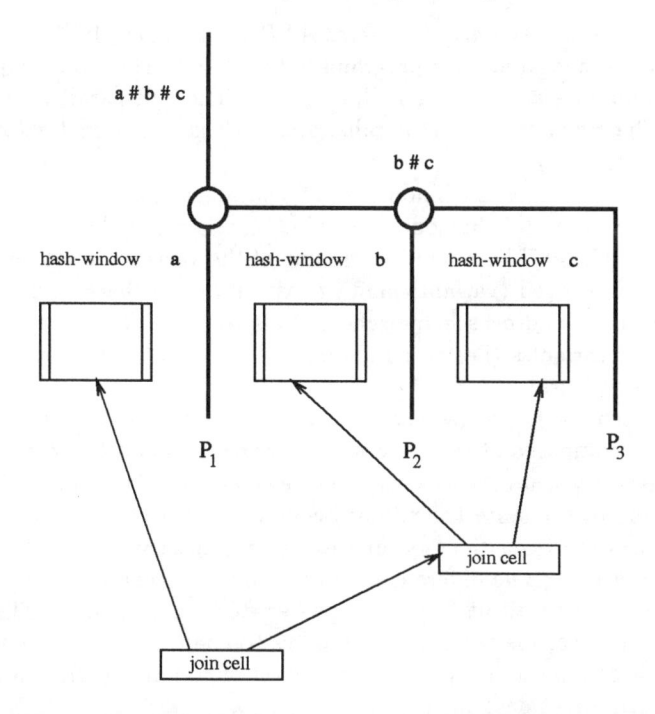

Figure 6: Cross Product by join-cells

The PEPSys language and its computational model have been validated; an implementation on a commercial multiprocessor, the Siemens MX-500, is available and running [Chas88a]. A Distributed Architecture was investigated for the execution of the PEPSys model [Baro88a]. The results from the MX-500 implementation show that the PEPSys model is well suited for shared memory architectures, and the multiple binding scheme used is efficient. The complete interaction between AND-/OR-parallelism has not been implemented; only deterministic independent AND-parallel execution was supported.

The Distributed Architecture is a multi-clustered architecture. Simulation results have shown that the multi-clustered machines increase the complexity of the system (e.g. they introduce an indirect memory addressing system, and communication latency plays an important role in the performance of the system), and that parallelism in the PEPSys model cannot be efficiently exploited.

Discussion: The PEPSys model was one of the first attempts to complete an extension of the sequential Prolog model for an AND/OR-parallel model. Although the exploitation of AND-parallelism is left open to the user, the amount of parallelism obtained is very restricted. The exploitation of OR-parallelism in PEPSys is quite efficient, as it is shown in the results presented in ([Baro88b],[Chas89a]).

The amount of recomputation allowed by the PEPSys model (due to backtracking) is compensated for by the high locality of reference of the model. Thus, if the model were to be implemented in an architecture with the communication between all the processing elements of the system constant and uniform, the model would yield better performance than that observed in the multi-clustered architecture.

2.2.3 Limited OR-Parallelism and Restricted AND-Parallelism In [Bisw88a], a combined model for non-annotated logic programs is presented. The model supports non-shared memory and message-passing architectures. The OR-parallelism is *demand driven* or *lazy*. The Restricted AND parallel approach is based on DeGroot's model [DeGr84a] (see section 1.4).

In the paper, the notion of *late* binding for OR-parallelism is introduced. Such concept describes the procedural behaviour of the binding scheme used (similar to Conery's closed environment [Cone87b]), where the binding of the variable is not performed until the goal has been proved (variable binding exportation or back unification). The description of the late binding scheme scheme fails to indicate the case of returned additional exported variables (i.e. when an exported variable is bound to a partially instantiated data structure).

The execution scheme is process-based. Every clause corresponds to a *major* process, which itself is composed of two processes: a *foreground* and *background* one. The foreground process represents the execution of the compiled code, and the background process corresponds to the state transitions occurring in the management of the *major* process. These state transitions occur through the interpretation of the different messages received or sent. The different states are: busy, accept and wait. The *accept* state represents a process waiting for a child process to give an answer. The *wait* state means a child process waiting for a parent process to change to the accept state, and the *busy* state indicates an active process. The level of communication in this system occurs only between direct descendents.

The results presented are based on a Transputer implementation, with the PEs connected on a torus ring manner. The processes of the benchmarks considered were allocated statically, due to the lack of support for dynamic processes in Occam. The mapping of the processes at the LORAP level to the Occam level was one to one. Super-linear speed-ups were observed in some cases. The explanation given by the authors is that the overhead for managing several parallel processes per Transputer increases with the number of active processes per PE. Thus, in a configuration with more transputers, each one has fewer active processes and represents, as a whole, less overhead. The performance of the implementation in one PE (Transputer) is more than an order of magnitude slower than SEPIA version 2.1 (ECRC Prolog system) on a Sun-3/50, a medium performance Prolog system. The full prototype is, with 16 PEs, still slower than SEPIA.

Discussion: This is an example of a model integrating different approaches and at the same time, minimising the overhead due to the management of parallelism. The research reported shows that parallelism can be exploited, but leaving open the question about how high performance can be achieved within the framework presented. The main motivation should be to attain high performance on a scalable parallel machine.

2.2.4 A Data-Driven Parallel Execution Model

This data flow execution model features *S-streams* for the management of the combined computation of Restricted AND-/OR-parallelism [Tsen88a]. The Restricted AND-parallelism is based on Conditional Graph Expressions (CGE) [DeGr84a].

The underlying abstract architecture is a dynamic data-flow machine which allows multiple activations of the same data-flow graph. A node in the data-flow graph is activated when all its related inputs are available; to identify each activation all its inputs should have the same colour or tag. A specific architecture has been designed for the dynamic data-flow machine, for further details please refer to [Tsen88a].

The *S-streams* are streams of streams and are not-strict data structures. They are represented by specialised data cells. An S-stream is composed of other S-streams and/or a list of variable bindings, the so-called *binding environment frames (BE)*. An S-stream is terminated with an End-of-Stream (eos) cell. A binding environment frame represents a set of arguments for any goal call.

The CGEs are compiled into a data-flow graph for execution on the dynamic data-flow machine. Each clause graph is composed of a unification block, a body expression graph (compiled CGEs) and a return block. The return block combines the output generated by the body expression and returing it to the parent goal.

The body expression itself is composed of another set of graphs. Every goal call is expanded into a procedure graph, for the evaluation of the different clauses. Its input is a BE frame, which is replicated for the different clauses in the procedure. The output is an S-stream, the set of solutions of the procedure. A parallel graph is created every time the independence or ground test succeeds (part of the RAP model, section 1.4). The input for each of these parallel graphs is also a BE frame, and their output is an S-stream formed by the Cartesian product of the different solutions produced by the AND parallel goals. Sequential evaluations are also required, the first input of a sequence of sequential graphs is a BE; the rest can be S-streams.

Forward execution proceeds by generating data-flow graphs which are completely executed as soon as leaves of the search tree are computed. The computation cycle in each graph requires the decomposition of a S-stream into the different BEs needed for the graph evaluation. Once a graph has been evaluated, a process collects all the different BEs and re-creates an S-stream for the next execution step.

The BE frame is represented in a vectorised form. Variables are identified as indices to the vector. The BE represents all the variables required by the computation of the clause.

The status of this research is at the simulation level, so far no information about the performance has yet been disclosed. A compiler of the OR-parallel version of the abstract machine is currently being developed.

Discussion: The work presented in this model is very similar to the work in [Li86a] and in [Take89a]. All these approaches have in common the processing of streams of streams for the parallel evaluation of AND-/OR-parallelism. The present model, and [Li86a], is based on a data-flow concept. The main difference between them concerns the management of the streams and the establishment of the data-flow graphs. In [Li86a] the data-flow graphs are constructed dynamically, and in [Tsen88a] a compiled approach is used. Another common feature of these two models concerns the handling of the Cartesian product when independent AND-parallelism can be exploited.

The model aims at fine grain parallelism but reduces the costs for its evaluation. All the information in the data-flow graphs are based on static information generated at compile time although the construction of the data-flow is conditional, depending on the status of the variables at run-time. The amount of parallelism that can be extracted with such method [DeGr84a] is not optimal.

The basic data-flow model follows the computation of process based models, which have well-known characteristics. The amount of computation required for the management of S-streams is a constant overhead involved in every clause execution.

3 SUMMARY

The use of compile-time analysis is of increasing importance for the current improvements on the RAP computational models. The compilation techniques developed can statically perform part of what was previously considered part of the computational model. Abstract interpretation of logic languages is not only effective in reducing the search space and in generating mode inferencing, but it can be a powerful tool to evaluate other features, e.g. data-dependency analysis. This is an important development which has made efficient implementations of AND-parallelism more feasible.

Considering the RAP models described in this section, it seems that the works presented in ([Xia88a],[Herm90a],[Muth90a]) indicate the route to follow for the future development of restricted AND-parallelism. All the work on hybrid models has been inspired by the research presented in [DeGr84a], a simple idea containing lots of implications. Another advantege about the implementation of these approaches is that they closely follow the *don't-know* non-determinism of logic programs.

This section has also presented the trends in the definitions of computational models for combined AND-/OR-parallelism in logic languages. This section focuses on Restricted AND-parallelism combined with OR-parallelism. The combination of different sources of parallelism in logic programs has always been an interesting research niche.

The combination calls for OR-parallel binding environment mechanisms. The approach made by most of the reviewed research is based on the concept of a non-shared memory space which directs the computational model towards a process based model. But the need for an OR-parallel binding environment can only be eliminated if one OR-branch per procedure needs to be active at once (lazy evaluation). This is exemplified in some of the reviewed papers (e.g. Biswas' LORAP model). Such combined approaches aim at eliminating most of the recomputation of the search space (done by naive OR-parallel scheme or by naive backtracking).

The driving force behind the trend towards non-shared memory models is the idea that *highly* parallel architectures will be based on non-shared physical memory. Advances in technology may show that even in these highly parallel architectures, shared memory can be efficiently simulated [Dall87a]. A trade-off must be established to determine which of approaches generates less overhead. Evaluation studies are required to compare both approaches in an architecture which can support them. Only in such an environment it seems possible to draw specific conclusions about their relative performance.

From the view point of languages, most of the logic languages that have AND-/OR-parallelism permit annotations. These are normally used to restrict the complexity of computation and the amount of search, i.e. to be able to implement the computational model. A general view is that compile-time analysis is beneficial to generating code which is more efficient and follows the restrictions imposed by the annotated programs.

ACKNOWLEDGEMENTS

The review presented in this chapter is an updated version of one section of the Tech. Report *Computational Models of Parallel Logic Languages*[Delg89a], written by the author at ECRC GmbH, Munich, Germany. Special thanks are due to: Uri Baron, Andy Cheese, Michel Dorochevsky, Kees Schuerman, André Véron, Jiyang Xu, Andrzej Ciepielewski, Kam-Fai Wong and Michael Ratcliffe for useful comments on earlier drafts.

7 An AND-Parallel Distributed Prolog Executor

A. Verden and **H. Glaser**

University of Southampton, UK

ABSTRACT

This chapter presents an execution scheme based on the independent and–parallel execution of Prolog. The parallel execution is exploited on a distributed memory machine.

When bindings are communicated from one processor to another, additional runtime information is derived for communicated variables concerning their current level of binding instantiation. The extra information is incorporated into the execution and is used to improve both the distributed execution and the backtracking.

Our executor is most notably derived from the execution schemes of Hermenegildo [Herm86a, Herm86b, Herm90a, Herm90b] and Lin [Lin88a] although both these other schemes are implemented for shared memory machines.

We present an incremental algorithm to support clause level intelligent backtracking. In our scheme intelligent backtracking will both select subgoal(s) attributable to the failure and prevent unnecessary re-execution of subgoals independent of the failure.

The effectiveness of our execution scheme and intelligent backtracking is demonstrated by an implementation based on an array of transputer processors.

1. INTRODUCTION

This research considers parallelism implicit in Prolog's computation rule known as and–parallelism. The unrestricted form of and–parallelism must solve the *binding conflict problem* which occurs when two or more subgoals executed in parallel generate different bindings for the same logic variable in a clause. An and–parallel execution scheme must resolve this conflict returning only those solutions with consistent variable bindings.

An alternative to solving the binding conflict problem is to adopt a limited form of and–parallelism, such as *independent and–parallelism*, first proposed by De Groot [DeGr84] and then called *restricted and–parallelism*. In independent and–parallelism a variable cannot be shared between subgoals executed in parallel unless it is fully instantiated (*ground*), thus avoiding the binding conflict problem but reducing the amount of parallelism in a clause. To distinguish between clauses which are compiled for independent and–parallel execution and those which are compiled conventionally we refer to independent and–parallel clauses as *parallel clauses*.

The following example highlights the need for an execution strategy which is able to react to the runtime activation of the clause and determine when variables become fully instantiated during the clause execution. Also, we would like a scheme where the completion of $a(X,Y)$ will alone initiate the execution of $c(Y)$ independent of the completion of $b(X)$.

$$p(X,Y) :- a(X,Y), b(X), c(Y), d(X,Y).$$

In this example we assume that $p(X,Y)$ is executed with X *ground* and Y *unbound*. Initially subgoals $a(X,Y)$ and $b(X)$ can be executed in parallel as their only shared variable X is fully instantiated. When $a(X,Y)$ succeeds, $c(Y)$ can then be executed. $b(X)$ may still be executing. In addition, $d(X,Y)$ may also be executed in parallel with $c(Y)$ and $b(X)$ if Y is fully instantiated.

In other schemes further information is derived at run-time by traversing the incoming arguments for a call or performing ground and independence tests for specific variables [DeGr87a, Lin88a]. These tests must traverse the variable's binding structure to determine its *level of instantiation*; this overhead cannot normally be justified as the complexity of traversing these incoming structures is often more than the complexity of the clause they are intended to aid. Therefore, we would also like a way of obtaining this runtime information at little or no overhead to that already incurred from parallel execution.

Our destination architecture is a distributed memory machine. A Prolog executor is placed on each processor and is capable of receiving goals and spawning further subgoals to other processors. Each executor is realised as an extension to the *WAM* [Warr83a] used extensively in sequential Prolog execution.

When a task is spawned to another processor, variable bindings are passed from parent to child processors by passing the entire binding structure for the call. As we shall see, the communication costs alone justify this decision but further benefits follow that can improve the execution and increase the efficiency of the system as a whole. In particular the current level of variable instantiation can be determined for each communicated variable. Potentially, this information can be used in the execution of the parent parallel clause and provide activation information for the child subgoal.

The independent and–parallelism in a parallel clause is first encoded at compile-time as a worst-case approximation expressed as a data-dependency graph (*DDG*) [DeGr87a, Lin88a, Hwan89a, Xia89a]. The worst-case approximation arises as the DDG encoding must be able to execute every possible activation for the clause used in the program. In our scheme the actual execution of a parallel clause is determined at runtime from both the compile-time DDG and further information derived at runtime.

Much of the information derived to control the independent and–parallel forward execution can also be used to improve the backward execution. Backward execution is improved through *intelligent backtracking* which intelligently selects backtrack points [Chan85b, Borg86a, Kuma87a, Lin88a]. Later we refer to backtrack points as *redo subgoal(s)*. In our execution scheme, backward execution allows all parallel execution to continue unless directly affected by the chosen redo subgoal(s). The backward execution is improved by both skipping unnecessary backtracking and preventing subgoals from being re-executed with the identical variable bindings.

In this chapter, we first consider a more complex example to illustrate the mechanism required to support independent and–parallelism and intelligent backtracking.

Then we describe our system in greater depth by considering the cost of communicating bindings from one processor to another and discussing other influences on the system as a whole.

Our execution scheme combines compile-time information with runtime information derived from the communication of bindings to provide dynamic execution of parallel clauses. Additional data-structures are present in the extended WAM, which maintain the current status of the execution in a parallel clause. Next, we describe the mechanism to perform intelligent backtracking in parallel clauses. At the end of this chapter, we present performance results for execution on an array of Transputer processing elements.

2. AN EXAMPLE EXECUTION

To illustrate both independent and–parallel execution and intelligent backtracking in a parallel clause we consider the previous example with different semantics.

$$p(X,Y) :- a(X,Y), b(X), c(Y), d(X,Y).$$

In this example, $p(X,Y)$ is called with both variables X and Y *unbound* and *independent*. First subgoal $a(X,Y)$ is executed. No other subgoals can be executed in parallel as variables may only be shared if fully instantiated; both variables X and Y have been allocated to subgoal $a(X,Y)$. In our example, $a(X,Y)$ succeeds with variables X and Y not yet fully instantiated although they are still independent. The subgoal $a(X,Y)$ is designated a *generator* for variables X and Y. Next $b(X)$ and $c(Y)$ are executed in parallel; both further instantiate their respective variables and are also designated generators. When $b(X)$ and $c(Y)$ succeed $d(X,Y)$ is executed. Subgoal $d(X,Y)$ fails invoking the backward execution algorithm.

The failure of $d(X,Y)$ has *attributed cause variables* X and Y. A variable is an attributed cause variable if it was passed to the subgoal in an instantiated state (not *unbound*). Intelligent backtracking is used to select the redo subgoal(s). The last designated generator of any of the attributed cause variables is chosen rather than simply the previous subgoal.

Processing of the failure results in the selection of subgoal $c(Y)$ for redo; $c(Y)$ is redone but its execution fails, invoking the backward execution algorithm once more.

This time selecting the correct redo subgoal(s) is more complex. With no history of the failure's source the cause of the failure is attributed only to variable Y, resulting in the selection of subgoal $a(X,Y)$. This is incorrect. The original failure of $d(X,Y)$ attributed cause variables X and Y; clearly, at this point $b(X)$ should be redone rather than $a(X,Y)$.

A *failure history* must be maintained so that when $c(Y)$ fails the next redo subgoal is selected from the cause of $d(X,Y)$, the original failure which resulted in the selection of $c(Y)$. In our scheme the redo of $c(Y)$ is tagged with the original failure, $d(X,Y)$ and additional cause variables are added to the current set for the failure. In this case the variable Y is already in the set of attributed cause variables.

This example has illustrated the requirements to support independent and–parallel execution with intelligent backtracking. In the following sections we describe how our WAM has been extended to support these mechanisms. First, we turn our attention to the communication of variable bindings from parent task to child task.

3. COMMUNICATING VARIABLE BINDINGS

A descendent task for remote execution requires the communication of binding structure from the parent task. In a distributed memory environment the problem is one of communicating the binding structure to another processor. This will undoubtably incur a higher cost than in existing schemes for shared memory machines where memory can be switched from processor to processor.

Three basic strategies have emerged to communicate bindings:

- *demand driven.* Bindings are passed on demand, in component parts. Two messages are required for each component part of the structure, one message to request the binding and another to communicate the binding. As in the hash window scheme of Fagin [Fagi87a, Fagi90a].

- *Stack frame communication.* Bindings are passed by duplicating the WAM stacks onto the child processor in a single communication [Ali90a, Gupt91a].

- *Total binding communication.* Bindings are passed by completely traversing the dereferenced structure and communicating it as a single message [Verd90a].

A demand driven approach has the advantage that only bindings required by the descendent task are communicated. The main disadvantage is that the machine must be globally addressable to determine on which processor any binding structure lies. This non-duplicating approach may also lead to much contention for bindings held on the same processor. If implemented on a distributed memory machine the demand driven approach would also require that each processor has sufficient other tasks to execute while waiting for the binding requested by a suspended task.

Strategies which pass the entire binding structure for a call irrespective of whether the bindings are actually required by the descendent task pay a large cost in terms of memory usage. However, the cost of communicating bindings as a single message is often less than communicating the same structure with many messages.

In a distributed memory environment both demand driven and total binding communication schemes may be considered. Here we compare communicating bindings on demand and communicating the entire binding structure when the task is created. The latter approach differs from the passing stack frames approach because only dereferenced bindings on the stack are communicated. In the stack frame approach, the ability of a compiler to optimise heap usage directly affects the amount of garbage communicated with the bindings.

Figure 1 shows the ratio of cost between the demand driven (C_D) and total binding (C_T) schemes for binding communication. D is the diameter of the network, (the number of intermediate processors a message must cross to reach its destination). The communication cost ratio varies according to the percentage of the binding structure that is actually required by the child task. There is a break even point (BEP where $C_D/C_T = 1$) at which it becomes cheaper to communicate the whole binding structure than to communicate the required portion incrementally. Thus we can justify the use of the total binding scheme for binding communication above this percentage.

The cost of communicating messages across a network of processors is often dependent on more than simply the raw transfer of data from one processor to another. On a Transputer the cost of communicating a message across an intermediate Transputer (that is, a message which goes in via one link and out another one via an intermediate

C_D / C_T

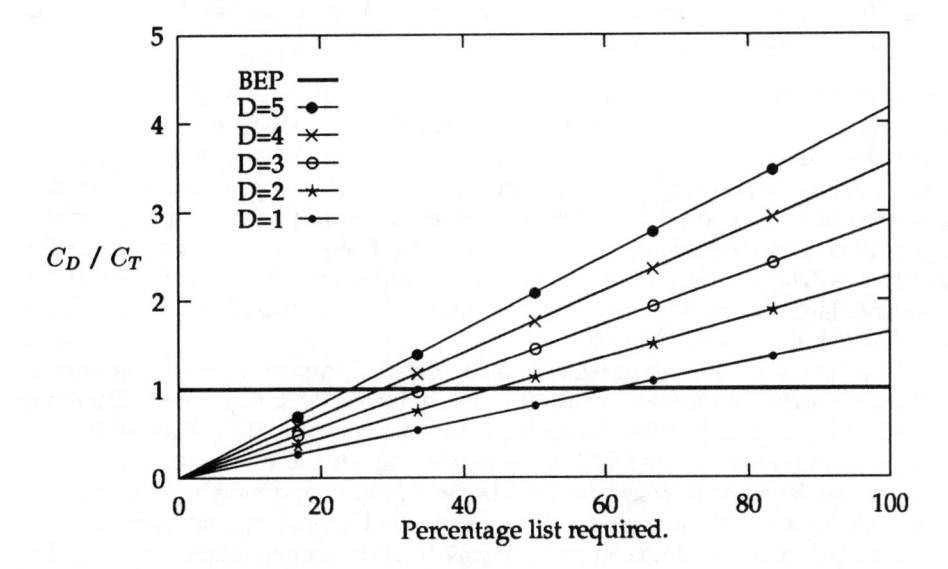

Figure 1: Communicating Bindings for Different Diameter Networks

message buffer) is not proportional to the message length. Once the communication has been established the transfer is handled by the link adapter itself and does not significantly impede the CPU. Therefore, the overall communications cost is dependent on both the amount of structure communicated and the number of messages used to communicate the binding structure.

We see from *figure 1* that to justify the communication of a task to another processor on a network of diameter 4 ($D = 4$) by total structure communication at least 30 percent of the total binding structure must be required by the child processor. The analysis presented here is described in greater detail in [Verd90a, Verd91b].

4. THE EXECUTION SCHEME

4.1 Introduction

The forward execution of a parallel clause is derived at run-time from the compile-time prediction held in the DDG together with the run-time activation determined from binding communication. The dynamic generation of the DDG was first proposed by Conery [Cone87a] and has been shown to be efficient in the implementation by Lin [Lin88a]. In our scheme the activation of the initial call on a processor is based on information communicated by the innitial binding structure. This information is propagated further through descendent parallel clauses. The dynamic information is also incorporated into the parallel clause from which the task was spawned.

The execution of each parallel clause switches dynamically between two modes of operation. The execution mode is selected automatically according to the demand for tasks on that processor.

- The *distribution mode* controls execution in a parallel clause so that tasks may be allocated to other processors as well as executed locally.

- The *serial mode* controls execution in a parallel clause optimised towards execution on a single processor.

It is important that an execution scheme be efficient in both modes. The distribution mode requires all the data–dependency information to spawn independent tasks. When all processors allocated to receive tasks from a processor have received tasks, any further parallel clauses are executed in serial mode. No data–dependency information need be constructed and a parallel clause is executed in a similar way to a conventional sequential clause. It is still possible to spawn further tasks from a serial mode parallel clause by switching the execution to distribution mode. The allocation of tasks is itself a sequential operation and as tasks are first offered for local execution, parallel clause execution is initially in serial mode.

The extra instructions to implement independent and-parallel execution provide table driven access to individual subgoal code. Information derived at compile-time for each subgoal in a parallel clause is held in the corresponding *static table*. The static table encodes both the DDG of the parallel clause and information describing the static prediction as to when variables become ground and remain unbound. The static table is part of the bytecode program and is not altered during execution. The selection algorithm uses both compile-time information from the static table and run-time information in the parallel frame to determine whether a subgoal can be executed independently.

4.2 Parallel Clause Execution

A subgoal traverses the states in *figure 2*. There are three types of execution that may take place in a parallel clause:

- *Forward Execution*. A subgoal has its state changed during forward execution when it is executed on a processor in the system. Forward execution always results in the subgoal finishing in one of the *Finished* states.

- Backward Execution. The subgoal execution state changes during backward execution when its own execution fails or the subgoal is redone.

- External Execution. A subgoal has its state changed externally when an another subgoal executing independently fails and is determined to be dependent on the outcome of the subgoal's execution.

A subgoal is initially marked in the *Dependent* state. A subgoal may then be executed locally or remotely. When a subgoal completes successfully it's state is changed according to whether any choice points (*CHPT*) or parallel frames (*PF*) were created on the local stack when the subgoal executed. If no choice points or parallel frames were created the completion is marked *Finished Nomore*. The *Finished Nomore* state saves unnecessary redo's which are particularly expensive if executed on a remote processor.

From the *Dependent, Executing Local* or *Executing Remote* states, a subgoal may have its state changed when another subgoal in the clause backtracks and is forced to wait for the outcome of the subgoal. The subgoal is then changed to the corresponding *To Redo On* state.

A subgoal which fails checks its current state. If marked *To Redo On* the dependent failure is processed together with the failure that occurred from the subgoal's own

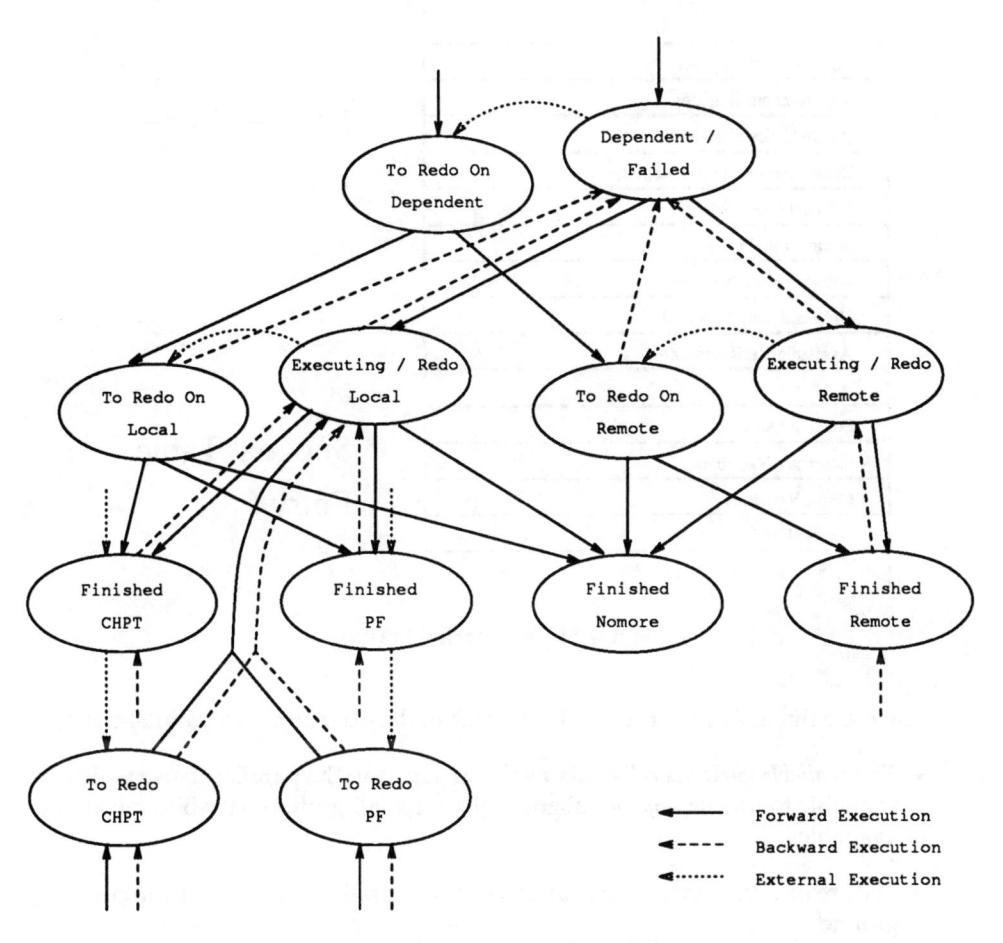

Figure 2: Subgoal Execution States

execution. The intelligent backtracking mechanism is described in detail in the next section.

The *To Redo* states are used to indicate that a task executed locally must be redone; the local processor is currently executing its own independent task and will encounter the subgoal marked *To Redo* when it completes its own task.

The state of execution in a parallel clause is held in a *parallel frame* (see *figure 3*). The parallel frame is a new data structure placed amid *choice points* and *environments* on the WAM *local* stack; our parallel frame is similar, in concept, to that of Hermenegildo [Herm86b]. A subcomponent of the parallel frame, the *subgoal table* is held for each subgoal in the parallel clause. The subgoal table holds information concerning the run-time status of individual subgoals.

The WAM choice point and environment registers are stored in the parallel frame when it is allocated. The *subgoal index* field denotes the subgoal on the active branch. Other new registers are held and are used to link parallel frames into a chain so that they may be traversed by the algorithms associated with task allocation and intelligent backtracking.

```
┌─────────────────────────────────┐
│ Choice Point Register           │
├─────────────────────────────────┤
│ Environment Register            │
├─────────────────────────────────┤
│ Parallel Frame Register         │
├─────────────────────────────────┤
│ Spawn Parallel Frame Register   │
├─────────────────────────────────┤
│ Subgoal Index Register          │
├─────────────────────────────────┤
│ Static Table Pointer            │
├─────────────────────────────────┤
│ Grounds Variables Cell          │
├─────────────────────────────────┤
│ Unbound Variables Cell          │
├─────────────────────────────────┤
│ Available Variables Cell        │
└─────────────────────────────────┘

┌─────────────────────────────────┐
│ Subgoal Status                  │
├─────────────────────────────────┤
│ Generator Variables             │
├─────────────────────────────────┤
│ Cause Variables                 │
├─────────────────────────────────┤
│ Pointer Field                   │
└─────────────────────────────────┘
```

Parallel Fame Body

Subgoal Table Entry

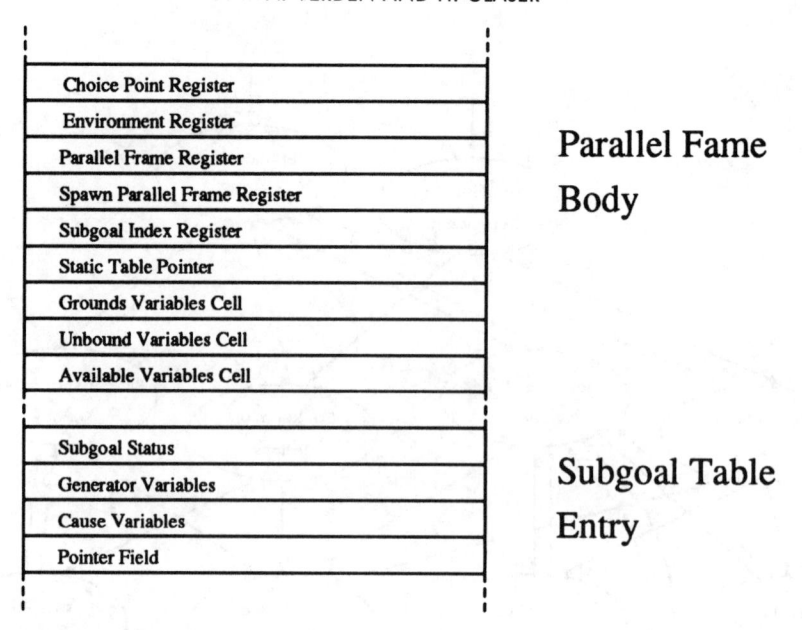

Figure 3: The Parallel Frame

There are three bit vector cells used to control the execution in a parallel clause:

- The *available variables cell* contains the variables in the parallel clause which are available to any *dependent* subgoal. Note that all ground variables are always available.

- The *grounds cell* contains the variables in the parallel clause which are currently ground.

- The *unbound cell* contains the variables in the parallel clause which are currently unbound.

Each bit vector has a bit assigned to each variable in the parallel clause. Simple *AND* and *OR* manipulation of the cells can determine when a subgoal is available for execution. During distribution mode execution the *Available Variables Cell* is masked with information in static table, to determine whether or not the subgoal can be executed independently. When a subgoal is executed the variables passed to the subgoal which are not ground are removed from the *Available Variables Cell*. When a subgoal completes all the variables passed to the subgoal returned to the *Available Variables Cell*. The *Ground Variables Cell* and the *Unbound Variables Cell* are updated from the static table. In serial mode the *Available Variables Cell* remains unused and instead the next subgoal is chosen as the next subgoal which has not already been executed.

There are several fields associated with each subgoal in a parallel clause held in its subgoal table:

- The *Subgoal Status* holds the status of the subgoal corresponding to those mentioned in *Figure 2*.

- The *Generator Variables* are those variables designated generators when the subgoal is executed. These are a safe approximation to the variables for which the subgoal may generate bindings.

- The *Cause Variables* are those which are passed to the subgoal and are not in the unbound state. These are a safe prediction to which variables could possibly cause failure should the subgoal fail.

- Another field is used to hold pointer values in the subgoal table so that completed subgoals can be redone. When a task completes a pointer to the choice point register, parallel frame register or, if the task was executed remotely, a pointer to its completion table is held. The field is also used to store the *failure history* bit vector.

A number of new registers have been added to the WAM; these control the parallel frames in their local stack.

PF   Pointer to the topmost parallel frame
sPF Pointer to the spawn parallel frame
tPF Pointer to the topmost spawn parallel frame

The *PF* register points to the parent parallel frame which is always the topmost locally active parallel frame. The *sPF* register points to the highest parallel frame searched when allocating tasks to waiting processors. The *tPF* register points to the highest parallel frame from which a task was allocated. A simple comparison between the *PF* register and the *tPF* register determines the execution mode. Serial mode occurs when ($PF > tPF$).

There are also a number of control flags which make forward execution more efficient, and support the *tail recursion optimisation* in parallel clauses. In serial mode, parallel frames can be efficiently operated without the need to re-traverse previous subgoal status's to find the next available subgoal. This significantly reduces the overhead of executing parallel code sequentially.

5. CLAUSE LEVEL INTELLIGENT BACKTRACKING

The backward execution algorithm is invoked when the forward execution algorithm has resulted in the failure of a subgoal. In Prolog the next alternative is selected according to the depth–first left–right procedural interpretation. In many Prolog programs this execution strategy will redo subgoals which are out of context with that of the failed subgoal and variables not attributable to the cause of failure are re-instantiated. In our backward execution algorithm we aim to improve the selection of redo subgoal(s) in a parallel clause by taking into account the cause of failure. Where possible forward execution is allowed to continue in parallel with backward execution. Subgoals are terminated only if they are dependent on a variable which has both been attributed to the cause of failure and is being re-instantiated by the redo subgoal(s).

In our scheme, processing of a failure is delayed until all subgoals to the left of the failed subgoal with variables in common have completed. Consider the clause:

p(X,Y) :– a(X,Y), b(X).

Assume subgoal p(X,Y) is called with variable X ground so that a(X,Y) and b(X) are executed independently in parallel. If b(X) fails before a(X,Y) has completed then in our scheme the processing of b(X)'s failure is delayed until a(X,Y) completes.

If subsequently a(X,Y) were to fail then the cause of the failure would be both variables X and Y (the cause variables) rather than just variable X. A subgoal with common variables to the left which contributes no further cause variables may be skipped. Delaying the processing of b(X)'s failure results in a more accurate selection of redo subgoals.

Our backward execution algorithm operates in two execution modes corresponding to the two execution modes of forward execution. Backward execution is simplified in serial mode because a serial mode parallel clause has only one executing subgoal. Therefore, there are no subgoals to terminate once the redo subgoal has been selected and the single possible failure can lead only to a single redo subgoal being selected.

In distribution mode the backward execution is more complex and is broken into three phases. Firstly, we determine which subgoals must be satisfied by the selection of redo subgoal(s). Next, we determine the set of subgoals that must be redone and finally, terminate all other subgoals dependent on any of the variables re-instantiated by any of the redo subgoals.

5.1 Supporting Failure History

The pointer field in the subgoal table for the redo subgoal is marked with the subgoal index(es) for all failed subgoals satisfied by the selection of this redo subgoal. Should the subgoal subsequently fail the original failed subgoal(s) is thus determined. The subgoal table *Cause Variables* for each satisfied subgoal is ANDed with the *Cause Variables* for the redo subgoal. In this way solutions generated indirectly through a previous redo subgoal will also be taken into account.

5.2 Failure in a Parallel Clause Distribution Mode

A search is made backwards through the parallel clause until all subgoals dependent on the failure are satisfied by the redo subgoal(s). The set of subgoals to be satisfied depends on the executing status of the completed subgoal (see *figure 2*). If a failure is an original failure, determined by the subgoal executing in *Executing* status rather than *Redo* status, the set of subgoals to be satisfied is simply the failed subgoal. If the subgoal is executing in *Redo* status then the set of subgoals to be satisfied are those which have previously selected the now failed subgoal.

The backtrack algorithm starts by searching backward through the parallel clause from the most recently failed subgoal; when the search encounters a subgoal in the following states the corresponding actions are taken:

- *Dependent* status means that the searched subgoal has not yet started executing. If there are variables in common with cause variables for any failed subgoals then the subgoal is marked *To Redo Dependent*. The potential generators for the subgoal are determined from the static table.

- *Executing* or *To Redo On* status means that a subgoal to the left has yet to complete. If the current subgoal has variables in common with any of the failed subgoals and upon its failure further cause variables would be added to the current cause variables, then the current failure is dependent on the outcome of this execution. The subgoal's index is added to the subgoal's table *Pointer Field* and the state of the searched subgoal is changed to *To Redo On*.

- *Finished PF*, *Finished CHPT* or *Finished Remote* status means there are further branches to be explored by redoing this subgoal. The subgoal is marked *To Redo* if it was executed locally and is immediately redone if it was executed remotely. The failure history is also updated.

- *Finished Nomore* status means that there are no further branches to be explored by redoing this subgoal. Actions are taken to emulate the subgoal being redone and subsequently failing.

Finally, other subgoals in the parallel clause are updated with the redo. If executing in parallel a subgoal may be dependent on variables re-instantiated by the redo and must be terminated. Completed subgoals may also be dependent on variables re-instantiated by the redo and must have their branches pruned. The dependent subgoal is then marked *Dependent*.

5.3 Intelligent Cutting

During backward execution, a subgoal which generates no variables is never selected for redoing. The only possibility is that the corresponding search space will be pruned if the subgoal is dependent upon the variables re-instantiated by any subgoals in the redo set. Subgoals which generate no variables when they complete can have all their associated search space *cut intelligently* from the WAM stacks.

In our execution scheme, we maintain a worst-case approximation for generated variables for each subgoal in a parallel clause. This is used during backward execution to select the last generator subgoal for the cause variables for any subgoal in the failed set. When the execution for the current subgoal completes, a simple test is made comparing the subgoal generators with *null*; if the subgoal execution generates no variable bindings then the search space can be discarded and the subgoal completes in *Finished Nomore* state.

This saving in search space is of particular relevance to the *generate and test* programming paradigm; all *test* subgoals have their search space removed once they have completed.

6. EVALUATION OF OUR IMPLEMENTATION

Our implementation places a Prolog bytecode emulator written in occam and capable of 8 KLIPS on each processor. Results were obtained on an array of Transputer processing elements using the *ECCL* communications harness [Surr89a].

We consider several aspects of our implementation: the efficiency of execution in serial mode and distribution mode, any benefit from intelligent backtracking and speedup of the parallel system as a whole.

6.1 Serial Mode vs Distribution Mode Execution

To compare serial mode and distribution mode execution we consider programs which exhibit varying degrees of potential parallelism in their execution. There is an overhead associated with executing parallel encoded clauses sequentially and we might expect this to shows up in the performance results where *fine grained* benchmark programs execute less efficiently than *course grained* programs.

Table 1: The Efficiency of Single Processor Execution

Benchmark Program	Sequential Code (msec)	Parallel Code Serial Mode (msec)	actual speedup	Parallel Code Distribution Mode (msec)	actual speedup	Intelligent Backtracking attrib. speedup
nfib	8761	10944	0.80	12160	0.72	
quicksort	7821	8576	0.91	9088	0.86	
reverse	63	63	1.00	63	1.00	
colour_A	4.48	4.41	1.01	4.93	0.91	1.25
colour_B	5.95	4.80	1.24	5.38	1.11	1.53
colour_C	9.47	9.28	1.02	10.94	0.87	1.26
colour_D	18.88	12.80	1.47	14.87	1.27	1.81

Table 1 gives results for the sequential execution of parallel clauses in serial mode and distribution mode.

The *nfib* program calculates the fibonacci number plus one at each recursive iteration, for *nfib(20)*. The program exhibits a large amount of parallelism preceded in each clause by simple arithmetic operations. The *quicksort* program exhibits similar divide and conquer parallelism but at each recursive iteration, the incoming argument list must first be split into two parts; a list of 200 random elements is sorted. The *reverse* benchmark reverses a list of 30 elements.

The results are very encouraging and show that even the finest granularity benchmark programs execute at above 80% WAM speed in serial mode and above 70% in distribution mode.

The use of two modes of execution has contributed approximately a 10% improvement over execution which derives all the data-dependency information. This is significant as it is vital to maintain a high efficiency for the sequential execution of parallel clauses.

To show the effectiveness of our intelligent backtracking scheme we consider four variations of a map colouring problem. We choose to colour a map of five regions with three colours (see *Appendix*). A more naive arrangement (*colour_D*) requires more backtracking to reach solution than a near optimal arrangement (*colour_A*).

A map colouring problem was chosen as each individual subgoal execution is as fine grained as is possible in Prolog execution. Any benefit in the execution is attributable only to the intelligent backtracking.

In the map colouring programs, significant speedup is attained for nearly all of the benchmarks. colour_C is unusual in that the intelligent backtracking also results in a rather naive execution. It is anticipated that for more *general* programs the intelligent backtracking will effectively pay for the parallel execution.

6.2 Parallel Execution

Figure 4 illustrates parallel execution for the *nfib(20)* and *quicksort* benchmark programs executing on a number of processing elements. The graph plots true speedup over sequential code execution.

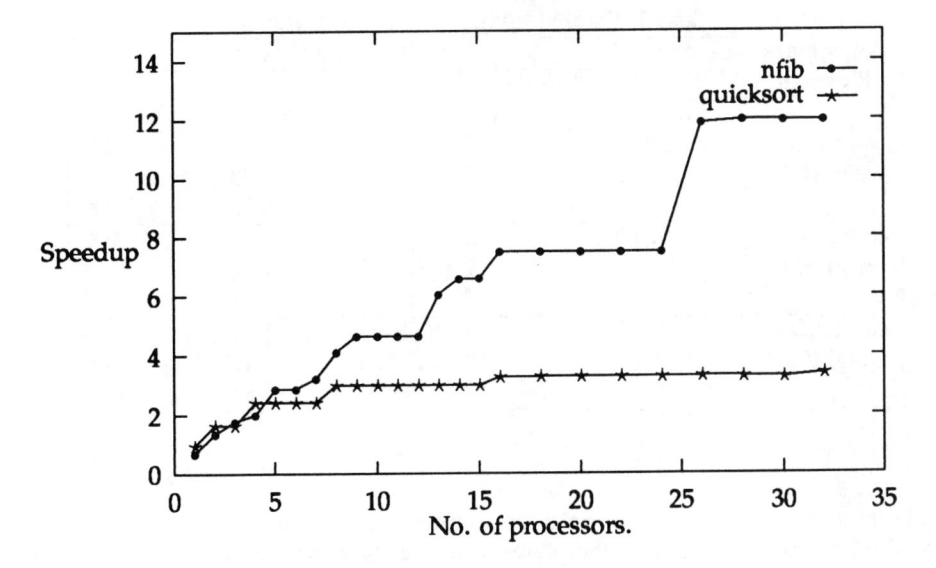

Figure 4: Parallel Execution

The *nfib* program performs significantly better than the *quicksort* program. This is due to a number of differences between the two executions.

- The cost of spawning tasks in *nfib* is less than in *quicksort* as the binding structure that is communicated is only a single integer rather than a list of elements. The same is true when the result is returned to the parent processor.

- The *quicksort* benchmark must first traverse the incoming list argument to form two sublists before any remote tasks can be spawned.

- The performance of *quicksort* depends greatly on the length of the list sorted.

From the graph it is interesting to note the apparent step function for the *nfib* benchmark, which illustrates the *balanced divide and conquer* nature of *nfib*. In *quicksort* it is encouraging to see that once the maximum speedup is achieved in the execution it is maintained despite adding further, potentially hindering, processors to the system.

6.3 Parallel Intelligent Backtracking

To measure the effectiveness of the combination of and–parallel execution and intelligent backtracking we consider the most complex map colouring problem *colour_D*. We consider the parallel execution with varying weight to the *next* subgoal. Weight is measured in recursive iterations; a weight of 5 corresponds to the *next* subgoal calling a procedure which performs 5 recursive iterations. This will provide us with some indication as to how the and–parallelism and intelligent backtracking behave in combination and also provide an indication of the complexity a task must have to justify its remote execution.

Table 2 gives results for the parallel execution of the *colour_D* benchmark. With no additional weighting to the *next* subgoal the performance degrades when executed on

Table 2: Parallel Intelligent Backtracking

Benchmark Program	Sequential Code (msec)	Number of Processors	(msec)	Speedup	Utilisation
colour_D weight(0)	18.88	1	12.80	1.47	100%
		2	57.01	0.33	56%
		3	51.26	0.37	40%
colour_D weight(5)	82.69	1	51.78	1.14	100%
		2	73.73	1.12	61%
		3	63.23	1.31	48%
colour_D weight(10)	143.42	1	88.90	1.61	100%
		2	100.74	1.42	66%
		3	86.72	1.65	51%

a parallel machine. The remote tasks are so fine grained that when 3 processors are used the first to receive a task completes it before the parent processor has finished allocating a task to the second. Execution continues in this way until no further tasks are available, only then is the parent able to execute its own task.

As the weight of the tasks is increased so the performance on the parallel machine is improved. Execution on 2 processors is never better than execution on 1 processor; this is probably due to the more efficient execution on 1 processor in serial mode.

From these results it is not possible to make an accurate measurement of the weight required to justify remote execution of a task, but the weight is believed to be around 5 recursive iterations.

7. CONCLUSIONS

We have demonstrated that independent and–parallel execution can be augmented with intelligent backtracking to provide an effective parallel execution scheme on a distributed memory machine. Our scheme aims to be both scalable and efficient so that Prolog programs can be executed dynamically on arbitrary numbers of processors.

Our intelligent backtracking algorithm gives surprisingly good results on a single processor, and may be capable of paying for the dynamic construction of DDG's in parallel clauses for more general programs.

The parallel benchmarks show that providing an excess amount of parallelism exists in the program, good utilisation can be made of the processors. By dynamically switching between serial mode and distribution mode the scheme also maintains 'near WAM performance' on each processor.

When the benchmark program constrains the amount of parallelism in the execution, it is encouraging to see that performance is maintained for increasing numbers of processors in the system.

In the future we intend to execute a number of more general Prolog programs and consider issues such as I/O and scheduling in greater detail.

APPENDIX

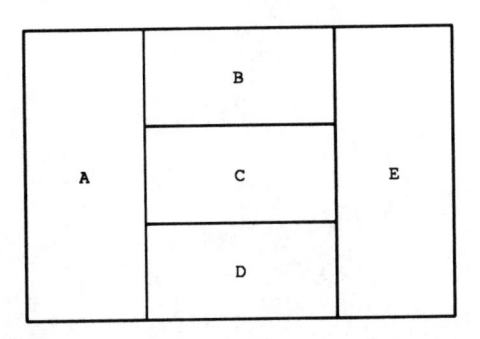

Figure 5: A Map Colouring of Five Regions

The following are Prolog clauses to colour the map in *figure 5*. The clauses differ in their strategy for solving the map colouring problem. The *next* subgoal is satisfied by all possible combinations of three different colours.

colour_A
  colour(A,B,C,D,E) :–next(A,B), next(A,C), next(A,D),next(B,C),
          next(C,D), next(B,E), next(C,E),next(D,E).
colour_B
  colour(A,B,C,D,E) :–next(A,B), next(B,E), next(A,C), next(C,E),
          next(A,D), next(D,E), next(B,C), next(C,D).
colour_C
  colour(A,B,C,D,E) :–next(A,B), next(D,E), next(B,C), next(C,D),
          next(A,C), next(C,E), next(A,D), next(B,E).
colour_D
  colour(A,B,C,D,E) :–next(C,D), next(A,B), next(D,E), next(A,D),
          next(B,C), next(C,E), next(B,E), next(A,C).

8 The OPAL Machine

J. S. Conery
University of Oregon, USA

ABSTRACT

This chapter describes OM, a virtual machine for languages with an operational semantics defined by the AND/OR Process Model. The machine differs from the WAM, the well-known virtual machine for Prolog programs, in two significant areas: the unification instructions build and access binding environments tailored for non-shared memory multiprocessors, and control instructions and the underlying kernel operations implement fine-grain parallelism. After some background information on the AND/OR model, the OPAL language, and a general overview of OM, the main body of the chapter focuses on the control and unification operations in the machine. Following that is a section that gives some performance figures, and the conclusion describes some areas for future improvement.

8.1 BACKGROUND: OPAL AND THE AND/OR MODEL

OPAL, the Oregon PArallel Logic language, is a pure Horn clause language augmented with predicates for arithmetic and simple operations such as testing to see if a term is an unbound variable or finding the functor of a term. A few more complex operations, such as I/O, can be implemented on the front-end host machine, but they are "cavalier" operations and no attempt is made to serialize programs through these constructs (for an example of a system that delays side effect predicates until all preceding side effects have been executed, see [HAUS90]).

Figure 8.1 shows three simple OPAL programs. The first is an OR-parallel program that searches for all even length paths in an acyclic graph. The parallelism comes from multiple arcs leaving a node that is being searched, and the overall effect is of a pipeline where shorter paths are reported first. The second program has an

Example 1: "path". There are 16 arcs, leading to 51 solutions, in the actual program (only three arcs are shown here).

```
goal <- epath(X,Y).

epath(A,C) <- arc(A,B) & arc(B,C).
epath(A,D) <- arc(A,B) & arc(B,C) & epath(C,D).

arc(0,1).
arc(0,2).
arc(0,4).
```

Example 2: "color". There are 12 clauses for next/2 in the actual program (only three are shown here).

```
goal <- color(A,B,C,D,E).

color(A,B,C,D,E) <-
            next(A,B) & next(C,D) & next(A,C) & next(A,D) &
            next(B,C) & next(B,E) & next(C,E) & next(D,E).

next(green,yellow).
next(green,blue).
next(green,red).
```

Example 3: some rules from the symbolic differentiation program.

```
d(U*V,X,P) <- functor(U,_,N) & product(N,U,V,X,P).

product(0,C,U,X,C*DU) <- C \== X & d(U,X,DU).
product(N,U,V,X,DV*U+DU*V) <- N > 0 & d(U,X,DU) & d(V,X,DV).
```

Figure 8.1 Three OPAL Programs

AND-parallel procedure that generates all possible colorings of a map with five regions and eight interior borders. The predicate next/2 colors a region if the name of the region is unbound in a call, but if both parameters are bound the call checks to see if the two regions have colors that can be adjacent (*i.e.* they are different colors). The third example is part of a program for symbolic differentiation and shows a combination of AND and OR parallelism. The two recursive calls to d/3 in the body of the rule that differentiates products can be done in parallel since X, the only common variable, will be bound when the body is invoked.

OPAL programs are executed according to the AND/OR Process Model, in which collections of asynchronous objects communicate solely via messages. The objects are AND and OR processes: an AND process solves the set of goals in the body of a clause, and an OR process coordinates the solution of a single goal with multiple definitions. Messages are used to start new processes for subgoals, report results, or perform control operations such as asking for another result or canceling a subgoal. A process will update its internal state only when it receives a message from another process, and process updates are nonpreemptible operations.

The OPAL implementation is based on a byte-coded virtual machine named OM (for the OPAL Machine). The OPAL compiler generates OM code for AND and OR processes from the clauses of the user program. It creates a code block for an AND process from the body of each nonunit clause in the program, and collects all the clause heads of a procedure into the code block for an OR process. At runtime, an instance of a process will be a data structure known as a *state vector* allocated from the local memory of one of the nodes. When a process is scheduled for execution, the machine will install frequently used parts of the state vector in OM registers, branch to the code block, and execute the instructions in the block. The instructions define a *process step* that will update the state vector and possibly create new processes and messages.

The compiler automatically creates parallel goals wherever it can. When a procedure is called, the resulting OR process will attempt to unify the call with every clause head, and each successful match with a nonunit clause leads to a new AND process. In AND-parallel goals, the compiler uses sharing and independence information extracted from an abstract interpreter to order the goals in a data dependency graph which will control the order of execution at run-time [SUNDA91].

8.2 MODULES OF AN OPAL IMPLEMENTATION

Our goals for OM were to define a machine that would support both AND and OR parallelism, be scalable by not relying on a single memory space, be portable to a wide range of commercial multiprocessors, and use compile time analysis of user programs wherever possible. Our strategy was to concentrate first on those parts of the system that would most clearly have an effect on performance, namely task switching in a fine grain parallel system and representing variable bindings in such a way that terms stored in one node would not depend on the values of terms stored in other nodes. The result is a system with efficient task switching and memory management within a node and interprocessor communication limited to starting new tasks and reporting results.

Figure 8.2 shows the software modules in a multiprocessor implementation of OPAL. At each node in the system there is a complete and independent interpreter, consisting of the OM virtual machine and a simple operating system module. The registers, instructions, and other structures of the virtual machine are all concerned with the execution of a single process, which we call the *current process*. The OS module implements inter-process communication; for example, if the current process executes an instruction that sends a message to its parent process, the instruction traps to the OS level where the message is created and sent.

The virtual machine and system modules are both machine independent. Supporting them is the host-dependent kernel, which implements memory management, all inter-processor communication, and other functions that depend on the structure of the host architecture. For example, the OS uses a kernel routine to decide if a message it is handling is to a local process, and traps to the kernel's interprocessor message router if the receiving process is on another node.

The user interacts with the system through an interface program that may reside on one of the nodes in the multiprocessor or on a separate host processor. The interface program invokes the OPAL compiler to generate virtual machine code from user programs and then downloads a copy of the compiled code to each module. Compiled queries are sent to one of the nodes, which starts an AND process for the query and begins execution.

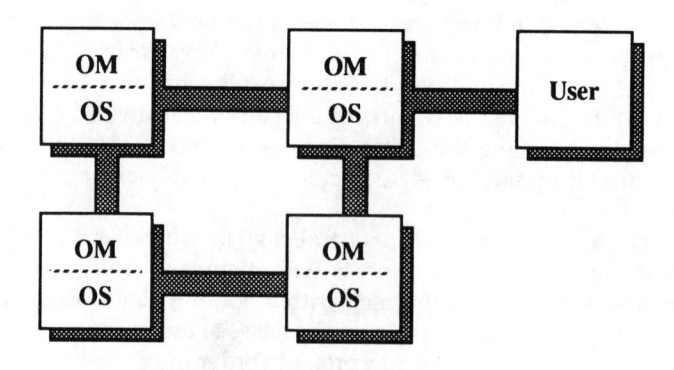

Figure 8.2 Modules in an OPAL Implementation

The main focus of this chapter is on the implementation of control structures and unification operations in OPAL. To set the context for the detailed discussion later in the chapter, the next two sections provide some background information on the kernel module and OM virtual machine registers.

8.2.1 Kernel Functions
One of the most important kernel functions is memory management. The OM kernel uses a block oriented heap-based memory allocator. All data structures — terms, binding environments, process states, messages, and miscellaneous structures — are built from blocks of contiguous words. Memory allocation and deallocation are based on the "fast fit" method, which arranges free blocks in linked lists indexed according to their size [STAN80]. Each kernel module is responsible for memory management in the local memory, so the system automatically does distributed garbage collection.

Another important kernel function is task distribution, which distributes processes to nodes in a multiprocessor implementation of OPAL. Throughout the OS and OM modules are hooks that are invoked at various times, for example when a new process is created or when the task queue in a node is empty. By changing the functions called via the hooks we can implement several different dynamic task allocation schemes.

Newly created process states are called *seeds*. When the new process receives a start message, the system expands the seed into a complete state vector before the virtual machine executes the code block for the start message. All of the strategies we have experimented with have two rules in common. Once a seed has been planted in a node, and expanded into a full process, it cannot move to another node in the multiprocessor; this way we avoid the overhead associated with forward addressing and other problems. The other constraint is that preference is given to messages bound for existing processes over start messages bound for seeds, giving the system a built-in bias against speculative work since the process might fail and cancel one or more seeds.

Mohamed's M.S. thesis describes the OM task distribution mechanisms in more detail, and contains some simulations of several different strategies [MOHA90]. A paper on the OM kernel designed for the HP Mayfly describes task allocation and other kernel functions for that host [CONE90].

8.2.2 OM Registers

The state vector of the currently executing process is stored in memory, in one or more blocks allocated when the process first begins execution. The virtual machine registers are used to provide fast access to the process, to the message that triggered this process step, and other frequently used information.

The two registers that point to structures used in the current process step are the **P** register and **M** register. **P** points to the current process state vector. For an AND process, the state vector holds the binding environment for the variables in the goal, a record of which goals from the body have been solved, the failure history, and other control information. An OR process state vector is simpler, but still needs information about the status of each descendant process and other control information.

M points to a message. When a process is started or resumed, **M** will point to the message that activated it. Later, when the process needs to send a message to another process, **M** will point to the message being built. In some cases the OS will allocate a new message block, but in others the process can reuse an existing message.

Where necessary in the remainder of the paper, we will use a Pascal-like record syntax with implied pointer references to refer to one of the fields of a structure pointed to by **P** or **M**. Some examples: **P.kind** is the entry in the current process state that says whether the process is an AND or OR process; **P.and.desc[i].marks** is the marks vector of the ith goal in the body of the current process (which must be an AND process for this expression to make sense); **M.from** is the process ID of the process that sent the current message.

Four registers that point to *frames*, or blocks of terms, are **E**, **A**, **R**, and **S**. The first entry (with index 0) in a frame is a descriptor that gives the size of the frame and other information. In the current implementations, the frames pointed to by one of these registers are always left in the heap, and we just use the value in the register as a base address of the frame. So although we speak of "register E[i]" or "the A registers" we are actually referring to a term or block of terms on the heap pointed to by one of these four registers.

E is the environment register. During the execution of an AND process, it points to the set of bindings for the variables of the process. **E** is just an alias for the environment of the current AND process, **P.and.env**, since the variables themselves remain in memory as part of the state vector of the process. When an OR process is running, it allocates and initializes a new environment for each descendant, and at these times **E** points to the newly allocated frame.

The **A** register points to the current set of procedure arguments. In preparation for making a procedure call, an AND process allocates a frame to hold the arguments, puts a pointer to the frame in **A**, and then fills the frame with the values to be passed to the called procedure. The pointer to the block is then passed as one of the parameters in the start message to the OR process. When an OR process is running, **A** points to the parameters passed from the parent AND process, and the OR tries to unify the compiled clause heads with the terms in the **A** registers.

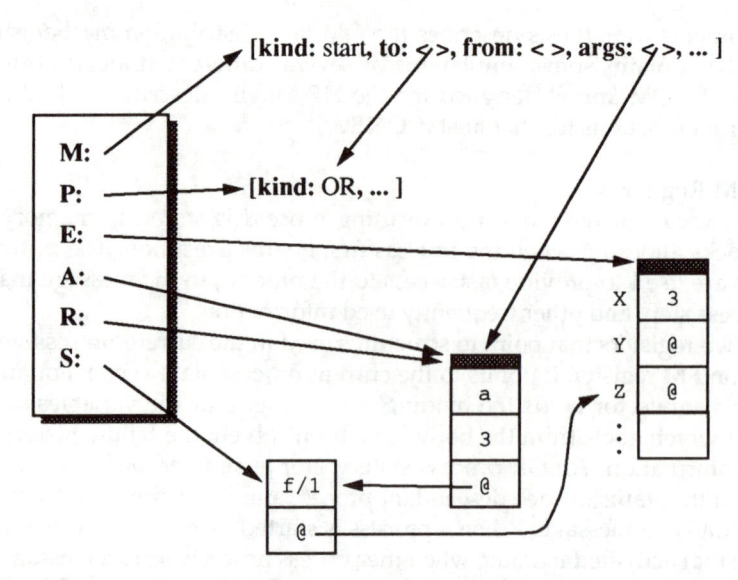

OM registers and the data blocks they point to during the unification of the call p(a,3,N) with the clause head p(a,X,f(Z)). **M** and **P** point to records that represent a message and process state, respectively. **E**, **A**, and **R** point to frames (vectors of terms), and **S** points to a term on the heap. When a variable (marked @) is unified with another term, it is bound to a pointer to that term.

Figure 8.3 *OM Registers During Head Unification*

The **R** register points to the *response frame*, which is the set of values that will be sent back to the AND process that originates a procedure call. In most cases the **A** and **R** frames are the same frame — an AND process sets up the arguments of a call and then expects the same frame (or a copy) as a result. However, when the compiler detects a case where last call optimization can be applied, the frames are different. The **A** registers will be filled with parameters of the call, but the **R** register will point to a frame that will be sent back to an ancestor goal. Details of when **A** frames are copied, and how and when **R** frames can be used, are presented in Section 8.3.5.

The **S** register is the structure register. Complex terms in OM are hierarchies of blocks, where each subterm of the form f/N has its own block of N+1 cells. The first cell identifies the functor and arity while the remaining cells hold the arguments. For example, p(a,(g(b,c),d) is represented by two blocks. The main term is a block of four cells, with the atom p in the first cell and atoms a and d in the first and third argument positions. The second argument is a pointer to another block which holds the representation of g(b,c). When structures are being manipulated, S points to the header cell of the corresponding block.

In addition to the registers described above, there are the usual program counter (**PC**) and instruction register (**IR**). A continuation pointer (**CP**) holds the address of the code for the next clause head when an OR process is in the middle of a procedure defined by more than one clause, and is zero when the process is unifying the head of the last clause. **DX** is the descendant index register. During the execution of an AND process it has the index of one of the literals in the clause body; for example, if the machine is setting up arguments to call the third subgoal (as defined by the linear ordering generated by the compiler) **DX** will be 3.

Two small stacks inside the processor hold information that is used within a single process activation. The information is not a permanent part of the state of any process, since it will not be needed when the process is resumed, and these stacks are reinitialized by each process that needs to use them. The *trail stack* holds pointers to parent variables bound during a unification step; the variables are either untrailed and/or copied before the process gives up control, so the trail does not have to be saved between process invocations. The *quad stack* holds quadruples that contain pointers to structures so the machine can more easily detect and mark ground terms as they are built. There are several other temporary registers that hold information used within a process step, but they are not mentioned in the explanations in the next two sections.

8.3 CONTROL: PROCESSES AND CONTINUATIONS

The execution of a process in the AND/OR model is defined by a sequence of discrete *steps*. Each step is an atomic operation, triggered by a message to a process. In the OM virtual machine, an instance of a process is defined by a state vector stored in the local heap of one of the processors. A step is executed by storing a pointer to the message that triggers the step in the **M** register, a pointer to the state vector of the process that will handle the message in the **P** register, and then resuming the machine so that it executes a code block compiled for the process. During the execution of the step the state vector is updated in place. In addition, the step might create new process seeds and send messages to other processes. The step ends when an instruction causes a task switch, which traps to the OS level so it can install the next process.

The details of how OM implements the control structures of the AND/OR model are presented in this section. First we will look at how code blocks are defined and how the OS implements efficient task switching, and then go into the details of code blocks for AND and OR processes. Following that we will see how OM improves the basic message passing patterns of the AND/OR model by using continuations in messages so that a process does not have to send a response to its immediate parent.

The OM control instructions described in the following sections are listed in Figure 8.4 and described in greater detail in the "appendix" at the end of the chapter (Section 8.8).

8.3.1 Port Instructions

The OPAL compiler generates code blocks for AND and OR processes from clause bodies and heads, respectively. Every code block starts with sequence of *port instructions*. There is one port instruction for each type of message and each type of process (see the definitions of the port instructions at the end of the chapter). When a process handles a message, the OS causes a branch to the port instruction for that type of message in that process' code block; the port instruction then loads more information into registers from the state vector, and then branches to a location in the body of the code block which will execute the rest of the process step.

As an example, suppose the message that triggers the next step is a success message to an AND process. The OS will set up a branch to the **and_success_port** instruction at the head of the code block. This instruction is basically a complicated N-way

Ports:

and_start_port N	Initialize new AND process with **N** descendants; continue.
and_success_port	Restore process state, branch to success block for solved literal (literal number in message).
and_redo_port Addr	Restore process state, branch to **Addr**.
and_fail_port	Restore process state, branch to fail block for failed literal (literal number in message).
or_start_port	Initialize a new OR process, continue.
or_redo_port	If results in queue, send one to parent and switch; else if active descendants, switch; else fail.
or_fail_port	If results in queue or active descendants remain, switch, else fail.

Messages:

start_and Addr	Create seed for new AND process with code block beginning at **Addr**.
start_or A1 A2 A3	Create seed for new OR process with code block at A1, success block at A2, fail block at A3
start_last_or A1 A3	Create seed for OR process with code at **A1**, fail block at **A3**.
succeed	Send success message to parent.
proceed	Append success message to OR process queue.
send_redo N	Send redo message to OR process for literal N.
send_cancel N	Cancel OR process for literal N.
send_fail	Send fail message to parent.
next_alternative A1	Code for next clause head starts at A1.
last_alternative	This is the last clause head.

Figure 8.4 OM Control Instructions

branch instruction. First it initializes the frame pointers **E**, **R**, and **A** from values stored in the state vector and message. Then it uses information in the message header to set the **DX** register to the index of the literal that was solved by the process that sent the message. Finally the instruction branches to code which will extract the bindings passed back in the message and apply them to the current environment.

8.3.2 Task Switches

Recall that processes do not move once they are expanded from seeds. This allows us to use the local address of a process as part of its permanent ID, a fact that will help in the implementation of fast task switching.

When a kernel expands a seed, it assigns the new process an ID that contains the processor number, the local address of the process state, and other information. Interprocessor message routers use the processor number field to forward the message to the node where the process lives, and the kernel at a node uses the local address field when it needs to find the process state, for example during a task switch.

Messages have three of these ID fields in their headers: one for the sender, one for the receiver, and a continuation ID which will be explained in a later section. Message headers also have a two-bit field which defines the message type (start, succeed, redo, or fail).

We now have enough information to explain how the OM kernel executes a task switch. When the current process traps to the kernel at the end of a process step, the kernel gets the next message from its local queue. It uses the local address field of the receiver ID to find the state vector of the new process. Finally it calculates the address of the next instruction to execute by adding the code address of the process (which is one of the fields of the state vector) to the message type, which gives the address of a port instruction in the code block:

```
M = next_message();
P = M->to.addr;
PC = M->kind + P->codeloc;
```

Since messages are stored in a linked list, the above steps require only a few pointer updates, and the entire task switch (modulo the execution of the port instruction) can be done in very few host machine instructions. If there are no messages in the local queue, the processor is idle until a message arrives from another node; this is where one of the hooks to the task allocation functions is placed, since many task allocation methods are based on idle nodes polling their neighbors for work.

8.3.3 Code Blocks for OR Processes

An OR process in OM does all of its real work when it is first started. Its purpose is to unify the terms in the **A** registers with the arguments of the compiled heads for each clause in the procedure. The result of a successful unification with a unit clause goes into a success message which will be returned either to the calling AND process or one of its ancestors. Each successful unification with a nonunit clause leads to a new AND process for the body of the clause. After all unifications are done, the process simply waits until all descendant ANDs have failed, and then sends a fail message to its parent.

The outline of a code block for a typical OR process is shown in Figure 8.5. The four port instructions are at the front of the block, followed by a set of instructions for each clause head. The fail and redo ports simply count messages and switch the process between waiting and gathering mode. Since the success port is never invoked, **or_success_port** is now an obsolete instruction, for reasons that will be explained later in the section on continuations. The **or_start_port** instruction allocates and initializes the state vector for the new process, and then falls through to the code for the first head.

The code for each head except the last begins with a **next_alternative** instruction, which sets the **CP** register to the address of the code for the next clause head. Each unification instruction is a conditional branch. If it successfully unifies a compiled term with a term passed in the **A** registers, it increments the **PC** so control passes the next argument. If the unification fails, it sets **PC** to the contents of **CP**, effectively branching to the next clause head. The code for each head ends with an instruction that carries out the action to be performed when all arguments have been unified. In

```
p/N:            or_fail_port                          % port instructions
                or_redo_port
                or_success_port
                or_start_port
p/N/0:          next_alternative      p/N/1           % addr of next clause head
                <unification instructions>
                proceed                               % when clause is a unit clause
p/N/1:          last_alternative                      % compiled for last clause
                <unification instructions>
                start_and             p/N/a1          % when clause has a body
```

Figure 8.5 Control Instructions in an OR Process

a unit clause, the **proceed** instruction loads the **R** registers into a success message; in nonunit clauses, the **start_and** instruction traps to the OS to create the seed of a new AND process. Currently an OR process does all unifications in one step, which means **proceed** and **start_and** do not cause task switches, but rather continue execution at the next clause.

The **last_alternative** compiled for the last clause sets **CP** to 0. When **CP** is 0, the other instructions in the head trap to the OS to do a task switch instead of branching to the next alternative when they are finished.

8.3.4 Code Blocks for AND Processes

AND processes are considerably more complex than OR processes, mainly because of the backtracking steps they take when processing a fail message. Unlike the WAM, which treats every failed unification the same way, OM invokes a section of compiled code to handle each failed procedure call. Instead of simply invoking a backtracking mechanism hidden inside the machine, OM executes a sequence of instructions that has been optimized for that call [MEYE90].

The code block for an AND process (Figure 8.6) starts with a set of port instructions. The **and_start_port** instruction initializes the state vector for the new process and then falls through into the body of the code block so the machine can make the first set of procedure calls. The success and fail ports are both N-way branch instructions. When the OR process for the ith body goal is started, the seed is given a key to use when it returns success and fail messages. The success and fail port instructions extract the literal number from the key, and then branch to code that handles the ith literal.

There are three sections of code for each literal. The first is executed to set up an OR process for the literal. It consists of a series of unification instructions that load arguments into a frame followed by a **start_or** instruction which traps to the OS to create the seed of a new OR process. The second is the *success block* for the literal, which is invoked when the OR process for the literal sends a success message to this AND process. The third is the *fail block*, invoked when the OR process sends a fail message. The addresses of the success and fail blocks are stored in the AND process state vector by the **start_or** instruction; later the port instructions perform a table lookup and branch to the proper block.

The success block contains instructions that extract bindings from a success message and apply them to the environment of the AND process; these instructions implement the environment closing operation that is part of the unification procedure

```
p/n/ai:       and_fail_port
              and_redo_port          andxfc
              and_success_port
              and_start_port
              <put instructions>                      % set up arguments for call
              start_or               p, psc, pfc
              <put instructions>
              start_or               q, qsc, qfc
              check_solved           [1,2]            % switch if both not solved

psc:          <cget instructions>                     % extract bindings from ...
              set_solved             1                % ... the success message
              check_solved           [1,2]
              succeed

pfc:          <backtracking instructions>             % determine backtrack literal
              send_cancel            2
```

Figure 8.6 Control Instructions in an AND Process

used in OM (these instructions and environment closing are described later in the chapter). The **set_solved** instruction adds the index of the newly solved literal to the set of solved literals. **check_solved** is a conditional instruction that causes a task switch if the set of literals in its argument is not a subset of the solved set.

The fail block consists of instructions that add the index of the failed literal to one or more sets of "marks" and then examine the marks on generators in other sets to determine a backtrack literal. Once a literal j has been chosen as the backtrack literal, the **send_redo** instruction is used to send a redo message to the OR process for literal j. Several other literals may have to be canceled at this time, and there is a sequence of **send_cancel** instructions for each of them.

AND-parallel calls depend on the fact that the goals are independent, *i.e.* their arguments have no unbound variables in common. The OPAL compiler analyzes pairs of goals, and if there is a chance they will have one or more common variables it will insert "check" instructions before the calling sequence of one of the goals. For example, if the compiler wants to call p(X) and q(X) in parallel, it will generate the code to make a call to p(X), as in the example, but before the code that sets up the call to q(X) there will be a **check_ground** instruction. If X is nonground, the instruction causes a branch and the call to q(X) is not made. Later, after p(X) has been solved, it will be possible to start q(X). Note that if the compiler determines that X will always be ground by the time the AND process is started, then the check instruction is omitted and the two goals are always started in parallel.

The control instructions that set and use marks, the check instructions, and the other AND process control instructions that deal with backtracking in parallel goals are described in detail in [MEYE90]. That paper also describes some compiler optimizations that show how effective it is to tailor a fail block for each literal instead of relying on a general purpose backtracking mechanism built into the virtual machine.

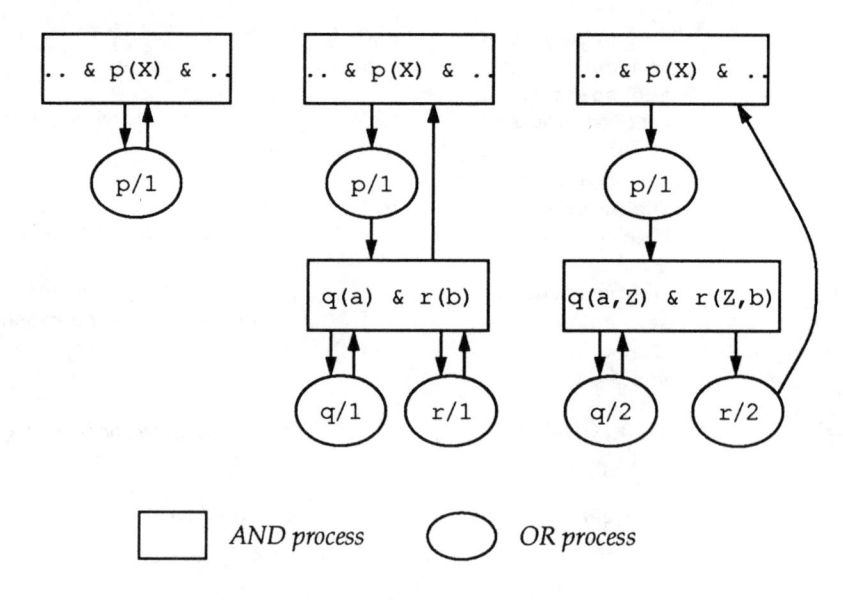

Figure 8.7 *Message Passing Patterns in OM*

8.3.5 Continuations

In the basic AND/OR model, a process communicates only with its parent or its immediate children. Communication patterns in OM improve the basic model by allowing a process to send a success message to an ancestor and bypass intervening steps that merely pass the result back up the process tree.

The message passing patterns in OM are shown in Figure 8.7. Downward pointing arrows indicate start messages, and upward pointing arrows are success messages. Redo messages are sent backwards along success arcs, and fail messages flow backwards along the start arcs. In the first example shown in the figure, an AND process calls a procedure that is defined only by unit clauses, and the OR process for the procedure responds directly to the AND process. In the second case, the procedure is defined by one or more nonunit clauses; when the AND process for the body of a clause in the called procedure has successfully solved all its goals, it responds directly to the process that made the original call, bypassing the OR process (this is why OR process success ports are no longer invoked).

The third case shows how *last call optimization* is implemented (for an introduction to last call optimization in Prolog, see [KOGG91]). The two calls in this goal are executed sequentially, since they share an unbound variable. If there is just one goal remaining to be solved by an AND process, the result of that call can be passed higher up in the process tree. If the results were returned to the AND process, it would just turn around and send a success to its parent, as it did in the second example; by having r/2 or one of its descendants send the results directly back we can avoid some unnecessary message handling.

The definition of a last call in OPAL is not the same as it is in Prolog. Intuitively, a call is the last call if we know that the entire goal statement will succeed if that call succeeds. The OPAL compiler can generate the instructions for a last call only when the data dependency graph for the clause body has exactly one call on the last level. Not every clause has a last call, as the middle example in Figure 8.7 shows. Here the data dependency graph has two independent goals on the last (only) level and the calls to q/1 and r/1 are made in parallel. Neither call is a last call since the AND process has to wait until it knows both have succeeded before it can send a success message to the calling process.

The message passing patterns are implemented through the use of *continuations*, which are the IDs of processes that should receive the results. The notion of a continuation is the same as that used in Actors systems [HEWI79]. However, continuations are not first class citizens of the OPAL language; they are only used by the underlying system to implement a more efficient control strategy.

When a new process is started, it is given two continuations from its parent: a success continuation and a fail continuation. When an AND process starts an OR process for an inner (not last) call, it gives its own ID to the OR process to use as a success continuation, since it needs to handle the results of the call. When starting an OR process for a last call, the success continuation of the AND process is passed down to the OR process. Refer to the descriptions of the **start_or**, **start_last_or**, and **succeed** instructions at the end of the chapter for more details on how success continuations are handled.

One of our current projects is to improve on the message passing patterns in deterministic programs. If the compiler knows a procedure is deterministic, or we can add some information to a success message indicating that there are no more solutions in the sending process, then we can use a different redo continuation in many cases and therefore might also be able to reuse process states. In the third example in Figure 8.7, if q/2 has only one solution, we can make two improvements when we start the last call for r/2: we can deallocate the AND process before the call, and we can designate the OR process for p/1 to be the redo continuation for successes sent to the top level from r/2.

8.4 UNIFICATION: CLOSED ENVIRONMENTS

One of the major problems that must be addressed by an OR-parallel system is how to represent variables so that subgoals have their own copies of unbound global variables. Several systems generate "cactus stacks" that allow each new subgoal at a parallel branch point to share the stack that exists before the branch. The systems differ in how they provide each new process with its own virtual copy of unbound variables in the shared portion of the stack [WARR87].

The *closed environment* representation solves the problem of unbound ancestor variables by copying nonground frames [CONE88b]. In a system based on closed environments, a binding environment is a collection of frames. A frame is *closed* if none of its variables is defined in terms of variables that belong to other frames. After each unification it is possible to close the frame that represents the environment of the called procedure by copying the parent goal's frame and rearranging the pointers that link variables in the new goal to variables in the parent goal. Another closing operation may be required when results are returned to the parent goal if the results are nonground.

The OPAL compiler makes the operations of the closed environment model more efficient in two ways. First, new frames for called goals are already in closed form as they are made, so there is no need for an explicit closing step after arguments are set up. Second, when results are returned, an optimized sequence of instructions extracts only the bindings that are necessary, avoiding the copying of nonground result frames.

OM implements the closed environment model through what we call *four phase unification*. The first two phases are similar to unification in the WAM. In the first phase, the parent goal loads parameters into argument registers. In the second phase, an OR process unifies the argument registers with the heads of clauses in the called procedure. The instructions that implement the first two phases are defined so that environment closing is folded in with unification; when a clause head is successfully unified, the environment of the new AND process for the body of the selected clause will be in closed form.

The last two phases implement the environment closing steps that are applied when the process for a subgoal returns a success message. This step is essentially a *back unification* step that unifies the still-unbound variables passed in the call with terms passed back in a success message [WISE86b]. Phase three is executed in the OR process, as it takes bindings from the environment of its descendant AND process and builds a success message to return to the calling process (when success continuations are used, OR processes are bypassed as results are communicated directly to the calling AND process, so our compiler no longer generates phase three instructions). In phase four, the calling AND process extracts bindings returned in the success message and applies them to its local variables.

The details of how OM implements unification and environment closing are presented in the next three sections. The first explains how the frames pointed to by the **A**, **E**, and **R** registers are passed between AND and OR processes when procedures are called and results are returned. The second describes the virtual machine instructions that carry out unification and closing. When lists and other complex terms contain unbound variables, the environment closing steps are more complicated; the third section below explains how environments are extended to contain these variables.

8.4.1 Registers as Message Arguments

Argument frames are the basic unit of communication between processes in OM. At the beginning of phase one, when an AND process is getting ready to make a procedure call, it allocates a new frame for the arguments of the call and puts the address of the frame in the A register. When results are returned, they will be in the form of copies of the argument frame. If the called procedure is deterministic, the same frame is returned, with variables replaced by bindings made in the solution of the called goal. If the procedure is nondeterministic, the returned frame may be a copy of the original. Either way, phase four instructions are used to apply bindings from the filled-in frame to the variables in the AND process environment.

The introduction of success continuations complicates the picture, since the process that returns the frame might not have the same number of arguments or same order of arguments as the original call. Consider the following simple case:

```
<- foo([a,b,c],L).
foo(X,Y) <- bar(X,[],Y).
```

THE OPAL MACHINE

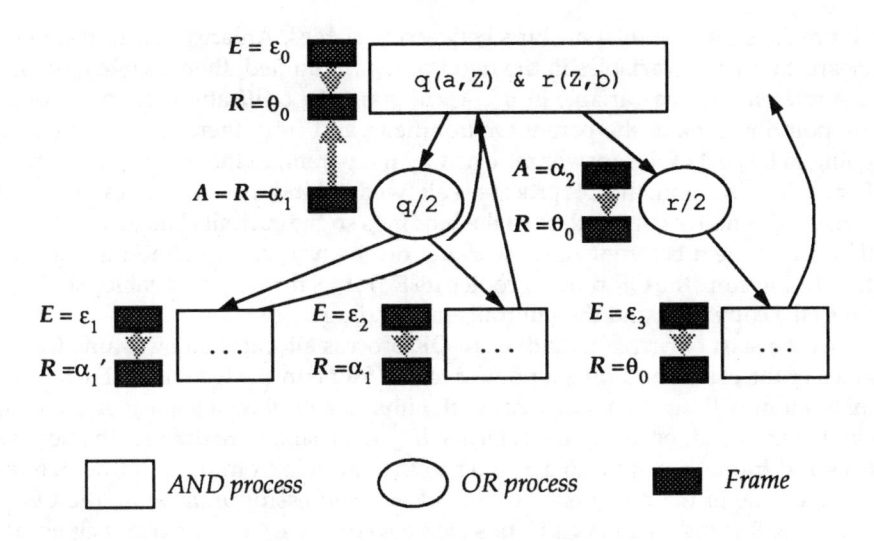

Figure 8.8 *Registers as Message Arguments*

Since bar/3 is the last call in the body of foo/2, solutions for bar/3 will be sent all the way back to the top level goal. However, that goal expects to find a value for L in the second argument in the returned frame, but solutions to bar/3 will have the result in the third argument position.

OM solves this problem by passing two frames in every call. When a start message is sent to a new OR process, it is given an *argument frame*, which holds the values of the parameters being passed to the procedure, and a *result frame*, which will be filled in and mailed back to the process specified in the success continuation.

Figure 8.8 shows how frames are passed as arguments in start and success messages. The frame pointed to by the **E** register when an AND process is running is the current environment, containing the bindings for the variables of the clause. Another frame owned by the AND process is pointed to by the **R** register; it is the response frame that this process returns in a success message when it succeeds. The process at the root of the portion of the tree shown in the figure owns frames ε_0 and θ_0.

When an AND process makes a procedure call, it allocates a new frame to hold the arguments of the call. When it is an inner (not last) call, the AND process expects either this frame or a copy when it receives a success message, so it passes the same block as both argument and result frame (the pointers in the start message both point to the same frame). In the figure, the call to q/2 is an inner call, so frame α_1 is both the argument and result frame. To set up a call to the last procedure in the body, the AND process allocates a new argument frame, as usual, but it passes its own response frame to the new OR process because the OR process or one of its descendants will respond directly to an ancestor. The call to r/2 in the figure is an example of a last call. Note that θ_0, the frame that the AND process at the root of this subtree is expected to fill in, is the frame passed back by the OR process for r/2.

Before explaining how an OR process creates **E** and **R** frames for its descendant AND processes, we need to see how variables are related within a closed environment (recall that an environment is a set of one or more frames). The light arrows in

Figure 8.8 show the relationships between variables. An arrow from frame σ_1 to σ_2 means that when variables in the two frames are unified, the variable in σ_1 is bound to a reference to the variable in σ_2. At the start of a unification, unbound arguments are pointing back to the parent environment, and from there, if a parent variable is going to be part of the answer returned by the parent, to the parent's response frame. For each unification, the OR process is allowed to bind these variables, but if there are further alternatives, it has to save the bindings so the current clause can use them and then undo them before it starts working on the next clause. Bindings are saved via the closing step: the OR process copies its **R** frame, renaming variables so they are local to the copy of **R**, and then untrails the bindings.

At the start of each alternative, an OR process allocates a new frame for the variables of the clause and puts a pointer to the frame in the **E** register. Each unification instruction will match one **A** term with either a compiled term (*e.g.* if there is a constant in the head) or one of the **E** terms. If two variables are unified, the new variable (in the **E** frame) is bound to a pointer to the variable from the call (the dereferenced value of one of the **A** terms). At the end of a successful unification, the OR process copies its **R** frame and closes it (this step also closes **E**). If the current clause is a unit clause, the **R** frame is put into a success message; otherwise the **E** register and **R** register are put into a start message that will be sent to an AND process for the body of the clause.

Returning to the figure, note that since **A** and **R** point to the same frame in the OR process for q/2, each of its descendants has its own copy of α_1 to use as its response frame. When these AND processes succeed, the copies of α_1 are sent back to the top AND process, which can then extract bindings for z. Since **E** variables point to **R** variables when they are unified, this latter step will fill a θ_0 slot in cases when z is a value to be returned. Since the call to r/2 is a last call, that OR process is given two different frames, and each descendant of r/2 is given its own copy of θ_0 which it can return higher in the tree.

As a final comment, when CP is zero, the OR process does not copy R, since there is no other alternative in the current procedure. Note also that if a procedure is deterministic, there is no need to untrail bindings made to the parent environment and phase four unification instructions can be omitted. We take advantage of this fact when compiling calls to built-in predicates, and are working on enhancements to the compiler to get it to detect when a user goal has just one solution.

8.4.2 Unification Instructions
Instructions that implement various steps in unification are listed in Figure 8.9 and described in greater detail in 8.8 at the end of the chapter. The first four instructions in the list initialize or reinitialize frames at the start of phase one or phase two. An AND process executes **make_args** to create a new argument frame before each call. The instruction specifies the size of the frame and also the index of the literal, since subsequent instructions need to record the literal number so it can be used in future backtracking steps. An OR process executes **make_env** to create the environment of each new alternative clause. The **store_args** instruction is executed once, just before the first alternative in a procedure that has more than one clause. It records the index of each nonground term in the argument list, since these are the terms that might need to be closed later after unification succeeds. **restore_args** is executed before each succeeding alternative to reinitialize the set of terms that actually need to be closed.

Initialization:

make_args I N	Allocate argument frame of size **I** for literal **N**.
make_env N	Allocate environment frame of size **N**.
store_args	Save index of every nonground argument, clear set of arguments to close.
restore_args	Clear set of arguments to close.

Phase One:

put_const c Aj	Load c to argument register **A[j]**.
put_var Ei Aj	Initialize variable **E[i]**, load it into **A[j]**
put_val Ei Aj	Load **E[i]** into **A[j]**.
put_struct f/n Aj	Allocate a new structure for f/n and put a pointer to it in S and **A[j]**.

Phase Two:

get_const c Aj	Unify c with **A[j]**.
get_var Ei Aj	Bind **E[i]** to **A[j]**.
get_val Ei Aj	Unify **E[i]** with **A[j]**.
get_struct f/n Aj	Unify f/n with **A[j]**.

Phase Four:

cget_var Ei Aj	Bind **E[i]** to **A[j]**.
cget_val Ei Aj	If **E[i]** was nonground, traverse it and bind every variable to the corresponding term from **A[j]**.
cget_struct Aj	Set S to **A[j]**.

Structures:

unify_const c Si	Unify c with **S[i]**.
unify_var Ei Sj	Bind **E[i]** to **S[j]**.
unify_val Ei Sj	Unify **E[i]** with **S[j]**.
unify_struct f/n Si	Unify f/n with **S[j]**.
cunify_var Ei Sj	Bind **E[i]** to **S[j]**.
cunify_val Ei Sj	If **E[i]** was nonground, traverse it and bind every variable to the corresponding term from **S[j]**.
cunify_struct Sj	Set S to **S[j]**.
set_struct N	Use top **N** entries from the quad stack to mark the corresponding structures as ground or nonground.
cset_struct N	Pop **N** entries from the quad stack, reset S.

Figure 8.9 OM Unification Instructions

The instructions that load terms into the argument registers in phase one all have names beginning with "put", and they are analogous to the instructions with the same names in the WAM. One difference is that when the term being loaded is nonground, the OM instructions need to record that fact for later backtracking steps. Also, as will be explained in the next section, structures are handled differently.

The phase two instructions that do the actual unification all have names beginning with "get". One argument of a **get** instruction specifies a term from the clause head; for example the **get_const** instruction has the index of an atom from the user program, and **get_var** has the index of a local variable from the current environment. The other argument is an index into the argument frame. The instruction unifies the two terms, and if it is successful, it increments the program counter. If it cannot unify the terms, it executes the *failure trap* which is common to all get instructions. This subroutine untrails bindings made since the last **[re]store_args** instruction and branches to the address in the **CP** register to begin the next alternative in the procedure. If there are no alternatives, a task switch occurs.

Another subroutine that is common to phase 2 instructions is the close operation executed by **proceed** or **start_and** when a unification is completed. This subroutine transforms the **E** frame so it is independent of any parent variables, and then it copies the **R** frame (the copy is either put into a success message by **proceed** or sent to the new AND process by **start_and**). The terms in the copy of the **R** frame are also transformed so they are independent.

Phases three and four implement the environment closing steps applied when results are returned to a calling process. This operation is a form of unification, so the instructions have names that start with "cput" and "cget." Since **cput** instructions are now obsolete (no results are returned to OR processes) only the **cget** instructions are listed in the figure.

A **cget** instruction is compiled for each argument that could be nonground at the time of the call. The goal of the instruction is to apply bindings found in the copy of the original argument to variables in the original, thus updating both the current environment (**E** frame) and the AND process' own response frame (**R** frame).

The unification instructions in the AND and OR process code for one of the clauses in the symbolic differentiation program is shown in Figure 8.10

8.4.3 Lists and Other Complex Terms

In the closed environment model, a frame is extended to contain slots for new variables if a term of the frame is bound to a complex term that contains variables from another frame. For example, consider the following call and procedure definition:

```
<- p(f(X),Y).

p(A,g(B)) <- ...
```

After unification, the variable A in the environment of the new AND process is bound to f(X). To close the E frame, we need to make a place for the AND process' own copy of X. Similarly, if the body does not create a binding for B, Y will be bound to a nonground term when the results are passed back, and the parent environment will have to be extended to contain a slot for B.

Rather than extend an already allocated frame to contain new slots, OM considers any variable that is reachable from a frame to be part of the frame. In the example, X

Code for the head of the clause (part of the OR process for d/3):

```
d/3/o5:
            next_alternative d/3/o4
            restore_args
            make_env 6            % This clause has 6 vars
            get_struct */2, 1
            unify_var 1, 1
            unify_var 2, 2
            set_struct 1
            get_var 3, 2
            get_var 4, 3
            start_and d/3/a5      % Env initialized; pass it to code for body
```

Code for the body of the clause; note last call instruction for second goal:

```
d/3/a5:
            <and port instructions>
            make_args 1, 3        % Arg frame for first body goal
            put_val 1, 1
            put_var 5, 2
            put_var 6, 3
            start_builtin 19, d/3/sc1, d/3/5fc1
            check_solved [1]      % Can be optimized away if goal is synchronous
            make_args 2, 5        % Arg frame for second goal
            put_val 6, 1
            put_val 1, 2
            put_val 2, 3
            put_val 3, 4
            put_val 4, 5
            start_last_or product/5, d/3/5fc2
```

Success continuation. Branch here when builtin done (or, in general, when success message arrives with results of solved subgoal).

```
d/3/sc1:
            cget_val 1, 1         % Can be optimized away if modes known
            cget_var 6, 3
            set_solved 1
            continue              % ... with code that sets up second call
```

Code from one of the clauses in the symbolic differentiation program:
d(U*V,X,P) <- functor(U,_,N) & product(N,U,V,X,P).

Figure 8.10   *Unification Instructions in an OPAL Program*

is reachable from the E frame after unification since E contains a pointer to the term f(X). This policy works if only one active or enabled process can reach a variable. In the AND/OR model, with its independent AND parallelism, this is a valid assumption, since a parent goal passes an unbound variable to only one subgoal at a time, and it will not try to access a variable again until after the subgoal that is using it has returned a success message.

OM structures are represented by a hierarchy of fixed size blocks. A term with functor f and arity N is always represented by a frame of size N+1. The first cell holds a representation of the constant f, and the remaining cells hold the arguments. If one of the arguments is itself a complex term, the corresponding slot in the frame holds a pointer to the term, *i.e.* terms are never flattened and stored in a single block. Lists are represented by "cons cells" with functor '.' and arity 2. In future versions we expect to introduce cdr-coded blocks for more efficient representations of lists [MOON87].

A top level structure will be created by either a **put_struct** instruction (if it occurs in the argument list in a literal in the body of a clause) or a **get_struct** instruction (if it is in the head of a clause and is unified with an unbound variable argument). A compiled argument of the instruction specifies the name and arity of the term, which is enough information to allocate and initialize the frame that will hold it. A pointer to the term is put into the S register.

As is the case in the WAM, when a new term is created, the machine is put into *write mode*. Arguments are then added to the term by unify instructions. Unlike the WAM, the unify instructions in OM name an argument position that is interpreted as an offset relative to the address in the S register. If a **get_struct** instruction finds an existing structure in an A register, the machine is put into *read mode* and S is set to a pointer to the existing term. The unify instructions then simply match the arguments of S with compiled arguments.

Because OM has to copy nonground terms, there is an advantage in knowing when a term is ground so it does not have to be copied. OM uses its quad stack to store descriptors of terms it is building so it can mark the terms as nonground as they are built. A quad is a tuple of the form <G,M,T,S> where G is a one-bit flag, M is a one-bit mode, and S and T are references to terms. When a new top level structure is created, the quad stack is initialized and the first quad is pushed. Then each time a **unify_struct** instruction builds a new inner term, a quad describing that term is pushed on the stack.

The G flag on the top of the quad stack is 1 if the term currently pointed to by the S register is ground. A new term is assumed ground, so the first quad has G initialized to 1. If a **unify** instruction puts a nonground argument into the current term, G is set to 0. The M flag is the machine's mode (read or write) when the quad is created; it is needed in case the machine has to switch back from write to read mode after building a new subterm for an already existing term.

The T and S entries in a quad point to terms. Whenever a new structure is created, it is because the machine is unifying a variable with the structure. T is a reference to that variable. Once the term is built, the variable will be overwritten with a reference to the new term. T is part of the quad stack because we want to mark the new reference with a bit that indicates whether the structure is ground or not. The S entry in the quad stack is the contents of the S register when the quad is built; it is saved because we need to restore the old S when we finish working on a subterm.

A **set_struct** instruction is used to pop the descriptor off of the quad stack when the machine reaches the end of a term. The term pointed to by **T** is a reference to the newly finished structure; the reference is tagged with the value of **G** from the popped quad. The **G** bit in the new top of the quad stack is ANDed with the **G** bit from the old quad — if the old structure is nonground, then by definition the enclosing term is nonground also. The **M** and **S** fields of the popped quad are used to reset the machine's mode and **S** register, respectively. To make handling of long lists more efficient, the **set_struct** instruction has an integer operand **N** which specifies how many quads to pop; this lets the compiler replace N consecutive **set_struct** instructions with a single instruction.

8.5 PERFORMANCE

The following two sections will present some data on how well a single OM interpreter executes OPAL programs. The first section describes a program that builds random AND/OR trees and simulates messages between nodes in the tree; this program was written to measure the efficiency of the low level kernel operations required to allocate process states and switch between tasks. The second section gives some data on how well OM runs some simple benchmark programs on a single processor workstation; in this implementation, the hooks that implement task distribution were disabled and all tasks stayed in the local heap. For data on how well OPAL runs on multiprocessor systems, see the paper on the Mayfly kernel [CONE90].

8.5.1 Kernel Operations

To measure the performance of the memory manager, message queue, and task switcher, we wrote a simulator that builds a random AND/OR tree. The "process" at a node does little more than use a random number to compute the number of descendants it will have, create those descendants, and then coordinate success and fail messages from descendants. Independent variables in the simulations were the maximum depth of the tree, the maximum number of descendants for each type of node, and a probability (which decreases with the depth of the tree) that an OR node will succeed.

The simulations were run on an HP 9000/835 workstation. The system has an HP-PA RISC processor with a 66.7ns instruction cycle time (rated at 14 Vax MIPS by HP), 128KB cache, and 32MB RAM. The operating system was HP-UX version 7.0

The performance ranged from 75,000 steps per second up to 98,000 steps per second. A step involves

- removing the first message from the queue and installing the receiving process as the current process (using the algorithm presented in the section on task switching).
- if the message is a start message, calling the random number generator to calculate how many new nodes to generate below this node, and putting start messages for each one in the queue.
- if the message is a success, sending a success message to the parent node.
- if the message is a fail, decrementing the active descendant counter for this node, and if that counter is now zero, sending a fail to the parent.

Each new process state and each new message required a call to the memory allocator to create a new block. Messages were deallocated as soon as they were used, and process states were deallocated as soon as the process failed.

The results tell us three things. At almost 100,000 steps per second (about 10 microseconds per step), task switching and memory allocation are reasonably efficient. Inspection of the code (the times we too short to measure accurately with an execution profiling tool) shows that about half this time was spent in task switching and memory allocation operations. Second, the shape of the tree affects the run times. The slower runs were on shallower, broader trees, which tended to have more nodes because of the higher branching factor. The slowdown undoubtedly comes from decreased cache hit rates, as operations invoked nodes at several different parts of the tree and process states fell out of cache before being used again. So even though using a heap-based memory allocator is not much slower than simply building new environments on top of a stack, the loss of locality of reference in a heap-based system will add to the inefficiency.

The third thing these figures give us is an upper bound on the number of LIPS a single interpreter is capable of executing in the straightforward AND/OR model. Since each procedure call will take two tasks — one to create the OR process and one to create the AND process for the body — the best we can hope for with one node running append/3 is 50 KLIPS on the HP 9000/835. Improvements will have to come from better compilation techniques (for example executing tail recursive code in iterative loops within a single process) and from using redo continuations for early deallocation of useless processes and better memory locality.

8.5.2 Single Processor Implementation

A kernel that has "stubs" in place of all the hooks that implement interprocessor communication was used to measure the performance of OM running on a single processor. This implementation is instructive because it allows us to compare OM with the WAM in order to gain a sense of how much overhead the AND/OR model, with its small-grain processes and heap-based operations, adds to different types of programs.

We compared several OPAL programs executed by OM with equivalent Prolog programs executed by the SICStus implementation of the WAM. We chose SICStus because it is generally considered to be one of the more efficient implementations of Prolog based on the same technology we used for OM, namely a byte-code interpreter written in C and running on Unix systems. SICStus is a much more polished system than OM, with sophisticated compiler optimizations and "call chains" to implement clause indexing [CARL90]. Still, it is necessary to compare our parallel system with the best sequential system to get a fair answer to the question, "what does it cost to run this program in parallel?"

The table in Figure 8.11 compares OM with the SICStus WAM on a few small benchmarks. The best, from our perspective, are the three nondeterministic programs listed first (path searches for even length paths in a graph, color is a map coloring program, and bid computes opening bids for a Bridge hand). The worst were the deterministic programs (a naive reverse of a list of 350 elements, and a quick-sort of 75 items), Part of the reason OM is so much slower due to our treatment of lists as cons cells, but the rest can be attributed to our inefficient execution of deterministic goals such as append.

Program	SICStus	OPAL	Ratio
path	.020	.078	3.9
color	.044	.224	5.1
bid	.070	.110	1.6
reverse	.010	.130	13.0
qsort	.060	.950	15.8

Times are in seconds, and are for all solutions. All programs were I/O bound when solutions were printed, so times were obtained by disabling I/O in OPAL and timing the failure of goals of the form `:- goal(), fail` *in Prolog.*

Figure 8.11 *Performance on a Single Processor*

Even with the improvements we have planned for clause indexing, lists, and redo continuations, it is unlikely OM will ever be better than two or three times as slow as the SICStus WAM. This may seem discouraging, especially when one considers that Aurora, an OR-parallel versions of SICStus, is roughly 1.25 times slower than SICStus ([CARL90, LUSK88]). However, Aurora requires a shared-memory multiprocessor and exploits OR parallelism only. OM will be an effective system for solving problems that exhibit both AND and OR parallelism on large nonshared memory machines.

8.6 ACKNOWLEDGMENTS

The OM virtual machine is the result of several years work by many different people, and the system described here is just the latest in a series that started with a "paper machine" defined jointly with David Meyer in 1987.

The first complete virtual machine and its compiler were implemented by Craig Thornley, who also got the first parallel implementation going early in 1988. Mike Stafford and David Meyer made some further improvements in the implementation of both parts of the system. All three contributed, directly and indirectly, to the evolution of the machine.

Compilation and execution of AND-parallel goals were defined by David Meyer. Efficient execution of goals with dynamic dependencies is unique to OM, and will be the topic of his Ph.D. thesis.

Renganathan Sundararajan has contributed significantly to the development of the compiler, especially in the area of abstract interpretation for sharing and groundness analysis.

Moataz Mohamed and David Keldsen also helped shape the project, and ideas they worked on will be included in later versions.

The main source of funding for the OPAL project was NSF grant CCR-8707177. We are also grateful for support from Sam Daniel and his group at Motorola GEG in Scottsdale, Arizona, and a generous equipment grant from Hewlett-Packard through the efforts of Roy D'Souza and Al Davis at HP Labs in Palo Alto.

8.7 THE OM INSTRUCTION SET

The OM instructions mentioned in this chapter are described below. The first two subsections list control instructions: message ports, instructions that generate messages, and a few miscellaneous instructions. The remaining subsections list unification instructions, including instructions that build and access complex terms. Also described under unification are the general purpose procedures that are invoked when two terms do not unify and when the unbound arguments of a call must be put into closed form.

8.7.1 Control Instructions

Ports:

and_start_port N
Allocate a state vector for an AND process with N descendants; set **E** to the frame in **M.args.af** and **R** to the frame in **M.args.rf**; allocate variable information records for each variable in the **E** frame.

and_success_port
Get the descendant index **DX** from **M.to.key**, and insert the message in the queue of results for this descendant. If **DX** is in **P.solved**, do a task switch, otherwise set **A** to the frame in **M.args.af**, restore **E** and **R** from the corresponding fields in the state vector, and branch to **P.sc[DX]**.

and_redo_port Addr
Restore **E** and **R** from the process state, then branch to **Addr**.

and_fail_port
Get the descendant index **DX** from **M.from.key**, and mark the descendant as failed. If **DX** is in **P.solved**, do a task switch, otherwise restore **E** and **R**, untrail the variables bound by this literal, and branch to **P.fc[DX]**.

or_start_port
Allocate a state vector for an OR process. Set **A** and **R** from **M.args.af** and **M.args.rf**, respectively, and set **E** to nil.

or_redo_port
If no active descendants remain, build a fail message in **M** and send it to **P.or.par**, otherwise set **P.or.mode** to **waiting**. Do a task switch.

or_fail_port
Decrement **P.or.active**. If it is now 0 and **P.or.mode** is **waiting** build a fail message and send it to **P.or.par**. Do a task switch.

Message Passing:

start_and Addr
Close the **R** frame. Set **M** to a new start message, set **M.args.af** to **E**, **M.args.rf** to **R**, and **M.args.pc** to **Addr**. If CP is nonzero, set **PC** to **CP**, else do a task switch.

start_or A1 A2 A3
Set **M** to a new start message. Set **M.rsvp** to **P.self**. Set **M.args.af** and **M.args.rf** to **A**, and **M.args.pc** to A1. Set **P.sc[DX]** to A2 and **P.fc[DX]** to A3. Set **P.marks[DX]** to the empty set.

THE OPAL MACHINE

start_last_or A1 A3
  Same as **start_or**, but **M.rsvp** is set to **P.rsvp** and **M.args.rf** is set to **P.rf**.

succeed
  Allocate a new success message. Set **M.to** to **P.rsvp**, and **M.args.af** to **P.rf**. Send the message and do a task switch.

proceed
  Close the **R** frame and send it in a success message to **P.rsvp**. If CP is nonzero, set PC to CP, otherwise do a task switch.

send_redo N
  Remove literal N from **P.solved** and send a redo message to its OR process.

send_cancel N
  Remove N from **P.solved**, trap to OS to cancel OR process and its descendants.

send_fail
  Send a fail message to **P.par**, deallocate P, do a task switch.

Miscellaneous:

next_alternative Addr
  Set CP to Addr.

last_alternative
  Set CP to 0.

8.7.2 Unification

Initialization:

make_args I N
  Set **A** to a new frame of size N, and set the descendant index **DX** to **I**.

make_env N
  Set **E** to a new frame of size N.

store_args
  Initialize **P.cset** with the index of every nonground term in **R**, reset the trail and quad stack, and set **P.eset** to the empty set.

restore_args
  Reset the trail and quad stack, set **P.eset** to the empty set.

Phase One:

put_const c Aj
  Store constant c in register A[j].

put_var Ei Aj
  Make a new unbound variable in E[i] and bind A[j] to E[i]. Record the fact that the current literal (**DX**) is the generator of variable E[i].

put_val Ei Aj
  Dereference E[i] and put the result in A[j]. If the term is a variable, record the fact that **DX** is its generator; if it is a nonground structure record the fact that **DX** is the generator for all the variables in the term.

put_struct f/n Aj
 Allocate a new structure for f/n and put a pointer to it in S and A[j]. Initialize the quad stack with A[j], and put the machine in write mode.

Phase Two:

get_const c Aj
 Unify A[j] with the constant **c**.

get_var Ei Aj
 Bind E[i] to the dereferenced contents of A[j]. If it is nonground, add **i** to **P.eset**.

get_val Ei Aj
 Unify E[i] with A[j]. If the result is nonground, add **i** to **P.eset**.

get_struct f/n Aj
 If A[j] dereferences to a variable, allocate a new structure for f/n, put a pointer to it in S, and put the machine in write mode. If A[j] points to an existing term with header f/n, set S to the existing term, and go into read mode. Initialize the quad stack with A[j].

Phase Four:

cget_var Ei Aj
 Dereference A[j] and put the result in E[i].

cget_val Ei Aj
 If E[i] was a variable, bind it to the (dereferenced) term in A[j]. If E[i] was a nonground complex term, then A[j] is a copy of it; traverse E[i] and bind each variable to the corresponding term in A[j].

cget_struct Aj
 Set S to A[j] and initialize the quad stack.

Structures:

unify_const c Si
 In write mode, bind S[i] to the constant **c**. In read mode, dereference S[i] and unify it with **c**.

unify_var Ei Sj
 In write mode, bind E[i] and S[j] to a new variable in S[j], mark the top of the quad stack as nonground, and record the fact that **DX** is the generator of E[i]. In read mode, dereference S[j]; if it is a variable, add **i** to **P.eset**. Unify E[i] and S[j]; if nonground, mark the top of the quad stack.

unify_val Ei Sj
 In write mode, dereference E[i]; if it is a nonground term, mark the top of the quad stack as nonground, record **DX** as the generator of variables in E[i], and bind S[j] to E[i]. In read mode, unify E[i] and S[j]; if the result is nonground, mark the top of the quad stack.

THE OPAL MACHINE

unify_struct f/n Si
   In write mode, push S[i] on the quad stack, bind S[i] to a new structure for f/n and then set S to the new structure. In read mode, dereference S[i]; if it is a variable, bind it to a new structure for f/n, set S to the new structure, and put the machine in write mode; if it is also a structure for f/n, push S[i] on the quad stack and set S to S[i]; otherwise fail the clause.

cunify_var Ei Sj
   Similar to **cget_var**, but use S[j] instead of A[j].

cunify_val Ei Sj
   Similar to **cget_val**, but use S[j].

cunify_struct Sj
   Push S on the quad stack, set S to S[j].

set_struct N
   Pop N entries from the quad stack and reset S. Set the ground flag on each structure reference popped.

cset_struct N
   Pop N entries from the quad stack, reset S.

Traps:

Failure:
   Deallocate the frame pointed to by **E**. If **CP** is nonzero, untrail each variable on the trail (pop each address and reset the term at that address to an unbound variable), set **PC** to **CP**, and resume execution. If **CP** is zero, do a task switch (if no clause heads matched, deallocate the **A** frame and send a fail message to the parent process first).

Close Frames:
   Copy the **R** frame. For each i in **P.cset**, close **R'**[i] (if the term is a variable, make sure the unbound term is in **R'**; if it is a complex term, copy it). For each i in **P.eset**, close **E**[i]. Reset each variable on the trail to unbound.

9 The Reduce-OR Process Model for Parallel Logic Programming on Non-shared Memory Machines

L. V. Kalé and **B. Ramkumar**

University of Illinois at Urbana-Champaign, USA

ABSTRACT

We describe the design and implementation of a parallel Prolog compiler called ROLOG for non-shared memory machines. It is based on the Reduce-OR process model for the AND and OR parallel execution of logic programs. This paper includes the design of a binding environment for the execution of parallel logic programs that is suitable for (shared and) non-shared memory multiprocessors. The binding environment supports full OR and independent AND parallelism on both types of machines. The term representation, the algorithms for unification and the join algorithms for parallel AND branches are presented. The abstract machine designed for the ROLOG compiler is also described. We provide performance data of ROLOG across a range of benchmark programs on the Intel iPSC/2, the NCUBE 2, the new Intel i860 hypercube, and a network of Sun Sparc 1 workstations.

1 INTRODUCTION

Logic programming languages, with pure Prolog as an example, are implicitly parallel languages. Such languages are useful for programming large-scale parallel machines, as they free the programmer from dealing with the extraction and management of parallelism. To run a logic program in parallel, it is necessary to efficiently break down its computation into parallel parts, provide algorithms and bookkeeping schemes to manage the parallel parts efficiently, while exploiting as much parallelism as possible from the program. It is also preferable to keep the management of parallellism *transparent* to the user.

Another factor affecting the design of parallel execution schemes for logic programs is the memory organisation of the system it is to be implemented on. Most of the parallel models proposed so far have been designed for shared memory multiprocessors or at least assume a global address space. However, we believe shared memory environments suffer from lack of scalability and will, in the long run, prove unsuitable for exploiting of all the available parallelism in logic programming applications. Large scale MIMD systems like the 1024 node NCUBE/2 hypercube are already commercially available today. There is also an increasing trend towards hybrid systems where small clusters

---

[1] This research was supported in part by a National Science Foundation grant number NSF-CCR 89 02496.

of processors share memories but no memory is shared between any two clusters in the system. Therefore, our approach makes no assumptions about the memory organisation of the target machine.

The contents of this chapter fall broadly into three parts: a description of the binding environment that is suitable for the parallel execution of Prolog programs [Kale88a], a description of the abstract machine designed for the ROLOG compiler, and the performance of the Reduce-OR process model (ROPM) [Kale85a],[Kale87a] for ROLOG, a compiler that runs on (shared and) non-shared parallel machines. We present the performance results the Intel iPSC/2, the NCUBE 2, the Intel i860 hypercube, and a network of Sun Sparc 1 workstations.[2] The binding environment proposed is suitable for exploiting both AND and OR parallellism in logic programs, on both shared and non-shared memory machines. ROPM is based on an alternate tree representation of logic computations called Reduce-OR trees, which is better suited for representing parallel evaluations than the AND-OR or SLD trees. We have shown elsewhere [Kale87b] that compared to most other schemes, ROPM is able to extract more parallelism from logic programs. It accomplishes that by handling the problems of interaction between AND and OR parallelism.

The compiler (ROLOG) described in this chapter for the parallel execution of Prolog programs is one of the first implementations of parallel Prolog to run on a variety of MIMD machines — shared-memory machines, message-passing machines, and a network of workstations. ROLOG supports full OR parallelism and independent AND parallelism. We demonstrate this with benchmarks exhibiting AND, OR and AND/OR parallelism. In the following section, we review the Reduce-OR process model and its implementation briefly. Section 3 describes our binding environment scheme that enables ROPM to exploit AND and OR parallelism on both shared memory and message passing machines. The abstract machine for the ROLOG compiler and compiled execution is discussed in Section 4. The performance of benchmarks programs on non-shared memory machines is discussed Section 5.

2 THE REDUCE-OR PROCESS MODEL

We use the example program shown in Figure 1 to briefly describe the behaviour of the Reduce-OR process model. A clause in the program can be either a fact, or a rule which consists of a head literal and a set of literals as its subgoals. For rules, it is not always efficient to compute all subgoals in parallel. Therefore, for each rule, a *Data Join Graph* (DJG) is used to give a partial ordering to solve the clause effectively.

Each arc in the DJG represents a literal of the rule, and each node denotes a joining point for the data produced by the literals on its incoming arcs. In the example DJG in Figure 1, the two arcs from node 1 to node 2 represent the subgoals $b(X, T)$ and $c(Y, S)$ respectively. Since there happen to be no data dependencies between these subgoals, they can be solved in parallel. The data dependency information may be obtained by some static analysis of the rule [Chan85a],[Debr89a], or may be provided by the programmer. Attached to each arc and each node in the DJG, there is a relation holding a set of *tuples* (partial solutions) which represent the variable bindings obtained

---

[2] ROLOG also runs on a range of shared memory machines like the Encore Multimax, the Sequent Symmetry and the Alliant FX/8.

Program 1:

?- p(U,V).

p(X,S) :- a(X,Y), b(X,T), c(Y,S), d(T,S).

a(x_1, y_1).   a(x_2, y_2).
b(x_1, t_1).   b(x_1, t_2).
b(x_2, t_3).   c(y_1, s_1).
c(y_1, s_2).   d(t_2, s_2).

A *Data Join Graph* for $p(X, S) : -a(X, Y), b(X, T), c(Y, S), d(T, S)$

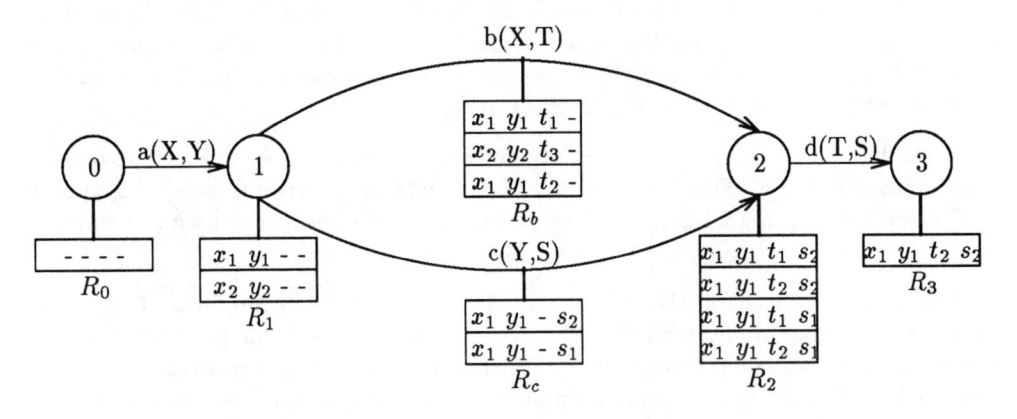

Figure 1: The behaviour of the Reduce-OR process model.

---

so far. If two or more arcs $A_1 \ldots A_k$, $k \geq 2$ are incident upon a node N, the *node-relation* of N represents the join of the *arc-relations* of A_i, $1 \leq i \leq k$. This is explained below with the help of the example in Figure 1.

In this example, the execution of ROPM starts with the query $p(U, V)$ as its top level goal, where the variables U and V are unbound. Upon successful unification of $p(U, V)$ with the head of clause $p(X, S)$, the tuple containing the bindings for the head variables in the clause are inserted into the relation for node 0. This initial tuple has one entry per variable in the clause (in this example there are 4 variables). Then, all subgoals corresponding to *parallel* arcs emanating from node 0 are fired. In the example, there is only one such arc, corresponding to the subgoal $a(X, Y)$. In general, as soon as a partial solution tuple is inserted into a node relation, all subgoals corresponding to arcs emanating from that node are fired.

When a solution tuple is returned for a subgoal S corresponding to an arc A of a DJG, two cases may arise. If the succeeding node N in the DJG (i.e. the node A is incident on) has only one incoming arc A, then the solution tuple is inserted in the node relation for node N and the arcs emanating from N are fired as before. If N has more than one incoming arc, the solution tuple is inserted in the arc-relation for A.

In the example, the node 1 has only one incoming arc for subgoal $a(X, Y)$. When the first solution (x_1, y_1) returns, the tuple $[x_1, y_1, -, -]$ is inserted in node-relation 1, and subgoals $b(x_1, T)$ and $c(y_1, S)$ are started in parallel. When subgoal a returns another solution (x_2, y_2), the tuple $[x_2, y_2, -, -]$ is inserted in node-relation 1, and the subgoals $b(x_2, T)$ and $c(y_2, S)$ are started in parallel again (even if the earlier subgoals $b(x_1, T)$ and $c(y_1, S)$ have not finished). The two b subgoals and two c subgoals may return solutions in any order. The arc relations in Figure 1 show a possible sequence in which the solutions arrive.

Notice that the node-relation associated with a node k is a relational join of all the arc-relations for the parallel arcs incident on node k. Whenever a solution tuple is inserted in an arc-relation of an arc A incident on node k, (a singleton relation with) this tuple is then joined with tuples in arc-relations of all arcs parallel to A and incident of k, to generate new tuples for node-relation k. In the example, when the solution (y_1, s_2) for subgoal c arrives, the tuple $[x_1, y_1, -, s_2]$ is inserted in R_c. A join of this tuple with relation R_b is computed, and tuples $[x_1, y_1, t_1, s_2]$ and $[x_1, y_1, t_2, s_2]$ resulting from successful join operations are inserted in R_2.

Since the last node of a DJG has no outgoing arcs, the tuple inserted here becomes a solution to the clause. The DJG for a fact is a single node (with no arcs). So, should unification between a goal G and a fact be successful, the resulting tuple is a solution for G.

In this simple example, all the subgoals in the rule for $p(X, S)$ are facts. In general, whenever a subgoal unifies with the head of a non-fact clause C, the DJG for C is used to generate other subgoals recursively. With that in mind, different forms of parallelism exploited by ROPM can be demonstrated with this simple example. When $a(X, Y)$ is fired, multiple clauses that match it may start looking for solutions to $a(X, Y)$ in parallel. This represents a simple form of OR parallelism. Full OR parallelism, that is exploited by a purely OR parallel scheme, includes a few other forms. For example, $a(X, Y)$ may return one solution, leading to the firing of an instance each of $b(X, T)$ and $c(Y, S)$ which can be executed in parallel with exploration of further solutions to $a(X, Y)$. More importantly, when the second solution to $a(X, Y)$ arrives, it leads to firing of two new instances of $b(X, T)$ and $c(Y, T)$, which execute in parallel with the b and c instances fired earlier. This last source of parallelism is called *consumer instance* parallelism and distinguishes ROPM from many other AND/OR schemes. Epilog [Wise86b] and the combined AND-OR model [Gupt89a] are notable exceptions. In addition to OR parallelism, AND parallelism is exploited by firing literals on two or more arcs of a DJG (b and c parallelism) whenever they are known to be independent at compile time[3].

Messages are used to represent new goals and responses to goals. The execution proceeds in a coarse grained *data-flow* style as follows. At every level in the problem space, the process model decomposes the problem at that level into subproblems that are represented by messages. An underlying kernel called the *Chare Kernel* [Kale90a],[Fent91a] is responsible for maintaining a pool of messages and of scheduling the messages across processors. When a processor is free, the *Chare Kernel* supplies a message M to it for

---

[3] Our model permits the exploitation of *non-strict* AND independence as defined by Hermenegildo in [Herm89b], where two or more literals in a clause body are AND independent if, for every variable V shared between them, at most one literal can bind V.

execution. M may be a message representing an instance of a body literal L (called a *goal* message) to be evaluated, or a *response* to L. The evaluation of M may result in the creation of more goal messages, or may produce one or more responses for M's parent process. Further details of the implementation can be found in [Ramk90a],[Ramk91a].

3 THE BINDING ENVIRONMENT

The binding environment described in this section is one of the first schemes supporting both AND and OR parallelism to be implemented on shared and non-shared memory multiprocessors. It has points of similarity with Conery's *closed environments* [Cone87b] scheme. In this section, we describe our scheme with emphasis on its differences from Conery's approach.

The unification scheme described here uses an idea similar to the importation and exportation of variables proposed by Lindstrom [Lind84a]. Crammond's experiments [Cram85a] show that this scheme is comparable in efficiency to the hash windows [Borg84a] approach and the directory trees [Ciep84a] approach. In Lindstrom's scheme, however, it is necessary to follow pointers through stack frames to dereference a term. This makes it difficult to implement it on a non-shared memory machine. In addition, the scheme as proposed in [Lind84a] handles only OR parallelism. We use the idea of importing and exporting variables but adapt it to handle both AND and OR parallelism. We also render it suitable for non-shared machines. Furthermore, it is not necessary in our scheme to have explicit import and export vectors as is required in Lindstrom's approach. In the following sections, we describe our binding scheme, and then discuss the differences between the two schemes.

3.1 Term Representation

A *goal term* is identified by a literal and a *current binding-environment tuple* (henceforth referred to as simply *tuple*). A literal comprises a functor followed by a list of (zero or more) terms. Each term may be a variable, an integer, a real, an atom (functor with arity 0) or a functor followed by a sequence of (sub)terms.

All terms and tuples are stored in a data area called *term space* which is a large contiguous collection of *slots*. Each slot contains a tag and one or more fields associated with the tag. A compound-term of arity n is stored in $n+1$ contiguous slots, where the zeroth slot identifies the functor (see Figure 2(a)) and slots 1-n contain subterms or references to subterms. As an optimising measure, the $n'th$ subterm is not referred to but is stored in place whenever possible (Figure 2(a)). Variables in a term are represented by indices to its associated tuple. All tuple indices occurring in the subterms also refer to the term's current tuple. Subterms may be referred to by absolute addresses, an index into *term space*, a relative index or as a bound variable (through a tuple). Some of the tags and the corresponding fields are listed in Figure 2(b).

A tuple is a contiguous sequence of slots. Its length is initially determined by the number of variables present in the clause. However, a tuple can be extended by the subgoals in the clause body and may therefore grow during the execution of the clause. Each slot can be tagged as *unbound*, bound to a term, or bound to another *tuple slot*. Figure 2(a) illustrates the term representation.

```
              X   Y   Z
    tuple: |   | - | 4 |        | g/2 | d | h/2 | b | $2 |
```

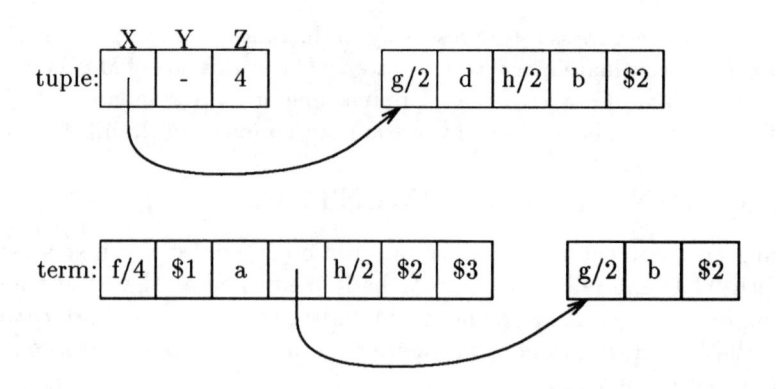

```
    term: | f/4 | $1 | a |   | h/2 | $2 | $3 |       | g/2 | b | $2 |
```

(a): Term Representation for f(X, a, g(b,Y), h(Y,Z)) where X is bound to g(d, h(b, Y)), Y is unbound and Z is bound to the integer 4. "$" is used to indicate a tuple index and "-" to indicate an unbound variable.

TAG	SLOT FIELDS
ATOM	pointer to sym. table, arity 0
CLOSED TERM	pointer to sym. table, arity
PURE CLOSED TERM	pointer to sym. table from program, arity
FUNCTOR	pointer to sym. table, arity
PURE FUNCTOR	pointer to sym. table from program, arity
INTEGER	integer
MOLECULE	pointer to a molecule
ABSOLUTE ADDRESS	pointer to a term
ABSOLUTE ADDRESS-2	pointer to a term that is to be interpreted in the *other* tuple's context
TUPLE INDEX	offset (from base of current tuple)
TUPLE INDEX-2	offset (from base of *other* tuple)
PURE CODE INDEX	offset (from base of pure code)

(b): Some tags and their interpretation

Figure 2: Tagged representation of terms.

3.2 The Unification Algorithm

The binding environment is described here with the help of the example in Figure 3. In the context of the Reduce-OR process model, a processor is assumed to have chosen for execution a goal spawned by a Reduce process. This goal is unified with all clause heads bearing the same predicate name and DJGs are created for all matching clauses as described in Section 2. The unification process is described below. The algorithm for combining bindings from AND parallel branches in a clause is described in Section 3.2.2.

Query:
  ?- Z = g(c), f(X,k(Y,a), g(Z)).

Clauses:
  f(h(A,c),B,C) :- p(A,C), q(B).
  p(g(h(E,F)),G).
  q(k(g(E),a)).

Data Join Graph for f(h(A,c),B,C):

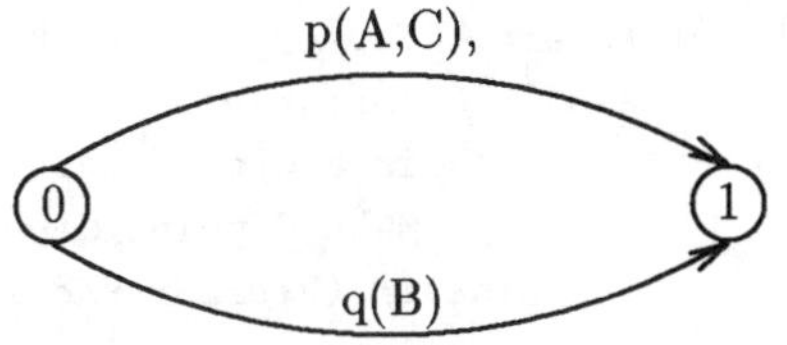

p(A,C),

(0) ⇄ (1)

q(B)

Figure 3: An example and its corresponding Data Join Graph.

3.2.1 Two-Phase Unification: When a goal matches a clause head, the goal and its tuple (called the *parent* tuple) and the clause head and its tuple (called the *child* tuple) are sent to the unification module. The treatment of facts and rules is slightly different. For facts, the procedure is quite simple and is discussed later. We first consider the algorithm for rules.

As in Conery's scheme, unification is implemented as a two phase operation. The first phase decides if the unification is successful, and if so, sets up the pointers between the tuples for the two terms being unified. The second phase *closes* the child's environment with respect to the parent's environment.

Our definition of *close* differs from that proposed by Conery [Cone87b]. Conery defines a *closed environment* to be a set of frames E such that no pointers or links originating in E refer to slots in frames that are not members of E. Our definition, however, permits pointers or links originating in E to refer to terms residing *outside* E in certain special cases. The justification for this choice of definition is provided below.

This difference in the definition of *close*, in conjunction with the use of tags in the term representation, permits several optimisations in the unification algorithm. In the *CloseTuple* phase, it may be necessary to copy terms to close one environment with respect to the other. However, it is not necessary to copy ground terms; they may be shared. Hence, among the tags for functors, a distinction is drawn between ground and nonground terms. In addition, ground terms themselves have two representations. The functor of a term is tagged as a *closed term* if all its subterms are bound and contain no references to tuples. For example, f(a,g(c)) is a closed term but f(a,$3) with $3 bound to g(c) is not. A ground term with tuple references (once recognised) is represented by a *molecule*[4]. A molecule is a pair of pointers that point to a term and a tuple (similar to molecules used in structure sharing implementations of sequential Prolog). To create a molecule, it is necessary to scan the term once to determine whether the term is ground. However, once the molecule has been created, the term is *known* to be ground. Hence, during subsequent unifications done in the same address space, molecules save additional scans through terms they point to. A goal that contains molecules may be shared by all the processes in a shared memory environment. On message passing machines, when they are sent across a processor boundary into a

---
[4] Note that this is a more restricted use of molecules than in standard structure sharing. Molecules are used here only when the term they point to are *known* to be ground.

```
PROCEDURE UnifyPhaseI(Rterm, RTuple, Cterm, CTuple, RtermGround) returns BOOLEAN
Deref [CTerm, CTuple] to get [C, CTuple']
Deref [RTerm, RTuple] to get [R, RTuple']
    Case C is variable:
        If R is a closed term
            Make C point directly to R; Tag T as CLOSED TERM
        Else if (RtermGround = TRUE)
            Create a molecule M = [R, RTuple']
            Make C point to Molecule M; Tag T as MOLECULE
        Else if R is an integer or atom
            Set C = R; Tag(C) = Tag(R)
        Else if R is a non-closed sub-term
            Make C point to R; Tag C as ABSOLUTE ADDRESS 2
        Else if R is a variable
            Set R to index of C in CTuple'; Tag R as TUPLE INDEX 2
        Else return FALSE
    Case R is a variable:
        :
        :
END UnifyPhaseI
```

Figure 4: Phase I of unification.

---

different address space, they are copied as closed terms. It is self-evident that the use of structure sharing and tags are instrumental in making these optimisations possible.

The first phase of unification proceeds along conventional lines (see Figure 4) except for the handling of ground terms. When a variable is unified with a closed term or a molecule, the variable points to it directly (using the ABSOLUTE ADDRESS tag in Figure 2(b)). When a variable is unified with a subterm T of a term that has been referenced through a molecule, the variable is bound to a new molecule that points to T and its corresponding tuple. No additional scanning or copying needs to be done in phase two, since T is *known* to be ground.

In the two <term, tuple> pairs being unified, a variable in one tuple may be bound to an unbound variable in the *other* tuple, or to a subterm that contains a reference to a variable in the *other* tuple. Tags are used to disambiguate this situation from one in which the context for the two "items" being bound is the same. These tags exist after the first phase of unification and are eliminated during the second phase (the close tuple phase) in the tuple being closed. In Figure 2(b) they are called TUPLE INDEX-2 and ABSOLUTE ADDRESS-2. When two unbound variables belonging to two different tuples are bound, the binding is represented as a pointer oriented from the parent tuple to the child tuple. However, if both variables belong to the same tuple, the orientation is arbitrary. Figures 5(a) and 5(b) show the state of the unification before and after phase I for the example described in Figure 3.

The second phase uses the *CloseTuple* algorithm (see Figure 6) to close the child tuple (a): Before unification.

(b): After phase one of unification.

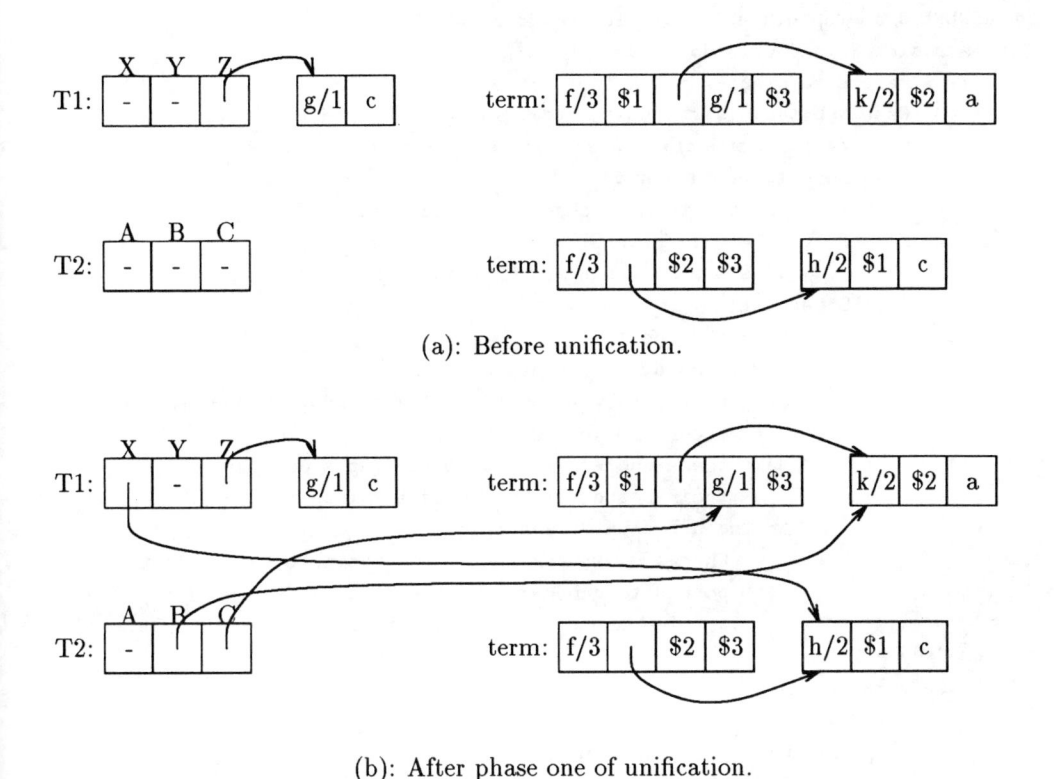

Figure 5: The bindings after Phase I of unification between f(X,k(Y,a),g(Z)) where X and Y are unbound and Z is bound to g(c), and f(h(A,c),B,C) where A, B and C are unbound.

---

with respect to the parent tuple. The child tuple may have references to terms that need to be interpreted in the context of the parent tuple. Every such term T is scanned to determine whether the term is ground or not. If T is ground, a molecule is created to point to the term and the parent tuple. For nonground terms, for every unbound variable in the parent tuple referenced by T, a new variable (slot) is created in the child tuple. These nonground terms are then copied and any references (tuple indices) to variables in the parent tuple that remain unbound *after* the first phase of unification are changed to references to their corresponding newly created variables of the child tuple. In addition, each reference to a variable of the parent tuple *bound to an unbound variable* of the child tuple, is replaced by a direct reference to the corresponding variable of the child tuple. For example, in Figure 5(b), the variable B in tuple T2, is bound to $k(Y, a)$ after the first phase of unification. Since Y is unbound, a new variable D is created in T2 to represent Y, and $k(Y, a)$ is copied as $k(D, A)$. This closes the child tuple with respect to the parent tuple, i.e. eliminates all references from the child to the parent. Figures 5(b) and 7(a) describe the state of the unification before and after the second phase. Figure 7(b) shows the use of a molecule for closing tuples that avoids copying as is shown in Figure 7(a).

```
PROCEDURE CloseTuple(RTuple, CTuple) returns TUPLE
For each slot S in CTuple do
    If S refers to a sub-term in the ''other'' term
        Case sub-term is variable, atom, integer, closed term:
            /* taken care of in Phase I, so this case does not arise */
        Case non-closed sub-term:
            Traverse the term to check if it is ground
            If the term is ground:
                Create a molecule and have it point to the term and Rtuple.
            Otherwise:
                Copy the sub-term
                Make S point to the new copy.
                Extend Ctuple by the number of distinct unbound variables
                    occurring in the sub-term.
                Make these unbound variables in Rtuple point to
                    their respective newly added slots in Ctuple.
                In the new copy of sub-term:
                    Change every reference to a variable in Rtuple that
                    points to unbound variable slot in Ctuple to
                    a reference to the corresponding slots in Ctuple.
return Ctuple
END CloseTuple
```

Figure 6: Phase II of unification – The Close Tuple Algorithm.

3.2.2 The Join Algorithm: When two or more branches meet in the DJG, the partial solutions coming from the parallel branches need to be combined. In Conery's AND/OR process model, at any point in time only one solution on each branch is available for the join operation. Should this set of partial solutions fail to produce a solution for the entire clause, backtracking (in the form of a "redo" message) is used to obtain other solutions for the AND parallel branches. The join can be accomplished using the *Close* algorithm as follows. When the AND parallel subgoals are encountered, only *one* tuple R is active and can be used to spawn these subgoals. Subsequently, when the solutions from the AND parallel subgoals arrive, R can be closed with each of these solutions in sequence. This is possible because R *must* be the common ancestor tuple for all the arrived AND parallel solutions by virtue of the fact that it was the only tuple active when the AND parallel subgoals were spawned. In addition, the closing of R with each of the AND parallel solutions in sequence may produce at most one active "joined tuple", since only one solution on any AND parallel branch may be active. This algorithm is not as simple as it appears; it requires additional bookkeeping in order to correctly handle variables imported from other clause instances, especially in the presence of backtracking over the AND parallel branches due to failure. At the time of writing of this chapter, we do not know of any description of this algorithm in the literature.

In the presence of *consumer instance* parallelism, the join algorithm becomes more

THE REDUCE-OR PROCESS MODEL

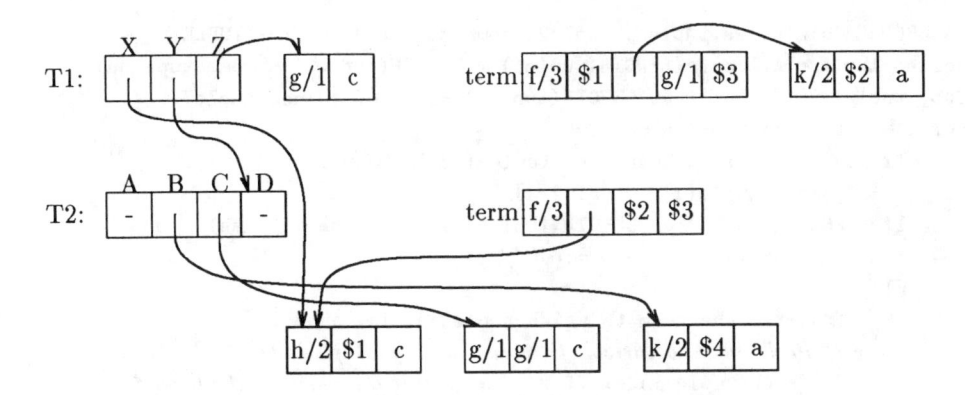

(a): After phase two of unification – without molecules.

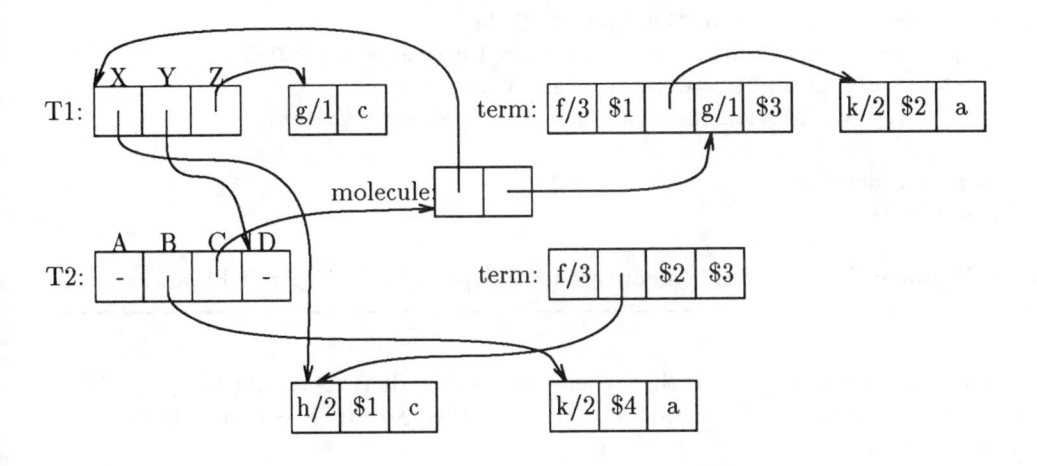

(b): After phase two of unification – with molecules.

Figure 7: Phase II of unification between f(X,k(Y,a),g(Z)) where X and Y are unbound and Z is bound to g(c), and f(h(A,c),B,C) where A, B and C are unbound.

---

complex. There may be several solutions at each AND parallel branch that need to be joined. These solutions can be combined incrementally as and when they are created (an *incremental* join), or a *full-relational* join can be done once all the solutions have arrived in both the branches. The Reduce-OR process model does an incremental join operation on solution tuples from AND parallel branches. Wise [Wise86b] describes the use of a full relational join in his Epilog process model. An incremental join operation is also used in the PEPSys approach by the ECRC group [West87a]. With either full or incremental join, the *join* can be computed by joining *all* the solution tuples in one parallel arc with *all* the solution tuples in each of the other parallel arcs[5]. However,

---

[5] In databases, a *sort-merge* is used to join relations. It cannot be used incrementally. Also, our join algorithm is more efficient since it is specialised for independent AND parallelism.

```
PROCEDURE JoinTuples(tuple1, tuple2, comm-tup-len) returns TUPLE
joined-tuple = Allocate(LENGTH(tuple1) + LENGTH(tuple2) - comm-tup-len)
Copy tuple1 into the first LENGTH(tuple1) slots of joined-tuple.
For i = 1 to comm-tup-len do
    If (tuple1[i] is unbound and tuple2[i] is bound)
        joined-tuple[i] = tuple2[i]
    If (LENGTH(tuple1) or LENGTH(tuple2) equals comm-tup-len)
        /* no renumbering is required */
    Else
        Traverse the term to which tuple2[i] is bound :
        /* In the term, a variable is represented by a tuple index */
        For each tuple index TI /* representing a variable in the term */ :
            If TI > comm-tup-len
                replace TI with (LENGTH(tuple1) + TI - comm-tup-len)

For i = comm-tup-len + 1 to LENGTH(tuple2) do
    joined-tuple[LENGTH(tuple1) + i - comm-tup-len] = tuple2[i]
    if a tuple index TI > comm-tup-len is encountered
        replace TI with (LENGTH(tuple1) + TI - comm-tup-len)

return joined-tuple
END JoinTuples
```

Figure 8: The Join Tuple algorithm for independent AND parallel branches.

---

such a 'comprehensive' join of this type is an overkill. It is clear that the join of two solution tuples will fail if a common variable in the two tuples is bound to different values.

So long as one is confined to independent AND parallelism, combining two solutions from different AND parallel branches may appear simple. As the two sides produce bindings for distinct variables, simply combining the two partial solutions appears sufficient. However, this operation is complicated by the fact that one or more of the partial solution tuples may have imported new variables in the course of being evaluated. These new variables are referred to using tuple indices only. If both branches have imported new variables, at least two distinct new variables (one from each branch) have the same tuple index. It is therefore necessary to assign distinct indices to such variables.

An algorithm for joining two solution tuples, each solution from a different parallel arc, is described in Figure 8. It assumes independence of AND parallel subgoals, and is called repeatedly to accomplish the join operation. The main operation performed in the algorithm is the extension of the partial solution tuple and a consequent possible renumbering of tuple indices. In the example being considered, suppose a solution tuple each for the subgoals p and q has arrived and is to be joined. Figure 9(a) shows two such possible solution tuples. One solution for p has the variable A bound to $g(h(E, F))$ where E and F are unbound. A solution for q has the variable D bound to (a): Two solution tuples, one for p and one for q being joined. The dotted tuple and term is the reference tuple to which a molecule points to. C was bound to this molecule before p and q were started.

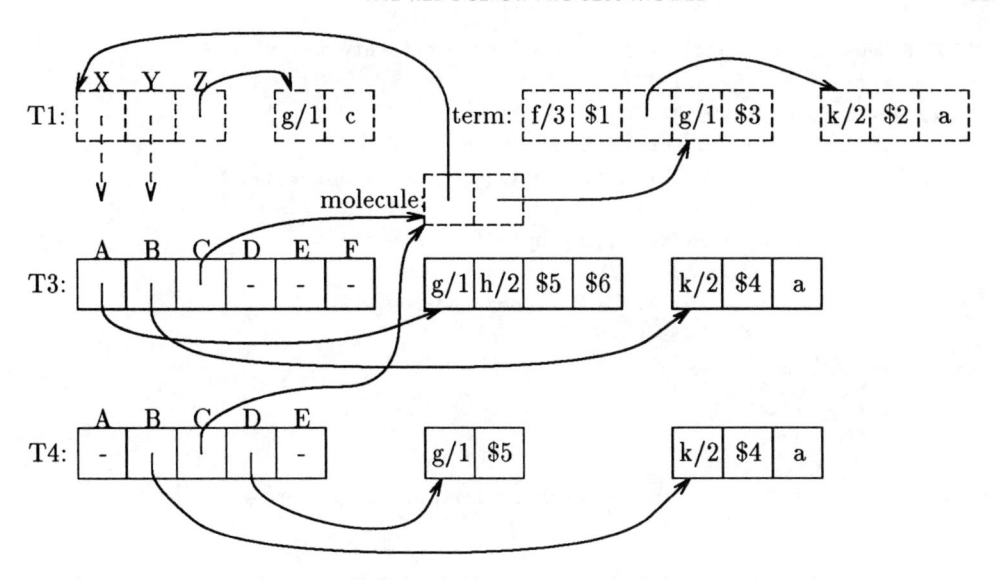

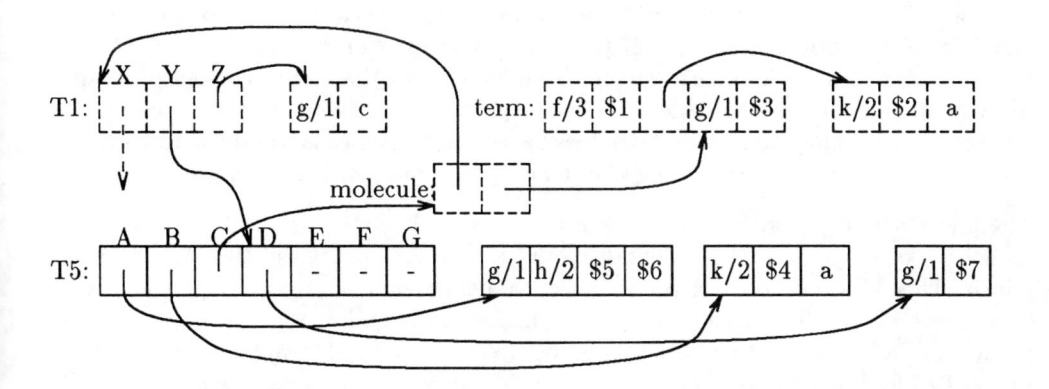

(b): The resulting tuple after the tuples in Figure 9(a) were joined.

Figure 9: The join of two tuples.

$g(E)$ where E is unbound. Note that the variable E being referred to is different in the two solutions. The dotted tuple (and term) is the parent tuple (and term) to which a molecule pointed following head unification. Figure 9(b) shows the state of the tuples after the join operation.

The comm-tup-len field passed to the *JoinTuple* procedure is the length of the partial solution tuple before the parallel AND branches were forked. At first glance, this field may appear unnecessary. A simple algorithm to join two tuples T_1 and T_2 in AND

```
PROCEDURE CommTupLen(tuple1, tuple2, original-len) returns INTEGER
    comm-tup-len = original-len
    For i = 1 to comm-tup-len do
        If tuple1[i] and tuple2[i] are both bound
            If (NOT Consistent(tuple1[i], tuple1, tuple2[i], tuple2))
                return "join failed"
        Traverse the term to which tuple1[i] is bound:
            If a tuple index TI is encountered,
                comm-tup-len = MAX(comm-tup-len, TI)
                /* Do not traverse TI further */
return comm-tup-len

END CommTupLen
```

Figure 10: An algorithm to compute the common tuple length for two tuples that need to be joined.

---

parallel branches would be to copy into the node-relation (into tuple T_n) whichever response tuple comes first (say T_1). Now T_n could be closed with T_2 when it arrives, using the algorithm in Figure 6. This may seem to work without using the comm-tup-len field, but it does not if consumer instance parallelism is to be exploited. For example, if T_1 extends the original tuple length by 2, and T_2 extends it by 3, the tuple resulting from the join of T_1 and T_2 must extend the comm-tup-len by 5 and must renumber the new variables in T_2 (or T_1). To recognise this, it is necessary to restrict the *close* operation to the variables present in the tuple *before* the parallel AND branches were forked. This can only be done if the comm-tup-len is known.

The above simple algorithm will work for Conery's scheme for the AND/OR process model by keeping track of the length of the ancestor tuple of the two tuples being joined. This does not pose a problem since, as mentioned before, at any point in time only one AND parallel solution on each branch is active and in the AND/OR process model, the AND parallel solutions *must* be descendants of the same ancestor tuple. In the Reduce-OR process model, since several tuples may be active when the AND parallel subgoals are spawned, it is incorrect to assume that the two tuples being joined are descendants of the same common ancestor tuple.

In the example in Figure 9, the comm-tup-len field is 4: the length of the tuple before p and q were initiated. Given p and q, this length must first be determined. A naive approach is to start with the number of variables in the original clause, (0 in the example being considered) and compute the common tuple length as described in Figure 10. This algorithm works for any arbitrary DJGs, but only with the assumption that the parallel AND subgoals are independent. An "optimized" join algorithm, described in [Kale87a], is employed in ROLOG developed using this binding scheme. This algorithm necessitates the use of some compile time analysis to determine common ancestors for the various join nodes in a DJG. This information is used with some run time bookkeeping to maintain *back pointers* to common ancestor tuples at the join arcs,

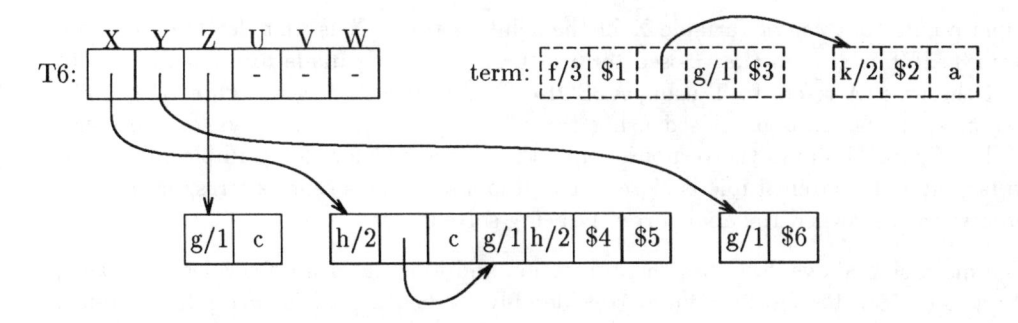

Figure 11: The response created after the parent tuple T1 is closed with respect to the solution tuple T5 in Figure 9(b).

---

and *forward pointers* at the common ancestor tuples to access the tuples that need to be joined at the join node(s). Details of the implementation of the optimised join algorithm can be found in [Ramk91a].

The algorithm in Figure 10 includes a consistency check which appears redundant. The following argument justifies its presence: Consider the case where both tuple1[i] and tuple2[i] are bound and i is in the range 1...comm-tup-len. If tuple1 and tuple2 have a common ancestor tuple, they must be bound to the same term since the same variable cannot be bound in the two parallel AND branches, which means that this variable must have been bound *before* the two branches were forked. If however, tuple1 and tuple2 do not share a common ancestor, then the above argument is not valid. This is best seen with an example:

```
c(1).     c(2).        e(1,5).    f(2,7).
?- c(Y), e(Y,Z), f(Y,T).
```

where subgoals e and f are executed in parallel after c returns a binding for Y. The solution tuple $\{Y = 1, Z = 5\}$ for e and the solution tuple $\{Y = 2, T = 7\}$ for f do *not* share a common ancestor. But Y is bound in both tuples. Without the check, the join will succeed and produce a response whereas it should have failed. (If the lowest common ancestor optimisation is used, two tuples are not even considered for join unless they share a common ancestor.)

For ease of description, only successful branches in the search tree are discussed here. In our scheme, since no backtracking is performed in ROPM, failure handling and termination is only important from the viewpoint of garbage collection. Termination detection is outside the scope of this chapter and can be found in [Ramk91a].

A tuple being inserted in the last node relation indicates that a solution to all the literals has been found. A copy of the parent tuple (T1 in Figure 5(b)) is closed with respect to this solution tuple (T5 in Figure 9(b)) thus eliminating pointers from the parent tuple to the solution tuple and incorporating the solution produced by the tuple. This is done as follows: First, the links from *unbound* variables in the parent tuple to unbound variables in the solution tuple are reversed. Also, if a variable A in the parent tuple points to a *bound* variable X in the solution tuple, X is first dereferenced to a term T. If T is ground (i.e. closed term or molecule), A is made to point directly to T. Otherwise, A refers to T using ABSOLUTE ADDRESS-2 (see Figure 2(b)). The parent tuple can now be closed using the *CloseTuple* algorithm to yield a response tuple. Figure 11 shows the response tuple that is created for the example considered so far, after the parent tuple is closed. The response tuple is sent as a response to the process that spawned the goal currently being solved.

The discussion above describes the unification and join algorithm for rules. For facts, the process can be short-circuited considerably. When a goal is successfully unified with a fact in the first phase of unification, the binding tuple for the goal is closed with respect to the binding tuple for the matching fact. This tuple is sent off as a response as before.

The join operation is described here in the context of the Reduce-OR process model. However, it must be emphasised that a join operation is necessary for all parallel process models for logic programs that exploit both AND and OR (*including* consumer instance) parallelism.

3.3 Comparison with Conery's Closed Environments

One of the major differences between our scheme and the closed environments scheme is a direct consequence of our use of structure sharing. Consider a simple *append* program, where two ground lists of size n and and m have to be appended. Consider the top level goal and its associated tuple. In Conery's scheme, since structure copying is used, at the call site before unification an instance of each of the two lists is constructed (and loaded into registers using *put* instructions). This cost of term construction is not incurred in our scheme. Moreover, Conery's scheme pays this cost even if unification fails.

Another significant difference is in the use of tags, which permit several optimisations to our (and Conery's) scheme. Some of the principal optimisations discussed above include the use of molecules and closed terms, notably absent in Conery's scheme. Closed terms in the input program are easily identified during parsing and obviate the need to scan terms to check whether there are unbound variables present. Closed terms can also be constructed dynamically using techniques similar to those proposed by DeGroot [DeGr84a]. While closing a tuple, no additional scanning and copying needs to be done if a variable is bound to a closed term in phase one. Molecules identify ground but nonclosed terms and save future scans to check for unbound variables. Consider the simple *append* program mentioned earlier, where two ground lists of size m and n are to be appended. Without the tags, for each new subgoal the close operation will involve copying the two lists in the current subgoal (this takes $O(n + m)$ time. Overall, n new subgoals are created to execute the program, thus leading to $O(n^2 + nm)$ time to execute the program. Using molecules, however, our algorithm reduces the execution time to $O(n+m)$ if the program is run on the same processor, or on a shared memory multiprocessor. This is because both input lists are ground terms, and for every subgoal, molecules obviate the need for copying (and scanning). Recognising ground terms and creating molecules for them at the first call takes $O(n + m)$ time. However, every subsequent unification takes constant time. This initial scan is avoided when *append* is a top level goal because the input lists are now closed terms. The execution time is now $O(n)$ since *every* unification takes constant time.

To a lesser extent, the use of these tags permits a similar reduction in execution time on non-shared memory multiprocessors as well. On most non-shared memory machines, it is necessary to send data from one processor to another in a contiguous buffer. Therefore, for data that is to be shipped off to another processor, it is necessary to pay the extra overhead of *packing* it into a contiguous buffer, and correspondingly, *unpacking* it at the destination processor. Due to this increased cost, an effort is made to keep all processors busy while leaving goals local to their processors as far as possible. For a reasonably large problem, a significant fraction of the goals are not sent out. This is because once the available processors are each given a node in the search tree to work on, to a large extent, the subtrees rooted at their respective nodes remain local to their corresponding processors. Thus, the cost of copying is only incurred for goals or responses that are actually sent off to other processors. The savings due to this optimisation are significant, since, for large programs, a sizeable proportion of goals are kept local to the processor they are created on. This optimisation is not done in Conery's scheme as discussed in [Cone87b],[Cone88a].

As mentioned in Section 2, an underlying kernel called the *Chare Kernel* is responsible for maintaining a pool of messages, load-balancing the messages between available processors and scheduling the available messages. The load-balancing strategy used by the kernel is called *adaptive-contracting-within-neighbourhood* (ACWN) [Kale87c]. Briefly, the system is deemed to be in *idle* state, *normal* state, or in *saturated* state based on pre-determined thresholds. For each processor, a *neighbourhood* of processors is defined for load-balancing purposes. A processor exchanges load information with other processors in its neighbourhood. In idle state, a message M is distributed, at random, to processors *outside* the neighbourhood of the processor on which M is created. In *normal* state, messages are load-balanced *within* the creating processor's neighbourhood. In the *saturated* state, all messages are kept local to the processor they are created on.

The structure sharing approach also permits a reduction in the amount of packing necessary. During initialisation, every processor is provided with a local copy of the skeletal (*pure*) code of the Prolog program. Now, when a goal is packed, any terms appearing in the *pure* code are simply sent as tagged indices (TERM SPACE INDEX in Figure 2(b)) into a pure code array. These indices are dereferenced to the same terms using the local copy of the pure code at the destination processor. An additional advantage stems from the tagged representation. If a goal is to be packed for shipping off to another processor, all terms referred through molecules are copied as closed terms, thus optimizing further accesses to such terms.

The copying of terms and the associated renumbering of embedded logical variables from other clause instances variables is a major source of overhead in Conery's scheme. Consider the term $k(Y, a)$ in the literal f of the query in Figure 3. $k(Y, a)$ is first constructed (in registers) by the AND process for the query and then copied as $k(Y', a)$ during the close phase of forward unification by the OR process created for f. Y' represents Y in the child environment. This copy is made available to the AND process created for the body of the clause for f. $k(Y', a)$ is loaded into registers before an OR process is created for q. The OR process for q first constructs the term $k(g(E), a)$ occurring in the head of the fact q during forward unification. It then constructs a new term $k(g(E), a)$ during the close phase of forward unification. A newly instantiated term $g(E')$ is constructed during the close operation of back unification, thereby renumbering E as E' in the context of the reference tuple for the OR process for q. These bindings are then sent to the AND process for the body of clause f. This AND process makes another copy of $k(g(E'),a)$ in order to renumber E' as E'' in the context of *its* current environment. This copy, $k(g(E''),a)$, is sent to the OR process for f which makes yet another copy of $k(g(E''),a)$ into registers and sends $k(g(E'''),a)$ to the AND process for the query. Finally, the query makes a copy of $k(g(E'''),a)$ to produce $k(g(E^{(iv)}),a)$ when its environment containing the local variable Y is closed during back unification. If Conery's scheme were to exploit AND parallelism, the join of the AND parallel solution would require yet more copying since further renumbering of variable indices in the AND parallel solutions is involved.

In contrast, in our scheme, when $f(X,k(Y,a),g(Z))$ and $f(h(A,c),B,C)$ are unified, $k(Y,a)$ is copied once in the close phase. This copy is made available to the OR process for $q(B)$. During back unification between $q(B)$ and the fact for q, the subterm $g(E)$ is copied (and renumbered) in the context of the environment tuple for the clause f. This copy of $g(E)$ is used in the join of the solutions of p and q and may need to be copied for renumbering reasons. (Note: This copy for renumbering is *not* necessary if p and q are not evaluated in parallel.). Finally, $g(E)$ is copied during the back unification between $f(X,k(Y,a),g(Z))$ and $f(h(A,c),B,C)$ to renumber the embedded variable E in the context of the query environment. Note that, unlike Conery's scheme, only one copy of $k(Y,a)$ is made during the initial forward unification; all other copies made are of $g(E)$.

In addition to the copying described above, both schemes incur the cost of *packing* goals before shipping them off to other processors for evaluation.

Another important difference is in the handling of the join of AND parallel solutions. The different phases in Conery's unification algorithm in a compiled context are described in [Cone88a]; neither the algorithm in [Cone87b] or the algorithm in [Cone88a] exploit AND-parallelism. However, as mentioned earlier, it is possible to use the *close* operation to join solutions from AND parallel branches in his scheme. In order to deal with embedded logical variables imported from the AND parallel branches during backward execution, it is necessary to trail additional information and modify the backward execution algorithm appropriately. Since the order of backtracking is statically determined, it cannot be assumed that it is the reverse of the arrival order of AND parallel solutions. This, in turn, implies even more copying of terms for renumbering of variable indices during backtracking.

Furthermore, Conery's scheme is clearly inadequate if consumer instance parallelism is to be exploited, since an implicit assumption of the scheme is that only one solution on each AND parallel branch is active at any time. By contrast, the join algorithm described in this chapter addresses the problem of handling multiple solutions on the AND parallel branches, thus making it possible to exploit consumer instance parallelism. The Reduce-OR process model is also capable of handling arbitrarily complex DJGs. Furthermore, the join algorithm described above works in the presence of arbitrarily complex DJGs. On the other hand, it is unclear how the close algorithm can be used for joining AND parallel solutions in Conery's scheme if arbitrarily complex data dependency graphs are permitted.

4 COMPILED EXECUTION

We now briefly describe how this model and this binding environment has been implemented in ROLOG. It was necessary to design an abstract machine specifically for this purpose which was quite different from the Warren Abstract Machine [Warr77a]. The primary reasons for this are differences in the execution model and the binding environment.

We limit the discussion of the abstract machine instructions here to those relating to the process model and the binding environment. A more detailed discussion of the abstract machine can be found in [Ramk91a].

4.1 The Process Model

In Section 2, we mentioned that the ROLOG compiler has been written using an underlying kernel (called the *Chare Kernel* that is responsible for maintaining a pool of messages. The role of the compiler is to create messages representing work to the kernel. The kernel then will processes the messages in its pool in turn.

Initially, a *new-goal* message is created for the top level goal (query) and put in the work pool. The entry point for the top level goal is supplied in the code in a predetermined location. One of two instructions – *GetFactEnv* and *GetClauseEnv*, sets up the parent and child environment registers for unification with the corresponding fact or clause head respectively. This also involves creating a tuple of the required length for the clause. Upon successful unification, a *CreateNewQuery* instruction creates the necessary run time data structures that represent the DJG for the clause, and subgoals in the body of the clause may be fired using *FireArc* instructions. A *FireArc* instruction creates a *new-goal* message to solve a subgoal (see Figure 12). The *FireArc* instruction supplies each *new-goal* message with a goal entry point - the entry point in the code for the newly created *goal* and a response entry point - i.e. the entry point for one or more *responses* from the newly created subgoal. The *FireArc* instruction is somewhat similar to the *call* instruction in the WAM. However, unlike the WAM, no *put* instructions need to be generated prior to a *FireArc* (due to structure sharing). All parallel arcs emanating from the "current" node (see Section 2) are fired, following which the *goal* suspends via a *Suspend* instruction and returns control to the *Chare Kernel*.

In Figure 12, we provide the code generated for the following *hanoi* program. The "&&" annotation is used to denote that the two subgoals are to be solved in parallel.

```
hanoi(1,From,Aux,To,[mv(From,To)]).
hanoi(N,From,Aux,To,[Offmvs,mv(From,To),Onmvs]) :- N > 1, N1 is N - 1,
        (hanoi(N1,From,To,Aux,Offmvs) && hanoi(N1,Aux,From,To,Onmvs)).
```

Code is generated to execute builtins (we consider only deterministic and small grained builtins here) in-line, since the overhead of creating *goals* and processing responses for such small granules of work is clearly unwarranted. Thus, the query is traversed, executing builtins in-line successively, until a nonbuiltin is encountered. This can be seen in lines 42-44 in Figure 12, for the *hanoi* program, where the ">" and "IS" builtins are executed in-line. Upon successful unification, code for the builtins is generated in-line, and a later node (i.e. not necessarily node 0) may possibly generate a *FireArc* for

```
---- Byte Code Disassembly ----
1    GetFactEnv      *ptr*, 3              /* set up env. (3 vars)
                :                             for unification         */
15   SendFactResp                          /* send soln. as response  */
16   GetClauseEnv    *ptr*, 7              /* setup clause env- 7 vars */
17   InitCTuple      slots=7
18   AllocateBlock   3                     /* for strcts, nest level 3 */
19   Unify1stVar     $1,fail=51
                :                          /* unify vars N,From,Aux,To */
22   Unify1stVar     $4,fail=51
23   UnifyStrct      nextArg=36,fail=51 /* [                         */
24   Unify1stVar     $5,fail=51            /*   Offmvs,               */
25   UnifyStrct      nextArg=35,fail=51 /*   [                       */
26   UnifyStrct      nextArg=30,fail=51 /*     mv(                   */
27   UnifyVar        $2,fail=51            /*       From,             */
28   UnifyVar        $4,fail=51            /*       To                */
29   PopStack                              /*     ),                  */
30   UnifyStrct      nextArg=34,fail=51 /*     [                     */
31   Unify1stVar     $6,fail=51            /*       Onmvs,            */
32   UnifyAtom       40c1ec, fail=51       /*       []                */
33   PopStack                              /*     ]                   */
34   PopStack                              /*   ]                     */
35   PopStack                              /* ]                       */
36   CloseCVar       $1
                :                          /* close variables in      */
41   CloseCVar       $6                    /*   clause head           */
42   GTVarInt        $1, 1, fail = 51
43   CopyVartoAcc    $1, 0                 /* do builtins in line     */
44   SubIntFromAcc   1, 0
45   ISVarAcc        $7, fail = 51
46   SetUpNodeTuple  2, 0, 2
47   CreateNewQuery  num_nodes=4,num_arcs=4,query_size=136
                                           /* create DJG for query    */
48   FireArc         goalE=1,respE=53,hanoi(...) /* fire subgoals     */
49   FireArc         goalE=1,respE=60,hanoi(...)
50   Succeed                               /* failure detection code  */
51   SendControlMsg
52   Suspend
53   /*   code for join */
           :
60   /*   code for join */
           :
```

Figure 12: Fragment of code for unification in the *hanoi* program.

a nonbuiltin. Also, all builtins invoked before the first *FireArc* for that query have the same fail address associated with them as for failed unification (see Figure 12). Should any of these builtins fail, the query is considered to have failed. Builtins occurring later in the query (i.e. have a *FireArc* preceding it) have to be treated differently. Should they fail, the current partial solution is discarded.

4.2 Unification

The unification algorithm described in Section 3 was specialised for compiled execution. For forward unification, instructions are generated for unification of the subterms of the head of the clause, much the same way as in the WAM except that the terms do not have to be constructed as in the structure copying scheme. However, once unification succeeds, for non-facts, instructions need to be generated for *closing* the variables in the child tuple. This is in keeping with the second phase of unification (Figure 6). Also, once a solution tuple for a query is generated, the parent (reference) tuple needs to be closed with the solution tuple to create a response. This is done in the *SendFactResp* and *SendClauseResp* instructions respectively.

During forward unification, some optimisations immediately follow due to compiled execution. It is only necessary to close the variables occurring in the head of the clause. Closing *all* tuple variables was unavoidable in the interpretive framework as it was not known which variables were "head" variables and which were not. During back unification, once again, only the variables in the parent tuple that were bound during forward unification need to be closed.

As with the WAM, separate instructions are generated for constants, variables and structures. However, due to structure sharing, structures are handled differently. It is possible that subterms within a structure may be referenced via *molecules*. This would mean that subterms may refer to tuples different from the current tuple. As a consequence, a stack of current tuples needs to be maintained while accessing a structure and its subterms. This poses no problem since the stack can only be as deep as the structure itself and the depth is known at compile time. Therefore, an instruction is generated to allocate space for a stack (*AllocateBlock*[6]) before unification for structures is carried out. Every *UnifyStruct* instruction pushes the current binding tuple address onto the stack. The "current" binding tuple can thus be different for subterms of the structure. Upon stepping out from depth d to a subterm at depth d-1 in the structure, an explicit *PopStack* instruction restores the binding tuple for depth d-1. The code for the *hanoi* program in Figure 12 also illustrates the code generated for structures.

During unification, compilation permits other optimisations that are not possible in interpretive execution. For example, registers can be used to represent the two binding tuples being unified. Should unification be successful, space can be allocated for the tuples. However, the overhead of memory allocation and deallocation is not paid should unification fail. Also, *CloseTuple* can now be performed with the tuple in registers. Since there is conceptually an infinite array of registers (they are currently set at 100), this permits the free growth of the tuple during unification, should any embedded variables present need to be imported.

5 PERFORMANCE

In Tables 1 – 5 we provide performance results on the Intel iPSC/2, Intel i860 and NCUBE 2 hypercubes, and a network of Sun Sparc 1 workstations. In Tables 1, 2, 3 and 5, column 2 gives the total number of messages generated during the execution of

---

[6] The code illustrating this in Figure 12 is not entirely accurate. For efficiency reasons, a fixed size stack is preallocated; the instruction is actually generated only if the block required exceeds that size.

Table 1: Performance of benchmark programs on the Intel iPSC/2.

Progs.	Msgs.	Time/msg	1	% Seq.	4	8	16
Queens1 (8)	386	52 ms	20.1	96%	(3.2)	(4.9)	(9.0)
Queens2 (8)	386	178 ms	68.8	99%	(3.8)	(6.4)	(10.2)
Knight	2050	137 ms	281.0	97%	(3.8)	(7.2)	(11.4)
12-Puzzle	2782	90 ms	250.5	98%	(3.4)	(4.3)	(6.1)
Primes	6144	48 ms	292.3	98%	(3.9)	(7.7)	(14.6)
Houses*20	166	164 ms	27.3	99%	(2.2)	(2.8)	(3.3)
Houses2*20	179	151 ms	27.1	99%	(2.8)	(3.9)	(6.5)
Farmer*100	1005	15 ms	15.2	87%	(1.7)	(2.3)	(3.3)
Farmer2*100	1100	14 ms	15.3	87%	(3.3)	(5.4)	(8.0)
Salt-Mustard	3856	2 ms	7.37	56%	–	(1.6)	(.17)

a program. Column 3 gives the average computation time per message, and column 4 gives the single processor execution time in seconds. Column 5 gives the percentage of time spent in sequential evaluation of a goal during uniprocessor execution. It is discussed later in this section. The remaining columns give speedups of the respective benchmark programs on the specified number of processors respectively. These speedups have been computed relative to the one processor execution time.

Queens1, *Queens2*, *Houses*20*, *Farmer*100* and *Salt-Mustard* are the ECRC benchmarks, also used in [Szer89a], [Ali90a]. "20" and "100" indicate the number of iterations of the problem. The data for *Houses*20* represents the time for 20 iterations. The *Knight* problem is an OR parallel benchmark that tries to find all possible knight's tour in a partially filled 6x6 chessboard. The *12-Puzzle* benchmark is another OR-Parallel benchmark that uses the IDA^* algorithm [Powl89a] to solve an instance of the 12-puzzle. *Pentomino* is a pentomino problem that was written in Prolog based on the ICOT *pentomino* benchmark. It involves fitting a given set of pieces exactly onto a given board. This too is an OR parallel benchmark. All the OR parallel benchmarks were run in all-solutions mode. *Primes* is an AND parallel benchmark that computes the number of primes up to a given limit using divide-and-conquer.

A point to note here is that *Houses*20* and *Farmer*100* were described in [Szer89a] as exhibiting medium and low parallelism respectively. Since the 20 and 100 iterations respectively were AND-independent, they were run in AND parallel as shown below:

```
repeat(0).
repeat(N) :- N > 0, N1 is N-1, ((go, fail) && repeat(N1)).
?- repeat(100). /* 20 for Houses */
```

They can be viewed as AND-OR parallel benchmarks in this light.

The data on these machines show that the *Queens* benchmarks, *Knight* and *Primes*

Table 2: Performance of benchmark programs on the Intel i860.

Progs.	Msgs.	Time/msg	1	% Seq.	4	8	16	32
Queens1(10)	5296	14.4 ms	76.5	98%	(3.9)	(7.1)	(11.0)	(18.2)
Queens2(10)	5296	60.5 ms	320.2	99%	(4.0)	(7.8)	(15.2)	(28.5)
Knight	2050	24.6 ms	50.4	98%	(3.7)	(5.9)	(10.0)	(15.0)
12-Puzzle	2782	16.8 ms	46.7	99%	(2.9)	(4.5)	(6.0)	(7.9)
Primes	6144	8.7 ms	53.5	99%	(3.8)	(7.1)	(13.5)	(19.5)
Houses*20	166	24.1 ms	4.0	99%	(1.6)	(2.4)	(2.7)	(4.6)
Houses2*20	179	22.3 ms	4.0	99%	(2.7)	(3.7)	(4.7)	(6.2)
Farmer*100	1005	2.8 ms	2.8	90%	(1.4)	(1.8)	(2.7)	(4.2)
Farmer2*100	1100	2.5 ms	2.8	89%	(2.9)	(4.4)	(7.1)	(9.5)

perform well, and *12-Puzzle* performs moderately well. *12-Puzzle* has less parallelism than the other programs due to the IDA^* algorithm implemented. Briefly[7], the IDA^* algorithm requires that the entire search space to a given depth is searched for solutions. If no solution is found, the depth is increased, and the entire search space upto the new depth is explored. When one or more solutions are found the program terminates after completing the search for that given depth. The synchronisation between iterations is achieved using *findall*. The *Salt-Mustard* program simply suffers from too small a grainsize. More than 3000 messages are created for a total single processor execution time of less than 8 seconds. The overhead of parallelisation is much too high to achieve much speedup. (This is no cause for concern since parallelisation of such small problems is less interesting.) It is more interesting in that *Houses*20* and *Farmer*100* benchmarks do not exhibit much speedup. This is partly due to the small execution time of the two benchmarks. A second reason is that, executing the iterations in AND parallel backfires somewhat because the resulting search space is skewed and interprocess communication during termination detection dominates the execution time. To demonstrate this, a second version (*Houses2*20* and *Farmer2*20*) of these two problems was run on the iPSC/2 where the search tree produced is more balanced:

```
    repeat(1) :- go, fail.
    repeat(N) :- N > 1, N1 is N/2, N2 is N-N1,
                 (repeat(N1) && repeat(N2)).
?- repeat(100). /* 20 for houses */
```

As can be seen in Tables 1, 2, 3 and 5, this yielded much better results. Table 4 also demonstrates that for large enough problems, it is possible to obtain good speedups on upto 256 processors. This shows that, if available, large amounts of parallelism in

---

[7] This is a simplified version of the algorithm. In reality, a cost function is used instead of simply using the depth of the search space.

Table 3: Performance of benchmark programs on the NCUBE 2.

\multicolumn{9}{c}{NCUBE 2}								
Progs.	Msgs.	Time/msg	1	% Seq.	4	8	16
Queens1 (9)	2068	93 ms	192.2	97%	(3.9)	(5.1)	(12.5)
Queens2 (9)	2068	335 ms	692.4	99%	(3.9)	(7.5)	(13.7)
Knight	2050	279 ms	571.2	98.5%	(3.6)	(6.7)	(11.0)
12Puzzle	2782	182 ms	506.3	98.5%	(3.0)	(4.0)	(5.6)
Primes	6144	91 ms	560.1	99%	(3.9)	(7.2)	(14.6)
Houses*20	166	285 ms	47.3	99.5%	(1.5)	(2.5)	(2.8)
Houses2*20	179	264 ms	47.3	99.5%	(2.5)	(4.0)	(5.0)
Farmer*100	1005	25 ms	25.5	91.5%	(1.5)	(2.7)	(3.9)
Farmer2*100	1100	23 ms	25.6	91%	(3.5)	(5.4)	(8.9)

Table 4: Performance of large benchmark programs on a 256 processor NCUBE 2. The figures with an asterix are conservative estimates of the speedups obtained from Table 3. The remaining speedup data in parenthesis has been computed based on these estimates.

\multicolumn{6}{c}{NCUBE 2}					
Program	16	32	64	128	256
Queens2 (11)	2918.3 (13.7*)	1465.60 (27.3)	825.05 (48.5)	437.33 (91.4)	223.30 (179.0)
Knight	632.54 (13.0*)	318.54 (25.7)	159.69 (51.3)	86.13 (95.2)	48.79 (168.0)
Queens1 (12)	3730.8 (12.5*)	2282.46 (20.4)	1195.59 (39.0)	624.54 (74.7)	323.32 (144.2)
Primes	— (14.6*)	—	77.06 (45.5)	42.87 (81.9)	24.69 (142.2)

Prolog programs can be exploited effectively on message passing machines. Table 5 demonstrates the versatility of the ROLOG implementation. A network of Sun Sparc 1 workstations were used as a non-shared memory machine. It was possible to get modest speedups on most of the benchmarks used. Loss of speedup is due to several reasons, including the context switching behaviour of the Unix kernel, swapping of memory to and from a file server on the network, and other network traffic.

An important point about the data is that it demonstrates the effectiveness of *grain-size* control. All these programs were run in parallel, creating thousands of messages representing parallel pieces of work, upto a certain threshold. In column 2 of Tables 1, 2, 3 and 5, the number of messages created during the course of execution of the respective benchmarks are provided. Currently, this threshold is specified using

Table 5: Performance of benchmark programs on a network of Sun Sparc 1 workstations.

Network of Sun Sparc 1 workstations							
Progs.	Msgs.	Time/msg	1	% Seq.	2	4	8
Queens1 (9)	2068	14 ms	28.3	96%	(1.7)	(2.8)	(4.2)
Queens2 (9)	2068	48 ms	98.4	99%	(1.6)	(2.9)	(4.3)
Knight	2050	39 ms	79.3	96%	(1.6)	(2.3)	(4.4)
12Puzzle	2782	27 ms	76.3	96%	(1.4)	(2.2)	(2.3)
Primes	6144	14 ms	84.0	96%	(1.6)	(2.7)	(5.1)
Houses2*20	179	41 ms	7.3	97.2%	(1.1)	(2.1)	(1.7)
Farmer2*100	1100	4 ms	4.9	78%	(1.0)	(1.4)	(1.4)

program annotations, though methods for grainsize analysis are currently being developed [Tick88b],[Debr90a] can be used in the future to generate such annotations automatically. When the threshold was reached for a goal message G, the bindings were copied across into a sequential component, which invoked a sequential Prolog compiler to evaluate the literal instance represented by G and returned solutions found to the parallel Prolog compiler. All solutions found by the sequential component are copied back into the parallel component. Using a simple property of trees, by ensuring that the amount of work done by the sequential component is approximately 10 times the amount of work done when decomposing a parallel goal into parallel subgoals, over 90% of the effort of evaluation is spent in the sequential component. In addition, predicates with no parallelism to offer are simply evaluated sequentially – they do not incur the overheads associated with parallelisation.

In column 5 of Tables 1, 2, 3 and 5, we present the percentage of time spent in the sequential component during evaluation on one processor. These figures represent *only* the cost of sequential evaluation by the sequential component of ROLOG; it *excludes* the cost of creating messages, and of full copying of terms and tuples back and forth across the sequential/parallel interface. As can be seen, in most of the benchmarks, more than 95% of the one processor execution time is spent in the sequential component. In general, our experiments have shown that a grainsize of approximately 50 ms is adequate to capture more than 95% of the execution time in the sequential component on both shared and non-shared memory machines. This is significant because it unequivocally demonstrates that the execution time of ROLOG is dominated by the speed of its sequential component and not due to parallelisation overheads.

The sequential component used in our compiler is a simple two-stack implementation of sequential Prolog developed to illustrate the parallel-sequential interface. It runs approximately 6-8 times slower than Quintus Prolog [Quin91a]. If a faster sequential compiler like Sicstus 0.7 [Carl88a] or the BAM compiler [VanR90a] developed at the University of California, Berkeley, is used to execute the sequential component, the results obtained will be significantly improved.

The interface between the parallel and sequential component is small and clean. We impose the restriction that calls from the sequential component to the parallel component are not permitted. Thus, the sequential component is independent of the parallel component, it can have a different binding representation and different data areas. Only three interface functions are required to accomplish this. One performs a full copy of a (sub)query and its bindings in the parallel component to the sequential component performing any conversions necessary. Another is required to start (or resume) sequential execution of the (sub)query. A third and final function is required to intercept solutions found by the sequential component and copy the bindings to the parallel component performing the necessary conversion of the binding environment.

6 SUMMARY

We have described the design and performance of a compiler for the parallel execution of logic programs. This included the design of a binding environment suitable for shared and non-shared memory machines. The process model and the binding environment are designed so that they work with both shared and non-shared memory organisations, and can scale up to thousands of processors, if the application program has sufficient parallelism. The performance data demonstrates that it is possible to write an efficient compiler for logic programs even on non-shared memory machines.

10 An Actor-oriented Computer for Logic and its Applications

C. Percebois, N. Signès and L. Selle

Université Paul Sabatier, France

ABSTRACT

The aim of the COALA (un Calculateur Orienté Acteurs pour la Logique et ses Applications - an Actor-Oriented Computer for Logic and its Applications) machine is to extract and make use of the parallelism inherent to Horn clauses i.e. without requiring programmer intervention. The COALA parallel execution model considers definition clauses as rewriting rules, indicating that a head literal can be rewritten by the corresponding body goal literals. The implementation of this goal rewriting model is based on R. Kowalski's AND/OR connection graph. This graph includes one arc for each pair of matching atoms on opposite sides of the implication symbol. Associated with an arc is the resolvent obtained by resolving the atoms connected by the arc.

With the connection graph, two levels of parallelism can be observed: the first one appears when building different intermediate goals and the second one is associated with the creation of different arcs for each intermediate goal. These two levels correspond respectively to OR- and AND- parallelism. Several extensions have been proposed and implemented, in particular independent AND-parallelism and SEARCH-parallelism.

In order to efficiently run large logic programs, an abstract machine closely tied to the COALA model and called CIAM (COALA Inference Abstract Machine) was designed. The main idea is to translate an arc and its behaviour into a sequence of CIAM instructions associated with the basic operations of the parallel connection-graph proof-procedure. A first version of the CIAM Abstract Machine is now running on a message-passing computer using Transputers, called HYPERTORE.

1. COMMITED-CHOICE LANGUAGES VS NON-DETERMINISTIC SYSTEMS

Parallel logic programming systems can be classified in two broad categories: committed-choice languages and non-deterministic systems. Committed-choice languages like Concurrent Prolog [Shap83a], Parlog [Clar84a] [Clar86a] and GHC

(Guarded Horn Clauses) [Ueda86a] are process-oriented languages based on guarded-command indeterminacy. On the other hand, non-deterministic systems like PEPSys [Baro88b], Aurora [Lusk88a] and Andorra [Hari88a] are designed to speed up existing logic programming systems while remaining as close as possible to Prolog. Because many execution models for non-deterministic systems have been proposed, we have defined [Perc90a] the following taxonomy: AND/OR process models e.g. [Cone83b] [Cone85a] ; multisequential models e.g. [Hari88a] [Lusk88a] and goal rewriting models e.g. [Ciep84a] [Goto84a] [Yasu84a].

1.1. AND/OR process models
In these models [Cone83b] [Cone85a], goal statements are solved by a set of processes. There are two types of processes: AND-processes which produce solutions for goal conjunctions and OR-processes which solve single goals. Communication paths between AND- and OR- processes create a dynamic AND/OR tree, with AND-processes forming the descendants of OR-processes and OR-processes forming the descendants of AND-processes. Processes communicate via messages only with their parents or descendants.

Messages that can be sent from a process to its parent are SUCCESS and FAIL. A SUCCESS message occurs when an AND-process solves all the goals in the conjunction, or when an OR-process unifies a unit clause. These messages pass upward in the tree. The amount of time required by this form of communication can be a severe drawback.

An important feature concerns the AND-parallel computation. In a conjunction, only one of the literals is designated to produce the value for a variable and is solved first. Complex algorithms are needed to determine which literals must be solved before others (the "ordering algorithm"), which literals must be examined to progress (the "forward execution algorithm"), and which literals must be re-solved (the "backward execution algorithm").

In these models, combining OR- and AND- parallelism is a difficult aim. Today, researchers are concerned with special forms of AND-parallelism such as Restricted AND-parallelism (RAP) [DeGr84a], Independent AND-parallelism (IAP) [Lin88d] and AND-parallelism based on intelligent backtracking [Codo89b]. In most cases, a compile-time analysis of clauses is involved and a limited amount of run-time support is required.

1.2. Multisequential models
Multisequential models [Baro88b] [Hari88a] [Lusk88a] are based on a very small number of processes, each one having weak interactions with other processes proceeding in parallel. The basic execution mode is sequential and implementations are usually extensions of the D.H.D. Warren Abstract Machine (WAM) [Warr83a].

In most cases, research is focused on OR-parallelism because of the suitability of large-grain parallelism. Sequential computations are retroactively converted to parallel on demand from idle processing elements. Furthermore, combining OR-parallelism and backtracking is an important feature. This strategy introduces an explicit control mechanism which restricts the parallelism to the number of available processors.

The issue of task scheduling is a crucial aspect of these approaches. The engine/schedule interface must reduce the cost of task switching without penalizing large-grain size computations. As an example, the Aurora project [Lusk88a] has defined and compared three quite different schedulers (Manchester, Argonne and Wavefront) [Cald89a].

First experimental results of multisequential models are encouraging [Baro88b] [Lusk88a]. However, using sequential techniques with large stack sizes implies the use of shared-memory multiprocessors. In the future, it would seem that these models are not well suited to take into account the scalability advantages of local-memory multiprocessors.

1.3. Goal rewriting models

These models [Ciep84a] [Goto84a] [Yasu84a] are based on a parallel search of goal statements. With such a parallel control method, goal statements can be distributed to independent processing elements. In this approach, a breadth-first traversal of the search tree usually replaces the backward execution algorithm.

At each choice point of the search tree, definition clauses are considered as rewriting rules, indicating that a head literal can be rewritten by corresponding body goal literals. First, a goal list is generated with the initial goal statement to resolve. After that, for each successful unification of a literal of the list against a clause head literal, the goal list is modified by adding new goal literals as next intermediate goals.

One can observe that this interpretation differs from the classical top-down interpretation for which clauses are considered as process descriptions that execute resolution and unification operations. In a goal rewriting model, a clause is rewritten as a new one through a resolution mechanism. Consequently, various proof strategies can be introduced. In particular, OR-parallelism refers to the simultaneous computation of intermediate goals and AND-parallelism to the simultaneous computation of the literals in an intermediate goal.

Goal rewriting models differ greatly from both AND/OR process models and multisequential models, mainly because they are not based on a process-oriented control mechanism. A highly parallel environment can be defined to support these models, not limited to shared-memory multiprocessors as is the case with the multisequential models.

2. THE COALA GOAL REWRITING SYSTEM

COALA is a goal-rewriting, non-deterministic system based on R. Kowalski's connection graphs [Kowa79a] and on C. Hewitt's actors [Hewi77a]. R. Kowalski's connection graphs refer to the proof procedure and C. Hewitt's actors refer to the computational model.

2.1. The AND/OR connection graph model

In the AND/OR connection graph model proposed by R. Kowalski [Kowa79a], clauses are stored in a graph and occurrences of matching atoms on opposite sides of the implication symbol are connected by arcs. An arc is labelled by the matching substitution. Associated with each arc in the graph is the resolvent obtained by rewriting the parent clauses connected by the arc.

Example: Assume the following set of clauses:
    p(X) :- q(X).
    p(X) :- r(X), s(X,Y).
    q(a).
    r(b).
    s(a,b).

and the goal: :- p(L). The corresponding AND/OR connection graph is given by Figure 1.

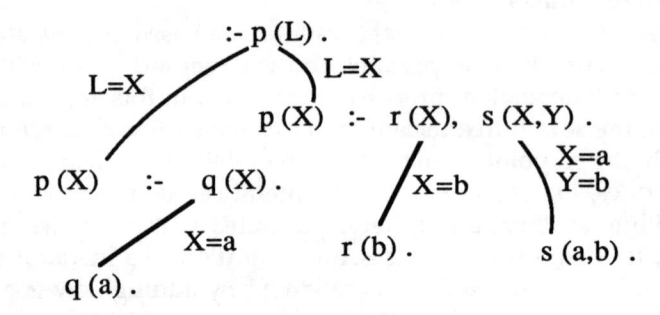

Figure 1 Initial connection graph

The selection of an arc and the construction of the associated resolvent is the main operation in the connection graph proof procedure. The selected arc is deleted and new arcs are added connecting the literals of the resolvent to the rest of the graph. If a clause contains an unlinked literal, the clause can be deleted with all of its arcs. For a head literal, this situation means that the clause will never be used, and for a body literal, this means that the literal cannot contribute to a resolution refutation because there are no clause-heads with which it may be unified.

Deleting a clause can lead to several clauses being removed. The effect of deleting clauses with unlinked literals can be illustrated by Figure 2, assuming that the assertion s(a,b) is deleted from the initial set of clauses.

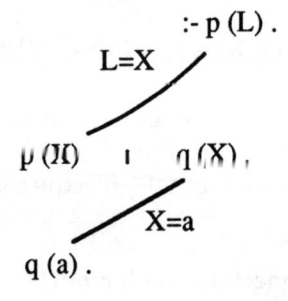

Figure 2 Deleting arcs and clauses

Let's continue with the initial example. When the arcs connecting atoms of the resolvent to atoms in the rest of the graph are added, we don't need to traverse the entire graph. Arcs are added by using matching substitutions attached to the arcs already connected to the atoms in the parent clauses. As an example, in the initial connection graph of Figure 1, we can evaluate the graph bottom-up by selecting the arc connecting the two atoms q(X) and q(a). A new resolvent p(a) is generated and added to the graph, as shown by Figure 3.

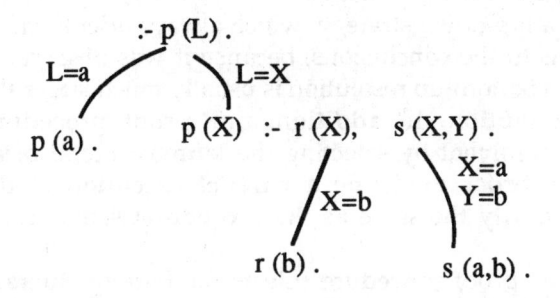

```
                    :- p (L) .
            L=a   /        \ L=X
         p (a) .      p (X) :- r (X),   s (X,Y) .
                            /                \ X=a
                          / X=b                \ Y=b
                        r (b) .              s (a,b) .
```

Figure 3 *Adding the resolvent p(a) in the initial graph*

The substitution L=a which labels the new arc connecting the atoms p(L) and p(a) is computed from the substitution L=X associated with the parent arc connecting the atoms p(L) and p(X), and the substitution X=a associated with the selected arc connecting the atoms q(X) and q(a).

If we continue this resolution process with the last generated graph, the selection of the arc descending from the body literals r(X) or s(X,Y) leads to the deletion of the selected arc and so to the deletion of the clause p(X) :- r(X), s(X,Y), as previously explained, because the substitutions X=a and X=b are incompatible. Finally, we obtain the graph of Figure 4.

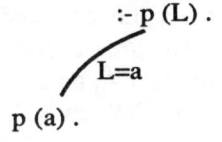

```
              :- p (L) .
             / L=a
           p (a) .
```

Figure 4 *Graph after resolving the literals r(X) and s(X,Y)*

Note that the top-level algorithm of the connection graph proof procedure can be summarized by the following pseudo-code:

```
repeat
    delete all the clauses containing unlinked atoms;
    select and delete any remaining arcs;
    add the new resolvent to the graph by adding links
       to its atoms;
until there are no more arcs in the graph
```

Each time the empty clause is generated as a new resolvent, the selected arc's environment is a solution to the initial problem. Resolution ends when there are no more arcs in the graph.

2.2. The COALA parallel execution model

Using the graphs, we can extract a form of parallelism which is different from the classical OR- and AND- parallelisms. For example, one can traverse the graph from different points and mix the bottom-up and top-down approaches. The large range of execution strategies afforded by connection graphs formed a basis for the COALA parallel rewriting model.

We chose a top-down strategy, which always orients the arcs of the graph from the conditions to the conclusions, because it was observed that the search space produced by a bottom-up resolution is usually much larger than that produced by a top-down resolution. In addition, our proof procedure always builds an intermediate resolvent by selecting the leftmost literal of a resolvent. We chose this literal in order to define a parallel execution model whose procedural semantics is nearly the same as the procedural semantics of an abstract Prolog interpreter.

The parallel proof procedure selects the leftmost literal of the resolvent and activates all the arcs descending from this literal. Each one can produce a resolvent which is added to the graph. This form of parallelism looks like OR-parallelism because the rewriting operations are applied in parallel to each clause with the same head predicate as the goal literal.

To build the resolvent of an arc, unification environments are consumed in parallel by all the arcs descending from other literals of the parent clauses. This form of parallelism looks like a restricted form of AND-parallelism because unification operations for each body literal of a resolvent are performed in parallel. Note that this solution avoids access conflicts to variable bindings and does not require a join algorithm, which is particularly inefficient when a set of partial solutions for a literal is large with respect to other literals.

In a top-down resolution, the arcs of the graph are directed from the conditions to the conclusions. Thus an arc connects two parent clauses: the *origin* (i.e. condition) clause and the *extremity* (i.e. conclusion) clause. If the arc Aj is selected for resolution, we note by Ai o Aj an arc produced by an arc Ai descending from the extremity clause and we note by Ai x Aj an arc produced by an arc Ai descending from the origin clause. For example, let's consider the graph of Figure 5.

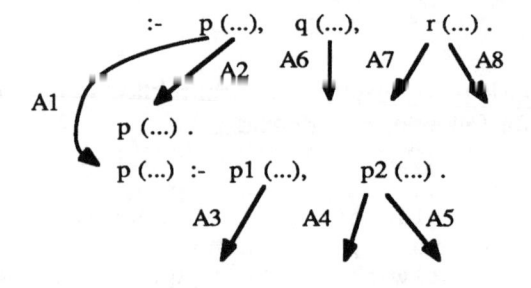

Figure 5 Graph with oriented arcs

AN ACTOR-ORIENTED COMPUTER 219

When the literal p is chosen by the resolution mechanism, the arcs A1 and A2 are activated and each produces a resolvent, as described by Figure 6. For the resolvent of the arc A1, the arcs are built from the arcs A3, A4, A5, A6, A7 and A8; for the arc A2, they are obtained from the arcs A6, A7 and A8.

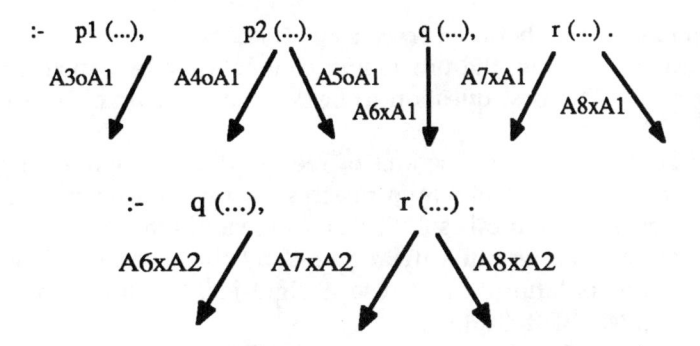

```
 :-    p1 (...),      p2 (...),         q (...),      r (...) .
       A3oA1 /    A4oA1 /  \ A5oA1    A7xA1 /
                              A6xA1 |           A8xA1 \


 :-      q (...),              r (...) .
      A6xA2 /      A7xA2 /        \ A8xA2
```

Figure 6 Resolvents of the arcs A1 and A2

Using this goal rewriting model based on R. Kowalski's connection graph, two levels of parallelism can be observed: the first one deals with generating different resolvents and the second one is associated with the generation of different arcs for each resolvent. These two levels can be compared respectively to OR- and AND-parallelism. Moreover, they are processed in the same way and don't refer to the AND/OR division of a given problem. In particular, broadcasting the matching substitutions of an arc to all its parent arcs leads to a breadth-first traversal of the clauses.

3. IMPLEMENTATION OF THE PARALLEL EXECUTION MODEL

3.1. Precompilation

A precompilation of a source Prolog program generates the initial connection graph. To represent the graph, we simply have to represent each of its arcs. An arc is defined by its matching substitutions called the *unification environment* and a list of links directed towards other remote arcs called *parent arcs*. In this list, we have to define the arcs descending from the literals of the extremity clauses called *son arcs*, and the arcs descending from the literals of the origin clauses, called *brother arcs*. Note that the association of the son and brother arcs together forms the parent arcs.

In the unification environment of an arc, two subsets of variable bindings are defined: the *origin environment* for the variables of the origin clause and the *extremity environment* for the variables of the extremity clause. The origin environment will be sent during unifications to brother arcs and the extremity environment during unifications to son arcs.

In fact, the precompilation step of the Prolog program can only generate the arcs of the initial graph i.e. all the son arcs of the different clauses, denoted as Ai (basic arcs). The dynamic evolution of the graph when goals are rewritten prevents the brother arcs from being generated during the precompilation step.

These brother arcs form the resolvent and contain bindings dynamically updated each time the resolution is in progress. So, they will be communicated to the literal chosen by the resolution process, when it is selected. These arcs are denoted as Ri (resolution arcs).

3.2. Communication between processing elements

In our parallel machine, the processing elements try to transform the graph by rewriting goals. The first question to be resolved is where the arcs are to lie in relation to the processors.

The first solution stores the arcs of the graph in a memory shared by all the processors, assuming free and uniform access by the multiple processes running on the processors. Although this solution is simple and attractive, its main drawback is related to the task granularity required by the memory. Fine-grain shared-memory implementations can cause a significant bottle-neck in the parallel machine [Ciep84a] [Goto84a].

The second solution is to store one part of the graph in a private local memory called *Graph Memory*. With this solution, each processing element is an independent worker which transforms the graph in his own memory. A processing element can reference a remote arc by the duplex form <PE,address> where PE is the processing element whose memory contains the referenced arc and address is the address of the arc in that local memory. This solution reduces the bottle-neck due to a shared memory where contention effectively swamps the benefits obtained from the parallelism [Hewi84a].

In the same way, we have preferred a task queue distributed among the processing elements to a centralized task queue, from which processors seek work. If a processor wants to perform an operation on a remote arc, it forms a request packet containing the address of the arc to be accessed, the type of the operation and the parameters for the task (if they are necessary) [Kell79a]. The dialogue must be taken into account by switches which deal with the routing of packets. The communication network topology is arbitrary, but must obviously ensure the reliable transmission of requests from one processor to another. The general structure of a request packet is given by Figure 7.

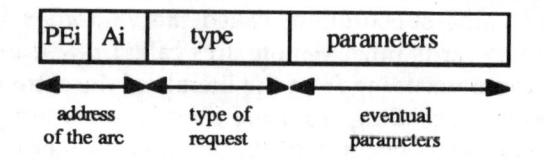

PEi	Ai	type	parameters

address of the arc — type of request — eventual parameters

Figure 7 General structure of a request packet

The task associated with an incoming message is performed by an actor [Hewi77a] associated with the addressed arc. The actor concept is quite different from the well-known process concept. An actor is entirely defined by its behaviour when it receives a message: ending a job, sending messages to other actors, creating new actors, and so on. To dynamically update the AND/OR connection graph, several actors are required to cooperate. Each one performs, independently and locally, a small transformation on the graph. In our case, these transformations concern the basic operations of an abstract Prolog interpreter: resolution, unification and garbage collection.

3.2.1. Resolution. When a literal is selected for resolution, a RESOLVE-REQ request is sent to each arc descending from this literal. This request contains the identification of all brother arcs of the selected literal, so as to ensure the upkeep of the graph. An arc receiving this request sends its unification environment to each of its sons and brothers through UNIFY-REQ requests. The replies corresponding to the UNIFY-REQ requests are either UNIFY-ACK in case of success, or UNIFY-NACK in case of failure.

When a successful unification has occurred, a new arc is generated and allocated in the same local memory as the arc which has received the UNIFY-REQ request. We chose this solution because the physical representation of the newly created arc is nearly the same as the parent arc.

When a resolvent has successfully been computed, the resolution proceeds with the selection of a new literal to be resolved. The resolution of an arc having neither brother nor son corresponds to the empty clause. Thus an arc's environment is a solution to the initial goal statement.

3.2.2. Unification. The UNIFY-REQ request triggers the unification between two environments: the environment in the request and that of the arc to which the request is addressed. Note that the same form of request is received both by a son and a brother arc of a parent arc, without distinction. This property allows an easy breadth-first traversal of the AND/OR connection graph.

3.2.3. Garbage Collection. Throughout the resolution of a goal statement, the graph is dynamically being updated. New arcs are added and others are deleted. The memory location associated with a deleted arc must be garbage collected during the resolution process. Two messages in the model ensure the complete garbage collection of the graph: DESTROY-REQ and BROTHERS-REQ. These messages collect remote arcs.

Imagine a resolution arc which wants to build an intermediate goal. When all the UNIFY-REQ requests have definitely been processed by the parent arcs and when all the UNIFY-ACK and/or UNIFY-NACK acknowledgements have been returned, the resolution proceeds depending on the intermediate goal computation:

    i) If at least one literal of the intermediate goal has no connection with the rest of the graph, the computation of the intermediate goal is unsuccessful and needless arcs generated for other literals of this intermediate goal are deleted by DESTROY-REQ requests sent by the resolution arc. No further intermediate goals are built from this step.

    ii) If all the literals of an intermediate goal are connected with the rest of the graph through at least one arc, the computation to this point is successful and the resolution arc can build the next intermediate goals by sending RESOLVE-REQ and BROTHERS-REQ requests. A brother arc of a resolution arc is deleted after receiving all the unification environments of the literal currently in resolution. The BROTHERS-REQ request is used to inform the brother arc of the number of resolvents in progress.

Using the DESTROY-REQ and BROTHERS-REQ requests and a reference counter associated with each arc, the intermediate resolvents can be garbage collected once they are not required for the forward resolution algorithm.

As an arc always belongs to only one resolvent, BROTHERS-REQ requests and RESOLVE-REQ requests can be sent in parallel. Therefore, an arc is able to count the number of resolvents in progress (BROTHERS-REQ request) while at the same time unifying its environment against the received environments (UNIFY-REQ requests). Note that an arc can first receive either a BROTHERS-REQ request or a UNIFY-REQ request. However, because an arc processes only one communication at a time, arrival ordering of the two requests does not matter. An arc receiving a BROTHERS-REQ request increments its reference counter; similarly, when the arc receives a UNIFY-REQ request, a decrement operation is performed. If the reference counter of an arc is decremented to zero, the arc can be garbage collected.

3.3. Evaluation

In order to evaluate the COALA approach, we wrote two simulators: a functional simulator which simulates the functional aspects of the distributed model within a monoprocessor environment, and a system simulator which compares the impact of the number of processors and different network topologies on the machine's overall performance [Futo86a]. Our simulation considers that a processing element has a buffer of sufficient size, that a communication channel has a 10 Mbps transfer rate with full-duplex links and that the network is not ideal in the sense that conflicts may occur.

For purposes of comparison, we introduced programs operating on simple data structures such as constants and variables ('map', 'ibm-pc database',...) and programs operating on large data structures such as lists, n-tuples and compound terms ('4-queens', 'quick-sort',...). Usually, programs operating on simple data structures occur in *database applications* with a large number of unit clauses (>10K) and a small number of deductive definitions (<200). On the other hand, programs operating on large data structures occur in *computational algorithms* with multiple clauses (<100) and many complex definitions (<1000).

As additional processing elements are used, the duration of the execution of all bench-marks decreases. Then it levels off; between 9 and 18 processors, the duration of the execution is nearly the same. However, this saturation only depends on the application size and we assume that the number of processors does not give rise to a bottle-neck situation on the overall performances of COALA [Perc87a]. Better results are obtained with database programs: on 9 processors and for the non-deterministic *ibm-pc database* bench-mark, the speed-up is improved by 6 times. However, for the *4-queens* bench-mark, the model achieves no more than 3 times speed-up.

Simulation showed that the topology does not have a significant effect upon the performance results: completely connected networks, rings, trees, hypercubes, and so on, are similar with respect to our parallel execution model. A completely connected network would seem ideal, but the number of switching elements renders the topology unrealizable. However, this topology was used as a reference for the relative speed-up of the parallel model.

Furthermore, processor load balancing does not require dynamic process allocation as in many other approaches. In our model, the distribution of the arcs is equivalent to the distribution of the tasks among the processors. Unfortunately, for computational programs operating on large data structures, the results are not as good as for database programs operating on simple data structures. We can explain this behaviour by the small number of definitions of the same clause for computational programs.

Although we have only tested our implementation up to 36 processors, it is clear that non-deterministic programs operating on many definition clauses are better suited to our model. In particular, we are investigating classes of programs that can benefit of the goal rewriting mechanism. We think, as indicated in the section 5, that several improvements can be incorporated in the model and that a knowledge base machine can be an objective of future research [Perc87a].

4. INDEPENDENT AND-PARALLELISM

4.1. Dependency tables

The original model can be improved by generating only as many arcs as necessary and by executing independent sub-resolvents in parallel. In particular, it is unnecessary to send a UNIFY-REQ request from an arc to a parent arc if they don't share a variable. Furthermore, if brother literals do not share any variables, independent AND-parallelism can be performed [Perc88a].

The proposed method handles dynamic detection of dependencies within a resolvent. A *dependency table* is associated with each intermediate resolvent built by the rewriting algorithm. This dependency table records the list of literals in which a variable of the resolvent occurs and is updated at the end of the resolution of a literal to reflect the change of binding conditions. The unification environment of the resolved arc descending from the selected literal defines the dependency table's evolution. The method is quite similar to the one developed by Y. Lin [Lin88d], except that their bit-vectors associated with the body clauses are replaced by our dependency table associated with the literals of a resolvent.

Let T_r denote a dependency table of a resolvent r composed of literals L. Assume that we have $T_r[i,j]$ = '+' if the variable V_j occurs in the literal L_i, and $T_r[i,j]$ = '-' if the variable V_j does not occur in the literal L_i. It is easy to incorporate this additional information during compilation of the clauses. At execution-time, when the rewriting algorithm replaces a head literal by the corresponding body goal literals, one must dynamically construct a new dependency table corresponding to the next resolvent, according to the internal unification environment of the arc receiving the RESOLVE-REQ request.

The dependency tables update algorithm is the following:

i) If the unification environment of an arc contains a variable V_j bound to a ground term, the variable's description $T_r[i,j]$ is set to '-', since V_j is replaced by the ground term in the resolvent.

ii) If two variables V_j and V_k become dependent, then both descriptions of V_j and V_k are updated to '+'. This means that $T_r[i,j]$ = '-' is changed to $T_r[i,j]$ = '+', $\forall$ $T_r[i,j]$ for which $T_r[i,k]$ = '+', and that $T_r[i,k]$ = '-' is changed to $T_r[i,k]$ = '+', $\forall$ $T_r[i,k]$ for which $T_r[i,j]$ = '+'.

iii) Finally, if the variable V_j is replaced by a compound term, we recursively annotate all the variables within the term using the algorithm.

4.2. Independent AND-parallelism

Extraction of sub-resolvents is performed each time an intermediate resolvent is successfully built. The resolution process algorithm, with independent sub-resolvent detection, is the following:

i) Send UNIFY-REQ requests to all the literals L_i of the resolvent, as usual.

ii) Wait for UNIFY-ACK and UNIFY-NACK replies.

iii) Try to select the new sub-resolvents $sr_1, sr_2, ..., sr_p$ if the resolvent r has been added to the rest of the graph.

iv) Each sr_j is composed of literals L_i and is constructed using the following property: if $sr_j = \{L_{1j}, L_{2j}, ..., L_{ij}\}$ and if the variable V_m occurs in sr_j, then $\forall\ k \in [1,i]$ such that $T_r[k,m] = \,'+'$, $\exists\ p \in [1,i] - \{k\}$, such that $T_r[p,m] = \,'+'$.

If independent sub-resolvents do not exist, resolution proceeds as usual. When independent sub-resolvents have been detected by a resolution arc, the arc includes its identification within the RESOLVE-REQ request and waits for answering messages dealing with the success or the failure of the partial resolutions it has activated. During this process, if an arc receives a resolution request including a sender arc, the sender arc's identification is stored by the addressee and normal resolution steps are performed, with the possible detection of new sub-resolvents.

At the end of a resolution step, if the empty clause is generated, a RESOLVE-ACK message with partial solutions of the activated sub-resolvent is sent back to the resolution arc; otherwise, if a failure occurs during an intermediate goal computation, a RESOLVE-NACK message is sent back. The reply corresponding to a RESOLVE-REQ request is a RESOLVE-ACK answer in case of success, or a RESOLVE-NACK answer in case of failure. If a RESOLVE-NACK answer is sent back to a resolvent, the corresponding sub-resolvent fails, entailing a complete failure of the original resolvent. An arc which detects independent AND-parallelism builds the solutions of the resolvent by using the cross-product of the partial solutions sent back by the RESOLVE-ACK answers.

4.3. Example

Suppose we have the Prolog program described by Figure 8.

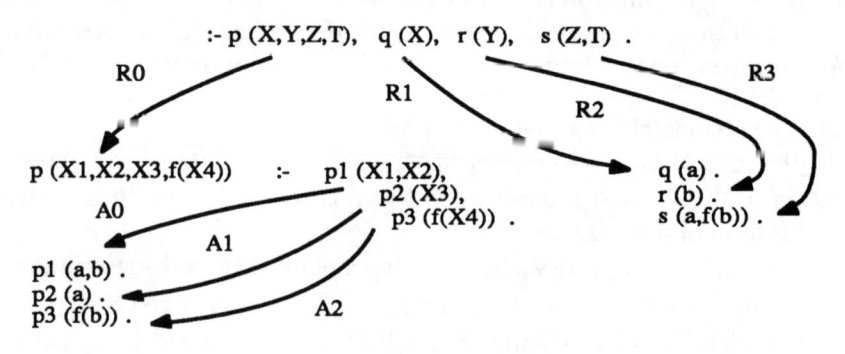

Figure 8 Initial graph

A table $T_{cl.p}$ is associated with the literals p1, p2 and p3, while a table T_{goal} corresponds to the literals q, r and s. When a RESOLVE-REQ request is sent to the arc R0, a new table T_{R0} is generated by adding the table $T_{cl.p}$ to the table T_{goal}. As the unification environment of the arc R0 is composed of the bindings X=X1, Y=X2, Z=X3 and T=f(X4), we obtain the modified table T_{R0} described by Figure 9. For instance, from the binding X=X1 and applying the marking algorithm, $T_{R0}[A0,X]$ is set to '+' since the variable X1 belongs to the arc A0; symmetrically, $T_{R0}[R1,X1]$ is set to '+' since the variable X belongs to the arc R1.

T_{R0}	X1	X2	X3	X4	X	Y	Z	T
A0	+	+	-	-	+	+	-	-
A1	-	-	+	-	-	-	+	-
A2	-	-	-	+	-	-	-	+
R1	+	-	-	-	+	-	-	-
R2	-	+	-	-	-	+	-	-
R3	-	-	+	+	-	-	+	+

Figure 9 Dependency table associated with the arc R0

UNIFY-REQ requests are sent to the arcs A0, A1, A2, R1, R2 and R3 with their respective environments. All these unification requests succeed and UNIFY-ACK answers are sent back to the arc R0 with newly generated arcs A0', A1', A2', R1', R2' and R3' associated with the future resolvent. The arcs A0', R1', R2' and the arcs A1', A2', R3' have no shared variables. Their corresponding sub-resolvents ':- p1(X1,X2), q(X1), r(X2).' and ':- p2(X3), p3(f(X4)), s(X3,f(X4)).' can be resolved in parallel. So RESOLVE-REQ requests are sent in parallel to the arc A0', with the brother table $T_{A0'}$, and to the arc A1', with the brother table $T_{A1'}$. These two dependency tables are given at Figure 10.

$T_{A0'}$	X1	X2
A0'	+	+
R1'	+	-
R2'	-	+

$T_{A1'}$	X3	X4
A1'	+	-
A2'	-	+
R3'	+	+

Figure 10 Dependency tables associated with the arcs A0' and A1'

According to the independent sub-resolvent detection algorithm, the tables $T_{A0'}$ and $T_{A1'}$ were extracted from the table T_{R0} updated by the UNIFY-ACK answers. Figure 11 illustrates this algorithm.

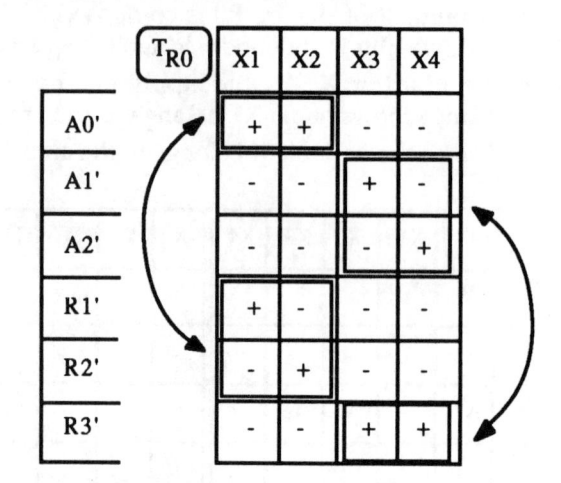

T_{R0}	X1	X2	X3	X4
A0'	+	+	-	-
A1'	-	-	+	-
A2'	-	-	-	+
R1'	+	-	-	-
R2'	-	+	-	-
R3'	-	-	+	+

Figure 11 *Extraction of the dependency tables associated with the arcs A0' and A1'*

When resolving the arcs A0' and A1', UNIFY-REQ requests are respectively sent to the arcs R1', R2' and to the arcs A2', R3'. After that, the parent arc R0 waits for two RESOLVE-ACK replies. Resolution of the arc A1' terminates when the arc R3' receives a RESOLVE-REQ request, immediately transforming it into a RESOLVE-ACK reply for the arc R0. Resolution of the arc A0' causes two sub-resolutions: one for the arc R1' and one for the arc R2'. When each of these arcs returns a RESOLVE-ACK answer to the arc A0', the arc A0' acknowledges the resolution by sending a RESOLVE-ACK message to the arc R0.

Note that our AND-parallelism does not need complex algorithms such as literal ordering, backtracking or join operations. When independent AND-parallelism occurs, the graph looks like a hierarchical tree and solutions are obtained by using the cross-product of partial solutions sent back by the RESOLVE-ACK replies.

4.4. Evaluation

The extension to COALA detailed above led to two new versions of the system: one incorporating dependency tables and one incorporating independent AND-parallelism. These versions have been compared with the original.

The dependency table strategy always reduces the search space created by the original model because unifications are restricted to those strictly necessary. The efficacy of the optimization relates to the number of unification requests and to the number of arcs generated to build intermediate resolvents. In most cases, the overall number of messages decreases, although a new message, BROTHERS-ACK, is required to acknowledge a BROTHERS-REQ increment-reference-counter request. Each time a selected literal of a resolvent does not send a unification request to other literals, the associated list of sons or brothers is not modified. As a result, an arc is now shared by several resolvents and the BROTHERS-ACK increment-reference-counter acknowledgement prevents the reference counter of a parent arc from being underestimated. In this way, an arc cannot restart a resolution step until the BROTHERS-REQ requests have definitely been processed.

With regard to independent AND-parallelism, our experiments do not lead to definitive conclusions. In programs which do not generate independent AND-parallelism, time is wasted trying to detect sub-resolvents. In these programs, a significant run-time overhead reduces the performance results, especially if the variables of the resolvent are bound to large structures.

Recursive programs, such as the 4-*queens* program, generate AND-parallelism. However, many useless computations are performed. In fact, such a parallelism should be controlled by the user [Ratc87a] or by compile-time analysis [Chan85a] to reduce these computations and hence reduce the overhead. In our method, an arc must entirely traverse a partial resolution before returning a success or a failure. This mechanism has a significant weakness when a sub-resolvent returns a failure while other sub-resolvents are still in progress. In other programs, such as the *ibm-pc database* program, independent AND-parallelism seems to be worthwhile. However, from our experiments, we cannot foresee if this form of AND-parallelism will be efficient in general [Perc88a].

5. SEARCH-PARALLELISM

5.1. Binding records

When a Prolog program uses a large number of unit clauses, the original model builds lists of sons and therefore lists of brothers which are far too long. With such a program, the processing time required to define the next intermediate resolvent is proportional to the number of UNIFY-ACK and UNIFY-NACK answers awaited by this resolvent. It is quite easy to modify the original representation by representing all the arcs for a procedure stored on the same processor using an extra arc called the *binding record*. The binding record contains the list of real addresses of the original arcs.

When a binding record receives a UNIFY-REQ request, it distributes this request among its real arcs. The algorithm used in treating the message is the same as the one for the original version, except that no message is sent directly. Instead, the addresses of the newly generated arcs update the old ones. If the new list of addresses contains at least one element, a UNIFY-ACK is sent to the resolvent; otherwise, if the list is empty, a UNIFY-NACK message is sent.

5.2. Evaluation

An advantage of this representation is that the list of sons of an arc contains only one arc per processing element instead of all the arcs defining the literal. This property greatly reduces the number of messages needed for the resolution process. Consequently, processing time required to define the next resolvent decreases and is about 12 times smaller than the original version, when about 100 clauses are considered.

Another feature of binding records is that the size of the resolution messages only depends on the number of processing elements. On the other hand, as the unification environment requests are restricted to constant or variable bindings, all the messages of the model have an acceptable size.

The binding record implementation does not require the introduction of new message types. The only modification concerns the UNIFY-ACK answer, which must now reply with the number of successes when unifying a request environment against all the unification environments of a record. This number, associated with a sub-list of sons or brothers, is used for garbage collection purposes.

Note that the dependency table and binding record strategies are two orthogonal concepts. This property allows us to effectively combine OR-parallelism and SEARCH-parallelism in the same parallel execution model.

6. THE CIAM ABSTRACT MACHINE

As mentioned above, several versions of the parallel execution model have been defined: OR-parallelism, independent AND-parallelism with dependency tables and SEARCH-parallelism with binding records. We chose to implement the original OR-version with dependency tables and binding records, mainly because OR-parallelism occurs across a wide range of applications and search processes are used in many applications, such as parsing a natural language or answering a database query. To achieve this, we defined an abstract machine closely tied to the COALA model, called CIAM (Coala Inference Abstract Machine) [Perc89a].

The main idea is to translate an arc and its behaviour into a sequence of CIAM instructions associated with the basic operations of the parallel connection graph proof procedure: resolution, unification and garbage collection. As a result, CIAM is not an extension of the Warren Abstract Machine (WAM) [Warr83a]. Other parallel implementations like ANLWAM (an OR-Parallel Prolog Architecture) [Cald89a] and RAP-WAM (a Restricted AND-Parallel Prolog Architecture) [Herm86a] are based on the WAM.

As an example, the RAP-WAM Machine [Herm86a] applies similar strategies to those used by Warren. In addition, a *Goal Stack* and the inclusion of *Parcall Frames* in the Local Stack of the WAM are proposed. The WAM instruction set is extended by special instructions for AND-parallelism, such as check instructions, goal scheduling instructions and control instructions. In our approach, the use of the connection graph and its proof procedure prevent the application of similar techniques.

6.1. The CIAM storage model

The CIAM storage model is composed of four main areas: the *message FIFO queue* for the incoming and outgoing messages, the *arc FIFO queue* holding the frames of the arcs, the *heap* holding the environments of the arcs and the *code space*, a static area holding the CIAM instructions. A block diagram of the CIAM storage model is shown in Figure 12.

Beside these areas, the CIAM abstract machine has a number of special locations called registers. Some registers are used to hold the data of an arc: OE (Origin Environment pointer), EE (Extremity Environment pointer), LS (List of

Sons pointer), LB (List of Brothers pointer), STS (Status: resolving, unifying or deleting), RCT (Reference Counter). These six registers, set by an *enter* instruction, define the context of an arc during the resolution, unification and garbage collection processes. In addition, the register A contains the address of the arc frame, composed of several item fields. The first field corresponds to the address of the first instruction in the code area to be executed by an arc when it receives a message.

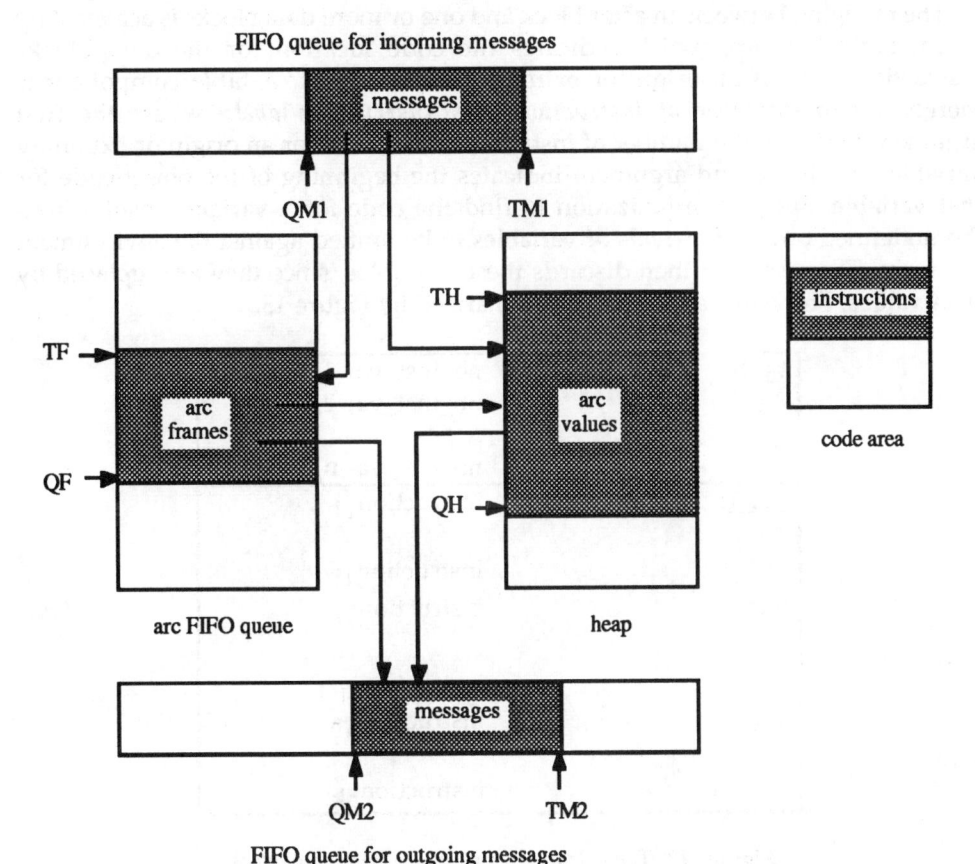

Figure 12 The CIAM storage model

6.2. The CIAM code blocks
The object-code produced by the compilation of the AND/OR connection graph is composed of independent code blocks called *actor blocks* and *data blocks*.

Actor blocks are scenarios. For the CIAM abstract machine, they correspond to the three behaviours of an arc: resolution, unification, or garbage collection. We defined a complete instruction set devoted to these behaviours. Each instruction performs a basic operation related to the parallel execution model such as allocating a new arc, sending requests to other arcs, modifying a list of sons or brothers, and so on. An arc executes these instructions each time it receives a request.

Data blocks are associated with the origin and extremity unification environments of an arc. For each variable of these environments, special instructions are generated depending on the type of the binding presented: constant, variable or compound term. These instructions perform specific actions related to the concerned variable such as unify a constant, copy a value into the message FIFO queue and update a dependency table. They are always activated by special actor block instructions.

The mapping between an actor block and one or more data blocks is achieved by a fast table look-up, which indicates the code location for the data blocks instructions within an origin or extremity environment. A table component is merely a pair <number of instructions, first instruction label> where the first argument indicates the number of instructions executed for an origin or extremity variable and the second argument indicates the beginning of the object-code for that variable. Such an organization to find the code for a variable results from the undefined order of arrivals of variables to be unified against the environment of an arc. The resolvent then discards these variables, since they are replaced by their values. This association can be summarized by Figure 13.

table:	nb_inst_var 1, var 1
	nb_inst_var 2, var 2
	.
	nb_inst_var n, var n
var 1:	$instruction_{11}$
	.
	$instruction_{1i}$
var 2:	$instruction_{21}$
	.
	$instruction_{2j}$
var n:	$instruction_{n1}$
	.
	$instruction_{nk}$

Figure 13 Table look-up and associated data block

The CIAM instruction set is composed of about 40 instructions. Each request for the parallel execution is handled by one or other actor block and its data blocks. Related to the resolution messages are the RESOLVE-REQ, UNIFY-ACK, UNIFY-NACK, and BROTHERS-ACK resolution blocks; unification of the environment of an arc is taken into account by the UNIFY-REQ block; finally, the BROTHERS-REQ and DESTROY-REQ blocks define the garbage collection mechanisms. We also defined two actor blocks, BD-RESOLVE-REQ and BD-UNIFY-REQ, related to binding records management.

6.3. Example: the UNIFY-REQ block

Unification of the environment of an arc against the received environment in a UNIFY-REQ request is the most important operation of the parallel model and is handled by the UNIFY-REQ block. As for the RESOLVE-REQ block, this block uses a table look-up to unify the variables of an arc. Instructions executed are the *unify_constant, unify_variable, re_unify_variable, unify_structure, get_constant, get_variable, assign_origin_variable* and *assign_extremity_variable* instructions.

In case of success, a new frame arc is allocated in the arc FIFO queue by the *allocate* instructions and a UNIFY-ACK message is sent via the *send_unify_ack* instruction to the caller arc; otherwise, a *send_unify_nack* instruction is produced.

The script and data of the UNIFY-REQ block are described by Figure 14.

unify-req:	switch_on_variable
success:	allocate_origin_variables
	allocate_extremity_variables
	allocate_new_arc
	send_unify_ack
L:	deallocate_arc
	return
fail:	send_unify_nack
	jump L

unify_constant
unify_variable
re_unify_variable
unify_structure
get_constant
get_variable
assign_origin_variable n
assign_extremity_variable n

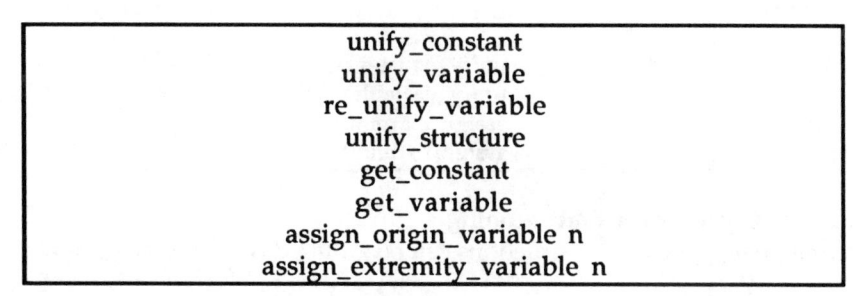

Figure 14 Script and data of the UNIFY-REQ block

The *unify* and *get* instructions access the dereferenced value of the variable designated by the *switch_on_variable* instruction and unify the term received in the message against this dereferenced value. If the unification fails, a branch to the label *fail* occurs; otherwise, the execution returns to the *switch_on_variable* instruction for unifying the next variable of the UNIFY-REQ message. This process repeats until there are no variables in the received environment. Two special registers, N and PS, are used by the *switch_on_variable* instruction to execute this repeating process. N is the number of variables received in the UNIFY-REQ request and PS maintains the address of the *switch_on_variable* instruction to restore the PC program counter when the unification succeeds.

Note that the newly created arc is allocated in the arc queue only when a unification is successfully completed. When the value of the register N is set to zero, execution continues with the instruction specified by the label *success* and the arc FIFO pointer QF is advanced by the *allocate* instructions.

Another interesting point of the unification process is the *assign_extremity_variable n* instruction. Execution of this instruction causes a new binding to be set for the extremity variable n. Assigning an extremity variable is necessary to catch the value of an origin variable, as only the origin environment of an arc is directly involved in the unification process. This instruction ensures communication between the two environments of an arc; values in the origin environment will later be sent via the extremity environment to son arcs.

As an example, let us consider the following sub-graph:

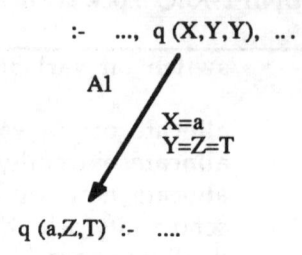

```
:-   ..., q (X,Y,Y), ... .
         A1
             X=a
             Y=Z=T

    q (a,Z,T) :-   .... .
```

Part of the UNIFY-REQ block for the arc A1 is:

V1:	1, var-X
	3, var-Y
	fail
var-X:	unify_constant
var-Y:	unify_variable
	assign_extremity_variable Z
	assign_extremity_variable T

6.4. The CIAM instruction encoding

To summarize, the CIAM instructions can be grouped into five categories:

6.4.1. The switch instructions. Switch instructions are used in the CIAM instruction encoding to support the message passing computation. These instructions act as multiway branches depending on the values of the received arguments. As an example, the *receive_message* and *switch_on_variable* instructions use table look-ups. A table consists of a sequence of labels pointing to arc codes. The switch instructions come in the following forms:

```
enter       A
return
continue    L
continue_or_jump      L1, L2, L3
jump        L
receive_message       Mi,n
switch_on_variable
switch_on_origin_variable         L
switch_on_extremity_variable      L
switch_on_unify_constant    fail
switch_on_put_constant
```

6.4.2. *The arc instructions*. These instructions manipulate the arcs in the arc FIFO queue. New arcs are created by *allocate* or *duplicate* instructions; deletion of arcs is performed by GC instructions. For garbage collection, a reference count field is associated with each arc. This is also used in the heap to remove useless structures. These instructions come in the following forms:

> *allocate_new_arc*
> *allocate_new_virtual_arc*
> *reallocate_arc*   L
> *build_arc*   L1, L2
> *deallocate_arc*
> *destroy_arc*
> *destroy_virtual_arc*
> *allocate_origin_variables*
> *allocate_extremity_variables*
> *increment_reference_counter*
> *decrement_reference_counter*   L
> *modify_son_or_brother*   L1,L2,L3
> *delete_son_or_brother*   L1,L2,L3
> *duplicate_list_of_sons*
> *duplicate_list_of_brothers*

6.4.3. *The unification instructions*. These instructions include *unify* and *get* instructions as found in the WAM [Warr83a]. They are used both to construct new structures and to decompose existing structures. The unification instructions come in the following forms:

> *unify_constant*
> *unify_variable*
> *re_unify_variable*
> *unify_structure*
> *get_constant*
> *get_variable*
> *assign_origin_variable*   n
> *assign_extremity_variable*   n

6.4.4. *The message instructions*. These instructions implement remote procedure calls. A remote procedure call is performed by a pair of messages: a request message and an acknowledgement message. Request instructions are directly tied to the parallel resolution and unification of the arcs. The message instructions come in the following forms:

> *send_resolve_req*
> *send_unify_req_to_sons*
> *send_unify_req_to_brothers*
> *send_brothers_req*
> *send_destroy_req*
> *send_unify_ack*
> *send_unify_nack*
> *send_brothers_ack*

6.4.5. The transfer instructions. These instructions copy arguments from the heap to the message FIFO queue for outgoing messages. There are used to incrementally build messages. They come in the following forms:

        put_constant
        put_variable
        put_first_variable
        re_put_variable
        put_structure
        put_list_of_sons
        put_list_of_brothers

7. PRELIMINARY RESULTS

To support our parallel execution model, we chose a three dimensional cube with the opposite faces identified. This network is a cartesian hypertorus, defined as a generalized hypercube. Each node of a cartesian hypertorus is connected to six other nodes using a three integer coordinate system: length, width and height. The hypertorus topology has a number of potential advantages, in particular homogeneity (no preferred locations) and isotropy (no preferred directions) [Hewi80a].

As the T800 Inmos Transputer is a "ready to use" processor, one can easily and quickly implement an hypertorus-like network. While the T800 solution appears to be a simple and efficient way to validate our approach, our network is only an approximation of the cartesian hypertorus since the T800 Transputer has only four links. An operational prototype, called HYPERTORE, and composed of 36 T800 Inmos Transputers with 4 MB DRAM per Transputer has been constructed. At the same time, we have developed a small communication system devoted to message and task management.

A first version of the CIAM Abstract Machine is now running on the HYPERTORE prototype. Table 1 shows times and speed-ups for different numbers of processors, up to 36. Bench-marks considered are *ibm-40* (a database about IBM personal computers), *map* (a program for colouring several countries) and *cousin* (a family tree). This version combines OR-parallelism with dependency tables and SEARCH-parallelism with binding records. Both strategies have been easily integrated into the same computational model.

Table 1 Times and speed-ups (in ms)

Program	MProlog Sun 3/50	CIAM (1)	CIAM (4)	CIAM (8)	CIAM (16)	CIAM (36)
ibm-40	300	332	175	149	137	104
map	920	732	660	625	593	524
cousin	360	459	230	144	129	131

As indicated by this table, the performance results are encouraging. On one processor, CIAM performances are nearly the same as MProlog performances (one of the fastest commercial systems) on a Sun 3/50: for the *map* colouring problem, we obtained 920 ms with MProlog and 732 ms with CIAM. On 4 processors, the execution is faster than the sequential implementation and absolute performances are obtained by increasing the number of processors. These performance results demonstrate the feasibility of the COALA model and are comparable to other prototypes like Aurora [Lusk88a] and PEPSys [Baro88b].

SUMMARY AND CONCLUSION

Our goal rewriting model, based on R. Kowalski's connection graph and C. Hewitt's actors, represents a new perspective on the parallel interpretation of Prolog programs. R. Kowalski's AND/OR graph and its proof procedure refer to the rewriting mechanism; C. Hewitt's actors refer to the computational model. As a result, the COALA model is not a process-oriented model.

OR-parallelism is obtained by rewriting the different intermediate resolvents during the resolution process. A restricted form of AND-parallelism occurs when building the literals of an intermediate resolvent. In addition, independent AND-parallelism is performed by the use of dependency tables which detect independent sub-resolvents. One can also combine OR-parallelism and SEARCH-parallelism by representing all the arcs of the same procedure stored on the same processor by a binding record. It appears that the first simulation results show that an acceptable performance is obtained while increasing the number of processors up to 36. Better speed-ups are observable for non-deterministic programs operating on numerous definition clauses.

Each arc is an actor composed of a unification environment and links towards other remote arcs. Associated with the behaviours of an arc are the CIAM actor and data blocks. Scripts of an arc specify the actions that the arc performs when it receives a message. All the CIAM abstract machine areas are FIFO queues, reducing the garbage collection process implementation. Garbage collection of memory blocks is based on reference counters, allowing a real-time algorithm. A first version of the CIAM abstract machine is now running on a message-passing computer using Transputers. First experimental results are encouraging and demonstrate the basic feasibility of the COALA approach.

ACKNOWLEDGEMENTS

We would like to thank our colleague Robert Wigetman for taking time to read this paper and comment on our discussion. We express our gratitude to Peter Kacsuk and Michael Wise for their helpful comments. We thank past members of Professor René Beaufils's team, manager of the Computer Architecture Group at the "Institut de Recherche en Informatique de Toulouse" Laboratory, University Paul Sabatier, Toulouse, France. This work has been supported by the "Gréco de Programmation du CNRS", France, since 1984.

PART III Committed Choice Languages

Probably the largest grouping of parallel Prolog implementations is those that have come to be called *Committed Choice*, or sometimes *Stream AND Parallel*. The basic idea behind all these languages is that the goals in a clause will be evaluated in parallel, but each (successful) goal must *commit* to a single set of bindings. That is, only a single set of bindings may be made to variables in the goal, which means that opportunities for OR parallelism are ignored. Variables shared by two or more goals provide the means by which values can be communicated between the sub-computations represented by each of the goals.

In particular, the values produced by a "producer" goal may be structures containing one or more unbound variables. These variables may subsequently be instantiated by a "consumer" goal. However the new set of bindings may also contain variables, which will be instantiated by a different consumer, and so on. Thus a stream is formed.

The choice of methods for synchronizing producers of values with consumers is one of the issues distinguishing the various implementations in this grouping. Included among the methods are the use of mode declarations and annotations on variables (indicating that evaluation of the corresponding goals must be suspended until certain conditions are met) or the use of evaluable predicates, which once again may be suspended until certain conditions are met.

These and other issues concerning the Stream AND Parallel/Committed Choice model are discussed in the excellent introduction that forms Chapter 11. The introduction should be of interest to anyone with an interest in models for parallel computation.

Chapter 12 describes the language RGDC (Reactive Guarded Definite Clauses) which brings the real-time processing capabilities of Occam into a committed choice language. This combination is particularly interesting; programs constructed using RGDC can be more abstract than is possible using Occam, but still exhibit real-time behaviour. This includes the ability to map processes to processors, the ability to set priorities for processes and the ability to enforce time-outs. RGDC is descended from PARLOG86 and somewhat resembles Flat GHC (Guarded Horn Clauses).

The following chapter describes an implementation of Flat Concurrent Prolog on a Transputer-based multiprocessor containing up to 320 nodes. This chapter describes an abstract FCP machine and addresses various issues arising from distributed implementation, in particular the design of a distributed reduction (i.e.

clause evaluation) algorithm. Also discussed are the distributed representation of data and the distributed detection of deadlock. Toward the end of the chapter, some performance results are presented.

The final chapter of the quartet making up this part describes the implementation of KL1, a language based on Flat GHC, on the Multi-PSI. The Multi-PSI is a distributed multiprocessor containing up to 64 nodes. After a brief overview of GHC and KL1, the architecture of the Multi-PSI is described. Following this is a discussion of the garbage collection techniques used, both within processors and between processors, and as with the previous chapter, there is a discussion of distributed unification and the management of distributed data. The chapter finishes with a number of performance measurements.

The three papers after this introduction cover the spectrum from language and semantic issues to implementation techniques. However, those readers more interested in the former aspects may prefer to read Chapter 12, while those more interested in implementation details may prefer Chapters 12 and 13.

11 Stream AND-Parallel Logic Computational Models

S. A. Delgado-Rannauro

Laboratoire Nacional de Informática Avanzada, Mexico

ABSTRACT

One of the prevalent forms of parallelism in logic languages is stream AND-parallelism. In this chapter, the different computational models developed for stream AND-parallelism are reviewed. First, the main concepts of the computational models for stream AND-parallelism are explained. Secondly, the basic notions of the underlying models for the Committed Choice Non-deterministic (CCND) logic languages, a family of stream AND-parallel languages, are described. Furthermore the different developments in compiler technology and the target architectures of the models will be described and reviewed in this chapter.

1 CONCEPTS

The stream AND-parallel computational model as defined in [Kibl85a] considers AND-shared variables in the body goals of a clause as communication channels between these goals. A producer-consumer relationship is needed between these AND-shared variables to establish the communication channel. These producer-consumer relationships are induced by the data-flow synchronisation semantics of the stream AND-parallel languages. Streams can be formed between the producer and consumer goals by using partially instantiated terms.

Annotations or an adequate programming methodology are used in each term of a clause to indicate the direction of the data-flow synchronisation. During the execution of the body goals of a clause, a goal cannot be executed until all its input arguments are available (i.e. all the input variables must be instantiated.).

Stream AND-parallelism can also be viewed as a way of implementing, within logic programming: reactive computation, perpetual processes and other forms of concurrent computation.

Fig. 1 shows an example of the implementation of a perpetual process in a stream AND-parallel program. In Fig. 1(a) a logic program that produces natural numbers is shown. Note that the mode declaration indicates the input and output conditions of the arguments to the clause *natural*. The execution of this program produces all the natural numbers from an initial input. Fig. 1 (b) shows a logic program that takes a natural number as its input and produces the double of the number as its output. A stream between these two programs can be formed, as illustrated in Fig. 1(d); where the *natural* goal produces all the natural numbers, the *double* goal consumes the natural numbers and produces the double of each consumed natural number.

The execution of the query to the programs of Fig. 1(c) attempts first to reduce the goal *double* but it is suspended because the input argument is not instantiated. Thus, the goal *natural* is reduced, it instantiates the variable that caused the suspension of *double*. After the reduction of *natural*, the reduction of *double* can continue with its execution, producing the double of the number and a new goal. The reduction of the new goal suspends, it will be activated as soon as the new goal *natural* binds a value to the variable that caused the suspension. The computation of the query continues perpetually in this form.

mode natural(input,output).

natural(X, [Xs|Y]):- Xs is X,
            Xo is X + 1,
            natural(Xo,Y).

a) A logic program that produces natural numbers.

mode double(input,output).

double([X|Y],Xd):- Xd is X * 2,
          double(Y,Xdd).

b) A logic program that doubles the input number.

?- double(X,Y),natural(0,X).

c) A query to the above programs.

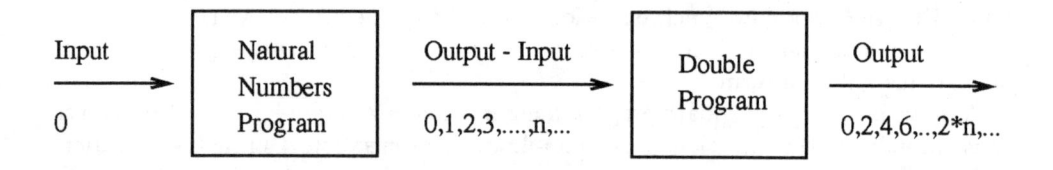

```
Input                Natural      Output - Input    Double       Output
────────▶            Numbers      ─────────────▶    Program      ──────────▶
0                    Program      0,1,2,3,....,n,...                0,2,4,6,...,2*n,...
```

d) A stream AND-parallel execution of the query.

Figure 1. The stream AND-parallel execution of logic programs

The logic languages based on stream AND-parallelism are known as *Committed Choice Non-Deterministic (CCND)* languages. These have abandoned the non-deterministic search provided by OR-parallelism, at least in their basic computational model. They use *don't-care* non-determinism instead, in which only one of the matched clauses of a relation is selected by an indeterministic choice. In section 2, the common features of the computational models are described for CCND languages and their differences are discussed in terms of their computational models. A comprehensive review of CCND languages can be found in [Shap89a].

1.1 Metrics

The different models of CCND languages reviewed in this chapter are compared with respect to their synchronisation mechanisms and unification algorithms.

- **Synchronisation.** With regard to data-flow synchronisation, the CCND languages have different requirements for synchronisation due to their program annotation or programming methodology used to enforce the communication channels through AND-shared variables.

- **Unification.** As a side effect of the *don't-care* non-determinism of these languages, in the evaluation of a specific set of body goal in the clause, unification of terms can be *atomic* or *non-atomic*. The importance of these different types of unification is even more obvious in implementation models for distributed parallel architectures or multi-cluster machines. In the following section, atomic and non-atomic unification are precisely defined within the context of CCND computational models.

2 CCND LANGUAGES

The family of CCND languages is mainly composed of three mainstream languages: **Parlog** [Clar86a], **Concurrent Prolog** [Shap83a] and **Guarded Horn Clause** (GHC) [Ueda86d]. In order to understand their computational model, their common features are described first: syntax, declarative semantics and operational semantics. Their different features in terms of synchronisation and unification will be discussed separately.

2.1 Common Features

2.1.1 Syntax These languages are based on the notion of guards [Dijk75a] and data-flow synchronisation principles. A program is a set of Horn clauses. The clauses are guarded and universally quantified. Their syntax[1] has the form:

H :- $G_1,\ldots,G_n$ | $B_1,\ldots,B_m$ n, m $\geq$ 0

where

G_i is a guard goal
B_j is a body goal
and | is the commit operator

2.1.2 Semantics The declarative semantics of these languages can be generalised as follows:
For all term values of the variables in the clause, H is true if both $G_1,\ldots,G_n$ and $B_1,\ldots, B_m$ are true.

An important issue of their operational semantics is the absence of *don't know* non-determinism; *don't care* non-determinism is used instead to select only one clause of a relation. If the clauses of a relation have proved their guard goals, only one of them is allowed to continue with the execution, the remainder are discarded. Which clause is selected is irrelevant. Once a clause is *committed* (i.e. selected) and any of its body

---
[1] This syntax is based on DEC-10 Prolog syntax.

goals fails, then the proof of the query also fails because there are no alternative paths to explore.

One way of expressing the operational semantics of CCND languages is to use a process-based model. Initially, an OR-process is created for every alternative clause in the relation of a goal call. These OR-processes are available for parallel execution. If some of them prove all their guard goals, then the execution of the commit operator in each OR-process attempts to abort all the other OR-processes in the relation (a mutually exclusive operation). Only the committed OR-process is allowed to proceed with the execution. The committed OR-process forks AND-processes as there are goals in the body of the clause and dies. A invocation of a relation fails if all the OR-processes fail. An AND-process represents a goal call. Therefore, several OR-processes can be spawned from its call.

2.1.3 Basic Computational Model All the CCND languages have adopted simpler definitions, yielding also simpler computational models. These **flat** versions are subsets of the original languages, in which the *guarded clauses* are restricted to a set of predefined predicates; user-defined predicates in the guards are no longer allowed. Thus, in the Flat CCNDs' computational models, guard evaluation is a very simple process. For this reason, the models have undergone a sequential guard evaluation to avoid the overhead caused by spawning OR-processes, for the alternative clauses in the relation; their lifetime would be too short to be worthwhile. This increases the computation grain, but at the expense of losing the non-determinism due to the commit operation.

The data-flow synchronisation of these languages is performed through unification. Synchronisation is achieved by the *Rule of Suspension*. In general, a process is suspended if certain conditions are not met while unifying a variable. Each language has its own set of suspension rules. A process is activated if the conditions which caused the suspension are no longer valid.

The computational model for the Flat CCNDs can be expressed in terms of *reduced* and *suspended* processes. The processes ready for reduction are kept in a *ready* queue. A *suspension* queue is maintained for a set of processes suspended on the same variable. Suspension occurs if an input variable cannot be unified due to its data-flow constraints.

The computation starts with the expansion of the query, producing a set of ready processes and placing them in the ready queue. The computation proceeds until there is at least one process in the ready queue, as shown below:

1. A ready process is de-queued and a reduction attempt is made by trying the clauses of the associated predicate, in the order given by the program (sequential guard evaluation).

2. If a clause is suspended, the suspended variable is placed in a *suspension table* and the next clause of the relation is processed.

3. If the guard goals of a clause succeed, then the clause is committed. The body goals of the clause are placed in the ready queue. All the suspended variables of the process are removed from the suspension table.

4. If all the attempts to commit fail and the suspension table is empty, then the calling goal fails. Otherwise, the process is suspended on the variables recorded in the suspension table.

The computational cycle described above shows the reduction process and how the constraints of the data-flow synchronisation suspend processes. The reactivation of processes is not explicitly mentioned in the computation steps. This activation varies according to the binding restrictions on variables imposed by each language. In the following sections the reactivation process will be described by the model of each language.

2.2 Parlog

Parlog adopts mode declarations at clause-level to enforce the direction in the unification of terms. All the relations defined in a Parlog program have to include their corresponding declaration. Every argument can be declared in input mode (?) or output mode (^). A clause is suspended if, during head unification, an attempt is made to unify a variable appearing in an argument position declared as input to a nonvariable term. Variables in output mode arguments can only be bound after a clause has been selected or committed. A Parlog program is shown in Fig. 2, it is the partition clause from the quicksort program. Note the mode declaration at relation-level, which provides a static definition of the program data-flow and synchronisation.

```
mode partition(?,?,^,^).

partition(X,[],[],[]).
partition(X,[Y|Z],[Y|Smaller],Larger):- X < Y |
    partition(X,Z,Smaller,Larger).
partition(X,[Y|Z],Smaller,[Y|Larger]):- X >= Y |
    partition(X,Z,Smaller,Larger).
```

Figure 2: A Parlog partition program

Compile-time analysis was necessary in the initial versions of Parlog [Greg85a] to ensure that a Parlog program was **safe**. A program is safe if no guard can bind variables appearing as input arguments. Program transformation techniques were used to translate Parlog programs to a *Kernel Parlog*; a simpler language which can be supported directly by different architectures.

The transformation process uses a set of one-way *unification primitives* to perform head unification. The need for mode declarations does not longer exist in Kernel Parlog, the binding conditions of the arguments are provided by the unification primitives. A definition of these primitives can be found in [Greg85a].

The use of these program transformation techniques in Parlog was one of the first steps taken to simplify the underlying computational model in a CCND language. The next step taken was the definition of a **flat** version of the language, in which the underlying computational model was simplified even further [Fost87a].

As mentioned in the definition of the basic computational model, Flat CCND languages have adopted the sequential evaluation of guards within a relation, Flat Parlog also uses the same mechanism. In Flat Parlog input variables cannot be bound during guard evaluation, this causes the suspension of the clause, i.e. the so-called Flat Parlog's Rule of Suspension. Output variables can only be bound after commitment,

```
partition(X,[],[],[]).
partition(X,[Y|Z],[Y|Smaller],Larger):- X < Y |
partition(X,Z?,Smaller,Larger).
partition(X,[Y|Z],Smaller,[Y|Larger]):- X >= Y |
partition(X,Z?,Smaller,Larger).
```

Figure 3: A Concurrent Prolog partition program

binding output variables may reactivate processes suspended on those variables.

2.3 Concurrent Prolog

Concurrent Prolog [Shap83a] adopts a *read-only* annotation at variable level as the data-flow constraint. The annotation is denoted by "?". Access to these variables is restricted to read-only mode. An attempt to instantiate a variable with read-only annotation causes the process to be suspended until the variable is instantiated by another process with permission to write to it, i.e. the same variable without read-only annotation. Read-only annotations must be handled in the general unification procedure, since read-only variables can appear anywhere in a term. The definition of the partition program written in Concurrent Prolog is shown in Fig. 3. Note that the read-only notation is used only when a goal is called.

The definition of Concurrent Prolog does not impose any restriction on the binding of variables. They can be bound at any time during processing the head, guard or body of clauses Due to this uncertainty about the binding operation in Concurrent Prolog, its unification must be exclusive. In order to achieve this property, the binding environments in the guards must be mutually exclusive in all the clauses of the same procedure (it requires the management of multiple bindings for the variables, similar to OR-parallel binding schemes). Thus, each clause upon evaluating the guard, must have a local environment for the isolation of variable bindings[2].

The initial description of Concurrent Prolog uses full unification in the guards, which led to the need for OR-parallel binding methods and a hierarchy of guard processes. This freedom made Concurrent Prolog a very flexible and expressive language, but at the expense of a complex computational model. Since Concurrent Prolog needs to manage multiple environments before committing, all the binding made during guard evaluation are kept in a local environment. After commitment the local environment is exported to the global environment.

Due to these complexities and the overhead caused in the unification algorithm by the read-only annotation, a new language was developed. This new version, *Flat Concurrent Prolog* (FCP) [Mier85a], eliminated the need for the management of multiple binding environments in the guard, As it is the case with all the Flat CCND languages, only predefined predicates are allowed in the guard. However FCP still supports variable bindings in the guard. Sequential guard evaluation is used and variable bindings made by the guard are undone on its failure. If a guard evaluation is suspended, all bindings made during the evaluation are undone before the next clause is processed,

---
[2]These variables are semantically the same as the OR-shared variables defined in [Delg92a]. In fact, the binding scheme used for the evaluation of guards in the initial definition of Concurrent Prolog is a copying environment scheme.

using a trail mechanism to record variable bindings. These variable bindings are re-computed once the process is re-activated since it would be more expensive to record them.

The name *atomic unification* has been coined to make the distinction between the method used in Concurrent Prolog and the ones used in Parlog and GHC. The method used in Parlog and GHC is referred to as *non-atomic unification*. Atomic unification refers to the evaluation of the guard in a clause, it must be performed as a single atomic action. This keeps other processes from attempting to bind the same variable while the guard evaluation is being performed.

Further developments in the language include distinctions in the predefined predicates of the guard, following considerations made by V. Saraswat [Sara86a]. These distinctions avoid the extensive use of atomic unification for simple equality tests required during guard evaluation. The guards are then divided in *ask* non-atomic unification and *tell* guards atomic unification [Klig88a]. This new definition of the language draws it closer to Flat Parlog and Flat GHC.

```
partition(X,[],Smaller,Larger):- true |
Smaller = [], Larger = [].
partition(X,[Y|Z],Sm,Larger]:- X < Y |
Sm = [Y|Smaller],
partition(X,Z,Smaller,Larger).
partition(X,[Y|Z],Smaller,Lr):- X >= Y |
Lr = [Y|Larger],
partition(X,Z,Smaller,Larger).
```

Figure 4: A GHC partition program

2.4 Guarded Horn Clause

Guarded Horn Clause (GHC) was developed as an alternative to Concurrent Prolog, it was designed overcome the problems highlighted in [Ueda86d]. The language does not use any direct and explicit annotation to restrict variable access. However, it uses the definition of the guard part to constrain access to variables in a goal. In GHC, during head unification and the computation of the guard, any attempt to instantiate a variable appearing in the head to a non-variable term causes the clause to suspend. All the unification of head variables to non-variable terms must be performed after the clause has been committed. The programming style is shown in Fig. 4 with the partition program.

GHC was designed to maintain a single binding environment. However, there is still a subtle problem (as mentioned in [Clar86a]); the unification must be able to detect whether a variable belongs to a guard conjunction or a body conjunction. A run-time check is required during unification. For this reason, the work on the language at the computational model level is being restricted to a Flat version. Flat GHC, called KL1, [Kimu87a] follows a similar direction to the other Flat CCNDs. Only predefined predicates are allowed in the guards and the suspension rule is very similar to that of Flat Parlog. If a variable in the goal is to be bound during guard evaluation, the clause is suspended. The guard evaluation is also sequential in Flat GHC.

3 ARQUITECTURAL MODELS FOR CCND LANGUAGES

The basic principles of the CCND models have been described but no assumptions been made about the underlying architectural model for the CCND models. In this section the different techniques used for the design of the corresponding computational models are described. These include compilation techniques and implementaion of the models, both in shared memory and distributed memory parallel machines.

The levels of complexity in these languages, at least at the computational model level, have been considerabley reduced by the definition of the **Flat** versions. In spite of being less expressive and powerful, they represent a compromise between efficiency and expressiveness. Some of the full versions can be mapped onto their corresponding flat versions without any problem. Along with the development of the flat versions, improvements in their compilation techniques have taken place. These developments have optimised further the underlying model.

3.1 Flat CCNDs Compilation Techniques

The new breed of Flat CCNDs can be characterised by non-atomic and atomic unifications. The latter belongs to the Flat Concurrent Prolog (FCP), and the former belongs to Flat Parlog and FGHC. The compilation techniques used for these languages can be classified as clause-level compilation or relation-level compilation. The clause-level compilation is a method adapted from the sequential Prolog techniques [Warr83a]. In Prolog, the clause-level compilation is required due to the embedded control strategy in the language, where the unification of arguments is repeated for every argument in each clause. Variable bindings must be undone during backtracking prior to the selection of the next candidate clause in the relation[3]. Flat CCND languages do not require such a control. Thus, the clause-level compilation is not completely needed. The relation-level compilation of [Klig88a] represents an alternative approach for the implementation of Flat CCNDs in which clause selection is coupled with sequential guard evaluation.

In [Klig88a] a new compilation technique is developed for another version of FCP, called FCP(:,|,?). This new language has two different sets of guard goals: ask and tell. The former only allows test unification (input unification) with the arguments of the goal, whereas the latter allows atomic unification. The decision-tree compilation method [Klig88a] improves the sequential execution part of the FCP(|,:,?) model. The approach compiles the entire relation into a control-flow decision-tree. Each node in the decision-tree either checks one of the arguments of the goal or performs an ask guard test. A leaf in the control decision-tree contains one of the following instructions:

- Instructions for performing the tell parts and the bodies of one or more clauses in the procedure. Each leaf corresponds to clauses with equivalent heads and ask guards. Reaching a leaf in the tree corresponds to a successful reduction of the ask part of the clause. In the other Flat CCND models such a leaf would imply successful reduction and commitment.

- A *fail* instruction

- A *suspend* instruction

---

[3] A relation-level compilation method is also needed in Prolog, but it is required for clause selection and efficient compilation of cut, i.e. as part of the indexing scheme ([Zhou90a],[Chen88a]).

The improvement of the decision-tree technique is achieved by generating the amalgamation of clause indexing with input unification, in the execution of the sequential part of the Flat CCNDs. Thus, it avoids the repetition of test instructions with the aid of the indexing scheme. It makes a global analysis of the procedure to find the shortest path to commitment and reduction. As a side-effect, it can also avoid unnecessary suspensions of variables which otherwise would have been performed.

3.2 Parallel Shared Memory Models for Flat CCNDs

3.2.1 Flat GHC The ICOT approach [Sato87a] towards a shared memory implementation is the basis of their Parallel Inference Machine, PIM. The target architecture is a multi-cluster machine in which each cluster itself is a shared memory machine. The main idea behind the design of such an architecture is to enhance locality of reference within cluster boundaries. The CCNDs impose a data-flow control that requires synchronisation. Therefore, the idea of using shared memory is to reduce the communication needed for the implementation of these data-flow controls. In a distributed architecture, one with only a single processing element per node, communication can be very expensive. However, in a distributed machine some other problems, such as load balancing, require a global approach which is normally easier to solve than in a system requiring consideration of the distances between processing nodes, as in the multi-cluster architecture.

The basic execution model of the PIM cluster is that each processing element PE has its own set of data structures to achieve locality; synchronisation is only required if variables are bound and for the management of the reduction queues (ready and suspended).

Each PE can abstractly be viewed as being composed of a *scheduler* process and a *reducer* process. The role of the scheduler is to select a *ready* goal and to invoke the reducer. The reducer performs the computation in three stages: *guard test, body unification*, and *body goal fork*. The execution of the three stages has the following order:

1. **Guard Test**: The test is done sequentially with all the guards of the procedure. The initial head unification of a clause is part of the guard test. The first guard evaluation to succeed is chosen and the reducer commits, i.e. it completes the clause selection phase. Any attempt to bind a variable in the guard causes the goal to be suspended on that variable before proceeding with the guard of the next clause. All suspended variables are recorded in a *suspension stack*. If there is no successful commitment, the reducer looks into the suspension stack for suspended variables. If empty, the goal reduction fails; otherwise, all the variables suspended are linked to the goal, forming suspension records. This mechanism provides a way of reactivating goals after the suspended variables are instantiated.

2. **Body Unification**: Unification, binding of variables in the goal being reduced, can only be allowed once a clause has been committed. If the unification instantiates a suspended variable, the reducer reactivates the suspended goals and places them in the ready queue.

3. **Body Goal Fork**: If there are any body goals in the clause, the reducer creates one record for each goal and places them in the ready queue. After that the reducer invokes the scheduler which selects the next *ready* goal. As an optimisation, to improve locality of reference and to develop a pseudo depth first search,

the reducer does not create a record for one of the goals but itself attempts the reduction at once. This has also the benefit of allowing the implementation of tail recursion optimisation (TRO), as in sequential Prolog.

Another important issue for the process of goal reduction is the distribution of goals. The basic scheduling mechanism is depth-first search which not only maintains locality but is more efficient since the PE's reducer process minimises memory accesses. The second scheduling level is performed on demand, i.e. only when a PE has its ready queue(s) empty. The advantage of such method is the elimination of wasteful inter-PE communication. The load distribution is achieved by means of user annotations. The user includes these designations, *pragmas*, in the program to balance the load. This process is called *On-Demand with Pragma (ODP) distribution*.

Each PE has two ready queues to distribute goals, one high priority and another low priority queue. The goals without pragmas are always placed in the former, whereas those with pragma are placed in the low priority queue, provided there are no requests pending from idle PEs. If there are idle PEs, the goal is placed in a message buffer instead and sent to the idle PE. Most of the time goals with pragmas are reduced by the owner PE. If there is an idle PE and the busy PE has goals in its low priority queue, the idle PE interrupts the busy one to request a goal. The busy PE then de-queues the goal from the low priority queue and places it in the message buffer of the idle PE.

Discussion: The pragma annotation mechanism could be advantegeous for machines with a small number of PEs but it seems to lack flexibility and puts an unnecessary burden on the user. It lacks flexibility if not enough goals with pragmas are generated. In the case of a large parallel system, the task granularity tends to be smaller and the amount of communication grows; hence enforcing too much locality has the disadvantage of producing starvation in other PEs while available work exists.

The amount of synchronisation is reduced considerably by localising the management of the ready queues, and using messages to transmit the reducible goal upon request. It could also be implemented in shared memory, but in this case, the ready queues memory area could be made global to all PEs and the need for explicit messages is obviated.

3.2.2 Shared Memory Management in Flat GHC The management of memory is crucial in all declarative languages; their memory consumption is well-known. Logic languages are no exception to the rule. However, one of the advantages of the control strategy followed by Prolog is the reduced amount of garbage collection required during execution. In Prolog, most of the memory is recovered while backtracking. Since Flat CCNDs do not support backtracking, the process of memory recovery has to employ other means. In ICOT, the importance of the problem has been realised and a garbage collector has been developed as an integral part of the abstract machine description of their language KL1 or Flat GHC.

In [Chik87a] a method based on incremental garbage collection is developed. The central idea is to recover quickly as much memory as possible. The method does not pretend to be a complete garbage collector[4], but aims at reducing the number of calls to a general garbage collector, while at the same time minimises the amount

---

[4]T. Chikayama in [Chik88b] gave an estimated overhead of a copying garbage collection algorithm in the PIM cluster. His calculations showed an overhead of 120% for this algorithm if the triggering point is at 50% of the heap memory used in the system. Therefore, if the number of calls to a general garbage collector is reduced, the overall performance of the system tends to be better. Thus, any

of allocated memory. This has important repercussions on several levels of machine design. Assume there is a parallel machine in which each PE has a local cache memory. First, by minimising the working set of the program, the cache hit rate is increased because the range of memory referred to is kept small. In the case of a virtual memory system, it would also reduce the amount of paging ratio. For further details about the behaviour of the model, the reader is directed to [Nish90a].

The garbage collection method used, *Multiple Reference Bit (MRB)*, uses one bit in each pointer to detect whenever multiple references are made to the referred data. The information is kept in the pointer rather than in the data itself to reduce the expensive management of reference counters, which in a parallel system would involve mutual exclusion for their updating. The MRB bit is set whenever more than one reference to a data cell is made. The method can only recover data when its MRB is zero, i.e. it has only one reference.

The abstract machine instruction set is augmented and modified to incorporate the MRB method. Instructions in the guard part are augmented to recover the memory space. The method is compiled into the execution model of the abstract machine architecture. Also the general unification algorithm is modified to cope with the MRB method.

3.3 Distributed Memory Models for Flat CCNDs

In this section, besides discussing pure distributed memory models, multi-cluster architectures are also included. Similar design considerations are necessary for inter-cluster processing or communication in distributed memory models ([Ichi87a],[Goto88a]).

In spite of a more efficient set of CCND languages defined, the implementation of their models in distributed architectures is by no means straight forward. Although many issues, such as non-determinate commitment, no longer need consideration. Issues such as distributed unification (to be explained in the following paragraph) and external references to suspended variables play an important role in the implementation of these languages in a distributed environment. Another important area of research for these distributed models is termination-detection and abortion algorithms. Each of the research groups addresses these issues in relation to their language implementation model.

The problem of distributed unification occurs whenever two different processes located in different PEs try to communicate via an AND-shared variable. A decision must be made to select the most suitable process to perform the unification of the AND-shared variable. The solution implies the specification of a communication protocol and also the use of some parameters to decide where the operation is to take place. Therefore, issues about locality of reference play an important role in the protocol definition. Distributed unification is also called as atomic, for FCP(:,|,?), and non-atomic, for Flat Parlog and Flat GHC.

3.3.1 Flat GHC The key issues with the distributed model for Flat GHC are the management of distributed processes and the development of an inter-processor communication protocol to avoid race conditions between simultaneous operations on the distributed AND-tree [Ichi87a]. First, the decisions made for the implementation in the Multi-PSI architecture are described. Then, A new enhanced model is described and discussed for the management of distributed unification and external references

---

effective measure of performance in these computational models should explain the overhead due to garbage collection.

[Ichi88a]. This enhanced model is geared towards the PIM machine, a multi-cluster architecture.

Multi-PSI Model [Ichi87a]: This system assumes the following specifications:

1. PEs are assigned unique identification numbers to be used in inter-PE communication and inter-PE data references.
2. PEs are interconnected by a high speed network
3. PEs have separate local memory spaces, but each PE can access external data by an inter-PE reference mechanism.
4. PEs communicate with each other by message passing via the network.

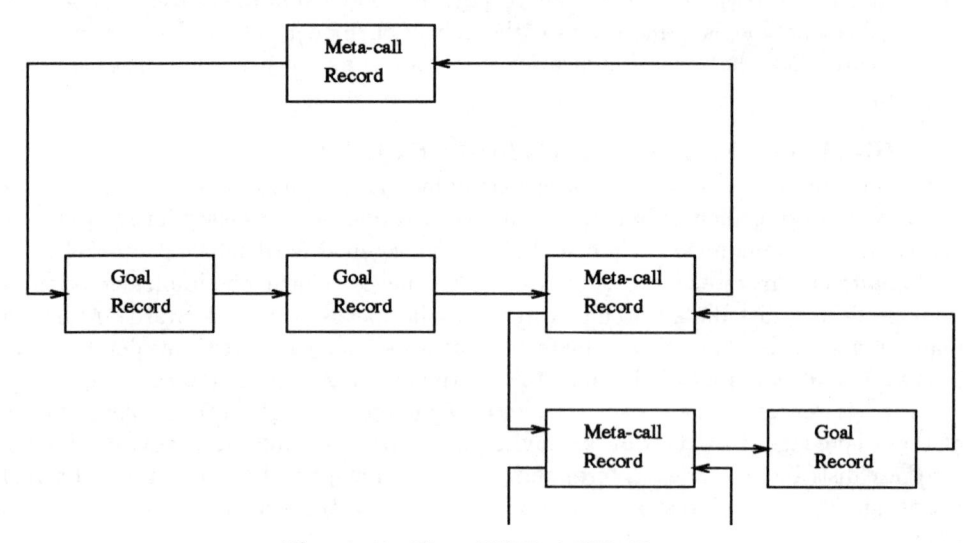

Figure 5: Flat GHC AND-Tree

The AND-Tree (Fig. 5) represents all goals under execution. The goals can be executed in different PEs, thus the AND-tree spawns over the active PEs in the system. If a goal is requested by an idle PE, the goal execution is considered to be external. The management of goals, which are executed externally, is achieved by a *meta-call record*. These records are the root of the subtrees generated by different PEs and represent the linking of the subtrees processed by each PE. The meta-call mechanism is also used for meta-level applications which can reason about programs as processes. For example, in operating system applications in which the concept of failure is different from logic programming (i.e. the implementation of the task or job concept in operating systems). A meta-call in the context of operating systems should be considered as a *process descriptor*, but with the subtle difference that the same abstraction the meta-call can be used at more than one implementation level, i.e. at system programming level and at program execution level.

A meta-call is of the form:

call (Goal,Result,Control).

Where **Goal** is the goal to be executed, **Result** is the result of the call and **Control** is an input stream for control messages *suspend, resume, stop*. The meta-call record in the computational model is divided into two records. One is maintained in the parent PE's local space, the *proxy record*, and the other is in the child PE's local space, *foster parent record*.

External references are represented by three element data cells: a read flag, the PE number and the cell identification number. The external reference is uniquely determined by the PE and the cell identification number. A cell which is referenced from outside the local PE is called *exported*. An export table is maintained in each PE to retrieve exported cells if their cell identification numbers are given as the key.

Distributed Unification in the model can occur at guard evaluation (*passive unification*) or body execution (*active unification*). Note that Flat GHC only allows equality tests (i.e. passive unification) in the guard, which means that variables appearing as input arguments cannot bind the input variables, they can only read values which may be external. The active unification can bind variables, therefore it may need to bind two terms which are not in the same PEs, thus requiring a distributed unification.

Tha passive unification may need to read external values. The algorithm used for reading external values consists of the following steps:

- If during guard evaluation an external cell is referenced, then the external access is delayed until the evaluation of all guards in the relation is completed. The externally referenced cell is treated as a suspended variable, i.e. pushed onto the *suspension stack*.

- If the goal has not yet been committed and there is an external reference in the suspension stack, then a *read_value* message is created to retrieve the desired value.

- When the external read transaction is completed, and if the goal has not yet been committed, then the goal is reactivated. In this case, if the externally read value does not enable the goal to commit, then the goal remains suspended.

Note that it does not matter whether the communication for the external message has been completed or not before attempting the commitment procedure. The latter brings back a non-deterministic behaviour in the guard evaluation, which is dependent on the availability of data.

The active unification part must avoid the race conditions when several PEs can potentially bind the same shared variable. The obvious and naive solution is to lock the variables while performing unification, but this would be too expensive in a distributed implementation and, on top of that, it would introduce new problems, such as deadlock avoidance. The solution found in this model is simply to avoid unifying if there is an external reference to a variable by explicitly generating a *unify message* to the foreign PE. The foreign PE will report whether the unification has succeeded or failed. For the case where there are two uninstantiated variables belonging to two different PEs, a *seniority rule* applies. The variable of the PE with the smaller PE number is made to point to the one with the larger PE number.

Multi-Cluster Architecture [Ichi88a]: The new external reference management and distributed unification models represent a step forward in the definition of the Parallel

Inference Machine, PIM. In this new scheme the realisation of incremental inter-PE garbage collection is discussed.

The incremental inter-PE garbage collection is a weighted garbage collector based on [Wats87a]. By assigning weighted reference counts to pointers as well as to referenced data, the race problem in a distributed environment has been solved. Some modifications to the basic model were done to customise it for the Flat GHC paradigm. The *Weighted External Counting (WEC)* scheme uses export tables, as defined in the Multi-PSI model, for making garbage collection independent. It also introduces *import* tables across PEs, to reduce the number of inter-PE read requests.

The distributed unification algorithm needs to be modified in the light of this new scheme. It turned out that the previous scheme [Ichi87a] could not prevent reference loops from being created.

In this scheme, the same abstract machine is used as in the Multi-PSI case. But furthermore, it is assumed that inter-PE communication is expensive and rare compared to local memory accesses. Those assumptions are to justify the "rather complicated external reference scheme adopted" (see Fig. 6).

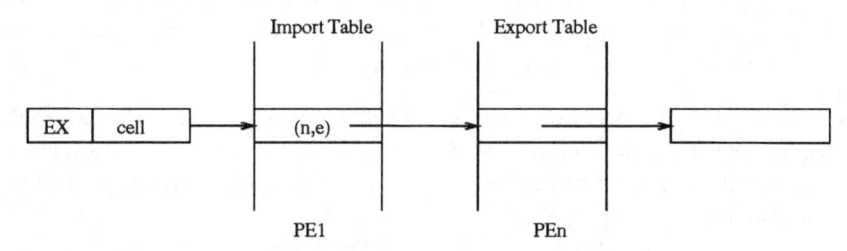

Figure 6: **External Reference Management in Distributed Flat GHC**

To manage external references, as in [Ichi87a], each PE has an *export* table to register all the data referred to externally. This makes it possible to localise the process of garbage collection by introducing an extra indirection in the address translation. In this case all the foreign PEs see external data with a unique identifier, although its physical address may change several times during the lifetime of the data cell.

As a measure to reduce the number of *external read* requests, each PE also has an *import* table associated with it. This table records all the external accesses made to foreign PEs. One could see this import table as a sort of cache, but equipped with extra functions needed for the proper implementation of the garbage collection scheme.

The WEC garbage collection scheme maintains a weight for each external reference (in both tables). In the first external reference, the corresponding entries in the export and import table receive a *maximum* weight. For every newly created reference pointing either to the import or the export tables, the weight is divided equally. The entry in the table and the new reference receive the divided weight. In this scheme the sum of all weights for a single external reference is the *initial* maximum weight (Fig. 7).

After references have been discarded, the WEC value of the discarded reference is subtracted from the WEC value of the cell being pointed at. When the WEC of a pointed cell reaches zero, the cell can be recovered.

If the WEC of an external cell can no longer be split (i.e. the operations on the WEC are integer. Thus, a WEC with value 1 can not be divided any longer), an *indirect exportation* is performed; an external reference with the maximum weight pointing to the cell with the minimum weight. The inconvenience of such an alternative is that it

a) first reference to D

b) second reference to D

c) deleting a reference to D

c) creating an indirect cell

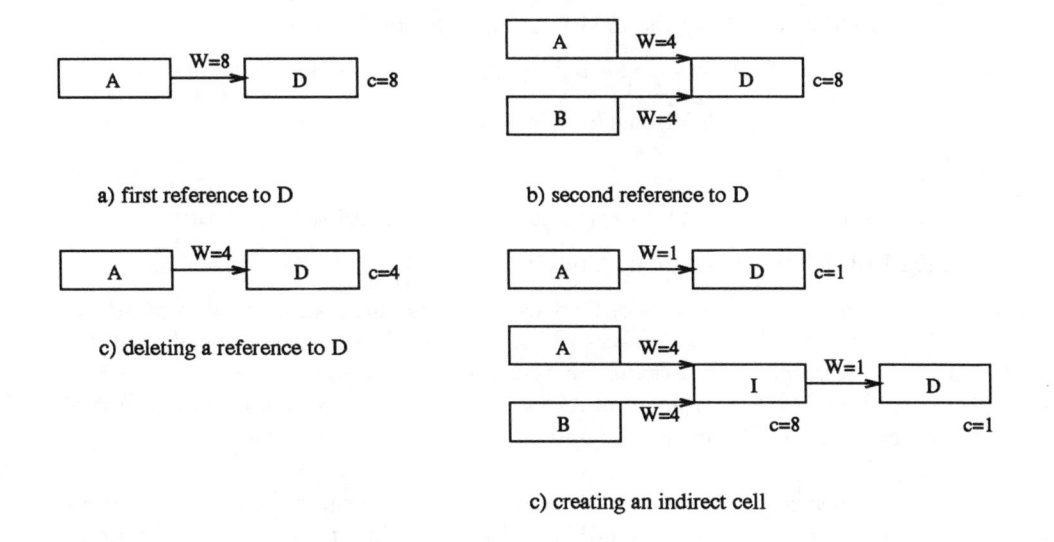

Figure 7: The Weighted External Garbage Collection scheme

makes the reference chain longer. Since the external reference chains are expected to be relatively short, the indirect exportation operation will rarely be applied.

However, the use of indirect exportation introduces an extra complexity for the distributed unification algorithm. The seniority rule employed in [Ichi87a] does not hold any more. Reference loops cannot be avoided with a simple PE numbering scheme. The notion of *safe* and *unsafe* external (E) references are introduced. A reference e is unsafe if and only if:

1. PE(from(E)) < PE(to(E)), or

2. PE(to(E)) is an unsafe external reference.

Discussion: The implementation schemes for Flat GHC in a distributed architecture assumes technological constraints on the access of memory cells. The external memory accesses are considered far more expensive than local memory accesses. The introduction of different levels of indirection in external memory access introduces a constant overhead, while minimising the amount of external communication in the system, either for normal external accesses or for the management of garbage collection. The WEC garbage collection algorithm localises, with the aid of the export and the import tables, in each PE the inter-PE garbage collection. As a side-effect, the WEC scheme increases the amount of locality of reference of the computational model.

The main criticism of the WEC scheme consists in the underlying assumptions about the cost ratio of external to local memory accesses. If such a cost ratio drops, the overhead for the management of external memory cells increases. Therefore, the management of the external cells should also be reduced.

3.3.2 Flat Parlog In [Fost88a] a distributed implementation model for Flat Parlog is described. This model tackles similar issues as those defined in [Ichi87a] and [Ichi88a]: external references, distributed unification and the *control call* (a similar role to the meta-call in [Ichi87a]).

The approach presented by the model assumes the following architecture:

- A number of nodes (PEs) connected by a reliable communication network,
- No global storage; each PE has local storage and
- PEs communicate by message passing.

The *control call* is an important component of Parlog and takes the form:

call(Module,Process,Status,Control)

It denotes the controlled execution of **Process** using the program defined in **Module**. **Control** is a stream of control messages which can cause **Process** to suspend, continue or abort the evaluation. The **Status**, another stream of messages, shows the current status of **Process**. The control call provides Parlog with the notion of *task*; a unit of computation which may be monitored and controlled as a single entity.

Distributed Unification. As in [Ichi87a] unification can be subdivided into a *read* algorithm (passive unification in Flat GHC) and a *unify* algorithm (active unification). The *read* algorithm is applied during guard evaluation. A test operation applied to a remote variable causes it to be suspended. If the reduction attempt is suspended, messages are generated to request the values of any remote variable encountered in the suspension stack. Then the process will be selected and placed in the ready queue upon receiving the requested remote term.

In Parlog, most of the guard tests are **strict**; they are suspended until all the input arguments are instantiated. A few tests are **non-strict**, like some equality and inequality primitives: $==$ and $=/=$; they can sometimes proceed if their input arguments are variables. Two types of read algorithm are considered to model the guard evaluation : *read* for strict test and *ns-read* for non-strict tests. The main difference between these two is that one can be completed only when the requested data is instantiated and the other can be completed if this is not the case.

The *unify* algorithm is executed once the goal is committed and the unification of the output arguments is to be performed at the *spawn* phase of the reduction process. If a unification operation encounters a remote reference, a **unify** message is generated to request PEs on which remote terms are located to continue the unification.

Consider the unification of two terms. If one of the terms is remote, then the unify message carries the value of the other term and the unification is performed by the remote PE. If both terms are remote references, a modified *unify1* message is sent. It is first dispatched to the PE where the first term is located; that PE forwards a unify message to the PE which has the second term, inlcuding the value of the first term.

A *failure* message is sent to the source PE so that the proper action is taken, such as reporting to the parent *control call* that the process has failed. This model does not seem to require a *success* message if the remote *unify* algorithm is completed, since in this scheme the success of the remote unification can be assumed because there is only one active path during the time active unification is performed. Therefore, the computation of the path can be continued without any delay.

The seniority rule of [Ichi87a] is applied for bindings made during distributed unification; that is, variables are bound according to their PE number, from low to high numbers. If an external variable is unified with a local variable and the external variable has its PE number smaller than the local PE, then a unify message is sent to the external PE so that the *binding order* is maintained.

Discussion: This Flat Parlog distributed model has incorporated the same ideas as [Ichi87a] which shows the similarity of the computational models of the two languages: Flat GHC and Flat Parlog, i.e. it could be said that they are semantically similar at the operational level, although their syntax is different. The Flat Parlog's distributed model is simpler than the current Flat GHC models because it does not incorporate any garbage collection algorithm. Although Flat Parlog's distributed model is simpler, there seems to be no indication of the reduction of inter-PE communication.

3.3.3 Flat Concurrent Prolog There are three distributed models for FCP described in the literature [Baro86a, Tayl87b, Tayl88a]. For the purposes of the present report, only [Tayl88a] is described and discussed since it is the most optimised version and has evolved from the preceding two.

The atomic unification in [Tayl88a] requires execution as a single atomic operation. Its implementation entails two additional subproblems: *deadlock* and *starvation*. In the context of FCP, deadlock may occur when multiple processes attempt to access shared variables. This is analogous to the concept of shared resources in operating systems. Starvation may occur if some deadlock prevention algorithm makes a process hold a lock on a variable indefinitely without ever writing to it. This may prevent other processes from accessing the variable.

The execution model presents a solution to the deadlock problem based on priority locking mechanisms. The model ensures that only a single occurrence of each variable exists. All other means of accessing the variable are made by local or external references to it. The notion of a global address space is implemented. It is composed of the PE number and the location within a PE.

Distributed Unification. The reduction algorithm is similar to the description of the basic CCND computational model, in which guard evaluation is performed sequentially. An external reference to a variable during guard evaluation causes the process, as in the Flat Parlog and Flat GHC distributed models, to be delayed. Communication is only performed if the guard evaluation cannot be reduced sequentially and there are external reference requests pending. The main difference is that FCP can have head unification operations during the guard evaluation, i.e. during atomic unification. All the data required to reduce a goal needs to be local. This ensures that even in the case of distributed atomic unification it is realised locally after all the information is brought in.

The reduction process deals with the external references in a similar way as with the suspension of read-only variables. There are two *tables* to be checked during the execution of the suspension phase, the *suspension* table and the *lock* table. The former is for local suspension records and the latter for external suspension records which require explicit communication.

The reduction process makes a further distinction between external *read* and *write* requests. The communication protocol for external *read* requests is simple because it does not require to be mutually exclusive. The *write* requests require locking since there can only be a single occurrence of variables. Remember that atomic unification is to be performed locally, regardless of external values. Therefore every time a goal reduction needs to write to an external reference, the external variable is to be localised, this is referred to as *variable migration*. Localising a variable is performed by swapping the value of the external variable with the local reference of the external variable.

The implementation of variable migration requires locking, which brings up the issue of deadlock prevention. The algorithm uses statically assigned priorities to PEs. The *locking* algorithm ensures that locks are always granted to PEs with higher priority. So, a PE with lower priority will always release the lock it holds when a higher priority PE requests the same variable. If a PE with lower priority requests access to a locked variable, the request is deferred until either the variable lock is removed or the variable is bound to a value. This algorithm ensures that eventually a PE will be granted all the locks it requires, except in the case of starvation.

When localising a variable, *variable migration*, several processes may be suspended on that variable, to reactivate all those externally suspended processes, a *broadcast note* is attached to the reply message. The note indicates which processes need to be activated as a result of unifying the variable. As an optimisation and to avoid the unnecessary creation of messages, the broadcast note only contains information of the destination of the variable.

3.3.4 Discussion of the Distributed Models for Flat CCNDs As previously stated the main difference between these computational models consists in the different language semantics: FCP allows head (output) unification at the guard level, calling for an atomic unification procedure. This mechanism requires an algorithm that ensures mutual exclusiveness if it involves access to external references. This characteristic is not required in the other two Flat CCNDs due to their more restricted data-flow synchronisation. Flat Parlog constraints the data-flow by annotated declarations at the relation-level, and Flat GHC ensures that no variable can be bound during guard evaluation.

In terms of performance, only one attempt has been made to compare Flat CCND languages [Fost87a]. This study only included Flat Parlog and FCP in a sequential environment. It was observed that Flat Parlog is about 10% more efficient than FCP due to the constant usage of general unification in the latter. Since then, attempts have been made to overcome such problems in the definition of FCP. A new language has been developed, FCP(:,?,|) [Klig88a], having a similar semantic behaviour to Flat Parlog and Flat GHC, but without losing the concept of read-only variables.

Although FCP seems to be the most complex model. The real performance differences in a distributed implementation can be minimal if the observed behaviour on external communication in [Tayl87b] occurs in most programs. It resulted that from the total number of external reference requests around 85% of them were read requests. External read requests do not need any synchronisation. Furthermore, optimisations such as the ones used in [Ichi88a] can also be introduced to reduce the number of external read requests in FCP. Therefore, the complexity of the algorithm for the atomic unification in FCP (which is now considerably simplified) is rarely used in the case of external communication. Thus, it may be concluded that, in practice, the difference in performance of the various computational models in a distributed environment is not as important as the first impression leads to believe.

4 SUMMARY

During the last decade, since the definition of Concurrent Prolog [Shap83a], the advances made in Committed Choice Non-Deterministic languages have been substantial: language issues, computational models, program transformation techniques, implementation issues, etc.. The development process of these languages has been influenced by the definition of computational and execution models. The first set of CCNDs, although expressively powerful for several applications, were difficult to implement because of the problems mentioned in the introductory paragraphs of this chapter. The development of the Flat CCNDs ushered a new era for the computational and execution models for stream AND-Parallelism. These new sub-sets are simpler but they have preserved most of the expressive power whereas at the computational level, they have considerably simplified and improved their efficiency and performance.

Another important area is the garbage collection. The research reported by ICOT has also tackled this issue. Their distributed approach involves the creation of several levels of addressing in order to isolate the different accessing mechanisms (import and export tables used in [Ichi88a]). However, the model does not guarantee the recovery of all data, as all the garbage collectors based on reference counting.

ACKNOWLEDGEMENTS

The review presented in this chapter is an updated version of one section of the Tech. Report *Computational Models of Parallel Logic Languages*[Delg89a], written by the author at ECRC GmbH, Munich, Germany. Special thanks are due to: Uri Baron, Andy Cheese, Michel Dorochevsky, Kees Schuerman, André Veron, Jiyang Xu, Andrzej Ciepielewski, Kam-Fai Wong and Michael Ratcliffe for useful comments on earlier drafts.

12 Logical Occam

D. Cohen, M. M. Huntbach and **G. A. Ringwood**

Queen Mary & Westfield College, UK

Abstract

For general portability to future generations of parallel machines, a concurrent programming language must be able to express relatively fine grain parallelism. The features of one such language RGDC, Reactive Guarded Definite Clauses is described. It is representative of a set of languages, the individuals being determined by the primitives provided. Such primitives include a stream interface to databases. RGDC is particularly suitable for applications of distributed and realtime AI.

The language is process based and can be thought of as an amalgam of Occam and Prolog. Process Scheduling and distribution are orthogonal to the language. Variations on the producer-consumer and the client-server prototypes can be programmed almost trivially. The language is particularly sympathetic to program construction using abstract data-types.

While the semantics of RGDC is drawn from Horn clause logic the computational model is significantly different from Prolog. Unlike Prolog, there is no concept of failure; this gives rise to an Open World Assumption in which each stage of the computation is viewed as a conditional answer.

Empathy with meta-interpretation and partial evaluation are two important, related attributes of symbolic languages. Using these techniques in conjunction with program analysis and parallel scheduling algorithms, arbitrary parallel architectures can be exploited. The meta-interpretation of Occam is illustrated.

1 Introduction

Distributed and realtime AI applications such as speech, natural language understanding, vision, computer supported cooperative work, intelligent control systems and robotics have inherent concurrency. For such applications, distributing the computational load over more than one processor promises to improve response time, fault tolerance and scalability. The choice of one programming language in preference to another is often put down to religious dogma. That this position is untenable is illustrated by the difference between Roman and Arabic numerals. In Roman representation, the multiplication of two numbers can hardly be done at all. In the Arabic system, the concept of positional representation makes complex arithmetic calculations tractable. A poor choice of representation can make common ideas difficult to express. Equally importantly, it can make them inefficient to compute. The strategic objectives of realtime, distributed AI applications are to predict and influence future events. The ease with which a programming language can represent real world situations and the efficiency with which this representation can be manipulated are, thus, of crucial import in this endeavour.

Extant programming languages can be categorized by six paradigms: imperative; concurrent; functional; object oriented; relational (database) and logic programming. The paradigms can be understood alternatively as abstractions of applications or reifications of computational models. Logic programming, for example, is a reification of the computational mechanism of deduction while imperative programming can be seen as an abstraction of the von Neumann computational model. Concurrent programming is an abstraction of operating and distributed systems.

An expressive programming language of itself is not sufficient. There are many different types of parallel hardware architecture and to be generally useful a program should be portable. The problem of portability of programs on conventional von Neumann machines is solved by high level languages, in particular C. For parallel machines, high level languages are only part of the solution. Bal et. al. [Bal89a] distinguishes two classes of distributed system: *closely coupled* and *loosely coupled*. In closely coupled systems the computation to communication cost ratio is low, e.g. Transputer arrays. In *loosely coupled distributed systems* the ratio is high, e.g. workstations connected by LANs. The technology of parallel machines is moving in the direction of increasing numbers of autonomous processors and reducing communications costs. If a language is to remain viable through this technological development it must have the potential to exploit relatively fine grain parallelism when it becomes available. A portable parallel language must not enforce any inessential sequentiality.

The price to be paid for portability through fine granularity is the overhead of process switching when the average number of processors is much less than the number of processors. The Transputer is a hardware advance that goes some way to reducing this overhead. Closely allied with the Transputer is the concurrent programming language Occam. Occam was born of CSP (Communicating Sequential Processes) [Hoar78a] out of Dijkstra's guarded commands [Dijk75a]. Occam is minimal and efficient on Transputers because of hardware support for process scheduling and synchronization. Yet, Occam has been described as Concurrent Fortran. Like Fortran, Occam is not ideally suited to symbolic, knowledge-based applications: the language is inflexible; it does not support recursion, abstract data types, dynamic data structures or dynamic process creation. Occam code is not a first class object. This means that the language is not well suited to advanced AI programming techniques such as: pattern matching; metaprogramming; partial evaluation and abstract interpretation.

According to Bal et al [Bal89a], the appropriate choice of distributed programming language depends on the application. In the 1980s the Logic Programming paradigm emerged as an appropriate knowledge manipulation language. While Logic Programming is superficially open to parallel exploitation, its prime exemplar, Prolog, is not well equipped to exploit distributed systems [Ring87a]. Concurrent logic programming is the result of joining (in a lattice theory sense) the concurrent programming paradigm and the logic programming paradigm. A representative concurrent logic programming language, RGDC (Reactive Guarded Definite Clauses), being developed at Queen Mary and Westfield College is described in this chapter. In language terms, RGDC could be described as an amalgam of Prolog and Occam.

The purpose of this chapter is to illustrate the suitability of the symbolic language RGDC for concurrent and distributed programming. Section One compares a prototypical producer-consumer in Occam with a corresponding RGDC program. In contrast to Occam, RGDC can be viewed as an asynchronous, process-based language. Section Two shows how more closely coupled forms of synchronization can easily be programmed from the primitive asynchronous one. The section continues with related issues of process priorities and process distribution. Section Three looks at another prototype of concurrent programming, the client-server. It illustrates how abstract data types and atomic actions are almost natural consequences of the language. It is then demonstrated how lazily instantiated lists are a natural means of communication with devices and files. Section Four explains the logical semantics of the language. Despite concurrency the logical semantics of RGDC is totally pure. This semantics is not the usual one of Prolog but one in which there is no notion of failure. In Section Five, an explanation is presented of how this semantics naturally leads to an additional control structure, *otherwise* clauses. Implementational issues are briefly discussed in Section Six, where it is explained how, contrary to popular belief, arrays are subsumed data structures of the language. Section Seven illustrates the symbolic programming features of RGDC with a brief description of an Occam meta-interpreter.

2 The producer-consumer prototype

One way of comparing languages is to contrast the coding of prototypical examples. An archetype of concurrent programming in Occam is the producer-consumer. In Occam 2 a simple producer-consumer system can be coded as follows:

```
PROC producer(CHAN OF BYTE channel) =
  VAL [] BYTE love.message IS "I love you!":
  WHILE TRUE
    channel ! [love.message FROM 0 FOR 11]
```

```
PROC consumer(CHAN OF BYTE channel) =
  [11] BYTE message:
  WHILE TRUE
    channel ? [message FROM 0 FOR 11]

CHAN OF BYTE pipe:
PAR
  producer(pipe)
  consumer(pipe)
```

In this program an amorous producer persistently sends love messages to a coy consumer, which receives but ignores them.

The philosophy of Occam is, as its name suggests, *Entia non sunt multiplicanda praeter necessitatem*: entities are not to be multiplied beyond necessity. RGDC can be understood as an amalgam of Occam and Prolog. For a third generation language programmer, Prolog appears to have a dearth of control constructs. A consequence of the union is that the philosophy of RGDC is, in the vernacular, *KISS*: keep it simple stupid. The RGDC code corresponding to the Occam amorous producer and coy consumer is:

```
producer(Message:Chan)<-true
  <-Message=msg("I love you!"),
  producer(Chan).

consumer(msg(Contents):Chan)<-true
  <-Chan=Message:Chan',
  consumer(Chan).

<-producer(Message:Pipe),consumer(Message:Pipe).
```

As with Prolog, variables are identified syntactically, beginning with an upper case letter. The functional programming language Miranda's right-associative, infix list constructor, : [Holy91a], is used in preference to the Prolog one. Unlike Prolog, where a comma denotes sequencing of procedure calls, in RGDC a comma denotes parallel process composition (corresponding to the Occam **PAR**). (As will be described later, the parallel process composition symbol, comma, has the same denotational semantics as in Prolog: logical conjunction.) Unlike Occam, there is no sequential process composition in RGDC. In order to better explain how this program works a somewhat simplified, although more verbose program will initially be considered.

```
eagerProducer(List)<-true
  <-List="I love you!":TailList,
  eagerProducer(TailList).

syncConsumer(List)<-List<<=Message:TailList
  <-syncConsumer(TailList).
```

```
<-eagerProducer(List),syncConsumer(List).
```

The reason for the change in names of the producer and consumer will become clear later when alternative forms of the producer-consumer program are derived. The program for the producer process describes how it can metamorphose into two other processes. It is important to distinguish this metamorphosis from process creation such as forking. The one process continues as two processes, as in biological cell division, the identity of the initial process is shared. The first of these processes, an equality process = (written infix) is a primitive process. For the moment it can be thought of as assignment but will be elaborated further in Section Four. The equality process instantiates its parent's argument variable, List, to a list with the constant "I love you!" as head. The other child process behaves like its parent except that it has the, as yet unknown, tail of its parent's list as argument. Like Prolog but unlike Occam, RGDC has dynamic data structures and recursion. Occam only has iteration. The recursion of RGDC is not, however, the recursion of a stack based implementation but a distinct process behaviour. This is not possible in Occam because it does not allow dynamic process creation.

Whereas in Occam communication is synchronous, in RGDC it is asynchronous. The producer is unconstrained, as the name **eagerProducer** suggests. But the consumer process blocks waiting for its argument to be instantiated to a list, as indicated by the *instance* constraint, <<=, in the code for the consumer. This constraint is satisfied when its left hand argument is an instance of its right. In other words, when the right hand argument subsumes the left hand. When this constraint is satisfied, the consumer process can, ignoring the head of the list, metamorphose into a similar process but with the tail of the list as parameter. The true constraint of the producer is a null constraint inserted to make the producer and consumer take the same syntactic form.

Simulating concurrency by interleaving process reductions, one possible evaluation scenario for the producer-consumer example is as follows:

```
<-eagerProducer(List),syncConsumer(List).
<-eagerProducer(TailList),
  List = "I love you!":TailList,syncConsumer(List).
<-eagerProducer(TailList),
  syncConsumer("I love you!":TailList).
<-eagerProducer(TailList),syncConsumer(TailList).
<-eagerProducer(TailList'),
  TailList="I love you!":TailList',syncConsumer(TailList).
<-eagerProducer(TailList'),
  syncConsumer("I love you!":TailList').
<-eagerProducer(TailList''),
  TailList'="I love you!":TailList'',
  syncConsumer("I love you!":TailList').
```

```
<-eagerProducer(TailList''),
  syncConsumer("I love you!":"I love you!":TailList'').
   .
   .
   .
```

In this scenario, the processes denoted in outline are blocked by constraints. A graphical notation for exploring scenarios and a graphical syntax for RGDC is described in [Ring89b].

The general symbolic syntax for describing process behaviours is given, as with Prolog procedures, using the notation of definite clauses:

<definite-clause> :: <guard> <- < process behaviour>;
<guard> :: <head> <- <constraints>

A consequence of this factorisation is that the infix implication symbol, <-, is taken to be left associative. (It will be shown later that the implication symbol does have the semantics of logical implication. In which case the formula (A <- B) <- C is logically equivalent to A <- B ∧ C, the more usual syntax for a definite clause.) As with Prolog, the scope of variables is limited to a clause. A guarded definite clause is the analogue Dijkstra's (and CSP and Occam's) guarded commands (and the functional language Miranda's guarded abstractions [Holy91a]) and hence the derivation of the name Guarded Definite Clauses. The extension *Reactive* is to account for the adoption of Occam's process priorities and primitive timer processes. The terminology reactive comes from Harel and Pnueli [Hare85a], where it is used to describe programs that are interactive as opposed to transformational. The head of a guard corresponds to the head of a Prolog clause, while the constraint is a conjunction of language primitives that only test the input parameters. The constraints are in the form of equations, inequations, comparisons, and type tests, an example is the instance constraint, <<=, in the consumer clause. If there are no constraints, this is indicated by the trivial constraint true. (In fact, the guard can be an arbitrary Boolean combination of constraints, not just conjunctions, but then the clause will not necessarily be definite, in the logical sense.) Primitive constraints that are not satisfied block processes from metamorphosing.

If the guard is satisfied, a definite clause describes how the process named by the head can metamorphose into the parallel composition of processes described by the process-behaviour. In general, the process behaviour specifies dynamic process creation.

```
process(...) <- <constraint>
  <- newProcess1(...), newProcess2(...), ...
```

In contrast to Occam, where processes can only be declared statically and are persistent, RGDC processes are dynamically created and can be ephemeral. In this respect, RGDC process behaviour is more like CCS [Miln80a] than CSP [Hoar78a].

The top level of an RGDC program takes the form of a negative clause.

<- < process behaviour>

As the producer consumer system invocation indicates

`<-eagerProducer(List),syncConsumer(List).`

a process behaviour describes a network of concurrent processes communicating via variables shared between the processes. These variables are not the usual form of shared variables but are more like the channels of Occam. In concurrent programming two alternatives are offered as mechanisms for communication: shared mutable data and message passing. With shared address spaces, many processes can potentially assign the same variable. As is well known, competing processes trying to write to the same variable have race conditions e.g. Tanenbaum, 1987a]. This can cause inconsistency in the final value of a variable, the final value being determined by which process last assigns to it. In systems programming several solutions have emerged to this problem, such as semaphores [Tane80a].

Communication by shared variables is an abstraction of processors sharing the same address space. As Bal et al [Bal89a] points out, it is possible for a distributed programming language to have a logically shared memory while being implemented on a distributed system (where processors have distinct address spaces). Message passing is an abstraction of communication between processors that do not share the same address space. Message passing does not have race conditions as it is essentially data copying rather than data sharing. Data is copied from the address space of one process to that of the other. Consequently, message passing can be up to a 100 times less efficient than data sharing [Henn90a].

Whereas with communication by shared variables, a variable can be assigned any number of times, messages can only be assigned once. There is only one writer of each message but possibly many readers. The logical-variable of RGDC lies somewhere between the two extremes of shared variables and messages. Logical-variables like messages can only be assigned once but there can be any (finite) number of potential writers. Whereas a message writer is determined at compiletime, the writer of a logical-variable is determined at runtime. This, of course, leads to race conditions as discussed later. Only one process in a behaviour which shares a logic-variable can write to it. After assignment of a logic-variable, all other processes sharing it will necessarily be readers; this is similar to multicasting. In a broadcast message system any process can read any message. In multicast message systems only a prescribed subset of processes can be readers. In RGDC only the equality primitive process (illustrated in use above) can, in fact, assign logical-variables. Of the competing equality processes, the successful writer is the one that gets there first (in contrast to shared multi-assignment variables where it is the one that assigns last). With single assignment (logic) variables, the race condition still exists but is less of a problem than it is with multiply assignable variables. The race condition can only occur once. Exactly how such race conditions are dealt with in RGDC is described in Section Six.

Traditionally the proponents of Logic Programming have emphasized its stateless, side-effect-free nature. This emphasis is justified when the problem to be solved can be declared without reference to the state of the computation. In concurrent programming, the very nature of the problem usually contains references to the state of the system. In RGDC a process cannot change its state but only metamorphose (reduce) itself into other processes. From an intuitive point of view a process that reincarnates itself recursively can be thought of as a long-lived process. Simulating long-lived processes by ephemeral recursive calls allows interpretation of local (unshared variables) as states of a process. In the following skeleton process definition:

```
process(State,InList,...,OutList)
   <-InList<<=Message:TailInList,
   <otherConditions(State, Message)>
   <-computeStateResponse(State,Message,NewState,Response),
   OutList=Response:TailOutList,
   process(NewState,TailInList,...,TailOutList).
```

the new state and the response, in general, depend on the initial state and the message. This skeleton suggests how, in a side-effect-free way, local variables and recursive ephemeral processes effect long-lived processes that can change state.

In this and the previous example the effective processes are not just long lived but persistent - they never die. Processes can be terminated by specifying an empty process behaviour, denoted by the constant **true**:

```
process(...)<-<constraints>
   <-true.
```

The appearance of the constant **true** can be contrasted with the Occam SKIP and STOP processes. The constraints specify the conditions under which the long lived process is allowed to terminate.

A modification of the producer-consumer example that illustrates both state and process termination is as follows:

```
finiteEagerProducer(N,List)<-N>0,N1:=N-1
   <-List="I love you!":TailList,
   finiteEagerProducer(N1,TailList);
finiteEagerProducer(N,List)<-N<=0
   <-List=[].

terminatingSyncConsumer(List)
   <-List<<=Message:TailList
   <-terminatingSyncConsumer(TailList);
```

```
terminatingSyncConsumer(List)<-List<<=[]
  <-true.

<-finiteEagerProducer(5,List),
  terminatingSyncConsumer(List).
```

The producer only issues five devotions before it withers and dies. The state of this producer is the number of outstanding messages. The constant [] is used as a list terminator. The producer commits suicide when it has sent the specified number of unrequieted love tokens. This program modification introduces multiple clauses to describe alternative process behaviours. Alternative guards correspond to the Occam priority alternative construct, **PRI ALT**. In the above program the guards are mutually exclusive but this is not necessarily the case. There is no nonprioritized **ALT** construct in RGDC as there is in Occam but, as will be seen later, this is not detrimental. The arithmetic infix primitive := in the first clause of the producer blocks until its right hand argument is ground to an arithmetic expression (all variables instantiated). When ground it evaluates the expression and binds the value to the variable in the left hand argument. The left hand argument is not allowed to be a variable appearing in the head of the clause. In this way, expression evaluation does not cause any effect observable by other processes before the appropriate clause to reduce the process has been determined. Upon receipt of knowledge of its suitor's demise (the list terminator []) the consumer mortally regrets the rejection of its suitor.

3 Synchronous from asynchronous

The behaviour of an RGDC process is described by semicolon separated, alternative definite clauses, each clause of which has an identical head. As a notational convenience the syntactic instance constraint, denoted <<=, in the guard of the consumer will be represented by a pattern in the head of the clause. Thus, the RGDC clause for the original consumer of Section One

```
syncConsumer(List)<-List<<=Message:TailList)
  <-syncConsumer(TailList).
```

will be replaced by the more compact and readable

```
syncConsumer(Message:TailList)<-true
  <-syncConsumer(TailList).
```

The behaviour of a consumer process is as it was before. It will block until the process-call arguments pattern-match the head of some clause and satisfy any additional explicit guard constraints of that clause. Note, this is unlike Prolog where the head of the clause is used for unification, i.e both input and output. With RGDC the head of the clause is used only for input. Output bindings can only be effected using the equality primitive process.

The only form of synchronization in RGDC is condition synchronization as specified by the guard of a clause. This condition is composed of matching the pattern in the head of the clause, dataflow synchronization, and constraint satisfaction of the other explicit primitives in the guard. The list dynamic data structure used in the RGDC producer-consumer example of Section One behaves like an infinite message buffer. With such asynchronous communication, if the processes do not reduce at the same rate, producers can run ahead of the consumers. This situation is suggested by the reduction scenario of Section One. In this example, the producer is totally unconstrained while the consumer blocks waiting for data. This program will work as intended if the consumer consumes faster than the producer produces. If not, the list, a theoretically infinite buffer, will eat-up all the finite physical store.

RGDC programs have a fine grain which permits a very high degree of parallelism, and hence it is eminently portable. In conventional distributed systems the amount of parallelism available in the language usually exceeds the limited number of physical processors. In such circumstances processes are time-shared. The problem of the eager producer can be solved by giving the consumer a higher priority than the producer. The relative order of priority is determined by the order of processes in the invocation.

```
<-syncConsumer(List),eagerProducer(List).
```

In order to sustain this beyond the first generation a priority annotation is used.

```
<-eagerProducer(List,-1)@priority(-1),
  syncConsumer(List).
```

In RGDC, nonblocked processes are scheduled according to their priority. This corresponds to the Occam prioritized parallel composition construct, **PRI PAR**. In RGDC, processors with the same priority form a FIFO queue in order of creation. The priority of a child process, unless otherwise specified by an @priority annotation, reverts to the default priority for the user. Dynamic control over priorities may be effected by passing the priority from parents to children as in:

```
eagerProducer(List,Priority)<-true
  <-List="I love you!":TailList,
  eagerProducer(TailList,Priority)@priority(Priority).
```

explaining the seemingly redundant second argument in the initial process invocation above. This form of control is particularly useful for speculative search [Hunt91a].

When the number of processes exceeds the number of processors (which is usually the case) or where the communication overhead would outweigh the benefits of distribution, some judicious mapping of processes to processors needs to be made. The problem of mapping processes to processors in RGDC is, as it should be for maximum portability, orthogonal to the language. There are many ways in which process distribution might be achieved in sympathy with the language. One possibility is to map a conceptual tree of processes onto a physical network of processors [Hunt88a]. One can contemplate dynamic load balancing in shared memory systems or closely coupled distributed systems, where the cost of communication is low. In loosely coupled systems it may be desirable for the programmer to express some control of the distribution of processes.

Although communication in Transputer networks is, compared to LANs, relatively inexpensive, it is not without cost. Occam provides placement instructions to enable the programmer to distribute processes over processors. In a similar way RGDC provides programmer annotations to facilitate process distribution. By default, processes are scheduled on the processor on which their parent ran. Processor mapping annotations can be direct (specifying a particular processor) or indirect (specifying the *direction*, assuming some topology, of a nearest neighbour to migrate to). An example is :

```
foo(State,...)
    <-<determineProcessor(State, NextProcessor)>
    <-bar1(...)@processor(4),      %spawn on specified processor
    bar2(...)@processor(next),     %next processor ring topology
    bar3(...)@processor(east),     %mesh topology
    bar4(...),                     %stay put
    bar5(...)@processor(NextProc). %determined dynamically
```

Note that `NextProcessor` is determined dynamically in the guard from the process `State`. Partitioning processors among processors and scheduling is essentially orthogonal to the language. By coupling partial evaluation [Hunt89a] with partitioning scheduling techniques it is expected that parallel architectures can be better exploited. Partial evaluation transforms a general program into a specialized program by taking advantage of information available at compiletime. Such information could include processor topology. This differs from conventional compilation techniques. Conventional compilers seek to optimize the execution of procedure calls and data-structure manipulations. Partial evaluation seeks to eliminate such operations by performing them in advance of runtime.

Process priority will not solve the problem of the over eager producer if the producer and consumer are run on different processors. As an alternative, if the producer is known to be faster than the consumer the role of the producer and consumer can be reversed as in the program:

```
syncProducer(Message:List)<-true
    <-Message="I love you!",
    syncProducer(List).

eagerConsumer(List)<-true
    <-List=Message:TailList,
    eagerConsumer(TailList).

<-syncProducer(List),eagerConsumer(List).
```

In this reversal, the consumer solicits devotions from the producer by forming a list of message variables for the producer to instantiate on receipt. Now, the consumer can run arbitrarily far ahead of the producer.

If it is not known which of the producer and consumer is the faster, synchronous communication can be programmed by giving both the producer and consumer a pattern matching constraint:

```
syncProducer(Message:List)<-true
  <-Message=msg("I love you!"),
  syncProducer(List).

syncConsumer(msg(Contents):List)<-true
  <-List=Message:TailList,
  syncConsumer(TailList).

<-syncConsumer(Message:List), syncProducer(Message:List).
```

Here the producer and consumer have to be hand started, otherwise they would both block (deadlock). With this program there is only one possible execution scenario:

```
<-syncProducer(Message:List),syncConsumer(Message:List).
<-syncProducer(List),Message=msg("I love you!"),
  syncConsumer(Message:List).
<-syncProducer(List),
  syncConsumer(msg("I love you!"):List).
<-syncProducer(List),List=Message':List',
  syncConsumer(Message':List').
<-syncProducer(Message':List'),
  syncConsumer(Message':List').
<-syncProducer(List'),Message'=msg("I love you!"),
  syncConsumer(Message':List').
<-syncProducer(List'),
  syncConsumer(msg("I love you!"):List').
<-syncProducer(List'),List'=Message'':List'',
  syncConsumer(Message'':List'').
<-syncProducer(Message'':List''),
  syncConsumer(Message'':List'').
    •
    •
    •
```

In this scenario the producer and consumer are alternately blocked and progress lock-step. The synchronous producer-consumer is essentially the program given as the one corresponding to the Occam program of Section One.

The synchronous communication programmed above in terms of asynchronous communication effectively turns the infinite *List* buffer into a one slot buffer. Given that there is only one consumer in this situation, a used slot can be garbage collected straight away and the old slot can even be reutilized. It is possible to build some housekeeping of this kind into the compiler [Kemp90a]. Still, it is unlikely that all garbage collection can be done in this way and some runtime scavenging will be necessary.

A multislot buffer can be produced by further modifying the code for the consumer in the one-slot-buffer program.

```
buffConsumer(msg(Contents):Buffer-EndBuff)<-true
   <-EndBuff=_:NewEndBuff,
   buffConsumer(Buffer-NewEndBuff).

<-Buffer=_:_:_:_:EndBuff,
   buffConsumer(Buffer-EndBuff),syncProducer(Buffer).
```

This program uses the Prolog notation of an underscore to denote an anonymous variable; repeated anonymous variables are distinct. The familiar Prolog technique of a difference list (e.g. [O'Ke90a]), denoted by an infix functor -, at the consumer end acts as an N slot buffer. (The list functor, :, is assumed to bind tighter than the overloaded, -.) The equality process in the initial process invocation initializes N to four. The consumer maintains the length of the buffer by producing a new slot for every message consumed. Again garbage collection and slot reuse could be compiled into the consumer.

For larger buffers, the slots may be generated by an auxiliary process:

```
genBuffer(N,Buffer,EndBuff)<-N>0,N1:=N-1
   <-Buffer=_:TailBuff,
   genBuffer(N1,TailBuff,EndBuff);
genBuffer(0,Buffer,EndBuff)<-true
   <-Buffer=EndBuff.

<-genBuffer(25,Buffer,EndBuff),
   buffConsumer(Buffer-EndBuff),syncProducer(Buffer).
```

4 The client-server prototype

Another important prototype of concurrent programming is the client-server. Many problems occur in systems programming in which several processes share a common resource.

```
server(Transaction:MoreTransactions,Data)<-true
   <-respond(Transaction,Data,NewData),
   server(MoreTransactions,NewData).
```

Of the two arguments of **server**, the first is a stream of transactions from a client and the second a data structure administered by the server. This data structure is to be manipulated according to the form of transaction stipulated in the transaction message.

Alternative clauses for the server show how abstract data types can be naturally implemented in RGDC. A bank account accumulator provides a well exercised example of an abstract data type.

```
accumulator(deposit(Amount):More,Total)
   <-NewTotal:=Total+Amount
   <-accumulator(More,NewTotal).
accumulator(debit(Amount):More,Total);
   <-NewTotal:=Total-Amount,NewTotal>=0
   <-accumulator(More,NewTotal);
accumulator(balance(Amount):More,Total)<-true
   <-Amount=total(Total),accumulator(More,Total).
```

For the sake of simplicity the number of modes of access and functionality of the transactions has been kept small. In particular, the second clause, unrealistically, blocks indefinitely if the amount to be debited is greater than the balance. The third clause for accumulator illustrates how the server replies to its clients. The client provides the server with a logical-variable as a return-message slot.

A client using the account server facility might appear:

```
client(...,ToServer)<-...
   <-ToServer=balance(Amount).NewToServer,
   takeAction(Amount),
   client(...,NewToServer)

takeAction(total(Total))<-true
   <-...
```

Here the client program interrogates the account held by the server with the incomplete message *balance(Amount)*. It spawns a child process to take appropriate action (earning some more money or asking for credit) dependent on the return information. Note the `takeAction` process will block until its argument is instantiated to `total(Total)`.

Prolog primitives for reading from the keyboard and writing to the screen are side-effected. The sequencing of goals in the body of a Prolog clause is crucial in getting the required external behaviour. In RGDC input/output is implemented in a natural way using primitive server processes. For example, a naive user defined process **double**:

```
double(N:InList,OutList)<-N2:=N+N
   <-OutList=N2:TailOutList,
   double(InList,TailOutList);
double([],OutList)<-true
   <-OutList=[].
```

which takes a list of integers and doubles them, can be configured to take input from the keyboard and produce output on the screen with an initial invocation:

```
<-stdIn("integers in",InList),
   double(InList,OutList),
   stdOut("integers out",OutList).
```

The primitive process **stdIn** instantiates a list of carriage-return separated terms typed at the keyboard. The input is closed by the constant term `[]`. The primitive process **stdOut** prints on the screen space separated terms that appear as list items on its argument. In a system where a user can invoke parallel processes a multiwindowing environment is natural. In such an environment, each invoked **stdIn** process would have its own input window (called "integers in" in the above example) and each **stdOut** process will have its own output window (called "integers out"). Positioning the input/output primitives in the top level process invocation saves them from cluttering and interfering with the semantics of the program in the lowest levels, as they generally do with Prolog. This is a very modular approach to the problem of input/output in declarative languages.

The lazily instantiated dynamic data structure of a list used in RGDC server communication is ideal for input/output as it behaves like an infinite message buffer. Lists used in this way correctly sequence the output to the windows though there is no sequential process control construct in the language. Lazily instantiated sequences of records, *streams*, were first introduced into programming by Landin [Land65a] in the context of functional programming. Streams are a particularly clean and natural way to deal with input/output and reactive systems. The relevance of streams to interactive data analysis in the context of Prolog has recently been elaborated by Parker [Park90a].

Each client of a server could be allocated its own stream for communicating with a resource. More usually, it is convenient (particularly with input/output) to determine or change at runtime the number of processes communicating with the server. In functional stream-languages this presents semantic difficulties. Because RGDC is a relational language, there is no such semantic difficulty here:

```
merge([],Stream,Stream1)<-true
  <-Stream1=Stream;
merge(Stream,[],Stream1)<-true
  <-Stream1=Stream;
merge(Item:Stream1,Stream2,Stream3)<-true
  <-Stream3=Item:OutStream,
  merge(Stream2, Stream1, OutStream);
merge(Stream1,Item:Stream2,Stream3)<-true
  <-Stream3=Item:OutStream,
  merge(Stream2,Stream1,OutStream).
```

A **merge** process can be used to merge messages from two clients to a server. In a message passing system the order of arrival of messages is not necessarily the order in which they were sent. However, with the merge process, above, the relative order of terms produced by sources is preserved. With Occam there is no guarantee of fairness with the alternative branches of an **ALT** construction. As noted previously, the guards of RGDC really correspond to the priority alternative **PRI ALT** of Occam. Given that at such choice points only one alternative is chosen, in order to avoid inappropriate choices, it is only reasonable that the programmer should be able to specify a preference. If several guards are satisfied by a process the one that appears textually first is selected to reduce the process. While this means that clause choice is not fair it does not prevent argument fairness from being programmed. To avoid starvation, when there are elements on the two input streams of the merge process the arguments are reversed in recursive process calls. With prioritized alternatives, changing the order of arguments causes the list from which an element is taken to alternate and serves to effect fairness of input arguments. This will adversely affect a compilers ability to produce optimised code for merge but this is a small price to pay for fairness.

The transaction facilities of RGDC can be used for many purposes; below is a client of the bank balance server that sends a pair of abstract datatype transactions to double the current account total:

```
client( ,ToServer)<-...
  <-ToServer=balance(Amount)+withdraw(Amount):NewToServer,
  client(...,NewToServer).
```

Underlying the doubling operation is some sophisticated synchronization: the two messages are both sent with the same uninstantiated argument. Once the server has received the first transaction it may receive the second before the reply to the first has been instantiated. This is legitimate because the condition synchronization of the arithmetic primitives ensures that Amount will not be added to the balance until it is ground. The use of RGDC clearly allows the programmer to express higher levels of abstraction without having explicitly to code the synchronization.

This example raises the spectre of atomic transactions. If the streams from the above client and any other clients (joint accounts) are merged as above, there is the possibility that another transaction, say a withdrawal, could sneak, God forbid, between the two parts of the double transaction. In such a situation, if the amount to be debited is greater than the current balance the transaction will deadlock. Whereas, if the amount to be debited was less than twice the total and the double transaction had taken effect atomically it could have paid out the requested amount. This is a variation on the "lost update" problem. A general approach to the problem is the provision of an atomic transaction protocol for the server. Transactions that must be processed atomically are bundled together into a single compound transaction:

```
client(...,ToServer)<-...
  <-ToServer=[balance(Amount),add(Amount)]:NewToServer,
  client(...,NewToServer).
```

([a,b] is an alternative Miranda notation for the list a:b:[]) which is unbundled by an additional server clause:

```
accumulator((X:Y):Rest,Total)<-true
  <-concatenate(X:Y,Rest,Stream),
  accumulator(Stream,Total).

concatenate([],Stream,TotalStream)<-true
  <-TotalStream=Stream;
concatenate(Item:Stream1,Stream2,TotalStream)
  <-true
  <-TotalStream=Item:TailStream,
  concatenate(Stream1,Stream2,TailStream).
```

The contrast between the alternatives of merging and concatenating streams are important for input/output. Note, as with Prolog, difference lists can be used to produce the effect of concatenation in constant time.

5 Semantics

The state of an RGDC computation is described by a triple <R, B, I> of multisets of reducible, blocked and irreducible processes, where the terminology will be explained. In the initial state, R, B and I are a partition of the processes in the initial network invocation:

<- $a_1, a_2,...a_n$.

Excluding for the moment the equality primitive processes, the reducible set R consists of those processes that satisfy the guard of some clause; that is, for each nonequality process a_i in R there is an instance of some clause

   h <- <constraint> <- b_1, b_2,...b_m.

in the program for which a_i and h are syntactically identical and the constraint <constraint> is satisfiable. The blocked set B contains those processes a_i that are not reducible but have a reducible instance, a_i'. These processes are blocked waiting for variables which they share to be instantiated by equality processes. All other nonequality processes are members of the irreducible set, I. For them, there is no instance of the process and clause of the program for which the guard is satisfiable.

There are no equality primitive processes allowed in B. If a_i is an equality primitive of the form f =f or $f(t_1,... t_k) = f(t_1',...t_k')$, with k non zero, then it is reducible and a member of R. If a_i is an equality primitive of the form X = t or t = X with X a variable and t a term not containing X as a subterm (occur check) and there is another occurrence of X in another process in R, B or I, then it is reducible and a member of R. Otherwise, the equality primitive is irreducible and a member of I.

A computation step is one of the following:
   i) For a nonequality process a_i in R and an instance

   h <- <constraint> <- b_1, b_2,...b_m.

of some clause in the program for which a_i and h are syntactically identical, a_i is removed from R and the instance of the behaviour of the clause, $b_1, b_2,...b_m$, is partitioned appropriately between the subsets R, B and I.
   ii) An equality primitive f=f or $f(t_1,... t_k) = f(t_1',...t_k')$ in R is removed and the network of primitive equality processes $t_1 = t_1',...t_k = t_k'$ are appropriately partitioned between R and I. Thus, in RGDC the equality process is a unification process that reduces implicitly and in parallel.
   iii) Equality primitives of the form X = t or t = X in R are transferred to I and for all other occurrences of X in the sets R, B and I are substituted by the term t. This is accompanied by a relocation of those nonequality processes from B to R, which as a result of the substitution have become reducible. At the same time, other equality primitives move from R to I, if the substitution has made them irreducible.

The denotation of each RGDC process is a logical atom. Primitive constraints can be thought of as semantic attachments in the sense of Weyrauch [Weyr80a]. The primitive equality process, which implements syntactic equality also can be thought of as a semantic attachment. In the same way, the primitive input/output processes are semantic attachments. Each clause denotes a first order, universally quantified, logic formula. Each step of the computation denotes a deduction. The deduction steps are complex, the like of paramodulation. Computation steps can be described as guarded complex deductions by analogy with Dijkstra's guarded commands. The denotation of the initial process network:

<- $a_1, a_2, ... a_n$.

is the conditional answer

$a_1 \wedge a_2 \wedge ... a_n$ <- $a_1 \wedge a_2 \wedge ... a_n$.

and resolvents form a denotation of subsequent program states.

$a_1 \wedge a_2 \wedge ... a_n$ <- R ∧ B ∧ I

Abusing notation, ∧ will be assumed to distribute over sets of atoms. The process reduction scenarios depicted in previous sections denote derivations. A program is thus denoted by the set of possible derivations. As such, RGDC programs are amenable to formal reasoning and program transformation. More precisely, RGDC programs are easy to reason about and transform because variables may be freely replaced by their values (single assignment).

6 Open worlds

A computation terminates when R is empty (denoted by the process **true**), but unlike Prolog, an RGDC computation may never terminate. (Conditional answer semantics for concurrent logic programs were first introduced to provide a semantics for perpetual processes in [Ring87a].) Unlike Prolog, with conditional answer semantics there is no concept of goal failure. If at any stage of the computation the irreducible set I contains an equality of, say, the form morningstar=eveningstar a Prolog computation would have been deemed to have failed. In RGDC the conclusion to be drawn is that morningstar and eveningstar are different names for the same entity, that is, aliases. The equalities of the irreducible set I establish a congruence relation on the Herbrand base. Since no inequality constraints appear, this set of equalities will always be satisfiable.

The term *reducible equality* is used in the sense of Herbrand's (syntactic) equality axioms over a universally quantified term algebra. If at any stage of the computation I contains an equality of the form X = t, where X is a variable and t is a term that contains X and t is not equal to X, the usual logic program would have been deemed to have failed. (This is not so for Prolog where the occur check is, usually, not included.) This means that, in general, it will be necessary to go beyond Herbrand interpretations and consider interpretations over functions with fixed points. Alternatively, such conclusions could be used to indicate a declarative error in the program [Hunt87a]

It will generally be the case that constraints in I can be further reduced by additional substitution axioms. For example, the constraints:

{f(f(f(f(f(a))))=a,f(f(f(a)))=b}
could be further reduced to
{f(f(b))=a,f(f(f(a)))=b}
by substituting the second constraint in the first. There exist fast decision procedures for determining the congruence closure of quantifier free equations [e.g. Nels80a] and these could be provided as a user defined extension of the equality primitive, but this idea will not be pursued here.

If at any stage of the computation the irreducible multiset of processes, *I*, contains predicates other than equalities, the corresponding Prolog program would have failed. The irreducible user defined goals are not assumed to be false, as is the case with negation as failure, but form part of the conditional answer. This has been called the *Open-World Assumption* [Ring87a] and is a desirable semantics where recovery from hardware failure is a promised attribute of distributed systems [Bal89a].

An additional control mechanism can be added to prevent nonequality processes becoming members of the irreducible set. This is the *otherwise guard* illustrated as follows:

process(State,Message:InStream,...,OutStream)
  <-<constraint(State,Message)>
  <-**computeStateResponse**(State,Message,NewState,Response),
  OutStream=Response:TailOutStream,
  process(NewState,InStream,...,OutStream);
process(State,InStream,...,OutStream)<-otherwise
  <-**exceptionHandl**(State,InStream,...,OutStream).

The otherwise clause is only used for process reduction if all other clause guards for the process are unsatisfiable. (It corresponds to the otherwise guard in Miranda [e.g. Holy91a].) That is, were it not for the otherwise clause the process would be irreducible. A process that has an exception clause can never be a member of the irreducible set, I, but it can be a member of the blocked multiset B. A situation in which this might be needed is to handle exceptions. The guard of the otherwise clause is, in effect, the negation of the conjunction of the guards of all the other clauses describing the possible process behaviours. Otherwise negation does not have the problems of Prolog's Negation as Failure. This is because all the guard constraints are decidable primitives. Guard constraints only test the input, they do not cause any bindings to the call variables.

If, at a stage of the computation the multiset of reducible processes, R, is empty, there may still be processes that are not irreducible yet have instances which are reducible. These processes will be in B. Such a state is called *deadlock termination*; the processes in the multiset B are waiting for conditions that will never hold. This predicament may occur because of cycles in the dataflow [Burt88a], or because of incomplete guards or because a node of the distributed system fails. Another time-out control mechanism could be introduced in the guard to ensure that processes do not remain indefinitely in B. This would correspond to the *after* guard of Occam. An alternative device more sympathetic to the semantics of RGDC is to introduce primitive timer processes.

```
<-timer(5,Ticks),...
   criticalProcess(...,Ticks,...)@priority(1).

criticalProcess(...,Ticks,...)<-
 .
 .
criticalProcess(...,tick:RestTicks,...)<-...
```

The primitive timer process instantiates a list of `ticks` at time intervals determined by its first argument. The `criticalProcess` has a clause whose only constraint is waiting for a tick message. In this way, it will not be delayed indefinitely. In this way, as with input, external events are turned into instantiation events in the language computational model.

7 Implementation issues

A functor of the form f(X1,...XN) is represented internally in RGDC as a tuple {f,X1,...XN}; that is a contiguous block of N+1 references in memory, numbered from zero. Access to the elements of tuples so far has been by pattern matching but for large or unknown tuples this is impractical. For such tuples two primitive processes and two primitive constraints can be provided to effect indexed array access. (Mechanisms for handling arrays in logic programming have been around for some time [e.g. Erik84a].) What is different in RGDC is that two of the primitives are provided as constraints.) The primitive process `isArray(FA,?NA,A)` is used to create an array. It blocks until NA is instantiated to a natural number. This is indicated by the question mark annotation. (Note a programmer would not use this annotation. It is used, merely, to assist the verbal description of primitives.) When this condition is satisfied the variable A is instantiated to an array {FA,A1,...AN}.

Dual to this primitive processes is the type checking constraint `functor(?A,FA,NA)` which causes a process to block until A is instantiated to a nonvariable term. When this holds, FA is instantiated to the name (functor) of the array (term) and NA to the arity. The use of this primitive is restricted in that FA and NA must be variables that are not contained in the head of the clause. This is similar to the restriction on the use of arithmetic constraint, :=. (This restriction is, really, the issue of *guard safety* [Ring87a]. When the guards are flat, as they are in RGDC, safety is decidable.) If A is a constant (functor of arity 0) then FA is bound to the same constant and NA is bound to zero.

The constraint primitive `arg(?A,?N,AN)` provides indexed access to the elements of an array without pattern matching. The argument A is the array and the argument N is the index of the array element being sought. Both these variables must be bound if the process is not to block. When this condition is satisfied, the arg primitive binds the variable AN to the Nth element of the array A. Like the constraints functor and expression evaluation, :=, the use of arg is restricted in that AN is not allowed to be a variable occurring in the head of the clause. This process is complemented by the primitive process arrayUpdate(?OldA,?NA,?Value,NewA) for updating an array. NewA is the same as OldA, except at the index NA which is Value.

The cost of representing arrays in this way is the need to copy nearly all the array to update a single element. If the old element value is not required by any other process it can be garbage collected and its storage reused by the new. This will require the somewhat sophisticated program analysis envisaged in [Kemp90a] if it is to compete with the efficiency of mutable arrays.

With the above primitive array constraints the proposed attachment semantics of equality is almost implementable in RGDC.

```
X=Y
    <-functor(X,FX,NX),functor(Y,FY,NY),NX=:=NY,FX<<=FY,
    <-equalArgs(X,Y,NX);
X=Y
    <-testCommitAndSet(X,Y)
    <-true;
X=Y
    <-testCommitAndSet(Y,X)
    <-true.

equalArgs(X,Y,0)<-true
    <-true;
equalArgs(X,Y,N)
    <-N>0,arg(N,X,XN),arg(N,Y,YN),N1:=N-1
    <-XN=YN,
    equalArgs(X,Y,N1).
```

The unexplained testCommitAndSet in the second and third clause for the equality process is a manifestation of the race condition associated with shared variables noted in Section One. If such a primitive were to be provided for programmers it would correspond to an atomic variable test-commit-and-set action. It tests to see whether the first argument is a variable and if so commits the clause and instantiates the first argument with the second argument as an all-or-nothing action. The idea of this primitive was first introduced by Burt and Ringwood [Burt88a]. It violates a previous programmer-level rule that guards cannot instantiate variables in the call. This condition has to be modified to allow instantiation of a process variable only as part of an atomic guard-variable test, clause commit and variable instantiation. (This in no way conflicts with the semantics where the guard is assumed to be atomic.)

In a distributed implementation, the atomic testCommitAndSet action is achieved is realised as follows. Each as yet unbound variable, X, occurs only once in the distributed system, at the node where it was first created. All other references to it are indirections. An equality process of the form x=t has to migrate to the node where the variable x is stored in order to bind it.

8 Meta-interpretation and partial evaluation of Occam

As a symbolic language RGDC is well-suited for writing meta-interpreters. Since RGDC code is a first class object, circular meta-interpreters.

```
reduce([])<-true
   <-true;
reduce(A=B:ProcessQueue)<-true
   <-A=B,
   reduce(ProcessQueue);
reduce(process(Goal):ProcessQueue)<-true
   <-clause(head(Goal),Behaviour),
   reduce(Behaviour),
   reduce(ProcessQueue).
```

Here a clause of the form h<-<constraint><-b$_1$,...b$_m$ is represented in the meta-interpreter by

```
clause(head(h),T)  <-<constraint>
   <-T=[process(b1),...process(bm)].
```

Using enhanced meta-interpreters (flavours) one can implement a wide spectrum of programming environments and debuggers for RGDC [Hunt87a]. Given the close correspondence between Occam and RGDC, a meta-interpreter can form the basis of an Occam interpreter. A brief description of how this may be done follows:

Occam is, like Fortran, an imperative language so multiple assignment to variables is the norm. As is usual in declarative languages, this may be simulated by representing the environment explicitly as a collection of {Variable,Value} pairs. The following is a simple interpreter for the mutable variables of Occam:

```
execute(env(Env),Variable:=Expression,NewEnv)<-true
   <-evaluate(Env,Expression,Value),
   update(Env,{Variable,Value},NewEnv);
```

The **evaluate** process relates an expression to its value with respect to a given environment. The **update** process relates the prior and post environments with respect to the change in the value of an Occam variable. When the update completes NewEnv is instanced by env(New) which as will be seen provides synchronization for sequential process composition.

The Occam **PRI ALT** structure maps onto alternative guarded clauses, though the implementation is made rather more complex by the need to support environments. Conditionals can be simulated using the guard construct.

```
execute(env(Env),if(Condition,Code1,Code2),NewEnv)<-true
   <-evaluate(Env,Condition,Value),
   branch(env(Env),{Value,Code1,Code2},NewEnv);

branch(env(Env),{true,Code1,Code2},NewEnv)<-true
   <-execute(env(Env),Code1,NewEnv);
branch(env(Env),{false,Code1,Code2},NewEnv)<-true
   <-execute(env(Env),Code2,NewEnv).
```

Iteration is simulated by recursion as is usual in declarative languages.

```
execute(env(Env),while(Cond,Code),NewEnv)<-true
   <-execute(env(Env),
      if(Cond,seq(Code,while(Cond,Code)),skip),NewEnv);
execute(env(Env),skip,NewEnv)<-true
   <-NewEnv=env(Env);
```

Since there is no sequencing of processes in RGDC, a sequence of Occam processes has to be treated as a continuation. Occam processes can be built pairwise from parallel and sequential process constructors. Sequencing is effected by chaining processes together with successive environments.

```
execute(env(Env),seq(P,Q),NewEnv)<-true
   <-execute(env(Env),P,IntEnv),
   execute(IntEnv,Q,NewEnv).
```

This idea is similar to the short circuit technique ([Take83a, Ring89b]), but in this situation the processes are effectively sequenced because the **execute** process blocks until its environment is instantiated.

The Occam **PAR** construct carries straight over to RGDC parallel process composition but allowance has to be made for channel communication.

```
execute(env(Env),par(P,Q),NewEnv)<-true
   <-initChan(Env,ChanEnv),
   execute(env(ChanEnv),P,_),
   execute(env(ChanEnv),Q,_),
   NewEnv=env(Env);
```

Occam allows read-only access to variables shared between processes. This is modelled by copying the environment and ignoring any subsequent changes to it. This copy is intialized with any channels used for communication between parallel processes. As described in Section 3, a synchronised producer-consumer pair may be realised in RGDC using streams. For this not to deadlock the initial stream associated with an Occam channel must be of the form Mess:Stream. This prototype leads to the following interpretation of synchronised communication:

```
execute(env(Env),Chan?Variable,NewEnv)<-true<-
  evaluate(Env,Chan,Stream),
  syncReceive(Env,{Chan,Stream,Variable},NewEnv);
execute(env(Env),Chan!Expression,NewEnv)<-true<-
  evaluate(Env,Expression,Value),
  evaluate(Env,Chan,Stream)
  syncSend(Env,{Chan,Stream,Value},NewEnv).

syncReceive(Env,{Chan,msg(Value):Stream,Variable},NewEnv)
  <-true
  <-Stream=Message:TailStream,
  update(Env,{Variable,Value},NewEnv),
  update(Env,{Chan,Stream},NewEnv).

syncSend(Env,{Chan,Mess:Stream,Value},NewEnv)<-true
  Mess=msg(Value),
  update(Env,{Chan,Stream},NewEnv).
```

A fuller description of this interpreter is given in Huntbach [Hunt91b].

The use of meta-interpreters offers a powerful programming technique in which applications can be constructed by writing layers of enhanced meta-interpreters, the enhancement in each layer concentrating on some reification of the application abstraction. For example, the process to processor mapping problem could be accomplished by having one layer of meta-interpretation interpret a virtual tree machine, and another layer to interpret the virtual tree on physical architecture [Tayl87a].

The problem with meta-interpretation as a means of implementation is that each layer of interpretation gives rise to additional overheads on the efficiency of the program. This can to a large extent be overcome by partially evaluating the interpreter with respect to the program it is interpreting [Gall86a]. Partial evaluation refers to executing code with the input only partially defined and constructing specialised versions of the code for those parts where there is not sufficient input for execution to complete. If an interpreter I is partially evaluated against a program P as input, but P's input is not fully instantiated, the code that remains will be a program that executes P but has the additional functionality introduced by I. The simple semantics, restricted syntax and symbolic nature of RGDC mean that partial evaluation may be expressed in terms of a small number of rules [Hunt89a].

Given an interpreter for Occam written in RGDC, as described above, and partially evaluating this interpreter with an Occam program as input would give an RGDC program that behaved as the Occam program but without the overhead of interpretation. A demonstration that this is feasible is given in [Hunt91b], where an interpreter that covers the essential features of Occam is given together with some examples showing the transformation of Occam-like code into RGDC. As described by Huntbach [Hunt91b], the Occam **ALT** structure can be coded as a set of RGDC clauses and again, while the details of handling this in the interpreter are complex, partial evaluation removes the complexities. Although cumbersome, the explicit representation of the environment also disappears during partial evaluation.

9 Conclusions

It would be uncommon, but not impossible, for an AI program to be written in C. The more usual choice programmers are offered is between Lisp and Prolog. Since Lisp is to some extent based on lambda calculus and Prolog is based on Horn clause calculus, they are both reifications of computational models. Nevertheless, they betray the underlying architecture of the conventional sequential machines they were designed for: stack-based machines. Neither Lisp nor Prolog is well adapted for distributed architectures and reactive programming. A more appropriate language abstraction for the hardware of distributed systems is the concurrent programming paradigm. Occam is an example of this class but such languages are not well suited to the task of AI programming. The concurrent logic languages are an attempt to weld together the best of both paradigms. A comparative review of the variations in concurrent logic languages is given in [Ring89a]. A representative of this class, Reactive Guarded Definite Clauses (RGDC) has been outlined in this chapter The kernel of the Japanese Fifth generation initiative is another representative of this family, FGHC (Flat Guarded Horn Clauses); a retrospective analysis of the Japanese influence on this on this subclass of languages is given in [Ring88b].

RGDC is a logic programming language that has been distilled by programming and implementation experience over a period of seven years from an initial amalgam of Prolog and CSP. Compromises have been made between expressiveness, ease of implementation and efficiency. It is a declarative language with a Horn-clause semantics that is purer than that of Prolog: input/output is defined in a side effect free way using streams; there are no dubious, *negation as failure, assert, retract* nor *var* primitives in RGDC.

If the constraints provided by the system are insufficient, or inappropriate, new ones can be user defined in a lower level language and linked into the system. Primitive processes can also be defined by the user as required and added to the system. In this respect RGDC is like ISWIM [Land66a], in that it is really a family of languages, the individuals being determined by the set of guard constraints and primitives processes provided as semantic attachments. An SERC/DTI supported research project is under way at Queen Mary and Westfield College to provide stream based database primitives that will allow integration of commercial databases such as Ingres and Oracle. This representative of concurrent logic languages will provide an implementation tool that is well suited for applications in distributed knowledge bases.

The genealogy of RGDC is as follows. Parlog86 [Ring88a] was an attempt to clean-up the syntax and semantics of Parlog84 [Clar86a]. As a result of the experience of implementing Parlog86 [Fost86a] an almost minimal subset was isolated as a viable programming language by one of the authors in the first quarter of 1986. This language was called *Flat Parlog with Assignment* and, although unpublished, a commercial version appeared under the trade name of Strand88 marketed by AI Ltd. Because of the collapse of AI Ltd, Strand88 is now marketed by Strand Software Technologies Ltd (SSTL). FGDC (Flat Guarded Definite Clauses) [Ring87a] was the result of restoring the logical semantics to *Flat Parlog with Assignment*, without the loss of any of its efficiency gains over Parlog86. RGDC is an extension of FGDC with priorities and timer primitive processes in line with those of Occam.

RGDC is, like Occam, a condition synchronised language with a process based computational model; this makes it suitable for embedded intelligent control systems. An RGDC process corresponds to an Occam process; a conjunction of RGDC goals corresponds to an Occam **PAR** directive; the guards of RGDC correspond to the Occam **PRI ALT** directive. RGDC can be understood as a guarded deduction language in analogy with Occam, a guarded command (a procedural concept) language. Unlike CSP and Occam, for RGDC channels (logical-variables) are first class objects that can be passed as data. (Huntbach [Hunt91c] gives an algorithm which is simple to express in RGDC for this very reason, but is difficult to express in other concurrent languages.) Given its process computational model, RGDC shares Occam's affinity for realtime embedded systems. As such, RGDC finds hardware support in the Transputer yet inherits Prolog's capacity for symbolic processing. RGDC's potential for reactive programming comes from the use of streams. Functional languages, such as Miranda [e.g. Holy91a], have noted that streams provide an elegant way to extend declarative languages to reactive applications. But, functional languages have some semantic difficulties with streams such as merge processes. On the other hand, RGDC, being a relational language does not have to make any semantic compromises in the use of streams.

Being a declarative language, RGDC is ideal for metaprogramming realtime embedded intelligent control systems. As such it should not be regarded as an object language, as is Prolog, but as a metalogic language. The language also shows promise for the programming of mutable neural nets [Koza90a]. If Occam is the Transputer's Fortran then RGDC is the Transputer's Lisp (or hopefully, somewhat better than Lisp). Given its close relationship with Occam, RGDC is ideally suited to benefit from direct implementation on Transputers.

13 A Distributed Implementation of Flat Concurrent Prolog on Multi-transputer Environments

U. Glässer
Paderborn University, Germany

ABSTRACT

This chapter describes a distributed implementation of the concurrent logic programming language Flat Concurrent Prolog (FCP) on Transputer networks, which has been developed at Paderborn University (FRG). Based on the general concept of an abstract Prolog machine, a parallel FCP machine is realized as a network of asynchronously operating sequential FCP machines. The applied parallel machine architecture easily scales for arbitrary network sizes as well as arbitrary network topologies. Substantial design issues including the applied distributed reduction algorithm as well as the integration of the different communication models – the one for the application language and the one for the target architecture – are considered in detail. Performance results from our prototype implementation running on a Parsytec Supercluster multi-Transputer system with up to 320 Transputer nodes are also presented.

1 INTRODUCTION

Flat Concurrent Prolog (FCP) is a general purpose logic programming language designed for concurrent programming and parallel execution. FCP was developed at the Weizmann Institute of Science in 1985 [Mier85a]. A uniprocessor version has been used for implementing the Logix programming system [Silv87a].

The computational model of FCP is based on the process reading of logic programs ([Shap86a], [Take86a]). Its basic control mechanisms are data-flow synchronization and guarded-command indeterminacy. From a practical point of view, FCP is representative of a whole class of concurrent logic programming languages, all based on stream-parallel execution. In particular, it has been shown that almost all other languages of the same class can be naturally and elegantly embedded in FCP [Shap89a].

Moreover, due to its powerful synchronization primitives, FCP offers certain high level programming techniques which are not available in most of the other languages. In order to achieve the same expressiveness as provided by FCP, some of these languages apply additional constructs that are not established in their abstract computational model. However, the more simple the synchronization primitives of a concurrent logic programming language are, the more easy its implementation is.

Our objective is to investigate the possibilities of embedding concurrent logic application languages on large Transputer networks. Essentially, we are concerned with the question of how features inherent to these languages can be matched with those inherent to Transputer architectures in order to utilize maximum parallelism. An issue particularly being addressed is the concept of integrating two different communication models. Asynchronous communication via shared logical variables, as applied in concurrent logic programming languages, has to be realized on a synchronous communication architecture. The language's basic primitives for interprocess communication and synchronization thus have to be transformed into corresponding primitives for the Transputer. The latter ones are defined by the message-passing model of CSP [Hoar78a].

Parallel execution of FCP programs on multi-Transputers basically requires a **distributed reduction algorithm** to be combined with a **dynamic load balancing policy**. At the same time, there are a number of related problems that need to be handled in order to implement a runnable system. The most important of these are: distributed termination detection, distributed garbage collection, livelock and deadlock prevention, and distributed debugging. Within this chapter we concentrate on the distributed reduction algorithm as well as the data structures used to realize it. The algorithm operates on a particular distributed representation scheme for shared logical variables, which is embodied in the design of our parallel FCP machine. However, mayor aspects concerning livelock and deadlock prevention and distributed termination detection are also considered.

The whole parallel machine is organized as a network of asynchronously operating sequential FCP machines. Each sequential machine component is called a *reduction unit*. It executes compiled FCP code similar to Warren's *Abstract Prolog Machine* [Warr83a] but has the additional capability to cooperate with other reduction units as required when performing a distributed computation. In the absence of a physically shared memory, any interaction between reduction units rests upon message-passing communication protocols.

The overall design of the parallel FCP machine is oriented towards **scalability**. It easily adapts to arbitrary network sizes as well as arbitrary network topologies with respect to the underlying target machine architecture. A most important issue in the design of the sequential FCP machine components was to maintain uniprocessor performance as far as possible. In contrast to a purely sequential FCP machine, a reduction unit's FCP machine component requires to handle a single additional pointer type for the representation of globally shared data objects.

The basic mechanisms for processing remote data objects are realized as part of the machine's distributed run-time system in such a way that they are not visible at the application language layer. For an FCP program effective parallelization appears transparent. As a consequence, the parallel machine becomes enabled to run code which has been generated by a compiler for a sequential FCP machine.

A prototype of the parallel machine has been implemented on a *Parsytec Supercluster* multi-Transputer system using the parallel programming language Par.C [Pars89a]. The system is composed of T800 Transputers with 4 MByte local RAM on each Transputer node. Several application examples have been tested with different network topologies and network sizes up to 320 Transputer nodes.

Closely related to our work is a distributed implementation of FCP on an iPSC Hypercube which has been developed at the Weizmann Institute ([Tayl86a], [Tayl89a]). However, this approach is different from ours in several ways. Beside using a different distributed representation scheme for logical variables, the reduction algorithm is more complex due to the variable locking mechanism it applies.

Furthermore, as the target architecture offers asynchronous communication, there is no need to cope with the integration of different communication models. Although using a highly optimizing compiler, the performance results presented in [Tayl89a] are comparable to ours. Unfortunately, these results are only given for very limited network sizes up to 16 processing nodes.

Another concurrent logic programming language that has also been implemented on Transputer networks is Strand [Fost90a]. Compared to FCP, this language has several substantial restrictions leading to a completely different programming approach. As it lacks for the ability to perform automatic load balancing, the programmer has to specify all activities concerning dynamic load balancing explicitly in the program. This includes the partitioning of process networks as well as the mapping of processes to processors.

The remainder of this chapter is organized as follows. Section 2 describes the abstract computational model of concurrent logic programming, the data-flow synchronization mechanism of FCP, and the computation of an FCP program. Section 3 briefly introduces the basic concept of a sequential FCP machine as it is embodied in the reduction units. The abstract system architecture of the parallel machine is specified in section 4. Based on this model, the distributed representation scheme for shared logical variables as well as the fundamentals of the distributed reduction algorithm are explained. This is followed by a discussion of livelock and deadlock prevention. Section 5 presents the parallel FCP machine architecture and its implementation in some detail. Some general conclusions are given in section 6.

2 CONCURRENT LOGIC PROGRAMMING

2.1 Process Interpretation of Logic Programs

Process interpretation of logic programs establishes the abstract computational model of concurrent logic programming in which the active objects of a computation are conceived as *concurrent processes*. Process interpretation, generally, is in contrast to procedural interpretation of logic programs [Ueda89a]. The latter one provides the abstract computational model of conventional (sequential) Prolog, as introduced by Kowalski in [Kowa79a].

2.1.1 The Process Model. Process interpretation of logic programs means that the conjunctive goal of a computation is viewed as a concurrent *process network*. The concurrent processes communicate and synchronize via shared logical variables according to an asynchronous communication model. Based on this concept various kinds of interprocess communication can be implemented. Shared logical variables therefore provide a simple way to build up the required communication channels, which specify the network's interconnection structure.

A process reads from input variables and writes onto output variables in such a way as process execution is blocked until all values required from process input variables are available. When being executed, a process produces results by instantiating output variables. This way, unification realizes both, the basic data manipulation operation as well as a universal mechanism for communication. This allows to describe communication implicitly by natural language constructs rather than explicitly by additional communication control constructs.

An individual process is represented by a goal atom of the form $p(A_1, A_2, ..., A_k)$. The goal atom's predicate symbol p/k identifies the process type, where k denotes the arity of p. The list of terms $A_1, A_2, ..., A_k$ in the argument of p/k is interpreted as a collection of process data registers reflecting the current process *data state*.

2.1.2 Dynamic Process Behaviour. A process can perform a single operation, called *process reduction*. When to reduce a process and how to reduce it depends on the actual process argument values. Regarding a *logic program* $\mathcal{P}$, the behaviour of a process $p(A_1, A_2, ..., A_k)$ is determined by the finite subset $C^{p/k}$ of *program clauses*, $C^{p/k} = \{C_1^{p/k}, C_2^{p/k}, ..., C_l^{p/k}\} \subseteq \mathcal{P}$, collectively defining predicate p/k. The set $C^{p/k}$ is also called a *process procedure*. Each clause $C_i^{p/k} \in C^{p/k}$ represents a rewrite rule for goal atoms of type p/k. It has the general structure of a guarded Horn clause as defined below, where A, the G_i, and the B_j respectively represent atoms:

$$\underbrace{A}_{Head} \leftarrow \underbrace{G_1, G_2, ..., G_m}_{Guard} \mid \underbrace{B_1, B_2, ..., B_n}_{Body} \qquad (m, n \geq 0)$$

The guard part $G_1, G_2, ..., G_m$ is read as a conjunction of predicates controlling clause selection. Guard predicates state conditions referring to process argument values. In order to perform a reduction on a process A' using some program clause $A \leftarrow G_1, ..., G_m \mid B_1, ..., B_n$, the goal atom A' must unify with the clause's head atom A and, in addition, evaluation of the guard must succeed; that is, all the guard predicates $G_1, ..., G_m$ must be fulfilled, simultaneously. The usage of guards in guarded Horn clauses with respect to the resulting impact on program control is closely related to the effect of a guard in the *alternative construct* of Dijkstra's guarded command [Dijk75a].

The body part $B_1, B_2, ..., B_n$ is read as a collection of atoms defining a multiset of concurrent subprocesses. As a result of a successful reduction step, these subprocesses spawn a local subnetwork replacing the reduced process within the global process network. Due to unification of respective variables in the environment of the process and the newly created subprocesses, the global network state is updated, accordingly.

A process reduction operation is *enabled* if the related process procedure contains one or more enabling clauses; i.e. clauses that can be applied to reduce the process. In order to find an enabling clause, all clauses of the process procedure are tried in parallel. When there are several clauses applicable at a time, clause selection proceeds under the control of the *commit operator* '|'.

Upon successful head unification and guard evaluation, a clause is definitively chosen for reduction after its commit operator has been processed. At the same moment all alternative choices concurrently being regarded are discarded. Clause selection thus provides some form of restricted OR-parallelism. The resulting behaviour is called *guarded-command indeterminacy* [Dijk75a] or *don't-care nondeterminism* in contrast to *don't-know nondeterminism* as applied in the computational model of Prolog ([Shap89a], [Ueda89a]).

According to their dynamic behaviour, we can identify two basic kinds of processes: *iterative processes* and *general processes*. Thereby, the behaviour of a process when being reduced primarily depends on the structure of the reducing clause. Referring to the implied process behaviour, clauses can be classified into three different categories, namely:

general clauses: $\quad A \leftarrow G_1, G_2, ..., G_m \mid B_1, B_2, ..., B_n \quad (m \geq 0,\ n \geq 2)$

iterative clauses: $\quad A \leftarrow G_1, G_2, ..., G_m \mid B_1 \quad\quad\quad\quad\ \ (m \geq 0,\ n = 1)$

unit clauses: $\quad\quad\ \ A \leftarrow G_1, G_2, ..., G_m \mid true \quad\quad\quad (m \geq 0,\ n = 0)$

A general clause specifies a *process fork* into a network of concurrent subprocesses, as defined by the body atoms $B_1, B_2, ..., B_n$. An iterative clause specifies a *state transition*, i.e. a modification of process argument values. A reduction by means of a unit clause, finally, results in a process *termination*. The term *true* represents the empty process network.

With respect to the complexity of guard predicates, concurrent logic programming follows two distinct approaches. A more general approach permits the usage of arbitrary complex guard predicates [Take86a]. In particular, it allows guard predicates themselves to be defined by application program procedures. As a consequence, the evaluation of guards may spawn arbitrary complex subprocesses and the reduction of these subprocesses in turn may require the evaluation of complex guards.

The execution of a program this way can result in an unbounded hierarchy of guard process calls. In a distributed implementation this may require rather complex control mechanisms, for instance, to perform distributed commit operations. Languages following this approach, e.g. are Concurrent Prolog [Shap83a], Guarded Horn Clauses (GHC) [Ueda85a], and PARLOG [Clar84a].

Alternatively, so-called *flat languages* restrict the use of guard predicates to a predefined set of primitive and built-in test operations. The advantage of this approach results from a significant decrease in program control complexity. Guard test predicates can be evaluated, immediately, i.e. without performing complex subcomputations. In the execution of a flat language, the goal therefore corresponds to a flat collection of processes.

For almost all concurrent logic programming languages flat language subsets have been defined and studied. These are considered to be more suitable for efficient implementations due to their simplicity, while the loss of expressiveness when restricting on the flat subset of a concurrent logic language seems to be relatively small. Examples of flat languages are Flat Concurrent Prolog (FCP), Flat GHC, or Flat Parlog. A detailed overview on flat languages is presented in [Shap89a].

2.2 Dataflow Synchronization

The basic synchronization concept of concurrent logic programming is to delay reduction operations depending on the instantiation state of variables in the argument of processes. This can be realized by means of a process suspension mechanism.

An attempt to reduce a process results in a *suspension* of that process if it cannot be decided, definitively, whether the process is reducable or not. That means, as the argument variables of the process have not been sufficiently instantiated, it is neither possible to determine a reducing clause nor to recognize that none of the potential clauses is applicable at all. A suspension therefore indicates that certain input data required for the process to be reduced is not yet available but can propably be obtained as the result of reducing some other processes.

When the process variables causing the process suspension have been instantiated further, a repeated reduction attempt may yield a definite result; i.e. the process either is successfully reduced, or otherwise, a *reduction failure* occurs. In the later case neither of the clauses would enable a reduction regardless of whatever the process variables are instantiated to.

FCP applies a reduction delaying mechanism based on the concept of *read-only* variables. In contrast to ordinary variables, which are refered to as *writable* variables, there is no write access to read-only variables, except by instantiating their writable counterparts. Using the *read-only operator* '?' as a dataflow synchronization primitive, various occurrences of the same variable can be supplied with different access modes. Thus, a writable variable 'X' as well as any read-only variable '$X?$' belonging to '$X?$', always refer to the same physical variable-instance.

In the execution model of FCP asynchronous interprocess communication through shared logical variables is controlled by application of a simple rule. Any attempt to reduce a process using a clause that would affect a read-only variable within the process argument results in a process suspension. However, the same attempt might be successful later on in the computation.

In combination, the variables X and $X?$ form a *communication channel*, where the direction of communication goes from X to $X?$. If X is located in the argument of some process $p(..., X, ...)$ while $X?$ is located in the argument of some other process $q(..., X?, ...)$, then both processes share this communication channel. Information that process p produces on output channel X is received by process q on input channel $X?$.

Though, any single variable – due to the single-assignment nature of logic variables – must be instantiated at most once, a communication channels as described above actually allows to transfer an infinite sequence of messages. This is achieved by instantiating the initial variable of the sender process with a compound term containing the message as well as an uninstantiated variable. The new variable in turn can be used to transfer a subsequent message the same way. In addition to each message being transferred, some new variable is created by extending some recursively defined data structure.

An example using the Prolog list structure as a framework for constructing communication channels is presented below. A sequence consisting of n dummy messages, one by one, goes along the channel from X to $X?$. When the last message has passed the sender, the channel is closed as X_n becomes instantiated with a ground term.

	Sender			Receiver	
	X		$X?$		
Step 0	X	$= [message_1	X_1]$	$X?$	$= [message_1	X_1?]$
Step 1	X_1	$= [message_2	X_2]$	$X_1?$	$= [message_2	X_2?]$
...					
Step n	X_{n-1}	$= [message_n	X_n]$	$X_{n-1}?$	$= [message_n	X_n?]$
Step $n+1$	X_n	$= [\,]$	$X_n?$	$= [\,]$

2.3 Computation of an FCP Program

Depending on the granularity of operations being observed, there are a number of distinct layers for describing computations performed by concurrent logic programs. Basically, these are *unification, clause try operations, reduction operations*, and the computation as a whole. When refering to the control-flow and data-flow in the execution of a program, the most interesting layer is the one dealing with reduction operations.

A computation $\mathcal{C}$ an FCP program $\mathcal{P}$ performs on a given set of input processes, which is represented by the initial resolvent $\mathcal{R}_0$, proceeds as a sequence of process reduction steps. Starting from the initial state $< start\ ; \mathcal{R}_0\ ; \epsilon >$, where *start* corresponds to the computation mode and ϵ denotes the empty substitution set, a finite computation eventually reaches one of three possible *terminal* states $< x\ ; \mathcal{R}_s\ ; \theta >$, $x \in \{succeed, suspend, fail\ \}$ ([Shap89a], [Tayl89a]). In a terminal state no further reduction is enabled.

If $x = succeed$, then $\mathcal{R}_s = \emptyset$ and θ represents the *answer substitution*, i.e. the final set of computed variable/sustitution pairs restricted on the variables in $\mathcal{R}_0$. If $x = suspend$, then $\mathcal{R}_s$ is nonempty but all the remaining processes are suspened. Finally, if $x = fail$, a reduction fail has occured.

3 DESIGN OF AN ABSTRACT FCP MACHINE

3.1 The Process Reduction Mechanism

The central operation in the execution of an FCP program is the process reduction. Under the objective to increase efficiency in processing program code, main efforts therefore concentrate on improving the process reduction mechanism.

Efficiency, with respect to program execution time, is principally a matter of clause selection and clause evaluation techniques. More precisely, it depends on the costs of head unification, guard evaluation, and of spawning new subprocesses. In general, several clauses from the same process procedure are tried for reduction until eventually an applicable clause reduces the process. In case of a delayed reduction, where a process becomes suspended on one or more read-only variables, clause selection is even more complex, since it may be required to evaluate a process procedure more than once. However, when using an appropriate process suspension mechanism, which avoids that suspended processes are scheduled for reduction (*busy waiting*), this overhead can be reduced significantly.

The execution of a process procedure $C^{p/k} = \{C_1^{p/k}, C_2^{p/k}, ..., C_r^{p/k}\}$ in an attempt to reduce a process $p(A_1, A_2, ..., A_k)$ naturally divides into a number of single clause tries. Each clause try again separates into three basic steps, as shown below:

(0) select some clause $C_i^{p/k}$ from $C^{p/k}$

(1) $unify(\ head(C_i^{p/k}),\ p(A_1, A_2, ..., A_k)\ )$

(2) $evaluate(\ guard\ (C_i^{p/k}),\ mgu(\ head(C_i^{p/k}),\ p(A_1, A_2, ..., A_k))\ )$

Clause selection. The abstract computational model of FCP assumes a nondeterministic clause selection mechanism, which would also allow to try all clauses belonging to the same program procedure in parallel. Any concrete realization of this model on a uniprocessor, however, needs to specify some deterministic clause selection policy. A straightforward policy would be to select the clauses from the process procedure $C^{p/k}$ following the textual order they appear in the program. Somewhat more sophisticated approaches take into account the relative frequency a certain clause type contributes to a reduction. For instance, an iterative process may be reduced arbitrary often using iterative clauses; by means of a unit clause, it can be reduced only once. In any case, the implemented clause selection policy is transparent for programmer.

Head unification. Step (1) handles the unification of the process structure with the head of some selected clause $C_i^{p/k}$. As the result of a successful unification we obtain the *most general unifier (mgu)* of the clause's head $head\ (C_i^{p/k})$ and the process structure $p(A_1, A_2, ..., A_k)$. This is an expression of the form $\{X_1 = T_1, X_2 = T_2, ..., X_l = T_l\}$, where the $X_i's$ denote variables and the $T_i's$ denote terms, such that $X_i \neq X_j$ if $i \neq j$. Each pair $X_i = T_i$ means that the variable X_i is instantiated with the term T_i and X_i does not occur in T_i.

The *mgu* specifies data-flow relations between input and output channels of the process to be reduced and the corresponding channels of its substituting subprocesses. At the same time, it provides input values for the guard predicates.

Guard evaluation. The guard part of a clause defines restrictions with respect to the process data state. Using the outcome of step (1), these conditions are checked in step (2). If a violation is detected, the clause attempt using $C_i^{p/k}$ fails immediately.

On reaching the commit operator after all predicates have been tested successfully, clause $C_i^{p/k}$ becomes a potential candidate for reducing the process. However, a definitive commitment to select $C_i^{p/k}$ is not made before its commit operator has been processed.

A considerable amount of the work devoted to clause selection is spent on unification. The complexity of unification operations being performed in order to select a reducing clause at least depends on four facts:

- the number r of clauses building up a process procedure $C^{p/k}$
- the arity and argument structure of each clause head
- the complexity of the guards
- the structure and type of the actual process arguments

As we have already seen, FCP restricts the usage of guard predicates to a predefined set of primitive test operations. These test operations like arithmetic comparison, type checking, term comparison, etc., do not require any complex subcomputations but can be computed, immediately. For that reason, we can understand guard evaluation as some kind of extended head unification. In principle, these operations could also be embodied in a general unification algorithm.

Following this approach, an appropriate interleaving of step (1) and step (2) – head unification and guard evaluation – would result in a simple but effective optimization. Due to the simplicity of guard testing, the compatibility of the process state with a clause's guard should be checked in parallel with head unification. In particular, it is often possible to extract information relevant to guard testing prior to thorough unifications of complex argument structures. This technique eliminates a significant amount of superfluous unification overhead.

3.2 The Abstract Machine Model

Based on the regular clause structure and the typical data manipulation operations in processing clauses, a process reduction cycle logically divides into two subsequent phases.

$$\underbrace{H \leftarrow G_1, G_2, ..., G_m}_{Phase\ 1:\ Unification}\ |\ \underbrace{B_1, B_2, ..., B_n}_{Phase\ 2:\ Process\ creation} \qquad (m, n \geq 0)$$

The unification phase handles a unification of the process structure with the clause head as well as guard predicate evaluation. The process creation phase spawns a set of parallel subprocesses replacing the process currently being reduced.

An efficient way of processing sequential Prolog code was proposed by Warren [Warr83a] and has become known as the *Warren Abstract Machine (WAM)*. The individual program clauses are compiled into sequences of primitive unification and goal creation instructions for an abstract Prolog machine. Because the granularity of operations decreases while the flexibility increases, the run-time overhead for processing program clauses is reduced.

The abstract machine approach, especially, the technique of compiling unification operations also works for concurrent logic programming languages. An extension of this general optimization technique to read-only unification primitives allows the design of an abstract FCP machine. Compared to sequential Prolog, the abstract machine for a flat concurrent language like FCP is less complex as it does not need the rather complex stack management in order to handle backtracking efficiently. On the other hand, it has to be supplied with an appropriate process suspension mechanism to avoid busy waiting.

An instruction set for a sequential FCP machine was first proposed by Houri and Shapiro [Hour87a]. In the design and implementation of our machine we use a different instruction set as well as different representations for FCP data structures.

4 CONCEPTS FOR A DISTRIBUTED IMPLEMENTATION

4.1 Abstract System Architecture

In order to point out substantial design issues of the parallel FCP machine, this section introduces the underlying abstract machine architecture in terms of a generic model. The resulting machine specification provides a general framework within which the various techniques used for exploiting and controlling parallelism are discussed. How to map the abstract architecture onto the real target architecture, then is presented in section 5.

The whole parallel machine is organized as a network consisting of $n+1$ asynchronously operating processing elements. According to the function they realize, the processing elements separate into n so-called *reduction units* $RU_0, ..., RU_{n-1}$, and a single *host unit*. While the uniformly constructed reduction units represent the machine's basic building blocks, the additional host unit takes the role of a central supervisor. Via a *communication network (CN)* built up from bidirectional point-to-point links, the reduction units as well as the host unit are clustered as shown in Figure 1.

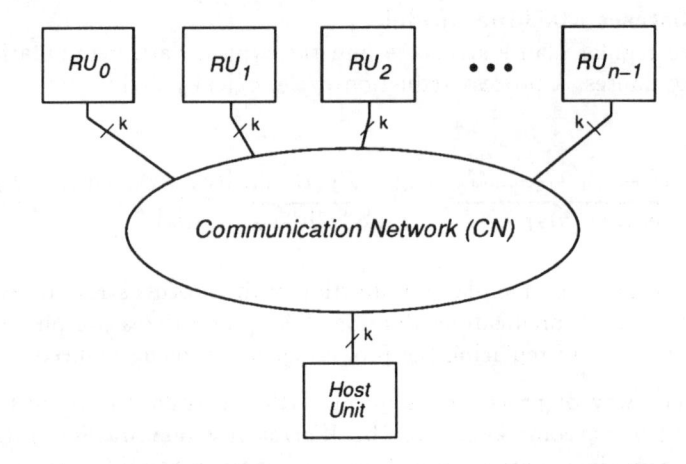

Figure 1: Abstract Architecture of the Parallel FCP Machine

An individual reduction unit essentially provides the functionality of a sequentially operating FCP machine, but has some extra capabilities to co-operate with other reduction units. Its core component executes compiled FCP code on a private local memory.

4.1.1 Parallelization. The parallel FCP machine offers parallelization at the process reduction layer, i.e. the basic *unit of parallelism* is the FCP process. When performing a distributed computation, each reduction unit RU_i runs an identical copy $\mathcal{P}_i$ of the same FCP program $\mathcal{P}$. By partitioning the global resolvent $\mathcal{R}$ into n subsets representing the subresolvents $\mathcal{R}_0, ..., \mathcal{R}_{n-1}$, the global computation becomes broken up into a corresponding number of local subcomputations, each of which is assigned to one of the reduction units $RU_0, ..., RU_{n-1}$.

Dynamic work load balancing ensures that local subresolvents are continuously reorganized during a computation. Processes therefore are enabled to migrate between reduction units. By means of a dynamic load balancing algorithm process migration is initiated and controlled according to frequently computed local load indices. However, all load balancing activities remain completely decentralized.

The described computation scheme corresponds to an *AND-parallel* execution model, i.e. the concurrently executed subcomputations operate on a common set of global variables. With respect to general design concepts of distributed systems and parallel machine architectures, the way a distributed computation on the parallel FCP machine is organized reflects the MIMD scheme. Though all units run the same program, each unit effectively executes a different stream of instructions on a different stream of data.

4.1.2 Scalability. A main objective in the design of the parallel machine is scalability. The proposed architecture easily scales for different network sizes. A minimal configuration is a network consisting of a single reduction unit together with the host unit ($n = 1$). Such a configuration actually realizes a sequential FCP machine. As there is only one reduction unit keeping all data local, any synchronization overhead is completely avoided.

The maximum value for n, however, is a limitation placed by the specific target hardware architecture. It merely depends on the number of processors that are available. Similarly, the maximum number of interconnecting links forming the communication network is determined by the hardware system.

Furthermore, the parallel machine does not require any particular network topology, such as a hypercube, a torus, etc. The system dynamically adapts to arbitrary network configurations (as long as the network remains connected). Starting the system on some unknown network, the network is explored first and a reduction unit is installed on each processor being reached.

4.2 Distributed Data Representation

The parallel machine architecture in principal realizes a *physically distributed system* with a *logically shared memory*. While the concept of a physically distributed system reflects the view at the parallel machine layer, the concept of a logically shared memory corresponds to the view at the application language layer. In the implementation of the parallel machine the logically shared memory has to be simulated in such a way that any physical distribution of data is transparent for the application program. For a reduction unit's sequential machine component a data object always appears to be accessible through a reference into a global memory.

Data representation at the machine layer is concerned with two basically different types of data objects: *local data objects* and *global data objects*. In contrast to local ones, global data objects need to be accessible by more than one reduction unit at a time. However, it is convenient to represent both kinds of data objects within a homogeneous global address space. Such a global address space is obtained by combining the local address spaces of the individual reduction units. A global address x then has the form $x = (i, j)$, $0 \leq i \leq n - 1$, where i identifies the reduction unit and j a corresponding local address.

With respect to the distributed representation of globally shared data, it is important to realize how the single assignment nature of logical variables is preserved in the execution model of concurrent logic programming languages. As no backtracking is applied, any variable bindings that are computed when performing a reduction operation become permanent as soon as the commit-operator has been processed. In fact, this means that any non-variable term can be treated as an *immutable data object*. For that reason, the resulting terms can be replicated and distributed to all reduction units referring to these variables. This is even possible for terms that consist of structures itself containing variables. In the copied structure these variables are replaced by corresponding remote references.

4.2.1 Representation of Non-Variable Terms. In general, replication of immutable data provides an appropriate means to reduce the access time to global data within a distributed environment. However, for complex data structures the resulting communication costs must also be taken into consideration. These costs can be reduced when using *data distribution by demand-driven structure copying*. Instead of replicating complex data structures as a whole, they are copied incrementally.

For the unification algorithm it is often sufficient to know the type and the top level arguments of a deeply nested data structure. This allows to split up complex structures by copying only a fixed number of levels in one step. When further levels are required, they are copied on demand. In contrast to the approach described in [Tayl89a], the first k levels are always copied by default, i.e. without explicit request. This provides a simple and efficient way to realize a distributed process suspension mechanism, as discussed in the subsequent section.

4.2.2 Representation of Logical Variables. For globally shared variables a special *distributed representation scheme* has to be applied. In combination with a set of rules controlling its dynamic evaluation, the distributed representation scheme ensures the following important features concerning the behaviour of the distributed reduction algorithm:

- Whenever two or more reduction units attempt to modify the same variable, concurrently, **mutual exclusive write access** is guaranteed.

- The operation of binding a writable variable to a non-variable term or another variable is performed as an **atomic action.**

To perform variable bindings as atomic action means, that any attempt to affect a variable during head unification or guard evaluation will have one of two definite results; the attempt either fails without leaving any trace or, in case it succeeds, any occurrence of this variable, independent of its location, is affected in the same way.

Formally, the distributed representation scheme of a logical variable 'X' corresponds to a *directed acyclic graph (DAG)* $G_X = (V, E, attr)$, which is extended by additional node attributes. The vertex set V together with the set of directed edges E define the distributed structure of X. To each vertex $v \in V$ an attribute identifying the particular vertex type is assigned using the function $attr : V \longrightarrow \{local, remote, read\text{-}only\}$.

Definition. Let $G_X = (V, E, attr)$ specify the *distributed representation scheme* of a globally shared variable X. For some subset of vertices $\{v_1, v_2, ..., v_k\} \subseteq V$ let $v_1 \stackrel{x}{\rightsquigarrow} v_k$, $x \in \{remote, read\text{-}only\}$, denote a path $v_1 \rightarrow v_2 \rightarrow ... \rightarrow v_k$ in G_X, such that the following property holds:

$$(\forall i)\ 1 \le i \le k-1 : (v_i, v_{i+1}) \in E \text{ and } attr(v_i) = attr(v_k) = x.$$

A legal representation scheme must satisfy the three conditions defined below, where $\hat{u}$ denotes a particular vertex in V and $V' = V - \{\hat{u}\}$:

1. $(\exists! \hat{u})\ \hat{u} \in V :\ attr(\hat{u}) = local\quad (\Rightarrow\ (\forall v)\ v \in V' :\ attr(v) \ne local\ )$
2. $(\forall u)\ u \in V'$:
    $attr(u) = remote \Rightarrow (\exists u')\ u' \in V :\ u \stackrel{remote}{\rightsquigarrow} u' \rightarrow \hat{u}$ is a path in G_X.
3. $(\forall v)\ v \in V'$:
    $attr(v) = read\text{-}only \Rightarrow (\exists v')\ v' \in V' :\ \hat{u} \rightarrow v' \stackrel{read-only}{\rightsquigarrow} v$ is a path in G_X.

The unique *local* vertex $\hat{u}$ identifies the current physical location of the variable X. Initially, this is the location where the variable is created. Additional writable occurrences of X on remote reduction units then are represented by means of remote references pointing to the physical variable location.

More precisely, a remote reference may either point to the physical variable location, immediately, or it may point to another remote reference. In the latter case, recursive evaluation of remote references eventually identifies the physical location. In the graph G_X remote references are reflected by *remote* vertices.

The third vertex type, the *read-only* vertices, correspond to the read-only occurrences $X?$ of the variable X. In fact, they also represent remote references similarly to *remote* vertices. Together with the *remote* vertex $\hat{u}$, the *read-only* vertices form a directed subtree in G_X, where $\hat{u}$ represents the root of this subtree (Figure 2).

With respect to the defined variable representation scheme, the following notation applies to reduction units. The reduction unit keeping the writable variable occurrence corresponding to the *local* vertex $\hat{u}$ is called the *variable owner;* whereas reduction units that hold writable occurrences corresponding to *remote* vertices are denoted as *variable members*.

Using this owner/member relationship the variable owner and the variable members respectively operate in different access modes. Immediate access to a variable, in order to bind it with another variable or to instantiate it to a non-variable term, is solely permitted to the variable owner. Any reduction unit other than the variable owner causes a process suspension when attempting to access this variable.

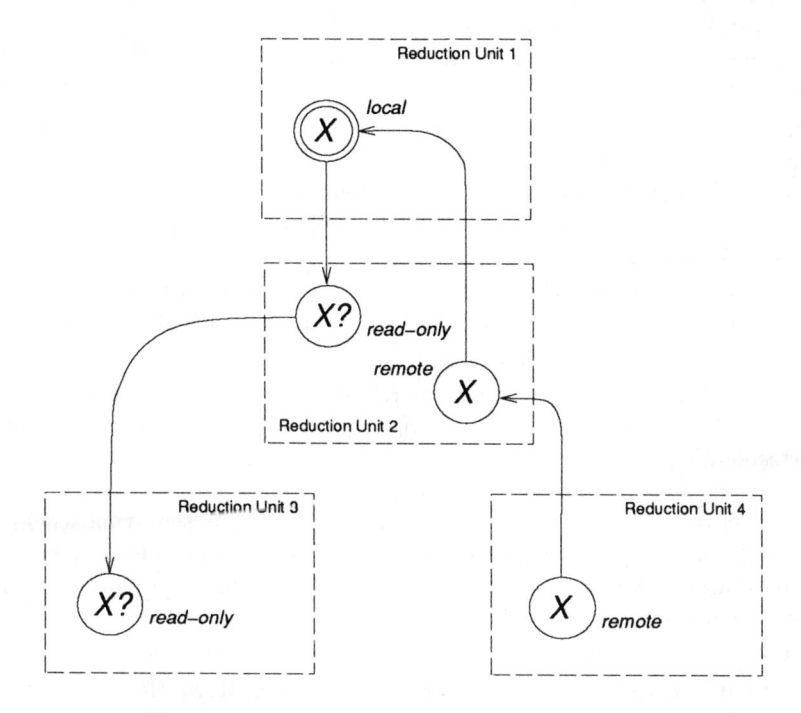

Figure 2: Distributed Variable Representation

4.3 The Distributed Reduction Algorithm

The basic model of the parallel FCP machine is a network consisting of asynchronously operating reduction units. However, in a distributed computation there frequently occur situations where certain operations have to be synchronized. As far as the distributed reduction algorithm is concerned, there are essentially two events which require some form of direct interaction between reduction units.

The first one occurs when a reduction unit encounters a remote reference in an attempt to access a variable. The second one occurs when a variable becomes instantiated and there are remote read-only occurrences for this variable. Both events need to be handled by message-passing based communication protocols. The protocols as well as their effect on distributed process synchronization are explained below.

4.3.1 Variable Migration. A variable member must not change its member relationship into an owner relationship on its own, but it may do so under control of the current variable owner. The operation is initiated by sending a request for ownership to the variable owner. The applied variable representation scheme ensures that there always exists a path along remote references from each variable member RU_j to the current variable owner RU_i. Variable requests thus can be forwarded accordingly. A successful operation transferring variable membership into variable ownership is denoted as *variable migration.*

Receiving a variable request for variable X from reduction unit RU_j, the reaction of the owner reduction unit RU_i depends on the actual state of X, which is referred as $value_i(X)$. If X is yet an unbound variable, then $value_i(X)$ represents a pointer to possibly existing read-only occurrences of X. That means, $value_i(X)$ either identifies the location of some read-only occurrence $X?$ or $value_i(X) = NIL$ in case read-only occurrences do not exist.

An unbound variable X causes RU_i to return $value_i(X)$ to RU_j. Now, RU_j replaces its remote reference $value_j(X)$ by the read-only variable pointer $value_i(X)$. On the other hand, RU_i substitutes $value_i(X)$ by a remote reference pointing on the current location of X on RU_j. At the same time, RU_i and RU_j respectively change the attributes of X from *local* to *remote* and vice versa. As a consequence, RU_j effectively becomes the new owner of variable X. Using the example shown in Figure 2, the effect of a variable migration operation which is initiated by RU_2 is illustrated in Figure 3.

Otherwise, if X has already been bound to a non-variable term, RU_i returns a copy of this term in order to replace the remote reference on RU_j. Since the term itself may contain variables, in the structure being copied each of this variables has to be replaced by a corresponding remote reference.

4.3.2 Process Synchronization. The applied variable representation scheme in combination with mode dependent access restrictions ensures mutual exclusive write access to globally shared variables. Based on this feature, concurrent process reductions that are jointly operating on a global variable set can be synchronized by implementing reduction operations as *atomic actions.*

With regard to the general structure of a guarded Horn clause and the typical data manipulation operations in processing it, a *process reduction cycle* consists of a number of clause try operations. Each clause try operation logically divides into two subsequent phases. The first phase handles *head unification* as well as *guard evaluation*

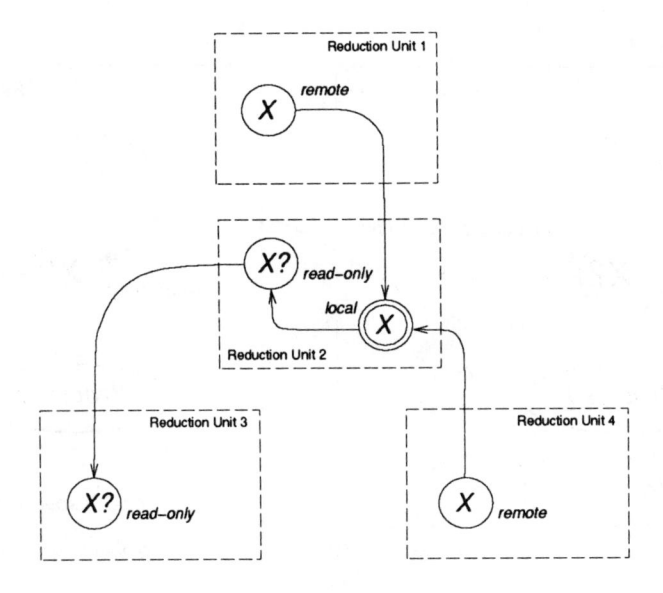

Figure 3: Effect of Variable Migration

prior to commitment; the second phase spawns new subprocesses as defined in the clause's body.

When performing a process reduction cycle, a reduction unit must not be interrupted before one of the following stable states is reached. It either has completed the second phase of a successful clause try operation or it has restored its old data state by releasing any computed variable bindings in case the process becomes suspended. This feature must be ensured by the implementation of the process reduction mechanism.

During the first phase of a reduction cycle variables are affected only within a reduction unit's local environment. If a clause try fails, these effects can easily be undone using a trail stack. The trail stack identifies all writable and read-only variables that have been modified during a reduction attempt. For each of this variables there is a trail stack entry containing the type, the pointer value, and the location of the variable.

In fact, a reduction unit is able to affect a variable, only if it is the current variable owner; otherwise, the reduction would be aborted and the process suspended. A successful clause try reaching the commit operator thus requires the reduction unit to be owner of all variables being involved in the reduction. At the same time, no other reduction unit can become owner of any of these variables, since the reduction cannot be interrupted. As a result, a reduction globally modifies all involved variables in case it succeeds, while it does not affect any variable neither globally nor locally when a suspension occurs; hence, it is *atomic*.

4.3.3 Distributed Process Suspension. When a writable variable X becomes instantiated, $value(X)$ is propagated to all related read-only occurrences $X?$. Due to the variable representation scheme, there always exists a path along references from the location of X on the owner reduction unit RU_i to each occurrence $X?$ residing on reduction units $RU_{j_1}, RU_{j_2}, ..., RU_{j_k}$ (not necessarily being member units).

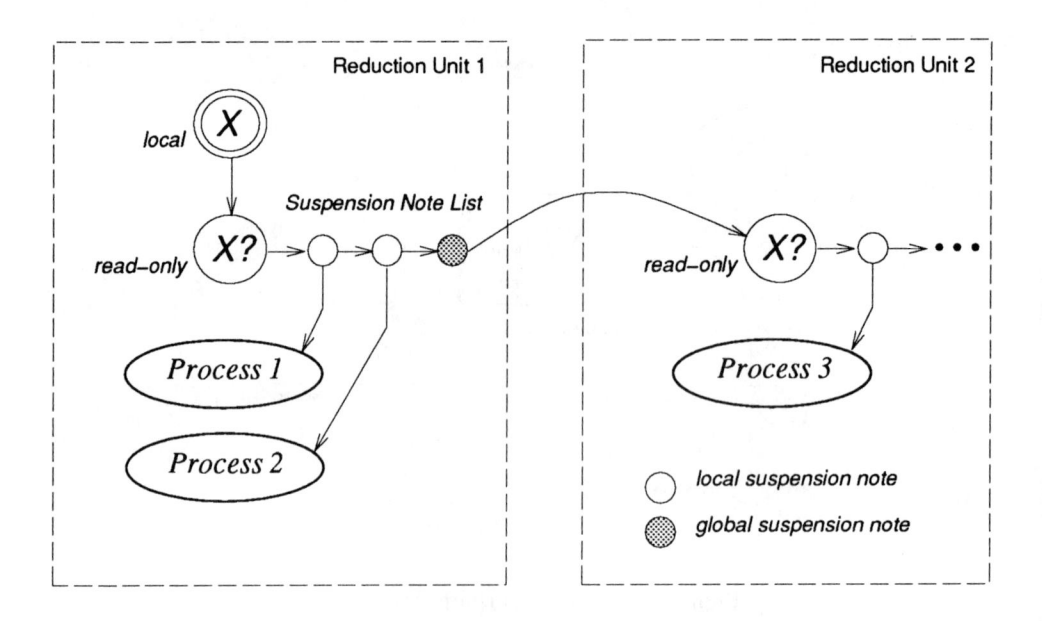

Figure 4: Distributed Process Suspension

With each $X?$ we associate a list of so-called *process suspension notes*. A *suspension note list (snl)* is attached to a read-only variable occurrence $X?$ by storing a pointer to $snl(X?)$ in $value(X?)$. Each entry in $snl(X?)$ identifies a process which has been suspended on $X?$. Traversal of the process suspension note list then allows these processes to be woken up.

Just the same way as for read-only occurrences, suspension notes are used in combination with remote references. Since a variable request should be only started for the first process attempting to write a remote reference, its value field thereafter becomes available to store a suspension note list address. Additional suspension notes can be included if necessary. When a remote reference is changed into a local variable, evaluation of the attached suspension note list again activates processes that have been suspended on this remote reference.

Furthermore, suspension note lists also provide a mean to handle *remote instantiations*, i.e. to wake up processes outside a local environment. Remote instantiations become necessary when instantiating a variable which owns read-only occurrences outside its local environment. For that reason, so called *remote suspension notes* identify related read-only occurrences in the environment of remote reduction units. Remote suspension notes are simply included into suspension note lists together with local suspension notes.

The evaluation of a remote suspension note S, which occurs in $snl(X?)$ on RU_i while referring to another $X?$ on RU_j, causes $value(X)$ to be transferred from RU_i to RU_j. On receiving $value(X)$, RU_j instantiates $X?$ and in turn starts evaluation of the attached suspension note list. Figure 4 gives an example for distributed process suspension.

4.4 Deadlock and Livelock Prevention

Livelock and deadlock prevention is a most important issue in distributed implementations of concurrent logic languages. Deadlocks as well as livelocks both may occur only in programs which allow several processes to write on the same variables *(multiple-writer programs)*.

A livelock corresponds to a situation where two or more reduction units perform some kind of circular 'variable stealing.' As none of the reduction units achieves simultaneous ownership of all the variables it requires in a certain reduction, they are iterating the same sequence of variable migration operations to infinity. In order to resolve livelocks, usually, a mechanism for locking variables against migration is applied [Tayl89a].

Unfortunately, an implementation of variable migration using variable locking usually results in rather complex protocols in order to avoid deadlocks. On the other hand, the detection of livelocks is relatively simple. A livelock can be detected by monitoring the variable requests on each reduction unit. When a livelock occurs, there are at least two reduction units requesting the same variables infinitely often. In a computation which is free of livelocks, however, there appear only a small number of variable requests on the same remote reference location. Usually, there is just a single request.

As livelocks do not occur very frequently and it is possible to detect them, we propose to attack the problem by means of a two-phase algorithm. The first phase operates without variable locking but it ensures a livelock to be detected.

If a livelock occurs, the algorithm switches to the second phase. Now it operates in a mode allowing reduction units to lock variables. Attaching different priorities to each reduction unit guarantees that at least one reduction unit will be enabled to perform reductions. A reduction unit always obtains ownership of variables which have been locked if the priority of the requesting unit is higher than that of the current variable owner. Upon successfully instantiating the variables that have been involved in the livelock, the reduction units again switch back to the non-locking mode.

The advantage of the two-phase algorithm rests upon the fact, that the overhead paid for livelock detection is relatively small compared to a deadlock prevention algorithm. However, the maximum number of variable requests on the same remote reference before a switch should be chosen carefully.

4.5 Distributed Termination Detection

In the current version of the parallel FCP machine, distributed termination detection is realized by means of a simple 2-phase termination detection algorithm. Basically, this algorithm is an extension of the one proposed by Dijkstra et al. [Dijk83a]. The extension allows to detect both, the successful termination of a computation as well as a computation suspension due to a situation, where all remaining processes have been suspended.

Operating as a central supervisor, the host unit starts a termination detection cycle by generating some initial token. This token then is propagated over all reduction units back to the host unit. From the information contained in the received token, the host unit recognizes the global computation state. Depending on this state, it either signals that the computation has been terminated or suspended or, otherwise, it continues by generating a new token for the next termination cycle.

The performance degradation caused by the described termination detection algorithm is quite small, since the token always rests on a busy reduction unit until this unit runs out of work. However, there is a significant drawback as the algorithm in its current version does not handle several computations at a time.

5 A MULTI-TRANSPUTER IMPLEMENTATION OF FCP

5.1 Parallel Machine Architecture

While the global system architecture has already been introduced in section 4.1, a description of the individual subcomponents of the parallel machine architecture is presented here. A somewhat more detailed description can be found in [Glae90a].

5.1.1 Reduction Unit Architecture. The uniformly constructed reduction units each consist of three basic subunits, namely: *a reducer, a distributor,* and *a router* as shown in Figure 5. These subunits are implemented as concurrently operating sequential processes running on the same Transputer node. The router acts as network interface unit, which is required for sending, receiving, and forwarding messages. Using a local routing matrix in combination with unique unit identifiers, messages always go along shortest paths. When booting the machine network, the unit identifiers as well as the corresponding local routing matrices are generated automatically, i.e. the necessary information about the actual network size and its topology is computed at run-time.

The core component of a reduction unit is the reducer. Essentially, it provides the function of a sequentially operating FCP machine with the additional capability to handle remote references. As already described in section 4, an attempt to access a remote reference results in a process suspension. Therefore, a remote reference affects the behaviour of the reducer almost the same way a read-only variable does. Using this relationship, the unification algorithm treats remote references exactly like read-only variables, except for the variable request that has to be generated when encountering a remote reference. However, the reducer has no direct internetwork communication facilities.

Any communication with other reduction units or the host unit remains under control of the distributor. Running the desired network protocols for the reducer, the distributor also needs to access the reducer data. Possible conflicts are avoided by explicitly synchronizing both units. None of these units is able to interrupt the other one while this is active. With respect to the atomicity of reduction operations, this mechanism also ensures that the reducer cannot be interrupted during a reduction cycle. In addition to reducer initiated communication activities, the distributor runs the dynamic work load balancing algorithm and the utilities for termination detection.

5.1.2 Host Unit Architecture. Instead of the reducer subunit of a reduction unit, the host unit is supplied with additional components for controlling I/O operations, global termination detection, network boot facilities, and evaluation of run-time statistics. In principal, the host unit could also be integrated into one of the reduction units. For symmetry reasons, however, it is more preferable to use an extra Transputer node.

```
                    External Links
                        ║║║
                                              Reduction Unit
    ┌─────────────────────────────────────────────────────────────┐
    │   ┌─────────────────────────────────┬─────────────────┐     │
    │   │                                 │   Local         │     │
    │   │         Router                  │   Routing       │     │
    │   │                                 │   Matrix        │     │
    │   └─────────────────────────────────┴─────────────────┘     │
    │                    ↕ Data                                    │
    │   ┌─────────────────────────────┐                            │
    │   │        Distributor          │                            │
    │   │ ┌─────────────────────────┐ │                            │
    │   │ │ Internetwork Communication │       ┌──────────────────┐│
    │   │ │      Protocols          │ │←─────→│     Reducer      ││
    │   │ └─────────────────────────┘ │Control│┌────────────────┐││
    │   │ ┌─────────────────────────┐ │       ││Sequential FCP  │││
    │   │ │  Work Load Balancing    │ │       ││Machine Component││
    │   │ └─────────────────────────┘ │       │└────────────────┘││
    │   │ ┌─────────────────────────┐ │       └──────────────────┘│
    │   │ │ Local Termination Detection│                          │
    │   │ └─────────────────────────┘ │                            │
    │   └─────────────────────────────┘                            │
    │              ↕ Data                        ↕ Data            │
    │   ┌─────────────────────────────────────────────────────┐   │
    │   │         Local Memory (Resolvent)                    │   │
    │   └─────────────────────────────────────────────────────┘   │
    └─────────────────────────────────────────────────────────────┘
```

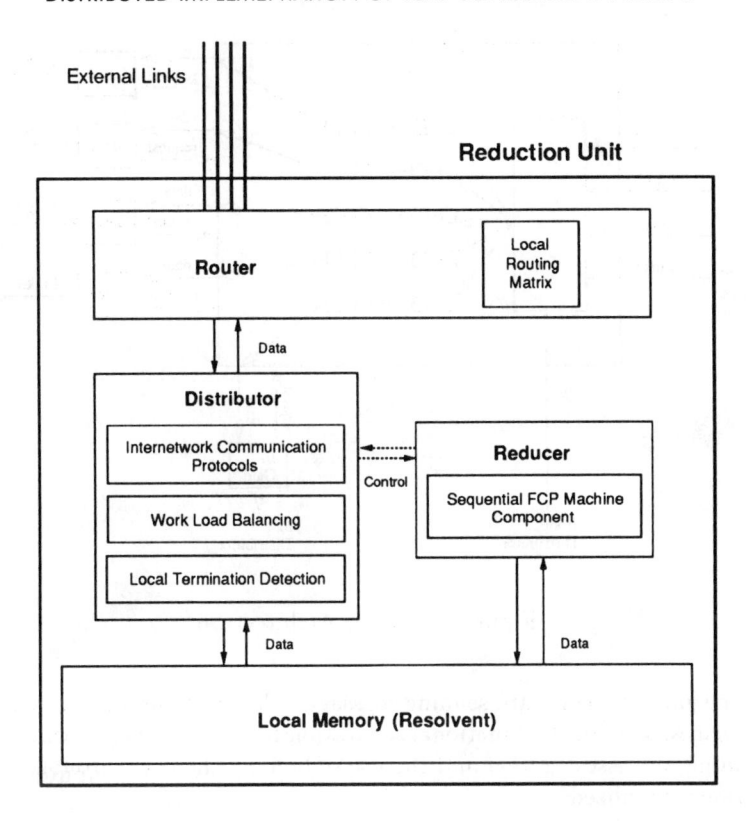

Figure 5: Reduction Unit Architecture

5.2 Integration of Communication Models

Implementing FCP on a synchronous communication architecture requires an efficient transformation of asynchronous communication behaviour into synchronous communication behaviour. Within a reduction unit the basic facilities for network communication management are embedded in the router (Figure 6). The router thus provides the interface where this transformation has to be done. The router function therefore is realized by a set of parallel processes.

Beside two internal ports to the reduction unit's distributor there are eight external ports connecting the router to a maximum of four neighbour reduction units (Figure 6). A single *depot process* receives all messages either being received on one of the external input ports $Link0,...,Link3$ or delivered by the local distributor. By means of a routing matrix in combination with unique unit identifiers, the depot process determines a corresponding output FIFO-queue to enqueue the message.

From the output queues the messages, one by one, are passed to *gate processes* $Gate0,...,Gate3$ controlling the output ports. The gate processes then perform the actual send operation handling one process at a time. Upon completion of a send operation, a gate process explicitly requests the next message by sending a signal to the depot process via the request channel. The depot process performs a dequeue and delivers the resulting message to the gate process via the data channel.

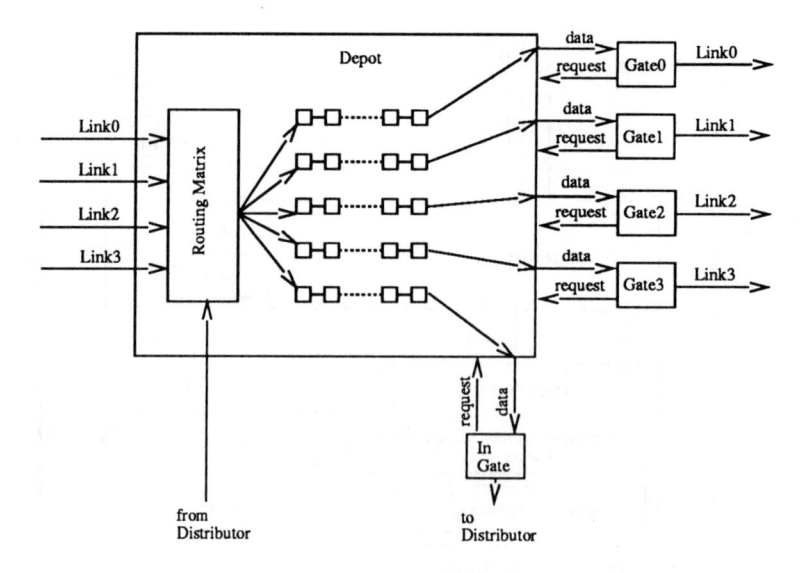

Figure 6: Router Architecture

While the gate processes are sending messages, the depot process may concurrently receive messages. Due to the functional separation into a receiving process (depot) and several sending processes (gates) and the use of buffers, the asynchronous communication behaviour is realized.

An additional aspect in the design of the router is *fairness*. Both, fairness with respect to the order in which incoming messages are processed as well as the way in which gate requests are served should be taken into consideration. In the current version of the router this is achieved as the depot process serves the input ports and output ports, respectively, in a round robin fashion.

5.3 Performance Measurements

The prototype implementation of our parallel FCP machine comprises about 12,000 lines of Par.C code. It has been tested on a Parsytec Supercluster with different network sizes and different network topologies using several smaller FCP example programs. The current version of the Supercluster offers networks up to 320 T800 Transputer nodes.

In combination with the prototype various work load balancing strategies have been tested. Due to the clear separation of its functional components, a replacement of the dynamic load balancing algorithm only requires to replace the corresponding subunit of the distributor. The resulting speed-up behaviour using a local-search-local-distribution load balancing strategy with the example programs *Matrix-Multiplication* and *Towers of Hanoi* is presented in the diagrams below. Speed-up here is defined as the runtime being required on a single processor network divided by the runtime being required on an n processor network ($n > 1$). The diagrams show this relationship for different problem sizes in contrast to different network sizes. For each test the network topology for *Matrix-Multiplication* has been a twisted torus of the appropriate dimension, while *Towers of Hanoi* has been tested on DeBruijn networks.

/* Towers of Hanoi: */

```
hanoi(N,From,To,(Before,(From,To),After)) <-
   N>1 |
   sub(N,1,N1),
   free(From,To,Free),
   hanoi(N1,From,Free?,Before),
   hanoi(N1,Free?,To,After).
hanoi(1,From,To,(From,To)).

free(a,b,c).
free(a,c,b).
free(b,a,c).
free(c,a,b).
free(b,c,a).
free(c,b,a).
```

/* Matrix-Multiplication: */

```
mm([Xv|Xm],Ym,[Zv|Zm]) <-
   vm(Xv,Ym,Zv),
   mm(Xm,Ym,Zm).
mm([],_,[]).

vm(Xv,[Yv|Ym],[Z|Zv]) <-
   ip(Xv,Yv,0,Z),
   vm(Xv,Ym,Zv).
vm(_,[],[]).

ip([X|Xs],[Y|Ys],P,S) <-
   P1 := P+X*Y,
   ip(Xs,Ys,P1?,S).
ip([],[],P,P).
```

Towers of Hanoi

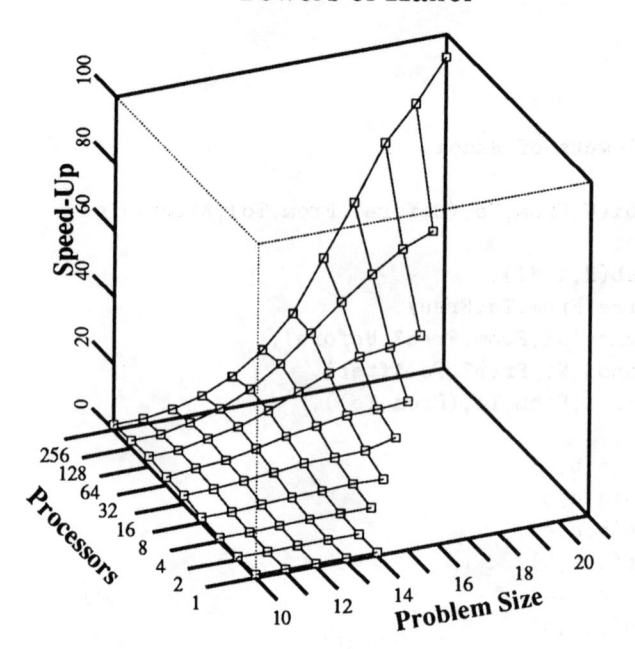

Matrix Multiplication

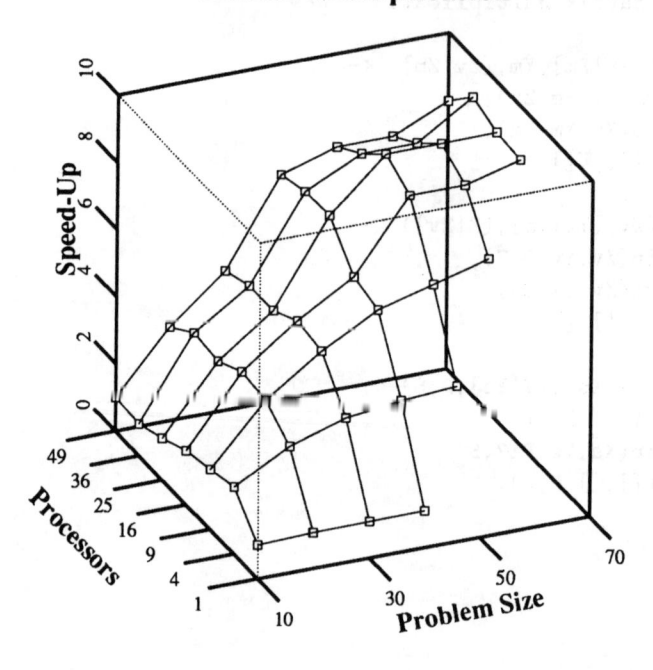

6 CONCLUSIONS

We have presented a concept for a distributed implementation of the concurrent logic programming language FCP on multi-Transputer environments. A most important aspect in the design of our parallel FCP machine is scalability with respect to the network size and network topology. Its functional architecture is oriented towards an efficient integration of the different communication models for the application language and the Transputer hardware.

Though the current prototype implementation has not been highly optimized, it already demonstrates the suitability of Transputer systems as target architectures for concurrent logic programming languages. An additional aspect encouraging this approach is the enhancement of Transputer communication facilities due to new technologies and further developments [May90a]. Automatic routing facilities, support for virtual links, and a general increase in communication speed will match the communication demands of our design.

An important issue not being discussed here, is the question of dynamic work load balancing. Beside the overall load balancing policy, an appropriate dynamic load balancing algorithm must also take into account the locality of computation and communication. Thus, one is concerned with at least two aspects: the *dynamic load balancing policy* and the *dynamic process selection policy*. While there are already a number of existing solutions to attack the first problem, the second one is more or less unsolved, especially, when dealing with large processor networks. Main activities for optimizing the prototype implementation currently concentrate on the development of improved load balancing algorithms.

14 Distributed Implementation of KL1 on the Multi-PSI

K. Nakajima

Mitsubishi Electric Corp., Japan

Abstract

KL1, a committed choice language based on Flat GHC, was implemented on a distributed memory multi-processor, the Multi-PSI, which has up to 64 processing elements (PEs) connected by a message passing network.

The key issues for a distributed implementation of KL1 are: (1) how to reduce the amount of inter-PE communication, (2) how to achieve efficient intra-PE and inter-PE garbage collection, and (3) how to avoid making redundant copies of data objects over many processors.

The well-defined semantics of KL1 allows incremental intra-PE garbage collection by the Multiple Reference Bit (MRB) technique and incremental inter-PE garbage collection by the Weighted Export Counting (WEC) technique. A global structure management mechanism is also introduced to avoid making duplicate copies of large data objects such as program codes. The communication required for inter-PE process control is minimized by the Weighted Throw Counting (WTC) scheme.

The implementation has been completed and the performance of inter-PE communication was evaluated. Although the cost for inter-PE message handling is high, the effective overhead in the benchmark programs remains within 20% on 64 PEs.

1. Introduction

KL1 is a committed choice language based on Flat GHC ([Ueda86a],[Chik88a]). It was designed in ICOT [Ueda90a] as an interface to fill the gap between the knowledge processing software and the hardware of the parallel inference machine(PIM) [Goto88a]. It is used as a system description language as well as an application language on the PIM.

---

*This chapter is an extended version of the paper titled "Distributed Implementation of KL1 on the Multi-PSI/V2" in Proceedings of International Conference on Logic Programming, 1989.

Section 7 was derived from the paper titled "Evaluation of Inter-processor Communication in the KL1 Implementation on the Multi-PSI" by K. Nakajima and N. Ichiyoshi in Proceedings of International Conference on Parallel Processing Vol.I (Univeristy Park: The Pennsylvania State University Press, 1990), pp 613–4. Copyright 1990 by The Pennsylvania State University. Reproduced by permission of the publisher.

The Multi-PSI system ([Taki88a],[Nakj89a]) was developed as a prototype machine for the PIM, having the purpose of serving as a testbed for implementing the parallel language KL1 on a scalable multiprocessor architecture. It is a distributed memory multiprocessor, whose processing elements (PEs) are the CPUs of the personal sequential inference (PSI) machine [Naks87a]. Up to 64 PEs are connected by an 8 × 8 mesh network with wormhole routing. The two-dimensional mesh network has a dense and simple implementation, and is scalable in that network node degree stays a constant (4) as the number of nodes increases. The PEs are microprogrammable and have an architecture suitable for executing logic programming languages efficiently.

A distributed KL1 implementation was developed on the machine. It is written in microcode for performance reason. The design rationale was to obtain a high overall performance, taking account of garbage collection overhead, and to decentralize management information for scalability.

Some performance measurements have been done so far especially on the inter-PE operations in the system, both in absolute terms (cost of primitive operations) and in relative terms (rate of communication overhead in non-trivial benchmark programs), which reveal the bottlenecks in the performance of inter-PE operations.

2. GHC and KL1

2.1 GHC and Flat GHC

GHC (Guarded Horn Clauses) is one of the committed choice AND-parallel languages. A GHC program is made up of a collection of guarded horn clauses, whose form is:

$$\underbrace{H :- G_1, \ldots, G_m}_{\text{guard}} \mid \underbrace{B_1, \ldots, B_n}_{\text{body}}. \ (m > 0, \ n > 0)$$

where H is called the *head*, G_i the *guard goal*, that are collectively called the *guard part*. The B_i are the *body goal* and the vertical bar (|) is called the *commitment operator*.

The guard part can be considered as test. If there are alternative clauses, their guard parts may be tested concurrently (OR-parallel). However, only one clause can commit even if more than one clauses can meet the test condition. The execution of the rest of the clauses is canceled. The caller goal is reduced to the body goals of the committed clause. These body goals are executed concurrently (AND-parallel). Body goals may be a unification goal of the form "$term_1 = term_2$," which may perform a binding to a variable. A body goal may, otherwise, be a user-defined goal which represents the rest of the work. Body goals communicate with each other through their common variables, which often represent a *stream* in the form of difference list.

In the guard part, binding to a caller variable is not allowed and the attempted binding causes a clause suspension. If there is no clause to commit and at least one clause is suspended, the predicate call itself suspends. This serves as a synchronization mechanism between GHC goals.

In Flat GHC, only predefined predicates are allowed as guard goals. This restriction does not decrease the expressive power of the language as the guard goals are a kind of auxiliary conditions for the clause [Ueda90a], while it makes the implementation much easier and more efficient.

2.2 KL1

KL1 is designed as a system and application language on the PIM. It is based on Flat GHC, and is extended to have process and resource management mechanisms and user-programmable mapping capabilities (load distribution and scheduling based on execution priorities).

(1) Shōen mechanism: A shōen is a meta-logical unit for controlling and monitoring KL1 goals. It corresponds to a "task" or a "process" in ordinary operating systems. A shōen consists of all the goals descended from the given initial goal of the shōen.

Shōen has a pair of input and output streams for interfacing with the outside. The input stream named the *control stream* is used to start, stop or abort the execution of the shōen from outside. Special events that occurred inside a shōen, such as termination of all goals, a failure or an exception, are reported on the output stream named the *report stream*. Shōen can be nested to form a tree-like structure (shōen tree) whose leaves are KL1 goals.

(2) Resource management: The upper limit of the resource that can be consumed by a shōen can be specified by a control message through its control stream. This mechanism prevents programs with bugs to go on running erroneously as in an infinite loop, wasting system resources. Resource shortages are notified on the report stream, and additional amount of resource can be selectively given. Currently, resource is measured by the number of reductions.

(3) Priority pragma ($\ldots, B@priority(Prio), \ldots$) : Scheduling by using *priority* contributes to efficient problem solving. The shōen has a priority range and each goal inside it can have an individual priority within this range. The priority is specified by a priority pragma with a relative value in the allowed range.

(4) Throw-goal pragma ($\ldots, B@processor(PE), \ldots$) : A throw-goal pragma in the program denotes load distribution. It also contributes to efficient execution on a multi-processor machine.

The priority and processor pragmas are merely guidelines of the execution and may not strictly be obeyed. The control such as an abortion in a shōen may not be immediately performed. Therefore, the pragmas make an efficient distributed implementation much easier without affecting correctness.

KL1 is also furnished with various predefined predicates for such as vector/string handling and arithmetic operations in the guard and body parts.

3. Architecture of the Multi-PSI

3.1 Processing Elements

The processing element (PE) of the Multi-PSI is the CPU of the sequential inference machine, the PSI-II [Naks87a]. It is a 40-bit (8-bit for tag, 32-bit for data) CISC processor controlled by horizontal micro-instructions. Microcoding enables a flexible implementation suited for incrementally enhancing the performance and adding various functions. The cycle time is 200 ns. It has up to 16 Mwords of local memory and a 4-Kword direct-map cache memory.

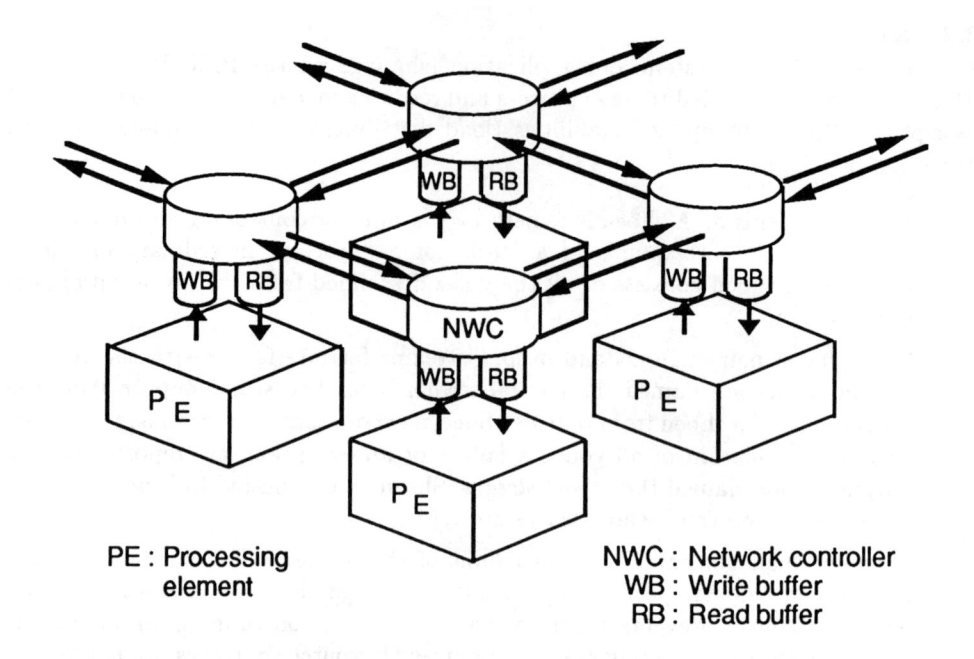

Figure 1: Processor Inter-connections of the Multi-PSI System

3.2 Network Controller

Each PE is paired with a specially designed network controller to support message-passing communication between PEs. The network controller has five pairs of input/output channels connected to the four adjacent network nodes and to the PE of the node (Figure 1). Each channel consists of 11 bits, 9 bits for data, one for a parity and one for a busy-acknowledge signal of the opposite direction.

The cycle time is 200 ns and the bandwidth of each channel is 5 Mbytes/s. Each output channel has a 48-byte buffer (*Output Buffer*) to retain messages when the destination node is busy. Each input and output channel for the PE of the node has a 4-Kbyte buffer (*Write Buffer* and *Read Buffer*) to reduce disturbance of processing in the PE. As soon as a complete message (from a message header to a tail) is written by the PE in the Write Buffer, it is shipped out by the controller unless the transmitting channel is busy. When a complete message is taken into the Read Buffer by the controller, the PE is informed by an interrupt signal.

The controller has the wormhole routing capability. It can route messages according to the PE number in the message header (Figure 2). A software-defined table called the *path table* is looked up to determine transmission direction. A fixed routing strategy called *prioritized coordinate ordering* is adopted. Using this strategy, a message is transmitted along the *x-coordinate* until the distance in the coordinate becomes zero. It is then transmitted along the *y-coordinate*. As long as messages are taken into the destination PE, network deadlocks never arise because there can be no cyclic chain of messages in transit blocking one another.

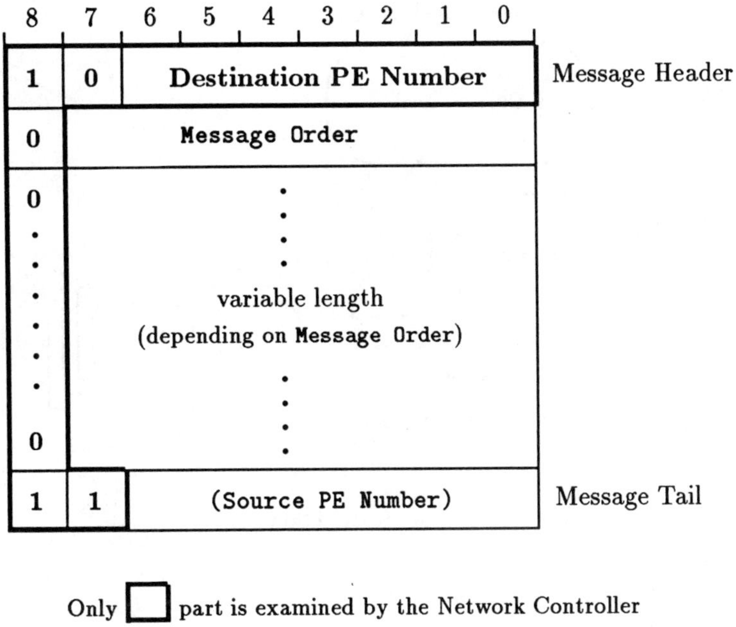

```
    8   7   6   5   4   3   2   1   0
  ┌───┬───┬───────────────────────────┐
  │ 1 │ 0 │   Destination PE Number   │  Message Header
  ├───┼───┴───────────────────────────┤
  │ 0 │         Message Order         │
  ├───┼───────────────────────────────┤
  │ 0 │                               │
  │ · │                               │
  │ · │         variable length       │
  │ · │    (depending on Message Order)│
  │ · │                               │
  │ 0 │                               │
  ├───┬───┬───────────────────────────┤
  │ 1 │ 1 │      (Source PE Number)   │  Message Tail
  └───┴───┴───────────────────────────┘
```

Only ▢ part is examined by the Network Controller

Figure 2: Message Packet Format

3.3 Message Handling in a PE

The read/write of *Read Buffer* and *Write Buffer* are done by microcode. A low level microcoded routine in the PE is responsible for handling messages to and from the network controller. The microcoded routine performs decomposition and composition of message packets such as handling the message header and tail (Figure 2), and constructing a 32-bit data item in the PE from/to four byte serial data in the Read/Write Buffer.

The interrupt signal of informing a message arrival invokes a micro routine to decode it just before starting the next reduction. This timing is called *slit-check* and is suitable for breaking the current execution sequence, because the processor has the minimum context at this timing.

The micro routine decodes all the messages arrived before starting a next reduction. Before decoding each message, the micro routine examines the size of the empty space in the Read Buffer. If it is below the fixed value, the micro routine moves the messages, instead of decoding, from the Read Buffer to a large memory area, called the *Read Packet Buffer*. It allows to take in further incoming messages and avoids traffic disturbance in the network. After the movement of the messages, the micro routine resumes decoding from the Read Packet Buffer.

On sending a message, if there is not enough room to put the whole message in the Write Buffer, the micro routine will wait until more room becomes available.

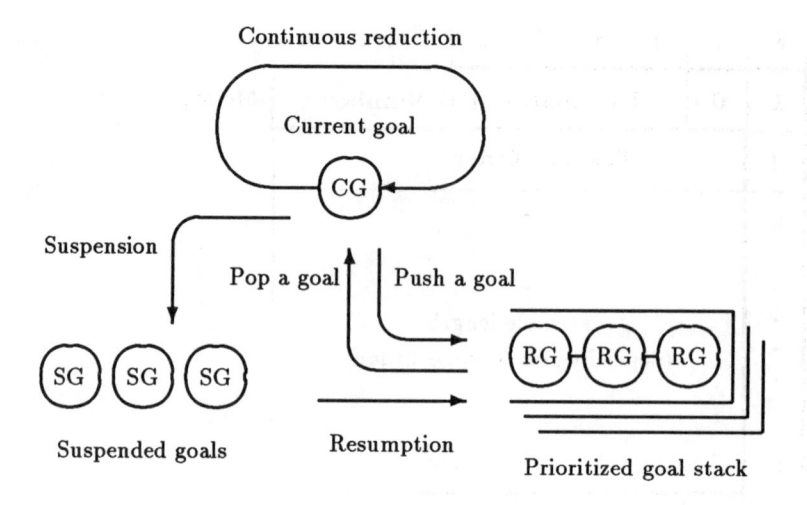

Figure 3: Goal State Transition

4. Intra-PE Processing

4.1 Execution Model of KL1 goals

KL1 programs are compiled into the sequence of WAM [Warr83a]-like abstract machine instructions named KL1-B [Kimu87a]. KL1-B is a register-based instruction set and serves as an efficient interface between the language and the machine architecture.

Goals are categorized as: (1) *ready goals* which are waiting for execution, (2) *current goal* which is being executed, or (3) *suspended goals* which are hooked on variables yet to be instantiated (Figure 3).

In this implementation, each PE has its own goal stack. Scheduling is performed on each PE individually. A reduction cycle at each PE is as follows. When a current goal calls a predicate, the guard parts of the clauses for the predicate are tested. In spite of the language allowing simultaneous evaluation of alternative clauses, guard unification is performed one by one for efficiency reasons. Non busy-wait suspension is employed. That is, if the predicate call suspends, the goal is hooked on the variable(s) that caused the suspension. If no clause commits and there are no suspended clauses, a *failure* is reported together with the goal information on the report stream of the shōen. In either case, another goal is popped from the goal stack to be evaluated. If one of the clauses commits, all the user-defined body goals, except for the unification goals and the leftmost user goal in the clause, are pushed to the goal stacks according to the priority pragmas attached to the goals. Unification goals are executed immediately. The leftmost user goal is chosen as the next one to be evaluated unless a goal stack with higher priority has a goal. When a clause without body goals commits, another goal is popped from the goal stack.

At the slit-check timing, request for stop-and-copying garbage collection (see 4.4) and message arrival from the network are checked, and processed if necessary.

4.2 KL1-B Execution

The KL1-B instructions, including approximately one hundred instructions for predefined predicates, are directly interpreted by the microcode to attain high execution speed.

The microcode of the PE can perform various functions in parallel, such as tag insertion, two-way or multi-way branching on a tag, specially prepared counter and flag operations, ALU operations and memory access operations. The arguments for the unification are fetched into the registers every reduction cycle. Control information, such as the priority and the shōen resource, remains in the registers as long as the execution context remains unchanged.

4.3 Local Goal Scheduling

If the strict ordering of goal priorities are to be kept on a multiprocessor, only a single prioritized goal stack will be used by the system. However, the access contention on such a global resource leads to serious performance degradation.

As KL1's priority pragma is a guideline for efficiency, each PE may have a prioritized goal stack, while sacrificing merely scheduling strictness. Even such local scheduling is known to be efficient enough to control the execution in most cases. However, the maldistribution of high priority goals over PEs is possible and problematic. A dynamic load balancing by software is necessary in such a case.

4.4 Memory Management

4.4.1 Two Local (Intra-PE) Garbage Collectors   As goals may not be executed in a last-in-first-out manner, the stack mechanism used in most Prolog implementations is not suitable for a KL1 implementation. Therefore, heap-based memory management must be used for flexible memory use, although memory reclamation is generally inefficient with this scheme. The time spent in garbage collection may seriously affect the system performance. Thus, efficient garbage collection is vital in a KL1 implementation.

In this KL1 implementation, two intra-PE garbage collectors were adopted. One reclaims *most* of garbage incrementally, and the other collects the rest of garbage by using conventional stop-and-copying scheme when a semi-space (half of the heap memory) is used up.

Although the stop-and-copying garbage collector may not be called very frequently, the time spent by it can be a big factor in the total performance because other PEs requesting a response from the garbage collecting PE have to wait for its termination[1]. One solution to improve the garbage collection time is *generation scavenging* ([Lieb83a], [Nakj88a]), which avoids moving long-life objects at every garbage collection. This is worth while investigating but not implemented yet.

4.4.2 Incremental Garbage Collection by MRB   Goal contexts are maintained in a *goal record*, which contains the predicate code address, arguments, priority and etc. Goal records are reclaimed at the beginning of its reduction if it is known not to be reused for one of the subgoals. They are linked into a free goal record list. On the other hand, variable cells or record areas for structured data are difficult to reclaim because they may be shared by two or more pointers. Incremental garbage collection by

---

[1] Messages sent to the garbage collecting PE are taken into the Read Packet Buffer of the PE.

(a) Single-referenced object (b) Multi-referenced object

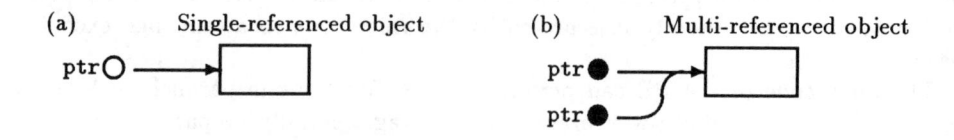

Figure 4: References in the MRB Scheme

reference counting is desirable because of its access locality and high hit-rate of cache memory. However, in reference counting, each word cell must have a reference counter field for the whole memory space. In addition, the cost of updating the reference counter is high, because data objects must always be accessed.

Several methods were proposed to reduce these overheads relying on the fact that very few data objects have more than one reference to them [Deut76a]. The *Multiple Reference Bit* (MRB) method was proposed [Chik87a] as an incremental garbage collection method for concurrent logic programming languages.

The MRB method maintains one-bit information in pointers indicating whether the pointed data object has multiple references to it or not. This multiple reference information makes it possible to reclaim storage areas that are no longer used.

Figure 4 shows the data representation in the MRB scheme. A single-referenced object (a) and a multi-referenced object (b) can be distinguished by the MRB flag on the pointers, *off-MRB* by ○ and *on-MRB* by ● .

The MRB method has the following two advantages;

- By keeping MRB information in the pointers rather than in the pointed objects, no extra memory access is required for reference information maintenance.

- On updating an *off-MRB* array, destructive assignment can be performed.

As variables in logic languages like KL1 can not be overwritten, updated array should not be identical to its original one. Each update causes a copy of the whole array with one element modified. However, in the case of a single-referenced array, the original array can be reused as a new one by modifying the element destructively.

The MRB information is also used and maintained through the unification. When a unification consumes a reference path to a single-referenced data object, the storage area can be reclaimed after the unification. It is known that even with the one-bit counter, more than 60% of the garbage cells are collected in various benchmark programs. Collected cells are linked into the free lists to be reused. Several individual free-lists for records of various sizes are prepared for them[2].

When records in a free-list are exhausted, a pre-determined number of new records are created on the heap-top and linked to the free-list. In the current implementation, fragmentation among the free-lists is resolved only by stop-and-copying garbage collection, because free-list handling operations are too frequent to employ fragment reconstruction techniques such as the buddy system [Know65a].

---

[2]In the current implementation, the sizes are from 1 to 8, 16, 32, 64, 128 and 256. A record over 256 words is allocated on the heap-top.

5. Inter-PE Processing

5.1 Implementation Issues for KL1

Because this KL1 implementation was aimed at a scalable system on a distributed memory multiprocessor, the following were the most important issues.

Reducing Message Communication: Message passing communication is more expensive than communication on a shared memory. The communication delay is also large. Reducing the amount of inter-PE communication and maintaining quick responses are major subjects in the implementation.

Efficient Inter-PE Memory Reclamation: As stated in 4.4, garbage collection is the key point in the implementation of concurrent languages like KL1.

Instead of implementing a single global garbage collector, an incremental inter-PE garbage collector and two intra-PE garbage collectors were implemented. This is because, stop-and-sweep type global garbage collection generates a lot of marking messages and is expected to take a long time.

Reference counting scheme must be employed for incremental inter-PE garbage collection. It should be implemented to minimize the number of reference counting messages and the runtime overhead by the counting operation.

Efficient Inter-PE Data Management: KL1 has a property where data objects that have been instantiated once can be copied, while keeping the program logic. To allow local access, data shared by PEs should be copied. However, uncontrolled copying leads to unnecessary data transfer.

5.2 Goal Distribution and Distributed Unification by Inter-PE Messages

5.2.1 Goal Distribution

A KL1 goal specified with a throw-goal pragma is distributed to another PE. The goal information in the goal record such as predicate code, goal arguments and execution priority are encoded into %throw_goal message. If the goal argument is an atomic data, it is encoded directly. If it is a structured data such as vector or string, or uninstantiated variable, it is encoded as an *external pointer*. The predicate code address is encoded to a pair of an external pointer representing code module and an offset representing the code position in the module. The code module handling will be explained in 5.4.8.

At the destination PE, the message is decoded, and a goal record is composed and is put in a goal stack according to its priority.

5.2.2 Guard Unification

As binding to caller variable is not allowed in the guard part, guard unification with an external pointer is suspended until its value is known.

If there are no other clauses to commit, a %read message is sent to get the value of the external pointer to the PE which has the data. A %read message has two arguments: the external pointer to read and a return address where to be replied to. The later is also an external pointer pointing to the cell which substitutes the former external pointer and will be instantiated by the value returned by %answer_value message. The suspended goal is hooked on the cell until it is instantiated.

At the PE where %read is received, an %answer_value message is immediately returned if the sought term has been instantiated. If the value is a structured data, the surface level (that is, the elements of the array or list) are encoded. If these elements

Table 1: Typical Inter-PE Messages

Message Order	Note
%throw_goal(PE,Code,Args, Priority,etc.)	Move the goal to specified PE
%read(Ext,Return)	Request to reply the value of an external pointer
%answer_value(Val,Return)	Respond to a %read message
%unify(Ext,Val)	Request to unify with an external pointer and an argument
%terminated(Shoen)	Report a local shoen termination in a PE
%release(WEC)	Return WEC value of an external pointer (see 5.4.3)

are themselves structured data, they are encoded as external pointers. On the other hand, if the exported data is still an uninstantiated (unbound) variable, the reply is suspended by hooking the received %read message on the variable. The arguments of %answer_value are the destination and the sought value.

5.2.3 Body Unification When one of the arguments in a body unification is an external pointer, the operation varies according to the other argument as follows;

- If the other argument is an instantiated data, it is encoded into %unify message and sent to the PE (exporting PE) which has the data cell of the external pointer. It corresponds to a write operation in this case.

- If the other argument is an unbound variable, either (1) the variable is bound to the external pointer or (2) a %unify message is sent to the exporting PE (carrying the reference to the variable). Which action is chosen is decided according to the *binding order* rule, which is designed to prevent the creation of a loop of references over PEs. Basically, the binding order is determined by comparing the exporting PE number with the self PE number.

- If a PE attempts to perform a body unification between two external pointers, it sends a %unify message to shift the work to one of the exporting PEs. The direction is also determined by the PE numbers.

Table 1 summarizes the typical inter-PE messages. A %terminated message reports a local shoen termination in a PE. A %release message carries a reference count information. They are explained in the following sections.

5.3 Distributed Goal Control
5.3.1 Creating KL1 Shōen A shōen is created by the following predefined predicate execute/6:

$$execute(Goal, ControlStream, ReportStream, MinPrio, MaxPrio, Mask)$$

Goal is the initial goal to execute inside the shōen. *MinPrio* and *MaxPrio* specify the range of the execution priority allowed in the shōen. *ControlStream* is used to start, stop or abort the execution inside from outside the shōen. It is also used to

DISTRIBUTED IMPLEMENTATION OF KL1

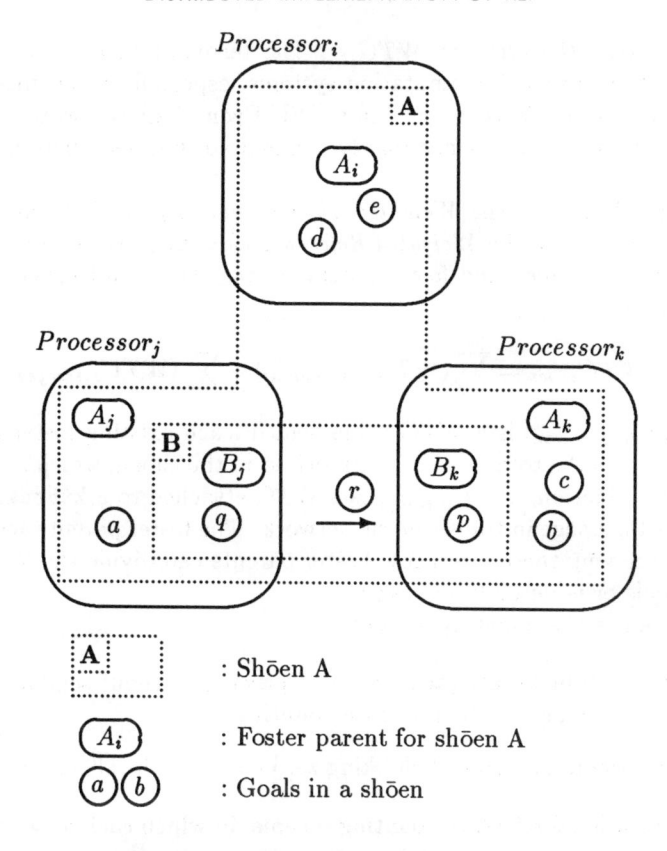

Figure 5: Shōen and Foster Parents

supply execution resources. From *ReportStream*, the events inside the shōen such as exceptions, resource shortages and the termination of the execution can be observed. Shōen itself never fails even if one of the goals inside the shōen would fail. The failure is treated as an exception and reported in the *ReportStream*. *Mask* is a bit-map to specify which exceptions should be reported.

Shōens can be nested. A child shōen is treated as one of the goals in the parent shōen.

5.3.2 Shōen and Foster Parent Goals which belong to the same shōen may be distributed over many PEs. Every event at each goal should be reported to the shōen staying at the PE where it is created. To reduce the message traffic towards a shōen, a cache technique is employed. When a goal is moved from the shōen PE (the PE that contains the shōen) to another, a *foster parent* is created on the PE to which the goal migrated [Ichi87a]. Only one foster parent is created for the shōen on each of the PEs which have goals belonging to the shōen (Figure 5).

The foster parents have the *shōen status* (*running, stopped or aborted*), the *child count* (the number of child goals created on the PE), and the cached resource information of the shōen. Goal termination is checked at the shōen only when one of the foster parents sends a %terminated message to report that its goal count has reached zero.

5.3.3 Termination Detection by WTC   The termination detection is one of the difficult subjects in parallel computation systems, especially when messages may be in transit on the network as in the Multi-PSI. Even if all the foster parents report %terminated, the shōen is not necessarily terminated, because there may be goals in transit.

One of the solutions is the *Weighted Throw Counting* (WTC) scheme [Roku88a], which is an application of the *Weighted Reference Counting* (WRC) scheme [Wats87a]. In this scheme, each shōen and foster parent manage the count called WTC and the following invariant is kept:

$$WTC_{shoen} = \sum(WTC_{fosterparent}) + \sum(WTC_{message})$$

where $WTC_{fosterparent}$ is a WTC value held in each existing foster parent for the shōen. WTC_{shoen} is the total of WTC memorized in the shōen, which is to be returned at the shōen termination. $WTC_{message}$ is a WTC attached to a %throw_goal, %unify or %terminated message in transit in the network. The foster parents accumulate their WTCs when receiving these messages. Foster parents can divide the WTC when they throw child goals or issue unify messages.

This scheme has the following features.

- WTC can be split locally (at each foster parent), without sending a message (to the shōen) to maintain the reference counting.

- No racing occurs in terms of checking zero count at the shōen.

With a conventional reference counting scheme, in which each foster parent reports the increase or decrease of the goal count to the shōen, the shōen may happen to observe zero count in total if decrease messages reach to the shōen earlier than increase ones (racing). WTC scheme does not create this situation.

5.4 Inter-PE Data Management

5.4.1 Copying Shared Data   When a goal is thrown to another PE, its arguments are also transmitted. If the argument is an atomic value, the value itself is sent with the goal. If it is an unbound variable, a pointer to the variable is created and carried. For a structure argument, there are three reasonable choices. One is to create and carry a pointer to the structure (0-level copying). The contents will be read when they are actually to be used in a unification. The second is to copy all the elements of the structure including all nested substructures (infinite-level copying). The third is to copy all the elements at the surface level (1-level copying).

In a distributed system like the Multi-PSI where the cost of the inter-PE reference is relatively high, it is better to copy data for later access in many cases. However, an infinite-level copying may cause unnecessary duplication because the passive or active unification for the structure might fail at any level in the destination PE.

Following the policy of *on-demand* copying, the 0-level copying is done for the arguments of thrown goals and the 1-level copying for those of unifications (for the Val of %answer_value and %unify in Table 1). It is one of the design decisions to be evaluated. At least, if it is known that the element of a structure will be read sooner or later (such as the next element of a stream), it is better to copy the elements at one time as long as they are bound to a value. This is left as a future optimization.

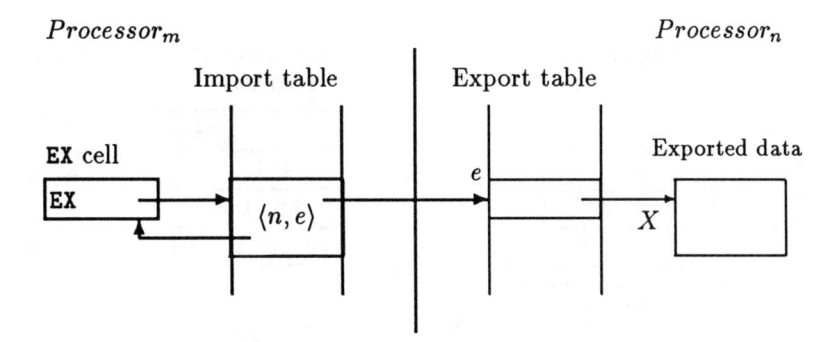

Figure 6: Export Table and Import Table

5.4.2 Export and Import Tables When a PE exhausts a semi-space, garbage collection must be performed. If the PE does not know whether a cell is referenced from other PEs or it is garbage, the PE cannot perform garbage collection for its memory without cooperation by all PEs. Global garbage collection, where all PEs perform garbage reclamation at one time by exchanging marking messages and indicating the movements of object cells [Ali86a], can be a solution, but it is expected to be very time consuming.

In a large scale distributed memory multiprocessor, local (intra-PE) garbage collection is desirable in terms of the system performance.

Local stop-and-copying garbage collection can be performed if the object cells referenced from outside PE are represented by global identifiers for the external PEs. A translation table called the *export table* (Figure 6) is used to associate the identifiers with the local object addresses. In a stop-and-copying garbage collection, the garbage collecting PE needs only to maintain the export table according to the local object movements.

The object cells referenced from the external PEs are said to be *exported*, and on the referencing side, they are said to be *imported*. The global identifier is represented in the form $< pe, entry >$, where pe is a PE number and $entry$ is the entry position of the export table. The global identifier is called the *external ID*.

5.4.3 Incremental Inter-PE Garbage Collection by WEC To collect the garbage cells pointed to by the export table, the entries in the table must be reclaimed when they become useless. The *weighted export counting* (WEC) method [Ichi88a] is employed to perform inter-PE incremental garbage collection. This scheme is also based on the WRC principle.

An integer representing a WEC value is attached to an exported pointer and is stored in the *import table entry* (Figure 7). In this scheme, the total of WEC value of the imported or to be imported pointers is kept equal to the value at the exporting PE (Figure 8).

Inter-PE incremental garbage collection is performed as follows.

WEC values are accumulated in each import table entry when the same pointers are imported. The number of imports, the *import count*, is also counted in the entry. When an imported external pointer becomes useless, the export-import relation is broken off. A %release message is sent to the exporting PE to return the amount of the WEC. A %release message is sent when : (1) the import count reaches zero by incremental garbage collection by using the MRB mechanism, or (2) an imported pointer is known

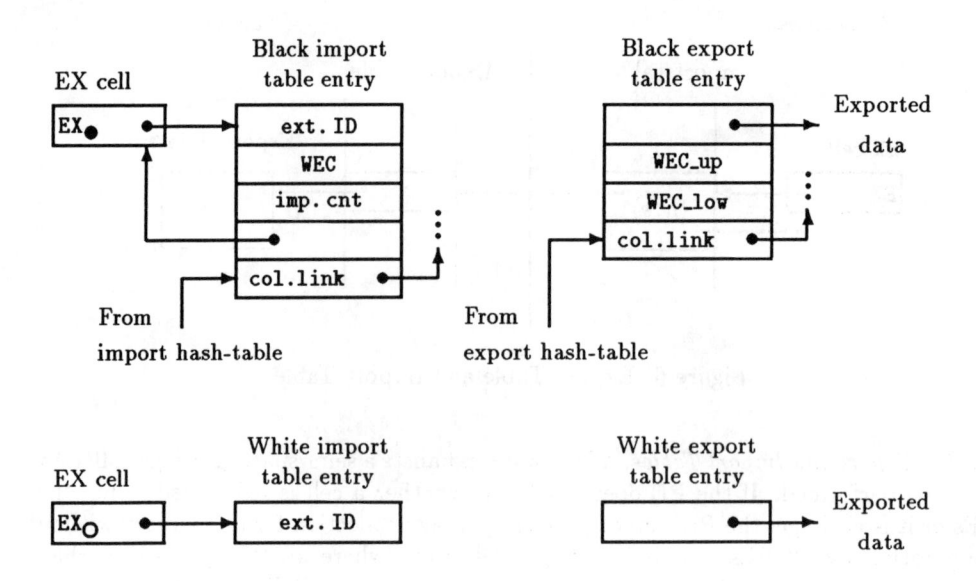

Figure 7: Export and Import Table Entries

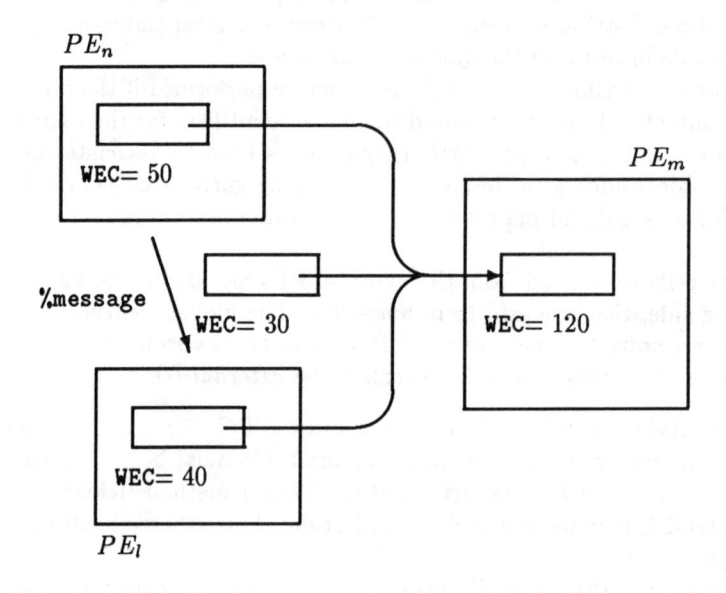

Figure 8: Weighted Reference Counting Scheme

to be garbage after a stop-and-copying garbage collection in the importing PE (see 5.4.4), or (3) an instantiated value (a copy of the sought term) is returned by an %answer_value message in response to a %read message. The last one may establish other export-import relations for the elements if the answered value is a structured data.

When an export entry receives a %release message, the WEC in the entry is decremented. If it becomes zero, the entry is reclaimed. In this case, the exported object cell itself may also be reclaimed when the export table entry is known to be the single reference to the cell by the MRB mechanism.

5.4.4   Releasing WEC in Stop-and-Copying Garbage Collection   The stop-and-copying garbage collector moves all data cells reachable from the prioritized goal stacks and the export tables to a new semi-space. After copying, valid entries in the import tables are swept. If unmarked entries are found, %release messages are sent to the exporting PEs to return their WECs.

5.4.5   Re-exporting   It is possible that a variable may be exported to the same PE more than once. If the re-exported pointer to a variable is given a different external identifier, it appears to be a different variable. Therefore, the importing PE may send %read messages twice, and if the object is a structure data, its copy is brought twice by %answer_value. This can be avoided by reusing the same export and import table entries. For this purpose, the *export hash-table* and *import hash-table* are provided on each side. The export hash-table associates the exported object addresses with their external identifiers, and the import hash-table associates the imported external identifiers and the import table entry.

5.4.6   White and Black Exports   This external reference management using the WEC has overhead in terms of maintaining both the WEC and import count, and in terms of looking up the hash-table to check for re-exporting. Fortunately, the MRB mechanism can be used to optimize both. To export a single reference pointer at a low cost, a simplified pair of export and import tables, called the *white export* and *white import* tables, are used (Figure 7). The original tables are called the *black export* and *black import* tables. Pointers that were duplicated once will mostly be copied again later. In contrast, a single reference pointer is not likely to be duplicated after being exported. Thus, the white export and import tables do not have hash-tables because the exported pointers are rarely exported again, for the same reason.

A white import table can be considered as an import table for the pointers whose WECs and import counts equal one, and whose entries are released immediately when the imported pointers are collected by an intra-PE incremental garbage collection[3]. The white export entries are also released only when a %release message is received. The effectiveness of this optimization depends heavily on the programs; however, the average characteristics are expected to be similar to that of the MRB inside a PE.

5.4.7   Global Structure Management   In this export system, the external ID originates from the exporting PE. For example, if PE_B has a copy of the structure in PE_A, and PE_C has external references to both the original structure in PE_A and the copy in PE_B, their external IDs are not the same. PE_C will have two copies after reading them. If the structure is big and will live long, it is inefficient in terms of both the memory space and the data transfer overhead. In the worst case, copies are created at each import if a pair of mutually linked structures are read alternately in a loop.

The *structure ID* solves this problem for such structures. It is a global identifier attached to an instantiated structure. By using this, what was originally the same structure is duplicated at most once in a PE even if it is imported from different PEs more than once.

---

[3] If an imported pointer is copied, the MRB of both pointers, the original and its copy, are turned on so that the import table entry is not released when one of the pointers becomes garbage.

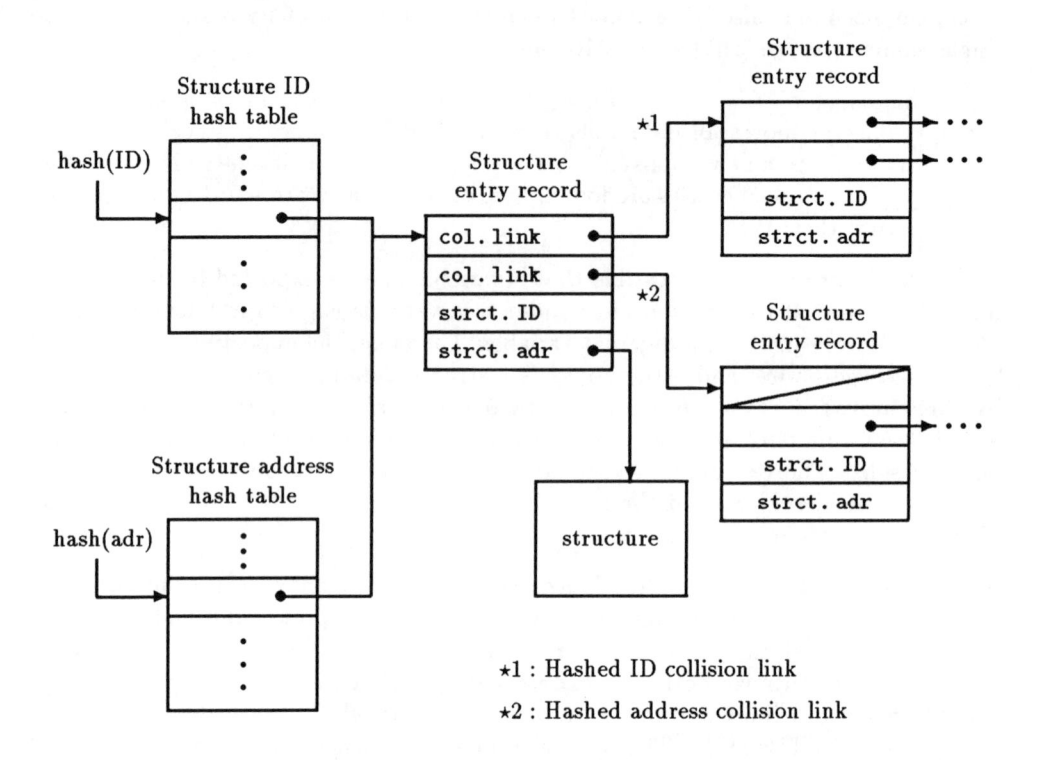

Figure 9: Structure Entry Records and Hash-Tables

When a %read message is sent to a PE for a structure with a structure ID, only the identifier is returned in the %answer_value message. If the %read sending PE receives only the ID, it looks up the *structure ID hash-table* (Figure 9) with the ID to search for the structure address if the PE already has the structure. If it is not found, a %read message is sent again to copy it. Another hash-table, the *structure address hash-table*, is used to get the structure ID from the structure address when the PE returns the ID instead of the structure itself in the %answer_value message.

The global structure management mechanism is used for the program code, because code pieces in a program are connected to each other and references to the same code piece can be imported from various PEs. The problem in this scheme is the collection of the no more use identifiers, which needs a kind of global garbage collection, and is not implemented yet.

5.4.8 *Program Code Management*   KL1 programs are described as a collection of *modules* which may contain several KL1 predicates. A module is the unit of compilation and is also used as the unit of code distribution to PEs.

The predicate calls within a module are represented by relative pointers. As they are constants in the module, they are free of maintenance when the module is relocated in a stop-and-copying garbage collection or is copied to send to other PEs. Only the inter-module predicate calls use absolute address pointers which require address maintenance in data transfers.

Absolute address pointers in a module are gathered at the top region in the module to reduce the size of sweeping for maintenance during stop-and-copying garbage collection. The rest (and the greater part) of the module contains only atomic data, that is, KL1-B instructions (with the relative address operand if any) followed by their full-word constant operands if any.

On a distributed memory multiprocessor with many PEs an on-demand loading mechanism for the program code is essential to save the memory area in the system. It is realized in the following way.

When a goal is thrown to another PE, the code address for the goal is encoded as a tuple of < *module, offset, structure ID* >, where *module* is an external reference to the code module in the exporting PE, and *offset* is the code location in the module.

At the destination PE, *structure ID* is used to check whether the same module exists or not. If it does, the code address is calculated with *offset*. If it does not, a %read message is sent to the exporting PE. The received goal is hooked on a newly created variable which will receive the module.

6. Programming Environment Support

The Multi-PSI together with the parallel inference machine operating system, *PIMOS* [Chik88a], provides a programming environment for developing application programs of practical sizes. It offers various functions for debugging parallel software and improving its performance. The KL1 implementation supports these PIMOS functions so that the runtime overhead is minimized.

6.1 Trace and Spy

The implementation supports the tracing and spying of goals.

KL1 goals are colored with **normal** or **traced**. The reduction of a "traced" goal results in a *trace exception* with the information of all the subgoals to be forked. The monitor process for the shōen will report them and the user can specify which subgoals are to be traced next.

The spy function is also realized by coloring goals. The user can fork a goal with **spying** color with a spied predicate information (the name and arity of the predicate to be spied). This information is inherited by the child goals. If a subgoal for calling the spied predicate is created, a *spy exception* is raised reporting details of the parent goal.

6.2 Deadlock Detection

One of the most common and distressful situations in debugging parallel programs is deadlock. Often, deadlock is known to the user only after all other executable goals have terminated, at which time there remain few clues for finding the cause of the deadlock. The basic functions for deadlock should be to detect deadlocks and to show their causes.

In the KL1 implementation, deadlocks inside a PE are all detected at a stop-and-copying garbage collection [Inam90a]. Typically, when a program falls inactive and seems to be deadlocked, the user will invoke the garbage collection.

At the garbage collection, the suspended goals that are not reachable from active goals are perpetually suspended. These goals are copied to the new semi-space and examined further by traversing the "causality graph" (goals and variables connected by reference and hook pointers) to find the maximal goal in the causality. *Deadlock exception* is raised to the report stream for the maximal goal. This concise information usually helps locate the real cause of the deadlock.

The MRB scheme enables early deadlock detection. This is a common merit of reference counting scheme. If an MRB-off pointer, that points to an unbound variable with suspended goals hooked on it, is found to be discarded at the commitment of a clause, the suspended goals are known to become perpetually suspended. Reporting a deadlock exception on the spot is generally more helpful than postmortem detection in a stop-and-copying garbage collection, because the clause in execution may be precisely the cause of the deadlock.

6.3 Profiling

Two kinds of profiling facilities are provided. *Shōen Profiler* counts the number of reductions of each predicate in the shōen. The control of profiling such as start, stop and collect data is done via the control stream of the shōen.

Processor Profiler measures various dynamic characteristics at each processor. It records the time stamp each time the processor idles or performs garbage collection. It also counts each inter-PE message frequency and the total time spent for message handling. Furthermore, it can record the user-defined events with time stamps. Predefined predicates are used to start and stop the profiling, and to record the user-defined events.

7. Evaluation

This section presents measurements of the costs of inter-PE operations in the system. Actual communication overheads in two benchmark programs are also shown.

7.1 Cost of Communication Primitives

In typical KL1 programs, fine-grain processes (*goals*) communicate with each other via logical variables. In the Multi-PSI system, goal distribution is realized by %throw_goal message and inter-PE reading of values is realized by %read & %answer_value protocols.

Figure 10 shows the cost of handling those three messages at both sending and receiving PE.

In Figure 10, Copy_RPKB stands for the time for copying a message packet from the Read Buffer to the Read Packet Buffer when a message is received (see 3.3). Basic message handling routine corresponds to the rest of the functions stated in 3.3, that is, puts byte-serial messages in the Write Buffer cutting from tagged words in encoding, or gets byte-serial messages from the Read Buffer and constructs tagged words for decoding.

Encode/decode KL1 term, etc. is for encoding internal KL1 term into a word sequence for export (by translating each element of the term to appropriate representation if it is a structured data and the encoding level is 1, see 5.4.1), or decoding a word sequence in a message packet form into the internal representation of KL1 term for import.

DISTRIBUTED IMPLEMENTATION OF KL1

Send_throw (goal (atom,EXREF,EXREF)) [65 bytes]
(a) 85 μsec (419 steps)

Receive_throw
(b) 130 μsec (637 steps)

Send_read (EXREF) [14 bytes]
(c) 25 μsec (117 steps)

Receive_read
(d) 35 μsec (175 steps)

Send_answer_value ([atom | EXREF]) [24 bytes]
(e) 42 μsec (208 steps)

Receive_answer_value
(f) 80 μsec (397 steps)

0   20   40   60   80   100   120   140   (μsec)

EXREF   External pointer
■   Copy_to_RPKB
▧   Basic message handling routine
☐   Encode/decode KL1 term, etc.

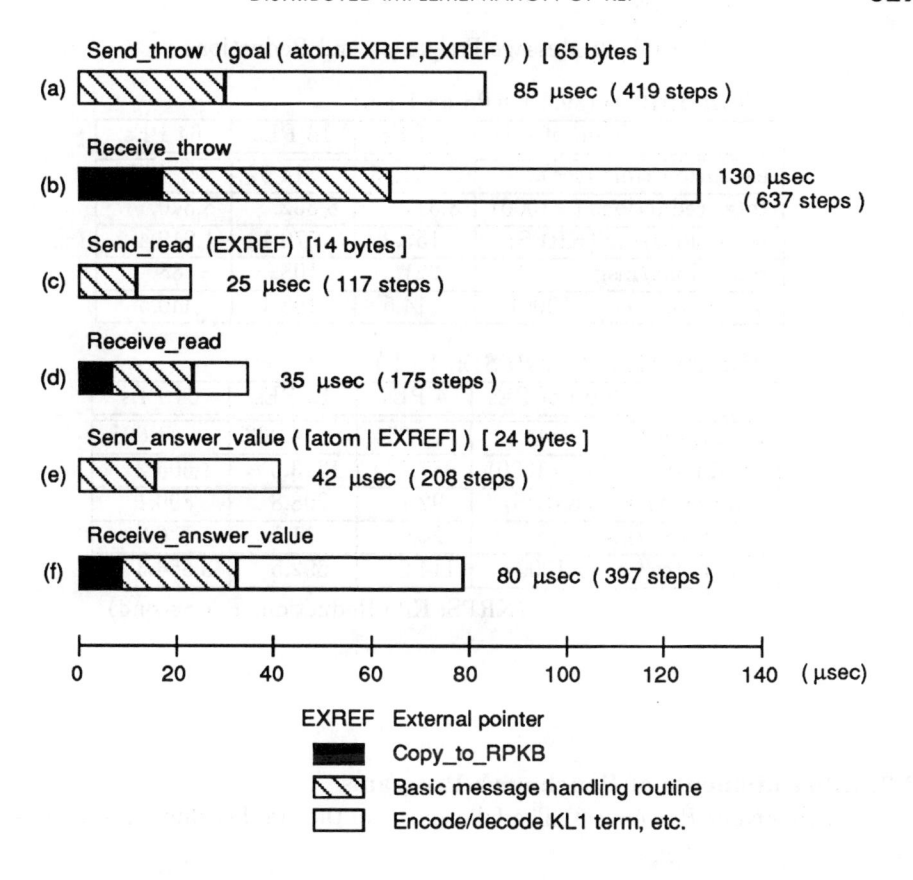

Figure 10: Message Handling Cost

Send_throw (a) shows the cost of sending a 65 byte %throw_goal message for a three argument spawned goal. It takes 419 micro-instruction steps or 85 μs (cycle time = 200 ns). Receive_throw (b) shows the cost of receiving the same %throw_goal message and storing it in a goal stack.

The bar graphs (c), (d), (e) and (f) describe the cost of sending and receiving a %read message and %answer_value message. The returned data in this case is a list whose CAR is an atomic data and the CDR is an external pointer. %read and %answer_value are the two most frequent messages in typical KL1 programs. The costs for %unify message, though not in the figure, are almost same as those of %answer_value.

In all operations, one third to half of the time is spent by Basic message handling routine. For example, it takes about 12 μs in Basic message handling routine for handling 14 bytes in (c). It is four times more than that for receiving them from the network channel. This demonstrates that the hardware support for message composing/decomposing is not sufficient and that the microcode is forced to do much work.

Encode/decode KL1 term, etc. occupies more than half of the time and same thing can be said compared with the network bandwidth. Possible support hardware would be for manipulating export/import tables and their hash tables. It can be a dedicated small processor.

Table 2: Message Frequency and Reductions

Pentomino (39.3 KRPS on 1 PE)

Num of PEs	4 PEs	16 PEs	64 PEs
execution time (sec)	54.63	14.62	4.35
total reductions (×1000)	8,317.	8,332.	8,340.
reductions/sec (KRPS)	152.2	570.1	1,919.4
reductions/msg	221.	108.	88.
msg bytes/sec (×1000)	14.5	108.1	440.5

Bestpath (23.4 KRPS on 1 PE)

Num of PEs	4 PEs	16 PEs	64 PEs
execution time (sec)	10.655	4.062	1.691
total reductions (×1000)	987.7	1213.6	1,505.2
reductions/sec (KRPS)	92.7	298.8	890.1
reductions/msg	21.9	11.7	6.2
msg bytes/sec (×1000)	114.0	692.5	3,854.3

(KRPS: Kilo Reductions Per Second)

7.2 Measurements of Benchmark Programs

7.2.1 Benchmark Programs   The followings are the two benchmark programs used here.

- **Pentomino:** A program to find out all solutions of a packing piece puzzle (Pentomino) by exploring the whole OR tree. Two-level dynamic load balancing is employed [Furu90a].

- **Bestpath:** A 160 × 160 grid graph is given together with non-negative edge costs. The program determines the lowest cost path from a given vertex to all vertices of the graph by performing a distributed shortest path algorithm. The vertices are represented by KL1 processes, and they exchange shortest path information along the edges.

7.2.2 Message & Reduction Profile   Table 2 shows the execution time, the reduction and message rates, etc. The message sending rates on 64 PEs are: one message per 88 reductions in Pentomino, and one per 6 reductions in Bestpath.

The average network traffic can be calculated from these figures. Relative to the 5 Mbyte/s network channel bandwidth, the average traffic on a channel is very small: 0.08% (Pentomino) and 0.3% (Bestpath) of the bandwidth.

7.2.3 Communication Overhead   By counting the number of executed steps and logging the time of entering and exiting from idle status at each PE, the execution time is broken down as follows; (1) the total executed steps for reductions (**Computing**) and (2) for message handling (**Msg handling**), both of which exclude cache-miss penalty, (3) the total cache-miss penalty (**Cache miss**), and (4) the total idling time (**Idle**).

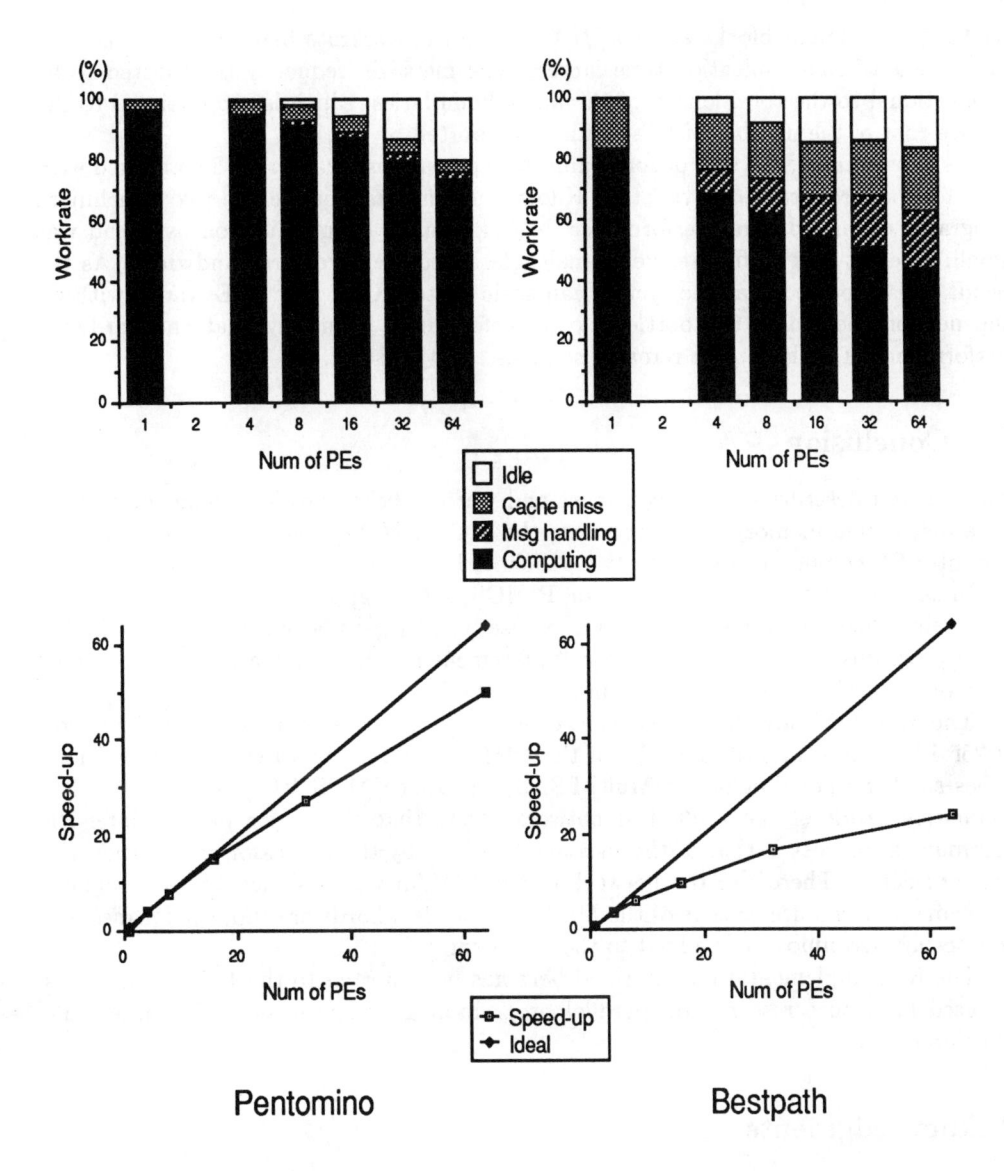

Figure 11: Decomposition of Processor Time and Speed-up

Figure 11 shows the average of the above figures of all PEs and the resultant speed-up shown with the ideal one. In Pentomino, the overhead generated by the message handling and cache misses is very small and the speed-up degradation was mainly due to idling time.

In Bestpath, while the idling ratio of 64 PEs is smaller than that of Pentomino, the computing ratio is rather low. Not only the overhead of the inter-PE communication, but also the cache-miss penalty is very large because of the large working set. As the number of PEs grows, the grid graph is divided into smaller blocks (5×5-grid block for

64 PEs, 16 different blocks at each PE) to keep the workrate high, and it makes the percentage of communication time larger. The message frequency is expected to be proportional to the total length of the block boundaries, which is proportional to the square root of the number of PEs. This is supported by Table 2.

As shown in 7.1, the cost of communication primitives is rather high compared with that for local reduction (25 μs at 40 Kilo reductions/s). However, in two benchmark programs examined here, performance degradation by communication overhead was small. The network traffic was very small relative to the hardware bandwidth. As the result, it is expected that the system can scale up to 1K ($2^5 \times 2^5$) PEs range without the network becoming the bottleneck in performance, assuming that the hardware performance of each element remains same as the Multi-PSI.

8. Conclusion

This chapter described the design issues and various techniques in implementing KL1 on a distributed memory multiprocessor, the Multi-PSI. Several evaluation results on the inter-PE communication with two benchmark programs were also shown.

In addition to the operating system, PIMOS, several application programs such as a protein sequence alignment program, a case-based legal reasoning system and LSI-CAD programs (a logic simulator, a cell placement program, and a routing program) have been developed and are now running on the Multi-PSI.

The Multi-PSI now has a successor, called PIM/m, whose maximum configuration is 256-PE (16×16 mesh). The PE of the PIM/m is more than twice faster and four times smaller than that of the Multi-PSI by utilizing CMOS VLSI technology. The evaluation result of the Multi-PSI network shows that the major part of inter-PE communication cost is that of the message handling by the processor rather than the network delay. Therefore, the network of the PIM/m was designed to have roughly the same performance as that of the Multi-PSI, while a hardware support for message composing/decomposing is added to the processor.

The KL1 implementation described here has been ported to the PIM/m, and will be used for future research on parallel programming and processing for large scale multiprocessors.

Acknowledgments

This KL1 implementation was developed by the author and the research members of ICOT, Mitsubishi Electric and other related companies in the fifth generation computer project. The author would like to thank all the people, who collaborated in the design and development of the Multi-PSI and its KL1 implementation.

PART IV Process-oriented Prolog Languages

Part IV, on Process Oriented Prologs, does not begin with an introduction. The reason for this is quite simple: until relatively recently (around 1989) there was only a single system — Delta Prolog — that could be called "Process Oriented". The term *Process Oriented* is being used here in the following sense. Most parallel Prolog systems, such as those described in the first three parts of this book, employ combinations of AND and OR parallelism to extract parallelism from logic programs. Clearly, the more parallelism there is in a particular algorithm, the more these systems will find. At an extreme, however, these systems may try to extract parallelism when little or none is available, e.g. when evaluating singly recursive predicates such as "append", with the result that the turn-around time may actually increase. At the other extreme these systems may be overwhelmed by the amount of parallelism available, e.g. in multiply recursive, divide-and-conquer algorithms. Further, if much of this work is "speculative" in nature, i.e. spent evaluating branches of the proof-tree that ultimately fail, the excess of unnecessary computation may cause the substantive computations to be delayed due to increased congestion. (This is particularly arguable in the case of distributed systems.) By contrast, the Process Oriented Prologs could also be called "Communicating Sequential Prolog Processes" (after Hoare's Communicating Sequential Processes), in that their processes are essentially pieces of sequential Prolog which are explicitly forked. Once forked, these Prolog processes communicate via the explict transmission and receipt of messages.

Chapter 15 describes Delta Prolog, the oldest of this new class of systems. (In fact, Delta Prolog was one of the first parallel Prolog systems to appear in the literature, first appearing in 1983.) In Delta Prolog, new processes are created using a *split goal* and communicate using *event goals*. The event goals are of particular interest; to send a term X to another process, a process executes X?E:C while the receiving process would execute Y?F:D. For the transmission to succeed, the variables E and F must be the same Prolog atom (called the *event name*), the terms X and Y must be unifiable and side conditions (i.e. predicates) C and D must succeed. Delta Prolog also has the concept of a *choice goal*, which is a list of literals separated by "::". A choice goal succeeds when one of the constituent literals successfully unifies with an appropriate clause-head. In the case where more than one constituent goals succeeds in this fashion, one is randomly chosen. It should be noted that split, event and choice goals may fail, triggering backtracking.

Distributed backtracking strategies are described in this chapter. The chapter also provides an operational semantics for Delta Prolog.

The following chapter describes a more recent system, CS-Prolog. What is interesting about this system is that it, too, is actually one of the earlier Prolog systems, being based on T-Prolog, a system for performing simulations in Prolog. T-Prolog first appeared in the literature in 1984. In CS-Prolog processes are forked using the builtin "new", which returns as one of its terms a process-descriptor for use in subsequent interactions. There is also a builtin for explicitly terminating processes. Communication occurs between named processes using the asynchronous builtins "send" and "wait_for"; non-blocking versions of these builtins are also available. Interestingly, non-backtrackable versions of the interprocess communications' primitives are available, because, like Delta-Prolog, subsequent failure can result in backtracking over a communication. Finally, a mechanism reminiscent of guarded commands is available to encode non-determinism. After outlining the features of CS-Prolog, the chapter discusses how completeness can be ensured in a distributed environment. This is followed by a discussion of the system's use for simulation and a discussion of some implementation issues, including distributed backtracking.

Chapter 17 describes PMS-Prolog. In this system, formally defined processes, each containing one or more clauses, are explicitly forked using the builtin "fork". These process definitions resemble modules, in that information hiding is facilitated. The forked processes communicate using the builtins "transmit" and "receive". The communication can be either synchronous or asynchronous (this is implementation dependent), but unlike the previous two models, there is no backtracking on communication. Communication is point-to-point via channels, which are passed to the processes as they are created. It is also possible, using "poll", to perform a non-blocking test of a channel to see if a transmitter is queued, awaiting a "receive". After describing the features of the language, the chapter gives some details of how the system is implemented on a Transputer-based multiprocess. In particular, methods for distributing the database of clauses are addressed.

It is in the final chapter, describing PADMAVATI Prolog, that one sees the clearest connection with OCCAM/CSP. PADMAVATI Prolog, or "Padamalog", is designed for the Padamavati architecture, a Transputer-based multiprocessor. The chapter begins with an overview of the Padamavati system. In this system the number of processes is set up in a configuration file, and is structured in the first instance as a Master process with the other processes being Workers. (The functions of the processes can be altered within a Prolog program.) Processes can create *ports* and have these registered with a name-server, so that processes can obtain a process's port knowing the processes's identifier. Interprocess communication occurs via the ports using the asynchronous primitives "send" and "receive", and like PMS-Prolog there is no backtracking over communications. This chapter provides details of the parallel and sequential aspects of the implementation and finishes with some performance measurements.

15 Delta Prolog: A Distributed Logic Programming Language and its Implementation on Distributed Memory Multiprocessors

J. C. Cunha, P. D. Medeiros, M. B. Carvalhosa and L. M. Pereira

Universidade Nova de Lisboa, Portugal

ABSTRACT

Delta Prolog is a logic programming language extending Prolog with constructs for sequential and parallel composition of goals, interprocess communication and synchronization, and external non-determinism. We present sequential and parallel search strategies for the language, based on the notion of derivations space. They rely upon distributed backtracking, a mechanism supporting the coordinated execution of multiple communicating Delta Prolog processes in their joint search for the solutions to a given problem. Then we describe an execution environment for Delta Prolog based on an abstract machine and discuss implementation issues for distributed memory Transputer-based multiprocessors.

1 INTRODUCTION

Delta Prolog (ΔP) is a parallel extension to Prolog inspired by Monteiro's Distributed Logic. The theory of Distributed Logic ([Mont83a], [Mont86a]) extends Horn Clause Logic (HCL) with constructs for the specification of distributed systems. As a distinctive feature, the ΔP model relies on the programmer to specify the sequentiality constraints and the desirable parallelism existing in each problem, together with the corresponding communication schemes ([Pere84a],[Cunh89a]).

The presentation is organized as follows. In section 2, we discuss the programming model and give an example. A discussion of the ΔP sequential and parallel execution models is made in section 3. Then, in section 4, we discuss implementation issues of the parallel execution models and outline the implementation on a Transputer-based distributed memory multi-computer (Meiko Computing Surface). Finally, in section 5, we present some conclusions and current work.

2 THE PROGRAMMING MODEL

In this section we discuss the ΔP language, focusing on the programming model, the language syntax and semantics, and give an example.

2.1 Language constructs

A ΔP program is a sequence of clauses of the form:

$H \text{ :- } G_1, \ldots, G_n. (n \geq 0)$.

H is a Prolog goal and each G_i may be either a Prolog or a ΔP goal. The latter are either *split*, *event*, or *choice* goals, described below. The *comma* is the *sequential* composition operator.

Declaratively, the truth of goals in ΔP is time-dependant, so H is true if $G_1, \ldots, G_n$ are true in succession (see section 2.2 below).

Operationally, to solve goal H is to solve successively goals $G_1, \ldots, G_n$.

An important aspect is that a ΔP program without ΔP goals is a Prolog program, and so ΔP is a true extension to Prolog.

2.1.1 Split goals Split goals are of the form $S_1//S_2$, where $//$ is a right associative *parallel* composition operator and S_1 and S_2 are arbitrary ΔP goal expressions. To solve $S_1//S_2$ is to solve S_1 and S_2 within concurrent processes. Declaratively, $S_1 // S_2$ is true iff S_1 and S_2 are jointly true.

The abstract execution models for the language do not require that the processes solving these two goals share memory. So if S_1 and S_2 share logical variables, the variables must be unified whenever both processes terminate. Failure to unify those variables, failure to solve S_1 or S_2, or failure of a subsequent goal and backtracking into the split goal, trigger *distributed backtracking*. Distributed backtracking extends the backtrack-based strategy of sequential Prolog systems as required to deal with concurrent processes.

2.1.2 Event goals Event goals are of the form $X?E : C$ or $X!E : C$, where X is a term (the *message*), ? and ! are infix binary predicate symbols (the *communication modes*), E is bound to a Prolog atom (the *event name*), and C is a goal expression (the *event condition*), which can not evaluate ΔP goals.

Two event goals, e.g. $X?E : C$ and $X!E : C$, are *complementary* iff they have the same event name, and different communication modes (i.e. one of type ? and the other of type !). If C and D are the atom *true*, we write $X?E$ and $X!E$. The two event goals execute successfully iff X and Y unify and the conditions C and D evaluate to true. An *event* is the outcome of the successful resolution of a pair of complementary event goals.

An event goal can only be said to be true when it has been successfully solved with its complementary goal. Thus the declarative semantics of ΔP states that a goal is true for some combinations of sequences of events.

An event goal, like $X?E : C$, suspends until a complementary event goal, like $Y!E : D$, is available in a concurrent process. When they are simultaneously available, their joint resolution may be intrepreted as a two-way exchange of messages followed by unification of X and Y and evaluation of conditions C and D. This form of rendezvous mechanism is a generalisation of Hoare's and Milner's synchronous communication ([Hoar85a], [Miln80a]) as it takes advantage of term unification for exchanging messages. The only significance of the communication modes ! and ? is that they are complementary in the sense described above.

Failure of an event goal, or backtracking into one, causes distributed backtracking.

2.1.3 Choice goals The choice operator :: was introduced for modelling *external* or *global non-determinism* ([Fran79a], [Hoar85a]).

In ΔP the selection of the clauses for resolution with a selected Prolog goal is like in Prolog sequential systems (i.e. it uses the textual occurrence of the clauses in the program), and is independent of the state of the environment. Choice goals allow the programming of applications where multiple communication alternatives may be simultaneously available and whose selection depends (non-deterministically) on the environment.

These goals have the form $A_1 :: A_2 :: \ldots :: A_i :: \ldots :: A_n (n \geq 2)$, where :: is the choice operator. Each $A_i (i : 1..n)$, is an alternative of the goal of the form H_e, B, where H_e is an event goal (the head of the alternative), sequentially conjuncted with a, possibly empty, goal expression B (the body of the alternative).

Declaratively a choice goal is true iff at least one alternative is true.

Solving a choice goal consists of solving the head of any one alternative (whose choice is governed by the availability of a complementary goal for its H_e), and then solving its body B. If no complementary event goals are available for any alternative the choice goal suspends. Failure of the selected alternative or backtracking into the choice goal triggers distributed backtracking.

2.2 Declarative Semantics

In ΔP, a goal may be true for some event sequences (traces) and false for others. In [Mont86a] a rigorous exposition is given of a declarative semantics for ΔP in which event sequences are modeled by finite sequences of events or "traces". Given an arbitrary goal expression S and supposing $X_1, \ldots, X_k$ are the variables that occur in S, the relation defined by S and a given program, according to the declarative semantics, is the set of all k-tuples $(X_1\theta, \ldots, X_k\theta)$, for all substitutions θ such that $S\theta$ is ground and is true in the minimal model of the program for the null trace (i.e. the empty event sequence).

The declarative, refutation and fixed point semantics of ΔP programs are defined and proved equivalent in [Mont86a].

2.3 An example

Below we give an example of an air-line reservation system. For more examples see ([Butl86a], [Cunh89a]). The description uses C-Prolog and assumes that the operators for split and event goals are defined as follows:

```
?- op(230, xfy, //).
?- op(200, xfx, [!, ?]).
```

Consider the following top goal:

```
topgoal :- terminal(t1)//terminal(t2)//terminal(t3)//
          database([112,256,68]).
```

A database process is responsible for the management of an air-line reservation system with multiple terminal processes. The database process handles a list (DB) with the current state of available seats for each flight, and solves, e.g. a top goal of the form `database([112,256,68])`, for three flights with the given number of seats.

It processes user requests of one of the forms:

```
info(FlightNumber, NumberOfAvailableSeats )
reserve(FlightNumber, NoOfRequestedSeats, Answer )
```

`NumberOfAvailableSeats` gives the available seats on the flight, and `Answer` is 'YES' or 'NO'.

Sequentiality is imposed by having the database process first receive the terminal name for a user process through an event goal named data. Then a single event goal is used to support the reception of a request, its processing (within the event condition) and the return of the results to the user. The name of the synchronous event goal is the terminal name for each user process.

Each terminal process solves the top goal `terminal(ttyn)` where ttyn is the terminal name. It uses event goals that are complementary to the ones that are used in the database process.

```
terminal(Tty) :- read(X), Tty ! data, X ! Tty, write(X), nl,
                 terminal(Tty).
database(DB) :- Tty ? data, database(DB, Tty).
database(DB, Tty) :-
                 Request ? Tty : dbprocess(Request, Tty, DB, NewDB),
                 database(NewDB).
dbprocess(info(Flight, Seats), Tty, DB, DB) :-
                 information(DB, Flight, Seats).
dbprocess(reserve(Flight,Seats,Resp),Tty, DB, NewDB) :-
                 reserve(Flight, Seats, DB, Response, NewDB).
dbprocess(Request, Next, DB, DB) :-
                 write('unknown command from '),write(Next), nl.
```

The interaction between the database process and each user process may use asynchronous event goals and only requires a 'send and receive' communication model. So, for efficiency's sake, one may use another type of ΔP goals, asynchronous event goals, with the forms

```
Tty !! data (instead of Tty ! data)
Tty ?? data (instead of Tty ? data)
```

where `Tty !! data` does not wait for `Tty ?? data`, but not vice-versa. Their semantics is defined in a way comparable, respectively, to the semantics for "write" and "read" in i/o streams. No distributed backtracking applies to event goals of this type.

3 OPERATIONAL SEMANTICS

In this section we discuss abstract execution models for the language. This includes a discussion of the ΔP derivations space, computation and search strategies, the parallel search of the derivation space - its forward and backward components (with focus on distributed backtracking) - and a presentation of the sequential and parallel execution models for the language.

3.1 Delta Prolog derivations and resolution rules

We present a formal definition of the derivations space that is defined by each ΔP program and top goal, which allows a rigorous definition of the *process* concept as well as other suitable abstractions for the specification of the forward and backward control. Each derivation in a ΔP program is visualized as a binary tree, rooted in the top goal, where an interpretation in terms of processes may be defined for the exploration of distinct paths. These abstractions are essential devices for the specification of the basic mechanisms being supported by a ΔP abstract machine. Intuitively, each ΔP computation is sliced down into well defined derivation segments (on the above mentioned tree) which are delimited by the resolution of ΔP goals. Each search strategy must define some ordering among the derivation segments so that it will guide the search in the derivations space.

3.1.1 Derivations A derivation is a finite non-empty ordered binary tree, which is developed by expanding one or more of its (non-suspended) leaves. Each leaf has an associated process, which expands it into its offspring. A binary node is expanded by the splitting of a process into two, while the expansion of a unary node corresponds to a computation step of the associated process.

Each process is identified by a *dyadic number*, that is a word over $\{1,2\}$ such that the initial process has number 1. Whenever a process with number P splits, its offspring are identified by P1 and P2. Q is a *sub-process* of a process P iff P is a prefix of Q. The left-right ordering of processes (denoted by $<<$) is their lexicographic ordering as words over $\{1,2\}$. For example, P1Q $<<$ P2R.

Nodes are labeled by a *resolvent sequence*, $S_1 \# P_1 \bullet S_2 \# P_2 \bullet \ldots \bullet S_k \# P_k (k > 0)$, of pairs of goal expressions S_i and processes P_i. The meaning of $S_i \# P_i$ is to solve S_i within process P_i. The resolvent sequence is solved from left to right, having the structure of a stack. P_1 is the *active process* at the node, subsequent processes being activated as soon as their predecessor terminates. If S_1 has the form $G_1, G_2, \ldots, G_n$ where G_1 is a split goal $H_1//H_2$, the parent process P_1 splits into two children. The left child label is $H_1 \# P_1 1 \bullet G_2, \ldots, G_n \# P_1 \bullet S_2 \# P_2 \bullet \ldots \bullet S_k \# P_k (k > 0)$ and the right child label is $H_2 \# P_1 2$.

For example, in a node with the pair $p//q, s\#1$, first solve $p//q$ in process 1 and then s in the same process. Two processes are spawned to solve $p//q$, identified by 11 and 12. Only when they both terminate should 1 start to solve s. This is expressed by defining the left and right offspring as, respectively, $p\#11 \bullet s\#1$ and $q \# 12$. When 11 terminates solving p, the left node is $[]\#11 \bullet s\#1$, where $[]$ stands for the empty resolvent. This node next reduces to $s\#1$, its parent's continuation, only when 12 also terminates solving q, i.e. the right node is $[]\#12$.

3.1.2 Definition of derivation Given a top goal S, the root of a derivation is the pair $S\#1$. A derivation generates another derivation by expanding its leaves, according to the following rules:

- A leaf with a single pair and empty resolvent is *successful*, and not further expanded. A derivation is successful and terminates iff all its leaves are successful. This occurs whenever process 1 is terminated, i.e. there is a leaf $[]\#1$ in the derivation.

- Other leaves have the form $S_1\#P_1 \bullet \ldots \bullet S_k\#P_k (k > 0)$, where S_1 is the goal expression $G_1, \ldots, G_n (n \geq 0)$. If $n > 0$, we call G_1 the *leading goal* of the leaf. If $n = 0$, we have $S_1 = []$.

For each leaf with $S_1 \neq []$ the leftmost (Prolog or ΔP) goal of its leading pair $(S_1\#P_1)$ is the one to be considered for resolution by the associated process. The resolution proceeds according to the rules given in the following three subsections. If expansion is impossible, a strategy for exploring alternative derivations must be invoked.

3.1.3 Resolution of Prolog goals Given a resolvent $G_1, G_2, \ldots, G_n (n > 0)$ where G_1 is a Prolog goal, find a clause $H :\text{-} B_1, \ldots, B_m$ such that G_1 matches H, with most general unifier θ. The leaf expands to a single child, $S_1'\#P_1 \bullet \ldots \bullet S_k'\#P_k$, where S_1' is the goal expression $(B_1, \ldots, B_m, G_2, \ldots, G_n)\theta$ that *reduces* G_1, and $S_i' = S_i\theta (k > 1)$. If no such clause exif no such clause exists, then G_1 is not reducible and the leaf is not expandable.

3.1.4 Resolution of split goals Given a resolvent $G_1, G_2, \ldots, G_n$ where G_1 is a split goal $H_1//H_2$, the left child process of this binary node must solve H_1 while the right child must solve H_2'. H_2' is H_2 with its variables renamed so as not to share variables with H_1 (*activation* of the split). Actually, the left child is $H_1\#P_11 \bullet (G_2, \ldots, G_n)\#P_1 \bullet S_2\#P_2 \bullet \ldots \bullet S_k\#P_k$ and the right child is $H_2'\#P_12$.

For the *completion* of the split, resolvents of the form $S_1\#P_1 \bullet \ldots \bullet S_k\#P_k (k > 0)$ where $S_1 = []$, must be derived:

- if $k > 1$, we have $P_1 = P_21$ (the left child of P_2). Expansion of this leaf suspends till the right child P_22 terminates, i.e. till there is a leaf $[]\#P_22$.

- if $k = 1$ and $P_1 \neq 1$ we have $P_1 = P_22$ (the right child of P_2). Expansion of this leaf suspends till the left child P_21 terminates, i.e. till there is a leaf $[]\#P_11 \bullet (G_2, \ldots, G_n)\#P_1 \bullet S_2\#P_2 \bullet \ldots \bullet S_k\#P_k$.

The two cases above occur when both goals H_1 and H_2' were successfully solved. Then their corresponding variables, which were previously renamed, must now be unified for the completion of the split to be successful. If an associated unifier θ exists, there is a continuation resolvent $(G_2, \ldots, G_n)\theta\#P_1 \bullet (S_2'\#P_2 \bullet \ldots \bullet S_k'\#P_k)$, where each $S_i' = S_i\theta (i > 1)$ and the right child process is *terminated*. If such unification fails, the expansion is not possible.

3.1.5 Resolution of event goals Consider a derivation with two leaves of the form:

i) $X?E : C, G_2, \ldots, G_n \# P_1 \bullet S_2 \# P_2 \bullet \ldots \bullet S_k \# P_k (k > 0, n \geq 1)$

ii) $Y!E : D, G'_2, \ldots, G'_m \# Q_1 \bullet S'_2 \# Q_2 \bullet \ldots \bullet S'_l \# Q_l (l > 0, m \geq 1)$

Event goals $X?E : C$ and $Y!E : D$ resolve with unifier θ obtained by first unifying X and Y and then solving C and D.

The leaves i) and ii) expand, respectively, to leaves i') and ii'):

i') $(G_2, \ldots, G_n)\theta \# P_1 \bullet S_2\theta \# P_2 \bullet \ldots \bullet S_k\theta \# P_k (k > 0, n \geq 1)$

ii') $(G'_2, \ldots, G'_m)\theta \# Q_1 \bullet S'_2\theta \# Q_2 \bullet \ldots \bullet S'_l\theta \# Q_l (l > 0, m \geq 1)$

Thus the rule defines a joint derivation step that involves the "simultaneous" expansion of a pair of branches in a derivation tree. If the conditions for event success are not fulfilled, the corresponding derivation tree is not expandable any further, i.e. a search strategy must abandon it and try to explore alternative derivations. Note that a similar situation arises when an unification failure occurs at the completion of a split goal (see above).

3.1.6 Resolution of choice goals If G_1 is a choice goal $A_1 :: A_2 :: \ldots :: A_j :: \ldots :: A_m$, the leaf is expanded by first replacing G_1 by some A_j $(j : 1..m)$ and then proceeding as in the resolution of event goals. Choosing A_j is determined by the existence of some other leaf with a leading complementary event goal. Unavailability of complementary event goals for any of the alternatives causes the choice goal to suspend. On failure of the head of the elected alternative, only the untried ones remain available for solving the choice. The expansion is impossible when no alternatives remain.

3.2 Searching the derivations space

We discuss distinct computation strategies for the language, including both sequential (suitable for uniprocessor machines) and parallel execution models (suitable for multiprocessors). The search strategy for ΔP extends the depth-first with backtracking search strategy of sequential Prolog systems in order to coordinate multiple communicating processes.

Given a ΔP program and top goal S, the *space of derivations* is the set of all derivations with root $S\#1$. The space is a graph, with an arc from derivation D_1 to derivation D_2 if D_2 can be obtained from D_1 by one of the rules described earlier.

Each strategy must impose some ordering that guides the search process so that it may preserve completeness and correctness. However, we only provide a semi-complete search strategy for the derivations space, due to the fact that ΔP subsumes Prolog, and so it may engage in infinite searches, if the derivations space is infinite.

Each path leading from the root of the derivation tree is sliced down into well defined derivation *segments* (defined in 3.4.2 below) which are delimited by the resolution of ΔP goals.

We define the notion of *executor* as an interpretative device, capable of executing derivation steps according to the ΔP resolution rules.

The problem of actually producing computations (i.e. sequences of derivation steps) is dependant on the availability of distinct executors. A sequential strategy is based on a single executor which is responsible for searching the derivation space using a depth-first strategy similar to Prolog. A parallel strategy allows the parallel expansion of several branches of a derivation by distinct executors.

Thus we distinguish two classes of execution models for ΔP, using coroutining or parallel processing.

3.3 Sequential execution strategy

The single executor tries to expand the leftmost branch in the current derivation, until it derives the empty resolvent for process #1 (and a successful derivation has been found), or an empty resolvent corresponding to a split goal for which completion is not possible yet (i.e. one of the subprocesses has not terminated), or an event or choice goal for which no complementary goal exists in another leaf. If the current branch suspends on one of the conditions above, the next leftmost active branch must be expanded by the single executor. This amounts to a left-right depth-first traversal of the graph defining the derivations space.

3.3.1 An example Consider the following program and top goal

```
?- a // b.
a :- t ! e.      b :- t ? e.
a.               b.
```

This strategy may be illustrated through a simplified model where a single stack of resolvents is used, as shown below for a successful derivation. For each resolvent, the selected goal is underlined, and the corresponding pending alternatives are shown. If

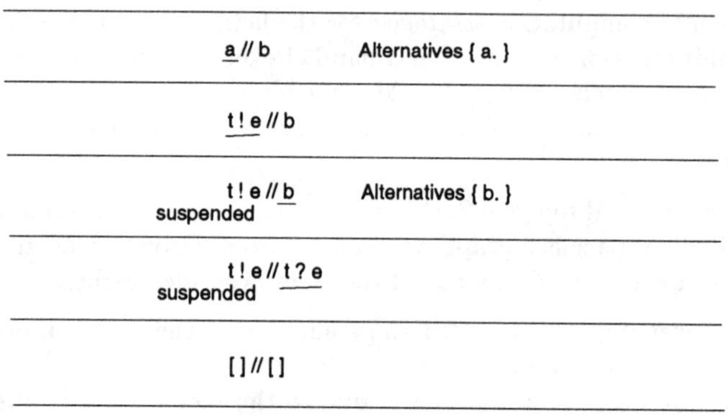

a // b	Alternatives { a. }
t ! e // b	
t ! e // b suspended	Alternatives { b. }
t ! e // t ? e suspended	
[ ] // [ ]	

Figure 1: Single stack model

two leaves have leading event goals with the same name, we assume it is impossible to expand another (third) leaf in the current resolvent such that a leaf will appear with a leading event goal with that name.

Given the derivation space defined by a ΔP program and a top goal, we assume that there is no derivation where more than two processes simultaneously try to communicate through an event with a given name. A consequence of this assumption is that if the expansion of a pair of complementary event goals fails, neither of them can be resolved with a third, and backtracking can start.

This restriction greatly simplifies the computation strategies for the language, at the cost of affecting the programming model. We have found it easy to program in ΔP assuming this restriction, for simple examples. However, this is a topic where further investigation is needed.

3.3.2 Deadlock detection and recovery   In the sequential strategy, when an unsuccessful derivation has all its leaves suspended there is a deadlock. The sequential strategy detects this situation and recovers by backtracking.

3.3.3 The coroutining algorithm   In this section we describe the implementation of a sequential execution model for ΔP programs. We have experimented with two different approaches: a Prolog interpreter based approach and a compiler plus abstract machine based approach [Carv91a]. Both techniques use a coroutining control strategy based on a depth-first search of the derivation space by a single executor. They also rely upon the notion of top of the *resolvent* [Mont83a], which is reviewed below.

The existence of the split goals and the comma operator induce a partial order relation on the goals of the current resolvent. The *top of a resolvent* indicates the set of goals in a resolvent which may be solved concurrently (i.e. either through coroutining or in parallel).

Definition. Let p and q be goal expressions not containing split goals. The top of the resolvent p is the leftmost goal of p. The top of the resolvent q is the leftmost goal of q. The top of the resolvent $p \; // \; q$ is the set {leftmost goal of p, leftmost goal of q }.

The ΔP coroutining strategy is described in a simplified way where, for simplicity, we do not consider the existence of choice goals in the resolvent (choice goals are handled according to the resolution rule given in 3.1.6).

The algorithm is as follows:

- Assumptions:
    - Let **S** be a stack (initially empty).
    - Let **R** be a resolvent.
    - Associated with each goal $\mathbf{G_i}$ of the resolvent **R** there is an attribute called *state* and denoted by $\mathbf{StateG_i}$ whose domain is the set { SUSPENDED, NOTSUSPENDED}.
- Pass1: /* *initializations* */
    - Let **R** become the top goal.
    - For every goal $\mathbf{G_i}$ in **R** let its state $StateG_i$ become NOTSUSPENDED.
- Pass2: /**choosing a goal* */
    - If there are no goals $\mathbf{G_i}$ in **R** such that $\mathbf{StateG_i}$ = NOTSUSPENDED then goto *Backtrack*. /**a deadlock was detected**/

- Select the leftmost goal whose state is NOTSUSPENDED from the top of the resolvent **R**. Denote this goal by **A** (i.e. the "selected atom") and its state by **StateA**.
- If **A** is an event goal then goto *Pass3*,
  else if **A** is a Prolog goal then goto *Pass4*.

- Pass3: /*event goals */
  - If there is not a complementary event goal in **R** for **A**, then **StateA** := SUSPENDED and goto *Pass2*.
  - Solve the event goal **A** with its complementary goal. If the solving does not succeed then goto *Backtrack*.
  - Goto *Pass5*.

- Pass4: /*Prolog goals */
  - Let **Alt** be the set of all clauses defining **A** (i.e. its alternatives).
  - If **Alt** is empty then goto *Backtrack*.

- NextTry:
  - Let **C** (i.e. the "selected clause") be the first element of **Alt** (according to the textual order as in Prolog) and let **Alt'** be **Alt** − {**C**}.
  - If **Alt'** is not empty then create a choice point by pushing onto **S** the triple {**R**, **A**, **Alt'**}.
  - Unify **A** with **C**. If the unification does not succeed then goto *Backtrack*; else obtain the new resolvent **R** where, for each goal G_i of the body of **C** do $StateG_i$:= NOTSUSPENDED.
  - Goto *Pass5*.

- Pass5: /* next goal */
  - If **R** is empty then notify the user (as in Prolog) with the final substitution and terminate the algorithm. /* a successful derivation was found */
  - Goto *Pass2*. /* R is not empty */

- Backtrack: /*failure or other solutions */
  - If **S** is empty there are no more successful derivations. Therefore notify the user and terminate the algorithm. /* failure */
  - Restore a previous choice state by popping **S** and updating **R**, **A** and **Alt** with the popped value. /* other solutions */
  - Goto *NextTry*.

3.4 Parallel execution strategies

With regard to the derivation tree, execution begins with an initial process for the top goal and proceeds depth-first till a split goal is found. In our models, a parallel thread of control is spawned for the right subgoal in the split, corresponding to the right child process in the derivation tree. The left subgoal is associated with the left child process in the derivation, which is executed by the same thread of control as the parent process.

3.4.1 Interaction points An *interaction point* between two processes is:

- a split point: a split goal was executed;
- an event point: two complementary event goals were activated.

The search strategy must find the next derivation in the space of possible derivations. We are modelling the expansion of branches in the tree by processes, each one following Prolog's sequential search strategy, so the mechanism for searching alternative derivations involves two aspects:

- A local search is performed by each process, relative to the doing and undoing of derivation steps for Prolog goals. This corresponds to Prolog's depth-first search and uses local backtracking within each process.
- A global coordination of the search is required whenever a joint derivation step (involving an event, a choice or a split goal) must be done or undone.

At any stage, some processes may be executing in the forward mode (it corresponds to the successful expansion of leaves in a derivation) while others are executing in the backward mode (corresponding to the failure of a leaf expansion). No interaction occurs as long as all processes are evaluating alternatives to Prolog goals, and do not reach interaction points.

We assume the restriction previously explained in 3.3.1, prohibiting the simultaneous use of an event name by more than two processes.

The main purpose of the distributed backtracking strategy is to implement an exhaustive search for the set of successful derivations defined by a program and a goal, where a distinction between local and global search is made and no centralized control component is required.

In the following we explain the principles behind the distibuted backtracking strategy by introducing the notion of segment of a derivation.

3.4.2 Segments of a derivation To show the coordination strategy of ΔP, we define the following abstraction on the derivation trees. The computation path of each process is subdivided into consecutive *segments of a derivation*. This concept allows us to ignore local backtracking within segments, and consider only interaction points. An *interaction node* is a node of the derivation tree whose associated resolvent sequence begins with a solved ΔP goal or the empty resolvent. A segment is a path of the derivation tree, satisfying the attributes below, where we identify two special nodes: the *start* node and the *end* node. A segment is a completed segment or an open segment.

A *completed segment* of a derivation is any path satisfying the following conditions:

1. Its end node is an interaction node.
2. The path includes only one interaction node.
3. It is the maximal path satisfying these conditions.

An *open segment* is a path satisfying the following conditions:

1. Its start node is the root of the derivation tree or a son of an interaction node.

2. It is not a completed segment.

3. It is the maximal path satisfying these conditions.

An open segment may become completed, on successful resolution of ΔP goals or on successful termination of a computation (producing the resolvent []#1). Open segments are currently being expanded (as in forward or backward execution modes of a Prolog computation), or are suspended resolutions in event goals or awaiting the completion of split goals (see 3.1.4). A completed segment belongs to the process containing its end node. An open segment belongs to the process containing its start node.

3.4.3 Total order among the segments of a derivation Consider the top goal (a//b//c),d and the following program:

```
a :- T!e1, U!e2, f.
b :- t?e1.
c :- u?e2.
d.
f.
```

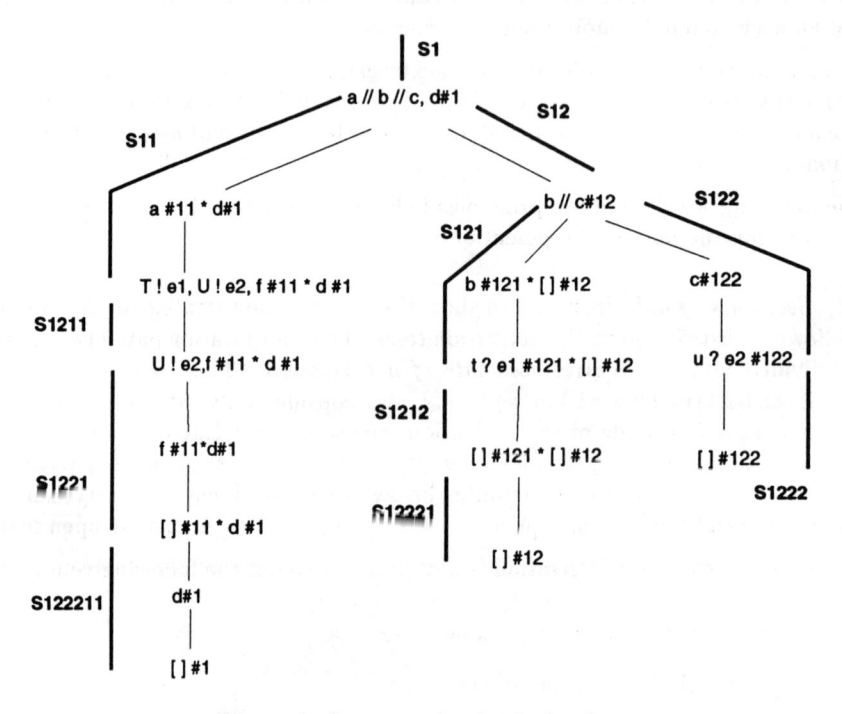

Figure 2: Segments in the derivation

A lexicographic order, denoted by $<$, of words over $\{1,2\}$, is defined over the segments of a derivation (as exemplified by the numbering scheme in figure 2). The relation $<$ defines a total order among the segments in a derivation which is used to guide the search strategy. The root of the derivation tree corresponds to an initial segment numbered 1 (we prefix S to segment numbers to distinguish them from process numbers). Next consider the cases:

1. *Split goal segment*:

    (a) a segment S_i ending in a split goal has two successor segments, where $S_l = S_i 1$ corresponds to the beginning of the left child process and $S_r = S_i 2$ to the beginning of the right child;

    (b) for segments, S_l and S_r, of the child processes that jointly complete a split goal, with $S_l < S_r$, their only successor (corresponding to the continuation of the father process where the split goal was activated) is numbered $S_f = S_r 1$ (see example in figure 3: $S_l = S1212, S_r = S1222, S_f = S12221$).

2. *Event goal segment*: segments S_i and S_j (in processes P and Q, P $<<$ Q) ending in complementary event goals(see figure 3), with $S_i < S_j$, have successor segments numbered $S_p = S_j 1$ (in P) and $S_q = S_j 2$ (in Q). There are cases where P $<<$ Q

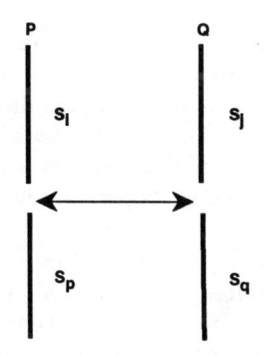

Figure 3: Segments in a event

but $S_j < S_i$, so $S_p = S_i 1$ (in P) and $S_q = S_i 2$ (in Q).

3. *Choice goal segment*: as the choice is replaced by a selected alternative, this reduces to the case of an event goal (the head of the chosen alternative).

3.5 Distributed backtracking strategies

When an expansion is impossible, a distributed backtracking mechanism is invoked, in order to search for alternative successful derivations. Starting from the current failed segment, the strategy selects the next one to be expanded, after reconfiguring the derivation tree.

Let $S_1, S_2 \ldots S_i \ldots S_k \ldots S_n$ be the order on the segments of the current derivations, and S_i be the segment corresponding to a failed expansion.

Each derivation tree can be explored sequentially, starting with the first segment in the ordering, switching execution to the next when the previous one became suspended at an interaction point. On a failure of S_i, a naïve strategy would select segment S_{i-1} and start looking there for alternatives.

However, if expansion of a derivation tree proceeds in parallel, on the failure of S_i some of its followers $(S_{i+1} \ldots S_k \ldots S_n)$ might be active already, because unrelated subtrees are being expanded in parallel. A selective strategy still uses the order over segments, but does not automatically affect all the segments to the right of the failed one. It does so only for those segments that have become related to the failing one in interaction points. The strategy uses a form of intelligent backtracking in the selection of the segment where alternatives will be sought such that segments that would repeat failure are ignored ([Bruy84a], [Pere84b], [Cunh88a]).

First, a centralized implementation of this strategy was experimented relying upon a global data structure to keep the information on the segments in the current derivation. This may be an interesting approach for shared-memory multiprocessors, but not for distributed-memory architectures. A different approach has been followed by us, relying upon a distribution of the data structures representing the current derivation, among the processes involved in the execution. This strategy allows more parallelism in both forward and backward execution because it does not require the use of locking techniques as in the first approach. This approach is briefly described in the following.

3.5.1 Outline of the decentralized strategy The main issue in this approach is the requirement for each process (possibly placed at a specific node of a (multi-)computer network) to be able to make decisions regarding the distributed backtracking strategy by relying on local information only. Instead of a global structure that keeps the total ordering among the segments in a derivation, each process is responsible for managing only the segments that were involved in its previous interaction points:

1. When an interaction point is reached in forward execution, the two involved processes exchange the required information about the corresponding segments. This exchange implies no additional cost to the message traffic generated by the distributed backtracking strategy, because it is performed by appending some control information to the exchanged data (i.e. subgoals of a split, event terms of an event goal, variable bindings at the completion of a split) that is required by the resolution of ΔP goals.

2. When local backtracking within a process reaches a previous interaction point, the process is able to decide which segments must be affected by this failure. They do necessarily directly or indirectly relate to previous interactions involving this process, so the required information was already collected by the process.

The segment numbering for each pair of segments involved in an interaction point is enough to establish their relative positions in the segment ordering. Also, the corresponding pair of involved processes is able to generate the correct numbers for the new segments that may arise from that interaction point.

On failure of segment S_i in process P_k, execution of the following steps is triggered:

1. Select a candidate segment S_j where search for alternatives will resume; this is a local decision made by process P_k.

2. Reconfigure the current (unsuccessful) derivation tree, such that only those segments related to S_i's failure are affected. This demands the coordination of the execution of the processes that contain the affected segments. It is performed by a distributed algorithm based on message-passing, whose initiator is the process containing the candidate segment S_j, after having received a message from P_k.

3. Backtrack into S_j in the newly reconfigured derivation tree.

3.5.2 Selecting a candidate segment for backtracking Each segment S_i in the tree has a list of backtrack nodes, denoted by L_i, which are those segments that are directly ou indirectly related to S_i by ΔP goals. The list is updated by the execution of these goals, according to simple rules which are summarized below [Cunh88a]. The segments in L_i are kept in the reverse order of $<$, so that on S_i's failure the first segment in L_i is the selected candidate segment S_j. In order not to miss currently unexplored alternatives, represented by the segments in L_i's tail, the identification of these segments must be passed to the process containing S_j, and inserted in S_j's list of backtrack nodes.

3.5.3 Updating of the lists of backtrack nodes The case for each ΔP goal is described separately:

- (a) *Split goal.* On activation of a split goal ending in segment S_i, the lists for S_i's sucessor segments (S_L and S_R, respectively in the left child process and in the right child process for the split) are set to $\{S_i\}$.

   The split goal fails iff S_L or S_R fail, and S_i is the candidate segment. Thereupon, the segments S_L and S_R in the derivation tree are cancelled, and S_i initiates backtracking, with its list L_i augmented with the tail of the list from the failed segment.

   - (a1) *Failure at the completion of a split goal*: This is due to a failure to unify the common-named variables that occur in the arguments of the split goal, on the completion of its execution. Let S_m and S_n, with $S_m < S_n$, be the segments respectively terminating the child processes P and Q for the split, and assume $P << Q$. In this situation, the lower segment in the order, S_m, suspends at the split goal completion, while the other segment, S_n, is the selected candidate, its list L_n being augmented with $\{S_m\}$. The reasoning behind this is that, on a later failure by S_n, S_m may still contribute with alternatives for the unification in the split's completion. When S_n fails and S_m is the selected candidate from its list, S_n restarts anew, in order to reopen all its alternatives for any unexplored alternative from S_m.

   - (a2) *Successful resolution of a split goal*: After success is obtained in the completion of the split, execution resumes in the parent process with a new segment $S_f = S_n 1$, whose list L_f is set to $\{S_n, S_m\}$. The computation states of both child processes are retained, as further alternatives may be required (as explained in the following case).

- (a3) *Failure into a solved split goal*: If backtracking within the parent process reaches the completion of a split, due to failure of S_f, segment S_n is always the selected candidate. The list L_n of segment S_n is updated with the remaining elements in S_f's list, and left segment S_m suspends at the split goal's completion as in (a1).

- (b) *Event goal*: Consider the interaction between processes P and Q, and segments S_i and S_j (see figure 3), regarding complementary event goals, and assume $S_i < S_j$.

    - (b1) *Failure in the unification of event terms or in the evaluation of the event conditions*: The lower segment in the order, S_i, suspends at its event goal while the other segment, S_j, is the selected candidate. The list L_j of S_j is augmented with $\{S_i\}$. The reasoning behind this is the same as given in (a1) above.

    - (b2) *Successful joint resolution of a pair of event goals*: In this case, execution proceeds in both processes, two new segments being activated: S_p in P and S_q in Q. The identifications of these segments are defined as explained in 3.4.3, and their lists L_p and L_q are set to $\{S_j, S_i\}$.

    - (b3) *Failure into a solved event*: This occurs iff S_p or S_q fail, and S_j is the selected candidate (given the assumption that $S_i < S_j$). The list L_j of segment S_j is augmented with the tail of the list of the failed segment. Before S_j starts backtracking, both segments S_p and S_q are *cancelled*, and left segment S_i suspends at its event goal. If, on a later failure by S_j, segment S_i is first in S_j's list, then S_i is the selected candidate. In this situation Sj restarts anew, thus keeping all its alternatives available again. However, other situations may arise on subsequent S_j failure, where $S_k (k \neq i)$ is first in S_j's backtrack list instead. This is shown in figure 4 where S_i is S11, S_j is S1221, and S_k is S122 and where S_j's backtrack list is $\{S122, S121, S11\}$. In such cases, S_i remains suspended, S_j is cancelled, and S_k backtracks in search of alternatives (its backtrack list updated with all backtrack candidates in the list of the failed S_j, including S_i as in figure 4). The rationale is that the greater segment in the order always backtracks first, so that search is exhaustive; and $S_i < S_k$, otherwise S_i would be first on S_j's list.

- (c) *Choice goal*: The above cases for event goals (in (b)) also apply to the head event goal of the selected alternative of a choice goal. Whenever backtracking should take place from the failed head event goal of the currently selected alternative, the remaining alternatives of the choice are tried instead, and execution of the choice resumes in the forward direction. Only when no untried choice alternatives remain, must backtracking from the choice goal begin.

3.5.4 Reconfiguring the failed derivation In the above description, given a failure by segment S_i, we have briefly indicated which are the segments that are directly or indirectly related to S_i. We also have assumed the existence of the following operations on segments, which are needed for the reconfiguration of a failed derivation tree:

- *Suspend*: A segment becomes suspended.

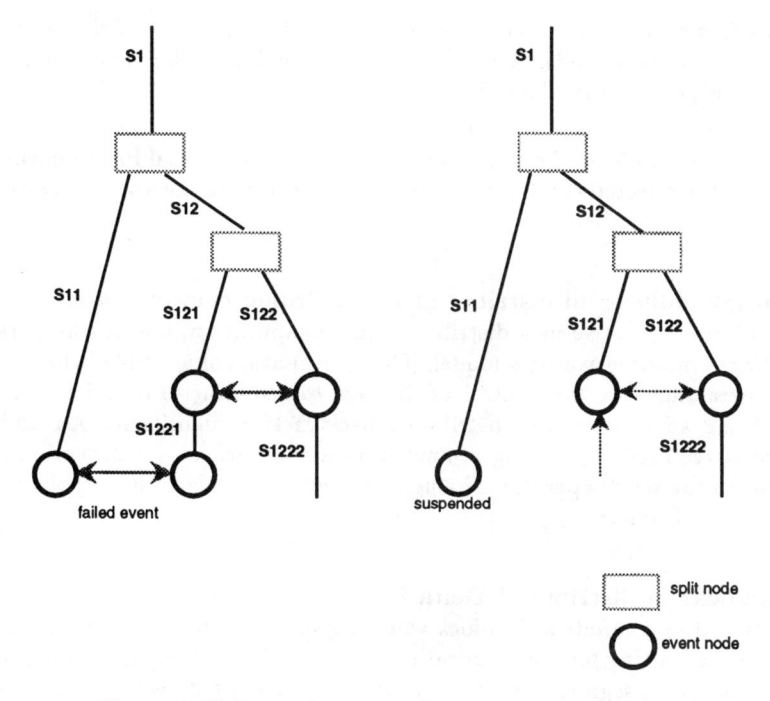

Figure 4: Failure of segment S1221 into a solved event

- *Redo*: Associated with each segment, there is a stack of choice points corresponding to the alternatives of the Prolog derivation leading from the start node to the end node of the segment.

  The redo operation is applied to a completed segment, or to a segment that was previously suspended. That segment becomes open, which corresponds to the search for alternative expansions. This can be achieved by forcing its owner process to start backtracking past the end node of the redone segment.

- *Restart* : The expansion of the segment is restarted anew. The segment becomes open and its computation starts from the very beginning, i.e. all possible derivations originating in its start node are again taken under consideration.

- *Cancel*: A segment is completely eliminated. The implementation of this operation must restore the state of the Prolog computation previous to the start node of the cancelled segment.

By cancelling or restarting a segment its descendants in the same process (and in its child processes) are also cancelled, with other possible side-effects on any segments that are related to the cancelled ones. For example, by cancelling a segment ending in a split, the initial segments for its child processes are cancelled, as well as their descendents. By cancelling (or restarting) a segment ending in an event goal, the segments activated when the event succeeded are cancelled. Additionally, the segment ending in the complementary event goal may have to be affected, depending on the fact that its computation state is in general dependant on that of the cancelled one, due to previous backtracking (after a redo operation) caused by a failure of the segment now being cancelled (or restarted). A more detailed discussion of the algorithm is beyond the scope of this document [Cunh88a].

3.5.5 Backtrack into S_j in the reconfigured derivation tree Usual Prolog backtracking begins within the selected candidate segment S_j, to continue the search (see operation redo).

3.6 Multiple failures in distributed Delta Prolog computations

Multiple failures may arise in a distributed ΔP computation, due to the parallelism provided by the multiple executor model. The coordination of multiple failures requires suitable abstractions for the control of distinct *backtracking waves*, i.e. the set of segments being affected by the distributed backtracking algorithm. An underlying mechanism is required supporting atomic transactions, where a transaction roughly corresponds to the set of operations being triggered by the algorithm on the failure of a given segment [Cunh88a].

3.7 Deadlocks in distributed Delta Prolog computations

A ΔP computation exhibits a deadlock when a non-successful derivation is obtained, all processes are waiting for communication at interaction points, and no pair of complementary and open segments exists. The strategies for the detection and recovery of such deadlocks, assuming a parallel execution model, depend on the degree of centralization of control [Cunh88a]:

- If centralized control is used, a global state of a deadlocked computation may be detected through the global data structure, via a supervisor process. Recovery must force the backtracking (via redo operation) in the rightmost segment (using $<$) in the deadlocked derivation, so that completeness of search is preserved.

- In a decentralized strategy, a distributed algorithm for deadlock detection must be used. This may be based on the passing of control tokens or may use the paradigm of diffused computations proposed in [Dijk80a]. Recovery proceeds by applying the decentralized algorithm (as outlined above), assuming that the failed segment (S_i in 3.5.1) is the rightmost in the deadlocked derivation.

4 IMPLEMENTING THE PARALLEL MODELS

In this section we discuss implementation issues of the above parallel execution models. We assume a multiple executor environment where there is no shared memory between executors. The described environment was used in our experimentation with an implementation for a Transputer-based distributed memory multi-computer (Meiko Computing Surface).

4.1 Implementation layers

We have defined an abstract machine for ΔP (called the DAM), by starting with a Prolog abstract machine, the WAM [Warr83a], and extending it with the internal structures and mechanisms to support ΔP [Carv91a]. In this approach, an existing Prolog compiler to the WAM is modified in order to generate code for the new instructions when ΔP goals are involved.

A two-layered system was designed:

- a *language level*, supporting the abstractions for the ΔP operational model, namely logical processes in a derivation, segments, ΔP goal resolution rules and distributed backtracking. This layer manages the internal structures of the DAM and supports its new instructions. It uses the services of a low-level system layer.

- a *system level*, supporting an interface to an operating system environment, namely for the management of multiple processes, communication and synchronization primitives and the mapping of logical processes into system processes.

A more detailed description of each layer is given below.

4.2 Language layer

This layer implements a basic machine supporting the mechanisms for the interpretation of Prolog and ΔP goals. We will center on the DAM instructions that support ΔP goals, as the machine behaves like the WAM when interpreting Prolog goals.

4.2.1 Support for split goals Two DAM instructions are provided: *Spawn* and *Join*. Corresponding to the activation of a split goal like g1(X)//g2(X), the *Spawn* instruction creates a new execution context. The new execution context consists of the set of data structures for representing the local stack, the heap, the trail and some state variables. Then a system process is allocated from a pool of executors, which will be responsible for the progress of the new execution context where the interpretation of the right goal in the split is performed.

The left goal in the split is executed in the parent context, i.e. the one invoking the split goal.

A copy of the right goal of the split must be passed to the new context. The right process inherits an independent and local copy of each variable that is shared by the subgoals (e.g. given the shared variable X in subgoals g1(X) and g2(X), we have the local instance X', copy of X, in the new context). The communication that must be established between the creator and created contexts for the sending of that goal is supported by a system level facility.

For simplicity, we are ommiting here the details of how a specific set of clauses, corresponding to the ΔP program, is sent to the newly created context.

The *Join* instruction supports the completion of the split goal, by performing the synchronization of the parent process and its offspring after they have sucessfully solved, respectively, the left and the right subgoals. Then, the compatibility of the instances representing the shared variables in the split is checked through unification (for example, between X and X' in the example above). On success, the parent process proceeds after the split goal, while the right process awaits backtracking commands (see 3.1.3, the process is terminated).

On failure, the distributed backtracking mechanism is triggered.

4.2.2 Support for event goals Event goals are supported by the *MeetAndExchange* and *Compute* instructions. The *MeetAndExchange* instruction suspends the caller's execution context until a complementary *MeetAndExchange* is invoked within another execution context. Two *MeetAndExchange* calls are complementary if their first arguments (the event name, which must be grounded) are equal and their second arguments (the event type, i.e. type_! or type_?) are different. The third and fourth arguments (the event terms), respectively input and output, are used for an exchange of terms between the two contexts, i.e. the fourth argument of *MeetAndExchange* is a copy of the third argument of its complementary predicate. This predicate never fails.

The unification of the exchanged terms is locally performed in each process by executing the *Compute* instruction.

It should be noted that a ΔP implementation requires no modification to the unification mechanisms of a Prolog abstract machine.

On success, both processes proceed after the respective event goals. On failure, the distributed backtracking mechanism is triggered.

4.2.3 Support for choice goals A DAM instruction, called *Choice*, supports the semantics of choice goals.

4.2.4 Support for distributed backtracking The backtracking mechanism of the WAM was extended in order to support distributed backtracking. The extensions to the WAM support segments and their interdependencies as well as internal primitives for the management of the execution stacks corresponding to the multiple contexts. The WAM execution model was also extended in order to incorporate a built-in interrupt handling mechanism that is used for the implementation of distributed backtracking.

4.3 System layer

This layer was designed in order to provide adequate system mechanisms to allow experimentation with concurrency and parallelism in a logic programming framework, namely the support of ΔP. Versions of this layer were implemented on distinct operating systems environments :

- in one processor, under UNIX, using SystemV mechanisms;
- in a network of UNIX machines using BSD sockets;
- in a Transputer-based multicomputer, using a kernel designed at our department [Bara90a];
- in a Meiko Computing Surface using the CSTools facilities [Meik90b].

Below we present the basic entities handled and the corresponding primitives of the system interface.

4.3.1 Executors At this level, an executor provides support for the execution of a DAM instance. In our implementation on the Meiko Computing Surface, on each node of the transputer network we launch a fixed number of instances of a specialized ΔP

executor. The operation *creatP* grabs one of the free executors and sends it (using the communication facilities) the clauses of the program and the initial goal. The operation *killP* returns the process to the pool of free executors.

4.3.2 Virtual channels Sending goals to a newly spawned process, getting back the corresponding results or a failure indication, as well as the exchange of terms in an event, all use a system mechanism, called *virtual channels*, for the passing of messages (Prolog terms) between executors. The basic operations allow the creation and deletion of channels, and the sending and receiving of Prolog terms through existing channels. Each channel is mapped to a CSTool port.

4.3.3 Support of distributed backtracking Operations on segments belonging to a certain process require low-level control of the DAM execution stacks, so that one may identify a frame in the execution stack corresponding to the activation of a given goal, and then perform the restart, cancel, suspend and redo operations, as described in 3.5.4.

Operations on segments belonging to other processes, distinct from the one where failure of a segment occurred, require the interruption of a DAM executor.

The system interface provides a mechanism for the sending of signals to DAM executors [Cunh87a]. It is possible to define an interrupt handler written in Prolog, used for the processing of the control messages originated by the distributed backtracking algorithm. The interrupt handler in each DAM executor receives a Prolog term from a channel, containing information on the interrupt cause and associated information. In our Transputer-based implementation under CSTools, there is a pre-defined CSTool port associated with each process, used to receive the interrupt messages.

5 CONCLUSIONS AND FUTURE WORK

Parallelism, communication and non-determinism are supported by ΔP.

The language has well defined declarative, denotational and operational semantics which are partly based on Distributed Logic, and these semantic models are proven equivalent. When ΔP goals are not used in a program, its semantics are exactly the same as pure Prolog's. A refutational semantics exists for the language, extending HCL with the resolution rules for ΔP goals, and satisfying the properties of completeness and correctness ([Mont83a], [Mont86a]). The corresponding resolution procedure exhibits several forms of non-determinism, namely at the atom selection and at clause selection levels, and at the event resolution level, which allow the definition of alternative computation and search strategies.

The event-based communication model is suitable for distributed implementations of the language, the exchange of terms in an event being supported by message-passing at the system level. Communicating sequential Prolog processes, in a CSP-like style [Hoar85a], are automatically supported by the language model, allowing the programming of distributed applications consisting of multiple Prolog agents. Efficient implementations on dedicated architectures (e.g. Transputer-based) have been achieved when the application does not require the power of distributed backtracking.

The computation strategies that have been devised for the language extend the backtrack-based search of Prolog sequential systems in order to support the additional ΔP goals and their parallel execution. Distributed backtracking is a built-in mechanism that supports the coordinated (forward and backward) execution of multiple concurrent ΔP processes in their joint search for the solutions to a given problem. The cooperating ΔP processes must achieve agreement on the (possibly intermediate) results of their local computations, by exchanging unifiable terms at communication points (events). If they do not reach this agreement, or if one of them locally backtracks to a previous communication point, a strategy has been devised where alternative local computations are tried, aiming to provide a solution to a top goal (i.e. the original problem to be solved). Experimentation with this novel strategy for distributed backtracking finds its motivation in Distributed Artificial Intelligence applications where a coordination is required for systems of cooperating problem solvers (each written in Prolog style). The main difficulty regards the complexity of the computations that may be defined by each program and top goal. One important topic of research is the improvement of the search strategy by the definition and use of more selective distributed backtracking algorithms, following the approach proposed in [Bruy84a]. We have experimented with distributed backtracking for simple programs, and we feel that in order to make feasible the programming of large realistic applications, further research must be pursued towards refining the language model, particularly the inclusion of modules.

Efforts at the implementation level on Transputers are currently addressing the design and implementation of the system layer, aiming at the support of flexible and efficient mechanisms, suitable for further experimentation with the language extensions.

ACKNOWLEDGMENTS

This work has been supported by the Instituto Nacional de Investigação Científica (INIC), the Artificial Intelligence Centre of UNINOVA and the ESPRIT Parallel Computing Action Project 4136. Special thanks are due to Peter Kacsuk and Michael Wise for their comments and sugestions for improving this document.

16 CS-Prolog: A Communicating Sequential Prolog

Sz. Ferenczi and I. Futó

MULTILOGIC Computing Ltd, Budapest, Hungary

ABSTRACT

A distributed version of Prolog, called CS-Prolog, is described. CS-Prolog programs are given both procedural and declarative meanings. A unique feature of CS-Prolog among distributed Prolog languages is that it ensures an exhaustive search for all solutions in case of distributed Prolog programs as well. This is achieved through search tree partitioning and subtree unifying or, from the procedural side, through AND-parallelism and distributed backtracking. By the explicit language tools of CS-Prolog both don't know and don't care nondeterminism of logic programs can be expressed. Beside being a true distributed Prolog language, CS-Prolog provides tools for distributed programming and high level intelligent simulation tasks too. The language tools of CS-Prolog and their justification are detailed. A short overview of the implementation details of the language is also shown in the text.

1. INTRODUCTION

This chapter demonstrates how Prolog, i.e. conventional Prolog, can be modified to get **distributed Prolog** and even preserve the declarative logic feature of the language. The solution combines the most useful results of logic programming and concurrent programming, so that coarse grain parallelism of logic programs can be achieved. It is also shown that explicit message communication of logic programs can be given a declarative reading too.

An extension of Prolog, called Communicating Sequential Prolog (CS-Prolog for short), is described. The aim of CS-Prolog is to provide a Prolog system in distributed multiprocessor environments. CS-Prolog supports both intelligent simulation and explicit parallelism in logic programs, being an unrestricted Prolog with an extended set of built-in predicates to support parallel execution and communication. A distinguishing feature of CS-Prolog among parallel Prologs is that, similarly to sequential Prolog, it fully supports **exhaustive search** through the logical state space. It is achieved by a kind of restricted AND-parallel execution and by distributed backtracking. CS-Prolog, the successor of T-Prolog [Futo84a], is already published elsewhere in literature, described by procedural terms [Futo89a] [Kacs90b], but the first time is it given a declarative interpretation as well. Throughout this chapter, the language will be described from both procedural and nonprocedural aspects, although, CS–Prolog has actually built-in predicates for the procedural interpretation only.

From the declarative point of view, CS–Prolog explicitly *permits* parallelism by declaring certain goals to be *hypotheses* in the course of the proof procedure. It means that the goals annotated to be hypotheses can be accepted true without proof and be proved by an independent proof procedure, hence remaining in the area of declarative logic programming while permitting simultaneous proof processes. The relative speed of the proof processes of hypotheses is only partially determined by the language. The only restriction is that the proof process of a hypothesis must succeed before the initial goal statement is accepted true. However, if a hypothesis cannot be proved true, all the consequences drawn upon that particular hypothesis must be rejected. In procedural terms, the computation of the whole system must be rolled back to the point where the false hypothesis was set, to keep the whole system consistent.

Communication in CS–Prolog can also be expressed in a nonprocedural way. Communication is reduced to search tree unification and further to **generalized** dynamic database handling. Message sending corresponds to asserting and message awaiting to retracting from a dynamic database. However, the dynamic database that serves for information exchange has a special role, since it stores those facts that could be deduced from the facts and rules of the program; and hence called *the database of theorems*. The term 'theorem' is chosen to emphasize that partial results can be deduced during the proof and these partial results logically follow from the static facts and rules of the program, therefore, they can also be added to the set of facts and used in other related proof processes as true facts. However, in CS–Prolog theorems can be redrawn, i.e. removed from the set of true facts, but in this case all the proof processes that have ever applied the particular theorem are forced to backtrack as if the theorem had never been available.

As opposed to languages executing Prolog programs by implicit parallelism (e.g. Aurora [Lusk88a]), CS–Prolog has explicit language tools for describing separate threads of proof procedures and arranging their interactions: parallelism and communication. In contrast to other concurrent or distributed Prologs which use stream communication (e.g. Concurrent Prolog (CP) [Shap86a], Guarded Horn Clauses (GHC) [Ueda86c], Parlog [Clar86a] and Strand [Fost90b]), communication among Prolog processes (Prolog objects), in CS–Prolog, is based on **generalized** database-manipulating built-in predicates of Prolog; and no communication by logical variables exists among the simultaneously executed program parts. It is similar to the message communication of other distributed Prologs (e.g. Delta Prolog [Pere86a] and Amoeba–Prolog [Shu290a]). Furthermore, CS–Prolog applies the concept of Guarded Commands to handle nondeterminism that arises from interactions among the resolution processes of different hypotheses.

2. CONCEPTS OF CS–PROLOG

On a conceptual level, the CS–Prolog system can be considered as a set of Prolog Inference Machines (PIMs) working **simultaneously** and **communicating** by messages. The activity of a PIM results in a single *process*. In a CS–Prolog system, the number of PIMs changes dynamically during execution. PIMs can do **backtracking** as it is usual in Prolog. However, backtracking may be influenced by messages the PIMs have accepted and emitted; communication is backtrackable in CS–Prolog. **Deadlock** may occur among CS–Prolog processes, however, it presents no problem in a Prolog environment because, after it is detected, it also activates backtracking. To solve deadlock problems and to control backtracking a distributed backtracking algorithm is introduced (Section 6.4).

The component PIMs communicate by messages. Messages form a message space that can be mapped into the dynamic database of Prolog. The entire database used for communication among PIMs is partitioned. A *partition* consists of facts having the same functor. Each partition must be associated with one of the PIMs that result in Prolog objects. Since Prolog is very much bound to sequential control, i.e. Left to Right Deep First (LRDF) control strategy, it must be given up at certain points (guarded alternatives) to let real parallelism work, as will be described later in this chapter.

In addition to the above mentioned features, the component processes of a CS–Prolog program can use the full power of Prolog. They can assert and retract clauses or maintain values in their own scopes and can use cuts to control execution; everything a Prolog program can do. Note, however, that a local database asserted by one of the PIMs is not accessible to any of the others. Neither can they communicate by global values.

2.1 CS–Prolog processes

CS–Prolog processes can be understood both procedurally and declaratively as follows from the logical (Prolog) nature. In Section 2.1(1) processes will be described by procedural terminology, while in Section 2.1(2) they are described from nonprocedural aspect.

1. *Prolog processes – a procedural view*:   The basic concept of CS–Prolog is *the process*. A process is defined by the clauses of the CS–Prolog program, a goal and the resolution rules. Using CS–Prolog, it is possible to solve several subgoals simultaneously with other goals. The solutions for these goals are ensured conceptually by separate PIMs realizing *parallel processes* while resolving the initial goals; just like separate Prolog programs.

Processes in CS–Prolog can be created by special metacalls. The built-in metapredicate **new(G,P,N)** or **new_unb(G,P,N)** create a process named P with initial goal G on processor N. Goal G cannot contain unbound variables. Process name P will be used in communication (see Section 2.2). Suffix _unb indicates a nonbacktrackable version. However, these metapredicates can have actually 1, 2, or 3 parameters. If the third one is missing, it means "any processor", while in case of a missing second parameter, a name is automatically generated.

A process terminates when it has resolved its initial goal G. Explicit termination is possible by executing the built-in predicate call **delete_process(P)** or **delete_process_unb(P)** by any of the processes in the system, where P is the process to be deleted. An additional built-in predicate **active_process(AP)** is available that returns in AP the name of the currently executed process, i.e. the name of the process that has issued the call. The built-in predicate **max_processor(MP)** returns in MP the number of available processors in the system. The successful termination of a CS–Prolog program requires the successful termination of all of its component processes.

The following example illustrates the creation of three processes by three metacalls to build up a producer-consumer configuration.

```
:- new(producer(10),prod,1),
   new(consumer(10),cons,2),
   new(buffer(3),buff,3).
```

The effect of this program part is similar to the following Prolog piece of program:

```
:- producer(10),
   buffer(3),
   consumer(10).
```

The difference is that the Prolog definition specifies an ordered evaluation of the goals (see LRDF), while the CS-Prolog solution lets the order be unspecified, i.e. permits parallelism. CS-Prolog processes are delayed AND-processes (cf. restricted AND-parallelism).

The AND-parallel goals cannot contain unbound variables in CS-Prolog. This is why binding conflicts do not occur, therefore, conflict resolution is not necessary. It is possible, however, to explicitly establish the consistency of the values of two different variables at two different AND-parallel processes: The values must be communicated by explicit message exchange. It resembles to a *distributed binding* where the value for a variable binding is derived at one process and is bound at another one. The sending of a value and an accepting of the same value yields a **single binding action**.[1]

2. *Hypotheses – Parallelism is permitted in Prolog:* The process concept of CS-Prolog, being a kind of Prolog, can be interpreted from a nonprocedural aspect too. To distinguish between procedural and nonprocedural usage, the terminology and the metapredicates are renamed. The new(G,P) metapredicate is renamed to assume(H,T) where H is called a *hypothetically true goal* or *hypothesis* and T refers to the functor of the *theorems* that are applicable during the proof of H; to have a logic-like flavour.[2] However, assume(H,T) can also be considered to be an annotation mark. An annotated goal (H) can be assumed to be true and might be proved independently from others using the associated theorems (T).

In Prolog, the PIM cannot continue as long as the current subgoal is not proved. In case of CS-Prolog, however, certain subgoals can be assumed to be true without proof and hence the PIM can immediately continue. *These special subgoals are called hypotheses.* Before CS-Prolog answers the initial goal, all the bypassed hypotheses must be proved as well. All the static clauses of the program and the specific theorems can be applied in the hypothesis proving process. A hypothesis is indicated in the clause bodies by using a special metapredicate: assume(H,T). The first argument is the subgoal to be accepted true, i.e. the working hypothesis, and the second argument, if present, associates a dynamic partition of the database from which the hypothesis can apply theorems (see later in Section 2.2(2)). The declarative reading is the following: assume(G) is true if G is true.

---

1) Just the same as with OCCAM [Inmo88d]: the parallel output of a value and the input of the same value yields a parallel or distributed assignment.
2) Note that process names of pocedural CS-Prolog are transformed into principal functors of the terms used in communication and, furthermore, the partition of these terms as dynamic facts is attached to that process.

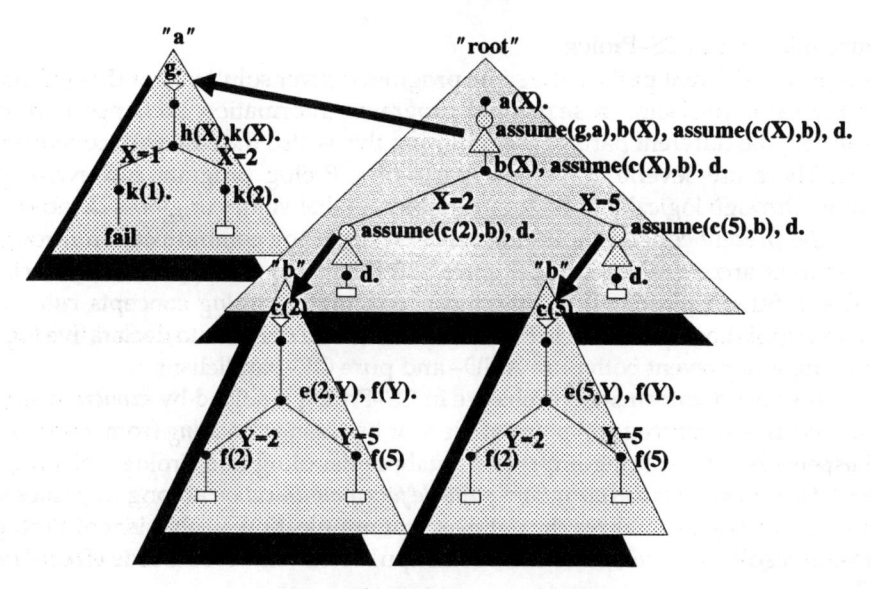

Figure 1 *A search forest.*

A hypothesis is also represented by the search space underlaying to the goal, i.e. a search tree. The search tree of a hypothesis can be constructed given the initial goal, the clauses of the database and the resolution rules. The nodes representing hypotheses, in the search tree, can be considered as a folds inserted into a tree.[3] On the other side, folds appear as individual search trees and together they build up a search forest. A sample search forest for the program below can be seen in Figure 1.

```
a(X)   :- assume(g,a), b(X), assume(c(X),b), d.
c(X)   :- e(X,Y), f(Y).
g      :- h(X), k(X).
b(2).              e(2,5).            f(2).
b(5).              e(X,X).            f(5).
h(1).              k(2).              d.
h(2).              k(3).
```

The declarative reading of the first clause is the same as that of the corresponding Prolog clause without the assume annotation: for all X, a(X) is true if **g and b(X) and c(X) and d** are true. During the proof of goal a(X), subgoals g and c(X) are accepted to be true immediately without any proof and, therefore, goal a(X) is reduced to b(X),d. Before the program terminates, however, goals g and c(X) must be proved too. The proof procedures of goals g and c(X) denote separate Prolog programs, hence processes.

Note that with the introduction of independent proof processes in the form of hypotheses the **declarative nature** of Prolog is **preserved**.

---

3) A PIM skips a fold and the skipped part can be traversed by another PIM.

2.2 Communication in CS-Prolog

In any program, different parts of the same program deliver solutions for the different parts of the same problem. In sequential programs information exchange is often needed among the different parts of the program; this is also the case with concurrent programs. There are several ways how parts of a Prolog program can exchange information: through logical (i.e. Prolog) variables, global values or global database.

Most of the present concurrent Prolog concepts are using communication through logical variables among AND-parallel goals (CP [Shap86a], GHC [Ueda86c], Parlog [Clar86a] and Strand [Fost90b]). Furthermore, concurrent Prolog concepts rule out database manipulation operations because they bring side effects into declarative logic programming and prevent both pure AND- and pure OR-parallelism.

On the other hand, information exchange in CS-Prolog is solved by *explicit message communication* from a procedural point of view or by *theorem handling* from a nonprocedural aspect. Theorems bring improved database handling into Prolog. CS-Prolog *makes the database manipulation operations suitable for communication* among hypotheses. Therefore, CS-Prolog generalizes the database communication mechanism of Prolog. As a pleasant result, however, the database manipulations will become **side effect-free** as well.[4]

1. *Message communication:* CS-Prolog processes can do everything a Prolog program can do and even more; the processes can also cooperate with each other. Processes can contain *communication points*. These are procedure calls sending messages to and awaiting from other processes.

The built-in predicates send(M,PL) and send_unb(M,PL) serve to broadcast message M to the processes on the list PL. On the other side, the built-in predicates wait_for(M), wait_for_unb(M), wait_for_dnd(M) and wait_for_dnd_unb(M) serve to accept any message that **matches** with M. The predicate wait_for/1 is a backtrackable and deterministic one. Suffix _unb indicates unbacktrackable procedure, while _dnd means nondeterministic built-in procedure. Message sending is a nonblocking operation while awaiting messages might cause a delay in the evaluation of the process that issued the call in case the message requested is not yet available. Thus, message exchange is **asynchronous** in CS-Prolog. The emitted message can be any ground term.[5] The receiver process can specify either ground terms or nonground terms to select from a number of available messages.[6] In case the receiver specifies a nonground term, the free variables will be bound during communication. A single message can be accepted by a single wait_forxx predicate.

For example, a process can send a piece of information represented by the term bag(hardware, keyboard) to processes named customer(1) and customer(4) as follows:

send(bag(hardware, keyboard), [customer(1), customer(4)])

The processes customer(X) can explicitly receive this message by issuing a built-in predicate call with a matching term to await any piece of 'hardware':

---

4) It is irrelevant when the database element becomes available. It is semantically the same if the database elements are present right from the beginning, similarly to the static clauses of Prolog, or they are asserted at any time.
5) A ground term cannot contain uninstantiated variables.
6) CS-Prolog, similarly to CSP [Hoar78a], uses pattern matching in communication. This specific feature of CSP is very seldom inherited by its ancestors.

[Figure 2: Hypotheses and Theorems. Diagram showing a logic layer with global static database (facts and rules) at the top, a control layer in the middle with local dynamic state spaces and proof processes of hypotheses (labeled "a", "b", "c"), and a logic layer at the bottom with theorems organized into partition "a", partition "b", and partition "c".]

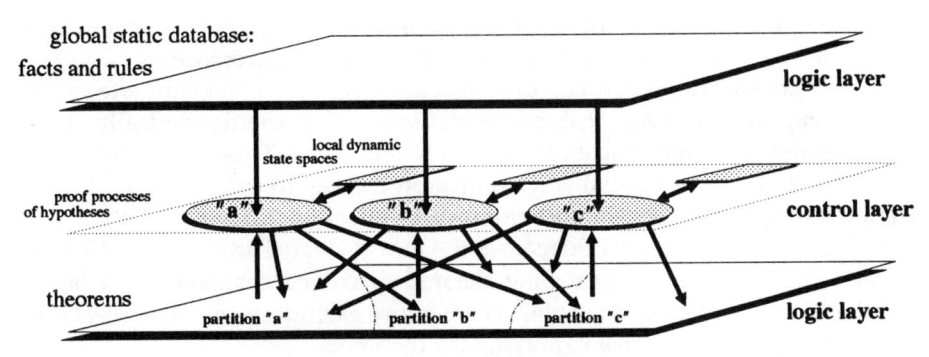

Figure 2 *Hypotheses and Theorems.*

```
wait_for( bag(hardware, Piece) )
```

or by issuing the following call to await any piece of any type:

```
wait_for( bag(Type, Piece) )
```

The second awaiting method is useful if any piece of any type is guaranteed to be acceptable though only a single message can be accepted. It will definitely accept **the first** arrived and **not redrawn**[7] matching message. Moreover, if more messages can be acceptable but the order of them is only partially determined and not known in advance (don't know nondeterminism), the **wait_for_dnd/1** is to be used. The following built-in predicate call is a nondeterministic one:

```
wait_for_dnd( bag(Type, Piece) )
```

If the message that the caller process receives during this call turns out to be unacceptable later on, the process can backtrack and pick up another matching message, if available, or wait for one to arrive.[8] If, however, **wait_forxxx** predicates have to be backtracked for any reason, the message accepted earlier is restored in the message space (except for predicates with **_unb** suffix) and is available for the same process to pick it up again at any other part of its execution.

If the **send/2** predicates have to be backtracked by the corresponding processes for any reason, the target processes having consumed the emitted messages are also **forced** to backtrack. This can only be avoided using the unbacktrackable versions of the predicates, if necessary.

2. Using theorems for information exchange in logic programs: The truth value of a hypothesis is derived both from the static Prolog database and from a specific partition of theorems which is part of the global dynamic database (Figure 2). Although the partition of theorems is built up during the evolution process of the whole system, from the hypothesis proving process aspect, it makes no difference; the theorems, i.e. the elements of the partition could have been present right from the beginning. Due to the

---

7) A message might be redrawn, in the course of the computation, if the sender backtracks through a backtrackable send operation.
8) This is illustrated in the buyer–vendor example, see later in Section 4.1

modification of the LRDF control strategy at guarded alternatives (see later in Section 2.3(2)), the order the theorems become available, makes no difference.

Some restrictions are necessarily introduced to get rid of the side effects of the database manipulations. One of these restrictions is that the dynamically changed database serving for communication consists of only facts. These are called *theorems* and must be handled in a special way: in metapredicates. In contrast to Prolog rules, unification attempt of a theorem **does not result in backtracking** if the database does not contain any matching clause but causes the PIM to **delay further evaluation** of the particular hypothesis until a matching theorem becomes available, or it becomes evident that it will never be available. This feature excludes time dependency from database manipulations, i.e. from applying the theorems.

Furthermore, the database of theorems used for communication is **partitioned**[10] and for each such partition special relations are declared that determine for which hypotheses the theorems apply to. Usually, a single hypothesis is related to a specific partition for unifying from it but any hypotheses can assert theorems to any partition (Figure 2). Partitions of theorems and their associated hypotheses form *Prolog objects* and they can be allocated to different processing elements of a distributed computer. The allocation can either be automatic or controlled by the programmer.

The message sendin primitives of procedural CS–Prolog are transformed into additional metapredicates that perform theorem access: **assert_theorem(C)**, **theorem(C)** and **retract_theorem(C)**, where C can be any term. However, in case of asserting theorems, the term cannot contain unbound variables. Beside being asserted and retracted, a theorem can simply be unified with a Prolog term if given in a **theorem/1** metacall. Since theorem handling is derived from message handling of procedural CS–Prolog, the theorem handling built-in metapredicates are similar to the message handling predicates. The **assert_theorem(C)** is derived from **send(M, PL)** so that the functor of term C is the same as an atom from the list PL[11] and the single argument of C corresponds to M. Similarly, **retract_theorem(T)** resembles **wait_for_dnd(T)** and **theorem(T)** is the same as **retract_theorem(T)**, except T is not removed from the partition of theorems, but it rather remains reusable. Note that while messages are addressed to the receiver process, theorems are asserted into the proper partition. Furthermore, the built-in predicate **attached_metapartition(P)** is a synonym for **active_process(P)**. So, the examples of the previous section look like these:

```
assert_theorem( customer1(bag(hardware,keyboard)))
assert_theorem( customer2(bag(hardware,keyboard)))
retract_theorem( bag(hardware, K) )
theorem( bag(hardware, K) )
```

Note that the terms are not the same in assertion and in retraction. This is because a partition of theorems are already attached to a hypothesis, i e a hypothesis proving process. To substitute addressing of procedural CS–Prolog the assertion must be placed into the proper partition (see **customer1/1** or **customer2/1**). Retracting or unification of theorems, however, is performed automatically from the proper partition due to a

---

9) The delay mechanism of CS–Prolog is similar to the rule of suspension of GHC. While GHC suspends execution if it cannot bind a variable, CS–Prolog suspends execution if it cannot find a matching theorem.
10) According to the functor of the facts, see Section 2.
11) Except that the elements of PL can be any Prolog term but the functor of C has to be an atom.

former association: e.g. the term given as bag(hardware,K) is transformed to customer1(bag(hardware,K)) if the former association is assume(..., customer1).

Theorem unification (theorem(Theorem)) resembles to Prolog unification (call(X)). Validating the declarative feature of **assert_theorem/1**, it needs some transforming. The **assert_theorem(Theorem)**, in principle, can be reduced to a Prolog rule that has **Theorem** as a head and all the AND-goals in the body that are necessary for the **Theorem** to be valid. Theorem assertions, therefore, correspond to Prolog rules from a nonprocedural aspect.

A communication event as a whole is built up from the **parallel** assertion and unification of a theorem, as two half-operations.[12] Thus, communication is reduced to *distributed unification*. Furthermore, asserting and retracting theorems are backtrackable operations to ensure exhaustive search and to exclude time dependency.

With the help of the dynamic database of theorems, information can be transferred in a Prolog-like style. The difference between the static Prolog database and the dynamic database of theorems is that the elements of the former are available at the beginning of the proof process, while the elements of the latter become available at indefinite points of time in the course of the proof (nondeterminism). Nevertheless, a hypothesis is proved from **both** the static database and the dynamic database of theorems (Figure 2). Special attention is given, however, to the exclusion of time dependencies from the dynamic database. This is why the evaluation of a hypothesis is delayed rather than failed in case a requested element of the dynamic database is not available. Thus, the time component of the side effect is eliminated.

2.3 Handling nondeterminism

In this section, a language tool is introduced that is not part of procedural CS-Prolog. Nevertheless, the new tool can be constructed from the lower level tools of procedural CS-Prolog (as will be shown in Section 2.3(2)).

In case of CS–Prolog, having distributed Prolog processes that bring concurrency into the scene, the language has to be modified so that at certain points the LRDF control strategy of Prolog can be changed to real nondeterministic control. The Prolog equivalent of Dijkstra's Guarded Commands construction is used as it is a well established tool both in procedural programming (see Distributed Processes [Brin78a] and Communicating Sequential Processes (CSP) [Hoar78a]) and in concurrent logic programming (see CP [Shap86a], GHC [Ueda86c], Parlog [Clar86a], Strand [Fost90b] etc.)

1. *Control mechanism for database communications:* If applying database manipulations for communication, some modifications to the usual LRDF control strategy must be made. Because there is only one single control stream during the resolution of a Prolog program, failure and then backtracking are quite reasonable for those attempts of database inquiries (i.e. unification attempts) for which there are no matches in the

---

12) As follows from the nature of Prolog database manipulating operations, communication is asynchronous in CS–Prolog.

database. The reason for this decision is that once a database element is not available, it will certainly never be available, since the database is not likely to change automatically: *'once false, always false'*.[13] But this is not true in case of multiple threads of control, i.e. concurrent processes, where the concurrent processes operate in an overlapped state space.[14] In a multiple programming environment the relative speeds of asynchronous processes are not predictable. Similarly, the **order** of their interactions (communications) is not fully determined from the program specification. Therefore, if the expected piece of data is not available, delaying the execution of the current thread is quite reasonable (see EWD554 in [Dijk82a]).

In case of processes with single control threads, it is also necessary to have language tools for accepting arbitrary interactions from a number of possible ones: a nondeterministic control structure. In Prolog, the means for expressing nondeterminism is the construction of alternative clauses. The alternative clauses of Prolog represent don't know nondeterminism, and by definition (LRDF) they are evaluated sequentially in the order written. If, however, the alternative clauses are used to control communication of asynchronous computing processes so that parts of the clause body (Guard, see later) refer to common state space where the state space changes unpredictably (concurrency), the construction must also be able to express nondeterminism (resulting from concurrency). This is contrasted to the predetermined LRDF control of Prolog. The main point is that the language tools **should not determine the order** of the communication events of a single thread of control, since they are likely to **occur in a nondeterministic order**. This can be achieved, among other tools, by a nondeterministic program construction such as the Guarded Commands of Dijkstra. This is why the alternative clauses of Prolog are merged with the Guarded Commands construction.

2. *Guarded Alternative:* Based on the tools and concepts introduced so far, a new language construction can be introduced into distributed logic programming for accepting information from a number of resources (processes): the combination of Dijkstra's Guarded Commands construction [Dijk75a] and alternative clauses of Prolog. This is called *guarded alternative clauses*. It is a general language tool so that **both don't care and don't know nondeterminism** can be expressed with it. The main difference between the guarded alternative and the Prolog alternative is in their **control strategy**. The guarded alternative means real *declarative OR–relation*, i.e. without the textual order being significant.[15]

While the operator :– denotes normal Prolog alternative, let the operator ?:– denote guarded alternatives. Bar (|) substitutes comma (,) between the guard and the body parts:

    Head ?:- Guard | Body.

13) In single program systems the control is sequential, so that the next operation cannot start until the previous one is not finished. Thus, a single program cannot solve scanning of the state space and changing it simultaneously.
14) Note that in this respect one-way channels of communicating systems like OCCAM [Inmo88d] or CSP [Hoar85a] can be regarded as common variables with special access rights: A channel is a common variable that a single process can write and another one can read.
15) Although the same is true for pure Prolog, it is not at all the case for conventional Prolog. However, it is close to guarded Horn clauses.

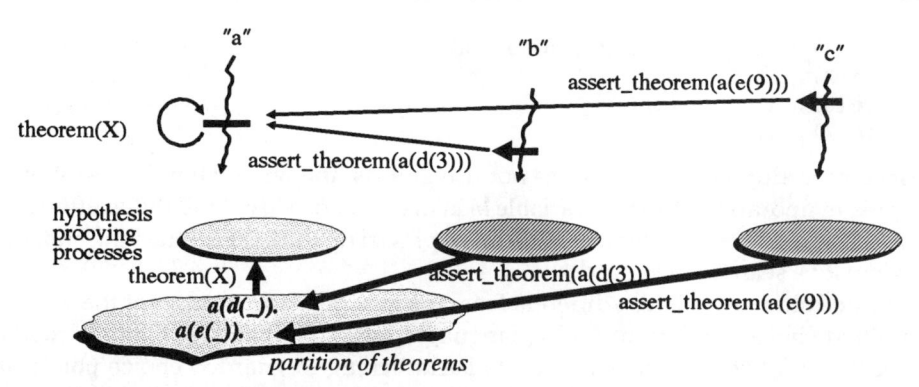

Figure 3 *Nondeterministic communication.*

Guards refer to theorems and the presence of the specified theorem is necessary for selection of the clause. When resolving a goal with guarded alternative clauses, any of the alternatives can be selected. The choice depends on the match between the goal and the head of the guarded alternative clause and on the truth value of the guard part. A guarded alternative clause is *selectable* if it has a matching head and a true guard. Any of the selectable alternatives might be chosen. Through backtracking the PIM can choose another selectable guarded alternative until an exhaustive search is achieved.[16] Another important feature is that if there is no selectable guarded alternative, the proof process of the hypothesis is delayed rather than failed. Let us take the following example:

```
a(X) ?:- theorem(d(X)) | c(X), f(X).
a(X) ?:- theorem(e(5)) | b(X).
a(X) ?:- theorem(e(X)) | noteq(X,5), g(X).
```

A process resolving goal a(G) and finding applicable guarded alternative clauses (procedure a(X)) in the database (as illustrated above), first determines the selectable clauses. There might be facts d/1 and e/1 asserted into its associated partition of theorems (Figure 3). If none of the requested facts is asserted yet, the resolution process is delayed. If, for example, the only fact e(9) is already asserted when the procedure a(X) is resolved, the third clause is selectable and will certainly be selected, since this is the only one. Finally, if both facts d(3) and e(9) are already asserted, both the first and the third clauses are selectable and one of them will be actually selected. The choice is really not determined by the rules of the language. It is up to the implementation, which alternative is chosen.[17] If the computation fails with a selected clause, another selectable one can be chosen during backtracking, since the former choice was a random one.

Using procedural CS–Prolog, the same construction can be expressed as follows:

---

16) This is different from the LRDF control strategy, where the order of the alternatives to be chosen at execution time is **determined by the program text** and consequently prohibits nondeterministic interaction.
17) Practically, however, most implementations will choose the first selectable one. Nevertheless, it completely satisfies the specification: "one of them".

```
a(X)      :- wait_for_dnd(M), a1(M, X).
a1(d(X), X) :- c(X), f(X).
a1(e(5), X) :- b(X).
a1(e(X), X) :- g(X).
```

Since procedural CS-Prolog does not use guards, the potential messages must be accepted temporarily into a free variable M in the order of arrival and tested afterwards (a1/2). If the test fails, another message can be picked up during backtracking and, thus, an exhaustive search is achieved.

Guarded alternative is also different from the guarded Horn clauses of the so-called committed choice concurrent Prolog languages (see CP [Shap86a], GHC [Ueda86c], Parlog [Clar86a] etc.) because it permits backtracking to guarded choice points and thus **realizes an exhaustive search** while achieving distributed execution. If, however, **don't care** alternatives must be specified, the guards should be formed accordingly[18] and cuts must be inserted to prohibit alternatives. By using the cut built-in predicate the alternatives of a guarded alternative can be pruned similarly to the cut and cavalier commit of Aurora Or-Parallel Prolog [Lusk88a].

3. ENSURING DISTRIBUTED COMPLETENESS

A logic program defines a set of solutions but does not specify the way how the solutions can be obtained. This is reflected by the famous equation:

Algorithm = Logic + Control

A distributed logic program, such as a CS-Prolog one, also defines a set of solutions and does not define the way how these solutions can be obtained as well. The distribution means that the truth value of certain goals cannot be obtained directly from the clauses of the program but the information for this is rather distributed **in space** as well as **in computation** dimensions (see also Section 2). These goals are the so-called theorem goals. While theorem goals are in AND-relation with the other goals of the same clause body, the resolution strategy must be changed at theorems. Instead of giving the exact resolution rules here, it is rather reduced to tree unification. It is achieved through patterns along the branches. Patterns are represented by special nodes, called half nodes. Furthermore, half nodes correspond to theorems.

The task of an abstract CS-Prolog Inference Machine (CSPIM) is to unify the matching half nodes of the individual search trees and find a successful branch on every search trees of the search forest so that all the half nodes are bound along a successful branch and the full nodes are successful too. Therefore, the CSPIM *unifies search trees by half nodes* in the search forest along their branches.

3.1 Search trees of communicating Prolog processes

A component search tree of a CS-Prolog search forest is built both from **normal Prolog nodes** and from **CS-Prolog nodes**. CS-Prolog nodes correspond to the additional built-in metapredicates. An **assume/2** metapredicate appears as a fold indicator along

---

18) See weakest precondition [Dijk75a]. The guard must be formulated so that if the guard denotes true, the associated body is guaranteed to terminate and ensures the proper postcondition.

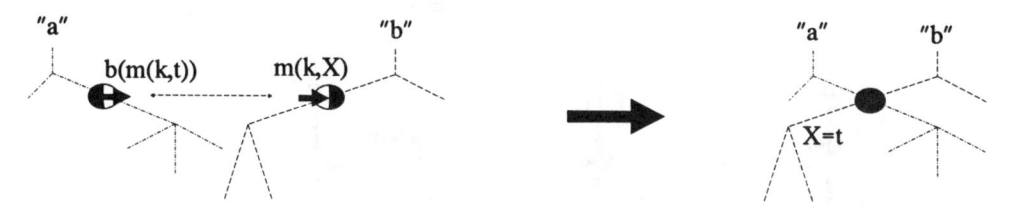

Figure 4 *Unifying half nodes.*

a search tree and points to a separate search tree that is regarded as if it was inserted as a fold into the current tree (fold node), see Figure 1. The denoted search tree wears the label corresponding to the functor of the associated theorems. Furthermore, theorem handling metapredicates are represented by *half nodes* along the branches of the trees, whereas normal Prolog predicates result in *full nodes*. A PIM resolves a full node from the static database during traversing the tree. However, half nodes can only be resolved by help of the CSPIM. A half node can be resolved if it can be unified with a corresponding other half node. (Figure 4)

There are three types of half nodes: *emitting, accepting* and *inquiring type* ones representing assert_theorem/1, retract_theorem/1 and theorem/1 respectively. A half node is marked by a Prolog term (theorem) which represents the argument of the corresponding metapredicate. An emitting type half node denotes a target search tree by the functor of its term but an accepting or an inquiring type one does not. An emitting type half node is unifyable with an accepting or an inquiring type one if the emitting type half node denotes the holding tree of the accepting or inquiring type half node by the functor of its term and the argument term of the emitting type half node matches with the term of the accepting or inquiring one. For example the emitting type half node b(m(k,t)) matches with an accepting type half node m(k,X) in the tree b. If these two half nodes are unified, however, X is bound to t.

3.2 Tree unification in the search forest

Given an initial goal and the clauses of the CS-Prolog program, a search forest is defined so that the processes of a CS-Prolog program correspond to the individual search trees. These search trees are not independent, however, since they are related through communication patterns.

A CS-Prolog program is successful if a single branch for each of the trees of the system can be found so that the following conditions are met:

- Along a successful branch all the normal Prolog nodes are successful;
- For every fold node, a successful branch can be found in the associated subtree;
- For every accepting type half node, an **exclusive** emitting type half node is found, so that it is situated along a successful branch;
- For every inquiring type half node, an emitting type half node is found, so that it is situated along a successful branch and is not bound to any accepting type half node along the same branch above.

An example tree unification is illustrated in Figure 5. The branches drawn by bold lines are matching ones. Note that every accepting and inquiring type of half nodes

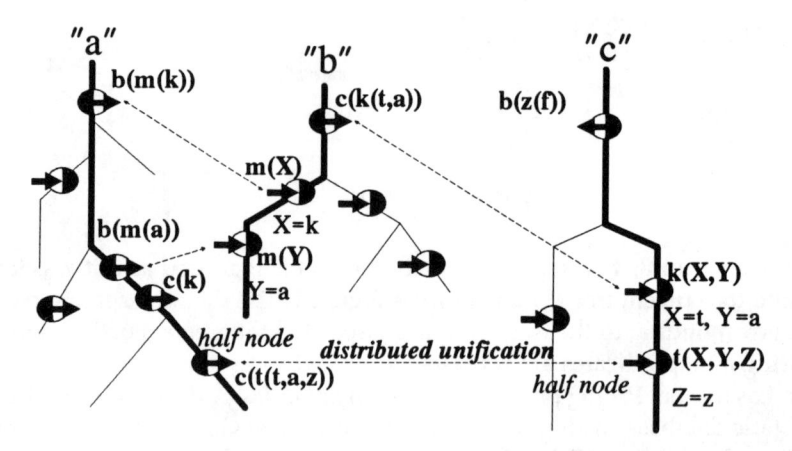

Figure 5 *Tree unification in the search forest.*

must be bound but emitting type half nodes may be left unbound along successful branches. In other words, some asserted theorems may remain unused.

4. EXAMPLES

4.1 The Buyer–Vendors problem

Consider the following example. Somebody wants to by a PC. In his note book he has information about vendors and computer prices (limits). He sends requests to all the vendors and waits for the quotations. If the quotation is under the limit, he buys the PC. The vendors are waiting for requests. Receiving a request, they look for the required PC in their stock and make a bid.

1. Solution: The solution for the buyer–vendors problem described above results in a parallel program.
A.) Using the procedural notation of CS–Prolog, the following main program can be derived where process creations are indicated by the goals called as a metacalls in **new/2** built-in metapredicates.

```
:- notebook( suppliers( Vendors ) ),
   suppliers( Vendors ),
   new( buyers_action, buyer ).
suppliers( [] ).
suppliers( [Vendor|Rest] ) :-
   new( suppliers_action( Vendor ), Vendor ),
   suppliers( Rest ).
```

B.) However, the parallel activities, i.e. the behaviors of the buyer and the vendors, can also be expressed using hypotheses. The goals representing hypotheses are declared in the first parameter of the **assume/2** built-in metapredicate and are accepted true during the proof and proved later based on the Prolog database and the associated dynamic partition.

```
:- notebook( suppliers( Vendors ) ),
   suppliers( Vendors ),
   assume( buyers_action, buyer ).
suppliers( [] ).
suppliers( [Vendor|Rest] ) :-
   assume( suppliers_action( Vendor ), Vendor ),
   suppliers( Rest ).
```

As demonstrated, the main program sets up the search forest and lets the CSPIM perform tree unification in the search forest.

2. *The definition of the buyer:* The activity of the buyer takes place simultaneously with the activities of other processes of the program. For both approaches, the following definitions apply:

```
buyers_action :-
   decision_on_buying( Computer, PriceLimit, Suppliers ),
   broadcast_messages( Computer, Suppliers, Buyer),
   accept_an_offer( PriceLimit, Price ),
   write( buyer( Buyer, chosen( Computer, Price ) ) ).
decision_on_buying( Computer, PriceLimit, Suppliers ) :-
   note_book( suppliers( Suppliers ) ),
   note_book( computer( Computer, PriceLimit ) ).
```

A.) Procedurally, this is interpreted as follows: The preparation step for buying consists of inquires in the global static database which contains information about addresses of potential vendors and determines the buyer's ideas about the computer to be purchased. Having assembled the necessary information the next step is to let each vendor know about the demand. For broadcasting messages and accepting answers, special built-in predicates are used.

```
broadcast_messages( Computer, Suppliers, Buyer) :-
   active_process( Buyer ),
   send( request( Computer, Buyer ), Suppliers ).
accept_an_offer( PriceLimit, Price ) :-
   wait_for_dnd( offer( Price ) ),
   Price <= PriceLimit.
```

As wait_for_dnd/1 is nondeterministic, the different quotations are tried by backtracking until an acceptable one (Price <= PriceLimit) is found.

B.) Declaratively speaking, the buyer is assumed to be successful, so that a hypothesis can be set that the subgoal buyers_action can be proved true from the program. Broadcasting messages correspond to putting forward theorems. Since there are several vendors to notify, the assert_theorem_comp/1 serves for repeatedly composing the proper term for the assert_theorem/1 built-in metapredicate and performing remote assertions of theorems for supporting other hypotheses. The built-in predicate attached_meta_partition/1 is used here to obtain the functor of the associated partition of theorems into a free variable.

```
broadcast_messages( Computer, Vendors, Buyer ) :-
   attached_meta_partition( Buyer ),
   broadcast_messages1( Computer, Vendors, Buyer ).
broadcast_messages1( _, [], _ ).
broadcast_messages1( Computer, [Vendor|Rest], Buyer ) :-
```

```
assert_theorem_comp( [Vendor, request( Computer, Buyer)] ),
broadcast_messages1( Computer, Rest, Buyer ).
```

A further clause only makes the asserting of theorems easier.

```
assert_theorem_comp( [Functor, Arg] ) :-
   MetaPart =.. [Functor, Arg],
   assert_theorem( MetaPart ).
```

While other processes are being executed, the one acting on behalf of the buyer attempts to unify a term with a theorem. The process is held up until a remote process asserts a matching theorem into its associated partition. If the binding made by theorem unification causes a failure, new theorems can be unified until a proper binding is made.

```
accept_an_offer( PriceLimit, Price ) ?:-
   theorem( offer( Price ) )  |  Price <= PriceLimit, !.
```

3. *The definition of the vendor:* The activity of the vendor takes place simultaneously with the activities of other processes of the program.

A.) The procedural definition of the vendor is as follows:

```
suppliers_action( Supplier ) :-
   wait_for( request( Computer, Buyer ) ),
   stock( Supplier, Computer, Price ),
   send( offer( Price ), [Buyer] ).
```

B.) The hypothesis **suppliers_action** is proved from the following definition. Note that, at the subgoals where theorems are used, the proof process of the hypothesis might be delayed.

```
suppliers_action( Supplier ) ?:-
   theorem( request( Computer, Buyer ) )  |
   stock( Supplier, Computer, Price ),
   assert_theorem_comp( [Buyer, offer( Price ) ] ).
```

4. *Miscellaneous definitions for both approaches:* The remaining definitions, the **note-book/1** and **stock/3** partitions, are common to both the procedural and the nonprocedural notation, since they are normal Prolog clauses.

```
note_book( suppliers([megatronic, monotronic, multitronic])).
note_book( computer( ibm_original, 10000 ) ).
note_book( computer( ibm_compatible, 5000 ) ).
note_book( computer( sun_workstation, 12000 ) ).

stock( megatronic, ibm_original, 12000 ).
stock( megatronic, ibm_compatible, 6000 ).
stock( megatronic, sun_workstation, 14000 ).
stock( megatronic, dec_workstation, 10000 ).
stock( monotronic, ibm_original, 11000 ).
stock( monotronic, ibm_compatible, 5000 ).
stock( monotronic, dec_workstation, 12000 ).
stock( multitronic, ibm_original, 11000 ).
stock( multitronic, ibm_compatible, 6000 ).
stock( multitronic, dec_workstation, 12000 ).
```

4.2 Bounded Buffer

Let us see how a bounded buffer can be defined (using difference lists to realize a First In First Out – FIFO – buffer). A bounded buffer is useful for smoothing the variations in the speed of producers and consumers of a concurrent program. One of the main tasks of a bounded buffer is to keep up a producer in case the buffer is full and keep up a consumer if the buffer is empty.

An empty buffer with a bound of ten is initiated in procedural CS–Prolog by the metacall:

```
..., new( buffer( B-B, 10 ), buff ), ...
```

and the same is achieved in declarative CS–Prolog with the assumption that the goal **buffer(B–B, 10)** can be proved true (i.e. a hypothesis):

```
..., assume( buffer( B-B, 10 ), buff ), ...
```

A.) The definition of the buffer, in procedural CS–Prolog, looks like this:

```
buffer( B, Max ) :-
   wait_for_dnd( M ),
   accept( M, B, B1, Max ),
   buffer( B1, Max ).
accept( put( Msg, Sender ), B-[Msg|B1], B-B1, Limit ) :-
   list_length( B, Len ),
   Len < Limit, !,
   send( ack, [Sender] ).
accept( get( Sender ), [Msg|B]-B1, B-B1, _ ) :- !,
   send( ack( Msg ), [Sender] ).
```

B.) Although a bounded buffer is not a logical phenomenon, using the declarative notation it might be expressed like this:

```
buffer( B-[Msg|B1], Max ) ?:-
   list_length( B, Len ),
   Len < Max,
   retract_theorem( put( Msg, Sender ) ) |
   !, assert_theorem_comp( [Sender, ack] )
   buffer( B-B1, Max ).
buffer( [Msg|B]-B1, Max ) ?:-
   retract_theorem( get( Sender ) ) |
   !, assert_theorem_comp( [Sender, ack( Msg )] )
   buffer( B-B1, Max ).
```

A producer can use the buffer by **put/1** and a consumer by **get/1** predicates, where these predicates are implemented as follows (only the nonprocedural version is given here and the procedural one is left to the reader):

```
put (Msg ) :-
   attached_meta_partition( Sender ),
   assert_theorem( buff( put( Msg, Sender ) ) ),
   retract_theorem( ack ).
get( Msg ) :-
   attached_meta_partition( Sender ),
   assert_theorem( buff( get( Sender ) ) ),
   retract_theorem( ack( Msg ) ).
```

5. SYSTEM SIMULATION IN CS–PROLOG

In CS–Prolog it is possible to make discrete and continuous system simulation. As the basic system is running in a distributed multiprocessor environment (Transputer networks) the implementation supports distributed discrete simulation.

In case of **distributed simulation** two scheduling algorithms can be used; **optimistic** (Time Warp [Jeff85a]) or **conservative** [Chan81a]. In CS–Prolog both algorithms are implemented, however, only the optimistic approach will be explained here (see also in [Futo90a]).

To support system simulation, the notion of *simulated time* is introduced. Real life processes have time durations. If such processes are to be modelled, durations have to be assigned to the activities of a process and they have to be synchronized in time. In discrete event simulation, time changes at discrete moments. Time durations are assigned to activities expressed in a given time unit (sec, hour, day etc). The simulation software should have a clock which measures the "age" of the processes. The duration can be measured by a global clock or by local clocks belonging to the processes. The global time shows the common system time while a local clock shows the private time of a process. In case of monoprocessor simulation systems, these two clocks are the same.

The most widely used scheduling algorithm in the monoprocessor world is the so-called Next Event algorithm. Its multiprocessor equivalent is the so-called **Time Warp** algorithm. Time Warp can be briefly explained as follows. Each process has a local clock. These local clocks can show different times. As long as no communication occurs among the processes, there is no need for the synchronization of these local clocks.

When messages are exchanged the clocks are to be synchronized (send time <= receive time). To make synchronization possible, messages carry their send time expressed in the local time of the sender process and the receive time of the message expressed in the local time of the receiver process. When receiving a message a process can be in one of the following two states:

(i) its local time is less or equal to the receive time of the message,

(ii) its local time is more than the receive time of the message.

In the first case at the moment of the message receipt, the local clock of the receiver process is set to the receive time of the message and the synchronization of the clocks is achieved. The receiver can continue its activities.

In the second case the situation is different. As the local time of the receiver process is more than the receive time of the message, when the local time of the receiver was equal to the receive time of the message the message was not physically available for the receiver and the receiver could not take into account the content of the message in the course of its following activities. Time Warp says that in this case the receiver should return (roll-back) to before the prescribed receive time in its local time, and then continue its activities taking the message into account. CS–Prolog has a modified Time Warp algorithm to permit distributed discrete event simulation.

Additional built-in predicates serve simulation purposes. In a monoprocessor implementation the built-in predicate hold(T) suspends a process for T simulated global time unit. Similarly, in the Time Warp model the built-in predicate advance(T) is available to set the local time of a process to current time + T

Special versions of the process creating built-in metapredicates are extended with the possibility to define the time limits in simulated time. The built-in metapredicates new(G,P,ST,ET,N) and new_unb(G,P,ST,ET,N) both start a new CS–Prolog process as described in Section 2.1(1) and set the starting simulation time of the processes to ST. If the evaluation of the processes are not finished until their simulation time reaches ET, local failure and backtracking is generated in order to find a new solution and, therefore, to fit into the simulation time limits.

For a more detailed description, please consult the book 'AI in Simulation' [Futo90b].

6. IMPLEMENTATION ISSUES

CS–Prolog is implemented on distributed multiprocessor systems, i.e. on Transputer networks. Although the architecture of CS–Prolog highly suits for distributed systems, some implementation issues are still remained to discuss. One of these is how tree unification is achieved in distributed environment (see Distributed Control Mechanism), and another one is how the functions and properties are distributed throughout the system.

6.1 Function distribution

A distributed system consists of Processing Elements (PEs). The static clauses of the entire CS–Prolog program are replicated at each PE in the system.[19] A PIM, a hypothesis and a partition of theorems form a Prolog object and is statically allocated to a PE. Administration information such as the content of Process Allocationn Table is also replicated at each PE.

6.2 Distributed Control Mechanism[20]

The control component of CS–Prolog is defined by a distributed control mechanism. In a CS–Prolog program, many PIMs work simultaneously. The component PIMs are exploring the individual search trees of the search forest. Each PIM can conclude failure and perform backtracking in scope of its associated component search tree. Arranging the harmonious cooperation of the component PIMs is the task of the CS–Prolog Inference Machine (CSPIM). Similarly to PIMs which explore individual search trees, the CSPIM explores the search forest by *unifying search trees* along communication patterns of the branches. A communication pattern is given by both the assertion and the successful unification of a theorem.

Deadlock may occur in the scope of the search forest too. Distributed deadlock detection and control of systematic backtracking is also the job of the CSPIM. A distributed deadlock situation is detected when not all the component PIMs have finished the proof process but these are delaying their activities at communication nodes. This deadlock situation is similar to the failure of Prolog executions which is indicated by fail leaves in the search tree; this is indicated by deadlock. The reaction of

---

19) The language rules of CS–Prolog make it hopeless to distribute the clauses unless some heuristic solutions are adapted. As soon as the language becomes modular, the distribution of the program clauses will be possible.
20) It is already described for message communication in [Kacs90b] and, therefore, only theorems are used here.

the PIM of a conventional Prolog at such a situation is the start of backtracking, i.e. undoing the previous bindings until a new alternative is found. So is it with CSPIM in case of a distributed deadlock: it starts to backtrack one of the PIMs to unbind half nodes until a new alternative in tree binding can be found by any PIM.

6.3 Forward execution

Since the proof process for a hypothesis is like a Prolog program, a PIM resolves the hypothesis based on the Prolog database and the associated theorems. During forward execution, a PIM asserts theorems at the proper PE according to a copy of the so-called Process Allocation Table (PAT). New Prolog objects are created and allocated to the proper PE at hypothesis nodes. The location of the new object is broadcasted and administered into the PATs. At theorem unification attempts, a PIM may delay its work until at least one matching theorem is asserted. If more than one matching theorems are available, the first arrived one is selected.

6.4 Distributed Backtracking

A PIM can start backtracking if it arrives at a fail leaf in the search tree, as usual in Prolog programs. This is called *failure backtracking*. In CS–Prolog programs, there is another source of backtracking: a deadlock situation. It involves *deadlock backtracking*.

1. Failure backtracking: It is always started locally to a specific PIM, however, any PIMs can do failure backtracking **simultaneously**. During failure backtracking all the asserted theorems and hypotheses should be redrawn. This means that the PIMs having accepted theorems and proceeded based on this theorem is forced to backtrack to the consumption point (i.e. rolled-back). Similarly, the created Prolog objects are forced to backtrack and then removed. Failure backtracking is finished when the backtracking PIM reaches the first previous theorem unification. Here, the backtracking is delayed and either it turns into forward execution or into deadlock backtracking depending on the further behaviour of the environment.

The reason is again time dependency and completeness. To meet the rules of tree unification, theorem unification should scan not only the available theorems at a given stage of the execution but all the theorems which can ever be asserted. More theorems are either asserted in forward execution or deadlock backtracking forces the system to find new alternatives.

2. Deadlock backtracking: A deadlock situation is detected if each PIM is either succeeded or being delayed at theorem unification. It activates backtracking to let the PIMs search for new alternative tree bindings.

Distributed backtracking is **sequential**; there is always a single PIM doing backtracking. With respect to distributed backtracking, PIMs are set in some order. The last PIM starts backtracking and the other PIMs are waiting for explicit activation. If a PIM arrives at a previous theorem or hypothesis assertion, during deadlock backtracking, it suspends backtracking and the previously activated PIM has to carry on backtracking until it passes this duty on to other PIMs or back to the activator. However, if any PIM finds an alternative way and can proceed forward, deadlock backtracking is finished. If no PIM is left to activate and the first PIM has already undone everything, the CS–Prolog system is failed.

6.5 Coding issues

Each PE realizes an Extended Prolog Machine (EPM).[21] An EPM can evaluate one or more CS–Prolog processes, hence, an EPM implements one or more PIMs. EPMs communicate with each other by implementation messages to manage CS–Prolog process. EPMs form a many-to-many network. They are implemented in C, i.e. Parallel C on Transputers. The program of a PE consists of several layers to make it modular and manageable.

Communication Subsystem Layer (CSL), the lowest layer of the program, builds a general network from the Transputer elements having only four next neighbours. CSL provides a simple packet transfer mechanism from any EPM to any EPM. The size of the packettes are limited to 250 bytes.

Communication Control Layer (CCL) extends the facilities of CSL based on its basic services. CCL provides transfer of messages of unlimited size, broadcasting messages and distributed deadlock detection.

Prolog Control Layer (PCL) manages the handling and administration of PIM messages. It maintains a Process Allocation Table which helps to find the destination EPM of emitted PIM messages.

Prolog Interpreter Layer (PIL) contains an efficient Prolog machine extended with communication facilities to meet the requirements of CS–Prolog.

7. ASSESSMENT OF CS–PROLOG

Compared to the AND– and OR–parallelisms of other parallel Prologs, the specification of concurrency in CS–Prolog is as unstructured forking. However, the introduction of structured concurrency is necessary and will be the feature of a modular distributed Prolog model which is under investigation (Fere91a). While the concepts described here correspond to the concepts of the early CSP [Hoar78a], the modular distributed Prolog model is going to make use of the concepts of the advanced CSP [Hoar85a].

The reduction of communication to the well-known database manipulating makes it quite familiar to Prolog programmers and at the same time the database handling is given a more declarative and more logical meaning. As a consequence, if database handling is accepted to be necessary for real Prolog programs, it follows that CS–Prolog should be accepted a distributed version of real Prolog as well. The adaptation of the Guarded Commands construction [Dijk75a] merged with the Prolog alternative seems to be an attractive solution because applying it, both don't care and don't know nondeterminism can be defined in Prolog programs with the help of the same language tool.[22] It further means returning to the original declarative meaning of the alternative clauses of logic programs rather than connecting it with a sequential evaluation strategy like the depth first search strategy of Prolog. Still, the language is expected to be easy for Prolog programmers to learn.

---

21) Note that these Extended Prolog Machines are not the same as PIMs mentioned earlier.
22) P–Prolog achieves the same [Yang86a] but not with a single language construction. Rather, it can use different language constructions for don't care and don't know nondeterminism in a mixed way throughout the same program.

The declarative side of logic programs is **preserved**. The assertion of a hypothesis corresponds to AND-relation of the goals. The assertion of a theorem is a **logical consequence** of the Prolog facts and rules. Time dependency is excluded from theorem unification by the evaluation rules of the language, hence the **timeless** world of logic is preserved.

The practical application programs should be built in a way not to use distributed backtracking heavily because it rather reduces efficiency of the execution. Nevertheless, it is available in cases when efficiency is less important than completeness. Moreover, the unbacktrackable versions of the built-in predicates are available for practical applications to make efficient programs, while the backtrackable ones are remained for pure CS-Prolog ensuring completeness of distributed logic programs.

The private dynamic databases and sets of global values of the hypotheses are not directly accessible to the others. Hence, information hiding, a very important requirement of concurrent systems, is available.

The concepts described here are already implemented in a number of sequential machines and in Transputer networks [Kacs90b]. CS-Prolog can be used in applications which can be partitioned into coarse grained parallel processes, where the processes can be realized by large pieces of Prolog programs. With the help of CS-Prolog, existing Prolog applications can easily be transformed and executed on distributed parallel machines.

ACKNOWLEDGEMENTS

We would like to thank Péter Kacsuk for his contribution to the design and our presentation of declarative CS-Prolog. We are grateful to Michael J Wise for his valuable suggestions and criticisms to the various parts of the draft and to György Totisz for the careful proofreadings.

17 PMS-Prolog: A Distributed, Coarse-grain-parallel Prolog with Processes, Modules and Streams

M. J. Wise[†], D. G. Jones[†] and T. Hintz[‡]

[†] *University of Sydney, Australia*
[‡] *University of Technology, Sydney, Australia*

ABSTRACT

The aim of the PMS-Prolog project[1] is the implementation of Prolog on a message-passing multiprocessor. The model is based on the definition of *Prolog processes*, which form the smallest unit for parallel execution.

It is the principal thesis of the new system that the level of granularity used by many multiprocessor implementations of Prolog is too fine, with the result that gains achieved through increased parallel computation are largely offset by communications overheads. This is particularly a problem for distributed architectures. The new system therefore aims to ignore the vast amount of low-level, fine-grain parallelism apparent in many Prolog programs, and concentrate instead on the coarser-grained, algorithmic parallelism that may be available higher up in a program's proof-tree.

The definition of the new model begins with the addition of modules into standard Prolog [Wise89a]. A Prolog process is then defined as a special Prolog module, which can execute "indefinitely" through the use of tail-recursion, and which communicates with other processes using streams (messages). The model is therefore "loosely coupled" in the communication sense, but "tightly coupled" in a problem solving sense. Processes are explicitly forked.

Based on a *strong concept of process*, the new model avoids many of the pitfalls associated with the earlier research because its parallelism is much coarser grained. This means that communicated values will generally have a much higher information content – being the result of larger computations – and unnecessary communication will be avoided. Finally, apart from aspects related to the definition of the processes and their communication, the operation of the new model remains close to that of standard Prolog. The target architecture for the new model is one based on the INMOS Transputer.

---

1. The project is supported by grants from the Australian Research Council and the University of Technology, Sydney, and the University of Sydney.

1. INTRODUCTION AND DESIDERATA

Over the last several years, since about 1980, there have been a number of proposals for implementing logic programming languages on multiprocessor architectures. Some of the earlier ones are reviewed in [Wise86b]. Of the proposals, a number have been simulated on uniprocessors, while a few have been implemented on multiprocessors, e.g. the systems of Disz et al. [Disz87a], Ichiyoshi et al. [Ichi87a], Lusk et al. [Lusk88a] and Taylor et al [Tayl86a]. From the latter list, the second and the fourth have been implemented on non-shared-memory architectures.

The field appears to have split into two main camps which one can loosely label as "Committed Choice And-Parallel" and "Or-Parallel/Restricted And-Parallel". The Committed Choice group contains, among others, Parlog [Greg87a], Concurrent Prolog [Shap87a] and Flat Concurrent Prolog [Tayl86a] and GHC (Guarded Horn Clauses) [Ueda86c] and Flat GHC [Ichi87a], while among the Or-Parallel/Restricted And-Parallel implementations one can include those of Hermenegildo [Herm86a] and Disz et al. [Disz87a], and the Aurora [Lusk88a] and Andorra [Hari90a] projects. PEPSYS [West87a], the Reduce-Or model [Kale87a] and the author's own EPILOG [Wise86b] attempt to find ways of integrating both And- and Or-Parallel models of computation. While some impressive results have been returned for shared-memory implementations, this paper will focus on a technique, quite different from those represented in the above list, that is well suited to non-shared-memory architectures.

Motivating this new focus is the notion that non-shared-memory architectures present an interesting alternative to the more common shared-memory architectures and hence are worthy of study in their own right. However, there is also some evidence that Prolog in general, and concurrent implementations of Prolog in particular, may ultimately not be well suited to shared-memory architectures. This evidence is provided by [Tick88a] and [Goto89a]. (Other indirect evidence may be found in [Egge89a].)

In [Tick88a] Tick reports the results from various experiments measuring memory reference patterns of some typical Prolog programs. While he comments that Prolog programs exhibit a greater locality of data reference than was anticipated at the time WAM was devised, when compared to the memory reference patterns of Pascal Tick states, "These results indicate that the Pascal working set is smaller and locality is higher. The Prolog storage model is more complex than the Pascal storage model, entailing a heap, stack, and trail. In addition, the heap and stack can grow large ... Even with garbage collection, the Prolog storage areas will grow erratically, still giving a larger working set than Pascal." This would imply that, if there is some inherent limit to the number of processors one can add to cache-coherence architectures when running programs written in conventional languages such as Pascal or C, the limit would be lower when running Prolog because less locality of reference implies more cache-misses, and hence greater bus contention. (Software techniques aimed at increasing locality would tend to ameliorate the above situation, but not remedy it.)

In [Goto89a], an analysis similar to [Tick88a] is carried out for a shared memory architecture (ICOT's PIM) running KL1, a language based on flat GHC. The conclusions there indicate a memory reference pattern approaching that of Prolog, but not as severe due to the absence of backtracking.

Looking at the literature, a number of general themes are becoming apparent. The first is that for all these models, but particularly the Or-Parallel and mixed And/Or Parallel models, the granularity of parallelism may be as small as a single unification. In other words, without programmer intervention such systems may create a "process" to evaluate a literal, only to have the process perform a single unification (albeit in parallel with other unifications). For example, in an And-Parallel system, the goals:

... p(X, Y), q(X, Z) ...

will be evaluated in parallel, particularly if X is ground. However, this will be a costly exercise if p is defined by a single literal or a clause defining a simple test.[2] (Similar examples could be created for each of the extant models.) In the end, if the context is to be non-shared-memory architectures, we are likely to see potential increases in speed due to the parallel computation being offset by communication overheads. In the context of shared-memory architectures, the result may well be increased bus-contention.

Indeed, the need to increase the grain-size of parallel execution is already acknowledged in many of the implementations. For example, in the Aurora system [Lusk88a] a design goal was 'to allow **any choicepoint** to be a candidate for **parallel execution**' (my emphasis). As this could lead to trivial tasks (processes) the Aurora schedulers are set up so that they will not make a node (choicepoint) public, i.e. release work for other workers (virtual processors) within five calls of the start of a task. Szeredi [Szer89a] also proposes the tactic, "lazy release of work", in which work is only released for other workers if one is free to accept it. Both these measures serve to increase the granularity of parallel computation, but as each is largely tactical neither takes any account of the algorithm being executed; as far as possible, tasks are created to fill the available workers, even if little parallelism is available in the algorithm. In the latter case, the tasks that are created are very small and context switching times approximately equal the computation times. The result is that throughput might actually decrease as the number of workers increases [Szer89a].

What is lacking is some form of syntactic aggregate-structure, larger than a single clause, which will force the granularity of parallelism to be larger than a single unification. For static Prolog clauses modules have been defined. (See [Wise89a], among many others). PMS-Prolog goes one further and defines *Prolog Processes*. Of course, the idea of defining aggregate constructs is nothing new. For example, many of those working with functional programming languages defined in terms of combinators have turned their attention to supercombinators [Hugh82a], while in

---

2. Quite apart from its impact on memory bandwidth, the effort spent creating a large number of small processes may itself be a problem, as is argued in [Fagi87a].

dataflow research there have been High Level Dataflow nodes [Hugs82a], Macro-Actors [Gaud86a] and more recently, Strongly Connected Blocks [Saka89a].

The problems with the Committed Choice implementations are somewhat different. The first point of contention is whether they are logic programming languages at all. The paper by Westpahl et al. [West87a] takes the view that they are not. Whatever else may be said, they are certainly not like Prolog; backtracking for alternative solutions is not permitted because only a single clause may be "committed to" out of several that may otherwise be evaluated by a literal. To this extent, committed-choice implementations resemble functional programming languages such as Miranda.[3] In fact, Ringwood [Ring88a] suggests that an appropriate domain for Parlog86 is concurrent programming, which the author defines as "an inclusive term for system-type software". The point is that, in this view, programming will be done at a level in the proof-tree where backtracking for alternative solutions is no longer an issue.

On the positive side, committed choice languages do have a concept of "process". First coined by Warren [Warr82a], a *perpetual process* is created when a tail-recursive predicate is allowed to recurse indefinitely. The process state is maintained by passing it from one recursion-step to the next. Two problems arise with this strategy, however. Firstly, these processes are weakened by the fact that predicates within a process are still visible to clauses outside the process – there is no information hiding.[4] Secondly, a perpetual process has at least one variable in the clause-head which represents the state that is being maintained. However, in order to facilitate communication between this and other processes, the clause-head must also include at least one variable which at the top-level is shared with the other processes. This variable must be passed to each child clause that is to participate in the communication. In other words, a clause-head representing a perpetual process will have (essentially private) variables for maintaining state as well as variables for communicating with other processes. It can be argued that the combination prejudices information hiding, and at the very least is liable to cause confusion.

A final problem with the committed-choice model is that it would appear to be limited to shared-memory architectures by the fact that most implementations allow "incomplete messages" or "back-communication". That is, one process sends to another process a compound-term containing one or more unbound variables. The intention is that the receiver should instantiate the unbound variables, and that these instantiations should be reflected back to the sender. However, back-communication is very difficult to implement on a distributed system. (See discussion in [Wise86a].)

---

3. There have recently been a number of proposals aimed at simulating the lost Or-Parallelism ([Shap87b], [Ueda86b],[Ueda87a]) but this is often achieved at high cost.
4. Recent systems built using committed choice languages, e.g. the Polka system [Davi87a] constructed on top of Parlog, go some way towards remedying this problem.

The remainder of this paper is falls roughly into three parts. The first part covers Section 2 to Section 7. In Section 2, the assumptions underlying the PMS-Prolog model are presented, followed by a brief overview of PMS-Prolog's module subsystem (in Section 3). Sections 4, 5 and 6 then describe in detail the semantics of PMS-Prolog's process subsystem.

The second part, in Section 8, discusses the implementation of PMS-Prolog, both on a conventional uniprocessor and on two Transputer-based multiprocessors. The third, concluding part of the paper includes a discussion of two longer PMS-Prolog programs that form an appendix to the paper. Section 10 then has a review of some related projects.

2. ASSUMPTIONS UNDERLYING PMS-PROLOG

With the above points in mind, the following assumptions underlie the PMS-Prolog model.

- The target architecture is assumed to be a non-shared-memory architecture.
- The implementation will be based on a form of coarse-grain parallelism in which the user defines those static objects that, once invoked, will become *Prolog Processes*.
- The process definitions will be of a *strong form*. That is, information hiding will be enforced both in the static descriptions of the processes and in the run-time objects created from them; the contents of processes will be invisible except through well-defined interfaces.
- Processes will be explicitly spawned. The granularity of parallel execution will be set at the level of a Prolog process.
- Processes will be able to spawn other processes.
- Within each process, there should be a separation of state-maintenance from communication State will still be maintained using tail-recursive predicates. On the other hand, communication between processes will be via special predicates for transmitting and receiving terms. Communication will be point-to-point and unidirectional.
- There will be no backtracking on communication.
- With the exception of the new built-ins for process management and for interprocess communication, each process will be a conventional Prolog program.

In short, the model is one of communicating, sequential (Prolog) processes and shares many features with OCCAM [Wexl89a].

Support for such a model is to be found in [Wise86b], which reports on experiments that were carried out on the EPILOG model.[5] Surveying these results it was found that, among other things, the best improvements in speed were achieved when most of the work was being carried out on the initiating processor, with only a rump being sent away to remote processors. It was therefore suggested that, while ideally the decision to send work away to a remote processor should be based on some notion of relative processor loadings, in any case these decisions should be made well up the proof tree, where the "work" involves the evaluation of entire subtrees of the proof-tree, rather than single nodes . Interestingly, the Aurora schedulers [Lusk88a] adopt a similar strategy for similar reasons; when chosing a node to make public, preference is given to nodes further up the proof-tree. The intent of these strategies is the same; by sending away larger computations one amortizes the costs of creating processes and establishing the communication channels.

The higher levels of a proof-tree also can be seen as the places where *algorithmic parallelism* is likely to be found, i.e. those opportunities for parallel execution that are evident in the algorithm itself. In the context of the current system, it is argued that it is quite reasonable to ask the algorithm designer to express the parallelism formally in terms of explicit 'fork' commands.[6] Further, it is very often the case that at these higher levels in the proof-tree the presence of CUTs prevents backtracking for alternate solutions and the presence of evaluable predicates (such as 'is') prevents predicates from being evaluated "backwards" (i.e. where inputs become outputs, and vice-versa). In other words, evaluation at this level is generally "functional". Therefore, at this higher, algorithmic level it is reasonable to define perpetual processes based on tail-recursion, to insist on unidirectional communication and to prohibit backtracking. However, eliminating backtracking at all levels in a computation – down to the lowest – as do the Committed Choice systems, is unduly restrictive.

Support for the new model also comes from an extensive performance analysis of various (restricted) And– and Or-Parallel programs reported by Fagin and Despain [Fagi90a]. Among other things, they conclude that:

- Restricted And-Parallelism is effective, but only for larger programs (with a number of large subtrees).

- Shallow Or-Parallelism is not effective, i.e. Or-Parallelism only involving the unification of clause-heads in parallel.

- Deep Or-Parallelism can be effective (i.e. the search for alternate solutions in parallel, where this also involves evaluation of clause-body literals).

In view of the latter two conclusions, together with the twin observations that:

---

5. The EPILOG model used both And– and Or-Parallelism, with additional control annotations supplied by the user. The purpose of the annotations is to limit the combinatorial explosion that inevitably flows from the unrestricted use of combined And– and Or-Parallelism. Execution of this model was simulated for a number of distributed computer architectures.

6. This has the immediate effect of eliminating "speculative parallelism" [Lusk88a].

1. a large number of Prolog programs only produce a single solution or the order in which multiple solutions are returned is significant, and
2. Or-Parallelism is more costly than And-Parallelism,

the authors argue that Or-Parallelism is of limited utility. The authors do not examine stream parallelism.

PMS-Prolog does not support Or-Parallelism. However, there is nothing to prevent a programmer from setting up parallel processes to search different parts of a solution space.

3. PRELIMINARIES – ADDING MODULES TO PROLOG

A precursor to the implementation the PMS-Prolog model was the introduction of Modula-2 style modules into UNSW-Prolog [Samm83b]. A complete description of this module system can be found in [Wise89a], while [Liu90a] provides a semantic model for the system. However, some of the new built-ins are relevant to the current discussion and so will be outlined here.

3.1 *module* M !
This declares the start of a new module, i.e. a set of Prolog procedures which is distinct from sets appearing in other modules or in the Prolog Environment. Modules may appear within other modules, forming a structure similar to the directory structure used in UNIX. The argument to 'module', here represented by the variable M, may be either an atom (which is the new module's name) or a compound-term, in which case the functor is the module-name. When argument M is a compound-term the included terms are restricted to being (unique) variables, e.g.

    module   m1(MoL) !

These variables act as *free-variables* (cf. LISP) whose scope is the entire module in which they appear. The presence of free-variables means that when an atom representing a variable is found during the compilation of a clause, the list of free-variables for the enclosing module is first checked to see whether the putative variable is included in the list. If it is, a reference to a free-variable has been found; if not, the variable is added to the list of variables for that clause in the usual way. (Free-variables also have precedence over clause-variables during computation.)

3.2 *end_module* M !
This closes the module that was most recently opened.

3.3 *export* P !
The atom or a list of atoms represented by P is exported, i.e. each of the predicates to be exported is first made *visible* to sibling modules and then added to relevant clause-lists in the parent environment.

3.4 *import* P !
Import introduces a predicate (or list of predicates) P from the current module's parent environment into the current module. The clauses defining these predicates are added to the clause-lists of the corresponding local predicates.

3.5 *export_qualified* P !

The built-in 'export_qualified' makes the atom (or list of atoms) P visible but does not promote them, i.e. the clauses defining each predicate are added to the clause-lists of corresponding predicates in the *parent environment*. The "parent environment" is the enclosing module if one exists, or the Prolog Environment, and a "corresponding predicate" is generally one with the same name as the predicate being exported.

3.6 *import* P *from* M !

In this case, the predicates represented by P are being imported from a sibling module, M, rather than the parent environment. The variable M represents the intended source module's name, and can be either an atom or a compound-term. In the case where M is a compound-term the functor of the compound-term is the module-name. In particular, **if M is a compound-term and the corresponding source-module argument is also a compound-term of the same arity, the terms of the import-request are bound to the free-variables appearing as terms in the source-module argument.** In this way, different instances of a module are created each time an import from the module is performed, e.g.

        import p from m1(42) !

Note that all the terms of the import-request must be ground at the time the import is performed.

3.7 @ and @@

These infix operators are used to perform "dynamic imports", in contrast to the imports described above, which are essentially static in nature. Instead of formally importing a (previously exported) predicate into a module, importing is done on-the-fly and only affects the clause containing the predicate. The duration of the dynamic import is the evaluation of the surrounding clause, after which it disappears. Dynamic imports can take one of two possible forms, corresponding to the two ways in which predicates may be introduced into a module – from a sibling module or from a child module. If a predicate from a child module is to be evaluated (one that could otherwise be exported up), the call has the format:

        ...., predicate(<terms>) @ module_name(<module_parameters>), ...

A call to a predicate from a sibling module substitutes '@@' in place of the former call's '@'. For example, assuming the prior definition of module m1 above, a typical call might be:

        p(X) @ m1(42) ?

One can also view this as a request to evaluate p(X), as defined in module m1, in a context where free-variable MoL has binding 42. Note that, once again, all the calling module arguments must be ground at the time '@' is executed.

4. ADDING PROCESSES AND STREAMS – AN OVERVIEW

The most notable aspect of the module system, from the point of view of the current exposition, is the fact that modules may be parameterized, giving the effect of *free-*

variables whose scope is the enclosing module. A static *Prolog Process* is a module which has an exported, top-level predicate, generally of arity zero, with the same name as the process-name. Processes, like modules, can have processes (or modules) defined within them. The following simple process prints out the numbers from 20 down to 0.

```
process ints(ID) !

ints:- p(20).
p(N):- N >= 0,
   print("In process ", ID, " N: ", N),
   N1 is N - 1,
   p(N1),  !.
p(_).

end_process ints !
```

Note that processes, like modules can have free-variables (in this case just an identifier for the process).

Processes are explicitly invoked using the built-in, *fork*. For example, assuming there is already in existence a definition for process 'proc1', the command:

```
fork  proc1 !
```

spawns the process proc1. This is taken to mean that execution commences for predicate proc1 in module proc1. Note that, during a *fork*, the parent process suspends. Note also that the Prolog Environment is assumed to live in a zeroth process. The command:

```
fork  proc1 // proc2 !
```

states that processes proc1 and proc2 will be spawned at the same time and run in parallel.

Any free-variables defined in the process-header receive a value when the process is spawned. For example, assuming the process definition for 'ints' above, the command:

```
fork  ints(42) !
```

creates an instance of ints, but now in a context where the free-variable ID has binding 42.

However, one particular kind of binding for free-variables in processes is of particular interest. Processes communicate via named *channels* using the commands *transmit* and *receive*. (More will be said of these presently.) The channels are unidirectional, point-to-point communication pathways similar to UNIX pipes, and are represented by pairs of *channel-structures*. An output channel-structure is a compound-term consisting of a variable, say CHAN, followed by the postfix operator '^^'. The input channel-structure has the postfix operator '??'. The channel, which is notionally under the control of the receiver, is assumed to contain a buffer whose capacity is implementation dependent (though it is generally zero). Zero buffering implies synchronous communication; otherwise communication is asynchronous up to the capacity of the buffering. For example, if process proc1 above is a producer and process proc2 a consumer, the *fork* command would now look like:

    `fork   proc1 (CHAN^^ ) // proc2 (CHAN??)`

This time, apart from spawning the two processes (and blocking the parent), one of the tasks undertaken by *fork* will be to create a physical channel one end of which is attached to the transmitting process and the other end to the receiving process. The physical channel is represented by a special Prolog atom, the *channel-atom*, which is bound to the shared variable CHAN. Among other things, the channel-atom contains whatever buffering there is to be between the sender and the receiver.

The communication built-ins *transmit* and *receive* to some extent resemble the existing Prolog built-ins *read* and *print*, except for the obvious difference that communication is no longer via standard input and output, but rather via a named channel (more precisely, channel-structure) which is given as the first argument. A transmit is a call of the form:

    transmit(< channel-structure >, < term >)

For example, in proc1 there might appear:

    transmit(CHANNEL, g(9, a))

In this case, the compound-term 'g(9, a)' is sent out on the (output) channel-structure pointed to by CHANNEL.

To receive an item sent by another process, a process executes a call of the form:

    receive(< channel-structure >, < term >)

For example, in proc2 there might appear:

    receive(C, g(X, Y))

The incoming term is taken from the channel-structure pointed to by C and unified with 'g(X, Y)'. Note that this unification may succeed or fail, (and therefore 'receive' may succeed or fail), but the receipt is never undone.

More details will be given of transmit, receive and fork in Section 6.

A new built-in atom *eos* is used to mark the end of a sequence of transmissions in the same way that Prolog built-in *end_of_file* marks the end of a file.

5. A SIMPLE EXAMPLE: THE PRODUCER– CONSUMER PROBLEM

The code below for the Producer – Consumer Problem illustrates how the new built-ins may be used.

```
process producer(C) !

producer:- p(20).
p(N):- N >= 0,
   transmit(C, N),
   N1 is N - 1,
   p(N1), !.
p(_).

end_process producer !


process consumer(C) !

consumer:-
   receive(C, Item),
   Item /= eos, !,
   print(Item),
   consumer.
consumer.

end_process consumer !

fork producer(C^^) // consumer(C??) !
```

6. MORE DETAILS ON *fork*, *transmit* AND *receive*

Having presented an overview of the communication subsystem of PMS-Prolog, it is now appropriate to fill in the details about the new commands. The interested reader may also wish to consult [Wise90a].

6.1 fork

The process-oriented built-in *fork* is implemented in terms of the module built-in '@'. Remember that '@' is used to indicate that a predicate defined in a child module is to be evaluated, e.g. p @ q states that literal p from child module q is to be evaluated. Based on the definition of '@', the final step in the execution of a fork command is to recast each process-name, p, as a call to predicate p in process p, i.e. p @ p. For example,

```
fork producer(C^^) // consumer(C??) !
```

is recast as:

```
fork  producer @ producer(C^^)
     // consumer @ consumer(C??) !
```

In other words, the final step in forking process 'producer' (for example) is to execute producer @ producer – go to (child) process producer and execute predicate producer. Before this occurs, however, new instances of the two processes, 'producer' and 'consumer', have to be created. This means that an entire new environment is created within PMS-Prolog for each of the processes, including the various stacks and their associated pointers. The channel-atoms connecting pairs of new processes are also created and bound to C, so that when the call to '@' finally occurs, the complete, ground channel-structures will be passed to their respective processes.[7]

The semantics of fork is AND. That is, if one of the child processes terminates unsuccessfully, the fork itself will fail – but not immediately. Failure will be returned by a 'fork' once all its child processes have returned and the parent (forking) process is awakened. In particular, failure – and termination – of a child process does not force sibling processes to be terminated because down-stream processes may still be working on previous, valid values generated by the now failed processes. This is most clearly seen for process pipelines controlled by the first process, e.g. the Crypt-Arithmetic program in [Wise91a]. Process pipelines controlled by the final process, e.g. the Prime-Numbers-Sieve pipeline defined in the Appendix could indeed profit from abrupt termination on failure, but this is hardly a clean solution. Note, however, that whichever scheme is adopted the AND semantics is preserved.

In the PMS-Prolog model the intention is that processes will generally communicate via the transmission and receipt of messages; processes themselves merely succeed or fail. However, there are times when it would be desirable for a process to return a value to the surrounding Prolog program. For example, it may be useful for a process to return an exit status, which is a little more informative then simple success or failure, say in the form of an atom.

To achieve this, the following must happen. Firstly, instead of executing the original producer-consumer fork and having the system recast consumer as consumer @ consumer, the programmer will use '@' directly, e.g.

```
fork producer(C^^)
     // consumer(Exit_Status)@consumer(C??) !
```

In this case, predicate consumer in process consumer is assumed to be of arity 1. It should be noted that bindings by child processes, such as consumer, to calling variables (Exit_Status) are only returned to the parent after the child process has (successfully) terminated, and because the child process is in a different context to its parent, a sequence of actions similar to *transmit..receive* must occur between child and parent process. In particular, the terms returned from the child process are *back-unified* with the corresponding calling terms. (A back unification may, of course, fail if two child processes sharing an unbound parent variable attempt to bind non-unifiable terms to that variable. In that case the parent process will have failed, as if one of the child processes had failed.)

---

[7] It is also possible for a channel-structure belonging to a parent process to be passed to one of the child processes. (See Appendix 1.) In that case the child process "takes over" the channel while the parent process blocks. The assumption is that the child process will be acting (in some sense) as the parent process' agent.

This extended form of fork can also be used when a process is first invoked, to provide some starting state (rather than using the module-arguments, which are intended for context information). The sequence of events is essentially the same as that described above. The producer – consumer fork may now look like:

```
fork producer(20) @ producer(C^^)
     // consumer(Exit_Status) @ consumer(C??) !
```

In this case, predicate producer is assumed to be of arity 1, and at the outset its argument (N) will be unified with 20.

6.2 Process Termination

When a process terminates, either successfully or after a failure, the channels to and from the process are closed if they are "owned" by the process; otherwise they are returned to the parent process.[8] Furthermore, an *eos* term is transmitted on each of the process' own output channels just before they are shut.

6.3 transmit

Transmit is the simplest of the new built-ins and is very similar to the existing built-in *print*. That is, the term to be transmitted is copied (dereferencing variables where possible) and the copy sent out on the channel given as the first argument. If the term to be transmitted is an unbound variable, a string of the form:

< underscore >< stack_location >

is sent, e.g. "_34". *Transmit* will block if there is no room left in the output channel's buffer, and it will fail if the channel indicates that the receiving process has terminated.

6.4 receive

Receive differs rather more from its Prolog counterpart, *read* than does transmit from print. In particular, when *read* reads a term that is syntactically a variable it is none-the-less rendered as an atom. (It becomes a true variable when asserted as part of a clause.) On the other hand when *receive* receives a term of the form "_N" it creates a genuine variable of that name. To understand why this must be the case, consider the following example.

Imagine that process p, the producer, transmits the term g(X, X) to process q. Assume also that at the time of transmission X is unbound, so a string something like "g(_34,_34)" is sent. Finally, assume that the receiving process, q, execute: 'receive(CHAN, g(9, 9))'.

The string is received by process q, which reconstitutes the compound-term and then tries to unify it with g(9, 9). If the variables-as-strings were to remain, unification would fail, whereas it would have succeeded had unification been

---

8. A process owns the channels that were created with it; it does not own channels that were passed to it by its parent as it was being created.

attempted in the transmitting process. The point, therefore, is that transmitted unbound variables act as place-holders, either in the sense of Prolog's "anonymous variable" or in order to signal the presence of a shared variable. For either of these events to occur, terms that previously were unbound variables need to be reconstituted as variables on arrival at the receiver. Note, however, that nothing that is bound to the reconstituted forms of transmitted variables in the receiving process will ever be reflected back at the transmitting process.

It should also be noted that because the variables created due to *receive* cannot be anticipated at the time the clauses for the process are being compiled, no space can be reserved for them on the stack. Instead, a separate stack called the *Temp Stack* has been created for them, and these variables are called *Temp Vars*.

As one would expect, *receive* will block if the input channel's buffer is empty, and it will fail if the channel indicates that the transmitting process has terminated.

Finally, a second form of *receive* is also provided. In this form, the channel that is otherwise supplied as the first argument is replaced by a list of channels. As happens with the other form of 'receive', if no channel in the list has anything buffered 'receive' blocks, while if only a single channel has something buffered, a receipt occurs from that channel. However, if more than one channel is ready, one is chosen at random and a receipt takes place from that channel. Finally, if all the incoming channels have been closed, 'receive' will fail. In the absence of shared channels, this second form of 'receive' allows streams of tokens arriving on a number of channels to be merged non-deterministicly. A simple example appears in the next section.

6.5 A Second Example
A process for merging a number of incoming channels can be written as follows:

```
process merge(Channellist, Cout) !

merge:-
    receive(Channellist, Item),% failure implies channels closed
    test_transmit(Item),
    merge.
merge.

test_transmit(eos):- !.
test_transmit(Item) :
    transmit(Cout, Item).

end_process merge !
```

Assuming the definitions of 'producer' and 'consumer' similar to those above (except that an extra free-variable representing the process identifier has been added to process producer), 'merge' could be used as follows:

```
fork    producer(1, C1^^ )
     // producer(2, C2^^ )
     // merge([C1??, C2??], Cout^^)
     // consumer(Cout?? ) !
```

7. TWO OTHER BUILT-INS

It has been found useful to define two further built-ins, *poll*, and *suspend_process*.

7.1 Poll

An essential part of the definition of *receive* is that, if nothing is bufferred, a call to *receive* blocks. However, there are occasions, for example in the list-of-primes generator (Appendix 3), where one wishes to test whether there is something buffered, without committing oneself to a *receive*. This is achieved by the second definition of 'receive' to some extent, but if one wishes to implement another form of multi-channel 'receive', for example a regime that gives priority to certain channels, one is stuck once again.

The built-in *poll* allows a user-program to test a channel. *Poll* takes two arguments: a channel to be examined, and a variable to record the result. Evaluation of *poll* will have one of the following terms unified with the second argument:

- 'no', if the channel being polled is closed at the transmitting end.
- 'nil', if the channel is open, but the buffer is empty.
- 'eos', if *eos* is the only thing left in the buffer.
- 'true', if there is something (other than *eos*) in the buffer.

7.2 Suspend_process

An obvious assumption underlying *receive*'s blocking behaviour is that it is pointless continuing execution without data having been received from the nominated channel. However, there are other circumstances when it also would be worthwhile suspending execution. For example, if one wishes to construct an alternative to the second form of 'receive', e.g. based on assigning different priorities to the various incoming channels (cf. OCCAM's PRI ALT), evaluation will at some time reach a point where a number of (input) channels are still open, but none of them have any data buffered. In that case, evaluation of the calling clause may loop uselessly because no other process (on that processor) can transmit data as long as the current process is executing.

Faced with this, a programmer may wish to use *suspend_process* to suspend the current process. The process will again be runnable once data has been placed in any of the receive-buffers for that process.

8. UNIPROCESSOR AND MULTIPROCESSOR PMS-PROLOG

Initially, PMS-Prolog was implemented on a UNIX-based uniprocessor (a Sun 3/60). To the basic, interpreter model of UNSW-Prolog [Samm83a] were added a number of new structures, initially to deal with modules [Wise89a], and later to deal with processes. In particular, the variables defining the "state" of a computation in PMS-Prolog were isolated and moulded into a 'process structure', one process structure for each instantiation of a (static) process. Some of the other new structures are:

- Module Stack – Processes (and modules) can contain modules nested to any depth, so as execution moves between parent and child modules it is important to maintain a record of the contexts that have been traversed (parent modules' free-variables must be available in child contexts).

- Temporary Variable Stack – When variables are transmitted from one process to another they must be reconstituted as they arrive at the receiver. However, no space can be set aside for these new variables at compile-time, so the new stack is used to hold their bindings.

- Process Queue – The Process Queue directly supports the parallel extensions to the language model. In PMS-Prolog, the scheduler on each processor maintains a queue containing all processes on that processor that are currently "alive", and services each on a round-robin basis.

Prolog processes resident on a processor are scheduled for execution by a scheduler internal to PMS-Prolog. The scheduler is conventional; there are four states: Running, Blocked/Waiting (due to *fork*, *transmit*, *receive* or *suspend_process*), Ready (initially or after returning from being blocked) and Zombie. A Prolog process that does not participate in any communication, self-imposed suspension or forking operates as a typical Prolog program, so it is plausible that such a process may execute perpetually or until exhaustion of its resources. The PMS-Prolog scheduler ensures that no process consumes more than its "fair share" of CPU time on a given processor. A simple method for achieving this time-slice scheduling is by pre-empting processes after a predefined number of Prolog goals have been executed. The present value is arbitrarily set to 100. The Prolog Environment becomes the 'zeroth' process.

Our multiprocessor implementations have been based on two hardware and software environments utilising the INMOS Transputer [INMO88a]. The discussion in this section will be restricted to the Transtech/NiCHE multi-Transputer system running Genesys II. A second implementation, for a multi-Transputer system made by INMOS running the Logical Systems C, is discussed in a later section. In both cases the Transputer system acts as a back-end to a host computer, respectively a Sun 3/280 and an IBM PC. Both systems are conceptually the same; the issues discussed in the following sections relate to support by the Transputer environment for the PMS-Prolog model, and to interactions between the Transputer and host environments.

The Transputer is a message-passing processor capable of supporting, in hardware, process scheduling and both inter-process and inter-processor communication using Occam's channel concept. Networks of arbitrary topology may be constructed using these processors, providing a freedom to experiment with and optimise parallel architectures for a given application. This is restricted by the number of physical links on the Transputers in the network. Presently each processor has four links [INMO88a].

The Transputer has an internal scheduler that supports a two-level priority scheme. Processes executing at the lower priority are scheduled 'round-robin' and are given a fixed time-slice to execute in. Processes that execute at the higher priority may run without interruption until completion or until they suspend themselves by attempting communication.

Inter-process and inter-processor (unbuffered synchronous) communication is handled efficiently by the Transputer through the combination of its internal scheduler with DMA hardware support for the physical links. Message-passing can take place between adjacent processors without consuming CPU time. Processes attempting to send or receive messages are removed from execution and placed on the waiting queue until the communication operation is complete.

The Transputer was chosen because of this efficiency, and its flexibility in constructing multiprocessor topologies. While Transputer-based multiprocessors are representative of the class of distributed multiprocessors, they are also relatively inexpensive in comparison to other multiprocessor systems.

8.1 Core Services Present on each Transputer

Because the software environments have to support conventional Prolog across a network of Transputers, it is necessary for user and filesystem I/O to have access to these environments. Furthermore, support for inter-processor communication on more than a point-to-point basis is required; information may have to be sent across the network to arbitrary locations, but in the Prolog program this must appear point-to-point. A number of other facilities must also be present:

- Prolog dynamically uses memory while executing a program. Each processor must therefore be able to manage memory for the processes resident on it.

- Because the PMS-Prolog implementation will utilise dynamic process creation it is necessary for the environment to support process creation and management on each processor.

- A Prolog "Core" must be present on each processor to provide the environment required to execute PMS-Prolog processes. To address this, identical versions of PMS-Prolog have been placed on each processor and a version that includes an user-input handler has been placed on the host.

- For any program to run on a MIMD (Multiple Instruction Multiple Data) system, consideration of process creation, distribution and access is an important issue. The designer of a PMS-Prolog program must choose the appropriate algorithm, process granularity and communication patterns for the problem at hand. In particular, because of the difficulty in determining a priori the physical placement of processes, it is assumed that the run-time system will place newly spawned processes in such a way as to provide optimal performance.

The following sections outline some of the more important execution issues we have uncovered in implementing PMS-Prolog on these Transputer-based systems.

8.2 Distribution of Processes

In PMS-Prolog, the placement of Prolog processes affects the computational and communication efficiency of execution. (Some evidence of this may be found in [Wise86b].) The programmer has control over the granularity of the processes (and thus the degree of parallelism) but the PMS-Prolog model regards the computational resource as a single processor pool. From this arises a trade-off between the system overheads and the clarity and expressiveness of the programming language and its portability across various systems and topologies. This trade-off, true for all high-level-language implementations, applies a fortiori in parallel implementations.

To help deal with this trade-off, a numbering scheme is applied to each processor in the network, related to its location. A first-pass attempt uses a simple linear numbering method for each processor. Stated simply, proximity in identification number corresponds to a proximity in the processor network. This is appropriate for topologies such as pipelines or rings. The process distribution algorithms to be described later take this heuristic into consideration when forking sibling processes. Note that the distance from a parent process to any of its children is not critical, in general, because information only flows between the parent process and its child during forking and when the child process terminates (and *back-unification* occurs – a term that was coined in [Wise82a]). Note however that in circumstances when a child process inherits one or more of its parent's channels, the distance of the child from an "uncle" process may be an issue.

8.3 Multiprocessor Load Sharing Algorithms

PMS-Prolog executes on both uniprocessor and multiprocessor architectures. When PMS-Prolog is executing on a multiprocessor, the scheduler inherits all the properties of the uniprocessor version but communications abilities are extended to a network-wide scale and a load-sharing algorithm is applied at the time of process forking.

At any time, the total loading on a processor can be determined by the number of runnable processes plus 1 (for the process currently running). The network loading is then the sum of the processor loads across the network.

In shared memory systems it is common to treat loading information as globally accessible, allowing load balancing decisions to be performed realistically and reliably. However, calculations of relative load are generally of tenuous value in distributed systems because they are very dependent upon the process granularity and the communication characteristics of the entire network. For example, the load characteristic in a fine-grained system may have altered considerably between when a request for information is broadcast and when it is received and processed.

In the initial multiprocessor implementations of PMS-Prolog the decision was made that this simple metric would nonetheless be adequate because;

- Process granularity is suitably coarse
- The network size is small
- Communication between processors is relatively fast (20Mbit/sec, less system overhead)
- The metric is easily computed

When a process is being forked, the processor loads are used in the following way to determine the site for the new process.

Every processor maintains a table of loadings (Processor Load Table, or "PLT") for each processor with which it may communicate. The ordering of the information in the table defines the preferential order in which remote processors are accessed.

This is important when a process is forked. The following algorithm is used to maintain the PLT for a single processor.

Initially the space in the table for each processor is set to NO_INFO. Then, at various times, a Query_Processor message is issued to one or more processors, requesting the process-loading value from those processors. The result is added to the PLT. If 'Query_Processor' fails, the processor is suspected to be DEAD.

Because information in a PLT only changes slowly over time, the values recorded there cannot be considered as being definitive, but they are useful nonetheless (due to the assumption that the system consists of coarse-grained processes).

8.4 Prolog Database Distribution

When a Prolog Process is forked to a remote processor, it is necessary for the clauses defining that process to be present on the remote node (together with the Prolog Core). Three simple approaches can be taken:

1. Install the entire database on all processors. – **Common Instancing**
2. Pass the process description to the receiving processor at fork time – **Sparse Process Instancing**
3. Fork only to processors containing the process description – **Cached Instancing**

While more will be said of these below, it should be noted that the first is the simplest to implement, and has been done successfully. The second is presently under construction. For each approach, the scheduler needs to be adapted to meet the requirements of that strategy. In particular, message protocols must be changed and the database of clauses added to the relevant processors.

Each algorithm is defined in terms of a *Query Protocol* and a *Forking Protocol*. The query protocol determines which processor a new process will be spawned on; the forking protocol then performs the fork.

8.4.1 Common Instancing

Pass 1: When a 'fork' predicate is executed, the scheduler examines each of the legal processors in the PLT. The first value found with a loading less than or equal to the forking processor is then queried for its current loading value. This value is used to update the PLT, and if the values is less than the local load, the process is forked to that location.

Pass 2: If no processor was identified with a lower processing load by using the "search-table-and-query-processor" method above, all other processors that have not been recently queried are checked in turn (i.e. they are issued a Query Processor request).

Default: If no remote processor is found, the goals are forked locally.

Once a remote processor has been found to execute a new process, the forking protocol is used to pass the relevant information to it. This includes: the Parent Address, the Full Goal Description and the Full Hierarchical Name of the new process. The parent, in return, is sent the forked processes' address.

8.4.2 Sparse Instancing The forking algorithm for Sparse Instancing is virtually the same as for Common Instancing, with only minor changes to the query and forking protocols. The Query Protocol must include the full (static) hierarchical name of process and the reply now includes a boolean indicating whether that process exists within the remote database. The Forking Protocol then includes the process description if the process description does not exist remotely. Of course, if no remote processor is found, the goals are forked locally.

8.4.3 Cached Instancing This is similar to Sparse Instancing but a history of fork locations for each process is maintained. Cached Instancing is not currently implemented.

8.4.4 A Note About Database Instancing Because PMS-Prolog organises processes and modules hierarchically, at any point in execution, the existence of a process description for the current process implies the existence of a process description for the current process' (statically nested) children. For this reason, any parent that attempts to fork a process must have the complete details of that child process. The process can **always** execute the process locally (or send complete information for that process to a remote node). This is a valuable property of the language, but it also implies that, to send the process to a remote location, it must send the **whole** descendent process tree, regardless of the relevance of whole portions (for this goal).

Another disadvantage with techniques other than Common Instancing is that lower branches of a process tree may exist on a remote node, but if a higher branch of that tree is forked to that node, the scheduler would attempt to send the whole process tree. This results in a duplication of the lower process tree on the remote node.

Another option would be to only send partial process descriptions (because there may already be part on the remote node). This has not yet been investigated because the Sparse and Cached Instancing methods have not been completed.

8.5 Interprocess Communication

As mentioned above, PMS-Prolog's interprocess communication mechanism is entirely through predicates that support unbuffered, unidirectional pipes. There is provision in the model for buffered communication [Wise90a] but at present only blocking communication is supported. The addition of the 'poll' predicate allows a receiving process to perform a non-blocking check on a channel.

The communication predicates are implemented in terms of the underlying Transputer systems' communication facilities. In particular, communication must appear to be point-to-point irrespective of whether the communicating processes are sited on the same processor or across the network.

8.6 Constraints and Difficulties Common to Both Implementations

At present, PMS-Prolog has no dynamic load balancing capabilities apart from a limited survey of network loadings which is taken each time the forking of a process occurs. As was argued above, this strategy is probably adequate for a system containing large grained processes, but may be inadequate if smaller grained process are extensively used.

Secondly, a process that attempts to fork processes remotely cannot be descheduled (by the PMS-Prolog Scheduler) until the sequence of actions involved in the fork is complete. This means that any PMS-Prolog activities (for example, other processes) are halted whilst the scheduler waits for messages from remote nodes. The reason for this is the way the PMS-Prolog scheduler has been implemented: PMS-Prolog runs as a single low-priority process on each Transputer node so Prolog processes are invisible to the Transputer's scheduler. As a result, when the scheduler communicates with other PMS-Prolog kernels during fork, the whole of PMS-Prolog is descheduled by the Transputer's scheduler. This may seem an awkward design decision but has been done (in these prototypes) to simplify the coding that is required due to the differences between the Transputer and Prolog process models. It is hoped that in the future, the two may be matched more appropriately, fully utilising the Transputer's internal scheduler.

On the other hand, it is important to note that communication between PMS-Prolog processes is achieved via a separate (low-priority) Transputer process that handles the network communications. This means that PMS-Prolog is not descheduled during interprocess communication.

8.7 Problems Specific to the Logical Systems/INMOS Implementation

Similar work to that described above for the Transtech/NiCHE system has been done using the Logical Systems 'C' compiler for the Transputer running on some of the INMOS range of Transputer hardware platforms. Most of the implementation issues discussed above apply equally to this implementation. (In fact, this is where the early work was done). The major differences concern interactions within the Transputer environment and between the Transputer and host environments. Two significant issues have been:

- Process Management and Network Messaging
  While the Logical Systems compiler supports the creation and control of processes on individual processors, there is no support for process control on remote processors. Secondly, the method of process control is achieved by Library calls, rather than Operating System routines, so they must be used prudently. Similarly, there is no support for inter-processor communication; library routines support inter-process communication and access to the Transputer's physical links, but without any protection or a facility for non point-to-point communication. Simply, the Logical Systems implementation lacks many of the facilities we require.

  For this reason, a small kernel was built to support these operations. The **Network Manager** [Jone89a] allows for inter-processor communication in a fixed (at run-time) topology network and the creation/control of processes across the network.

- Host System Interface
  Because the host machine for this system is an IBM PC and the operating system is MS-Dos, a console was implemented to facilitate communication between the multi-tasking environment of the Transputer system and the single-tasking environment of the PC. This was necessary because the PC would hang when arrival several messages arrived in quick succession. Use of the keyboard would also cause the system to block. The console supports the ability to toggle between the Prolog Environment and the Transputer Network Manager's environment [Jone89a].

9. DISCUSSION OF THE LONGER EXAMPLE

One longer example written in PMS-Prolog forms an appendix to this paper. Other examples may be found in [Wise91a].

The PMS-Prolog program in the appendix generates a list of the first N primes. According to the well-known algorithm, as each new prime is found it is added to the list of primes discovered to that point. This list is then used to test each new putative prime. What is interesting about the program is that it is implemented as a pipe-line of processes which lengthens as the list of primes gets longer. The first process generates odd integers that are not divisible by 3; the last process counts the primes as they are produced and signals the first process when the required number of primes has been produced. The middle process tests incoming putative primes against each of the primes found so far. If one of the putative primes turns out to be genuine, it is added to the list. This continues until the list reaches a maximum size (MAXLIST). At that point, the process forks two child process. The first process, which is not allowed to grow any further, is given the current list of primes; from now on it will act solely as a sieve for existing primes. The second process is given the most recent prime; further gathering of primes will take place in this process until it in turn grows too large and must split.

10. RELATED WORK

Of the original crop of projects aimed at implementing Prolog on multiprocessors, the one that comes closest to the model described above is Delta Prolog [Pere84a], [Mont84a], [Pere86a], [Cunh89a]. It has also been reviewed in [Wise86b]. In this model, the parallel evaluation of two literals is signalled by the connective '/', (more recently '//'), otherwise, sequential execution is assumed. Bracketing of groups of goals is permitted. When parallel evaluation is taking place, the processes running in parallel are able to communicate by the execution of *event goals*. That is, by evaluating a goal of the form

    G ! E

one process is able to send term G to another process via the mail-box represented by *event-name* E. The receiving process executes $G^* ? E$ to receive the term. For the transaction to be successfully completed G must unify with G^*. Because backtracking is a real possibility, and it is clearly undesirable to have needless backtracking over the transmission, G ! E is extended to G ! E:S and $G^* ? E$ to $G^* ? E:R$, where S and R are auxiliary goals that must also succeed for the transmission to be successful. If either the unification of G and G^* or the evaluation of S or R fails, the transmitting event-goal will fail, while the receiving event-goal will hang, waiting for the next transmission.[9]

---

9. The more recent articles, [Pere86a] and [Cunh89a], seem to complicate matters further by allowing *asynchronous event-goals* in which '!' and '?' are replaced by '!!' and '??'. These are similar to '!' and '?', except that the transmitting process is not forced to wait for the receiver.

Communication in this model is point-to-point. It is also unidirectional, but in a special sense. At the instant that a communication takes place and G is unified with G*, information can flow in **both** directions. That is, bindings can be made to sending variables as well as receiving variables. To some extent, this anticipates the concept of bidirectional message-passing (bi-io) [Lend88a]. However, it should be noted that back-communication, as per Parlog or Concurrent Prolog, is not possible.

While the Delta Prolog model has much to recommend it, the model does have some obvious problems. The first is that Delta Prolog, like the other models mentioned earlier, operates at the granularity of single unifications. In other words Delta Prolog operates at the level where backtracking is still a real issue. This complicates matters considerably, and clearly is the motivation for the addition of auxiliary goals. The second problem, related to the first, is that there is no aggregation construct larger than a single clause, so it is possible to perform trivial computations in parallel. Information hiding between processes remains the problem that it always was. Thirdly, the authors advocate the use of distributed backtracking [Pere86a] to perform exhaustive search in much the same way as backtracking is used in conventional Prolog implementations. Apart from adding considerably to the traffic of messages between sender and receiver, the ability to backtrack over communications will clearly make debugging of systems of modules much more difficult because they can not be decoupled and tested module-by-module. When several processes are involved the interactions now possible under this regime could become very complex indeed, resulting in an increased likelihood of deadlock. Finally, while the concept of communication-via-unification is of considerable interest (and should be investigated further), the implication for non-shared-memory systems is that the number of unifications would double because back-unification must be performed for each transmitter event-goal after unification has been completed with the receiver event-goal. (By way of comparison, in PMS-Prolog back-unification only occurs when one PMS-Prolog's relatively large and long-lived process terminates.)

Another early system which PMS-Prolog in some way resembles is T-Prolog [Futo82a], [Futo84a]. T-Prolog is a discrete-event simulation system, written as a module within M-Prolog [Szer82a]. The central idea is that if a simulation run on a particular model results in failure of the model, rather than having a human operator intervene, for example, to alter some parameters of the simulation, the system should backtrack and try alternative values. T-Prolog allows the user to define processes, and have them transmit and receive values. The primitives provided for this are:

- new(Goal, PID, Start-Time, End_Time) – Take goal Goal and create a process with name PID. The process will commence at time Start_Time and finish its activity at time End_Time.
- send(M) – Send message M, where M is a Prolog term (generally compound-term).
- wait_for(M) – Suspend processing until a message arrives that unifies with M.
- hold(T) – Suspend execution for T time-units.

The underlying model is a next-event queue (called by the authors "waiting queue"), supplemented with a queue of blocked processes. Processes move to the waiting queue when they are runnable, but if no process is runnable, or "activable", backtracking occurs.

This model is clearly intended to operate on a conventional machine. However, a descendant of T-Prolog, CS-Prolog has been implemented on a Transputer network [Kacs89a], [Futo89a]. In this implementation, the T-Prolog built-ins 'wait_for' and 'hold' have remained unaltered, but 'new' and 'send' are now:

- send(Message, Processlist) – Send message Message (a Prolog term) to the processes in Processlist.
- new(G, N, T) – Create a new process for goal G on Transputer T. The variable N represents the "name" of the process. If T is absent, the current Transputer is assumed.

Two further built-ins of note have been added:

- delete_process(P) – This deletes all processes whose names unify with P.
- run(G) – This indicates that concurrent computation is to be performed rather than serial, and sets up the zeroth process.

While it clearly is an attractive model, the T-Prolog/CS-Prolog model is not without its problems.

The main problem is that, although a notion of process has been defined, it is weaker than that of PMS-Prolog; any Prolog goal can be forged into a process, and process have no information hiding. Secondly, while the form of 'send' found in T-Prolog is clearly oriented to a shared-memory model, the 'send' in CS-Prolog still can be backtracked over and undone. In other words, in common with Delta Prolog, a form of distributed backtracking has been implemented [Futo89a], with the attendant problems outlined above. Finally, as things currently stand the allocation of processes is entirely up to the user; indeed, without the initial call to 'run', evaluation will be entirely sequential. Ideally, decisions about where to run a particular process should be made at runtime, when information is to hand regarding relative processor loadings. As runtime process allocation can be relatively costly, it would militate against smaller processes in favour of the larger, relatively long-lived processes supported by PMS-Prolog.

The last of the projects resembling PMS-Prolog is the Quintus Prolog Multiprocessing Package [Quin89a], which runs on the Sequent Balance shared-memory multiprocessor. In this system, a process is created by forking a Prolog goal using the built-in 'mp_fork'. This primitive is apparently based on the DYNIX *F primitive 'm_fork', so a separate DYNIX process is created for each Prolog process. Like PMS Prolog, interprocess communication is achieved via the transmission and receipt of messages along channels, however these may be shared by a number of processes. The implementation of the interprocess-communication primitives is based on UNIX System V messages [Bach86a]. In particular, channels

---

9. DYNIX is the implementation of UNIX found on Sequent multiprocessors.

(i.e. message queues) are explicitly created using the primitive 'mp_create_channel' and then passed to 'mp_fork'. Message passing then takes place using the blocking primitives 'mp_send' and 'mp_receive' or their non-blocking counterparts, 'mp_non_blocking_send' and 'mp_non_blocking_receive'. Also provided is the primitive 'mp_destroy_channel' for explicitly removing channels.

When compared with PMS-Prolog the following clear differences emerge. Firstly, the Quintus Multiprocessing Package clearly depends on system-wide facilities provided by UNIX in general, and Sequent's DYNIX in particular, and would therefore be difficult to move to other environments. Secondly, these facilities are much more heavy-weight than those provided by PMS-Prolog, and as a consequence strict limits apply to the number of processes. For example, without reconfiguring the system the number of processes is limited to 100 (governed by system constant MAXUPRC), the number of channels to 50 (MSGMNI) and the number of queued messages is limited to 40 (MSGTQL). Given these large processes, it is therefore unfortunate that there is no formal concept of 'process', and in fact any Prolog goal can be forked as a new process.

18 PADMAVATI Prolog

X. de Joybert and J. J. Monot
THOMSON-CSF/DOI, Colombes, France

ABSTRACT

This paper presents a "Process-oriented" parallel prolog, Padmalog, implemented on the Padmavati machine (Esprit project 1219/967). The architecture of Padmavati, based on Transputers, and the communication system layer are first presented. The model of parallelism, strongly based on the underlying hardware and system, is then described. The implementation of sequential and parallel aspects are detailed. The use of Padmalog is explained through examples : the N-queens problem, and the Padmalog compiler. Finally a discussion on performances tries to show the benefits and limits of the approach.

1. INTRODUCTION

The PADMAVATI (Parallel Associative Development Machine As a Vehicle For Artificial Intelligence) machine has been developed in the framework of ESPRIT project 1219 (967), funded at 50% by ECC. The aim of the project was to develop a parallel architecture with appropriate software environment for artificial intelligence applications. The project finished in March 1991 and has resulted in first prototypes. Inside this environment a Parallel Prolog (**Padmalog**) has been developed with original features inspired by the underlying hardware and software.

Actually the CSP (Communicating Sequential Processes) model [Hoar78a], on which the Transputer is based, has strongly influenced the Padmalog approach. Parallelism in Padmalog is obtained by running several sequential Prolog tasks concurrently. They synchronize and communicate through message passing. In Padmalog messages are Prolog terms. Communication is facilitated by the Padmavati network, which allows to dynamically connect any pair of machine nodes during execution.

The benefits one may expect from parallelism in such an implementation, are depending upon a combination of factors such as processor speed, quality of compiler generated code, efficiency of hardware and software communication support... The final discussion investigates the relations between all these elements.

2. THE PADMAVATI MACHINE

2.1. Architecture

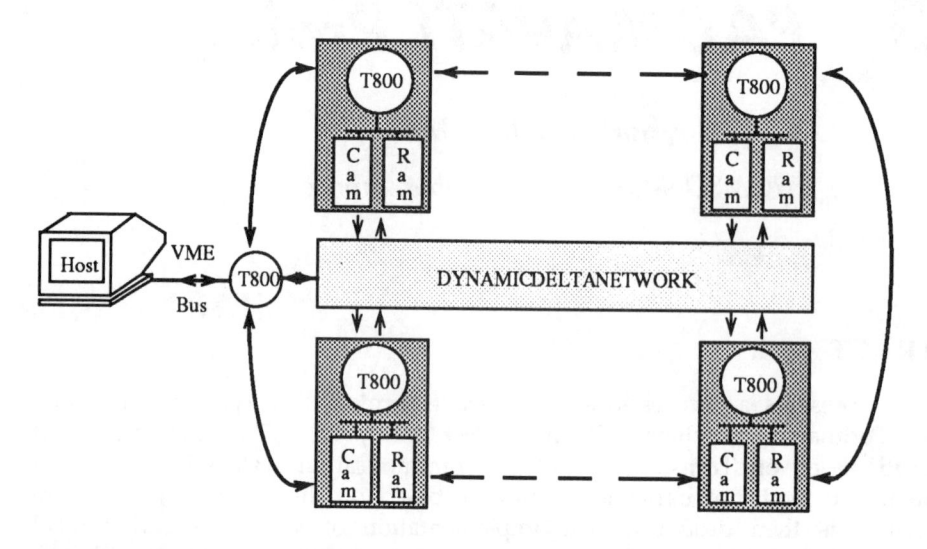

- PADMAVATI ARCHITECTURE -

PADMAVATI consists of a set of nodes (extensible from 8 to 256) interconnected by a dynamic network, and a ring of links. Each node is a Transputer (from INMOS Ltd) with 4 to 16 Mbytes of RAM, enhanced with CAM (48 Kbytes). The current prototype is composed of 16 T800 D-G20S (20 MHz, 10 Mips, 1.5 Mflops each). [Guic90a]

The interconexion network is based on a chip called Dynet (for DYnamic NETwork) developed during the project at Thomson-CSF (France). Dynet is a crossbar chip allowing the interconnection of 8 T800 processors. Dynet is cascadable in a delta fashion to form larger networks. Dynet dynamically establishes paths between nodes by using a very simple protocol : the first byte of a message represents the address of the target node. Connection is realised independently of already existing paths, and arbiters solve automatically any contention problem.

The CAM (Content Adressable Memory) is an optional device which can be plugged on the T800 bus where needed. It is based on a new Asic designed at GEC (UK). A part of the project has consisted of integrating the Cam into the interpretation of Prolog at the clause selection level. This aspect will not be taken into account here, as we shall focus on parallel aspects.

2.2. Run Time Support
The Run Time Support (RTS) is an interprocess communication system. It is implemented on top of synchronous and point-to-point communications provided by the Transputer, and extends this protocol to provide multi-point, asynchronous communications. It uses the functions provided by the dynamic network and hides the hardware by proposing to the user a communication model based on ports.

A port can be seen as a mail-box to which processes can send messages. Ports are created (and destroyed) dynamically by a process wanting to receive messages. They can be named or not. A system process called "name server" allows names of ports to be registered. This is useful when two processes new to each other want to start communication.

All software development has been carried out using the C development environment of 3L Ltd.

3. PROLOG PARALLELISM MODEL

The parallelism exploited by Padmalog is directly derived from Hoare's model : Communicating Sequential Processes. This is of course the basic model in Transputer-based machines and Padmavati follows the rule. Thus Padmalog relies on two concepts : Processes and Communications. The main difference with CSP is that the computation done by each process is specified by a Prolog program. It is essentially a two-level model :
- level 1 : the application is divided into several agents. At run-time they cooperate through message passing to achieve the desired goal.
- level 2 : each agent is given a behaviour through a Prolog program.

The advantage of this approach is its simplicity. The user, knowing the application very well, is in the best position to optimise processes and communication for his/her particular case. On the other hand the user supports all the burden of parallelisation.

Prolog adds its specificity to the resulting language. One must specially take care to correctly manage backtracking in the communication protocols. Each Prolog process executes a standard sequential Prolog extended with special predicates developed to support the model described. These extensions are now reviewed.

3.1. Process Handling

This section of Padmalog is intended to support level 1 of the model above. The user is given an abstract view of Padmavati where a Master process (the farmer) controls N slave processes (the workers) [May87a]. The number N is limited by the number of nodes of the Padmavati machine used, and the memory occupied by the Prolog processes. These processes are defined in a configuration file which is processed by the 3L configurer. The user specifies in this file the number of workers, which is a parameter of the farmer, and gives each worker a number. This static definition is the basis upon which Padmalog will work. A more flexible interface is made available to the user at the Prolog level.

In fact the farmer executes a Prolog program where the user may insert special predicates to manage workers. If no such predicates are used the farmer simply executes a sequential program. There are three main predicates : load/2, run/2, and signal/2.
- load(NoW,Code), net_load(Code) :
  load loads the program Code on worker NoW. Code must have been produced by the Padmalog compiler and linker.
  net_load replicates Code on every worker present on the machine.

- run(NoW, Goal) :
  run is used to explicitely start goal Goal on worker NoW. Workers may also begin processing immediately if a "startWorker" predicate is defined in their code.
- signal(NoW, Value) :
  signal enables the farmer to send a signal to worker NoW. Value may be an atom or an integer. This primitive may be useful for instance to stop some workers when an other one has found a solution.

The farmer/workers scheme does not imply that the user application must be parallelised in the same way. In fact the farmer may be used only to span processes on the machine and then become an ordinary process. An example described below shows the situation where, after loading, a pipe is set up with workers, and the farmer supports the last stage of the pipe. On the other hand, the farm of workers which is a rather common parallelisation scheme is ready for use with Padmalog.

3.2. Communication handling

Allowing Prolog processes to communicate means transferring information between two Prolog systems. The data exchanged are just Prolog terms. In the case of Padmavati the memory is fully distributed and all communications go through Dynet and the Transputer links. The format under which terms are passed cannot be the internal format found in the heap, as pointers loose their validity on a remote node. Thus a special format called intermediate format (between external and internal) has been studied. It is at the heart of the Padmalog implementation and is fully described in section 4.3.

The communication facilities of Padmalog are built on the Padmavati underlying system RTS presented above. Consequently the central notion of "port" surfaces at the Prolog level. In the same way that RTS enables processes to send and receive messages (byte arrays) on a port, Padmalog is able to send and receive terms on a port; Padmalog just changes them into intermediate format before passing them to RTS. The available primitives are as follows :

- **Port management** : create_port/1, create_port/2, name_port/2.
  Create_port(Port) allocates a new port Port. *Create_port*(Name, Port) does the same, but as a side effect an association (Name-Port) is registered in the machine by the "name server". The latter is a system process enabling processes which are new to each other to exchange their ports in order to start communication. *Name_port*(Name, Port) is the dual primitive allowing a process to find a port knowing its name. Port names are just integers.

- **Sending messages** ; send/2
  Send(Port, Term) sends the message Term to the port Port. The Padmavati communications are asynchronous, thus Term is kept in a buffer until corresponding reception occurs.

- **Receiving messages** : receive/2
  Receive(Port, Term) receives a message (let Mes) on the port Port. Upon reception Mes is unified with Term. Whatever is the result of unification Mes is taken out of the message queue of Port.

Some more primitives are available enabling the user to deal with tags and priorities in messages, to select messages from a particular sender amongst others and to test the status of a port (looking for a particular message) without getting blocked on receive.

Backtrack and send/receive : one difficulty in parallelising Prolog is to define the behaviour of the system upon backtracking. Two points are to be clarified : the management of processes (how they are run and stopped), and the way variables are bound and unbound. Different approaches exist in the current systems :
- adopting "don't care" non-determinism like the family of Concurrent Logic Programming Languages [Shap89a]
- using intelligent backtracking to register dependencies between variables and processes. [Bode89a] [Codo89a]
- defining a distributed backtrack algorithm [Pere84a] [Futo89a]

Our approach is different as there is no notion of "global backtracking" in Padmalog. All processes are fully independent and send/receive are deterministic predicates. They can be seen as classical read/write primitives, but instead of reading or writing on a file they read or write on a port. Sending and receiving terms are then pure side-effects relative to the resolution mechanism. On the other hand, our implementation (once special built-ins put aside) follows strictly the usual semantics of sequential Prolog.

This choice must be put back in the context of the Padmavati project, where the objective was to let rather coarse-grain tasks (possibly programmed in different languages) cooperate on a goal.

4. IMPLEMENTATION OF PARALLEL ASPECTS

This section has a double purpose : to review the implementation of the model and to give a first example using the primitives described above as the system is partly written in Padmalog.

4.1. Symbol table and printer

One implementation choice of Padmalog is to have a unique symbol table for the whole system, centralised on the farmer. As a consequence the reference attributed to a given symbol is unique and valid on any process. This allows to speed up communication as it is not necessary to register symbols on workers. An other consequence is that workers are not able to read and write terms by themselves. This has led to design a centralised process named Printer to which workers address requests for writing. Of course this is transparent to the user who uses a normal "write" in workers programs.

The printer process is placed on the same node as the farmer and has access to the symbol table which is placed in shared memory between both processes. There is no need for synchronisation on access to the table as, while the farmer modifies the table, the printer only consults it. Moreover an identifier only gets a reference after being fully installed in the table. This covers the risk that the printer tries to consult the table for an identifier which is currently being installed by the farmer.

In the current state of Padmalog there is no equivalent service for reading on a worker. Such needs must be explicitely programmed by letting the farmer read terms and send them to the relevant worker.

4.2. General organisation and predefined ports

In order to ease the programing of applications in Padmalog a set of predefined port-groups are created on each basic process. They are named *MyPorts* in the figure. They consist in three ports : user, system, and signal. The user port is at programer's disposal for application coding. The system one is used in Padmalog system procedures as described below. The signal port is used to implement the signal primitive. The latter two are not known at the user level.

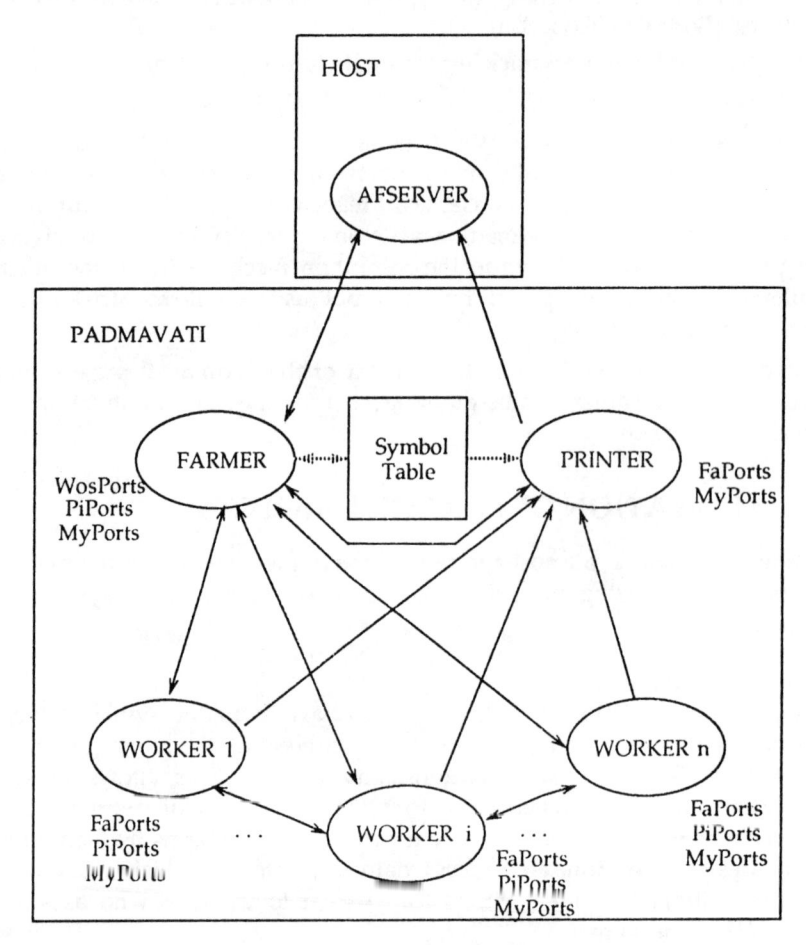

FaPorts :   Farmer's predefined ports
PiPorts :   Printer's predefined ports
WosPorts :   Worker's predefined ports array

MyPorts :   Process's localy predefined ports.

- PREDEFINED PORTS OF PADMALOG -

When Padmalog is run all the basic processes exchange information among which their local ports. During this initialisation phase, Padmalog uses the name-server supplied by RTS to communicate the adresses of locally created predefined ports. When it is over the situation is as follows :
- the farmer knows the number of workers, the ports of all the workers as well as the printer's ports.
- the printer knows the farmer's port.
- each worker knows its own identifier, the farmer's port and printer's port.

To allow the use of these data some extra primitives have been added. Between brackets are shown the processes on which these primitives are valid :
- **nb_workers(N)** [farmer] : returns the number of workers.
- **my_number(N)** [workers] : returns local worker-identifier.
- **my_port(P), my_system_port(P)** [all] : respectively returns user and system ports.
- **farmer_port(P), farmer_system_port(P)** [printer, workers] : respectively returns user and system ports of the farmer.
- **printer_port(P), printer_system_port(P)** [farmer, workers] : respectively returns user and system ports of the printer.
- **worker_port(N,P), worker_system_port(N,P)** [farmer] : respectively returns user and system ports of worker N.

After these initialisations each process enters a top-level loop. These top-level code segments are mainly written in Prolog except for the loading code on workers, which is still in C. A simplified version of these top-level codes is given below :

```
/* FARMER */

            farmer_toplevel(Prompt,Exit) :-
                repeat,
                    block(farmer_body(Prompt,Exit),
                          L,padma_exit_handler(L)), !.
            farmer_body(Prompt,Exit) :-
                write(Prompt),
                read(Goal),
                call(Goal),
                fail.

            padma_exit_handler :- ... /*exception handling*/
            /* Ask a worker to run a goal */
            run(Worker,Goal) :-
                worker_system_port(Worker,Port),
                send(Port,Goal).
```

The farmer top-level, being the interface with the user, is quite classical. The semantics of block(Goal,Label,handler(L)) is : first try to solve Goal ; if no exit_block(Value) is triggered during this execution behave as Goal ; otherwise if Value matches Label, execute handler(L). The primitive run is to be compared with worker_body described below.

```
/* WORKERS */

        worker_outerloop :-
            my_system_port(P),
            repeat,
                load_program_from_port(P),
                worker_toplevel.

        worker_toplevel :-
            my_system_port(P),
            repeat,
            block(worker_body(P),L,padma_exit_handler(L)), !.

        worker_body(P) :-
            receive(P,Goal),
            call(Goal),
            fail.
```

A worker starts and waits for a program to load from its system_port. This program is sent by the farmer on executing the primitive "load/2". When loaded, the worker then waits for a goal to execute, again on its system_port. These goals are sent by the farmer on executing the primitive "run/2". The primitive signal throws a block_exit to the concerned worker. If not already blocked, this block_exit will be processed by padma_exit_handler/1 and will possibly make the worker leave its top-level. It will then wait for a new program, and so on.

/* PRINTER */

The printer top_level is actually the same as worker's. Output requests generated by the workers are simply goals sent to Printer's system port. It is also possible to program the printer to make it implement some special service. An example of this is given in the description of the parallelisation of the compiler.

4.3. Intermediate Format

As already shown the communication between Padmalog processes has necessitated the design of an intermediate format for representing terms. This latter had to satisfy a number of constraints such as :
- independence from machine addresses used in internal representations,
- compactness as far as possible,
- easy conversion from or to internal format.

We call linearisation the transformation of the internal format to the intermediate format. Linearisation takes a term scattered in a heap and lines up its representation in the consecutive words of a buffer. The reverse operation is named delinearisation.

The intermediate representation of a term is quite close to the internal one except for two points :
- pointers in memory are replaced by offsets to the top of buffer.
- list elements are grouped in consecutive fields. This is known to be inefficient when used in an internal format, where pointers behave better. But it saves a lot of space in intermediate representations and a lot of time in communications.

A current limitation of this format is that it is difficult to build the representation incrementally, which can be useful if the size of the linearised term exceeds the buffer space. This format, originally designed for term transmission, has been in fact quite useful in other situations, e.g. database built-ins, reading and writing terms, C interface, and so on.

A C interface enables a Padmalog process to communicate with a C process through RTS. It is in fact a C library including two primitives "pro_send" and "pro_receive", which let a C program understand the Intermediate format of Padmalog, and exchange terms with Prolog.

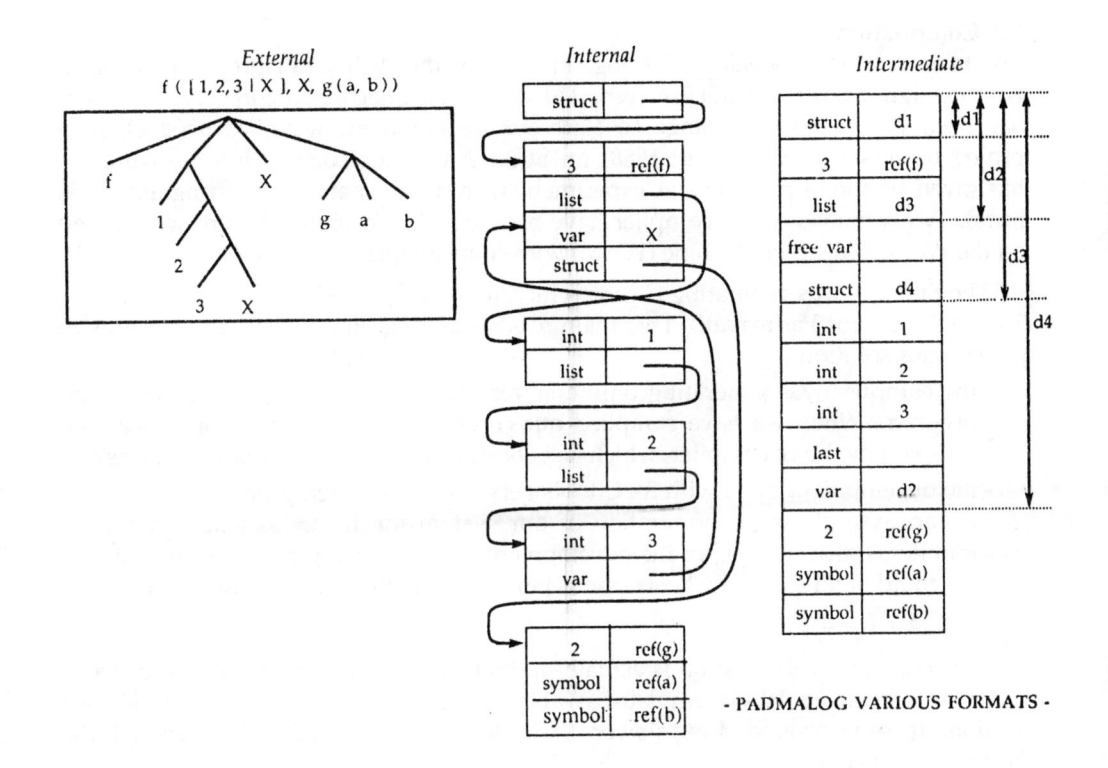

- PADMALOG VARIOUS FORMATS -

5. IMPLEMENTATION OF SEQUENTIAL ASPECTS

5.1. Interpretation in OCCAM

At the time when this project began (1986) the only language available on Transputers was Occam. So our first Prolog implementation was an interpreter coded in OccamII. Occam is a very pure and beautiful language for parallelism but is not very adequate for implementing another language. The main deficiency from this point of view is the lack of pointers.

An important choice was made at that time. In order to avoid latencies on communications it was decided to directly use a linear format for representing terms in the interpreter. This choice has given very bad results : unification became much more complex, slowing down the whole interpreter. As Padmalog is designed to have an efficient sequential implementation, with minimal overhead for parallelism, this was not adequate. It must be noticed that Prolog resolution usually builds large terms but with small pieces at a time. A linear form is quite unsuited for that.

But this interpreter enabled us to experiment with Transputers. A version of the interpreter split the code across two Transputers : one doing clause selection, the other resolution of goals. [Jary89a]

The performances of this interpreter was 1 klips for naive-reverse. The semi-compiler developed later in 3L C runs at 4.7 klips. It is likely that the relatively bad performance of 3L C versus Occam has limited the speed-up of compilation.

5.2. Compilation

The main reason to develop a Prolog compiler in the Padmavati project was that it is more significant to parallelise compiled code than interpreted code. The compiler has been developed in Prolog. To start our development we have used Delphia prolog (a version delivered in 1988) on SUN. After auto-compilation the compiler has given us the opportunity to experiment with a reasonably sized program (2250 lines). Two versions of the compiler have been developed. Both of them were based on the Warren Abstract Machine (WAM) with some adaptations.

The first one was generating C code which was then passed to a C compiler (cc for Sun, and 3L C for Padmavati). Two main reasons among others have convinced us to give up this solution :
  - the compiler was generating only one very large C main function for a Prolog program. When we have compiled our compiler, the C code obtained was not accepted by the cc compiler, which just aborted with an uninformative message.
  - the development cycle with 3L C tools gets very long when programs get bigger. As an example the configuration of our system for 16 nodes takes around 15 minutes. Introducing C in the development cycle of Prolog programs meant that we could handle around 3 corrections per hour, which makes debugging difficult.

The second implementation is actually a semi-compiler generating WAM pseudo-code. An associated WAM emulator is able to interpret this code. This is the last version. It runs around 40% slower than the previous version but has all the flexibility we needed.

6. PADMALOG THROUGH EXAMPLES

6.1. N-Queens problem
This problem is a classical one where one must place N queens on a NxN chessboard in such a way than they don't threaten each other. The program used only counts solutions without displaying them. To fix ideas the sequential version is described and then two ways of parallelising it.

Sequential Version

```
queen(N) :-
    columns(N,Lcol),
    queen(Lcol,1,[]).

queen([],_,Solution) :-
    count_solutions.
queen(Lcol, No, Lpos) :-
    solve(No, Lcol, Lpos, NewLcol, NewLpos),
    NewNo is No+1,
    queen(NewLcol, NewNo, NewLpos).

solve(I, L1, L2, NL1, [J,D1,D2|L2]) :-
    extract(J, L1, NL1),
    diagonals(I, J, D1, D2),
    verify(L2, D1, D2).

extract(X, [X|L], L).
extract(X, [Y|L], [Y|L1]) :-
    extract(X, L, L1).

diagonals(I, J, D1, D2) :-
    D1 is I+J,
    D2 is I-J.

verify([], _, _).
verify([_,DK1,DK2|L], DJ1, DJ2) :-
    DJ1 \== DK1,
    DJ2 \== DK2,
    verify(L, DJ1, DJ2).

columns(N,Lcol) :-
    columns(N,[],Lcol).
```

```
columns(0,L,L) :- !.
columns(N,L,Lcol) :-
    N1 is N-1,
    columns(N1,[N|L],Lcol).
```

The algorithm supposes each queen is placed on a different row in the beginning. Thus it computes for each queen the column on which it must be placed. A solution is then a list of N column numbers. This version starts by producing the list of integers between 1 and N (columns/2). Each solution is built progressively by extracting a possible number for the current queen (extract/3), computing the corresponding diagonal numbers (diagonals/4), and then verifying the new queen does not threaten an already placed one (verify/4). The current partial solution is retained in a list of triplets. Each triplet is made of the position of an already placed queen and its two diagonals numbers.

Pipe version The first scheme of parallelisation we have tried, is in fact an avatar of Erathostene sieve to compute prime numbers. Each queen is mapped on a process. These processes are organised in a pipe, where one can imagine at each level a queen trying to place itself on a row. Each level receives from its predecessor the partially computed solution, where all the preceeding queens have registered their position. It then looks for a safe place and, if successful, passes to its successor the partial solution augmented with its own position.

A pipe of queens :

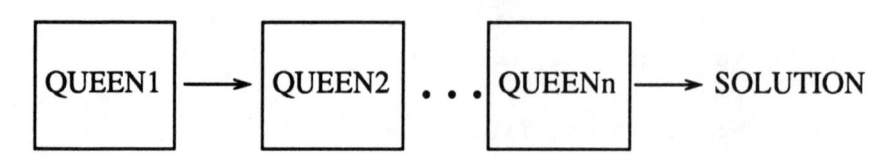

```
┌────────┐    ┌────────┐        ┌────────┐
│ QUEEN1 │──▶ │ QUEEN2 │  ...   │ QUEENn │──▶ SOLUTION
└────────┘    └────────┘        └────────┘
```

We give below the respective codes for Farmer and Workers :

```
/* FARMER */

pipe_queen(N) :-
    net_load(qpipe),
    queens(N, NbSol, Time).

queens(N, NbSol, Time) :-
    my_port(P),
    N1 is N-1,
    run_queens(N,N1,P),
    queenN(N,P).
```

```prolog
run_queens(_,0,_) :- !.
run_queens(N,I,Out) :-
    worker_port(I,In),
    run(I,queen(N,I,In,Out)),
    I1 is I-1,
    run_queens(N,I1,In).

queenN(N,Input) :-
    repeat,
        receive(Input, Message),
        traiteN(Message,N),
    Message = end, !.

traiteN(end,_).
traiteN(parsol(L1,L2),N) :-
    solve(N,L1,L2,NewL1,NewL2),
    count_solutions.
```

/* WORKERS */

```prolog
queen(N,1,_,Out) :- !,
    queen1(N,Out).
queen(N,I,In,Out) :-
    queenI(I,In,Out).

queen1(N,Output) :-
    columns(N,[],Lfree),
    extract(J, Lfree, Lcol),
    diagonals(1, J, D1, D2),
    send(Output, parsol(Lcol,[J,D1,D2])),
    fail.
queen1(_,Output) :-
    send(Output, end).

queenI(I,Input,Output) :-
    repeat,
        receive(Input, Message),
        traiteI(Message, I, Output),
    Message = end, !.

traiteI(end, I, Output) :-
    send(Output, end).
```

```
traiteI(parsol(L1,L2), I, Output):-
    solve(I, L1, L2, NewL1, NewL2),
    send(Output,parsol(NewL1,NewL2)).
```

The farmer first loads the workers with the program *qpipe*. Then it runs the appropriate goal on each level of the pipe. As it plays the role of last stage in the pipe, it ends by executing "queenN". Solve has the same definition as in the sequential version. The pipe is terminated when the last message "end" has gone through all levels.

This version presents a basic flaw : the load is not correctly balanced between the processors. For instance the first worker only finds its N possible places and has terminated. The last worker must do a full check on the N-1 positions already established which it receives, but most of the partial solutions are filtered by preceeding levels. The work is rather concentrated on the middle workers. An other path for parallelisation was then studied and is now described.

Distributed version The basic idea of this version is to use data parallelism. The farmer computes the positions of the first two queens and distributes them to the workers. Each worker presents itself to the farmer and ask for work, i.e. a partial solution with 2 queens placed. It then computes all the solutions depending on these 2 first positions. When finished it asks again the farmer for work and so on. In fact the complete search tree is splitted in pieces which are given to the workers at their demand. This is equivalent to classic Prolog OR-parallelism.

The number of partial solutions with the first 2 queens placed among N is (N-1)(N-2). For N=11 this makes 90 pieces. This allows, with 15 workers, a very good load balancing, with very few communications.

Splitting the chessboard :

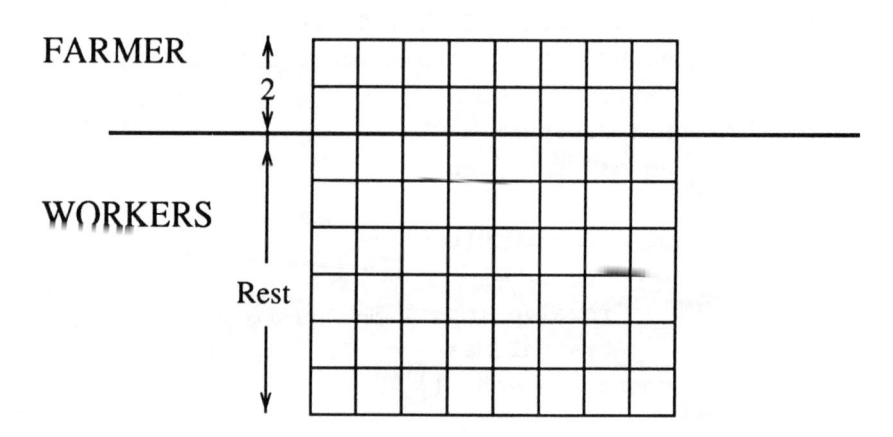

```
/* FARMER */

par_queen(N) :-
    net_load(qpar),
    queens(N).

queens(N) :-
    my_port(FarmPort),
    two_queens(N, Lcol, Lpos),
        receive(FarmPort,WorkPort),
        send(WorkPort,parsol(Lcol,Lpos)),
    fail.
queens(_) :-
    my_port(FarmPort),
    nb_workers(N),
    tell_workers(N).

two_queens(N, Lcol2, Lpos2) :-
    columns(N,[],Lfree),
    extract(J, Lfree, Lcol),
    diagonals(1, J, D1, D2),
    solve(2,Lcol,[J,D1,D2],Lcol2,Lpos2).
tell_workers(0) :- !.
tell_workers(N) :-
    worker_port(N,P),
    send(P, end),
    N1 is N-1,
    tell_workers(N1).

/* WORKERS */

startWorker :-
    my_number(N),
    my_port(WorkPort),
    farmer_port(FarmPort),
    repeat,
        send(FarmPort,WorkPort),
        receive(WorkPort,Order),
        execute(Order),
    Order = end, !.
```

```
execute(end) :- !.
execute(parsol(Lcol,Lpos)) :-
    queen(Lcol, 3, Lpos).

queen([],_,Solution) :-
    count_solutions.
queen(Lcol, No, Lpos) :-
    solve(No,Lcol,Lpos,NewLcol,NewLpos),
    NewNo is No+1,
    queen(NewLcol,NewNo,NewLpos).
```

The predicate "queen" executed by the worker is actually the same as in the sequential version.

6.2. Parallelising the compiler

The Padmalog compiler is a Prolog program, 2250 lines long. It is composed of several parts : pcomp, compil, gener, wam, util. *pcomp* is the main module taking care of file management, and input/output. *compil* takes a source prolog procedure and produces intermediate symbolic WAM code. *gener* takes this code and produces the final numeric code interpreted by the WAM interpreter. *wam* is a set of big facts defining for the compiler the WAM operation-codes and the builtins used in Padmalog. *util* is a set of general utility procedures.

Though much larger than "distributed queens" program the compiler has been parallelised using exactly the same method. In fact the farmer reads procedures from the input file and passes them to workers which compile them. Each worker gives the resulting code to Printer to be written into the output file. As in "distributed queens", workers present themselves to the farmer to obtain a procedure to compile. Dynamic load balancing is achieved with this mechanism where idle workers ask the farmer for work. The resulting mapping is a three stage pipe, whose middle stage is made of N workers :

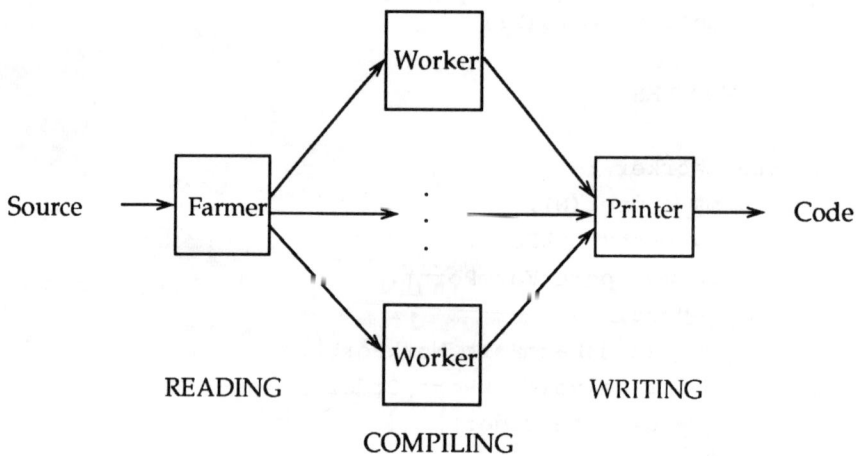

Source → Farmer → Worker ... Worker → Printer → Code

READING   COMPILING   WRITING

- SPLITTING THE COMPILER -

Starting from the sequential version of the compiler, the parallel version is realised by splitting the code in three : Farmer gets file mangement and input part of *pcomp*, Workers get the central part *(compil, gener* and *wam)*, Printer gets the output part of *pcomp. util* is distributed where necessary. Once this partitioning is done, communication between processes must be programmed in order to bring the whole structure to life.

The main procedure of the compiler, called "compileAllProcs", is now described. It has been slightly simplified to ease the explanation, removing unnecessary details. The parallelisation of the compiler is mainly embodied in this procedure.

```
compileAllProcs :-
    repeat,
        readOneProc( OneProc),
        compileProc(OneProc, SymbCode),
        genere(SymbCode, NumCode),
        writeCode(NumCode),
    end_of_file_reached, !.
```

/* AFTER SPLITTING */

/* FARMER */
```
compileAllProcs(_) :-
    reRecord(nbProcs,0),
    my_port(FarmPort),
    repeat,
        readOneProc(OneProc),
        countProc(nbProcs),
        receive(FarmPort,WorkPort),
        send(WorkPort,proc(OneProc)),
    end_of_file_reached, !,
    terminate(FarmPort).

terminate(FarmPort) :-
    recorded(nbProcs,N),
    receive(FarmPort, WorkPort),
    create_port(Port),
    send(WorkPort,end(N,Port)),
    receive(Port,end).
```

/* WORKERS */

```
startWorker :-
    my_number(N),
    my_port(WorkPort),
    farmer_port(FarmPort),
    printer_port(PrintPort),
    repeat,
        send(FarmPort,WorkPort),
        receive(WorkPort,Work),
        doit(Work,PrintPort).

doit(proc(oneProc),PrintPort) :-
    compileProc(OneProc, SymbCode),
    genere(SymbCode,NumCode),
    send(PrintPort,code(NumCode)).
doit(end(NbProcs,Port),PrintPort):-
    send(PrintPort,end(NbProcs,Port)).
```

/* PRINTER */

```
writeCodes(OutFile) :-
    my_port(PrintPort),
    reRecord(nbProcs,0),
    repeat,
        receive(PrintPort, Work),
        doit(Work,PrintPort,Cr),
        Cr = end, !,
    padma_close_obj.

doit(code(NumCode),_,goon) :-
    countProc(nbProcs),
    writeCode(NumCode).
doit(end(Nread,Port),PrintPort,end):-
    recorded(nbProcs,Ncomp),
    Rest is Nread-Ncomp,
    getRemainingCodes(Rest,PrintPort),
    send(Port, end).
```

```
getRemainingCodes(0,_) :- !.
getRemainingCodes(N,PrintPort) :-
    receive(PrintPort,result(NameAr,Code)),
    writeCode(NumCode),
    N1 is N-1,
    getRemainingCodes(N1,PrintPort).
```

An interesting point is the termination procedure used in the parallel version. The farmer counts the procedures which it reads (Nread). The printer counts the procedures for which it has written the generated code (Ncomp). When the whole program is read the farmer has finished. It then passes to the next ready worker a termination message "end(Nread,Port)". The worker then passes it to the printer. When the printer receives it there are still Nread-Ncomp procedures still being compiled at the worker's level. It has just then to wait for them and finish. An extra synchronisation is added between printer and farmer because the termination of a process placed on node 0 (like Farmer) provokes the ending of the whole program by aborting the server on the host. This RTS feature usually simplifies termination procedures but must be taken into account.

Prolog is usually appreciated for its declarativeness. The sequential version of the predicate "compileAllProcs" is nearly written as a person would explain the program. On the other hand it takes some time to convince oneself that the parallel version is equivalent. This bad result must be balanced by two remarks.

First, as stated before the compiler is 2250 lines long but all the parallel code is shown and fits on one page. This is due to the choice of coarse-grain parallelism : the effort of parallelisation is then concentrated on few procedures. The rest of program is standard sequential Prolog and may follow the usual taste of Prolog programmers. Moreover the compiler has needed 8 man-months development time but the parallelisation itself only about 4 hours. As shown later a speed-up of 4.18 is obtained for 5 nodes (reading time excluded). This is a good return for the extra development time invested.

Second the parallelisation method consisting of redistributing the code between the appropriate agents is rather straightforward. Thus there is scope here for a parallelisation tool taking charge of splitting the original procedure into the appropriate pieces. Of course no automatic parallelisation is envisaged here. The user would indicate to the tool the spot where to apply the transformation. The major difficulty foreseen is the fixing of the termination code. This is a well known problem of parallel programs and is far from being easily automatically generated.

7. DISCUSSION OF PERFORMANCE

Our current system executes naive-reverse in 58 ms (8.5 klips) on a Sun 3/260 and in 104 ms on a T800 (4.7 klips). We use two words to represent a Prolog atom. This choice penalizes the building of terms, but improves arithmetic. It has also been motivated by the fact that Transputers are not good at manipulating bytes.

The following table gives the results of the experimentation done with parallel Padmalog. These figures will then introduce a discussion on the possibilities and limits of our implementation.

Each square of the table presents two figures: the time (in seconds) taken for executing the program designated and a speed-up computed as the ratio between this time and the time taken to execute the same program on one Transputer.

Time (s.) / Ratio	Padmalog on 1 T800	Padmalog on 5 T800	Padmalog on 9 T800	Padmalog on 16 T800
11queens (pipelined)	1621 / 1.00			595 / 2.72
11queens (distributed)	1621 / 1.00	373 / 4.34	191 / 8.48	105 / 15.43
Compilation of Compiler	275.20 / 1.00	74.58 / 3.06	62.25 / 4.42	61.92 / 4.44
Reading without compiling	39.00 / 1.00	39.00 / 1.00	39.00 / 1.00	39.00 / 1.00
Compiling without reading	237.20 / 1.00	56.74 / 4.18	34.56 / 6.86	27.22 / 8.71

- PERFORMANCES IN PARALLEL EXPERIMENTS -

We find again reflected in these results the first comments of previous section. In the pipe version of queens the load is badly balanced, resulting in a 2.7 speed-up. This can now be compared with the distributed version, which obtains a speed-up of 15.43, thanks to the dynamic load balancing induced by the algorithm. Inputs/Outputs is also quite reduced as we only counted the number of solutions (2680 solutions for 11 queens).

On the other hand the results of the compiler parallelisation shows a different situation. The load balancing is as good as in distributed queens but I/O gains in importance. Indeed the compiler is a real program which reads a source file and produces a code file. The results of parallelisation are satisfying when speed-ups on pure compilation (+ output) are considered (last line of table). These figures have been obtained by reading the whole compiler from the source file into a list of procedures and then measuring the time taken to compile it (and write the resulting code). The time for reading the compiler has also been measured (4th line). It can be seen that it takes longer to read the file (39 sec.) than to compile it on 16 nodes (27 sec.). This explains the relative erosion of the speed-up curve when the whole process is considered (3rd line).

In fact I/O is a current bottleneck in Padmavati machine, and the reading process in our Prolog is rather slow (Delphia Prolog takes 7 sec. to read our compiler). This factor which is external to the parallelisation, is in fact a determinant of overall performance.

Another important matter is which grain of parallelism is "affordable" in a given implementation. This parameter represents the minimum size of code which must be executed to make up for the cost of communication introduced by parallelism. It depends on the cost of communication compared to the time taken to execute the code. These two factors depend on several more basic criteria. We try now to give some simple observations on these dependencies.

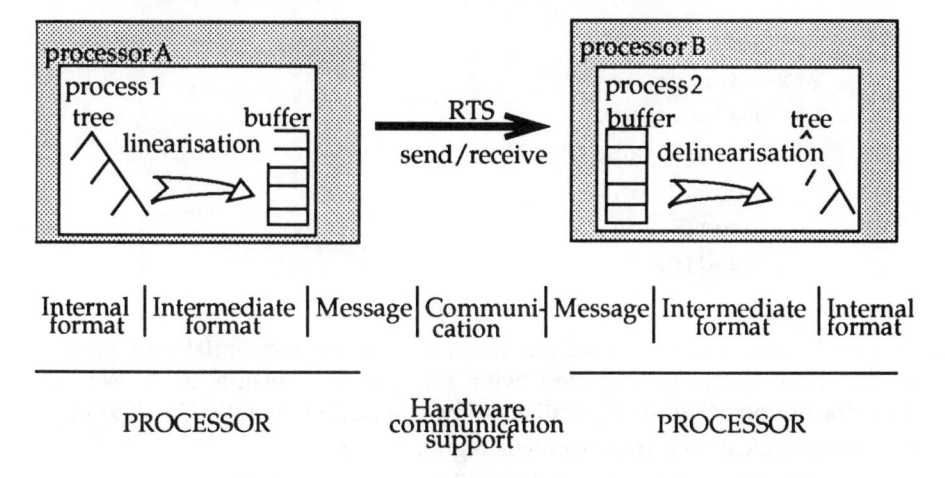

Internal format	Intermediate format	Message	Communication	Message	Intermediate format	Internal format

PROCESSOR	Hardware communication support	PROCESSOR

- COMMUNICATION COST IN PADMALOG -

This diagram tries to show the steps taken by a communication and the components involved : the processors and the network at the hardware level, and the linearisation/delinearisation routines and RunTimeSupport at the software level.

On the other hand, the time taken to execute a sequential piece of Prolog depends on the processor speed and the quality of the language implementation. This last parameter is usually measured in klips for Prolog. Alhough this criterion covers only a small part of a Prolog implementation we shall use it in our discussion.

Starting from the naive-reverse benchmark we construct an artificial problem to illustrate the situation. We suppose we have two lists of 30 elements to reverse. We compare two implementations : a sequential one, and a parallel one consisting of reversing each list on a separate processor.

```
/* SEQUENTIAL */
seq_rev :-
    list30(L),
    nrev(L,L1),
    nrev(L,L2).
```

```
/* PARALLEL */
/*FARMER */
par_rev :-
    my_port(F),
    worker_port(W),
    list30(L),
    send(W, L),
    nrev(L, L1),
    receive(F, L2).

/*WORKER */
startWorker :-
    my_port(W),
    farmer_port(F),
    receive(W,L),
    nrev(L,L2),
    send(F,L2).
```

Let us call Ts and Tp the respective times to execute sequential and parallel versions. The best speed-up expected with the parallel version is 2. We can approximate the notion of "grain of parallelism" by computing the ratio Gr = Tp/Ts :

Gr = 0.5 : communication is free, parallelism grain is fine.

0.5 < Gr < 1 : communication has a cost, parallelism grain is medium.

(Gr = 1 : communication is as costly as computing)

Gr >= 1 : communication is expensive, parallelism grain is coarse.

Gr is not an absolute criterion deciding for good or bad implementations. A very slow parallel prolog may have a very fine grain, whereas a fast one may have a very coarse grain. It is rather a criterion for deciding whether one can expect benefits for parallelising a given application on a given implementation.

On Padmalog the measures are as follows : Ts = 212 ms, Tp = 110 ms, giving Gr = 0.52. We try now to expand Ts and Tp to see how things may evolve :

Ts = 2*Nrev30

Tp = Nrev30 + Com = 109.6 ms

Nrev30 = 106 ms

Com = Send30 + Recv30 = 3639 μs

Send30 = Lin30 + Ovs + Ovd + Trans(296) = 1947 μs

Recv30 = Delin30 + Ovr + Ovd + Trans(296) = 1692 μs

Lin30 = "time to linearise a 30 elements list" = 685 μs

Delin30 = "time to delinearise a 30 elements list" = 1180 μs

Ovs = "RTS overhead to send a message" = 890 μs

Ovr = "RTS overhead to receive a message" = 140 μs

Ovd = "Dynet network overhead to establish a path" = 2 μs

Trans(N) = "time to transfer N bytes on a link (0.8 Mbytes/sec) = N/0.8 μs

Trans(296) = 370 μs

A linearised list of 30 elements occupies a buffer of 296 bytes. The second figure (109.6) given for Tp is synthesised from the elementary times given above. The difference with measured time (110 ms) comes from uncertainties in measurements. Synchronisation times between processes are also not taken into account in the detailled figures because they can vary a lot.

Now let us suppose we improve our compiler by a factor 5. Then Nrev30 will be 21 ms, Ts 42 ms, Tp 24.6 ms and Gr 0.58. Keeping this hypothesis we suppose now that we change our processors for ten times faster ones. Then Ts will be 4.2 ms, Tp 3.1 ms and Gr 0.74. But here the overhead of communication is made up by the transfer speed which we have not changed :

Com = (Lin30+Ovs+Delin30+Ovr)+(2*Trans(296)+Ovd)=289+744=1033 μs.

Finally the balance between all these parameters including I/O makes up the global "usability" of the parallelism offered by the machine.

8. CONCLUSION

The approach of Padmalog towards parallelism has been pragmatic and simple. The results obtained are quite satisfying in a context where the main concerns were distributed programming with heterogeneous languages and mixing symbolic and numeric computation, rather than pure parallel Prolog.

The expressiveness of Prolog has proven to be very useful in defining the protocols of communication between processes. Moreover the known ability of the language for rapid prototyping has allowed us to experiment very quickly with different parallel versions of programs, including the Padmalog compiler which was not an artificial toy example, but a useful program.

ACKNOWLEDGEMENTS :

Fabien Battini, Véronique Rajaud, Patricia Guichard-Jary, Jean-Louis Boisseaud, and Pierre Petit are gratefully acknowledged for their comments and contributions
This work has been granted at 50% by ECC.

References

[Abe87a] Abe, S., T. Bandoh, S. Yamaguchi, K. Kurosawa and K. Kiriyama, "High Performance Integrated Prolog Processor IPP", *14th International Symposium on Computer Architecture*, Pittsburgh, Pennsylvania, pp. 100–107, ACM (2–5 June, 1987).

[Ali86a] Ali, K. A. M. and S. Haridi, "Global Garbage Collection for Distributed Heap Storage Systems", *International Journal of Parallel Programming* 15(5), pp. 339–387 (1986).

[Ali87a] Ali, Khayri A. M., "OR-Parallel Execution of Prolog on a Multi-Sequential Machine", *International Journal of Parallel Programming* 15(3), pp. 189–214 (June 1987).

[Ali87b] Ali, Khayri A. M., "A Method for Implementing Cut in Parallel Execution of Prolog", *1987 International Symposium on Logic Programming*, San Francisco, CA, U.S.A., pp. 449–456, IEEE Computer Society Press (31 August – 4 September, 1987).

[Ali88a] Ali, Khayri A. M., "OR-Parallel Execution of Prolog on BC-Machine", *Fifth International Conference and Symposium on Logic Programming*, Seattle, Washington, ed. R. Kowalski and K. Bowen, pp. 1531–1545, MIT Press (15–19 August, 1988).

[Ali90a] Ali, K. A. M. and R. Karlsson, "The Muse Or-Parallel Prolog Model and its Performance", *North American Conference on Logic Programming*, Austin, USA, ed. Saumya Debray and Manuel Hermenegildo, pp. 747–768, MIT Press (October 29 – November 1, 1990).

[Alsh88a] Alshawi, H. and D. B. Moran, "The Delphi Model and Some Preliminary Experiments", *Fifth International Conference and Symposium on Logic Programming*, Seattle, Washington, ed. R. Kowalski and K. Bowen, pp. 1578–1589 (15–19 August, 1988).

[Ande90a] Anderson, Thomas E., "The Performance of Spin Lock Alternatives for Shared-Memory Multiprocessors", *IEEE Transactions on Parallel and Distributed Systems* 1(1), pp. 6–16, IEEE (January 1990).

[Apar88a] Aparício, Joaquim N., "Concurrency in Logic Programming", Technical Report, Universidade Nova de Lisboa, Departamento de Informática (1988) (MSc Thesis, in Portuguese).

[Arch86a] Archibald, James and Jean-Loup Baer, "Cache Coherence Protocols: Evaluation Using a Multiprocessor Simulation Model", *ACM Transactions on Computer*

Systems 4(4), pp. 273–98, ACM (November 1986).

[Arvi82a] Arvind and K. P. Gostelow, "The U-Interpreter", *IEEE Computer* 15(2), pp. 42–49 (February 1982).

[Avve91a] Avvenuti, Marco, "Parallel Interpretation of Prolog on Transputer Networks", *Transputing '91*, ed. Peter Welch, Dyke Stiles, Tosiyasu L. Kunii and Andre Bakkers, pp. 580–592, IOS Press (April 1991).

[Bach86a] Bach, Maurice J., *The Design of the UNIX Operating System*, Prentice Hall (1986).

[Bal89a] Bal, Henri E., Jennifer G. Steiner and Andrew S. Tanenbaum, "Programming Languages for Distributed Computing Systems", *ACM Computing Surveys* 21(3), pp. 261–322 (September 1989).

[Bara90a] Barata, Manuel M., José C. Cunha and A. Steiger-Garção, "Transputer Environment to Support Heterogeneous Systems in Robotics", *Transputer Applications 90 Conference*, Southampton, United Kingdom, pp. 327–334 (1990).

[Bark88a] Barklund, Jonas, Nils Hagner and Malik Wafin, "Condition Graphs", *Fifth International Conference and Symposium on Logic Programming*, Seattle, Washington, ed. R. Kowalski and K. Bowen, pp. 435–445 (15–19 August, 1988).

[Bark88b] Barklund, Jonas, Nils Hagner and Malik Wafin, "KL1 in Condition Graphs on a Connection Machine", *International Conference on Fifth Generation Computer Systems*, Tokyo, Japan, pp. 1041–1049, OMSHA and Springer-Verlag (November 28 – December 2 1988).

[Baro86a] Baron, Uri, *A Distributed Implementation of Flat Concurrent Prolog*, Weizmann Institute of Science (January 1986).

[Baro88a] Baron, Uri C., Bounthara Ing, Michael Ratcliffe and Philippe Robert, "A Distributed Architecture for the PEPSys Parallel Logic Programming System", *International Conference on Parallel Processing*, Chicago, USA, pp. 410–413 (August 15–18, 1988) (Volume 1 – Architecture).

[Baro88b] Baron, Uri, Jacques Chassin de Kergommeaux, Max Hailperin, Michael Ratcliffe, Philippe Robert, Jean-Claude Syre and Harald Westphal, "The Parallel ECRC Prolog System PEPSys: An Overview and Evaluation Results", *International Conference on Fifth Generation Computer Systems*, Tokyo, pp. 841–850, OMSHA and Springer-Verlag (November 28 – December 2, 1988).

[Baro89a] Baron, U. C., A. Cheese and M. Ratcliffe, "Parallel Logic Languages: State of the Art", CA-45, ECRC GmbH, Computer Architecture Group (April 1989).

[Beau90a] Beaumont, A., S. Muthu Raman, P. Szeredi and D.H.D. Warren, "Flexible Scheduling of OR-Parallelism in Aurora : The Bristol Scheduler", *Conference on Parallel Architectures and Languages Europe (PARLE'91)*, Eindhoven, pp. 403–420, Springer Verlag LNCS 506 (June 1991).

REFERENCES

[Bisw88a] Biswas, P. and C-C. Tseng, "LogDf: A Data Driven Abstract Machine Model for Parallel Execution of Logic Programs", *International Conference on Fifth Generation Computer Systems*, Tokyo, Japan, pp. 1059–1070, OMSHA and Springer-Verlag (November 28 – December 2, 1988).

[Bisw88b] Biswas, Prasenjit, Shyh-Chang Su and David Y. Y. Yun, "A Scalable Abstract Machine Model to Support Limited-OR(LOR)/Restricted-AND Parallelism (RAP) in Logic Programs", *Fifth International Conference and Symposium on Logic Programming*, Seattle, Washington, ed. R. Kowalski and K. Bowen, pp. 1160–1179 (15–19 August, 1988).

[Bode89a] Bodeveix, Jean-Paul, "Logarithm Un Modele De Prolog Parallele, Son Implementation Sur Transputers", Ph.D. dissertation, University of Paris-sud, Orsay (France) (January 1989) (In french).

[Borg84a] Borgwardt, Peter, "Parallel Prolog using Stack Segments on Shared-Memory Multiprocessors", *1984 International Symposium on Logic Programming*, Atlantic City, NJ, pp. 2–11 (6–9 February, 1984).

[Borg86a] Borgwardt, Peter and Doris Rea, "Distributed Semi-Intelligent Backtracking for a Stack-based AND-Parallel Prolog", *1986 Symposium on Logic Programming*, Salt Lake City, USA, pp. 211–222 (September 22–25, 1986).

[Bosc90a] Bosco, P. G., C. Cecchi, C. Moiso, M. Porta and G. Sofi, "Logic and Functional Programming on Distributed Memory Architectures", *7th International Conference on Logic Programming*, Jerusalem, pp. 325–339, MIT Press (June 1990).

[Bran88a] Brand, P. and J. Almgren, "Wave-front Model for Scheduling in OR-parallel Prolog", Internal Report, SICS (July 1988).

[Bria89a] Briat, J., M. Favre, D. Fort, Y. Langue and M. Santana, "Parx: a Parallel Operating System for Transputer-based Machine", *10th Occam User Group*, Enschede (The Nederlands), pp. 114–142, IOS (April 1989).

[Bria91a] Briat, J., M. Favre, C. Geyer and J. Chassin de Kergommeaux, "Scheduling of OR-parallel Prolog on a Scalable Reconfigurable, Distributed Memory Multiprocessor", *Conference on Parallel Architectures and Languages Europe, PARLE'91*, Eindhoven, pp. 385–402, Spinger Verlag LNCS 506 (June 1991).

[Brin78a] Brinch-Hansen, P., "Distributed Processes: A Concurrent Programming Concept", *Communications of the ACM* 21(11), pp. 932–941 (November 1978).

[Bruy84a] Bruynooghe, Maurice and Luís M. Pereira, "Deduction Revision by Intelligent Backtracking", *Implementations of Prolog*, ed. J. A. Campbell, pp. 194–215, Ellis Horwood (1984).

[Bruy87a] Bruynooghe, Maurice, Gerda Janssens, Alain Callebaut and Bart Demoe, "Abstract Interpretation: Towards the Global Optimisation of Prolog Programs", *1987 International Symposium on Logic Programming*, pp. 192–204, IEEE, San Francisco, USA (August 31 – September 4, 1987).

[Burt88a] Burt, A. and G. A. Ringwood, "The Binding Conflict Problem in Concurrent Logic Languages", TR Dept Computing PAR88/10, Imperial College, London,

UK (1988).

[Butl86a] Butler, R., E. Lusk, W. McCune and R. Overbeek, "Parallel Logic Programming for Numerical Applications", *Third International Conference on Logic Programming*, New York, pp. 357–388, Springer-Verlag (1986) (Lecture Notes in Computer Science No 225).

[Butl86b] Butler, R., E. L. Lusk, R. Olson and R. A. Overbeek, *ANLWAM – A Parallel Implementation of the Warren Abstract Machine*, Argonne National Laboratory, Argonne IL 60439 (1986).

[Butl88a] Butler, Ralph, Terry Disz, Ewing Lusk, Robert Olson, Ross Overbeek and Rick Stevens, "Scheduling OR-Parallelism: An Argonne Perspective", *Fifth International Conference and Symposium on Logic Programming*, Seattle, Washington, ed. R. Kowalski and K. Bowen, pp. 1590–1605 (15–19 August, 1988).

[Cald88a] Calderwood, A., *Scheduling Or-parallelism in Aurora – the Manchester scheduler*, Gigalips Project, U. Manchester (May 1988).

[Cald89a] Calderwood, Alan and Peter Szeredi, "Scheduling Or-parallelism in Aurora – the Manchester Scheduler", *Sixth International Conference on Logic Programming*, Lisbon, Portugal, ed. Giorgio Levi and Maurizio Martelli, pp. 419–435, MIT Press (19–23 June, 1989).

[Carl88a] Carlsson, Mats and J. Widen, "SICStus Prolog User Manual", Research Report R88007B, Swedish Institute of Computer Science (SICS), Kista, Sweden (October 1988).

[Carl88b] Carlsson, Mats, Ken Danhof and Ross Overbeek, "A Simplified Approach to the Implementation of AND-Parallelism in an OR-Parallel Environment", *Fifth International Conference and Symposium on Logic Programming*, Seattle, Washington, ed. R. Kowalski and K. Bowen, pp. 1565–1577, MIT Press (15–19 August, 1988).

[Carl90a] Carlsson, M., "Design and Implementation of an OR-Parallel Prolog Engine", Ph.D. Thesis, Royal Institute of Technology, Stockholm, Sweden (1990) (Tech Report TRITA-CS-9003).

[Carv91a] Carvalhosa, Manuel B., "Design and Implementation of an Abstract Machine for Delta Prolog", Technical Report, Universidade Nova de Lisboa, Departamento de Informática (1991) (MSc Thesis, in Portuguese).

[Cens78a] Censier, L. M. and P. Feautrier, "A New Solution to Cache Coherence Problems in Multicache Systems", *IEEE Transactions on Computers* C–27(12), pp. 1,112–8, IEEE (December 1978).

[Chai90a] Chaiken, David, Craig Fields, Kiyoshi Kurihara and Anant Agarwal, "Directory-Based Cache Coherence in Large-Scale Multiprocessors", *IEEE Computer* 23(6), pp. 49–58 (June 1990).

[Chan81a] Chandy, K. M. and J. Misra, "Asynchronous Distributed Simulation via a Sequence of Parallel Computations", *Communications of the ACM* 24(4), pp. 198–206 (April 1981).

REFERENCES

[Chan85a] Chang, J. H., Alvin M. Despain and Doug DeGroot, "AND-Parallelism of Logic Programs Based on a Static Data Dependency Analysis", *Twentieth IEEE Computer Society International Conference (COMPCON'85)*, San Francisco, USA, pp. 218–225 (February 25–28, 1985).

[Chan85b] Chang, Jung-Herng and Alvin M. Despain, "Semi-Intelligent Backtracking of Prolog Based on Static Data Dependency Analysis", *1985 Symposium on Logic Programming*, Boston, USA, pp. 10–21 (July 15–18, 1985).

[Chan85c] Chang, J.H., "High Performance Execution of Prolog Programs Based on A Static Data Dependency Analysis", UCB/CSD 86/263, University of California, Berkeley (October 1985).

[Chan86a] Chang, J. H., "High Performance Execution of Logic Programs based on a Static Data Dependency Analysis", UCB/CSD 86/283, University of California at Berkeley (1986).

[Chas87a] Kergommeaux, J. Chassin de, P. Robert and H. Westphal, "An Abstract Machine for the Implementation of the PEPSys Model", CA–26, ECRC GmbH, Computer Architecture Group (February 1987).

[Chas88a] Chassin, Jacques, Jean-Claude Syre and Harald Westphal, "Implementation of a Parallel Prolog System on a Commercial Multiprocessor", *8th European Conference on Artificial Intelligence*, Munich, Germany, pp. 278–283 (August 1–5, 1988).

[Chas89a] Kergommeaux, J. Chassin de, "Measures of the PEPSys Implementation on the MX500", Technical Report CA-44, European Computer-industry Research Centre, Munich (January 1989).

[Chen88a] Cheng, A. S. K., *An OR-Parallel Logic Programming Language: its Compiler and Abstract Machine*, Dept. of Computer Science, University of Essex (December 1988).

[Chik87a] Chikayama, T. and Y. Kimura, "Multiple Reference Management in Flat GHC", *Fourth International Conference on Logic Programming*, Melbourne, Australia, pp. 276–293 (May 25–29, 1987).

[Chik88a] Chikayama, T., H. Sato and T. Miyazaki, "Overview of the Parallel Inference Machine Operating System (PIMOS)", *International Conference on Fifth Generation Computer Systems*, Tokyo, Japan, pp. 230–251, OMSHA and Springer-Verlag (November 28 – December 2 1988).

[Chik88b] Chikayama, T., *PIM Architecture*, Gigalips Workshop at SICS (July 1988).

[Ciep83a] Ciepielewski, Andrzej and Seif Haridi, "A Formal Model for OR-Parallel Execution of Logic Programs", *Information Processing 83*, ed. R. E. A. Mason, pp. 299–305, Elsevier-North Holland (1983) (Proceedings of IFIP Conference, Paris, 1983).

[Ciep84a] Ciepielewski, Andrzej and Seif Haridi, "Control of Activities in the OR-Parallel Token Machine", *1984 International Symposium on Logic Programming*, Atlantic City, New Jersey, pp. 49–58 (6–9 February 1984).

[Ciep86a] Ciepielewski, Andrzej and Bogumil Hausmann, "Performance Evaluation of a Storage Model for OR-parallel Execution of Logic Programs", *1986 Symposium on Logic Programming*, pp. 246–257, IEEE Computer Society Press, Salt Lake City, Utah (September 22–25, 1986).

[Ciep89a] Ciepielewski, Andrzej, Seif Haridi and Bogumil Hausman, "OR-Parallel Prolog on Shared Memory Multiprocessors", *Journal of Logic Programming*, pp. 125–147, Elsevier Sciene Publisher Co. (September 1989).

[Clar78a] Clark, K., "Negation as Failure", *Logic and Databases*, ed. Herve Gallaire and Jack Minker, pp. 293–322, Plenum Press, New York (1978).

[Clar84a] Clark, Keith and Steve Gregory, "PARLOG: Parallel Programming in Logic", DOC Research Report 84/4, Department of Computing, Imperial College of Science and Technology (April 1984).

[Clar85a] Clark, K. and S. Gregory, "Notes on the Implementation of PARLOG", *Journal of Logic Programming* 2(1), pp. 17–42 (1985).

[Clar86a] Clark, K. L. and S. Gregory, "Parlog: Parallel Programming in Logic", *ACM Transactions on Programming Languages and Systems* 8(1), pp. 1–49 (January 1986).

[Clar87a] Clark, Keith and Steve Gregory, "PARLOG and Prolog United", *Fourth International Conference on Logic Programming*, pp. 927–961, MIT Press, Melbourne, Australia (May 25–29, 1987).

[Cloc86a] Clocksin, W.F. and H. Alshawi, *A Method for Efficiently Executing Horn Clause Programs Using Multiple Processors*, Computer Laboratory, University of Cambridge (May 1986).

[Clos84a] Clos, Charles, "A Study of Non Blocking Switching Networks", *Tutorial Interconnexion Networks for parallel and Distribued Processsing*, ed. Chuan-Lin Wu and Tse-Yun Fen, pp. IEEE Computer Society Press (1984) (Reprinted from The Bell System Technical Journal, March 1953 pp. 406–424).

[Codi86a] Codish, Michael and Ehud Shapiro, "Compiling OR-parallelism into AND-parallelism", *Third International Conference on Logic Programming*, London, pp. 283–297, Springer-Verlag (July 14–18, 1986) (Lecture Notes in Computer Science No. 225).

[Codo89a] Codognet, Philippe, "Intelligent Backtracking in Logic Programming : From Theory to Implementation and Application to Parallelism", Ph.D. dissertation, University of Bordeaux-I France (January 1989) (In french).

[Codo89b] Codognet, Christian and Philippe Codognet, "Non-deterministic Stream AND-Parallelism Based on Intelligent Backtracking", *Sixth International Conference on Logic Programming*, Lisbon, Portugal, pp. 63–79, MIT Press (19–23 June 1989).

[Cone81a] Conery, John S. and Dennis F. Kibler, "Parallel Interpretation of Logic Programs", *1981 Conference on Functional Programming Languages and Computer Architecture*, pp. 163–170, ACM (October 18–21, 1981).

REFERENCES

[Cone83a] Conery, J. S. and D. F. Kibler, "AND Parallelism in Logic Programs", *8th International Joint Conference on Artificial Intelligence*, Karlsruhe, West Germany (8–12 August 1983).

[Cone83b] Conery, John S., "The AND/OR Process Model for Parallel Execution of Logic Programs", Technical Report 204, Department Of Computer and Information Science, University of California, Irvine (June 1983).

[Cone85a] Conery, J. S. and D. F. Kibler, "AND Parallelism and Nondeterminism in Logic Programs", *New Generation Computing* 3(1), pp. 43–70 (1985).

[Cone87a] Conery, John S., *Parallel Execution of Logic Programs*, Kluwer Academic Publishers (1987).

[Cone87b] Conery, John S., "Binding Environments for Parallel Logic Programs in Non-Shared Memory Multiprocessors", *1987 Symposium on Logic Programming*, San Francisco, USA, pp. 457–467, IEEE Computer Society Press (August 31 – September 4, 1987).

[Cone88a] Conery, John, "OM: A Virtual Machine for the AND/OR Process Model", Internal report, University of Oregon (1988).

[Cone88b] Conery, J. S., "Binding Environments for Parallel Logic Programs in Non-Shared Memory Multiprocessors", *International Journal of Parallel Programming* 17(2), pp. 125–152 (April 1988).

[Cone90a] Conery, J. S., "Parallel Logic Programs on the HP Mayfly", Tech. Rep. CIS-TR-90-22, Univ. of Oregon (December, 1990.).

[Cors89a] Corsini, Paolo, Graziano Frosini and G. Speranza, "The Parallel Interpretation of Logic Programs in Distributed Architectures", *The Computer Journal* 32(1), pp. 29–35 (February 1989).

[Cost91a] Costa, Vitor Santos, Rong Yang and D. H. D. Warren, "The Andorra-I Engine: A Parallel Implementation of the Basic Andorra Model", *Eighth International Conference on Logic Programming*, Paris, MIT Press (25–28 June 1991) (To appear).

[Cram85a] Crammond, Jim, "A Comparative Study of Unification Algorithms for OR-Parallel Execution of Logic Languages", *IEEE Transactions on Computers* 34(10), pp. 911–917 (October 1985).

[Cunh87a] Cunha, José C., Pedro D. Medeiros and Manuel B. Carvalhosa, "Interfacing Prolog to an Operating System Environment: Mechanisms for Concurrency and Parallelism Control", Technical Report, Universidade Nova de Lisboa, Departamento de Informática (1987).

[Cunh88a] Cunha, José C., "Concurrent Execution of a Logic Programming Language", Technical Report, Universidade Nova de Lisboa, Departamento de Informática (1988) (PhD Thesis, in Portuguese).

[Cunh89a] Cunha, José C., Maria C. Ferreira and Luís M. Pereira, "Programming in Delta Prolog", *Sixth International Logic Programming Conference*, Lisbon, Portugal, pp. 487–502, MIT Press (19–23 June, 1989).

[Cunh89b] Cunha, José C., Maria C. Ferreira and Luís M. Pereira, "Delta Prolog User's Manual – Version 1.5", Technical Report, Universidade Nova de Lisboa, Departamento de Informática (1989).

[Dall87a] Dally, W., L. Chao, A. Chien, S. Hassoun, W. Horwat, J. Kaplan, P. Song, B. Totty and S. Wills, "Architecture of a Message-Driven Processor", *14th Annual International Symposium on Computer Architecture*, Pittsburgh, USA, pp. 189–196, IEEE (2–5 June,1987).

[Dall89a] Dally, W. J., A. Chien, S. Fiske, W. Horwat, J. Keen, M. Larivee, R. Lethin, P. Nuth, S. Wills, P. Carrick and G. Flyer, "The J-Machine: a Fine-Grain Concurrent Computer", *Information Processing 89*, pp. 1147–53, Elsevier Science (1989).

[Davi87a] Davison, Andrew, "Blackboard Systems in Polka", *International Journal of Parallel Programming* **16**(5), pp. 401–424 (October 1987).

[Debr89a] Debray, Saumya K., "Static Inference of Modes and Data Dependencies in Logic Programs", *ACM Transactions on Programming Languages and Systems* **11**(3), pp. 419–450 (July 1989).

[Debr90a] Debray, Saumya K., Nai-Wei Lin and Manuel Hermenegildo, "Task Granularity Analysis in Logic Programs", *ACM SIGPLAN-90 Conference on Programming Language Design and Implementation*, White Plains, New York, pp. 174–188 (June 1990).

[DeGr84a] DeGroot, Doug, "Restricted AND-Parallelism", *International Conference on Fifth Generation Computer Systems 1984*, Tokyo, Japan, pp. 471–478, North Holland and OHMSHA, Ltd (November 6–9, 1984).

[DeGr87a] DeGroot, D., "Restricted And-Parallelism and Side-Effects", *1987 Symposium on Logic Programming*, San Francisco, CA, U.S.A., pp. 80–89, IEEE Computer Society Press (31 August – 4 September, 1987).

[Delg88a] Delgado-Rannauro, S. A., T. J. Reynolds, A. S. K. Cheng and S. Marriot, "BRAVE Abstract Machine Definition", CSM–118, Department of Computer Science, University of Essex (March 1988).

[Delg89a] Delgado-Rannauro, Sergio A. and T. J. Reynolds, "A Message Driven OR-Parallel Logic Machine", *Third International Conference on Architectural Support for Programming Languages and Operating Systems (ASPLOS-III)*, Boston, USA, pp. 217–226, ACM (April 3–6, 1989).

[Delg89b] Delgado-Rannauro, Sergio A., "Computational Models of Parallel Logic Languages", CA-46, ECRC GmbH, Computer Architecture Group (May 1989).

[Delg91a] Delgado-Rannauro, Sergio A., Michael Dorochevsky, Kkees Schuerman, Andre Veron and Jiyang Xu, "A Shared Enviroment Parallel Logic Porgramming System on Distributed Memory Architectures", *2nd. European Distributed Memory Computing Conference*, Munich, Germany, ed. Arndt Bode, pp. 371–380, Springer-Verlag (April 22–24, 1991).

[Denn74a] Dennis, Jack B., "First Version of a Data Flow Procedure Language", *Programming Symposium (Colloque sur la Programmation)*, ed. B. Robinet, pp.

REFERENCES

362–376, Springer-Verlag (1974) (Lecture Notes in Computer Science 19).

[Deut76a] Deutsch, L. P. and D. G. Bobrow, "An Efficient, Incremental, Automatic Garbage Collector", *Commun. ACM* **19**(9), pp. 522–526 (1976).

[Dijk75a] Dijkstra, Edsger W., "Guarded Commands, Nondeterminacy, and Formal Derivation of Programs", *Communications of the ACM* **18**(8), pp. 453–457 (August 1975).

[Dijk80a] Dijsktra, E. W. and C. S. Scholten, "Termination Detection for Diffusion Computations", *Information Processing Letters* **11**(11), pp. 1–4 (1980).

[Dijk82a] Dijkstra, Edsger W., *Selected Writings in Computing: A Personal Perspective*, Springer–Verlag (1982).

[Disz87a] Disz, Terry, Ewing Lusk and Ross Overbeek, "Experiments with OR-Parallel Logic Programs", *Fourth International Conference on Logic Programming*, Melbourne, Australia, pp. 576–600, MIT Press (May 25–29, 1987).

[Dobr87a] Dobry, T., "A High Performance Architecture for Prolog", UUB/CSD 87/352, Computer Science Division EECS, University of California, Berkeley (May 1987).

[Egge89a] Eggers, Susan J. and Randy H. Katz, "The Effect of Sharing on the Cache and Bus Performance of Parallel Programs", *Third International Conference on Architectural Support for Programming Languages and Operating Systems*, Boston, Massachusetts, pp. 257–270 (3–6 April, 1989).

[Erik84a] Eriksson, Lars-Henrik and Manny Rayner, "Incorporating Mutable Arrays into Logic Programming", *Second International Logic Programming Conference*, Uppsala, Sweden, ed. S-A Tarnlund, pp. 101–114, Uppsala UP (July 2–6, 1984).

[Fagi87a] Fagin, Barry S. and Alvin M. Despain, "Performance Studies of a Parallel Prolog Architecture", *14th Annual International Symposium on Computer Architecture*, Pittsburgh, Pennsylvania, pp. 108–16 (2–5 June, 1987).

[Fagi87b] Fagin, B. S., "A Parallel Execution Model for Prolog", Ph.D. Thesis, University of California, Berkeley, California (1987).

[Fagi90a] Fagin, Barry S. and Alvin M. Despain, "The Performance of Parallel Prolog Programs", *IEEE Transactions on Computers* **39**(12), pp. 1434–1445 (December 1990).

[Fent91a] Fenton, Wayne, Balkrishna Ramkumar, Vikram A. Saletorc, Amitabh B. Sinha and Laxmikant V. Kale, "Supporting Machine Independent Programming on Diverse Parallel Architectures", *International Conference on Parallel Processing*, St. Charles, Illinois, pp. 193–201 (August 1991) (Volume 2 – Software).

[Fere91a] Ferenczi, Szabolcs, "Concepts for a Modular and Distributed Prolog Language", *Third International Symposium on Programming Language Implementation and Logic Programming (PLILP'91)*, Passau, Germany, ed. J. Maluszynski and M. Wirsing, pp. 159–170, Springer–Verlag (26–28 August 1991) (Lecture Notes in Computer Science No. 528, J. Maluszynski and M.

Wirsing (Eds)).

[Fost86a] Foster, Ian, Steve Gregory, Graem Ringwood and Ken Sayoh, "A Sequential Implementation of PARLOG", *Third International Conference on Logic Programming*, London, pp. 149–156, Springer-Verlag (July 14–18, 1986) (Lecture Notes in Computer Science No. 225).

[Fost87a] Foster, Ian and Stephen Taylor, *Flat Parlog: A Basis for Comparison*, Imperial College London and the Weizmann Institute (March 1987).

[Fost88a] Foster, I., "Parallel Implementation of Parlog", *International Conference on Parallel Processing*, St. Charles, USA, pp. 9–16 (15–19 August, 1988) (Volume 2 – Software).

[Fost89a] Foster, Ian and Stephen Taylor, *Strand: New Concepts in Parallel Programming*, Prentice–Hall, Englewood Cliffs, N.J. (1989).

[Fost90a] Foster, I., *Systems Programming in Parallel Logic Languages*, Prentice-Hall (1990).

[Fost90b] Foster, Ian and Stephen Taylor, *Strand: New Concepts in Parallel Programming*, Prentice–Hall, Englewood Cliffs, N.J. (1990).

[Fran79a] Francez, N., C. A. R. Hoare, D. J. Lehmann and W. P. Roever, "Semantics of Nondeterminism, Concurrency and Communication", *Journal of Computer Systems Science* (19), pp. 290–308 (1979).

[Furu90a] Furuichi, M., N. Ichiyoshi and K. Taki, "A Multi-Level Load Balancing Scheme for OR-Parallel Exhaustive Search Programs on the Multi-PSI", *Second ACM SIGPLAN Symposium on Principles and Practice of Parallel Programming (PPoPP)*, Seattle, Washington, pp. 50/-59 (14/-16 March, 1990) (ACM SIGPLAN NOTICES, Volume 25, Number 3, March 1990).

[Futo82a] Futó, Ivan and Janos Szeredi, "A Discrete Simulation System Based on Artificial Intelligence Methods", *Collection of Papers on Logic Programming*, pp. Paper 6, Institute for Co-ordination of Computer Techniques (Szki), Budapest, Hungary (May 1982), A, Javor (ed), North Holland 1982"" (Also appeared in "Discrete Simulation and Related Fields", A, Javor (ed), North Holland 1982).

[Futo84a] Futó, Iván and J. Szeredi, "System Simulation and Co-operating Problem-Solving on a Prolog Basis", *Implementations of Prolog*, ed. J. A. Campbell, pp. 163–174, Ellis Horwood Limited (1984) (Ellis Horwood Series In Artificial Intelligence).

[Futo86a] Futo, I., C. Percebois, I. Durand, C. Simon and B. Bonhoure, "Simulation Study of a Multiprocessor PROLOG Architecture", *First Italian Conference on Logic Programming*, Genova, Italy (March 1986).

[Futo89a] Futó, Iván and Peter Kacsuk, "CS-Prolog on multitransputer systems", *Microprocessors and Microsystems* 13(2), pp. 103–112 (March 1989).

[Futo90a] Futó, Iván, "The Modified Time Warp Mechanism of CS-Prolog", *European Simulation Multiconference*, Nuremberg, Germany, ed. Bernd Schmidt (June

REFERENCES

1990) (Proceedings of Modelling and Simulation).

[Futo90b] Futó, Iván and Futó Gergely, *Artificial Intelligence In Simulation*, Ellis Horwood Limited (1990) (Ellis Horwood Series In Artificial Intellignece).

[Gall86a] Gallagher, J., "Transforming Logic Programs by Specialising Interpreters", *7th European Conference on Artificial Intelligence*, Brighton, England, ed. Ben du Boulay, David Hogg and Luc Steels, pp. 313–326., North Holland (July 20–25, 1986).

[Gaud86a] Gaudiot, Jean-Luc, "Structure Handling in Data-Flow Systems", *IEEE Transactions on Computers* **35**(6), pp. 489–502 (June 1986).

[Glae90a] Glaesser, U. and G. Lehrenfeld, "A distributed implementation of Flat Concurrent Prolog on transputer architectures", *UNESCO Conference on Parallel Computing in Engeneering and Engeneering Education*, Paris, France, pp. 181–185 (October 8-12, 1990).

[Goto84a] Goto, A., H. Tanaka and T. Moto-Oka, "Highly Parallel Inference Engine PIE - Goal Rewriting Model and Machine Architecture", *New Generation Computing* **2**(1), pp. 37–58 (1984).

[Goto88a] Goto, A., M. Sato, K. Nakajima, K. Taki and A. Matsumoto, "Overview of the Parallel Inference Machine Architecture (PIM)", *International Conference on Fifth Generation Computer Systems*, Tokyo, Japan, pp. 208–229, OMSHA and Springer-Verlag (November 28 – December 2 1988).

[Goto89a] Goto, Atsuhiro, Akira Matsumoto and Evan Tick, "Design and Performance of a Coherent Cache for Parallel Logic Programming Architectures", *16th Annual International Symposium on Computer Architecture*, Jerusalem, Israel, pp. 25–33 (28 May – 1 June, 1989).

[Greg85a] Gregory, Steve, "Design, Application and Implementation of a Parallel Logic Programming Language", Ph.D. Thesis, Imperial College of Science and Technology (September 1985).

[Greg87a] Gregory, Steve, *Parallel Logic Programming in PARLOG*, Addison-Wesley (1987).

[Guic90a] Guichard-Jary, Patricia, "Padmavati Parallel Associative Development Machine as a Vehicle for Artificial Intelligence", *Annual ESPRIT Conference*, Brussels, pp. 227-241, Kluwer Academic (12-15 November 1990).

[Gupt89a] , Gopal Gupta and Bharat Jayaraman, "Compiled And-Or Parallelism on Shared Memory Multiprocessors", *North American Conference on Logic Programming*, Cleveland, Ohio, pp. 332–349 (October 1989).

[Gupt91a] Gupta, G. and M. Hermenegildo, "ACE: And/Or-Parallel Copying Based Execution of Logic Programs", *International Conference on Logic Programming Pre-Conference Workshop on Parallel Execution of Logic Programs*, Paris (June 24, 1991).

[Gurd85a] Gurd, J. R., C.C. Kircham and I. Watson, "The Manchester Prototype Dataflow Computer", *Communication of ACM* **28**(1), pp. 34–52 (January 1985).

[Hage89a] Hagersten, Erik and Seif Haridi, "The Cache Coherence Protocol of the Data Diffusion Machine", *Parallel Architectures and Languages Europe (PARLE'89)*, Eindhoven, The Netherlands, ed. E. Odijk, M. Rem and J-C. Syre, pp. 1–18, Springer Verlag (June 12–16, 1989).

[Hail86a] Hailperin, M. and H. Westphal, "A Computational Model for PEPSy", CA–16, ECRC GmbH, Computer Architecture Group (1986).

[Hali86a] Halim, Z., "A Data-Driven Machine for OR-Parallel Evaluation of Logic Programs", *New Generation Computing* 4, pp. 5–33 (1986).

[Hare85a] Harel, A. and A. Pnueli, "On the Development of Reactive Systems", *Logics and Models of Concurrent Systems*, ed. K. R. Apt, pp. 477–98, Springer-Verlag (1985).

[Hari88a] Haridi, Seif and Per Brand, "ANDORRA Prolog: An Integration of Prolog and Committed Choice Languages", *International Conference on Fifth Generation Computer Systems*, Tokyo, Japan, pp. 745–754, OMSHA and Springer-Verlag (November 28 – December 2 1988).

[Hari90a] Haridi, Seif and Sverker Janson, "Kernel Andorra Prolog and its Computational Model", *Seventh International Conference on Logic Programming*, Jerusalem, Israel, pp. 31–46 (18 – 20 June, 1990).

[Harp86a] Harp, J. G., C. R. Jesshope, T. Muntean and C. Whitby-Stevens, "The Development and Application of a Low Cost High Performance Multiprocessor Machine", *ESPRIT'86: Results and Achievements*, North Holland (1986).

[Haus87a] Hausman, Bogumil, Andrzej Ciepielewski and Seif Haridi, "OR-parallel Prolog Made Efficient on Shared Memory Multiprocessor", *1987 Symposium on Logic Programming*, San Francisco, USA, pp. 69–79, IEEE Computer Society Press (August 31 – September 4, 1987).

[Haus88a] Hausman, B., A. Ciepielewski and A. Calderwood, "Cut and Side-Effects in OR-parallel Prolog", *International Conference on Fifth Generation Computer Systems*, Tokyo, Japan, pp. 831–840, OMSHA and Springer-Verlag (November 28 – December 2 1988).

[Haus89a] Hausman, B., "Pruning and Scheduling Speculative Work in OR-parallel Prolog", *Parallel Architectures and Languages Europe (PARLE'89)*, Eindhoven, The Netherlands, ed. E. Odijk, M. Rem and J-C. Syre, pp. 133–150, Springer-Verlag (June 12–16, 1989) (Volume II - Parallel Languages).

[Haus90a] Hausman, B., "Pruning and Speculative Work in OR-Parallel Prolog", Ph.D. Thesis, Royal Institute of Technology, Stockholm, Sweden (1990) (Tech Report TRITA-CS-9002).

[Henn90a] Hennesy, J. L. and D. A. Patterson, *Computer Architecture: A Quantitative Approach*, Morgan Kaufmann (1990).

[Herm86a] Hermenegildo, M. V., "An Abstract Machine for Restricted AND-Parallel Execution of Logic Programs", *Third International Conference on Logic Programming*, London, U.K, pp. 25–39, Springer Verlag (14 – 18 July, 1986) (Lecture Notes in Computer Science No 225).

REFERENCES

[Herm86b] Hermenegildo, M. V. and R. I. Nasr, "Efficient Management of Backtracking in AND-parallelism", *Third International Conference on Logic Programming*, London, pp. 40–54, Springer-Verlag (July 14–18, 1986) (Lecture Notes in Computer Science No. 225).

[Herm86c] Hermenegildo, M. V., "An Abstract Machine Based Execution Model for Computer Architecture Design and Efficient Implementation of Logic Programs in Parallel", TR-86-20, Dept. of Computer Sciences, The University of Texas at Austin (August 1986).

[Herm87a] Hermenegildo, M. and E. Tick, "Performance evaluation of the RAP-WAM", PP-085-87, MCC (March 1987).

[Herm87b] Hermenegildo, M. V., "Relating goal scheduling, precedence and memory management in AND parallel execution of logic programs", *Fourth International Conference on Logic Programming*, Melbourne, Australia, pp. 556–575, MIT Press (May 25–29, 1987).

[Herm89a] Hermenegildo, M. and E. Tick, "Memory Referencing Characteristics and Caching Performance of AND-parallel Prolog on Shared-Memory Multiprocessors", *New Generation Computing* 7(1), pp. 37–58 (1989).

[Herm89b] Hermenegildo, Manuel and Francesca Rossi, "On the Correctness and Efficiency of Independent AND-Parallelism in Logic Programs", *North American Conference on Logic Programming*, Cleveland, Ohio, pp. 369–389 (16–20 October 1989).

[Herm90a] Hermenegildo, Manuel and Francesca Rossi, "Non-Strict Independent And-Parallelism", *Seventh International Conference on Logic Programming*, Jerusalem, Israel, ed. David H. D. Warren and Peter Szeridi, pp. 237–252, MIT Press (June 18–20, 1990).

[Herm90b] Hermenegildo, M. V. and K. J. Green, "&-Prolog and its Performance: Exploiting Independent And-Parallelism", *Seventh International Conference on Logic Programming*, Jerusalem, Israel, ed. David H. D. Warren and Peter Szeridi, pp. 253–268, MIT Press (June 18–20, 1990).

[Hewi77a] Hewitt, Carl, "Viewing Control Structures as Patterns of Passing Messages", *Artificial Intelligence* 8(3), pp. 323–364 (June 1987).

[Hewi79a] Hewitt, C. E., G. Attardi and H. Lieberman, "Specifying and proving properties of guardians for distributed systems", *Semantics of Concurrent Computation*, ed. G. Kahn, pp. 316–336., Springer-Verlag (1979) (Lecture Notes in Computer Science 70,).

[Hewi80a] Hewitt, C., "The Apiary Network Architecture for Knowledgeable Systems", *1980 LISP Conference*, Standford, U.S.A. (25–27 August 1980).

[Hewi84a] Hewitt, Carl and Henry Lieberman, "Design Issues in Parallel Architectures for Artificial Intelligence", *IEEE Computer Society International Conference (COMPCON'84)*, pp. 418–423 (February 1984).

[Hoar78a] Hoare, C. A. R., "Communicating Sequential Processes", *Communications of the ACM* 21(8), pp. 666–677 (August 1978).

[Hoar85a] Hoare, C. A. R., *Communicating Sequential Processes*, Prentice–Hall (1985).

[Holy91a] Holyer, I., *Functional Programming with Miranda*, Pitman (1991).

[Hour87a] Houri, Avshalom and Ehud Shapiro, "A Sequential Abstract Machine for Flat Concurrent Prolog", *Concurrent Prolog: Collected Papers*, ed. Ehud Shapiro, pp. 513–574, MIT Press Cambridge, Mass. (1987).

[Hugh82a] Hughes, R. J. M., "Super-Combinators: A New Implementation Method for Applicative Languages", *1982 ACM Symposium on Lisp and Functional Programming*, Pittsburgh, Pennsylvania, pp. 1–10 (15–18 August, 1982).

[Hugs82a] Hughes, Joseph L. A., "Implementing Control-Flow Structures in Dataflow Programs", *IEEE Computer Society International Conference (COMPCON'82)*, San Francisco, California, pp. 87–90 (22–25 February, 1982).

[Hunt87a] Huntbach, M. M., "Algorithmic Parlog Debugging", *1987 Symposium on Logic Programming*, San Francisco, CA, pp. 288–297, IEEE (31 August – 4 September, 1987).

[Hunt88a] Huntbach, M. M. and F. W. Burton, "Alpha-Beta Search on Virtual Tree Machines", *Information Sciences* **44**(1), pp. 3–17 (January 1988).

[Hunt89a] Huntbach, M. M., "Meta-Interpreters and Partial Evaluation in Parlog", *Formal Aspects of Computing* **1**(2), pp. 193–211 (April 1989).

[Hunt89b] M.Huntbach, M., "Implementing a Graph-Colouring Algorithm in Parlog", *SIGPLAN Notices* **24**(9), pp. 80–85 (September 1989).

[Hunt91a] Huntbach, M. M., "Speculative Computation and Priorities in Concurrent Logic Languages", TR Dept Computer Science NUMBER 520, Queen Mary and Westfield College, U of London, UK (January 1991) (Presented at the Third Conference of the UK Association for Logic Programming, Edinburgh (April 1991)).

[Hunt91b] Huntbach, M. M., "Automated Transaltion of Occam to RGDC", TR Dept Computer Science, Queen Mary and Westfield College, U of London (April 1991) (Presented at Workshop on Logic Programming and Transformation, Manchester (June 1991)).

[Hunt91c] Huntbach, M. M., "A Single-Message Distributed Algorithm for Minimal Spanning Trees", TR Dept Computer Science, Queen Mary and Westfield College, U of London (March 1991) (Presented at First International Conference of the Austrian Centre for Parallel Computation (October 1991)).

[Hwan89a] Hwang, Zhiyi and Shouren Hu, "A Compiling Approach for Exploiting AND-Parallelism in Parallel Logic Programming Systems", *Parallel Architectures and Languages Europe (PARLE'89)*, Eindhoven, The Netherlands, ed. E. Odijk, M. Rem and J-C. Syre **2**, pp. 335-345, Springer-Verlag (June 12-16, 1989).

[Ichi87a] Ichiyoshi, N., T. Miyazaki and K. Taki, "A Distributed Implementation of Flat GHC on the Multi-PSI", *Fourth International Conference on Logic Programming*, Melbourne, Australia, pp. 257–275, MIT Press (May 25–29, 1987).

REFERENCES

[Ichi88a] Ichiyoshi, Nobuyuki, Kazuaki Rokusawa, Katsuto Nakajima and Yu Inamura, "A New External Reference Management and Distributed Unification for KL1", *International Conference on Fifth Generation Computer Systems*, Tokyo, Japan, pp. 904–913, OMSHA and Springer-Verlag (November 28 – December 2 1988).

[Inam90a] Inamura, Y. and S. Onishi, "A Detection Algorithm of Perpetual Suspension in KL1", *Seventh International Conference on Logic Programming*, Jerusalem, Israel, pp. 18–30 (18–20 June, 1990).

[INMO88a] INMOS Limited, *The Transputer Databook*, INMOS Limited (November, 1988).

[INMO88b] INMOS Limited, *Transputer Instruction Set*, Prentice–Hall (1988).

[INMO88c] Limited, INMOS, *Transputer Reference Manual*, Prentice–Hall (1988).

[INMO88d] Limited, INMOS, *Occam-2 Reference Manual*, Prentice–Hall (1988).

[Jary89a] Jary, Patricia, Xavier de Joybert and Philippe Arsac, "Selection de Clauses en Prolog", *8th Seminar on Logic Programming*, Tregastel (France), pp. 499-521, CNET, France telecom (24-26 May 1989) (in french).

[Jeff85a] Jefferson, D. R., "Virtual Time", *ACM Transactions on Programming Languages* 7(3), pp. 404–405 (March 1985).

[Jone89a] Jones, David and Tom Hintz, "Implementation of a Parallel Prolog on Transputers", *Australian Transputer and Occam User Group Conference*, Melbourne, pp. 165–72, Centre for Advanced Technology in Telecommunications, Royal Melbourne Institute of Technology (6–7 July, 1989).

[Kacs87a] Kacsuk, P. and A. Bale, *DAP Prolog: A Set-oriented Approach to Prolog*, DAP Support Unit, Queen Mary College, University of London (June 1987).

[Kacs87b] Kacsuk, P., A. Bale and t02, *DAP Prolog*, DAP Support Unit, Queen Mary College, University of London (1987).

[Kacs89a] Kacsuk, P. and I. Futo, "Multi-transputer implementation of CS-Prolog", *Parallel Processing and Artificial Intelligence*, ed. Mike Reeve and Steven E. Zenith, pp. 131–48, John Wiley and Sons (1989).

[Kacs90a] Kacsuk, P., *Execution Models of Prolog for Parallel Computers*, Pitman Publishing (UK) (1990) (The MIT Press (USA)).

[Kacs90b] Kacsuk, Peter, Iván Futó and Szabolcs Ferenczi, "Implementing CS-Prolog on a communicating process architecture", *Journal of Microcomputer Applications* 13, pp. 19–41 (1990).

[Kacs91a] Kacsuk, P., "A Parallel Prolog Abstract Machine and Its Multi-Transputer Implementation", *The Computer Journal* 34(1), pp. 52–63 (February 1991).

[Kacs91b] Kacsuk, P., "Execution of Prolog on Massively Parallel Distributed Systems", SERC Technical Report, Centre for Parallel Computing, Queen Mary and Westfield College (1991).

REFERENCES

[Kahn84a]   Kahn, K., "A Primitive for the Control of Logic Programs", *1984 International Symposium on Logic Programming*, Atlantic City, USA, pp. 242–251, IEEE Computer Society (February 6–9, 1984).

[Kale85a]   Kale, Laxmikant V., "Parallel Architectures for Problem Solving", Ph.D. thesis, State University of New York, Stonybrook (December 1985).

[Kale87a]   Kale, L. V., "The REDUCE-OR Process Model for Parallel Evaluation of Logic Programs", *Fourth International Conference on Logic Programming*, Melbourne, Australia, ed. Jean-Louis Lassez, pp. 616–632, MIT Press (May 25-29, 1987).

[Kale87b]   Kale, Laxmikant V., "'Completeness' and 'Full Parallelism' of Parallel Logic Programming Schemes", *1987 Symposium on Logic Programming*, San Francisco, U.S.A., pp. 125–133 (August 31 – September 4, 1987).

[Kale87c]   Kale, Laxmikant V., "Comparing the Performance of Two Dynamic Load Distribution Methods", *International Conference on Parallel Processing*, St. Charles, Illinois, pp. 8–12 (August 1988) (Volume 1 – Architecture).

[Kale88a]   Kale, Laxmikant V., Balkrishna Ramkumar and Wennie Wei Shu, "A Memory Organisation Independent Binding Environment for AND and OR Parallel Execution of Logic Programs Programs", *Fifth International Conference and Symposium on Logic Programming*, Seattle, Washington, ed. R. Kowalski and K. Bowen, pp. 1223–1240, MIT Press (15–19 August, 1988).

[Kale90a]   Kale, Laxmikant V., "The Chare Kernel Parallel Programming System", *International Conference on Parallel Processing*, St. Charles, Illinois, pp. 17–20 (August 1990) (Volume 2 – Software).

[Kell79a]   Keller, R.M., G. Lindstrom and S. Patil, "A Loosely-coupled Applicative Multi-processing System", *National Computer Conference*, Arlington, U. S. A., pp. 613–622, AFIPS Press (1979).

[Kemp90a]   Kemp, R. S. and G. A. Ringwood, "Algebraic Framework for Abstract Interpretation of Definite Programs", *North American Logic Programming Conference 1990*, Austin, Texas, ed. S. Debray and M. Hermenegildo, pp. 516–530, MIT Press (1990).

[Kibl85a]   Kibler, Dennis F. and John Conery, "Parallelism in AI Programs", *Ninth International Joint Conference on Artificial Intelligence (IJCAI'85)*, Los Angeles, USA, pp. 53–56 (18–23 August, 1985).

[Kimu87a]   Kimura, Yasunori and Takashi Chikayama, "An Abstract KL1 Machine and its Instruction Set", *1987 Symposium on Logic Programming*, San Francisco, USA, pp. 468–477 (August 31 – September 4, 1987).

[Klig88a]   Kliger, Shmuel and Ehud Shapiro, "A Decision Tree Compilation Algorithm for FCP(|,:,?)", *Fifth International Conference and Symposium on Logic Programming*, Seattle, Washington, ed. R. Kowalski and K. Bowen, pp. 1315–1336, MIT Press (15–19 August, 1988).

[Know65a]   Knowlton., K. C., "A Fast Storage Allocator", *Communications of the ACM* **8**(10), pp. 623–625 (1965).

REFERENCES

[Kogg91a] Kogge, P. M., *The Architecture of Symbolic Computers*, McGraw-Hill (1991).

[Korf85a] Korf, R. E., "Depth-first Iterative-deepening: An Optimal Admissible Tree Search", *Artificial Intelligence* **27**, pp. 97–109 (1985).

[Kowa79a] Kowalski, R. A., *Logic for Problem Solving*, North-Holland (1979).

[Kowa79b] Kowalski, Robert, "Algorithm = Logic + Control", *Communications of the ACM* **22**(7), pp. 424–436 (1979).

[Koza90a] Kozato, F. and G. A. Ringwood, "Virtual Neural Networks", *Japanese Logic Programming Conference '90*, Tokyo, pp. 199–208, ICOT (July 1990).

[Kuma87a] Kumar, Vipin and Yow-Jian Lin, "An Intelligent Backtracking Scheme for Prolog", *1987 Symposium on Logic Programming*, San Francisco, pp. 406–414 (August 31 – September 4, 1987).

[Kumo86a] Kumon, Kouichi, Hideo Masuzawa and Akihiro Itashiki, "Kabu-Wake: A New Parallel Inference Method and its Evaluation", *Twenty-first IEEE Computer Society International Conference (COMPCON'86)*, San Francisco, pp. 168–172 (March 3–6, 1986).

[Land65a] Landin, P., "A Correspondence Between Algol 60 and Church's Lambda Notation, Part I", *Communications of the ACM* **8**(2), pp. 89–101 (1965).

[Land65b] Landin, P., "A Correspondence Between Algol 60 and Church's Lambda Notation, Part II", *Communications of the ACM* **8**(3), pp. 158–165 (1965).

[Land66a] Landin, P., "The Next 700 Programming Languages", *Communications of the ACM* **9**(3), pp. 157–166 (1966).

[Lend88a] Lenders, Patrick M., "A Generalized Message-Passing Mechanism for Communicating Sequential Processes", *IEEE Transactions on Computing* **37**(6), pp. 646–51 (June 1988).

[Leno90a] Lenoski, Dan, James Laudon, Kourosh Gharachorloo, Anoop Gupta and John Hennessy, "The Directory-based Cache Coherence Protocol for the DASH Multiprocessor", *Seventeenth Annual International Symposium on Computer Architecture*, Seattle, pp. 148–59, IEEE (28–31 May 1990).

[Li86a] Li, Peyyun Peggy and Alain J. Martin, "The Sync Model: A Parallel Execution Method for Logic Programming", *1986 Symposium on Logic Programming*, Salt Lake City, USA, pp. 223–234 (September 22–25, 1986).

[Li89a] Li, Kai and Paul Hudak, "Memory Coherence in Shared Virtual Memory Systems", *ACM Transactions on Computer Systems* **7**(4), pp. 321–59 (November 1989).

[Lieb83a] Lieberman, H. and C. Hewitt, "A Real-Time Garbage Collector Based on the Lifetimes of Objects", *Communications of the ACM* **26**(6), pp. 419–429 (1983).

[Lin86a] Lin, Yow-Jian, Vipin Kumar and Clement Leung, "An Intelligent Backtracking Algorithm for Parallel Execution of Logic Programs", *Third International Conference on Logic Programming*, London, pp. 55–68, Springer-Verlag (July 14–18, 1986) (Lecture Notes in Computer Science No. 225).

[Lin88a] Lin, Y. -J., "A Parallel Implementation of Logic Programs", PhD Thesis, University of Texas at Austin (1988).

[Lin88b] Lin, Yow-Jian and Vipin Kumar, "AND-parallel execution of Logic programs on a Shared Memory Multiprocessor: A Summary of Results", *Fifth International Conference and Symposium on Logic Programming*, Seattle, Washington, ed. R. Kowalski and K. Bowen, pp. 1123–1141, MIT Press (15–19 August, 1988).

[Lin88c] Lin, Yow-Jian and Vipin Kumar, "An Execution Model for Exploiting AND-Parallelism in Logic Programs", *New Generation Computing* 5(4), pp. 393–425 (May 1988).

[Lin88d] Lin, Yow-Jian and Vipin Kumar, "Performance of AND-Parallel Execution of Logic Programs on a Shared-Memory Multiprocessor", *International Conference on Fifth Generation Computer Systems*, Tokyo, Japan, pp. 851–860, ICOT (November 28 – December 2, 1988).

[Lind84a] Lindstrom, Gary, "OR-Parallelism on Applicative Architectures", *Second International Logic Programming Conference*, Uppsala, Sweden, pp. 159–170 (2–6 July 1984) (See also report of same name, Laboratory for Computer Science, MIT, January 1984).

[Liu90a] Liu, Chuchang, Norman Y. Foo and Michael J. Wise, "A Mathematical Semantics for Static Prolog Modules", Basser Department of Computer Science Technical Report, Sydney University (1990).

[Lusk88a] Lusk, Ewing, Ralph Butler, Terrence Disz, Robert Olson, Ross Overbeek, Rick Stevens, David H. D. Warren, Alan Calderwood, Peter Szeridi, Seif Haridi, Per Brand, Mats Carlsson, Andrzej Ciepielewski and Bogumil Hausman, "The Aurora OR-Parallel Prolog System", *International Conference on Fifth Generation Computer Systems*, Tokyo, pp. 819–30, OMSHA and Springer-Verlag (November 28 – December 2, 1988) (also New Generation Computing 7(2,3), 1990, pp. 243–271).

[Masu86a] Masuzawa, H., K. Kumon, A. Itashiki, K. Satoh and Y. Sohma, "Kabu Wake Parallel Inference Mechanism and its Evaluation", *Fifth Generation Computer Conference (FGCC)*, pp. 955–962, IEEE Computer Society Press (November 1986).

[May87a] May, David and Roger Shepherd, "Communicating Process Computers", Inmos technical note 22, INMOS Ltd (February 1987).

[May90a] May, D., "Future Directions in Transputer Technology", *UNESCO Conference on Parallel Computing in Engineering and Engineering Education*, Paris, France, pp. 193–203 (October 8-12, 1990).

[Meik90a] Meiko, *Computing Surface: CSTools for SunOS, Vols. 1 and 2*, Meiko Limited, Bristol (1990).

[Meik90b] Meiko, *CS-Tools for C Programmers*, Meiko (1990).

[Mell81a] Mellish, C. S., "Automatic Generation of Mode Declarations for Prolog Programs", Tech. Rep. 163, University of Edinburgh, Department of AI

(August 81).

[Mell86a] Mellish, C., "Abstract Interpretation of Prolog Programs", *Third International Conference on Logic Programming*, London, pp. 463–474, Springer-Verlag (July 14–18, 1986) (Lecture Notes in Computer Science No. 225).

[Meye90a] Meyer, David M. and John S. Conery, "Architected Failure Handling for AND-Parallel Logic Programs", *Seventh International Conference on Logic Programming*, Jerusalem, pp. 271–290 (June 18–20, 1990).

[Mier85a] Mierowsky, C., S. Taylor, E. Shapiro, J. Levy and S. Safra, "The Design and Implementation of Flat Concurrent Prolog", Tech. Report CS85-09, The Weizmann Institute of Science, Rehovot, Israel (1985).

[Mill89a] Mills, J. W., "A High-Performance Low Risc Machine for Logic Programming", *Journal of Logic Programming* 6(1), pp. 179–212, Elsesvier Science Pub. Co (March 1989).

[Miln80a] Milner,. J. R. G., *A Calculus of Communicating Systems*, Springer-Verlag (1980) (Lecture Notes in Computer Science, Vol. 92).

[Miya85a] Miyazaki, Toshihiko, Akikazu Takeuchi and Takashi Chikayama, "A Sequential Implementation of Concurrent Prolog Based on the Shallow Binding Scheme", *1985 Symposium on Logic Programming*, Boston, USA, pp. 110–118, IEEE (July 15–18, 1985).

[Moha90a] Mohamed, M. A., "Process Allocation and Load Balancing in Parallel Logic Programming", M.S. Thesis, University of Oregon (1990).

[Mont83a] Monteiro, Luís F., "A Logic for Distributed Processes", Technical Report, Universidade Nova de Lisboa, Departamento de Informática (1983) (PhD Thesis, in Portuguese).

[Mont84a] Monteiro, Luís F., "A Proposal for Distributed Programming in Logic", *Implementations of Prolog*, ed. J. A. Campbell, pp. 329–340, Ellis Horwood (1984).

[Mont86a] Monteiro, Luís F., "Distributed Logic: A Theory of Distributed Programming in Logic", Technical Report, Universidade Nova de Lisboa, Departamento de Informática (1986).

[Moon87a] Moon, David A., "Symbolics Architecture", *IEEE Computer* 20(1), pp. 43–52 (January 1987).

[Muda89a] Mudambi, Shyam, "Performance of Aurora on a Switch-Based Multiprocessor", *1989 North American Conference on Logic Programming*, Cleveland, Ohio, ed. E. Lusk and R. Overbeek, pp. 697–712, MIT Press (16–20 October 1989).

[Muth90a] Muthukumar, K. and M. V. Hermenegildo, "The CDG, UDG, and MEL Methods for Automatic Compile-time Parallelization of Logic Programs for Independent AND-parallelism", *Seventh International Conference on Logic Programming*, Jerusalem, Israel, ed. David H. D. Warren and Peter Szeridi, pp. 221–236, MIT Press (June 18–20, 1990).

REFERENCES

[Nais88a] Naish, Lee, "Parallelizing NU-Prolog", *Fifth International Conference and Symposium on Logic Programming*, Seattle, Washington, ed. R. Kowalski and K. Bowen, pp. 1546–1564, MIT Press (15–19 August, 1988).

[Nakj88a] Nakajima., K., "Piling GC – Efficient Garbage Collection for AI Languages", *Parallel Processing (Proceeding of the IFIP WG 10.3 Working Conference*, pp. 201–204, Elsevier Science Publishers B.V. (North-Holland) (1988) (Also in ICOT Technical Report TR-354, 1988).

[Nakj89a] Nakajima, K., Y. Inamura, N. Ichiyoshi, K. Rokusawa and T. Chikayama, "Distributed Implementation of KL1 on the Multi-PSI/V2", *Sixth International Conference on Logic Programming*, Lisbon, Portugal, pp. 436–451 (19–23 June, 1989).

[Naks87a] Nakashima, H. and K. Nakajima, "Hardware Architecture of the Sequential Inference Machine : PSI-II", *1987 Symposium on Logic Programming*, San Francisco, USA, pp. 104–113 (August 31 – September 4, 1987).

[Nels80a] Nelson, G. and D. Oppen, "Fast Decision Procedures Based on Congruence Closure", *Journal of the ACM* **27**(2), pp. 356–64 (1980).

[Nils86a] Nilsson, M. and H. Tanaka, "Fleng Prolog – The language which turns Supercomputers into Parallel Prolog Machines", *Fifth Logic Programming Conference (Logic Programming '86)*, ed. Eiiti Wada, pp. 170–179, Springer-Verlag (June 23–26, 1986) (Lecture Notes in Computer Science 264).

[Nils88a] Nilsson, Martin and Hidehiko Tanaka, "Massively Parallel Implementation of Flat GHC on the Connection Machine", *International Conference on Fifth Generation Computer Systems*, Tokyo, Japan, pp. 1031–1040, OMSHA and Springer-Verlag (November 28 – December 2 1988).

[Nils88b] Nilsson, M. and H. Tanaka, "A Flat GHC Implementation for Supercomputers", *Fifth International Conference and Symposium on Logic Programming*, Seattle, Washington, ed. R. Kowalski and K. Bowen, pp. 1337–1350, MIT Press (15–19 August, 1988).

[Nish90a] Nishida, Kenji, Yasunori Kimura, Akira Matsumoto and Atsuhiro Goto, "Evaluation of MRB Garbage Collection on Parallel Logic Programming Architectures", *Seventh International Conference on Logic Programming*, Jerusalem, Israel, ed. David H. D. Warren and Peter Szeridi, pp. 83–95, MIT Press (June 18–20, 1990).

[O'Ke85a] O'Keefe, Richard A., "On the Treatment of Cuts in Source-Level Tools", *1985 International Symposium on Logic Programming*, Boston, USA, pp. 68–72, IEEE Computer Society Press (July 15–18, 1985).

[O'Ke90a] O'Keefe, Richard A, *The Craft of Prolog*, MIT Press (1990).

[Okum87a] Okumura, Akira and Yuji Matsumoto, "Parallel Programming with Layered Streams", *1987 Symposium on Logic Programming*, San Francisco, CA, U.S.A., pp. 224–231, IEEE Computer Society Press (31 August – 4 September, 1987).

REFERENCES

[Park90a] Parker, D. S., "Stream Data Analysis in Prolog", *The Practice of Prolog*, ed. L. S. Sterling, pp. 249–301, MIT Press (1990).

[Pars89a] *Par.C System: User's Manual and Library Reference Version 1.22*, Parsec Developments, Leiden, The Netherlands (1989).

[Perc87a] Percebois, C., I. Futó, I. Durand, C. Simon and B. Bonhoure, "Simulation Results of a Multiprocessor PROLOG Architecture Based on a Distributed AND/OR Graph", *International Joint Conference on Theory and Practice of Software Development (TAPSOFT'87)*, Pisa, Italy, pp. 126–139, Springer–Verlag (March 23–27, 1987) (Lecture Notes in Computer Science No 250).

[Perc88a] Percebois, C., I. Durand and I. Futó, "Parallel Execution of Independent Subgoals", *International Symposium on Distributed Systems, Methods and Applications (IFAC-DIS'88)*, Varna, Bulgaria (June 1988).

[Perc89a] Percebois, C., Y. Beneteau and N. Signes, "Design of a Parallel Inference Abstract Machine", *Parallel Computing 89 Conference*, Leiden, The Netherlands, pp. 519–525 (29th August–1st September 1989).

[Perc90a] Percebois, C., "Definition et Evaluation d'un Modele d'Execution Repartie pour les Systemes Logiques Non-Deterministes", These de Doctorat d'Etat, Universite Paul Sabatier, Toulouse, France (Decembre 1990).

[Pere83a] Pereira, Fernando, "C-Prolog User's Manual", University of Edinburgh, Department of Artificial Intelligence (1983).

[Pere84a] Pereira, Luís M. and Roger Nasr, "Delta-Prolog: A Distributed Logic Programming Language", *International Conference on Fifth Generation Computer Systems*, Tokyo, Japan, pp. 283–91, North Holland and OHMSHA, Ltd (6–9 November, 1984).

[Pere84b] Pereira, Luís M. and António Porto, "Selective Backtracking", *Logic Programming*, ed. K. Clark and S-A. Tarnlund, pp. 107–114, Academic Press (1984).

[Pere86a] Pereira, Luís M., Luís Monteiro, José C. Cunha and Joaquim N. Aparício, "Delta-Prolog: A Distributed Backtracking Extension with Events", *Third International Conference on Logic Programming*, London, United Kingdom, pp. 69–83 (14–18 July, 1986) (Springer–Verlag Lecture Notes in Computer Science No. 225).

[Pere88a] Perera, Luís M., Luís Monteiro, José C. Cunha and Joaquim N. Aparício, "Concurrency and Communication in Delta Prolog", *IEE International Specialists Seminar on the Design and Applications of Parallel Digital Processors*, Lisbon, Portugal, pp. 94–104, IEE (1988).

[Pfis85a] Pfister, G. F., W. C. Brantley, D. A. George, S. L. Harvey, S. L. Kleinfelder, K. P. McAuliffe, E. A. Melton, V. A. Norton and J. Weis, "The IBM Research Parallel Processor Prototype (RP3): Introduction and Architecture", *International Conference on Parallel Processing*, pp. 764-771 (August 1985).

REFERENCES

[Poll81a] Pollard, George H., "Parallel Execution of Horn Clause Programs", PhD Thesis, University of London, Imperial College of Science and Technology.

[Powl89a] Powley, C. and R. E. Korf, "Single Agent Parallel Window Search: A Summary of Results", *International Joint Conference on Artificial Intelligence*, Detroit, Michigan, pp. 36–41 (August 1989).

[Quin89a] Quintus Computer Systems Inc, "Quintus Prolog Multiprocessing Package", Manual for Version 1.0, Quintus Computer Systems Inc (June 1989).

[Quin91a] Quintus Corporation, "Quintus Prolog 1: Programming Environment", Manual for Quintus Prolog Release 3.1, Quintus Corporation (February 1991).

[Rain90a] Raina, Sanjay, David H. D. Warren and James Cownie, "Shared Virtual Memory on the Computing Surface via the Data Diffusion Machine", *Thirteenth Occam User Group Conference*, York, England, pp. 322–30, IOS Press (18–20 September 1990).

[Ramk89a] Ramkumar, Balkrishna and Laxmikant V. Kale, "Compiled Execution of the Reduce-OR Process Model on Multiprocessors", *North American Logic Programming Conference*, Cleveland, Ohio, pp. 313–331 (16–20 October, 1989).

[Ramk90a] Ramkumar, Balkrishna and Laxmikant V. Kale, "A Chare Kernel Implementation of a Parallel Prolog Compiler", *ACM SIGPLAN Conference on Principles and Practice of Parallel Programming*, Seattle, Washington, pp. 99–108 (March 1990).

[Ramk91a] Ramkumar, Balkrishna, "Machine Independent "AND" and "OR" Parallel Execution of Logic Programs", Ph.D. thesis, Department of Computer Science, University of Illinois at Urbana-Champaign (1991).

[Ratc87a] Ratcliffe, M. and J.-C. Syre, "A Parallel Logic Programming Language for PEPSys", *10th International Joint Conference on Artificial Intelligence*, Milan, Italy, pp. 48–55 (August 23–28, 1987).

[Rayn88a] Raynal, Michel, *Networks and Distributed Computation. Concepts, Tools and Algorithms*, The MIT Press (1988) (Computer Systems Series).

[Reyn88a] Reynolds, T. J., A. J. Beaumont, A. S. K. Cheng, S. A. Delgado-Rannauro and L. A. Spacek, "BRAVE – A Parallel Logic Language for Artificial Intelligence", *Future Generations Computer Systems* 4, pp. 69–75 (1988).

[Reyn89a] Reynolds, T. J. and S. A. Delgado-Rannauro, "VLSI for Parallel Execution of Prolog", *VLSI for Artificial Intelligence*, ed. J. G. Delgado-Frias and W. Moore, pp. 38–46, Kluwer Academic (March 1989).

[Ring87a] Ringwood, G. A., "Pattern-Directed, Markovian, Linear Guarded Definite Clause Resolution", TR Dept Computing PAR87/10, Imperial College, LONDON (1987).

[Ring88a] Ringwood, G. A., "Parlog86 and the Dining Logicians", *Communications of the ACM* 31(1), pp. 10–25 (January 1988).

REFERENCES

[Ring88b] Ringwood, G. A., "Metalogic Machines: a Retrospective Rationale for the Japanese Fifth Generation", *Knowledge Engineering Review* 3(4), pp. 303–20 (1988).

[Ring89a] Ringwood, G. A., "A Comparative Exploration of Concurrent Logic Languages", *Knowledge Engineering Review* 4(4), pp. 305–32 (1989a).

[Ring89b] Ringwood, G. A., "Predicates and Pixels", *New Generation Computing* 7(1), pp. 59–80 (1989).

[Roku88a] Rokusawa, K., N. Ichiyoshi, T. Chikayama and H. Nakashima, "An Efficient Termination Detection and Abortion Algorithm for Distributed Processing Systems", *International Conference on Parallel Processing*, St. Charles, USA, pp. 18–22 (15–19 August, 1988) (Volume 1 – Architecture).

[Saka89a] Sakai, Shuichi, Yoshinori Yamaguchi, Kei Hiraki, Yuetsu Kodama and Toshitsugu Yuba, "An Architecture of a Dataflow Single Chip Processor", *16th Annual International Symposium on Computer Architecture*, Jerusalem, Israel, pp. 46–53 (May 28 – June 1, 1989).

[Samm83a] Sammut, C. A. and R. A. Sammut, "The Implementation of UNSW-PROLOG", *Australian Computer Journal* 15(2), pp. 58–64 (May 1983).

[Samm83b] Sammut, C. A., "UNSW Prolog User Manual", 8307, Department of Computer Science, University of New South Wales (July 1983).

[Sara85a] Saraswat, V. A., "Concurrent Logic Programming Languages", Thesis proposal, Computer Science Department, Carnegie-Mellon University (November 1985).

[Sara86a] Saraswat, V. A., "Problems with Concurrent Prolog", CMU-CS-86-100, Computer Science Department, Carnegie-Mellon University (January 1986).

[Sato87a] Sato, Masatoshi, Hajime Shimizu, Akira Matsumoto, Kazuaki Rokusawa and Atsuhiro Goto, "KL1 Execution Model for PIM Cluster with Shared Memory", *Forth International Conference on Logic Programming*, Melbourne, Australia, pp. 339–355, MIT Press (May 25–29, 1987).

[Shap83a] Shapiro, Ehud Y., "A Subset of Concurrent Prolog and its Interpreter", TR–003, ICOT – Institute for New Generation Computer Technology (February 1983) (Also in "Concurrent Prolog: Collected Papers", Ehud Shapiro (Ed), MIT Press, 1987).

[Shap86a] Shapiro, Ehud, "Concurrent Prolog: a progress report", *IEEE Computer* 19(8), pp. 44–58 (1986).

[Shap87a] Shapiro, Ehud, "Concurrent Prolog: A Progress Report", *Fundamentals of Artificial Intelligence*, ed. W. Bibel and Ph. Jorrand, pp. 277–313, Springer-Verlag (1987).

[Shap87b] Shapiro, Ehud, "An Or-Parallel Execution Algorithm for Prolog and its FCP Implementation", *Fourth International Conference on Logic Programming*, Melbourne, Australia, pp. 311–337 (May 25–29, 1987).

[Shap89a] Shapiro, Ehud, "The Family of Concurrent Logic Programming Languages", *ACM Computing Surveys* **21**(3), pp. 413-510 (September 1989).

[Shib88a] Shibayama, Takashi, Hiroyuki Sato and Toshihiko Miyazaki, "Overview of the Parallel Inference Machine Operating System PIMOS", *International Conference on Fifth Generation Computer Systems*, Tokyo, Japan, pp. 230–251, OMSHA and Springer-Verlag (November 28 – December 2 1988).

[Shin88a] Shinogi, Tsuyoshi, Kouichi Kumon, Akira Hattori, Atsuhiro Goto, Yasunori Kimura and Takashi Chikayama, "Macro-Call Instruction for the Efficient KL1 Implementation on PIM", *International Conference on Fifth Generation Computer Systems*, Tokyo, Japan, pp. 953–961, OMSHA and Springer-Verlag (November 28 – December 2 1988).

[Shiz90a] Shizgal, I., "The Amoeba-Prolog System", *The Computer Journal* **33**(6), pp. 508–517 (December 1990).

[Silv87a] Silverman, William, Michael Hirsch, Avshalom Houri and Ehud Shapiro, "The Logix System User Manual Version 1.21", *Concurrent Prolog: Collected Papers*, ed. Ehud Shapiro, pp. 46–77, MIT Press Cambridge, Mass. (1987).

[Sing91a] Singh, Jaswinder Pal, Wolf-Dietrich Weber and Anoop Gupta, "SPLASH: Stanford Parallel Applications for Shared-Memory", Technical Report, Computer Systems Laboratory, Stanford University (1991).

[Sohm85a] Sohma, Yukio, Ken Satoh, Koichi Kumon, Hideo Masuzawa and Akihiro Itashiki, "A New Parallel Inference Mechanism Based on Sequential Processing", *IFIP TC-10 Working Conference on Fifth Generation Computer Architecture*, Manchester (July 1985).

[Somo88a] Somogyi, Z., K. Ramamohanarao and J. Vaghani, "A Stream AND-Parallel Execution Algorithm with Backtracking", *Fifth International Conference and Symposium on Logic Programming*, Seattle, Washington, ed. R. Kowalski and K. Bowen, pp. 1142–1159, MIT Press (15–19 August, 1988).

[Stan80a] Standish, T. A., *Data Structure Techniques*, Addison-Wesley (1980).

[Stun91a] Stunkel, C. B., Bob Janssens and W. Kent Fuchs, "Address Tracing for Parallel Machines", *IEEE COMPUTER* **24**(1), pp. 31-38 (January 1991).

[Sugi88a] Sugie, M., M. Yoneyama, N. Ido and T. Tauri, "Load-Dispatching Strategy on Parallel Inference Machines", *International Conference on Fifth Generation Computer Systems*, Tokyo, Japan, pp. 987–993, OMSHA and Springer-Verlag (November 28 – December 2 1988).

[Sund91a] Sundararajan, R., "An Abstract Interpretation Scheme for Groundness, Freeness and Sharing Analysis of Logic Programs", Technical Report CIS-TR-91-06,, University of Oregon (March 1991).

[Surr89a] Surridge, M., "The Eulerian Channel Configuration Language and Message-Passing System", Report for E.M.R. Contract N2A-8R-1756 (Phase II), S.E.R.C./D.T.I. Transputer Initiative (1989).

REFERENCES

[Sven90a] Svensson, Anders, "Software Primitives for Emulation of Multiprocessor Architectures", *23rd Hawaii International Conference on System Sciences* (1990).

[Szer82a] Szeredi, Peter, "Module Concepts for Prolog", *Collection of Papers on Logic Programming*, Szki (Institute of Co-ordination of Computer Techniques), Budapest, Hungary (May 1982) (Presented at 'Workshop on Prolog Programming Environments', Linkoping, Sweden 24–26 March, 1982).

[Szer89a] Szeredi, Peter, "Performance Analysis of the Aurora Or-Parallel Prolog System", *North American Conference on Logic Programming*, Cleveland, Ohio, pp. 713–733, MIT Press (16–20 October, 1989).

[Takd88a] Takeda, Y., H. Nakashima, K. Masuda, T. Chikayama and K. Taki, "A Load Balancing Mechanism for Large Scale Multiprocessor Systems and its Implementation", *International Conference on Fifth Generation Computer Systems*, Tokyo, Japan, pp. 978–986, OMSHA and Springer-Verlag (November 28 – December 2 1988).

[Take83a] Takeuchi, A., *How to Solve it in Concurrent Prolog*, 1983.

[Take86a] Takeuchi, Akikazu and Koichi Furukawa, "Parallel Logic Programming Languages", *Third International Conference on Logic Programming*, London, pp. 242–254, Springer–Verlag (July 14–18, 1986) (Lecture Notes in Computer Science No. 225).

[Take88a] Takeda, Yasutaka, Hiroshi Nakashima, Kanae Masuda, Takashi Chikayama and Kazuo Taki, "A Load Balancing Mechanism for Large Scale Multiprocessor Systems and its Implementation", *International Conference on Fifth Generation Computer Systems*, Tokyo, Japan, pp. 978–986, OMSHA and Springer-Verlag (November 28 – December 2 1988).

[Take89a] Takeuchi, A., K. Takahashi and H. Shimizu, "A Parallel Problem Solving Language for Concurrent Systems", Tech. Report, ICOT (1989).

[Taki88a] Taki, K., "The Parallel Software Research and Development Tool: Multi-PSI system", *Programming of Future Generation Computers (France-Japan Artificial Intelligence and Computer Science Symposium 1987)*, pp. 411–426, Elsevier Science Publishers B.V. (North-Holland) (1988) (Also in ICOT Technical Report TR-237 and in Proceedings).

[Tane80a] Tanenbaum, A. S., *Operating Systems*, Prentice-Hall (1980).

[Tayl86a] Taylor, Stephen, Shmuel Safra and Ehud Shapiro, "A Parallel Implementation of Flat Concurrent Prolog", *International Journal of Parallel Programming* 15(3), pp. 245–75 (June 1986) (Also in "Concurrent Prolog: Collected Papers", Ehud Shapiro (ed), MIT Press 1987).

[Tayl87a] Taylor, S., E. Av-Ron and E. Shapiro, "A Layered Method for Process and Code Mapping", *New Generation Computing* 5(2), pp. 185–205. (1987).

[Tayl87b] Taylor, S. and E. Shapiro, *A Parallel Implementation of Flat Concurrent Prolog*, International Journal of Parallel Programming (1987).

[Tayl88a] Taylor, S. and E. Shapiro, "An Improved Parallel Execution Algorithm for Flat Concurrent Prolog", CS88-09, The Weizmann Institute of Science (June 1988).

[Tayl89a] Taylor, Stephen, *Parallel Logic Programming Techniques*, Prentice-Hall (1989).

[Tick88a] Tick, Evan, "Data Buffer Performance for Sequential Prolog Architectures", *15th Annual International Symposium on Computer Architecture*, Honolulu, Hawaii, pp. 434–442 (30 May – 2 June, 1988).

[Tick88b] Tick, Evan, "Compile-Time Granularity Analysis for Parallel Logic Programming Languages", *International Conference on Fifth Generation Computer Systems*, Tokyo, Japan, pp. 994–1000, OMSHA and Springer-Verlag (November 28 – December 2 1988).

[Tick88c] Tick, Evan, *Memory Performance of Prolog Architectures*, Kluwer Academic Publishers (1988).

[Tick89a] Tick, E., *A Performance Comparison of AND– and OR-Parallel logic Programming Architectures*, MIT Press, Lisbon, Portugal &J Sixth International Conference on Logic Programming (June 19–23, 1989).

[Tink87a] Tinker, Peter and Gary Lindstrom, "A Performance Oriented Design for OR-parallel Logic Programming", *Fourth International Conference on Logic Programming*, Melbourne, Australia, pp. 601–615 (May 25–29, 1987).

[Tsen88a] Tseng, Chien-Chao and Prasenjit Biswas, "A Data-driven Parallel Execution Model for Logic Programs", *Fifth International Conference and Symposium on Logic Programming*, Seattle, Washington, ed. R. Kowalski and K. Bowen, pp. 1204–1222, MIT Press (15–19 August, 1988).

[Ueda86a] Ueda, K., "Guarded Horn Clauses: A Parallel Logic Programming Language with the Concept of a Guard", ICOT Technical Report TR-208, ICOT (1986).

[Ueda86b] Ueda, Kazunori, "Making Exhaustive Search Programs Deterministic", *Third International Conference on Logic Programming*, London, pp. 270–82, Springer-Verlag (July 14–18, 1986) (Lecture Notes in Computer Science No. 225).

[Ueda86c] Ueda, Kazunori, "Guarded Horn Clauses", *Logic Programming '85*, ed. Eiiti Wada, pp. 168–179, Springer–Verlag (1986) (Lecture Notes in Computer Science No. 221).

[Ueda86d] Ueda, Kazunori, "Guarded Horn Clauses", PhD. Thesis, University of Tokyo (March 1986).

[Ueda87a] Ueda, Kazunori, "Making Exhaustive Search Programs Deterministic, Part II", *Fourth International Conference on Logic Programming*, Melbourne, Australia, pp. 356–75, MIT Press (May 25 – 29, 1987).

[Ueda89a] Ueda, K., "Parallelism in Logic Programming", *Information processing 89 (11th IFIP World Computer Congress)*, San Francisco, CA, pp. 957–964, North–Holland Amsterdam (August 28 – September 1, 1989).

[Ueda90a] Ueda, K. and T. Chikayama, "Design of the Kernel Language for the Parallel Inference Machine", *The Computer Journal* 33(6), pp. 494–500 (1990).

REFERENCES

[VanR87a] Roy, Peter Van, Bart Demeon and Yves D. Willems, "Improving the Execution Speed of Compiled Prolog with Modes, Clause Selection, and Determinism", *International Joint Conference on Theory and Practice of Software Development (TAPSOFT'87)*, Pisa, Italy, pp. 111–125, Springer-Verlag (March 23–27, 1987) (Lecture Notes in Computer Science No 250 – Volume 2).

[VanR90a] Roy, Peter Van, "Can Logic Programming Execute as Fast as Imperative Programming?", Ph.D. thesis, Computer Science Division (EECS), University of California at Berkeley (1990).

[Verd90a] Verden, A. R. and H. Glaser, "Independent AND-Parallel Prolog for Distributed Memory Architectures", 90-17, Dept. of Electronics and Computer Science, University of Southampton, Southampton, England (August 1990).

[Verd91a] Verden, A. R. and H. Glaser, "Intelligent Backtracking in And-Parallel Prolog", *Implementations of Prolog II*, ed. J. Cambell and P. Cox (1991) (Forthcoming).

[Verd91b] Verden, A. R., "And-Parallel Implementation of Prolog On Distributed Memory Machines", PhD Thesis, University of Southampton (1991).

[Vero91a] Veron, A., J. Xu, S. A. Delgado-Rannauro, K. Schuerman and M. Dorochevsky, "Virtual Memory Support for Parallel Logic Programming Systems (PARLE'91)", *Conference on Parallel Architectures and Languages Europe*, Einhoven, Netherlands, ed. E.H.L. Aarts, J. van Leeuwen and M. Rem, Springer-Verlag (June 10–13, 1991).

[Warr77a] Warren, David H.D., "Implementing Prolog – Compiling Predicate Logic Programs (Volume 1 and Volume 2)", D.A.I Research Reports 39 and 40, Department of Artificial Intelligence, University of Edinburgh (1977).

[Warr80a] Warren, David H. D., "An Improved Prolog Implementation which Optimizes Tail Recursion", *Logic Programming Workshop*, Debrecen, Hungary, pp. 1–11 (14–16 July 1980).

[Warr82a] Warren, David H. D., "Perpetual Processes – An Unexploited Prolog Technique", *Logic Programming Newsletter* (3), p. 2 (Summer 1982).

[Warr83a] Warren, David H. D., "An Abstract Prolog Instruction Set", Technical Note 309, Artificial Intelligence Center, SRI International (October 1983).

[Warr84a] Warren, D.S., "Efficient Prolog memory management for flexible control strategies", *New Generation computing* **2, 84**, pp. 361–369 (1984).

[Warr87a] Warren, David H. D., "The SRI Model for Or–parallel Execution of Prolog – Abstract Design and Implementation Issues", *1987 Symposium on Logic Programming*, San Fransisco, USA, pp. 92–102, IEEE Computer Society Press (August 31 - September 4, 1987).

[Warr87b] Warren,, David H. D., "OR-Parallel Execution Models of Prolog", *International Joint Conference on Theory and Practice of Software Development (TAPSOFT'87)*, Pisa, Italy **2**, pp. 243–259, Springer-Verlag (March 23–27, 1987) (Lecture Notes in Computer Science No 250).

[Warr88a] Warren, David H. D. and Seif Haridi, "The Data Diffusion Machine – a Scalable Shared Virtual Memory Multiprocessor", *International Conference on Fifth Generation Computer Systems*, Tokyo, pp. 943–52, OMSHA and Springer-Verlag (November 28 – December 2, 1988).

[Wars84a] Warren, D. S., "Efficient Prolog Memory Management for Flexible Control Strategies", *1984 International Symposium on Logic Programming*, Atlantic City, New Jersey, pp. 198–202, IEEE Computer Society Press (February 1984).

[Wats87a] Watson, P. and I. Watson, "An Efficient Garbage Collection Scheme for Parallel Computer Architectures", *Parallel Architectures and Languages Europe (PARLE'87)*, Eindhoven, The Netherlands, pp. 432–443, Springer Verlag (June 15–19, 1987).

[West87a] Westphal, Harald, Philippe Robert, Jacques Chassin and Jean-Claude Syre, "The PEPSys Model: Combining Backtracking, AND– and OR-parallelism", *1987 Symposium on Logic Programming*, San Francisco, U.S.A., pp. 436–48, IEEE Computer Society Press (August 31 – September 4, 1987).

[Wexl89a] Wexler, John, *Concurrent Programming in OCCAM 2*, Ellis Horwood (1989).

[Weyr80a] Weyrauch, R, "Prologemena to a Theory of Mechanical Formal Reasoning", *Artificial Intelligence* **13**, pp. 133–70 (1980).

[Wise82a] Wise, Michael J., "A Parallel Prolog: The Construction of a Data Driven Model", *1982 ACM Symposium on LISP and Functional Programming*, Pittsburgh, PA, USA, pp. 56–66 (15–18 August 1982).

[Wise86a] Wise, Michael J., "Experimenting with EPILOG: Some Results and Preliminary Conclusions", *Thirteenth Annual International Symposium on Computer Architecture*, Tokyo, Japan, pp. 130–9 (2–5 June 1986).

[Wise86b] Wise, Michael J., *Prolog Multiprocessors,* Prentice–Hall (Australia) (December 1986) (Japanese translation published by Keigaku Publishing Co, Tokyo, 1989).

[Wise89a] Wise, Michael J., "An Implementation of Modules in Prolog", *Australian Computer Journal* **21**(3), pp. 141–150 (November 1989) (Revision of Basser TR 324, May 1988).

[Wise90a] Wise, Michael J., "PMS-Prolog Programmer's Manual", Basser Department of Computer Science Technical Report, Sydney University (January 1990) (Includes UNSW-Prolog Versions 4.0 and 4.0M).

[Wise90b] Wise, Michael J., "PMS-Prolog: A Model for Parallel Prolog with Processes, Modules and Streams", *Open Distributed Processing Workshop*, Sydney, Australia (18 – 19 January, 1990) (Revision of Basser TR 337, Jan 1989).

[Wise91a] Wise, Michael J., "Experience with PMS-Prolog: A Distributed, Coarse-Grain-Parallel Prolog with Processes, Modules and Streams", Basser Department of Computer Science Technical Report (May 1991).

[Xia88a] Xia, H. and W. K. Giloi, "A Hybrid Scheme For Detecting AND-Parallelism In Prolog Programs", *International Conference on Supercomputing*, St. Malo, pp. 539–59, ACM press (July 1988).

[Xia89a]   Xia, H., "Analyzing Data Dependencies, Detecting AND-Parallelism and Optimizing Backtracking in Prolog Programs", PhD Thesis, University of Berlin, Berlin, Germany (April 1989).

[Yang86a]   Yang, Rong and Hideo Aiso, "P-Prolog: A Parallel Logic Language Based on Exclusive Relation", *Third International Conference on Logic Programming*, London, UK, ed. Ehud Shapiro, pp. 254–269, Springer–Verlag (July 1986).

[Yang86b]   Yang, R., "A Parallel Logic Programming Language and its Implementation", PhD. Thesis, Keio University (1986).

[Yang87a]   Yang, R. and H. Aiso, *Memory Management for Multiple Environments - Implementation of P-Prolog*, Keio University (January 1987).

[Yang88a]   Yang, R., "Solving Simple Substitution Ciphers in Parallel Logic System Andorra-I", Internal Report, University of Bristol (November 1988).

[Yang88b]   Yang, R., "Programming in Andorra-I", Internal Report, University of Bristol (September 1988).

[Yang88c]   Yang, R., "Implementation Notes on the Andorra Model", Internal Report, University of Bristol (November 1988).

[Yasu84a]   Yasuhara, H. and K. Nitadori, "ORBIT: a Parallel Computing Model of Prolog", *New Generation Computing* 2(3), pp. 277–288 (1984).

[Zhou90a]   Zhou, Neng-Fa, Toshihisa Takagi and Kazou Ushijima, "A Matching Tree Oriented Abstract Machine for Prolog", *Seventh International Conference on Logic Programming*, Jerusalem, Israel, ed. David H. D. Warren and Peter Szeridi, pp. 159–173, MIT Press (June 18–20, 1990).

Index

Abstract machines
  CIAM, 228–234
  CSPIM, 368, 375
  DAM, 352–355
  DDDPAM/3DPAM, 89–118
  FCP abstract machine, 288, 295
  OPAL machine, 159–185
  TWAM, 46
  WAM, compared with other machines, 101, 102, 103, 116, 168, 172, 180–181
  see also CIAM; DAM; FCP; OM; 3DPAM; TWAM; WAM
Activation messages, 76
Actor concept, 220
Actor-oriented model, 213–235
Adaptive-contracting-within-neighbourhood strategy, 203
Airline reservation system, Delta Prolog program for, 337–338
Ancestor stack, BOPLOG's use of, 14
AND nodes
  in DSG, 91, 94, 95, 105
  representation in 3DPAM, 106
AND operators, in 3DPAM, 105–106
AND/OR connection graph model, 215–218
  deleting of arcs and clauses in, 216
  example of connection graph, 216
AND/OR parallel implementations, 119–235
AND/OR parallel logic models, 132–140
  concepts, 132–133
  OPAL programs executed using, 160
  restricted AND/OR parallel models, 133–140
  upper bound on speed, 180
AND/OR parallelism
  distributed interpreter for, 65–85
  performance improvement using, 82
AND/OR process models, 214
AND parallel distributed Prolog executor, 143–157
AND parallel implementations, 119–235
AND parallelism
  binding conflicts in, 66
  combination with OR parallelism, 134–135
  meaning of term, 215
  performance improvement using, 82
  see also RAP models
AND processes, 214
  OPAL machine, 168–169
  in parallel execution model, 68, 77
Andorra-I system, 29
  run on DDM emulator, 41–42
    miss rates at local memories, 42
    traffic on each link in hierarchy, 42
Argument frames, in OPAL machine, 172, 173
Atomic transactions, 275
Atomic unification, 241, 245
Attributed cause variables, 145
Aurora system, 28
  compared with other systems, 41, 62, 181
  run on DDM emulator, 41–43
    miss rates at local memories, 42
    run-times on 4-processor emulator, 43
    traffic on each link in hierarchy, 42

Backtracking
  in CS-Prolog, 376, 402
  in Delta Prolog, 336, 356, 401, 402
  in Padmalog, 409
Back-unification, in PMS-Prolog, 390
Backward unification, 17, 18
Benchmarks
  Andorra-I, 41, 42
  Aurora, 41, 42
  COALA/CIAM, 222, 234
  distributed interpreter, 80–81
  KL1 implementation on multi-PSI, 330, 331
  OPAL, 181
  OPERA running in parallel, 60–61
  Padmalog, 424, 425–426
  programs listed, 86–87
  SICStus Prolog, 41, 181
  see also Bestpath...; Bid...; Color...; Deep Back...; Deriv...; Farmer...; Fibonacci number...; Hamilton...; Houses...; Knight...; Map colouring...; Matrix--Multiplication...; Mergesort...; Min-route...; Nand...; Nfib...; Nrev...; Path...; Pentomino...; Permute...; Primes...; Queens...; Query...; Quickdiff...; Quicksort...; Reverse...; Salt Mustard...; Test OR...; Tina...; Tree.; Turtles...; 12--puzzle...; Zebra benchmark program
Bibliography, 429–457
Bid benchmark program, 180, 181
Binding Array Model, 11–13
  advantages/disadvantages of, 13
Binding arrays
  meaning of term, 11, 12
  in SRI model, 11, 62

Binding conflict problem, 66, 143
Binding environment frames (BEs), 139
Binding environments
    AND and OR parallelism supported by, 191–204
    closed environments, 18–20
    handling in 3DPAM, 117
    shared environments, 6–16
Binding records, 227
Binding tree, meaning of term, 11, 12
Bit vector cells, execution in parallel clauses controlled by, 150
Bit vector model, 122–125
    performance results of, 14
    relationship between dependency-check and task granularity optimization, 125
Black export tables, 325
Black import tables, 325
Body goals, handling in 3DPAM, 105–107
BOPLOG (Butterfly OR-Parallel Prolog), 13
Bounded buffer (in CS-Prolog), 373
Bounded-depth backtracking, Delphi's use of, 23
BRAVE, binding array method in, 11
BUILT-IN nodes (in DSG), 91, 93
Butterfly parallel machine, shared environment models run on, 13, 16
Buyers–vendors problem
    definition of buyer, 371–372
    definition of vendor, 372
    solution in CS-Prolog, 370–371

Cache coherence protocols, 30, 32
Cached Instancing (in PMS-Prolog), 398
CCND (Committed Choice Non-Deterministic) languages, 240, 241–245
    architectural models for, 246–256
    basic computational model for, 242–243
    common features of, 241–243
    Concurrent Prolog, 244–245
    dataflow synchronisation of, 242
    flat versions of, 242, 243–244, 244–245
        compilation techniques for, 246–247
        distributed memory models for, 249–256
        shared memory models for, 247–249
    Guarded Horn Clause language, 116, 245
    Parlog, 243–244
    semantics of, 241–242
    syntax of, 241
    see also Concurrent Prolog; Flat CCND...; GHC...; Parlog
Centralized scheduling, 56
CGEs (conditional graph expressions)
    backtracking in/over CGEs, 130–131
    generation of, 128, 129, 139
Chare Kernel (in Reduce-OR model), 190, 203, 205
Choice goals (in Delta Prolog), 336
    resolution of, 341
    segments of, 347
    support in DAM, 354
    updating of lists of backtrack nodes for, 350
CIAM (COALA Inference Abstract Machine), 228–234
    see instructions, 233
    code blocks, 229–230

implementation on hypertorus, 234–235
instruction set, 230, 232–234
message instructions, 233
registers in, 228–229
storage model, 228–229
switch instructions, 232
transfer instructions, 234
unification instructions, 233
UNIFY-REQ block, 230–231
Clause selection, in FCP, 294
Clause-level compilation, flat CCND languages, 246
Client–server prototype, implementation in RGDC, 272–275
Closed binding environment OPC family, 16–20, 25
Closed binding methods, 16
Closed environments, 18–20
    Conery's scheme, 18, 193
        compared with Kalé's approach, 202–204
    in OPAL machine, 171–172
    in 3DPAM, 103, 112–115, 117
    see also Environment closing
Closed term, 193, 202
Closely coupled distributed systems, 260
CloseTuple algorithm, 196
COALA system, 215–219
    abstract machine, 228–234
        code blocks, 229–230
        instruction set, 230, 232–234
        results, 234–235
        storage model, 228–229
        see also CIAM
    parallel execution model, 218–219
        communication between processing elements, 220–222
        evaluation of, 222–223
        garbage collection in, 221–222
        implementation of, 219–223
        precompilation step, 219–220
        resolution operations in, 221
        unification operations in, 221, 230–232
Color benchmark programs, 154, 156, 157, 180, 181
Committed choice languages, 237–332, 380
    compared with non-deterministic systems, 213–215
    problems with, 382
    see also Concurrent Prolog; GHC; Parlog
Common Instancing (in PMS-Prolog), 397
Communicating Sequential Processes see CSP
Communicating Sequential Prolog, 357–378
    see also CS-Prolog
Compass (stable-state bit-vector), 34
Concurrent languages, 260
    see also Occam; RGDC
Concurrent logic programming, 261, 289–293
Concurrent Prolog, 244–245
    example program, 244
    flat version, 244–245, 287–309
    see also FCP
Conditional binding, 6
    in shared environment models, 10, 12, 14
Consumer instance parallelism, 190, 196
Context handling, in 3DPAM, 100–101, 102–103
Contexts, meaning of term, 7

Continuations
  meaning of term, 171
  use in OPAL, 170–171
Co-routining algorithm, in Delta Prolog, 343–344
Cousin benchmark program, 234
CS (Communicating Sequential) Prolog, 357–378, 402
  abstract machine, 368, 375
    half nodes resolved by, 369
  assessment of, 377–378
  communication in, 358, 359, 362–365
  distributed completeness ensured for, 368–370
  examples of use, 370–373
    bounded buffer, 373
    buyers–vendors problem, 370–372
  hypotheses in, 358, 360–361
  implementation issues, 375–377
    coding issues, 377
    distributed backtracking in, 376
    distributed control mechanism, 375–376
    forward execution, 376
    function distribution, 375
  non-determinism handling by, 365–368
  processes
    non-procedural aspects, 360–361
    procedural aspects, 359–360
  search trees of communicating processes, 368–369
  system simulation in, 374–375
  tree unification in search forest, 369–370
CSP (Communicating Sequential Processes)
  compared with Padmalog, 407
  languages influenced by, 260, 284, 377, 405, 407
  parallelism in Transputer-based machines derived from, 407
CSTools, Delta Prolog implemented under, 354, 355
CUT predicate, use in parallel execution model, 78–79

DAG (Directed Acyclic Graph), FCP data representation using, 298
DAM (Delta Abstract Machine), 352–355
  choice goals supported, 354
  distributed backtracking supported, 354
  event goals supported, 354
  instructions, 353, 354
  split goals supported, 353
DASH multiprocessor, 30
Data coherence, 30
Data dependency graph, 144
  see also DDG
Data Diffusion Machine, 31–32
  see also DDM
Data driven parallel execution model, 139–140
Data join graph, use in Reduce-OR model, 134, 188–189
Data parallelism, N-queens problem considered, 418–420
Data representation
  in FCP parallel machine, 297–299
  in 3DPAM, 99–100
Database communications, Control mechanism in CS-Prolog, 365–366
Database Instancing, in PMS-Prolog, 398
Dataflow computational models
  comparison of, 116
  graph representation used, 90–92
Dataflow Search Graph, 90
  see also DSG
Dataflow synchronization, in CCNDs, 242, 291–292
DDDPAM, 89–118
  see also 3DPAM
DDG (data dependency graph), 144
  dynamic generation of, 147
DDM (Data Diffusion Machine), 31–32
  cache coherence protocols of, 32, 33–34
  emulation of, 32–40
    Andorra-I and Aurora run on, 41–43
    coupling applications, 36–37
    design of emulator, 33–37
    implementation on Meiko Computing Surface, 37–40
    link-based protocol used, 33–35
    objectives of study, 33
    synchronization support for, 35–36
  hardware organization of, 31–32
Deadlock backtracking, in CS-Prolog, 376
Deadlock detection
  in CS-Prolog, 375
  in Delta Prolog, 343, 352
  in KL1, 327–328
Deadlock prevention
  in CS-Prolog, 359, 376
  in parallel FCP machine, 303
Deadlock termination, in RGDC, 278
Deep back benchmark program, 81, 82, 86
Deep binding, 10
Definite clauses, notation in RGDC, 264
DeGroot's RAP model, 127–130
Delphi model, 23–24
Delta Prolog, 335–356, 400–401
  abstract machine for, 352–355
  choice goals in, 337
    resolution of, 341
    segments of, 347
    updating of lists of backtrack nodes for, 350
  co-routining algorithm for, 343–344
  compared with PMS-Prolog, 401
  deadlock detection and recovery for, 343
  deadlocks in distributed computations, 352
  declarative semantics of, 337
  derivations in, 339–340
    segments of derivations, 345–346
  distributed backtracking strategies, 347–352
    decentralized strategy used, 348–349
    reconfiguring of failed derivation, 350–352
    selection of candidate segment for backtracking, 349
    updating of lists of backtrack nodes for, 349–350
  event goals in, 336–337
    resolution of, 341
    segments of, 347
    updating of lists of backtrack nodes for, 350
  example program, 337–338
  implementation on multi-processor, 352–355
    executors used, 354–355
    implementation layers, 352–353
    language layer, 353–354
    system layer, 354–355

Delta Prolog (cont.)
    virtual channels used, 355
    interaction points in, 345
    language constructs in, 336–337
    multiple failures in distributed computations, 352
    operational semantics of, 339–352
    parallel execution strategies in, 344–347
    programming model for, 335–338
    resolution rules in, 340–341
    searching of derivations space, 341–342
    semantics of, 337, 339–352
    sequential execution strategy for, 342–344
    split goals in, 336
        resolution of, 340
        segments of, 347
        updating of lists of backtrack nodes for, 349–350
    see also DAM
Dependency tables, 223–224
    update algorithm for, 223–224
Dereferencing of terms, 5
    in closed environment models, 18
    in shared environment models, 10, 11, 14
`Deriv` benchmark program, 60
Derivations, definition in Delta Prolog, 340
Directory based (cache coherence) protocols, 30, 33
Directory trees, 7–9
    advantages/disadvantages of, 7–8
Distributed backtracking
    in CS-Prolog, 376, 402
    in Delta Prolog, 336, 356, 401, 402
    strategies used, 347–352
    support in DAM, 354, 355
Distributed binding, in CS-Prolog, 360
Distributed control mechanism, CSPIM, 375–376
Distributed Data Driven Prolog Abstract Machine, 89–118
    see also THREE/3DPAM
Distributed environment, problems of implementing logic programming languages in, 117
Distributed interpreter
    benchmark performance of, 80–81
        programs used, 86–87
    future work on, 85
    implementation on Transputer-based hardware, 79–80
    inherent AND/OR parallelism, 65–85
    messages used, 76–77
    optimization of, 83–85
    parallel execution model working with, 72–79
    parallelism exploitation by, 81–83
    performance evaluation of, 80–83
    resource management for, 74–76
Distributed Logic, Delta Prolog inspired by, 335
Distributed logic program, meaning of term, 368
Distributed memory systems
    compared with shared memory systems, 29
    flat CCND languages used, 249–256, 311–332
    types of, 260
Distributed scheduling, 56
Don't-care non-determinism, 240, 290, 366
Don't-know non-determinism, 366
DSG (Dataflow Search Graph), 90, 91
    AND nodes, 91, 94, 95

BUILT-IN nodes, 91, 93
    dynamic work of, 94
    graphical notation of nodes, 91
    non-unit clause representation, 92
    OR nodes, 91, 93
    parallel execution using, 92–96
    predicate representation, 92
    representations used, 92
    UNIFY/AND ring, 94–95, 105
    UNIFY nodes, 91, 94
    UNIT nodes, 91, 93
Dynamic data dependency methods, for RAP models, 122–125
Dynet (DYnamic NETwork), T800 processors connected by, 406

ECDAM-2, 90, 91
    compound nodes defined in, 91, 104
    Dataflow Search Graphs generated by, 91–92
    pipeline parallelism in, 95–96
Environment closing
    in OPAL machine, 172
    in 3DPAM, 112–115
        algorithm for, 112
        before entering clause body, 112–113
        before exiting clause in UNIFY nodes, 114
        in UNIT nodes, 114–115
Environmental directories, 7
EPILOG model, 383, 384n
EPM (Extended Prolog Machine), 377
Event goals (in Delta Prolog), 336
    resolution of, 341
    segments of, 347
    support in DAM, 354
    updating of lists of backtrack nodes for, 350
Execution-driven simulation, 37
Export tables, in Flat-GHC/KL1 implementation of multi-PSI, 252, 323, 325
Exporter process, 49, 50
Extended Cellular-Dataflow Model, 90, 91
    see also ECDAM-2

Failure backtracking, in CS-Prolog, 376
Failure trap, OPAL machine, 176, 185
`Farmer` benchmark programs, 60, 208, 209, 210, 211
Farmer–worker scheme (in Padmalog), 407–412
    N-queens problem solved using, 416–420
    parallelization of compiler using, 420–423
FCP (Flat Concurrent Prolog), 244–245, 287
    abstract machine for, 288, 295
    clause selection in, 294
    compared with other flat CNND languages, 256
    compared with Strand, 289
    computational model of, 287
    control mechanisms used, 287
    dataflow synchronization for, 291–292
    distributed implementation of, 255–256, 295–304
        abstract system architecture, 295–297
        data representation in, 297–299
        deadlock prevention in, 303
        distributed reduction algorithm in, 300–302
        distributed unification in, 255
        livelock prevention in, 303

parallelization in, 296
process synchronization in, 300–301
reduction algorithm in, 300–302
representation of logical variables, 298–299
representation of non-variable terms, 297–298
scalability of, 288, 297
termination detection in, 303–304
variable migration in, 300
execution of FCP programs, 288, 293
guard evaluation in, 294
multi-Transputer implementation of, 288, 304–308
host unit architecture, 304
integration of communication models, 305–306
performance measurements, 306–308
reduction unit architecture, 304, 305
router architecture, 305, 306
process reduction mechanism in, 293–295
unification operations in, 294
FCP(:,?,—), 246, 256
FGDC (Flat Guarded Definite Clauses) language, 285
Fibonacci number benchmark programs, 41, 60, 154, 155
Flat CCND languages, 242, 243–244, 244-255, 291
comparison of, 256
compilation techniques for, 246–247
distributed memory models for, 249–256
garbage collection methods for, 248–249
parallel shared memory models for, 247–249
Flat Concurrent Prolog, 244–245, 287
comparison with other flat CCND languages, 256
distributed implementation, 255–256, 287–309
see also FCP
Flat GHC language, 245, 312
comparison with other flat CCND languages, 256
distributed memory model for, 249–253
external reference management in, 252
garbage collection in, 252
unification in, 251, 256
memory management in, 248–249
meta-call records in, 250–251
shared memory model for, 247–248
see also KL1 language
Flat Guarded Definite Clauses language, 285
Flat Guarded Horn Clauses language, 245, 312
see also Flat GHC...
Flat Parlog, 243–244
comparison with other flat CCND languages, 256
distributed memory model for, 253–255
distributed unification in, 254
Flat Parlog with Assignment, 285
Footsteps (transient-state bit-vectors), 34
Fork command (in PMS-Prolog), 387–388, 389–391

Garbage collection
in COALA system, 221–222
in KL1/Flat GHC implementations, 248–249, 252–253, 317–318, 323–325
Generation scavenging, 317
GHC (guarded Horn clause) language, 116, 245, 312
example program, 245
flat version, 245, 312
distributed memory models for, 249–253
memory management in, 248–249

shared memory models for, 247–248
see also Flat GHC; KL1
Goal rewriting models, 215
see also COALA
Grain size control, 55, 210
Graph representation (of Prolog programs), 90–92
Guard evaluation/test, in CCNDs, 247, 294
Guarded alternative clauses, 366–368
Guarded command indeterminacy, 290
Guarded Commands, CS-Prolog's use of, 358, 377
Guarded definite clause, meaning of term, 264
Guarded Horn Clause language, 116, 245
see also Flat Guarded...; GHC

Hamilton benchmark programs, 41, 60, 61
Hanoi program
code for unification in, 206
see also Towers of Hanoi benchmark program
Hash-windows, 9–11
in PEPSys model, 9, 10–11, 62, 135
Hermenegildo's RAP-WAM, 130–131
Hierarchical scheduling 56
Houses benchmark programs, 42, 208, 209, 210, 211
HYPERTORE, CIAM implemented on, 234
Hypotheses (in CS-Prolog), 360

IBM-40 benchmark program, 234
IDA* algorithm, 209
Import tables, in Flat-GHC/KL1 implementation on multi-PSI, 252, 323
Import vector creation, 17
Importer process, 49, 50
Incremental copying of stacks, OPERA's use of, 53–54
Incremental join, 197
Independent AND parallelism, 121–122, 136, 143–145, 224–226
example execution, 145
join operation in, 198–199
parallel clauses in, 144
see also RAP...models; Restricted AND parallel...
Inherent AND/OR parallelism, distributed interpreter for, 65–85
Inheritance binding mechanism, 13–15
advantage of, 15
disadvantages of, 14
INMOS Transputer see Transputer...
Instruction sets
CIAM, 230, 232–234
OM, 182–185
3DPAM, 101–112
Intel i860 hypercube, performance of ROLOG, 209
Intel iPSC hypercubes
FCP implementation on, 289
performance of ROLOG, 209
Intelligent backtracking, 144, 151–153
evaluation of effectiveness, 154, 155–156
example execution, 145
failure in parallel clause distribution mode, 152–153
support of failure history, 152

Intelligent cutting, 153
Interprocess communication, in PMS-Prolog, 398

J-machine, 30
Join binding algorithm, 135
Join cells, PEPSys' use of, 137
Join operation, 196–202
`JoinTuples` algorithm, 198

K-LEAF system, compared with OPERA, 62
Kabu-Wake system, 24
   compared with other systems, 61
   thread splitting procedure for, 25
Kernel Parlog, 243
KL1 language, 311, 313
   abstract machine instruction set, 116, 316
   implementation on multi-PSI, 311–332
      body unification by inter-PE messages, 320
      copying of shared data, 322
      cost of communication primitives, 328–330
      deadlock detection in, 327–328
      distributed goal control procedures, 320–322
      evaluation of, 328–332
      execution model of KL1 goals, 316
      export and import tables in, 323
      external reference management, 323, 325
      garbage collection in, 317–318, 322–325
      global structure management, 325–326
      goal distribution by inter-PE messages, 319
      guard unification by inter-PE messages, 319–320
      implementation issues, 319
      inter-PE data management, 322–327
      inter-PE processing, 319–327
      intra-PE processing, 316–318
      KL1-B execution, 317
      local goal scheduling, 317
      memory management for, 317–318
      message handling cost in, 328–329
      performance of benchmark programs, 330–332
      profiling facilities, 328
      program code management, 326–327
      programming environment support facilities used, 327–328
      spying-of-goals supported, 327
      termination detection in, 322
      tracing-of-goals supported, 327
   resource management in, 313
   shōen in, 313, 320
   see also Flat GHC
Knight benchmark program, 208, 209, 210, 211
Kowalski's AND/OR connection graph model, 215–218

Late binding, 138
Limited OR parallelism, combined with restricted AND parallelism, 138–139
Linearization, in Padmalog, 413
Lin's bit-vector model, 122–125
Livelock prevention, in parallel FCP machine, 303
Loosely coupled distributed systems, 260
LORAP, compared with SEPIA, 138–139
LRDF (Left-to-Right-Deep-First) control strategy, 359
   modification for database communication, 365–366

MAILBOX processes, 75
Map colouring benchmark programs
   Andorra-I, 41
   CIAM run on, 234
   OPAL, 181
   OPERA, 61
   parallel clause execution, 154
   parallel intelligent backtracking, 155–156
   TWAM, 60
`Matrix-Multiplication` benchmark program, 307, 308
Meganode, architecture of, 47
Meiko Computing Surface, 37–38
   DDM emulator implemented on, 39–40
   Delta Prolog implemented on, 352
   software development environment of, 38–39
Memory management metric, 4–5
   shared environment models, 8, 11, 14
`Mergesort` benchmark programs, 41
Message arguments, registers as, 172–174
Message communication, in CS-Prolog, 362–363
Message passing, 76–77, 265
Meta-interpreters, written in RGDC, 281–284
MIMD (Multiple Instruction Multiple Data) multiprocessors, 29
   CS-Prolog run on, 395
`Min route` benchmark program, 81, 82, 87
MRB (Multiple Reference Bit) garbage-collection method, 249, 317–318
   advantages of, 318
Multi-cluster architecture, flat GHC used, 251–253
Multiple binding algorithm, 135
Multiple depth-first execution (of search tree), 6–7
   advantages of, 7
Multiprocessor load sharing algorithms, in PMS-Prolog, 396–397
Multiprocessors, *see also* Transputer based...
Multi-PSI system, 312
   architecture of, 250, 313–315
   committed choice languages used, 249–250, 252, 311–332
   Flat-GHC/KL1 implementation on, external reference management in, 252, 323
   KL1 implemented on, 311–332
      evaluation of, 328–332
      inter-PE processing in, 319–327
      intra-PE processing in, 316–318
      programming environment support facilities used, 327–328
   message handling in processing element, 315
   network contoller of, 314
   processing elements of, 313
   processor inter-connections of, 314
   see also PIM
Multisequential approach, 20–22
   OPERA computational model, 46, 48–49
Multisequential models, 214–215
Multi-Transputer environments
   distributed implementation of FCP on, 304–309
   integration of communication models, 305–306
   parallel machine architecture, 304, 305, 306
   performance measurements, 306–308

INDEX

Muse (multi-sequential) parallel Prolog system, 22–23
  compared with other systems, 62
  incremental copying of stacks in, 53
  scheduling strategy in, 23, 62
MX-500 multiprocessor, PEPSys model implemented on, 137

Nand benchmark program, 42
NCUBE 2 hypercube, performance of benchmark programs using ROLOG, 210
Nfib benchmark program, 154, 155
Non-atomic unification, 241, 245
Non-determinism, handling in CS-Prolog, 365–368
Non-deterministic systems
  compared with committed choice languages, 213–215
  see also Andorra; Aurora; COALA; PEPSys
Nrev benchmark program, 60

Occam language
  characteristics of, 74, 260–261, 281, 414
  compared with RGDC language, 261–267, 281
  meta-interpretation of, 281–284
  Padmalog implementation coded in, 414
  philosophy of, 262
  producer–consumer system coded in, 261–262
ODP (On-Demand with Pragma) distribution process, 248
OM virtual machine
  code blocks for AND processes, 168–169
  code blocks for OR processes, 167–168
  compared with WAM, 168, 172, 180–181
  continuations in, 170–171
  control instructions for, 166, 182–183
  environment register in, 163
  initialization instructions for, 175, 183
  instruction set for, 182–185
  language used, 160
    see also OPAL
  last call optimization in, 170
  lists in, 176, 178–179
  memory management in, 162
  message-passing instructions for, 166, 182–183
  message-passing patterns in, 170
  performance of, 179–181
    kernel operations, 179–180
    single processor implementation, 180–181
  port instructions for, 165–166, 182
  procedure argument register in, 163
  read mode of, 178
  registers, 163–165
  response frame register in, 164
  structure register in, 164
  task allocation strategies in, 162–163
  task switches in, 166–167
  unification instructions for, 174–176, 183–184
  write mode of, 178
OPAL language, 159
  compiler, 160–161
  control operations in, 165–169
  implementation of, 161–165
    see also OM...
  interface program for, 161
  kernel functions of, 162–163
  modules of OPAL implementation, 161–165
  programs, 159–160
  unification operations in, 171–179
Open World Assumption, 278
OPERA, 45–63
  aim of project, 45, 46
  communication protocol used, 57–58
  compared with other systems, 61–63
  computational model, overview of, 48–49
  evaluation of glaobal state in, 57
  implementation of, 46, 59
  language supported by, 48
  parallel benchmarks used, 60–61
  scheduling of work in, 46, 54–59, 63
  sequential efficiency of, 59–60
  software structure of, 49, 50
  workers in
    classification of, 56
    evaluation of workload, 57
    process structure of, 49, 50
OR nodes, 3
  in DSG, 91, 93
  realization in 3DPAM, 109–110
OR parallel computational (OPC) models
  classification of, 5, 24, 380
  closed binding environment family, 16–20, 25
  recomputation family, 20–24, 25
  shared binding environment family, 6–16, 25
OR parallel implementations, 1–118
OR parallelism
  combination with AND parallelism, 134–135
  in DSG, 93
  meaning of term, 3–4, 215
  N-queens problem considered, 418–420
  performance improvement using, 82
  and PMS-Prolog, 385
OR processes, 16, 214
  OM
    code blocks for, 167–168
    control instructions in, 168
  in parallel execution model, 67, 77–78
OR shared variables, 3
OR trees, 4
  with hash-windows, 9
  representation in OPERA, 58–59
Oracles, use in Delphi model, 23
Oregon PArallel Logic language, 159
  see also OPAL
Otherwise guard, use in RGDC, 278

Padmalog, 405–427
  communication cost in, 425
  communication handling by, 408–409
  compiler used, 414
  examples
    N-queens problem, 415–420
    parallelizing of compiler, 420–423
  formats for term representation, 413
  general organization of, 410–412
  implementation using Occam, 414
  intermediate format for term representation, 412–413

Padmalog (cont.)
   parallelism in, 405, 407–409
   performance of, 423–427
   predefined ports for, 410–412
   printer process for, 409–410
   process handling by, 407–408
   reading process speed of, 425
   symbol table for, 409
PADMAVATI (Parallel Associative Development Machine As a Vehicle For Artificial Intelligence) machine, 405
   architecture of, 406
   parallel Prolog for, 405
   see also Padmalog
   Run Time Support for, 406–407
Parallel clauses, 144
   execution of, 147–151
      bit vector cells used to control, 150
      distribution mode used, 147
         evaluation of effectiveness, 154
         failure in, 152–153
      parallel frame used, 149, 150
      serial mode used, 148
         evaluation of effectiveness, 154
      subgoal execution states, 148–149
      types of execution, 148
Parallel execution models
   inherent AND/OR parallelism exploited by, 66–72
      AND processes, 68
         handling of environment in, 71
         structure of, 77
      CUT predicates handled in, 78–79
      environment of clauses in, 71–72
      example of use, 68–71
      interpreter working with, 72–79
      OR processes, 67
         handling of environment in, 71–72
         structure of, 77–78
      process hierarchy in, 67
      unification procedure in, 72
Parallel execution strategies, in Delta Prolog, 344–347
Parlog, 243, 284
   example program, 243
   flat versions of, 243–244, 285
Parsytec Supercluster multi-Transputer system, FCP abstract machine implemented on, 288, 306
Partition (in CS-Prolog), 359
PAT (Process Allocation Table), 376
Path benchmark program, 180, 181
Pentomino benchmark program, 208, 330
PEPSys model
   AND- combined with OR-parallelism, 135–138, 380
   compared with other systems, 62
   cross product using join cells, 137
   hash-windows in, 9, 10–11, 62, 135
   independent AND-parallel execution in, 136
Permute benchmark program, 81, 82, 86
PIM (Parallel Inference Machine)
   architecture of, 247
   flat CCND language used, 247, 312
   garbage collection in, 252
   multi-PSI system as prototype for, 312

PIMs (Prolog Inference Machines), CS-Prolog considered as set of, 358–359
Pipeline AND parallelism, 66
   exploitation using distributed interpreter, 82–83
Pipeline parallelism
   in ECDAM-2, 95–96
   N-queens problem considered, 416–418
   Padmalog compiler split, 420–423
PMS-Prolog, 379–403
   assumptions underlying, 383–385
   background to development, 380–382
   built-ins in, 387–388, 389–392, 393
   channel structures in, 387–388
   compared with other systems, 400–403
   database distribution, 397–398
   distribution of processes, 395–396
   examples, 388–389, 392–393
      channel merge, 392–393
      producer–consumer problem, 388–389
   fork command, 387, 388, 389–391
   implementation of, 393–399
      constraints and difficulties, 398–399
   interprocess communication, 398
   modules added to Prolog, 385–386
   multiprocessor implementation, 394–395
      core services present on each processor, 395
      database distribution, 397–398
      host system interface, 399
      load sharing algorithms, 396–397
      network messaging in, 399
      problems, 399
      process management in, 399
   OR-parallelism not supported by, 385
   poll command, 393
   process pipelines in, 390
   process termination in, 391
   processes added, 386–388
   receive command, 388, 391–392
   suspend-process command, 393
   transmit command, 388, 391
   uniprocessor implementation, 393–394
Port instructions, OM virtual machine, 165–166, 182
Ports, Padmalog's use of, 410–411
Pragma annotation mechanism, 248
Precompilation (of Prolog program), 219–220
Primes benchmark program, 208, 209, 210, 211
Process, meaning of term, 382
Process based computational models, 16
Process interpretation (of logic programs), 289–291
Process oriented Prolog languages, 333–427
   see also CS-Prolog; Delta Prolog; Padmalog; PMS-Prolog
Process suspension, in CCNDs, 242, 291–292, 301–302
Producer–consumer problem, PMS-Prolog used, 388–389
Producer–consumer system, Occam compared with RGDC, 261–267
Prolog abstract machines
   comparison of, 116–117
   see also Abstract machines
Prolog dataflow models, comparison of, 116
Prolog multi-sequential machine, 20–22

PSI processing element, 313
  see also Multi-PSI system

Quad stack, use in OPAL machine, 178
Queens1 benchmark program, 60, 61, 208, 209, 210, 211
Queens2 benchmark program, 61, 208, 209, 210, 211
Queens(N) problem
  distributed version, 418–420, 424
  pipelined version, 416–418, 424
  sequential version, 415–416
Query benchmark programs, 42, 60, 81, 82, 86
Quickdiff benchmark program, 60
Quicksort benchmark programs, 60, 154, 155, 181
Quintus Prolog
  compared with other systems, 61, 211
  Multiprocessing Package, 402–403
    compared with PMS-Prolog, 403

RAP (restricted AND parallel) models, 121–132
  dynamic data dependency method used, 122–125
  hybrid models, 122, 127–132
  static data dependency analysis used, 122, 125–127
RAP-WAM, 130–131
Reactive Guarded Definite Clauses language, 259–285
  see also RGDC...
Reactive programs, meaning of term, 264
Receive command (in PMS-Prolog), 388, 391–392
Recomputation OPC models, 20–24, 25
Redo subgoal(s), 144
Reduce-OR model, 134–135, 188–191, 380
  behaviour of, 189
  FireArc instruction in, 205–206
  forms of parallelism exploited by, 190
  join operations for, 196–202
  message passing in, 190–191
  parallel Prolog compiler based on, 188, 205–207
    see also ROLOG
  underlying kernel in, 190, 203, 205
  unification process in, 192–195, 207
Registers
  CIAM, 228–229
  OM, 163–165
  3DPAM, 101
Relation-level compilation, flat CCND languages, 246
Reply messages, 76
Resolution operations, in COALA parallel execution model, 221
Resolution rules, in Delta Prolog, 340–341
Restricted AND/OR parallel models, 133–140
Restricted AND parallel logic models, 121–132, 380
  combined with limited OR parallelism, 138–139
  see also RAP models
Reverse benchmark programs, 60, 81, 86, 154, 181, 425–426
RGDC (Reactive Guarded Definite Clauses) language, 259–285
  abstract data types implemented in, 272
  client–server prototype examined, 272–275
  compared with Occam language, 261–267
  control mechanisms for, 277–279
  implentation of, 279–281

input/output handling by, 273
meaning of name, 264
merge process in, 274
Occam meta-interpreter written in, 281–284
process distribution in, 268–269
process termination in, 266–267
producer–consumer prototype examined, 261–267
semantics of, 275–277
synchronization in, 267–271
syntax of, 264
transaction facilities of, 274–275
ROLOG compiler, 188
  join algorithm used, 200
  performance of, 207–212
  process model, 205–206
  unification procedures, 207
ROPM, 188–191
  see also Reduce-OR model
RTS (Run Time Support), Transputer interprocess communication using, 406–407

S streams, 139
Salt-mustard benchmark program, 41, 208, 209
Save-and-Restore technique, in 3DPAM, 96, 102–103
Scalable multiprocessors, parallel Prolog on, 27–63
Scheduling
  OPERA, 46, 54–59
  types of, 56
  see also Centralized...; Distributed...; Hierarchical scheduling
Scheduling algorithm, CS-Prolog's use of, 374–375
Scheduling capability, 5, 46
  closed environment models, 18, 20
  shared environment models, 9, 11, 13
SDDA (static data dependency analysis) method
  backward execution supported by, 126–127
  use in RAP models, 125–127
Search forest (in CS-Prolog), 361
  tree unification in, 369–370, 375
Search parallelism, 227–228
  advantage of representation, 227
Search trees, communicating Prolog processes, 368–369
SEPIA, compared with LORAP, 138–139
Sequent Balance shared-memory multiprocessor,
  Quintus Multiprocessing Package run on, 402, 403
Sequent Symmetry machine
  Andorra-I run on, 41
  Aurora run on, 41
  Versions-Vector run on, 16
Shallow binding, 10
Shared binding environment OPC models, 6–16, 25
  implementations of, 25
Shared binding mechanism, 6
Shared memory systems
  compared with distributed memory systems, 29
  flat CCND languages used, 247–249
Shared variables, communication in RGDC, 265
Shared virtual address space, 29
Shared virtual memory proposal, 30–31
Shōen (in KL1)
  control/report streams of, 313

Shōen (in KL1) (cont.)
    creation of, 320–321
    and foster parents, 321
    meaning of term, 313
    profiling facilities for, 328
SICStus Prolog
    compared with Aurora, 41, 62, 181
    compared with PEPSys, 62
    WAM implemented on, 180
        compared with OPAL machine, 181
Simulated time, 374
Slit-check timing mechanism, 315
Snoopy (cache coherence) protocols, 30, 32, 33
Solver process
    in OPERA, 49, 50
    in parallel execution model, 83–85
Sparse Instancing (in PMS-Prolog), 398
Speed-up
    CIAM, 234
    distributed interpreter, 80–81
    KL1 implementation on multi-PSI, 331
    OPERA compared with other systems, 63
    Padmalog, 424
    parallel clause execution, 154–156
Spin-locks, 35
Split goals (in Delta Prolog), 336
    resolution of, 340
    segments of, 347
    support in DAM, 353
    updating of lists of backtrack nodes for, 349–350
Spy exception, KL1 implementation on multi-PSI, 327
Spy process, 49, 50, 56, 57
SRI model
    binding array method in, 11, 62
    compared with other systems, 62
    extension to Andorra-I, 29
State vector, 161
Strand language, 285
    compared with FCP, 289
Stream AND-parallel computational models, 239–257
    concepts, 239–241
    see also Committed-choice languages
Stream AND-parallelism, 239
    languages based on, 240, 241–245
    see also CCND languages
Streams, use by RGDC, 273
Sun 4/60 processor, Prolog systems run on, 61
Sun Sparc 1 workstations, performance of benchmark programs using ROLOG, 211
Sun 3/50 processor, systems run on, 41, 61, 234
Sun 3/60 processor, PMS-Prolog run on, 393
Sun 3/260 processor, Padmalog run on, 423
Supernode
    architecture of, 47–48
    interconnection network for, 48
Suspension of processes, in CCNDs, 242, 291–292, 301–302
Symbol table, in Padmalog, 409
Synchronous communication, programmed by RGDC, 270–271
System simulation, in CS-Prolog, 374–375

T414-20
    distributed interpreter implemented using, 79
    see also Transputer
T800
    Andorra-I run on, 41
    Aurora run on, 41
    CIAM running on hypertorus using, 234
    PADMAVATI machine based on, 406
    Parsytec Supercluster based on, 288, 306
    SICStus Prolog run on, 41
    Supernode based on, 47
    see also Transputer
T-Prolog, 401–402
Task granularity (for Supernode/Meganode), 55
Task scheduling, 56, 215
    see also Scheduling
Term dereferencing, 5
    see also Dereference of terms
Term space, 191
Termination detection schemes, 322
Termination messages, 76
Test OR benchmark programs, 81, 82, 87
Theorems, information exchange using, 363–365
Thread, meaning of term, 5n, 135–136
3DPAM, 89–118
    abstract instruction set for, 101–112
    AND nodes represented in, 106
    AND operators in, 105–106
    argument preparation instructions in, 105
    body goal handling in, 105–107
    compared with other abstract machines, 116–117
    compared with other dataflow models, 116
    compared with other techniques, 115–117
    compared with WAM, 90
    context handling in, 100–101, 102–103
    data representation in, 99–100
    data structures for context handling, 100–101
    distributed implementation techniques used, 117
    environment handling in, 103, 117
    failure mechanism of, 116
    OR alternatives represented in, 109–110
    overview of, 97–98
    registers used, 101
    rule clauses represented in, 107–109
    term handling in, 102
    token representation in, 98–99
    unification procedure in, 101–102
    UNIFY nodes represented in, 103, 104
    variable bindings used, 112–115
Time out control mechanisms, use in RGDC, 278–279
Time stamping
    BOPLOG's use of, 13–14
    Kabu-Wake system's use of, 61
    OPERA's use of, 49, 50, 52
Time Warp algorithm, CS-Prolog's use of, 374–375
Tina benchmark program, 41, 42
Tnodes, 47
    speed of data exchange within/between, 48
Token colouring scheme, in 3DPAM, 96
Token representation, in 3DPAM, 98–99
Token streams, 93
Towers of Hanoi benchmark program, 307, 308
Trace driven simulators, 36

INDEX

Trace exception, KL1 implementation on multi-PSI, 327
Transmit command (in PMS-Prolog), 388, 391
Transputer based hypertorus, CIAM implemented on, 234
Transputer based multiprocessor
    Delta Prolog implemented on, 352
    distributed interpreter implemented on, 79–83
    emulation of DDM on, 32–40
        Andorra-I and Aurora run on, 41–43
        coupling applications to, 36–37
        design of emulator, 33–37
        implementation on Meiko Computing Surface, 37–40
        link-based protocol for, 33–35
        objectives of study, 33
        process structure of emulator, 39–40
        synchronization support for, 35–36
    PMS-Prolog implemented on, 394–395
    see also Supernode
Transputer based network
    CS-Prolog on, 375
    FCP on, 287–309
    PADMAVATI machine comprising, 406
Transputer Warren Abstract Machine *see* TWAM
Transputers
    characteristics of, 394–395
    multi-tasking on, 79
    Occam used on, 74, 260
`Tree` benchmark program, 81, 82, 87
`Turtles` benchmark program, 41
TWAM (Transputer Warren Abstract Machine), 46
    data structures of, 49–50
    example use of TWAM stacks, 51
    process structure of worker, 49, 50
    sequential efficiency of, 59–60
    stack copying in, 50–52
    synchronization of TWAM processes, 52
`12-puzzle` benchmark program, 208, 209, 210, 211

Unconditional binding, 6
Unification environment, 219
Unification instructions, OPAL machine, 174–176, 183–184
Unification operations
    in CCND languages, 245, 247, 251, 294
    in COALA parallel execution model, 221
    in CS-Prolog, 365, 369–370
    in FCP, 294
    four-phase unification, 172
    in KL1 implementation on multi-PSI, 319–320
    in OPAL machine, 171–179
    in parallel execution model, 72
    in 3DPAM, 101–102
    two-phase unification, 193–195
        first phase, 194
        second phase, 194–196
    in WAM, 102, 172

UNIFY/AND ring, 94–95, 105
    representation in 3DPAM, 107–108
UNIFY nodes
    in DSG, 91, 94
    code segments representing, 104
    as compound nodes, 104
    environment closing procedures, 112–115
    representation in 3DPAM, 103, 104
UNIT nodes
    in DSG, 91, 93
    realization in 3DPAM, 111
UNSW-Prolog, modules introduced into, 385–386

Value trail, compared with time stamping solution, 54
Variable bindings
    closed binding mechanisms, 16
    communication of, 146–147
        cost comparison of strategies, 146–147
        demand driven approach, 146
        total communiaction scheme, 146
    shared binding mechanisms, 6
    in 3DPAM, 112–115
    see also Closed...; Shared binding...
Variable importation method, 17–18
Variable migration, 255, 256
Variable migration (in FCP), 300
    effect of, 301
Verden and Glaser's AND parallel execution scheme, 143–157
Versions-Vector binding mechanism, 15–16
Virtual channels (in DAM), 355

WAM (Warren Abstract Machine), 295
    compared with OPAL machine, 168, 172, 180–181
    compared with 3DPAM, 101, 102, 103, 116
    DAM as extension of, 352–355
    environment handling in, 103
    failure mechanism of, 116
    Padmalog compilers based on, 414
    parallel frame added, 149
    RAP implemented on, 130–131
    registers added, 151
    term handling in, 102
    3DPAM as modification of, 89–118
    Transputer-based extension of, 46
    unification procedure in, 102, 172
WEC (Weighted Export/External Counting) garbage collection method, 252–253, 323–325
White export tables, 325
White import tables, 325
WRC (Weighted Reference Counting) termination detection method, 322
WTC (Weighted Throw Counting) termination detection method, 322

Xia's hybrid RAP model, 131–132

`Zebra` benchmark program, 41

Index compiled by Paul Nash